MASTERPLOTS

AMERICAN FICTION
SERIES

MASTERPLOTS

Revised Category Edition

AMERICAN FICTION SERIES

3

Rea-Z
Indexes

Edited by

FRANK N. MAGILL

SALEM PRESS
Englewood Cliffs, N.J.

Library of Congress Cataloging in Publication Data
Masterplots: revised category edition, American
fiction series.
   Includes index.
   1. America—Literatures—Stories, plots, etc.
2. America—Literatures—History and criti-
cism—Addresses, essays, lectures. 3. Fiction—
Stories, plots, etc. 4. Fiction—History and crit-
icism—Addresses, essays, lectures. I. Magill,
Frank Northen, 1907–
PN843.M15 1985   809.3   85-1936
ISBN 0-89356-500-8
ISBN 0-89356-503-2 (volume 3)

LIST OF TITLES IN VOLUME 3

LIST OF TITLES IN VOLUME III

MASTERPLOTS

AMERICAN FICTION
SERIES

THE REAL LIFE OF SEBASTIAN KNIGHT

Type of work: Novel
Author: Vladimir Nabokov (1899–1977)
Type of plot: Simulated biography
Time of plot: 1899–1938
Locale: England and Europe
First published: 1941
>*Principal character:*
>V., Sebastian Knight's brother and biographer

The Real Life of Sebastian Knight, written in Paris in 1938 but not published in the United States until 1941, is Vladimir Nabokov's first work in English; previously he had written in Russian. Although this earlier novel does not show quite the same ingenious conjuring with language as do *Lolita* and *Pale Fire*, it is, nevertheless, a brilliant, sometimes funny, and almost perversely complex book.

The novel is written as a biography of Sebastian Knight, a writer who has just died, by his younger half brother, who designates himself only as V. Beginning as an attempt to present the real Sebastian, V.'s biography becomes the quest of V. himself to understand the personality of the man revealed by his search. Two problems, therefore, run as concurrent themes through the novel: first, the problem of communication between a writer and his readers, the task of conveying reality with precision, and, second, the greater problem of what this reality is—the multiple views possible of the same thing and the necessarily unsuccessful attempt to capture anything so elusive as personal identity. The novel presents a dazzling series of masks, none of which may be removed completely because knowing more about Sebastian Knight does not help readers to understand him but rather increases his complexity.

Within the novel are three different literary attempts to portray Sebastian. The first is V.'s own earnest, painstaking effort to portray his brother objectively. At the opposite extreme is a slick, superficial biography, already published, by Mr. Goodman, Sebastian's former secretary. V. admits in quoting from it at length that even this book contains elements of truth. Somewhere in the middle are Sebastian's own novels, which reveal obliquely something of the man himself, even though we can never be sure of how much they disclose.

V.'s first-hand knowledge of Sebastian, colored by the adoration of a younger brother for the clever older one and by V.'s nostalgia for Russia, is confined to Sebastian's youth. Sebastian had been born in Russia; his English mother, a restless, romantic woman, deserted her husband and baby; his father remarried. Sebastian left Russia for Cambridge and remained in England, becoming almost a caricature of an Englishman and writing his novels in England. At this point in his biography, V. must search for people who knew Sebastian, for V. saw almost nothing of him after he left Russia, and their few meetings were cold and strained.

V.'s search for the truth becomes a kind of detective novel, but an enigmatic and paradoxical one. His elaborate quest is continually frustrated—by someone's inability to remember, by his own timidity, by his willingness to content himself with an intuitive impression, almost as if he does not wish to have any illusions shattered. One is reminded of Sebastian's own first novel, a parody of a detective story; indeed, the quotations from Sebastian's writing provide not only a glimpse of his real self but also an insight into this novel, for one might say of it that he employed parody as a means of achieving effects of serious thought and feeling. This novel of Sebastian's, called *The Prismatic Bezel*, also hints at the many-faceted obliquity of Nabokov's novel.

V.'s quest degenerates into a melodramatic farce. He finds the woman whom Sebastian loved and tricks her into an admission of her identity, but again he contents himself with his own impression of her and his own estimate of the effect she must have had on his brother. Nabokov weaves parallel situations from Sebastian's novels and from his and the narrator's life into a glittering web which conceals as much as it reveals. One cannot know another person because countless factors of which one is totally unaware intervene. His method is the juxtaposition of a series of glimpses, absurd and touching, like a series of sleight-of-hand tricks. One cannot tell what is the trickery of legerdemain and what is not.

Two incidents, one near the beginning, the other at the end of the book, illuminate its meaning. On one of his trips to Europe, Sebastian finds a village called Roquebrune, the town where his mother had died. He finds her house and sits for a long time in the garden, trying to find the mother whom he scarcely knew. At length, he can almost see her figure, like some pastel ghost, gliding up the stairs to the door. Much later, he discovers by accident that the Roquebrune he had found was not even the same town where his mother had lived, but another, many miles away. There is something funny and pathetic in his own deception, something that undercuts and transcends the experience. Its meaning is made clearer by the end of the book. V. had been in Marseilles when he received a telegram telling him Sebastian was seriously ill. After many delays, he finds the hospital, has some difficulties in making the porter understand him, but is eventually shown into the room where the Englishman, still alive, is sleeping. He spends only a few minutes there, but he feels he can at last express the kinship he has always felt with his brother, that at last these moments listening to the sound of his breathing have crystallized a whole series of other moments as words could not have done. Yet, on leaving the room, he discovers by chance that this man was not his brother at all, for Sebastian had died the day before. He says that later he found his life transformed by the short time he spent in the dying man's company. He now believed that the soul—any man's soul—is a way of being rather than a constant state; therefore, souls are constantly in flux and interchangeable. V. feels that he is Sebastian Knight; he wears his mask. Sebastian may even be V., or both may be someone they never knew. In this mood, he begins to write his brother's biography.

One cannot, of course, know another person completely, for one cannot know oneself. The fact that V. goes on to write Sebastian's biography proves that he has understood for only a moment; but the existence of a series of masks does not necessarily mean that nothing lies behind them, only that one can penetrate no further.

Nabokov's method is oblique, moving as does the chess knight who must leap in two directions and skip over intervening pieces, because the reader's knowledge of identity must be reached obliquely. This novel is at once a fascinating puzzle and a profound statement, whose depths are disguised as absurdities. It is technically not the *tour de force* that *Lolita* and *Pale Fire* are, but its discussions of the relationship between the writer and his art reveal much about the author's own technique. Its themes are similar to those of his other works, as is its deliberate comic view, which approaches within a hairbreadth of the tragic. This book is at once a witty bit of hocus-pocus and a fine and moving novel.

THE RED BADGE OF COURAGE

Type of work: Novel
Author: Stephen Crane (1871–1900)
Type of plot: Impressionistic realism
Time of plot: Civil War
Locale: A Civil War battlefield
First published: 1895

Principal characters:

HENRY FLEMING, a young recruit
JIM CONKLIN, a veteran
WILSON, another veteran

The Story:

The tall soldier, Jim Conklin, and the loud soldier, Wilson, argued bitterly over the rumor that the troops were about to move. Henry Fleming was impatient to experience his first battle, and as he listened to the quarreling of the seasoned soldiers, he wondered if he would become frightened and run away under gunfire. He questioned Wilson and Conklin, and each man stated that he would stand and fight no matter what happened.

Henry had come from a farm, where he had dreamed of battles and longed for army life. His mother had held him back at first. When she saw that her son was bored with the farm, she packed his woolen clothing and with a warning that he must not associate with the wicked kind of men who were in the military camps sent him off to join the Yankee troops.

One gray morning, Henry awoke to find that the regiment was about to move. With a hazy feeling that death would be a relief from dull and meaningless marching, Henry was again disappointed. The troops made only another march. He began to suspect that the generals were stupid fools, but the other men in his raw regiment scoffed at his idea and told him to shut up.

When the fighting suddenly began, there was very little action in it for Henry. He lay on the ground with the other men and watched for signs of the enemy. Some of the men around him were wounded. He could not see what was going on or what the battle was about. Then an attack came. Immediately Henry forgot all of his former confused thoughts, and he could only fire his rifle over and over; around him, men behaved in their own strange individual manners as they were wounded. Henry felt a close comradeship with the men at his side—men who were firing at the enemy with him.

Suddenly the attack ended. To Henry, it seemed strange that the sky above should still be blue after the guns had stopped firing. While the men were recovering from the attack, binding wounds, and gathering equipment, another surprise attack was launched from the enemy line. Unprepared and tired from the first fighting, the men retreated in panic. Henry, sharing their sudden terror, ran, too.

When the fearful retreat had ended, the fleeing men learned that the enemy had lost the battle. Now Henry felt a surge of guilt. Dreading to rejoin his companions, he fled into the forest. There he saw a squirrel run away from him in fright. The fleeing animal seemed to vindicate in Henry's mind his own cowardly flight; he had acted according to nature whose own creatures ran from danger. Then, seeing a dead man lying in a clearing, Henry hurried back into the retreating column of wounded men. Most were staggering along in helpless bewilderment, and some were being carried on stretchers. Henry realized that he had no wound and that he did not belong in that group of staggering men. There was one pitiful-looking man, covered with dirt and blood, wandering about dazed and alone. Everyone was staring at him and avoiding him. When Henry approached him, the young boy saw that the soldier was Jim Conklin. He was horrified at the sight of the tall soldier. He tried to help Jim, but with a wild motion of despair, Jim fell to the ground dead. Once more Henry fled.

His conscience was paining him. He wanted to return to his regiment to finish the fight, but he thought that his fellow soldiers would point to him as a deserter. He envied the dead men who were lying all about him. They were already heroes; he was a coward. Ahead he could hear the rumbling of artillery. As he neared the lines of his regiment, a retreating line of men broke from the trees ahead of him. The men ran fiercely, ignoring him or waving frantically at him as they shouted something he could not comprehend. He stood among the flying men, not knowing what to do. One man hit him on the head with the butt of a rifle.

Henry went on carefully, the wound in his head paining him a great deal. He walked for a long while until he met another soldier, who led Henry back to his regiment. The first familiar man Henry met was Wilson. Wilson, who had been a terrible braggart before the first battle, had given Henry a packet of letters to keep for him in case he was killed. Now Henry felt superior to Wilson. If the man asked him where he had been, Henry would remind him of the letters. Lost was Henry's feeling of guilt; he felt superior now, his deeds of cowardice almost forgotten. No one knew that he had run off in terror. Wilson had changed. He no longer was the swaggering, boastful man who had annoyed Henry in the beginning. The men in the regiment washed Henry's wound and told him to get some sleep.

The next morning, Wilson casually asked Henry for the letters. Half sorry that he had to yield them with no taunting remark, Henry returned the letters to his comrade. He felt sorry for Wilson's embarrassment. He felt himself a virtuous and heroic man.

Another battle started. This time Henry held his position doggedly and kept firing his rifle without thinking. Once he fell down, and for a panicky moment he thought that he had been shot, but he continued to fire his rifle blindly, loading and firing without even seeing the enemy. Finally someone shouted to him that he must stop shooting, that the battle was over. Then Henry looked up for the first time and saw that there were no enemy troops before him. Now he was a hero. Everyone stared at him when the lieutenant of the regiment complimented his fierce fighting. Henry realized that he had behaved like a demon.

Wilson and Henry, off in the woods looking for water, overheard two officers discussing the coming battle. They said that Henry's regiment fought like mule drivers, but that they would have to be used anyway. Then one officer said that probably not many of the regiment would live through the day's fighting. Soon after the attack started, the color-bearer was killed, and Henry took up the flag, with Wilson at his side. Although the regiment fought bravely, one of the commanding officers of the army said that the men had not gained the ground that they were expected to take. The same officer had complimented Henry for his courageous fighting. He began to feel that he knew the measure of his own courage and endurance.

His outfit fought one more engagement with the enemy. Henry was by that time a veteran, and the fighting held less meaning for him than had the earlier battles. When it was over, he and Wilson marched away with their victorious regiment.

Critical Evaluation:

The Red Badge of Courage, Stephen Crane's second novel (*Maggie: A Girl of the Streets* had appeared under a pseudonym in 1893) and his most famous work, has often been considered the first truly modern war novel. The war is the American Civil War, and the battle is presumed to be the one fought at Chancellorsville, though neither the war nor the battle is named in the novel. Further, there is no mention of Abraham Lincoln or the principal battle generals, Joseph Hooker (Union) and Robert E. Lee and "Stonewall" Jackson (Confederate). This is by design, since Crane was writing a different kind of war novel. He was not concerned with the causes of the war, the political and social implications of the prolonged and bloody conflict, the strategy and tactics of the commanding officers, or even the real outcome of the battle in which historically the combined losses were nearly thirty thousand men (including "Stonewall" Jackson, mistakenly shot in darkness by one of his own men).

From beginning to end the short novel focuses upon one Union Army volunteer. Though other characters enter the story and reappear intermittently, they are distinctly minor, and they are present primarily to show the relationship of Henry Fleming (usually called only "the youth") to one person, to a small group of soldiers, or to the complex war of which he is such an insignificant part.

Much of the story takes the reader into Henry's consciousness. Readers share his boyish dreams of glory, his excitement in anticipating battle action, his fear of showing fear, his cowardice and flight, his inner justification of what he has done, his wish for a wound to symbolize a courage he has not shown, the ironic gaining of his false "red badge," his secret knowledge of the badge's origin, his "earning" the badge as he later fights fiercely and instinctively, his joy in musing on his own bravery and valiant actions, his anger at an officer who fails to appreciate his soldiery, and his final feeling that "the great death" is, after all, not a thing to be feared so much. Now, he tells himself, he is a man. In centering the story within the consciousness of an inexperienced youth caught in a war situation whose meaning and complexities he cannot understand, Crane anticipates Ford Madox Ford, Ernest Hemingway, and other later novelists.

Crane has been called a Realist, a Naturalist, an Impressionist, and a Symbolist. He is all of these in *The Red Badge of Courage*. Though young Stephen Crane had never seen a battle when he wrote the novel, he had read about them; he had talked with veterans and had studied history under a Civil War general; and he had imagined what it would be like to be a frightened young man facing violent death amid the confusion, noise, and turmoil of a conflict that had no clear meaning to him. Intuitively, he wrote so realistically that several early reviewers concluded that only an experienced soldier could have written the book. After Crane had later seen the Greeks and Turks fighting in 1897 (he was a journalist reporting the war), he told Joseph Conrad, "My picture of war was all right! I have found it as I imagined it."

Although Naturalistic passages appear in the novel, Crane portrays in Henry Fleming not a helpless chip floating on the indifferent ocean of life but a youth sometimes impelled into action by society or by instinct yet also capable of consciously willed acts. Before the first skirmish, Henry wishes he could escape from his regiment and consider his plight: ". . . there were iron laws of tradition and law on four sides. He was in a moving box." In the second skirmish, he runs "like a rabbit." When a squirrel in the forest flees after Henry throws a pine cone at him, Henry justifies his own flight: "There was the law, he said. Nature had given him a sign." He is not, however, content to look upon himself as on the squirrel's level. He feels guilt over his cowardice. When he carries the flag in the later skirmishes, he is not a terrified chicken or rabbit or squirrel but a young man motivated by pride, by a sense of belonging to a group, and by a determination to show his courage to an officer who had scornfully called the soldiers in his group a lot of "mule drivers."

From the beginning, critics have both admired and complained about Crane's

Impressionistic writing and his use of imagery and symbols in *The Red Badge of Courage*. Edward Garnett in 1898 called Crane "the chief impressionist of our day" and praised his "wonderful fervour and freshness of style." Joseph Conrad (himself an Impressionist) was struck by Crane's "genuine verbal felicity, welding analysis and description in a continuous fascination of individual style," and Conrad saw Henry as "the symbol of all untried men." By contrast, one American critic in 1898 described the novel as "a mere riot of words" and condemned "the violent straining after effect" and the "absurd similes." Though H. G. Wells liked the book as a whole, he commented on "those chromatic splashes that at times deafen and confuse in the *Red Badge*, those images that astonish rather than enlighten."

Yet judging by the continuing popularity of *The Red Badge of Courage*, most readers are not repelled by Crane's repeated use of color—"blue demonstration," "red eyes," "red animal—war," "red sun"—or by his use of images—"dark shadows that moved like monsters," "The dragons were coming," guns that "belched and howled like brass devils guarding a gate." Only in a few passages does Crane indulge in "arty" writing—"The guns squatted in a row like savage chiefs. They argued with abrupt violence"—or drop into the pathetic fallacy—"The flag suddenly sank down as if dying. Its motion as it fell was a gesture of despair." Usually the Impressionistic phrasing is appropriate to the scene or to the emotional state of Henry Fleming at a particular moment, as when, after he has fought, he feels heroically, the sun shines "now bright and gay in the blue, enameled sky."

A brilliant work of the imagination, *The Red Badge of Courage* will endure as what Crane afterward wrote a friend he had intended it to be, "a psychological portrayal of fear."

THE RED ROVER

Type of work: Novel
Author: James Fenimore Cooper (1789–1851)
Type of plot: Historical romance
Time of plot: Mid-eighteenth century
Locale: Newport, Rhode Island, and the Atlantic Ocean
First published: 1827

Principal characters:

HARRY WILDER, formerly Henry Ark, actually Henry de
Lacy
THE RED ROVER, the captain of the *Dolphin*
DICK FID and
SCIPIO AFRICA, seamen and Harry Wilder's friends
GERTRUDE GRAYSON, General Grayson's daughter
MRS. WYLLYS, her governess

The Story:

While in the town of Newport, Rhode Island, Harry Wilder saw in the outer harbor a ship, the *Dolphin*, which interested him greatly. He decided to try to secure a berth on her for himself and his two friends, Dick Fid and Scipio Africa, a black sailor. His determination was strengthened after meeting a stranger who in effect dared him to try to obtain a berth there. That night, the three men rowed out to the ship lying at anchor, in order to give the vessel a closer inspection. Hailed by the watch on deck, Wilder went aboard her. There he learned that he had been expected and that if he were interested in sailing with her, he might go to see the captain. The captain was the mysterious, mocking stranger whom Wilder had met that afternoon in the town. Before Wilder signed on as a member of the ship's crew, however, the captain revealed the true nature of the ship and admitted that he himself was the Red Rover, the scourge of the sea. Wilder, who had formerly been an officer in the British Navy, was given the post of second in command. He persuaded the captain to sign on Dick and Scipio as well. He then returned to shore to settle his affairs in the town. The other two men remained aboard the *Dolphin*.

At the same time, the *Royal Caroline*, a merchantman trading along the coast and between the colonies and England, lay in the inner harbor ready to embark on the following day. Two ladies, Gertrude Grayson and her governess, Mrs. Wyllys, were to take passage on her to Charleston, South Carolina, Gertrude's home. Wilder met the ladies as if by chance and tried to dissuade them from sailing aboard the *Royal Caroline*. He hinted that the *Royal Caroline* was unsafe, but his words were discredited by an old seaman who insisted that there was nothing wrong with the ship. The ladies decided to sail in spite of Wilder's warnings. Then the master of the *Royal Caroline* fell from a cask and broke his leg, and a new captain had to be found immediately. The Red Rover sent a message ordering Wilder to apply for the vacant position. He did and was immediately hired.

The voyage of the *Royal Caroline* began with difficulties which continued as time went on. They were not long out of port when a ship was sighted on the horizon. It continued to keep its distance in approximately the same position, so that all aboard the *Royal Caroline* suspected that it was following them. In trying to outdistance the other ship, Wilder put on all sail possible, in spite of the threatening weather. A storm struck the ship and left her foundering in heavy seas. When Wilder commanded the crew to man the pumps, they refused and deserted the sinking ship in one of the boats. Only Wilder and the two women were left aboard the helpless *Royal Caroline*. Hoping to make land, they embarked in a longboat, but the wind blew them out to sea. They were sighted and picked up by the *Dolphin*.

Gertrude and Mrs. Wyllys were not long aboard the *Dolphin* before the true state of affairs became apparent to the women in spite of the kindly treatment afforded them. Mrs. Wyllys realized also that Roderick, the cabin boy, was in reality a woman; but this mystery was nothing when compared with that of Harry Wilder.

Dick Fid told the story of Harry Wilder's past history to the two ladies and the Red Rover, thus explaining the affection Wilder, Dick, and Scipio held for each other. Some twenty-four years earlier, Dick and Scipio had found a child and a dying woman, apparently a nurse, aboard an abandoned ship. After the woman died, the two seamen took care of the boy. They had only one clue to follow in their efforts to locate the child's relatives. This was the name Ark of Lynnhaven which had been painted on a ship's bucket and which Scipio had tattooed on Dick's arm. There was no ship of that name in any port registry, however, and so the search for the child's relatives was abandoned.

As Dick finished his story, another ship was sighted. It was the *Dart*, a British naval vessel on which Wilder, Dick, and Scipio had previously sailed. Wilder wanted the Red Rover to flee, but the captain had another plan for dealing with the *Dart*. After showing British colors, the Red Rover was invited by Captain Bignall of the *Dart* to come aboard his ship. There the pirate captain learned that Henry Ark, alias Harry Wilder, was absent from the *Dart* on a dangerous secret mission. The Red Rover realized that he had betrayed himself to his enemy. He went back to the *Dolphin* and then sent Wilder, Dick, Scipio, and the two women to the *Dart*.

Wilder had informed the Red Rover that once aboard his own ship, the *Dart*, he would be duty bound to reveal the true nature of the *Dolphin*. In telling Captain Bignall his story, Wilder begged for mercy for both the master and the crew of the pirate ship. Bignall agreed and sent Wilder back to the

Dolphin with lenient terms of surrender. The Red Rover refused them and told Wilder that if there were to be a fight, Captain Bignall would have to start it. As the *Dart* attacked the pirate ship, a sudden storm gave the *Dolphin* an unexpected advantage. Its crew boarded the *Dart*, killed Captain Bignall, and captured the ship. The crew of the *Dolphin* demanded the lives of Wilder, Dick, and Scipio as traitors, and the Red Rover handed them over to the crew. When the chaplain who was aboard the *Dart* came forward to plead for their lives, he saw the tattoo on Dick's arm. He told the story of the *Ark of Lynnhaven* and revealed that Harry Wilder must be the son of Paul de Lacy and Mrs. Wyllys, who had kept the marriage a secret because of parental disapproval and later because of Paul's death. Mrs. Wyllys then begged for the life of her son, whom she had thought dead all these years. The Red Rover dismissed his crew until the next morning, when he would announce his decision concerning the fate of the prisoners.

The next morning, the Red Rover put his crew and all the gold aboard the *Dolphin* into a coaster and sent them ashore. The crew of the *Dart*, Wilder, Dick, Scipio, and the women were put aboard the *Dart* and told to sail off. When they were some distance away, they saw the *Dolphin* catch fire and burn. None had been left aboard her but the Red Rover and Roderick. Some aboard the *Dart* thought they saw a small boat putting off from the burning ship, but none could be sure because of the billowing smoke.

Twenty years later, after the colonies had won their independence from England, the Red Rover, a veteran of the Revolutionary War, reappeared in Newport and made his way to the home of Captain Henry de Lacy, who had previously called himself Harry Wilder. Admitted, he identified himself as the long-lost brother of Mrs. Wyllys. Shortly thereafter the Red Rover, pirate and patriot, died.

Critical Evaluation:

Though *The Red Rover* has never been as popular as James Fenimore Cooper's two greatest sea romances, *The Pilot* (1824) and *The Two Admirals* (1842), it has its own sturdy merits as a suspenseful tale of intrigue and adventure. Superficially, the early scenes of the novel bring to mind the classic American sea novel, Melville's *Moby Dick* (1851). Harry Wilder, like Ishmael, is drawn mysteriously to a ship anchored in the harbor. Aboard the ship, Wilder encounters the notorious Red Rover, just as Ishmael meets the enigmatic Captain Ahab; and just as Ahab violates metaphysical laws in his pursuit of the White Whale, so the Red Rover is a law unto himself as he plunders merchant vessels in the period before the Revolutionary War. Beyond this point, the similarities between the novels are less clearly marked than the contrasts. Melville's novel is composed on an epic scale, with a profound sense of tragic drama. *The Red Rover*, quite the opposite, is an entertaining melodramatic romance, written without any pretensions to examine deeply the mysteries of man's place in the universe.

Nevertheless, the novel is interesting from points of view other than simply those of a sea adventure story. Considered from a psychological perspective, *The Red Rover* reveals Cooper's contradictory ideas about the structure and philosophical ideas of the work. In *Studies in Classic American Literature* (1923), D. H. Lawrence suggests that Cooper's "white novels," among which the sea stories may be included, betray the novelist's confusion about the superiority of democracy. Cooper, according to Lawrence, believes that the American is bound to assert his superior claims over other peoples, even if these claims are undeserved. This forceful assertion is a form of aggression, however, and Cooper, at least philosophically, is disturbed by aggressiveness. One side of him prefers gentle action; another, violent force. Without pressing Lawrence's suggestion too far, it is certainly true that in *The Red Rover* Cooper is both repelled by and attracted to the brutality of the captain of the *Dolphin*, just as he is ambivalent about his feelings concerning Wilder. For Wilder is at the same time the gentle, chivalrous comrade of the women, Gertrude Grayson and Mrs. Wyllys, and the tough-minded, rugged sailor-adventurer.

Cooper partially resolves the conflict between aggressive and gentle conduct through the mechanism of the Revolutionary War. The romantic rebel in the personage of the Red Rover emerges as the patriotic rebel, when the pirate reappears late in the book as a veteran and hero of the American Revolution. Now his violence has the sanction of patriotic duty; and Harry Wilder, formerly seaman, also changes roles. By the end of the novel, he is Captain Henry De Lacy, gentleman. Thus, on a psychological level, Cooper justifies the intrepid, violent action of the story from the viewpoint of its satisfactory conclusion: both the Red Rover and Wilder are seen as American heroes who have advanced the cause of freedom.

REDBURN

Type of work: Novel
Author: Herman Melville (1819–1891)
Type of plot: Adventure romance
Time of plot: Mid-nineteenth century
Locale: New York, the Atlantic Ocean, and England
First published: 1849

> *Principal characters:*
> WELLINGBOROUGH REDBURN, a young lad on his first voyage
> CAPTAIN RIGA, the master of the *Highlander*
> HARRY BOLTON, a young English prodigal

The Story:

Wellingborough Redburn's father had died, leaving the mother and children poorly provided for, although the father had been a highly successful merchant and at one time a wealthy man. When Redburn was in his middle teens, he decided to take some of the burden off his mother by going to sea. Given an old gun and a hunting jacket by an older brother, Redburn left his home by the Hudson River and went to New York to seek a berth on a ship.

A college friend of his older brother aided Redburn in finding a berth on a ship bound for Liverpool. Unfortunately, the friend had emphasized the fact that Redburn came from a good family and had wealthy relatives; consequently, Captain Riga, master of the *Highlander*, was able to hire the young lad for three dollars a month. Having spent all his money and unable to get an advance on his wages, Redburn had to pawn his gun for a shirt and cap to wear aboard ship.

During his first few days out of port, Redburn thought that he had made a dreadful mistake in going to sea. His fellow sailors jeered at him as a greenhorn; he made many silly mistakes; he became violently seasick; and he discovered that he did not even have a spoon with which to take his portion of the food from the pots and pans in which it was sent to the forecastle. Most horrifying of all was the suicide of a sailor who dived over the side of the ship in a fit of delirium tremens.

As the thirty-day cruise to Liverpool from New York wore on, Redburn learned how to make himself useful and comfortable aboard the ship. When he went aloft alone to release the topmost sails, he earned a little respect from his fellow seamen, although they never did, throughout the voyage, let him forget that he was still a green hand and had signed on as a "boy." Redburn found the sea fascinating in many ways; he also found it terrifying, as when the *Highlander* passed a derelict schooner on which three corpses were still bound to the railing.

For Redburn, one of the liveliest incidents of the voyage was the discovery of a little stowaway on board the *Highlander.* The small boy had been on board the vessel some months before, when the father had been a sailor signed on for a trip from Liverpool to New York. The father had since died, and the boy had stowed himself away in an effort to return to England. Everyone on the ship, including the usually irascible Captain Riga, took a liking to the homesick stowaway and made much of him.

Redburn had little in common with his fellow crew members, most of whom were rough fellows many years older than he. Through them, however, he received an education quite different from that which he had been given in school. At first he tried to talk about church and good books to them, but he soon discovered that such conversation only irritated them into more than their usual profanity and obscenity. Redburn thought that they were not really very bad men but that they had never had the chance to be good men. Most of all, he disliked them because they looked upon anyone who could not follow the seaman's trade as a fool.

A long, low skyline in the distance was Redburn's first glimpse of Ireland. He met his first true European when an Irish fisherman hailed the *Highlander* and asked for a line. When he had hauled fifteen or so fathoms of the line into his boat, the Irishman cut the line, laughed, and sailed away. Even though the rope was not Redburn's, he, boylike, felt that the man had played a scurvy trick.

When the *Highlander* arrived at Liverpool, Redburn decided that the English city was not a great deal different from New York. Sailors and ships, he found, were the same in one place as in another, with a few notable exceptions. His trips into the city, away from the waterfront, and excursions into the Lancashire countryside convinced him that he, as an alien, was not welcome. People distrusted him because of his ragged clothing, and he had no money to purchase a new outfit, even though Captain Riga had advanced him three dollars, one month's pay, upon the ship's arrival in port.

Redburn's greatest disappointment came when he tried to use for his excursions an old guidebook he had brought from his father's library. The guidebook, almost half a century old, was no longer reliable, for streets and structures it mentioned were no longer in existence. Redburn felt that the whole world must have changed since his father's time; he saw in the unreliable guidebook a hint that as the years passed the habits and ideals of youth had to be charted anew. Each generation, he learned, had to make its own guidebook through the world.

While in Liverpool, Redburn met Harry Bolton, a young Englishman of good family but a prodigal son. Bolton said that he had shipped on two voyages to the East Indies; now he wanted to emigrate to America. With Redburn's help, Harry Bolton was enrolled as a "boy" on the *Highlander* for its return trip to New York. The two boys, traveling on Bolton's money, made a quick excursion to London before the ship sailed, but they were back in Liverpool within forty-eight hours. Redburn saw little of England beyond the port where he had arrived.

On the return trip to America, the ship carried a load of Irish emigrants. Redburn quickly felt sorry for them but, at the same time, superior to the miserable wretches crowded between the decks. The steerage passengers suffered a great deal during the voyage. Their quarters were cramped at best, and during heavy weather, they could not remain on deck. For cooking they had a stove placed on one of the hatches, one stove for five hundred people. Worst of all, an epidemic of fever broke out, killing many of the emigrants and one of the sailors.

Bolton had a miserable trip, and Redburn was sorry for him, too. The English boy had lied in saying he had been at sea before. Because he could not bear to go aloft in the rigging, he, in place of Redburn, became the butt of all the jokes and horseplay that the crew devised.

After the ship reached America, however, the voyage seemed to both Redburn and Bolton to have been a good one. They discovered that they really hated to leave the vessel which had been home to them for several weeks. Their nostalgia for the vessel, however, was soon dissipated by Captain Riga. The Captain dismissed Redburn without any pay because the lad had left his duties for one day while the ship was at Liverpool. The Captain even told Redburn that he owed the ship money for tools he had dropped into the sea. Bolton was given a dollar and a half for his work; the pittance made him so angry that he threw it back on the Captain's desk. The two boys then left the ship, glad to be back on land once more.

Critical Evaluation:

Redburn, like much of Herman Melville's work, was based on his own life. The background of the Redburn family is very similar to that of the Melville family after the father's death. The trip on a merchant vessel is clearly based on a similar round trip to Liverpool which Melville himself had made while still in his teens. The incident of the guidebook, for example, and the guidebook itself, are taken directly from Melville's own experience. Again, like other of Melville's books, *Redburn* is authentic in its treatment of sailors and sea life. Melville saw seafaring life through the eyes of a common sailor who learned his trade the hard way and wrote his novel from the seaman's point of view. Also, readers find in *Redburn* the beginnings of the philosophical elements that made *Moby Dick*, Melville's masterpiece, one of the great novels of all time.

The best way to read *Redburn* is as a prologue to *Moby Dick*. The story of the white whale is anticipated by the tragic themes of the earlier novel: its relentless depiction of misery and cruelty on board Captain Riga's ship, as well as in Liverpool port, develops a universal consciousness of human suffering, of the crushing effect of experience on innocence. F. O. Matthiessen called *Redburn* "the most moving of its author's books before *Moby Dick.*" Redburn is abused by the other sailors for openly showing his fright when a man with delirium tremens throws himself over the side; the isolation makes him dread lest he become "a sort of Ishmael." He does, of course, become just that (and seems strengthened by the transformation) in *Moby Dick*, which was published two years after *Redburn* appeared.

Not only is Redburn similar to Melville's narrator in *Moby Dick*, but also the whole novel is strewn with anticipations of the great novel's themes and characterizations. The mad sailor Jackson foreshadows Ahab: "He was a Cain afloat; branded on his yellow brow with some inscrutable curse; and going about corrupting and searing every heart that beat near him." The friendship between Harry Bolton and Redburn is curiously similar to that between the cannibal Queequeg and Ishmael: Harry is the prodigal son of a genteel family and Queequeg a royal personage; Harry introduces Redburn to London, Queequeg introduces Ishmael to the *Pequod*; Harry is finally killed when he is crushed between a ship and a whale, while Queequeg dives into the heart of a whale to rescue Tashtego.

All these similarities indicate the direction of Melville's art. He was moving from a fiction of initiation and adventure to one of philosophical depth. The symbolic action of Redburn is a cruder version of the same superstructure that supports Melville's masterpiece.

THE REDSKINS
Or, Indian and Injin, Being the Conclusion of the Littlepage Manuscripts

Type of work: Novel
Author: James Fenimore Cooper (1789–1851)
Type of plot: Historical romance
Time of plot: 1842
Locale: Upstate New York
First published: 1846

> *Principal characters:*
> HUGH ROGER LITTLEPAGE, the narrator and the heir to Ravensnest
> HUGH ROGER LITTLEPAGE, called Uncle Ro, his uncle
> MARY WARREN, a friend of the Littlepage family
> THE REVEREND MR. WARREN, her father
> SENECA NEWCOME, an antirenter
> OPPORTUNITY NEWCOME, his sister
> MRS. URSULA LITTLEPAGE, Hugh's grandmother
> PATT LITTLEPAGE, Hugh's sister
> JOSHUA BRIGHAM, another antirenter
> SUSQUESUS, an old Onondaga Indian living at Ravensnest
> JAAP (JAAF), an old black servant at Ravensnest
> HALL, a mechanic

The Story:

Hugh Littlepage and his Uncle Ro, the owner of Satanstoe and Lilacsbush, had been traveling through Europe and the East for five years, and they had not heard from their family in America for eighteen months. Upon arriving at their apartment in Paris, they received a bundle of letters and packages from the family. Among other things, the letters told them that the Littlepages' Ravensnest estate was in danger from tenants who had formed a terrorist party known as the "Injins." Since Hugh was now master of the estate and the rents were due in the fall, he and his uncle decided to return home early, even though they were not expected before autumn. They decided to travel under the name of Davidson in order to keep their return a secret.

Arriving in New York, they went to see the Littlepage agent, Jack Dunning, who informed them that the estate was threatened from two sides. On the one hand, there were the Ravensnest tenants led by the demagogue lawyer Seneca Newcome; on the other, there were the Albany politicians, who depended on the tenants for votes. The politicians had already raised the taxes on the estate, and the tenants were petitioning for a removal of the rents and a chance to buy the property at their own low prices. To speed up the process, the tenants had resorted to terrorizing the landlords with tar buckets, rifles, and calico hoods. To mask their greed for land, they claimed that their activities were carried on in the name of liberty, equality, and justice.

Because it would be dangerous to visit Ravensnest openly, Hugh and his uncle disguised themselves as a watch peddler and an organ-grinder, acquired broken German accents, and started for Ravensnest. On the boat to Albany, they met Seneca Newcome, who, thinking that they might make good Injins, invited them to Ravensnest. They got off at Albany and went from there to Troy. In that city, they made the acquaintance of the Reverend Mr. Warren and his daughter Mary. In his new role as an organ-grinder, Hugh invented a false history for himself and his uncle, a story accepted by the Warrens. Hugh soon learned that the Warrens lived at Ravensnest, where Mr. Warren was an Episcopal clergyman, and that Mary was a close friend of Hugh's sister Patt. Mary proved to be a charming, well-bred girl in striking contrast to Opportunity Newcome, who was also present at the inn. After Seneca Newcome joined the group, the conversation turned from Opportunity's pretentious learning to antirentism. Mary and her father argued gracefully and well in marked contrast to Seneca's and Opportunity's ill-constructed logic.

After a journey by train and carriages, Hugh and his uncle arrived in Ravensnest. Still in their new roles as peddler and organ-grinder, they traveled about the area to see for themselves how matters stood. At the tavern where they stopped overnight, they heard two men arguing over antirentism. While a lawyer took a mild stand against it, Hall, a mechanic, stood firmly against it and the greed behind it.

After a day's walk, the travelers arrived at Ravensnest manor. They decided, however, to retain their disguises and visit the two old men on the place, the Indian, Susquesus, and the black servant, Jaap. While they were at the hut of these faithful old retainers, Hugh's grandmother, Mrs. Ursula Littlepage, his sister Patt, Mary Warren, and his uncle's two wards, Henrietta Coldbrook and Anne Marston, rode up. None penetrated the disguises. After the others had gone, Susquesus revealed that he knew who Hugh and his uncle were, but he promised secrecy.

The two also visited the Miller farm where they learned that Tom Miller was hostile to antirentism and that a farmhand of his strongly favored it. The farmhand, Joshua Brigham, was extremely greedy, Miller pointed out. While they were at the Miller farm, the five women again rode up, and Uncle Ro showed them some watches. Mrs. Littlepage, who wished to buy a very expensive watch for Mary, told them that they could receive payment for the watch at the manor.

That evening, still dressed as peddlers, they went to the Littlepage home. Hugh, asked to play his flute, performed very well, but when the flute was passed around, his grandmother recognized it. When she drew her grandson aside he confessed to the deception. Soon he and his uncle were reunited with Mrs. Littlepage and Patt, who also promised secrecy. Later that evening, Hugh slept in the Miller house next to Joshua Brigham. Drawn into a discussion on antirentism, the farmhand, thinking Hugh shared his sentiments, told of his plans for robbing the Littlepages of their land. He also revealed that the Injins were to hold a meeting the next day.

On the following day, Hugh and his uncle rode in a wagon to the meeting at the town of Ravensnest. They were stopped on the way by a gang of hooded Injins who wanted to know their business. Interrupted by the appearance of Mr. Warren and Mary, the hoodlums disappeared into the bushes. The Littlepages, trying to pacify the hiding Injins by expressing mild antirentist sentiments, provoked Mr. Warren to argue with them, whereupon the Injins came out of hiding. The Injins then drove Uncle Ro and Mr. Warren to the meeting, leaving Hugh to drive Mary. On the way, he disclosed to her his true identity and motives.

At the meetinghouse, the imported lecturer began to rant about liberty, equality, and justice, accused the Littlepage family of standing for slavery, aristocracy, and injustice, and declared that they were no better than other folks. When he had finished, Hall, the mechanic, got up to speak. He said that the true aristocrats of America were demagogues and newspaper editors, that the Littlepages had as much right to their ways as he did to his, and that if the Littlepage property should be divided, that of the tenants should be too. His speech was interrupted by several Injins who came whooping into the meetinghouse. Most of the people fled, but Mary, Hall, and the Littlepages remained, comporting themselves with dignity.

The Injins ran wild, stealing calico and wagons from their own sympathizers. After seeing the Warrens off, Hugh and his uncle got into their wagon and rode toward the manor. They could see a party of armed men following them. On the way, they met some antirenters who had been deprived of their wagon. They walked alongside, still talking about the virtues of antirentism. Suddenly a group of real Indians appeared in the road. Surprised, Uncle Ro forgot his German accent, and the antirenters, realizing who their companions were, ran into the bushes. The Littlepages learned that the Indians had come from Washington and were seeking Susquesus, the old Onondaga who lived at Ravensnest manor. When the terrorist Injins appeared, the real Indians let out a war whoop, and the Injins ran. Two, Joshua Brigham and Seneca Newcome, were captured but were soon released. The Littlepages invited the Indians to stay in an old farmhouse at the manor. When Hugh and his uncle arrived home, everyone knew who they really were, and there was great rejoicing.

That night the Indians held a conference on the lawn in which Susquesus was the center of attention. The Indians spoke about the old days, the coming of the white man, and the different types of men with force, eloquence, and reserve. Hugh felt that they were as much gentlemen in their own way as he and Uncle Ro were in theirs.

Later that night Hugh, looking from his bedroom window, saw Opportunity Newcome riding toward the house. The ostensible purpose of her visit was to tell him that the Injins were trying to get a legal charge against him and that they were planning arson. He immediately warned Mary to keep an eye out for trouble and then went to tell the Indians to do the same.

A short time later, Mary signaled to him as he was patrolling the grounds. She said that two Injins were setting fire to the kitchen. Hugh rushed to the kitchen window and fired a shot into the air as the men came out. He clubbed one over the head and fell grappling with the other. Hugh might have been overpowered if Mary had not come to his aid. At that moment the Indians, attracted by the shot, arrived on the scene. The prisoners turned out to be Joshua Brigham and Seneca Newcome. A short time later, a few Injins set fire to a load of hay and then ran off, the Indians close at their heels.

Sunday morning was peaceful. The Littlepages went to church and sat in the canopied pew that the tenants resented. After church, following a brief meeting down the road, three antirenters presented Hugh with a petition to remove the canopy; he refused. On the way home, Opportunity coyly asked Hugh to release her brother, but he was noncommittal. After leaving her, he learned that the canopy had been torn down and placed over the Miller pigpen. On arriving home, he was told that Seneca had tried to escape arson charges by proposing to each of the four young women at the manor.

Later that day, a final ceremony was held in honor of Susquesus. The peace pipe was passed around, and Jaap, the companion of Susquesus, was invited to make a speech. He was interrupted, however, by the appearance of a large group of Injins. While the Littlepages waited to see what was intended, Opportunity rode up, drew Hugh into the house, and told him that these Injins were not afraid of Indians. She said that Hugh was standing over an earthquake if he did not release her brother. Hugh was called outside again when it was discovered that the Injins had surrounded the Warrens. Mr. Warren and Mary maintained their composure, however, and managed to go free. The Injins were duly warned about the ferocity of the Indians, and the ceremony was continued. The Indians told how the white men broke their laws for selfish reasons and hid their shame under calico hoods, while the red men upheld their laws even at great personal sacrifice. The Injins were humiliated by this speech. While they were listening, Jack Dunning, the business agent, arrived with the sheriff and a posse to drive off the Injins. By this time, however, the Injins had lost public support and were thoroughly disgraced. Taking advantage of the confusion, Opportunity released her brother and Joshua Brigham, and the two were never seen in that part of the country again. The Supreme Court upheld the rights of the landlords, and the antirent wars ended.

Uncle Ro gave a good portion of his estate to Mary when she and Hugh were married. Hugh heard that Opportunity Newcome intended to sue him for breach of promise, but nothing ever came of that threat.

Critical Evaluation:

The Redskins: Or, Indian and Injin is the final novel in James Fenimore Cooper's Littlepage series. Like many of his novels, this work deals with the conflict between a cultured upper class of high principles and an uncultured middle class with no principles except those of self-interest. Cooper's characters are drawn in keeping with their sympathies, according to whether they sympathize with the rights of the landowning Littlepage family or with the grasping Newcome family. Cooper stacks the cards in favor of the landowners and makes the conflict one between the patroons and the poltroons. He tends to caricature his villains and to treat them with satire and irony. In spite of the rather restricted interest of the antirent controversy around which *The Redskins* centers, the novel has suspense, action, romance, villainy, conflict, and some sharp, if limited, insights into the structure of American society. Cooper clearly saw the perpetual struggle for power within America, and he described it with compelling logic. The reader will discern Cooper's belief that Jacksonian democracy had degenerated into an ill-conceived, leveling movement which threatened the genteel American ethic in the pre-Civil War period. Hugh Littlepage—gentleman, world traveler, and landowner—represented the ideal America which Cooper wanted to preserve from the opportunistic and materialistic self-interests of the middle class represented by Seneca Newcome.

The Redskins begins with an indirect approbation of the American leisure class and their values. The reader quickly learns that the Littlepage family had become wealthy in the course of two generations and were spending much of their leisure abroad. Their apartment in Paris and their recent return from faraway places set the tone for the Littlepages' adventurous spirit and cosmopolitan taste. At the same time, the news of trouble at Ravensnest serves as a means to depict Hugh and his Uncle Ro as representative American landowners who willingly accept their responsibilities as paternal but benevolent superiors.

While Hugh and his Uncle Ro are members of the landed class, however, they can also identify with the lesser classes as illustrated by the disguises they adopt when they return to New York to investigate Ravensnest's troubles. Incognito as immigrant artisans, the two members of Cooper's "natural" aristocracy learn about the real feelings, ideals, and fears of such individuals as: the Reverend Mr. Warren and his daughter, Mary, and the true nature of the antirenter, Seneca Newcome, and his crass sister, Opportunity Newcome.

Cooper's message is clear. Jacksonian democracy would work if America were a nation of Warrens who are basically honest, hardworking, and sensible. In reality, however, America also consisted of men like Newcome, who, under the guise of justice and reform, would tear down the American Republic and its noble principles and values. In *The Redskins*, these principles and values triumph at the ceremony where wise old Susquesus is reunited with the members of his tribe. Jaap, Susquesus' black companion, reveals the story behind the old prairie Indian's exile. This development illustrates Cooper's ideal values of benevolent paternalism and noble obligations as the antirenter movement dissipates by the moral force of Jaap's tale—and the physical presence of Susquesus' braves.

THE REIVERS
A Reminiscence

Type of work: Novel
Author: William Faulkner (1897–1962)
Type of plot: Psychological realism
Time of plot: May, 1905
Locale: Yoknapatawpha County, Mississippi, and Memphis and Parsham, Tennessee
First published: 1962

Principal characters:

LUCIUS PRIEST, the eleven-year-old narrator

BOON HOGGANBECK, a part-Chickasaw Indian and the poorest shot in the county

NED WILLIAM MCCASLIN, the Priests' coachman and a black member of the McCaslin and Priest families

LUCIUS QUINTUS PRIEST (BOSS), young Lucius' grandfather, a Jefferson banker, and owner of the stolen Winton Flyer

MISS SARAH, his wife

MAURY PRIEST, his son and Lucius' father

MISS ALISON, Maury Priest's wife

MISS REBA RIVERS, the proprietress of a Memphis brothel

EVERBE (MISS CORRIE) CORINTHIA, one of Miss Reba's girls and beloved of Boon Hogganbeck

MR. BINFORD, Miss Reba's landlord and protector

MINNIE, Miss Reba's maid

OTIS, Miss Corrie's delinquent nephew from Arkansas

SAM CALDWELL, a railroad brakeman and Boon's rival, who aids in transporting the stolen racehorse

UNCLE PARSHAM HOOD, a dignified old black man who befriends young Lucius Priest

LYCURGUS BRIGGINS, his grandson

BUTCH LOVEMAIDEN, a brutal deputy sheriff

MCWILLIE, the rider of Acheron

COLONEL LINSCOMB, the owner of Acheron

MR. VAN TOSCH, the owner of Coppermine, the stolen racehorse renamed Lightning

BOBO BEAUCHAMP, Mr. van Tosch's stableboy and Ned William McCaslin's cousin

DELPHINE, Ned's wife and the Priests' cook

Subtitled "A Reminiscence," *The Reivers* begins on a note of action recalled in memory, and about a fourth of the way through the novel (posthumously awarded the 1963 Pulitzer Prize for Fiction) readers come upon one of William Faulkner's most engaging yarns.

In 1905, eleven-year-old Lucius Priest, Boon Hogganbeck—a tough, faithful, but completely unpredictable and unreliable part-Chickasaw Indian mad about machinery—and freeloading Ned William McCaslin, the Priests' black coachman and handyman, are on their way to Memphis in the Winton Flyer owned by young Lucius' grandfather and "borrowed" for the excursion without the owner's permission or knowledge. Because of the condition of the roads, the truants are forced to make an overnight stop at Miss Ballenbaugh's, a small country store with a loft above it containing shuck mattresses for the convenience of fishermen and fox or coon hunters. The next morning, after one of the breakfasts for which Miss Ballenbaugh is famous, they start out early and soon reach Hell Creek bottom, the deepest, miriest mudhole in all Mississippi. There is no way around it: started in one direction, the travelers would end up in Alabama; head in the other, and they would fall into the Mississippi. Naturally, the automobile becomes mired and remains stuck in spite of their labors with shovel, barbed wire, block and tackle, and piled branches. Meanwhile on the gallery of a paintless cabin nearby, his two mules already harnessed in plow gear, a barefooted redneck watches and waits. This backwoods opportunist remarks that mud is one of the best crops in the region when the three give up in exasperation and he appears to pull the car out of the slough. Then follows some stiff bargaining. Boon claims that six dollars is too much for the job, all the more so because one of his passengers is a boy and the other is black. The man's only answer is that his mules are color-blind.

This is the tall-story idiom and spirit of Huck Finn brought forward in time, but its presence in *The Reivers* is not so much a matter of imitation as of a common source. For there is a sense in which Faulkner stands at the end of a literary tradition rather than, as many of his admirers claim, at the beginning of a new one. Through all of his writing runs a strain of broad folk humor and comic invention going back through Mark Twain to A. B. Longstreet's *Georgia Scenes* and George W. Harris' *Sut Lovingood's Yarns*, and beyond them to the Davy Crockett almanacs and the anonymous masters of oral anecdote who flourished in the old Southwest. The early American was by nature a storyteller. The realities of frontier life and his own hard comic sense created a literature of tall men and tall deeds repeated in the trading post, the groggery, the rafters' camp, wherever men met on the edge of the wilderness. These stories, shaped by the common experience and imagination, had a geography, a mythology, and a lingo of their own. Some were streaked with ballad sentiment. Others guffawed with bawdy humor; but mostly these tales were comic elaborations of character, of fantastic misadventures in which the frontiersman dramatized himself with shrewd appraisal and salty enjoyment. Through them goes a raggle-taggle procession of hunters, peddlers, horse traders, horse thieves, eagle orators, prophets, backwoods swains, land speculators, settlers—a picture of the country and the times.

Faulkner's Yoknapatawpha County lies, after all, in the same geographical belt with the Mississippi River and the Natchez Trace, and these are regions of history, folklore, and fantasy revealed in tall-story humor. This humor came into Faulkner's fiction as early as *Mosquitoes*, in the account of Old Hickory's descendant who tried raising sheep in the Louisiana swamps and eventually became so much at home in the water that he turned into a shark. It contributes to effects of grotesque outrage and exaggeration in *As I Lay Dying*, gives *Light in August* a warming pastoral glow, adds three episodes of pure comedy to *The Hamlet*, and provides illuminating comment on the rise and fall of Flem Snopes. Faulkner's habit in the past, however, was to subordinate his racier effects to the more serious concerns of man's mortality and the disorder of his moral universe. Not until he wrote *The Reivers* did he give free play to his talent for comedy of character and situation and, like Mark Twain in *The Adventures of Huckleberry Finn*, make it the master bias of structure and theme.

Other parallels with Twain's novel are not lacking. One is the unmistakable flavor of a style derived from the drawled tones of reminiscence. If readers turn back to the nineteenth chapter of *The Adventures of Huckleberry Finn* we see how this style was being shaped to reveal habits of thought and feeling in art, a truly colloquial style, marvelously tuned in pulse and improvisation, with the incorrectness of folk speech in its idiom as Lucius Priest tells his story to his grandson. In *The Reivers*, it is made to support both a burden of feeling within a boy's range of response and an old man's accumulation of a lifetime's reflections; and it can record sensory impressions with poetic finality.

Like *The Adventures of Huckleberry Finn*, too, *The Reivers* is a story of initiation, of innocence corrupted and evil exorcised. Both show the world through the eyes of childhood, an effective device when employed as a freshener of experience or a corrective of judgment, but between the two novels there is this important difference: Huck is protected by the earthy nonchalance of his own native shrewdness and resourcefulness from the contamination of the shore. Young Lucius Priest lives by the code of his class, the code of a gentleman, and he brings its values to the bordello, and to the racetrack. The true test is not innocence itself but what lies behind the mask of innocence. Grandfather Priest claims that when adults speak of childish innocence, they really mean ignorance. Actually, children are neither, in his opinion, for an eleven-year-old can envision any crime. If he possesses innocence, it is probably lack of appetite, just as his ignorance may be a lack of opportunity or ability.

So young Lucius Priest had only the gentleman's code to protect him when his grandfather, the president of a Jefferson bank and the owner of the second automobile ever seen in the county, goes to Louisiana to attend a funeral, and Boon Hogganbeck tempts the boy with a proposal that they drive the Winton Flyer to Memphis during its owner's absence. Lucius proves vulnerable to Boon's proposal, and after considerable conniving, they set out. On the way, they discover Ned William McCaslin hidden under a tarpaulin on the backseat. Having passed Hell Creek bottom, they arrive in Memphis, but instead of going to the Gayoso Hotel, as Lucius expected (the McCaslins and Priests always stayed at the Gayoso because a distant member of the family had in Civil War times galloped into the lobby in an effort to capture a Yankee general), Boon drives his passengers to Miss Reba's house on Catalpa Street. (This is the same Miss Reba, grown older, who figures in *Sanctuary*.) Boon had his reasons; Miss Corrie, one of Miss Reba's girls, shares with the Winton Flyer the affections of his crude but open and innocent heart. That night, Ned, a master of indirection and a reckless gambling man, trades the stolen automobile for a stolen racehorse never known to run any better than second. Before the three can return to Jefferson, it is necessary for young Lucius to turn jockey and win a race against a better horse, Colonel Linscomb's Acheron. Meanwhile, he has fought with Otis, the vicious nephew who slurred Miss Corrie, and his chivalric gesture restores her self-respect. Boon and Ned become involved in difficulties with the law as represented by Butch Lovemaiden, a corrupt deputy sheriff; it is discovered that Otis has stolen the gold tooth prized by Minnie, Miss Reba's maid; and Boon finds, and fights, rivals for Miss Corrie's charms. As a result of all this, Lucius, forced to assume a gentleman's responsibilities of courage and conduct, has lost the innocence of childhood before his grandfather appears to set matters straight. At times, the boy is close to despair, but he realizes that he has come too far, that to turn back now would not be homesickness but shame.

Lucius survives his ordeal, but at considerable cost to his conscience and peace of mind. Grandfather Priest has the final word on his escapade. When the boy asks how he can forget his folly and guilt, his grandfather tells him that he cannot because nothing in life is ever forgotten or lost. Lucius wants to know what he can do. His grandfather says that he must live with it. To the weeping boy's protests, he replies that a gentleman can live through anything because he must always accept the responsibility of his actions and the weight of their consequences. Grandfather Priest ends by telling Lucius to go wash his face; a gentleman may cry, but he washes his face afterward.

From these examples, it will be seen that, under its surface of fantastic invention and tall-story humor, *The Reivers* is another moral fable in the Faulknerian manner. Yet it is quite different in effect from the earlier, darker studies of manners and morals. In tragedy, and Faulkner was a great tragic artist, the soul of man stands naked before God, and He is not mocked. In comedy, it is not the possible in man that is revealed but the probable in conduct or belief. Thus, man in comedy is viewed in relation to some aspect of his society. In *The Reivers*—the title means plunderers or freebooters—a master of comedy was at work testing young Lucius Priest by the behavior of a gentleman in a world of evasion and deceit where it is easier to run from one's responsibilities than to stand up and face them.

In setting these matters straight, the triumph of the novel is in the manner of the telling. *The Reivers* is a story about a boy, but it is told by a man grown old enough and wise enough through the years of accumulated experience to look back on his adventure, relish it in all its qualities of adventure and fantasy and, at the same time, pass judgment on it. This judgment is never harsh. Lucius Priest, telling the story to *his* grandson, is revealed as a person of tolerance and understanding of much that is so deeply and irrevocably ingrained in the eternal condition of man, and his point of view gives the novel added depth and dimension.

Put beside the novels of his great period, *The Reivers* is minor Faulkner. At the same time, it is a good yarn in the tall-story tradition, skillfully told, comic in effect, shrewd in observation on manners, morals, politics, and the general cussedness and downright foolishness of mankind. More to the point, it broadens even if it does not deepen the reader's knowledge of Faulkner's legendary Mississippi county.

REMEMBRANCE ROCK

Type of work: Novel
Author: Carl Sandburg (1878–1967)
Type of plot: Historical chronicle
Time of plot: 1607–1945
Locale: England and America
First published: 1948

Principal characters:

ORVILLE BRAND WINDOM, former Justice of the United
 States Supreme Court
OLIVER BALL WINDROW, a woodcarver and philosopher
MARY WINDLING, a young Puritan
JOHN SPONG, her husband
REMEMBER SPONG, their daughter
ORTON WINGATE, a sojourner in Plymouth
PETER LADD, a seaman and gambler
RESOLVED WAYFARE, a follower of Roger Williams
ORDWAY WINSHORE, a Philadelphia printer
ROBERT WINSHORE, his older son
JOHN LOCKE WINSHORE, his younger son
MARINTHA (MIM) WILMING, a dressmaker's assistant
OATES ELWOOD, a friend of Robert and Locke
ANN, his sister and Locke's wife
OMRI WINWOLD, a former gambler
JOEL WIMBLER, an abolitionist
BROOKSANY, his wife
MILLICENT (MIBS), their daughter
RODNEY WAYMAN, Mib's husband and a Confederate
 officer

The Stories:

The rock stood in the cedar-shaded garden of former Supreme Court
Justice Orville Brand Windom, a giant boulder about which he had scattered
earth from Plymouth, Valley Forge, Gettysburg, the Argonne. The justice
was old, with a deep and brooding concern for the American land, its history,
its people. He spoke some of his ideas to the world in a radio broadcast he
made in 1944. He recorded others in three chronicles of the living past that
his grandson, Captain Raymond Windom, veteran of Okinawa, found in a
locked box after the old man's death. These tales, like the antique bronze

plaque inscribed with Roger Bacon's Four Stumbling Blocks to Truth, were Justice Windom's legacy of wisdom and love to his grandson, his grandson's wife, and their son, Joseph Stilwell Windom.

In the first, red-haired Oliver Ball Windrow, the woodcarver, had on one side of his face the look of a poet and dreamer and, on the other, a countenance of wrath and storm. A seeker and questioner, he loved Mary Windling, a girl only half his age and a member of the Separatist congregation that worshipped secretly at Scrooby, and for her, he made a small plaque of bronze, on which he inscribed Roger Bacon's Four Stumbling Blocks to Truth, to wear on a silver cord around her neck.

Mary liked his sudden whims and strange humors, but in the end, she married a young workman named John Spong. This happened in 1608, just before the Scrooby congregation escaped to Holland. For twelve years, Mary Spong and her husband lived in Leyden. Infrequent news came from England. Windrow had wed Matilda Bracken, the devoted mute who kept his house. Then, in 1620, he and his two daughters died of smallpox. Mary's sadness for her friend was lessened by promises and fears surrounding plans of the Puritans to try their fortunes in the new world.

The Spongs and their daughter Remember were passengers aboard the *Mayflower* when it sailed. Little Remember had only one memory of Plymouth. One day, while she was playing on the wharf, some boys began to torment her. Another boy came with an ax handle and beat them off. She forgot to ask his name.

Mary Spong, dying during that first terrible winter in the wilderness, gave her daughter the tarnished keepsake Windrow had made years before. Remember grew up in Plymouth, a cluster of houses between forest and sea, and those gaunt years of hardship and toil helped to shape her strong body, her resolute will, and her sober decorum that hid deep passions. Her father grew grim and silent as time passed. He disliked Orton Wingate, a sojourner in Plymouth, a man whose face showed peace and calm on one side, turmoil on the other. Wingate was Remember's friend, however, and came to sit with her from time to time. She knew without his saying that she could have had him for her husband. Restless and uncertain of her own mind, she waited.

Sometimes she rebelled against the harsh Puritan laws, as when she concealed Hode Latch, a convicted drunkard for whom constables were searching, and then she was afraid that she was damned. Perhaps Peter Ladd sensed that wild streak in her when he came courting. He was a young seaman who drifted into Plymouth, steadied himself for a while, and then fell once more into dissolute ways. When Remember refused him, he went away to make his fortune in the slave trade. Two years later, he was drowned in a wreck off the Virginia capes.

Roger Williams, a free-thinking preacher, lived in Plymouth for a time. Several years later, he was shaking the colonies with his liberal beliefs and teachings. A new age was beginning when Williams, a fugitive, built his own town beside Narragansett Bay, but Remember Spong could not know how far-reaching were to be his challenges to usages of authority and custom. She feared him most because he revealed the rebel in herself. For that reason, she was of two minds about Resolved Wayfare, a newcomer to the colony in 1638. Wayfare had crossed the ocean to learn for himself the meaning of Roger Williams' message. He was also the boy, grown to manhood, who had defended Remember on the Plymouth wharf.

After he saved John Spong's life during a blizzard, Remember nursed the young man back to health. During that time, there was a battle of wills between them. He wanted her to go with him to Providence, but she, like her father, held that the teachings of Roger Williams were of Satan. Although Wingate's wisdom and the cruel lashing of an unmarried mother finally convinced her of the folly and blindness of custom, she could not quite make up her mind to go with Wayfare on his journey. Yet she walked with him some distance into the forest, and before they parted, she gave him the bronze keepsake she had from her mother. Knowing that they would meet again, they vowed to be true as long as grass would grow or water flow. That was the solemn promise between them.

The second tale begins in March, 1775. Ordway Winshore, master printer, left Philadelphia to visit his sons in New York and Boston. Below rusty hair, his face on one side promised peace, on the other wrath and doom—a face half serious, half comic, making him a man easy to confide in. Among his fellow travelers were two young British lieutenants, Francis and George Frame. During a tavern halt, Francis Frame broke his hand by striking a blacksmith who had cursed King George. The Philadelphia printer felt that the war was beginning.

Winshore spent two days in New York with Locke, his younger son, a typesetter for Henry Tozzer, printer of Independence leaflets. Locke reported that his brother Robert was deep in the activities of Massachusetts patriots. He also hinted at Robert's romance with a dressmaker's assistant.

Another passenger in the coach to Boston was Marintha Wilming, to whom George Frame paid marked attention. Winshore liked her, not knowing, however, that she was the girl his older son loved.

Not far from Boston, Robert Winshore helped some Sons of Liberty to tar and feather Hobart Reggs, a prosperous Tory who had informed on a British deserter. Sapphira, Reggs's daughter, accidentally saw his face during the tarring.

Boston, Winshore found, was a seething, sullen city filled with British troops, Tories, Rebels, and neutrals. At the dress shop where Marintha Wilming worked, there was much talk of Ann Elwood, an innocent young girl who had been tricked into a false marriage by a Grenadier sergeant. Winshore met Marintha (Mim) again in Robert's company and visited the house where she lived with her aunt. He also encountered Isaiah Thomas, printer of the *Massachusetts Spy* and Robert's employer, and in Henry Knox's bookstore, he met Mary Burton, whom he, a widower, was to marry a short time later. One day, at the dress shop, Sapphira Reggs recognized Robert. When Lieutenant George Frame attempted to arrest him at the home of Mim's aunt, Robert escaped. Fleeing, he lost the old bronze plaque that had come to him from a great-granduncle and that he wore on a chain under his shirt.

Robert was with the Minutemen when the British marched on Lexington. Darius, Mim's brother, was killed in the fighting, and Lieutenant George Frame was crippled for life. Robert ventured into Boston to tell Mim of her brother's death, but the girl, distracted by his news and George Frame's injuries, declared that she wanted to forget him and his rebel violence.

Locke became a military courier. In Philadelphia, Winshore and his new wife read Paine's *Common Sense*. Robert and Oates Elwood, Ann's brother, marched with Benedict Arnold toward Quebec until they became ill with fever and were forced to turn back. The British evacuated Boston. Robert was invalided home. Locke and Elwood, carrying messages from General Greene to General Washington, spent a night with the Winshores in Philadelphia. Robert was there, a messenger at the Continental Congress. There was no time for Locke to tell his family that he had secretly married Ann Elwood. The next night, while riding to New York, Locke was shot by British scouts. Mim Wilming, working in a Philadelphia dress shop, delivered the shroud for his burial. Meeting Robert for the first time since the fighting at Lexington, she told him that she believed at last in the patriots' cause.

The years moved ahead with dates and names—July 4, 1776, and the Unanimous Declaration, Christmas night and Trenton, Valley Forge. Near Morristown, Ann Winshore gave birth to a son named after his dead father. Mim, nursing the sick and wounded at Bethlehem, became ill with putrid fever. Ordway Winshore drove through the British lines in Quaker clothes to take her back to his house and nurse her there. When word came that Robert had died at Valley Forge, she showed his father the plaque she had found after Robert's flight from arrest. Winshore told her it was hers to keep.

Summer came, and with it the British left Philadelphia. The Winshores hung out the flag which had been hidden under Mim's mattress during her illness. One day, Oates Elwood arrived with his sister and her baby. Mim told Winshore that his grandson, born in 1777, the Year of the Three Gallows, would see many dawns. He was the future.

The third tale revolves around Omri Winwold, who had been many things—tavern chore-boy, mill worker, lawyer's clerk, gambler. He was a man of easy manners but deep reserves, his brick-dust beard covering a face peacefully calm on one side, seamed with turmoil on the other. The person who understood him best was a distant cousin, Brooksany Wimbler, whose husband Joel was an abolitionist harness-maker in Arpa, New York.

For years Omri had dreamed of a farm in Illinois, and in 1836 he headed west by wagon with his wife Bee and their infant son, Andrew Marvel. Near Arpa, where he stopped to say good-bye to the Wimblers, he deserted his sluttish wife, taking the child with him, after she had behaved shamelessly with a bachelor. The Wimblers knew nothing of his plans, but they believed that he had continued his journey west.

All America seemed to move westward by highway and canal. Millicent Wimbler was a baby in arms when her parents went with a large party of neighbors to found the antislavery community of New Era, Illinois. Her childish nickname, Mibs, stuck, even after she grew into a beautiful young woman with a will of her own. She had two admirers. One was Hornsby Meadows, instructor at New Era College and a crusading Abolitionist. The other was Danny Hilton, a farmer and contractor. She went to church and to antislavery lectures with Hornsby, to dances and the Lincoln-Douglas debate in nearby Galesburg with Danny, but she would have neither. Hornsby finally married Fidelia Englehart, a village teacher. Danny went to Chicago. Then, in 1859, Rodney Wayman and his friend Nack Doss rode into New Era. Wayman was a cattle buyer from Atlas, Illinois. A Southerner, he had been a banjo player in a traveling minstrel show, a miner in California. Mibs married him without her parents' consent two weeks later.

In Pike County, meanwhile, Omri Winwold had prospered. Taking a gambler's chance on a charge of bigamy, he had married Sarah Prindle, a neighbor's daughter. After her death, he married her sister, Anne Moore, a widow. By 1857, his roomy farmhouse had eight children, from Andrew Marvel, who was twenty-two, to Robert, who was seven—a good muster, Omri felt, after his unsettled early years. In 1852, during a business trip to St. Louis, he ran into Bee again and also met her husband, Henry Flack. The husband never knew the truth about Omri and Bee. After Bee ran away to San Francisco and Anne Winwold died, Omri and Flack, both lonely, became close friends. When Rodney Wayman brought his bride home to Atlas, and Mibs and Omri had established their kinship, letters passed once more between Omri and Brooksany.

Storm clouds were gathering. John Brown raided Harper's Ferry. Clayborn Joel Wayman was born a few months before Lincoln was elected. Rodney was buying horses in Texas with Nack Doss when the war began. Both became captains in the Confederate Army. Doss was killed in a raid in Mississippi. Captured at Chickamauga, Rod was sent to the military prison at Camp Morton. Omri's boys who were old enough joined up. Rodney Wayman, Junior, was born that first year of the war, but his father never had word of him; he had escaped from Camp Morton and rejoined the troops. Joel Wimbler, commissioned in the commissary service, was furloughed home and lay dying in New Era. Brooksany died a few days after her husband. Going though their things, Mibs found in a trunk an ancient bronze plaque with

Roger Bacon's Four Stumbling Blocks to Truth inscribed on it in antique script. She hung the keepsake around her neck, under her dress.

At Fredericksburg, Rod was again wounded and taken prisoner. While he lay in a barn hospital, Colonel Hornsby Meadows died on the floor next to him. Rod lived in the filth and stench of Johnson's Island until Mibs came to get him through a prisoner exchange. One night, they went to have supper with Omri, and Rod lost some of his deep bitterness when he saw the younger Winwolds maimed and crippled in the war. Andrew Marvel, brevetted brigadier general, lacked an arm. Milton was paralyzed by a bullet in his spine. Holliday, starved in a prison camp, was dead.

The fighting ended, but deeper grief hung over the land when Lincoln's body was brought back to Springfield for burial. Mibs felt, however, that their days of storm and travail were almost over. Across the wide land, the arch of union, strength, and love still held firm.

Captain Raymond Windom and his wife knew that they, too, had seen years of crisis and destiny. To them it seemed only fitting that other earths, symbols of hardship and storm and stars coming after the storm, should be buried at the base of Remembrance Rock—gravel from Anzio, sand from Utah Beach in Normandy, black volcanic ash from Okinawa.

Critical Evaluation:

Remembrance Rock, a first novel published when its writer was seventy, is a work almost as sprawling and formless as the land it celebrates. The pattern is simple: three stories dealing with the settling of Plymouth, the American Revolution, and the Civil War, set between a prologue and an epilogue which have for background Washington in the years of World War II. Imperfect as a novel, the book is nevertheless a great American document, presenting in human terms and in the idiom of Carl Sandburg's "swift and furious people" the growth of the American Dream through more than three centuries of our national history. *Remembrance Rock* has been called a saga, a chronicle, a sermon, a collection of Chaucerian tales, a miscellany on folk themes; and it is all of these. By means of fable, paean, symbol, and style that ranges from the grave, proud language of Bunyan and Defoe to the downright slangy and boisterous, Sandburg has projected a poet historian's testament of American life. The result is a narrative as passionate and affirmative as the tough and mystic eloquence of his poetry. Unity of theme is provided by characters recurring in the major episodes and by symbolic reappearances of a bronze plaque bearing an inscription of Roger Bacon's Four Stumbling Blocks to Truth. First, the influence of fragile or unworthy authority; second, custom; third, the imperfection of undisciplined senses; and fourth, concealment of ignorance by ostentation of seeming wisdom.

Sandburg devoted five years to writing the book, his only novel. With his accustomed diligence, he researched the general social background of the

Pilgrims, both in England and America; of the Revolutionary period from
1775–1777; and of the pre-Civil War era up to the death of Lincoln, roughly
1836–1865. Sandburg's research, however, was not intended to treat actual
history, as he does in the Lincoln biographies; instead, he was concerned with
the spiritual heritage of the people. To be sure, real historical figures and
events crowd the pages of the novel; yet the major characters are clearly of
heroic proportions—the creations of myth, not fact. To provide a "frame"
for his narrative, Sandburg uses Justice Windom, a contemporary of the
1940's, as his mouthpiece for his own ideas. Thus, he examines four selective
but crucial moments in the history of the nation to answer four significant
questions: How did America come to be what it was in 1948? When and
where did it begin and develop? What is the "mysterious variable" that in
moments seems to be a constant in the moral history of the people? And
what is the "ever shifting and hazardous" principle that underlies the American Dream?

To answer these questions, Sandburg approaches American history as myth,
symbol, and unified design. In each of the four narratives (really brief novels
in themselves), he traces the lives of patriots who have inherited a 1607
medallion engraved with Roger Bacon's Four Stumbling Blocks to Truth.
Each Stumbling Block—or "Cause of Error"—corresponds to an adventure
of the narrative; the moral lesson of the history parallels that of Bacon's
warnings. For example, the Puritans in England oppose religious persecution,
thereby avoiding the first error—"the influence of fragile or unworthy authority." In America, however, the Puritans practice their own form of intolerance.
They fall prey to the second error, "custom." Fortunately, with the onset of
the Revolutionary War, old customs are swept aside as the patriots establish
a more humanistic morality. During the Civil War, patriots must overcome
the third error, that of "the imperfection of undisciplined senses." For the
fourth historical period, Sandburg's own, the patriot Justice Windom must
avoid the error of "concealment of ignorance by ostentation of seeming wisdom." In effect, the poet satirizes his own "ostentation" in creating the bom-
bastic rhetoric spoken by Windom. Thus, with gentle irony Sandburg concludes
his panoramic history: even he, the author patriot, has a Stumbling Block to
overcome.

In addition to Roger Bacon's Four Stumbling Blocks to Truth, Sandburg
uses other unifying devices in the novel. The similarity of the names of his
protagonists—Windom, Windling, Wingate, Winshore, Winwold—serves to
remind the reader both of the continuity and variety that marks the American
heritage. Windom (win-*doom*, the old word for *judgment*) is an appropriate
name for the former Supreme Court Justice; just as Orton Wingate is a "gate"
to the future, Ordway Winshore provides a shore-mooring for freedom, and
Omri Winwold (*wold* as *forest*) helps to clear the wilderness and bring civilization to mid-America. Sandburg's women characters are alike in their

patriotic devotion to the land; they, too, form a pattern of heroism. In each section of the novel, a woman treasures the Roger Bacon medallion. Typically, the author develops his stories around the relationship between a young girl (representing the future) and an older man (the past), or between the girl and her fiancé or husband (the present). The characters, then, are treated both realistically and symbolically, as protagonists in stories and as heroic figures of a national myth. Because of the symbolic patterns of the novel, its ideas cannot be appreciated fully from the perspective of a conventional work of either fiction or chronicle. In spite of its sentimentality, repetitiousness, and grandiloquence, *Remembrance Rock* attempts to commemorate, in a form approaching folk poetry, the very spirit of the nation.

REQUIEM FOR A NUN

Type of work: Novel-play
Author: William Faulkner (1897–1962)
Type of plot: Psychological melodrama
Time of plot: 1938
Locale: Jefferson, Yoknapatawpha County, Mississippi
First published: 1951

>   *Principal characters:*
>   TEMPLE DRAKE STEVENS, a woman in her late twenties
>   NANCY MANNIGOE, a black woman, about thirty,
>   condemned to die for murder
>   GOWAN STEVENS, Temple's husband
>   GAVIN STEVENS, a lawyer and Gowan's first cousin
>   THE GOVERNOR OF MISSISSIPPI
>   POPEYE (VITELLI), a psychopathic gangster, now dead
>   ALABAMA RED, Temple's lover eight years before
>   PETE, Red's brother and Temple's recent lover

Requiem for a Nun takes up the story of *Sanctuary* eight years after Temple Drake's "imprisonment" in a Memphis house of prostitution. The epic depiction of the past as an act of community self-discovery and the individual's anguished scrutiny of his personal history, in the context of the communal past, as an act of self-knowledge are central themes in William Faulkner's work. The obvious structure of this book graphically illustrates the dynamic interaction of these themes: In the long prose introductions to each of the three acts, Faulkner, as omniscient storyteller, gives readers the entire history of Yoknapatawpha County, using the method of scene and panorama. Against the reader's understanding of the community's past, Temple Drake, in the drama sections, acts out the climax of her personal story. Many of the major characters in Faulkner's works figure in the prose sections; their individual dramas are presented in other novels and stories.

In the prose sections, Temple's story is not mentioned, though it is symbolically predetermined; in the play sections, the town's history is not mentioned, though the configuration of Temple's drama is symbolic of the communal experience. The scenes in Temple's house (itself steeped in history) occur in the context of public institutions: courthouse, capitol building, jail. Thus, in the structure and in other aspects of the book as well, Faulkner uses the method of juxtaposition. His consistent use of repetition and of very long, complex, now contorted, now eloquent sentences and paragraphs in the prose sections and in Temple's speeches about her past suggests the labyrinthine course of a journey into the enigmatic past, with its elements of tragedy, folksy, hyperbolic humor, and banality.

Faulkner transcends certain conventions of the dramatic form. The play-wright must provide a scene description. Shakespeare does this in one line, Faulkner in twenty-six pages; but the importance of setting in Faulkner's works was never more dramatically illustrated. In bad plays, the lighting of cigarettes and the making of drinks are action-clichés, but in this book, such activity suggests the triviality of present physical action in contrast to the heroic action of the past and to Temple's spiritual anguish. There is more action and a sense of pace in Faulkner's use of rhetoric in the prose sections than there is theatrical action and pace in the play sections. The community history is presented in metaphors derived from the drama; for example, Faulk-ner explicitly presents the courthouse, then the capitol, then the jail as stages for the drama of the past and the consequent drama of the present. The lack of symmetry in the relation of the book's parts, in terms of length, is delib-erate, just as the account of the county's history is speeded up the nearer it approaches the present. Temple's story is ended quickly after her disclosure of her past; the last act of the play is twelve pages short. Faulkner forces the reader to attend to those incongruities of form, expecting a more profound understanding of content.

In act 1, "The Courthouse (A Name for the City)," Faulkner relates the history of the settlers, the creation of Jefferson simultaneously with the build-ing of the courthouse and the jail, the origin of which is comic, though its history is heroic. In this courthouse, in the fall of 1938, Nancy Mannigoe, town drunk, occasional prostitute, and dope fiend, is sentenced to hang in March for smothering Temple's six-month-old baby. As the courthouse is symbolic of the settlers' aspirations, Temple's actual sin is symbolic of the community's decline; and as the dispossession of the Indian and the enslave-ment of the black are related in the prose, the present situation of the black is dramatized in Nancy's predicament. In jail, years before, she had tried to hang herself in order to leave the white man's world, in which the black does the dirty work (this incident is related in "That Evening Sun"); now she is to be hanged for trying to save Temple's baby from a world made unfit for the innocent by Temple's sin.

In "The Golden Dome (Beginning Was the Word)," Faulkner tells of the creation of the state capitol, named after Andrew Jackson; in the Governor's office, Temple tells her personal story. Nancy's lawyer, county attorney Gavin Stevens, takes Temple to the Governor on the pretext that her testimony may save Nancy. To Gavin, however, death is not the problem; legally, Nancy is already dead, for he knows the Governor will not save her; thus, the law is satisfied, but truth and love are not, and therein lies the injustice.

Nancy's soul is alive; Temple's is dead. Gavin wants to save Temple's soul by persuading her to tell the truth, to undergo the purification of suffering-by-confession that must precede redemption. Other Faulkner characters suffer through telling, but Temple is the major character in his work who confesses to her fellow man. Stevens arranges for Gowan, Temple's husband, to hear that part of her story which he does not yet know—her recent affair with Pete, the brother of Red, Temple's lover in Memphis eight years before. Thus, Temple Drake, daughter of a judge, descendant of famous statesmen and soldiers, returns to Jackson, her hometown, to accuse, try, judge, and condemn herself. Her mission to save Nancy may end in her own salvation.

The flow of Faulkner's story of the past contrasts with Temple's shuddering struggle, without the benediction of tears, to tell her own story. Readers witness the validity of Stevens' claim that there is no immunity from the past because it is actual in the present. With both the absence and the assertion of human will, man's history moves through a chaotic complex of accident, chance, and design. Thus, in the past, the community set a pattern for the future, which one can perceive only by experiencing it. For example, male vanity and chastity are two cornerstones of the Southern social structure, built on bought land and a slave economy. Jefferson came into being and got its name because of the vanity of a pint-sized mail rider named Thomas Jefferson Pettigrew; the settlers bribed his complicity in a group act of deception by naming the town after him, though, ironically, he himself was named after Jefferson. It was vanity that compelled Gowan to marry Temple. As a contrast to Temple and Gowan, Faulkner tells the romantic story of a brave Civil War soldier and the virginal daughter of the county jailer. The minor indiscretions of a "foolish virgin" (Temple) and a drunken coward (Gowan) set in motion the further development of a pattern started in the past, the final act of which is Nancy's smothering the baby to save it from suffering and to show Temple the consequences of her sins. Temple's declaration that she places her love for the blackmailer Pete above love for her baby prompts Nancy's act. The personal catastrophes of the present emerge out of the antics and nightmares of history. The book is a reconstruction of this web of accident and design, which the reader alone, by listening to Faulkner, suffering with Temple, and evaluating with Stevens, is able fully to grasp.

In "The Jail (Not Even Yet Quite Relinquish—)," Faulkner brings the story of the county up to the present; the jail is the artifact that "witnesses" the town's swift and dubious progress. In the bullpen of the jail (the stink of which is the stink of Temple's sin that overwhelms her), Temple's personal story, and thus the community's history, reaches a climax in Temple's confrontation with Nancy, on the eve of the execution, to occur in the jail itself.

It is characteristic of Faulkner's use of Christian symbolism that the relation between the titles *Sanctuary* (Temple's "sanctuary" in a sporting house) and *Requiem for a Nun* (Nancy, a prostitute as a nun) is paradoxical and ironic. Nancy, who once held the Stevens family together as nurse, catalyst, confidante, and magnetic center, resembles other of Faulkner's black women; but she has "endured" only to be hanged, "crucified" for Temple's sins. The death of this mortal Christ forces Temple to atone all the more deeply herself.

Temple, as Mrs. Gowan Stevens, says in act 1, scene 1, that Temple Drake is dead; on the eve of Nancy's execution, Temple Drake truly dies in an act of painful self-recognition; Faulkner suggests that Nancy's goodness may be resurrected in Temple Stevens.

Having suffered the telling, Temple must ask Nancy's forgiveness. She wonders why Nancy and others must suffer because she decided to sneak off to a ballgame with Gowan eight years earlier. Stevens' answer is that good can, and must, come out of evil. Even if there were no God, evil would corrupt, as putrefaction taints. Temple knows now that one need only refuse to look on evil, for she thrilled to the evil of the impotent, perverted, murdering gangster, Popeye, who enjoyed watching her make love to his bodyguard, Red. Perhaps man must sin, then suffer, and thus make salvation possible. Nancy rejects hope, because in hoping to be free of the circumstances which make salvation possible, one may defer or miss it. She is certain she will go to Heaven; for just as she loved the baby she killed, God loves her, though he makes her suffer. In emulation of Nancy, Temple wants to experience the grace of Christ, but she fears that after suffering, there may be no God to forgive her. Nancy's exhortation is trust Jesus and believe. Faulkner leaves to the accidents and patterns of history the answer to the question of Temple's, and the South's, salvation.

RIP VAN WINKLE

Type of work: Tale
Author: Washington Irving (1783–1859)
Type of plot: Regional romance
Time of plot: Eighteenth century
Locale: New York State
First published: 1819–1820

> *Principal characters:*
>> RIP VAN WINKLE, a henpecked husband
>> DAME VAN WINKLE, his wife

The Story:

Along the reaches of the Hudson, not far from the Kaatskill mountains, there was a small, antique Dutch town. The mountains overshadowed the town, and there were times when the good Dutch burghers could see a hood of clouds hanging over the crests of the hills.

In that small town lived a man named Rip Van Winkle. He was beloved by all his neighbors, by the children and the dogs, but at home his life was made miserable by his shrewish wife. Though he was willing to help anyone else at any odd job that might be necessary, it was impossible for him to keep his own house or farm in repair. He was descended from a good old Dutch family, but he had none of the fine Dutch traits of thrift or energy.

He spent a great deal of his time at the village inn, under the sign of King George III, until his wife chased him from there. Then he took his gun and his dog Wolf and headed for the hills. Wolf was as happy as Rip to get away from home. When Dame Van Winkle berated the two of them, Rip raised his eyes silently to heaven, but Wolf tucked his tail between his legs and slunk out of the house.

One fine day in autumn, Rip and Wolf walked high into the Kaatskills after squirrels. As evening came on, he and his dog sat down to rest awhile before starting home. When Rip started down the mountainside, he heard his name called.

A short, square little man with a grizzled beard had called Rip to help carry a keg of liquor. The little man was dressed in antique Dutch clothes. Although he accepted Rip's help in carrying the keg, he carried on no conversation. As they ascended the mountain, Rip heard noises that sounded like claps of thunder. When they reached a sort of amphitheater near the top, Rip saw a band of little men, dressed and bearded like his companion, playing ninepins. One stout old gentleman, who seemed to be the leader, wore a laced doublet and a high-crowned hat with a feather.

The little men were no more companionable than the first one had been, and Rip felt somewhat depressed. Because they seemed to enjoy the liquor from the keg, Rip tasted it a few times while they were absorbed in their game. Then he fell into a deep sleep.

On waking, he looked in vain for the stout old gentleman and his companions. When he reached for his gun, he found only a rusty flintlock. His dog did not answer his call. He tried to find the amphitheater where the little men had played, but the way was blocked by a rushing stream.

The people he saw as he walked into town were all strangers to him. Since most of them, upon looking at him, stroked their chins, Rip unconsciously stroked his and found that his beard had grown a foot long.

The town itself looked different. At first, Rip thought the liquor from the keg had addled his head, for he had a hard time finding his own house. When he did locate it at last, he found it in a state of decay. Even the sign over the inn had been changed to one carrying the name of General Washington. The men gathered under the sign talked gibberish to him, and they accused him of trying to stir up trouble by coming armed to an election. When they let him ask for his old cronies, he named men who the loungers told him had moved away, or else they had been dead these twenty years.

Finally, an eager young woman pushed through the crowd to look at Rip. Her voice started a train of thought, and he asked who she was and who her father had been. When she claimed to be Rip Van Winkle's daughter Judith, he asked one more question about her mother. Judith told him that her mother had died after breaking a blood vessel in a fit of anger at a Yankee peddler. Rip breathed more freely.

Although another old woman claimed that she recognized him, the men at the inn only winked at his story until an old man, a descendant of the village historian, vouched for Rip's tale. He assured the men that he had it as a fact from his historian ancestor that Hendrick Hudson with his crew came to the mountains every twenty years to visit the scene of their exploits, and that the old historian had seen the crew in antique Dutch garb playing at ninepins just as Rip had related.

Rip spent the rest of his life happily telling his story at the inn until everyone knew it by heart. Even now when the inhabitants of the village hear thunder in the Kaatskills, they say that Hendrick Hudson and his crew are playing ninepins, and many a henpecked husband has wished in vain for a draught of Rip Van Winkle's quieting brew.

Critical Evaluation:

The Sketch Book of Geoffrey Crayon, Gent. made Washington Irving the first American author to enjoy international fame. "Rip Van Winkle" is perhaps the best example in the collection of Irving's artistic movement away from the neoclassic cosmic interests of his earlier satirical writing toward a localized and sentimental Romanticism. In a sense, Irving's Romanticism is more superficial than that of the great American Romantics such as Emerson and Poe. Irving is concerned more with capturing, through vivid description, moods and emotions than with probing introspectively into metaphysical states. Even his later writing follows his early stylistic models, Addison and Goldsmith. Although he did not develop a style peculiarly his own, Irving nonetheless wrote with undeniable clarity, grace, and charm—making the "regional romance" a noteworthy and enjoyable American genre.

The author's introductory note calls Rip's adventure "A Posthumous Writing of Diedrich Knickerbocker," the imaginary historian Irving invented earlier for his *A History of New York by Diedrich Knickerbocker* (1809). The narrator's droll references to his own "scrupulous accuracy" and "precise truth," as well as the "confirmation" provided by Peter Vandervonk (a figure from the past parallel to the Dutchmen Rip meets in the mountains), add subtlety to the humorous claim of veracity. Nevertheless, the story clearly combines the literature of folk-fable with that of antifeminism. Rip is depicted, almost heroically, as a kind of Socrates: "a simple good-natured man," a great rationalizer, always willing to help others (consequently henpecked, because unwilling to do his own work), ever found at the inn—"a kind of perpetual club of the sages." From this ironic-realistic basis the story leaps into myth, with the appearance of the strange little man carrying the keg, whose sullenness somehow enhances his mysterious character and the story's naïve credibility. When Rip awakens to present reality, himself now a fabulous figure from the past, he finds things much the same as before. Irving's satirical point is that political and social "revolutions" are superficial. Change is a myth.

With his Romantic, almost fantastic, tales of *The Sketch Book of Geoffrey Crayon, Gent.*, Irving made his earliest and most favorable impression on the English and American reading publics. He was living in England when he wrote these tales, but it is easy to see that the fascination of the American landscape was with him there. "Rip Van Winkle" is said to be based on a common European legend transferred to American soil; that is, Otmar's tale of "Peter Klaus" in the *Volkssagen*.

THE RISE OF SILAS LAPHAM

Type of work: Novel
Author: William Dean Howells (1837–1920)
Type of plot: Domestic realism
Time of plot: Nineteenth century
Locale: New England
First published: 1885

Principal characters:

SILAS LAPHAM, a self-made manufacturer
MRS. LAPHAM, his wife
PENELOPE and
IRENE, his daughters
TOM COREY, the Laphams' friend
MR. ROGERS, Mr. Lapham's former partner

The Story:

Silas Lapham was being interviewed for a Boston paper. The journalist was secretly mocking Lapham's way of life, but Lapham, content with his success, paid little attention to his interviewer as he proudly exhibited a photograph of his two daughters and his wife. He told how he had been brought up in a large family, how he had gone West with his brothers, how he had returned, bought a stage route, married the village schoolteacher, and finally hit upon making paint from a mineral his father had discovered on his farm.

The story of his success was a story of determination and hard work. During the Civil War, his wife had kept the paint works going, and after the war, he had taken a man named Rogers as a partner for a short time.

After the interview, Lapham and his wife drove out to see the site of a house they were building in a more fashionable part of Boston. Although both looked with pride upon the place soon to be their residence, they pretended not to want the house at all. They merely suggested the new home would be a greater advantage for Penelope and Irene when their friends came to call.

Neither Penelope nor Irene, however, anticipated with any great joy their coming change of living. They said they felt the present house was more convenient to the horsecars. Secretly, both realized that their parents were awkward in social life. At the same time, they themselves had never been brought up to feel comfortable in the presence of people whose families had been accustomed to wealth for generations.

One day, as Mr. and Mrs. Lapham were dismounting from their carriage, Lapham's former partner appeared unexpectedly. Rogers had furnished money to help Lapham get started, but later Lapham had crowded Rogers out.

Lapham insisted that what he had done had merely been good business. Mrs. Lapham, however, maintained that she never felt quite right about what had happened to Rogers, and seeing him again took all the happiness out of her plans for the new house.

The next time the family ventured out to visit the partly completed house, Irene was surprised by the arrival of Tom Corey, a young man who had shown some interest in her. Immediately Mr. Lapham took over the occasion, and by his bragging, he greatly embarrassed his daughters.

That evening, young Corey talked to his father about the Laphams. Bromfield Corey did not agree with his son's easy acceptance of the Laphams, but he did not object when his son announced his intention to apply for a position in Lapham's firm.

Young Corey visited Lapham in his office in order to ask for a job. Lapham was so pleased that he invited Corey to go with him to Nantasket where Mrs. Lapham and the girls were expecting Lapham for the weekend. At the Nantasket cottage, the girls and their mother could not understand what had brought young Corey for the weekend visit. They had thought Lapham's bragging would have kept him away forever.

That evening, Lapham discussed Corey with his wife. Mrs. Lapham contended that Corey was interested not in the paint but in Irene. Her husband commented that unless the young man were interested in the paint he would never get a chance to be interested in Irene. When Lapham said he intended to give the young man a chance, Mrs. Lapham warned him that he was playing with a situation which was bound to bring trouble.

Tom Corey's mother was concerned when she heard what her son had done. She admitted she would not object if he made a fortune from the paint business, but she did not want him to fall in love with either of the Lapham girls.

After Corey entered Lapham's employ, he was invited frequently to the Lapham home, for Irene was beginning to fall in love with him. Bromfield Corey grew more and more curious about the Laphams. He decided that he would encourage his wife to give a dinner for them in the autumn.

The cost of the new house worried Mrs. Lapham, and she asked her husband to stop his lavish spending. She learned that he had given a substantial loan to Rogers, his former partner.

When Mrs. Corey returned from Bar Harbor, she debated a long time about giving a dinner party for the Laphams. In the first place, the Laphams were newcomers. On the other hand, she wanted to give public recognition of the new connection between her son and the Lapham family. She finally decided to give a formal dinner early in the season, before her more prominent friends returned to the city.

On the night of the dinner, the Laphams tried to appear at ease. Penelope had refused to attend, thus causing her mother considerable embarrassment.

Lapham watched the other men carefully, feeling sure that he had not made too many social blunders. The next day, however, he was not so sure, for he had taken too much wine at dinner.

At the office, Lapham sought out Corey and mentioned with embarrassment his behavior of the night before. He offered Corey his liberty to seek another job, a position among gentlemen, but Corey refused to go, saying that Lapham's tipsy talk had been only an unfortunate accident. When they parted, Corey insisted that Lapham's conduct had been proper and entertaining.

That night, feeling that he had actually patronized Lapham, Corey resolved to go to his employer and apologize. Lapham was out, but Penelope received Corey. At the end of a long talk, he stammeringly confessed his love for her. In great confusion, he left without waiting to speak to Lapham.

The next day, Mrs. Lapham informed her husband that Corey had been coming to see Penelope all the time. She could only imagine what the shock would do to Irene. They felt, however, that Penelope would never permit Corey to become her suitor, for Penelope was convinced that he belonged to Irene.

Irene was informed of the situation by her mother that evening. Immediately she carried to her sister's room every memento of Corey's attentions that she possessed. After a few days, Lapham took her to his boyhood village in Vermont.

Corey called on the Laphams to present his explanation, saying that he had cared more for Penelope all the time. Penelope refused to give him any satisfaction. She said she owed more to her sister's hurt feelings.

At the same time, Lapham's finances were troubling him greatly. People who owed him money were unable to pay; his own creditors were pressing him. Lapham determined to take a trip west to inspect some mills held as security for his loan to Rogers. When he returned, he was even more concerned. Rogers had drawn him into a trap with his securities, for a railroad controlled the value of the property. Lapham decided it would be necessary to sell the new house unfinished. Learning of Lapham's difficulties, Corey offered to lend his employer thirty thousand dollars, but Lapham rejected the offer.

Lapham's affairs took a turn for the worse. An added blow was the destruction of the unfinished Back Bay house. Wandering through the house one night, he decided to test one of the chimneys and made a fire from blocks and shavings that the workmen had left scattered about. He thought the fire had burned out before he left. That night the house burned to the ground. The insurance policy had expired a week before.

Determined to raise money by selling everything he could, Lapham visited his competitors who were working on a new mineral paint. They were willing to merge with him if he could raise money to help develop their plant. While he was trying to secure a loan, he learned from Rogers that some English gentlemen were interested in buying the property which Rogers had put up as security and which Lapham had thought valueless. Lapham refused to sell the mills, however, because he believed a sale would be unethical as long as the railroad controlled their value.

He asked for time to think over the proposition. Shortly afterward, the railroad forced him to sell the mills at a ruinous figure. Lapham felt that his honesty, which had kept him from selling the property to the Englishmen, had been unjustly abused. Rogers claimed that Lapham had made it impossible for him to recover his losses. Lapham was now ruined, for he could not raise capital to merge with the rival paint firm.

Tom Corey was determined to marry Penelope in spite of her father's impending ruin. He did marry her after Lapham went into bankruptcy, and his family accepted her for their own sake as well as for his. Irene, who had returned as soon as she heard of her father's troubles, was pleased with her sister's happiness.

Lapham managed to save a part of his fortune, but more important to him was the belief that he had acted honestly in all his business dealings.

Critical Evaluation:

According to many critics, *The Rise of Silas Lapham* is the most important book William Dean Howells ever wrote. Howells, a prolific though never a brilliant writer, attempted to deal conscientiously with the everyday experiences of rather ordinary people. By presenting character and situation in a straightforward manner, he wrote novels characterized chiefly by their moral atmosphere and authentic domestic Realism.

The reputation of Howells suffered much from the charge of many critics that his scope was too limited to satisfy the requirements of complexity demanded by the sophisticated twentieth century reader. It is argued that his insights into man's social existence, for example, were based on tenets from a past age that are no longer viable in the face of reality; the absence of certain intense passions and obsessions in the novels, as well as Howells' failure to explore in depth such areas as human sexuality and man's capacity for violence, are cited as evidence. Similarly, *The Rise of Silas Lapham*—the author's most popular work and in many ways his masterpiece—has been adversely judged by some on the grounds that its plot is too slender to support the weight of its own implications. To support such charges, however, is either to misunderstand the nature of Howells' moral vision of life, or to overlook its depth and breadth, its universality, its applicability to all times and places.

Howells believed in the interdependence of people upon one another; he viewed each person's life as inextricably caught up with the lives of others, thus creating the web of interrelationships that forms societies. Such a belief meant that, for Howells, man's personal moral life and his life as a social being were fused; there was no such thing as a purely individual moral act, whether good or evil, since each personal act had its inevitable consequences in the interpersonal or social realm. This in turn led to the morally pragmatic stance that the proper course of action can often be chosen on the basis of which course will result in "the most good for the greatest number" of people. This utilitarian viewpoint is reflected in such concepts as "the economy of pain" principle, propounded by Howells through the character of David Sewell in the scene from *The Rise of Silas Lapham* in which Silas and his wife seek the minister's advice concerning the triangular love-complication between their two daughters and Tom Corey. He tells them that in such a situation, for which no one is to blame, the best solution is the one that will cause suffering to the fewest number of people. In this case, therefore, Penelope would be wrong to sacrifice Tom to Irene, which would make all three persons suffer miserably; she should marry him herself, which would result in the great happiness of two people and the temporary hurt of only one.

Underlying this moral outlook were three basic assumptions: that all aspects of human life, including the social, are infused with moral purpose, thus making society an extremely precious commodity; that the preservation of society depended upon man's overcoming destructive passions with reason; and that the function of art is to reveal the superiority of the civilized and reasoning side of man's nature over the primitive and ignorant side. Howells' first assumption was shared by most people in his age, but it was his fervent espousal of the last proposition that placed him at the philosophical head of a group of writers whose aim it was to reveal the morality of life through the use of Realism in their fiction. Yet Howells abhorred sermonizing and attacked the didactic element in writing wherever he encountered it.

This seeming paradox is cleared up, however, when one examines more closely Howells' theory of literature. What he objected to was not the presence of moral purpose in a work but rather any attempt by an author to force artificially his set of beliefs into a fictional structure without regard to the organic dictates of the work itself. When Howells was finally asked to summarize explicitly his theory of the moral purpose of literature, he began by identifying the three progressively worse stages of "immorality" often practiced in fiction. The first involves the obscuring of the reader's judgment through indulgence of his "gross appetite for the marvelous"; the second, the elevation of passion over principles; and the third (and most pernicious), the presentation of characters who commit serious sins but are left unpunished by the penalties which follow such sins in the real world. The true function of the writer, Howells argued, is first to reject any absolute standard of morality and then to portray lives of characters in honest and careful detail; as the characters meet each new situation in their everyday lives, as they are faced with decisions over what is right and what is wrong, they will respond as people do in life. Sometimes they will act in morally responsible ways and will be rewarded, if not with worldly success, with inner peace; at other times, they will commit wrongs and will suffer the inevitable consequences. Thus, Howells believed, all the author need do is describe reality truthfully, and the morality of life will come through the narrative naturally, as it does in life.

Howells carried out his theory to near-perfection in *The Rise of Silas Lapham*. This novel tells the story of a man who has been led astray from the true values in life by the corrupting influence of wealth. The action centers around Silas Lapham's fall into financial ruin, which turns out to be his salvation, his rise (hence the title) back into a morally healthy state. The plot is organic, reflecting the theme of the novel and growing out of the main character's growth. The beginning and end are linked masterfully, while the midway point in the story—the dinner party given by the Coreys—serves to converge all the threads spun out so far, suspend them momentarily for the reader's contemplation, and then direct them toward their climax and natural conclusion. In his interview with Bartley Hubbard at the opening of the novel, Silas is seen in all the glory of his material success: he is proud of his rise from humble beginnings, of his newly acquired social position, and of the new house he is just starting to build. The house becomes a symbol of Silas' fortunes; destined to be a magnificent mansion, it rises quickly until its construction is slowed down because of lack of funds. In the end, it is burned to the ground. The destruction of the house represents Silas' rebirth, however, since his moral regeneration can only occur after he has been stripped of the false trappings of materialism. In his talk with David Sewell at the end, Silas' transformation is set in dramatic contrast to his initial appearance in the Bartley interview: he has grown humble and honest; bragging has been replaced by sincerity.

Lapham has been able to reach this new stage of awareness by progressing through a series of moral "tests," culminating in the legal, but morally dishonest, deal urged upon him by Milton Rogers and the Englishmen; when he refuses to participate, both his financial ruin and his personal salvation are secured. He has painfully but steadily moved from the easiest stages of redemption—acts of unselfishness and generosity on a personal, one-to-one basis—through a wider area of commitment to people in large groups, and has finally reached the highest, most difficult to attain level of good action. This level involves an individual's commitment to the social body as a whole, to the welfare not of a personally known individual or group but of all men as they comprise society.

Although Howells' efforts to uncover the underlying morality of all human action by focusing on the commonplace and familiar in his fiction reached a pinnacle in *The Rise of Silas Lapham*, he was not fully conscious of the nature of his achievement until a year after the novel's publication. It was in that year—1886—that he began reading Tolstoy. His exposure to the Russian novelist was like a religious experience for him; of its effects he wrote, "What

I had instinctively known before, I now knew rationally." Following this illumination of his own motives and absorbing concerns as an artist, Howells was able to sum up the vision which inspired not only *The Rise of Silas Lapham* but all of his work as well: "Morality penetrates all things, it is the soul of all things."

RIVER OF EARTH

Type of work: Novel
Author: James Still (1906–   )
Type of plot: Regional romance
Time of plot: Early twentieth century
Locale: Kentucky
First published: 1940

> Principal characters:
> BRACK BALDRIDGE, a Kentucky mountaineer
> ALPHA BALDRIDGE, his wife
> BRACK'S OLDEST BOY, the narrator
> EULY, the narrator's sister
> GRANDMOTHER MIDDLETON, Alpha's mother
> UNCLE JOLLY, Alpha's brother

The Story:

When the mines closed in March, there was very little food left in the house. It was still a long time before the garden crops would be ready, and Alpha wanted Brack to tell his two cousins, Harl and Tibb Logan, to leave the house and find food for themselves; but Brack said that as long as he had food in his house, he would never turn his blood kin away. Then Uncle Samp came to live with them, and the mother saw her four children getting hungrier and leaner. Knowing that the kin would leave if there were no place for them to sleep, she calmly set fire to the house, first moving the children and the skimpy furniture to the smokehouse.

All spring, while the family lived in the smokehouse, they ate less and less and waited for the first vegetables. When the beans were almost ready and the whole family dreamed of having their stomachs full, three men came from the mining town to beg food for their families. Unable to turn down starving people, Brack sent the men into his garden. When they came out, the boy saw that they had taken every bean from the patch. He turned away, wanting to cry.

In May, Brack took the boy with him when he went to help a neighbor deliver a colt. The boy expected to get the colt for his own, as his father's fee, but the neighbor's son told him that no Baldridge was going to get the colt, that the Baldridges were cowards, and that after their Grandpa Middleton had been killed by Aus Coggins, no Baldridge had done anything about it. The boy fought with the neighbor's son. When the fight was over, they found that the colt was dead.

One day, Uncle Jolly arrived and brought them a pair of guineas from Grandmother Middleton. Uncle Jolly spent as much time in jail as out. It was said that he was avenging Grandpa's death by tormenting Aus Coggins—cutting his fences, breaking his dam, and doing other mischief.

Soon after Uncle Jolly left, Brack wanted to move the family down to Blackjack, for the mines were going to open again. The mother did not want to go because the smoky valley would be a bad place for her sickly baby; but she resigned herself to her husband's wishes.

In the middle of August, the boy and his sister Euly started to school. They were anxious to learn to read and write, the boy especially, because he did not want to be a miner. He hoped that someday he could be an animal doctor, as his father had always wanted to be. It seemed to the boy and Euly, however, that the most important thing they learned in school was how to smoke bats out of the building.

In late September, the boy was sent to stay with his Grandmother Middleton while Uncle Jolly served a term in jail. He was to stay with her only until Uncle Luce came, but the corn was husked and the other grain harvested before Uncle Luce arrived. The boy was astonished at his grandmother's ability to do heavy work, for she was very old. When she learned that Uncle Jolly had been sentenced to two years in the state penitentiary, she asked the boy to stay with her during the winter. As soon as the crops were in, she spent a great deal of time in bed. She spent hours telling him about her children and her husband. It was easy to see that Jolly was her favorite.

In January, Uncle Jolly came home. There had been a fire at the penitentiary, and Jolly had been so brave in helping to fight the fire that the governor had pardoned him. Grandmother Middleton said nothing when Uncle Jolly told her that he had started the fire.

Uncle Jolly also brought the news that the boy's family had moved at last to Blackjack, but there was no other word of his family. Visitors were scarce in the hills.

Spring and summer passed pleasantly for the boy. In October, Uncle Jolly was in jail again, this time for fighting. Uncle Toll came to bring Grandmother Middleton the news and he took the boy back to Hardin Town with him. They found Jolly content to be in jail except that he was lonesome. Uncle Toll begged him not to break out, for one more jailbreak would send him to the penitentiary for a long time. Toll left the boy at the jail so that Uncle Jolly would not break out for lack of companionship. The boy slept in the hall outside his uncle's cell. When Uncle Jolly thought he would have to break out of jail or die, he stole the keys from the deputy and told the boy to take the key of Jolly's cell to his mother and ask her to keep it until the remaining days of the sentence were served. In that way, the boy went back to his family.

In March, the family moved from Blackjack again, this time to a little rented farm on a hillside. There the baby died of croup. Another garden was planted, and in the summer, they had a funeral for the baby. The boy saw more relatives than he had known he had. At the end of summer, Brack decided to go back to the mines and moved his family to Blackjack and into a house with windows.

Uncle Samp and Harl and Tibb Logan came back to live with the family. Harl and Tibb worked in the mine, but Uncle Samp had never worked and did not intend to start now. Soon the mines began to close down, and men everywhere were laid off again. Brack was kept on, with only one or two days of work each week.

Harl and Tibb, angry because they were laid off, dynamited one of the veins. At first, it was thought that they were trapped in the mine and had died, but Uncle Samp and Brack rescued them. They left the Baldridge house after Harl and Tibb were kicked out by the mine boss, and Uncle Samp married a fortune-teller.

Food was scarce again, and the mother was sickly most of the time, her stomach swollen terribly. In March, Uncle Jolly brought Grandmother Middleton's body to the house. The old lady had died at last, and Jolly was taking her to her old home to be buried. While they were sitting with the body in the front room of the house, the boy noticed his father looking constantly at the closed door behind which the mother had been taken by a neighbor woman. In the morning, the boy knew what his father had been waiting for and why his mother had been so swollen. As he stood looking at the tracks the wagon had made as it carried his grandmother's body away for the last time, he heard a baby begin to cry.

Critical Evaluation:

James Still's richly evocative style, particularly the sensuousness of his imagery, brings to stirring life the full range of a young boy's introduction to experience. The anonymity of the boy narrator (readers never learn his Christian name) adds to the mythic dimension of his point of view. He recalls Wordsworth's persona in the early books of the poet's famous autobiography in verse, *The Prelude*: raised by the "ministries of beauty and fear," like the young Wordsworth, Brack's "boy" is initiated into the fullness of nature.

What distinguishes Still's novel from the Romantic nature myth is the book's stark realism. Wordsworth's child fears strange spirits that haunt dark coves; Still's narrator fears hunger. Nothing makes a greater impression in this book than the many descriptions of hunger and its psychological and moral implications. The primary urge is to get enough to eat, and it supplies almost all of the motivation and action.

At the beginning of the novel, Alpha announces to her husband: "We have enough bran for three more pans of bread. If the children eat it by themselves, it might last a week. It won't last us all more than three meals. Your kin will have to go today." With that kind of stark alternative, the story takes on the epic dimensions of a struggle for elemental survival. Later, when Brack brings home a table full of food, which he purchases on credit after being taken on at the coal mine, the family reacts as if he had returned from battle with an immense treasure: "We looked in wonder, not being able to speak, knowing only that a great hunger stirred inside us, and that our tongues were moistening our lips. The smell of meat and parched coffee hung in the room."

In addition to its realism, the story is marked by compassionate humor. Uncle Silas and his mysteriously clipped moustache together with Uncle Jolly, the hopeless but lovable jailbird, balance the boy's tragic education with joy.

THE RIVET IN GRANDFATHER'S NECK

Type of work: Novel
Author: James Branch Cabell (1879–1958)
Type of plot: Social satire
Time of plot: 1896–1927
Locale: Litchfield, not to be found on the map of Virginia
First published: 1915

> *Principal characters:*
> COLONEL RUDOLPH MUSGRAVE, a Southern gentleman
> MISS AGATHA MUSGRAVE, his sister
> PATRICIA STAPYLTON MUSGRAVE, his wife
> JOHN CHARTERIS, a novelist
> ANNE CHARTERIS, his wife
> MRS. CLARICE PENDOMER, Charteris' former mistress

The Story:

Colonel Rudolph Musgrave, family head of the Musgraves of Matocton in Litchfield, was forty years old in 1896. He was a consummate Southern gentleman: an aristocrat, a scholar, a lover, and an indifferent businessman. A bachelor, he lived with his sister Miss Agatha, who let nothing interfere with his comfort. His small income from his position as librarian of the Litchfield Historical Society was augmented by his genealogical research for people who were trying to establish a pedigree. The brother and sister lived quite comfortably on his earnings.

Both, however, had inherited Musgrave weaknesses. She tippled, and he fell in love with many women. The Colonel had a streak of chivalry in his nature which prompted him to make gallant gestures of renunciation for the sake of the lady in question. His most recent act of chivalry, which had provided Litchfield with amusing gossip, occurred when he had been overheard by Anne Charteris—whom he had loved and lost to the selfish novelist, John Charteris—while he was reprimanding her husband for getting Mrs. Pendomer pregnant. Anne, who blindly worshipped her husband, had misunderstood the situation, and she had supposed that Musgrave was the guilty party. Musgrave had accepted the blame in order to save Anne from learning that her husband was a philanderer. Privately, Musgrave delighted in the episode.

The Musgraves were visited by Patricia Stapylton, the twenty-one-year-old daughter of a second cousin once removed who had eloped with an overseer.

Roger Stapylton, the overseer, had become wealthy in the North, and Patricia was engaged to marry Lord Pevensey. Although Musgrave tried to impress Patricia with his most formal manner, she was not at all awed by him and immediately punctured his reserve. He spent a good deal of time with her, however, and once he read to her "The Shepherdess and the Chimney Sweep."

Musgrave, acting according to his code of honor, fell in love with Patricia and tried to renounce her; but she saw through his performance and jilted the Englishman. During the dinner at which their engagement was to be announced, Musgrave discovered that Patricia had fallen in love with Joe Parkinson. Musgrave made his grand gesture by announcing her engagement to the younger man. Patricia jilted Parkinson, however, and she married Musgrave.

At first their marriage was very happy, even though Patricia was troubled by her husband's reserve. Stapylton offered Musgrave a remunerative position in his business, but Musgrave refused it. Then Musgrave tried to make some quick money in the stock market but promptly lost all his savings. After that, they lived on Patricia's allowance, which was rather small because Stapylton was displeased by their refusal to leave Litchfield.

Patricia had inherited a deformed pelvis from her mother, who died in childbirth. When Patricia became pregnant, the doctors gave her the choice between losing the child or her life. Without telling her husband anything about the matter, she decided to have the child because she knew how much Musgrave wanted a son. Though she survived the birth of her son, she was never completely well afterward and had to have a series of operations. The son was named Roger after her father, and Stapylton settled almost all his money on the child.

Tensions began to develop between the Musgraves. Miss Agatha and Patricia had never got along well together because the spinster resented Patricia's role in Musgrave's life. Patricia, still young and lively, found her husband's formality increasingly annoying. Also, she was annoyed by his ineptness with money.

The crisis in their relationship came with the death of Miss Agatha. During one of her drinking spells, Miss Agatha had wandered out into a storm and had caught pneumonia. When she died, she was attended only by the black maid, Virginia, and Musgrave rebuked his wife for leaving the sick woman alone. Patricia said some bitter things about Miss Agatha and insisted that Virginia hated all the Musgraves because Musgrave's uncle had fathered her son, who had been lynched by a mob for becoming involved with a white woman. Patricia declared that Virginia frequently was the only one present when a Musgrave died. Musgrave insisted that this claim was nonsense. The quarrel ended bitterly, and their relationship was never quite the same afterward.

When their son was five, the Musgraves gave a house party at Matocton, the Musgrave ancestral estate. Among the guests were Anne and John Charteris. Patricia, finding Charteris a pleasing contrast to her husband, let him persuade her to run off with him. On his part, Charteris enjoyed the adoration of women and had been involved in many affairs. Though a successful novelist, he was not independently wealthy, and so he had always remained with Anne because she had a great deal of money. Now he was prepared to leave his wife because he thought he had found a richer woman.

Musgrave, discovering the plan, informed Charteris that Patricia had very little money of her own. Charteris then told Patricia that he could not take her away, giving her many hypocritical reasons for his change of heart.

Patricia was told by her doctor that her heart was weak and that she would not live long. Although she kept her own counsel, she was now determined to seek happiness with Charteris, and so she persuaded him to go through with their original plan. Charteris borrowed money from his wife to finance his desertion.

Musgrave, learning that Charteris and Patricia were going through with the elopement, attempted to dissuade Charteris by telling him that they were actually half brothers. According to Musgrave's code of honor, no gentleman would steal his brother's wife. Charteris was unmoved by the news. The next morning, Musgrave met the lovers as they were departing and struck Charteris. Patricia, realizing that Charteris was a coward, broke with him.

A few days later, Charteris was murdered by a jealous husband. On this occasion, for once, he was innocent. The newspaper story was brought to Patricia by Virginia, and Patricia died of a heart attack.

Anne Charteris, who had never seen through her husband, continued to adore him. Some five years after his death, she met Musgrave in the cemetery where Patricia and Charteris were buried. Musgrave had Mrs. Pendomer's son with him. At first, Anne was outraged by Musgrave's lack of taste in being seen in the company of his illegitimate child, but as she looked at the boy she realized that Charteris was the boy's real father. Although Musgrave tried to maintain the deception, Anne finally realized that her husband had been a scoundrel. There was now nothing to stand between Anne and Musgrave; they recognized, however, that their loyalties to their dead mates were too strong to let them marry.

In 1927, Colonel Rudolph Musgrave died dreaming of his first meeting with Patricia.

Critical Evaluation:

The Rivet in Grandfather's Neck, James Branch Cabell's third novel and the fourteenth volume in the Storisende Edition of his works, deals with the American descendants of Count Manuel of Poictesme. Subtitled "A Comedy of Limitations," the book satirizes the American South and its adherence to the code of chivalry. The title is taken from Hans Christian Andersen's fairy tale of "The Shepherdess and the Chimney Sweep," in which two porcelain figures who are in love attempt to escape after the shepherdess' grandfather, a porcelain Chinese figure with a nodding head, promises her to a wooden satyr. The shepherdess is frightened by the outside world, and they return. The grandfather had been broken while pursuing them, and his neck was riveted so that he could no longer nod agreement to the satyr's proposal. In the novel, Musgrave interprets this tale as an allegory about human limitations: everyone has a figurative rivet in his neck, and this signifies the action one cannot perform. Although the outmoded code by which Musgrave lives is satirized, the author also perceived that this code was not without grace and charm. The manner matches the matter. Cabell was an urbane stylist who seems closer to the English wits than to any American writer.

Cabell was a genteel Southern writer caught in the limbo between the crash of the old order following the Civil War and the rise of the Southern Literary Renaissance in the 1920's. A pragmatic Realist, he was too hard-nosed to indulge in the luxury of Romantic deception and accordingly felt constrained to satirize fantasies and idealizations that delude individuals and mock reality. Cabell wrote social satire that wanted to be romance.

Here lies the conflict in *The Rivet in Grandfather's Neck*. Cabell's protagonist, Colonel Rudolph Musgrave, thinks of the rivet in the fairy tale as that which makes people what they are: it symbolizes the limitations of character. A Southern aristocrat and conscious of his traditions and requisite obligations, Musgrave carries off self-sacrificing acts in the finest chivalric manner. However, the consequences are often tragic, comic, or absurd. Cabell relishes in deflating pretensions and neatly lampoons not only the Colonel's idealistic acts but also a wide range of pretensions, codes, and mannerisms characterizing the old South. Yet, Cabell also treats his material tenderly and fondly. He respects human dignity acting within human limitations, and is cautiously optimistic about man's potential. His style, moreover, is never heavy-handed. A suave, facile, and mannered—at times almost mandarin—style hovers over the novel constantly, bemusedly assessing and reevaluating the narrative experience. If some of the characters, particularly Colonel Musgrave, are ultimately unconvincing, it is because Cabell, cherishing what they are while parodying their limitations, burdens them too heavily with mannerisms.

Cabell's novel, which might seem to be a whimsical and elegant romance from aristocratic life, is also a pointed social satire. As much as the rivet in grandfather's neck led to happiness for the fairy tale figurines, the novel offers comfort and dignity through adherence to the way people are.

RODERICK HUDSON

Type of work: Novel
Author: Henry James (1843–1916)
Type of plot: Psychological realism
Time of plot: 1870's
Locale: Chiefly Rome, also Florence and Switzerland
First published: 1876

Principal characters:

RODERICK HUDSON, a young American sculptor
ROWLAND MALLET, a young, wealthy art patron
MRS. LIGHT, a vain and silly widow
CHRISTINA LIGHT, her beautiful daughter
THE CAVALIERE GIACOSA, Christina's father
PRINCE CASAMASSIMA, Christina's husband
SAM SINGLETON, an American painter
MRS. HUDSON, Roderick's insipid mother
MARY GARLAND, Roderick's American fiancée

The Story:

Rowland Mallet, expecting to sail for Europe in September, visited his cousin Cecilia in Northampton, Massachusetts. He was an idle bachelor, having inherited money, and he felt that he was leading a useless life. Having a passion for art, he was interested to learn of a young sculptor who lived in the town. On meeting the intense, impetuous Roderick Hudson and seeing proof of his talent, he offered to subsidize the young artist for a period of study in Rome. Rowland gained the assent of Hudson's widowed mother. At a farewell picnic, Rowland had a last talk with Mary Garland, a distant cousin of Mrs. Hudson, who had been visiting in Northampton. Rowland realized that he would not see her for perhaps three years. In their brief acquaintance, she had come to mean a great deal to him, but on the Atlantic voyage, Roderick Hudson told Rowland that he was engaged to Mary.

In Rome that autumn, as Rowland had expected, Roderick responded to the stimulus provided by the art treasures of the city. He assimilated experience readily and became eager to create masterpieces of his own. Rowland was pleased with his role as patron and nourisher of talent.

One day, while Roderick sat sketching in the Villa Ludovisi, the two companions observed a trio of passersby—a shabbily appearing man, a middle-aged woman, and a young girl with blue eyes, dusky hair, and perfect features. Roderick was enraptured and yearned to model her, but they did not stop.

Rowland began to introduce Roderick into society. The young and handsome sculptor, attractively impertinent and strident, became a favorite. He spent the days hard at work and the nights in Roman drawing rooms. His first work, a life-sized Adam, drew admirers to his studio. Among them were another sculptor, Gloriani, and a young American painter, Sam Singleton. Gloriani was skeptical of Roderick's staying power, while Singleton was an uncritical worshiper. Roderick frequently grew lyrical about his own brilliant future.

The onset of summer, however, brought Roderick to an impasse. His exuberance and inspiration departed. Rowland Mallet prescribed a change of scenery, and the two left Rome to ramble northward. Roderick desired to spend most of the summer alone.

In England, after a month with no word from Roderick, Rowland dispatched a letter. The reply was unsettling; Roderick had been gambling and was heavily in debt. When the two friends met in Geneva, Roderick admitted debauchery but felt no remorse. He had learned his susceptibility to the beauty and mystery of women.

Back in Rome, Roderick was discontented and worked only by fits and starts. Then one day, the man and woman and the beautiful young girl whom he had observed in the Ludovisi gardens burst into his studio. Madame Light, her daughter Christina, and the Cavaliere Giacosa had come to see the rising young sculptor and his works. Roderick insisted he must do a bust of Christina.

Mrs. Light was a vain, silly widow. She had picked up the old Cavaliere in her European ramblings and now lived solely to marry Christina to a fortune. Christina's beauty was supplemented by wit, will, and education.

During the winter, Roderick worked on his bust of Christina and became enamored of her. Rowland feared her influence on him. She seemed selfish and vicious, a complex person who demanded worship. Meanwhile, Christina's mother was becoming established in Roman society. Roderick took a commission from an American snob to create in marble the ideal of Intellectual Refinement.

The old Cavaliere became Rowland's confidant. Roderick would find his love unrequited, he said. Mrs. Light was determined that Christina should marry a man of wealth and position. Though Rowland and Christina disliked each other, they achieved a certain understanding. Christina confessed that she despised her own egotism and longed for someone to free her from herself. Roderick's adoration continued.

In an effort to cool the relationship, Rowland informed Christina of Roderick's engagement. Roderick's subsequent anger revealed something to Rowland: his friend lacked a feeling heart; he did not mind hurting Mary. Rowland's faith in Roderick's potential had been foolish. The artistic temperament was amoral.

Winter brought a new personage on the scene. Prince Casamassima was seen with the Light entourage. He was Mrs. Light's choice for Christina.

Rowland encountered Christina at various places in Rome, and their exchange of frank confidences continued. Rowland requested her to leave

Roderick alone. She seemed to desire Rowland's respect, but when she left Rome briefly, Roderick followed.

Despite Roderick's interlude of riotous living in Naples, Rowland's fondness for him was undiminished. Even when he stopped work on Intellectual Refinement, Rowland tried to understand.

Christina's engagement to Prince Casamassima was announced, but Roderick continued his pursuit. Rowland admitted himself disgusted with people. His good deed had turned sour; Mrs. Hudson and Mary Garland would be hurt to learn the truth about Roderick. His thoughts kept going back to Mary.

Hoping to save the situation, he cabled for Mrs. Hudson and Mary. Roderick greeted Mary in a state of drunkenness. To Rowland, she was more attractive than before.

Although Christina's wedding date was set for June, Roderick's infatuation continued. Rowland was astonished to learn from Madame Grandoni that his own love for Mary Garland was perfectly evident. Then Christina broke off with the Prince. Roderick isolated himself in his quarters for a week to contemplate this good fortune. Mrs. Light summoned Rowland to talk sense to Christina. Mrs. Hudson and Mary, still unaware of the complex situation, suffered in silence.

Rowland unwillingly conversed with Christina. Although Prince Casamassima's money did not excite her, she refused to accept Roderick's proposal of marriage. Three days later, Christina and the Prince were suddenly and privately married. Simultaneously, a secret came to light: Christina's father had been Mrs. Light's lover, the Cavaliere. Christina had married quickly before such a scandal could cause the Prince to break with her.

Roderick, angry, disappointed, and miserable, was ready to leave Rome. He placed himself entirely in Rowland's hands. Rowland agreed when Roderick confessed to his mother and Mary that he was a failure. Mrs. Hudson was appalled to learn that the uncompleted Intellectual Refinement was a five-thousand-dollar commission.

They all went to Europe for the summer. Rowland vaguely hoped that Roderick could still pull himself together. Rowland admired Mary more and more. After an idle, dreary summer, they moved on to Switzerland. Roderick's perceptions of beauty were as acute as ever, but he was unable to do anything constructive.

Rowland pressed the point about Roderick's engagement. Mary did not interest him, but he did not break it off. Roderick saw no point in Rowland's desire to keep his admiration for Mary a secret.

In one of their daily rambles, Roderick and Rowland encountered the Prince and Princess Casamassima. Christina detested her husband. Hitherto petulant and unforgiving of her, Roderick turned to pursuit again. The next day, he asked Rowland for one thousand francs to meet her at Interlaken. He got some money from Mary when Rowland, at the end of his patience, refused the request. He chided Rowland for moralizing, but Rowland admitted his love for Mary.

Roderick then disappeared. A spectacular mountain thunderstorm arose in the afternoon. He had not returned by dawn the next day. Sam Singleton, who had been diligently sketching all the while Roderick had idled, had stopped for a visit. He and Rowland went to look for Roderick. His body lay beneath a high cliff three hours' walk from the inn. He had fallen, apparently, on his way to Interlaken.

Mrs. Hudson and Mary Garland went back to Northampton. Rowland, with his inexhaustible patience, frequently came to call on Mary.

Critical Evaluation:

Roderick Hudson, the first novel of Henry James, is significant for two major reasons. First and most important, it is a readable and interesting book in its own right. The main characters are few and vivid, if exasperating. The main action, Roderick's ultimately tragic plunge into life's fullness, is easily followed, and its implications for the other characters are easily assessed.

Second, James here accumulates a great many of the themes, characters, and artistic devices which will appear in his work for three decades to come. The title character, Hudson, is one of the many sensitive artists and writers who populate James's fiction. He is also the impressionable American who discovers himself while in the process of discovering Europe, as do Christopher Newman, Isabel Archer, and Lambert Strether, in the better-known novels. Furthermore, the satellite characters include certain typical Jamesian figures: a member of the minor European nobility (Prince Casamassima), highly moralistic Americans (Rowland Mallet, Mrs. Hudson), and an energetic conniver (Mrs. Light).

Here, too, are the unmistakable Jamesian themes: the cultured but decadent Europeans set against the moralistic but naïve Americans, the intelligent young person who undergoes a process of self-discovery, the unpleasant and even tragic nature of the confrontation with reality, and the moral dilemmas of an overly sensitive soul.

Artistically, James adopts one of his favorite narrative devices. He puts himself, as the storyteller, inside the consciousness of a single person, Hudson's friend Rowland Mallet. The novel is, then, an account of Rowland's observations and judgments, while at the same time, James keeps Roderick as the main character.

According to his custom, James provides slow and careful development of character, with great attention to nuance of relationship. The reader becomes fascinated, for example, by what appears to be Roderick's callous treatment of his fiancée, and by the tenacious good will of Rowland toward the undeserving Roderick. Even more compelling is Roderick's half-crazed pursuit of the enigmatic Christina Light. (James himself was so taken by her that he made her the focus of a later novel, *The Princess Casamassima*.)

Two differences are likely to be noted between this novel and James's other work: the relative simplicity of style (even in the final revised version) and an unusually full and sensuous evocation of setting in Italy and Switzerland.

Roderick Hudson may be viewed as a signal achievement of American literary independence, as a reflection of the clash between the old world and the new, or as a story of the corruption of innocence by decadence. It is also important to note that *Roderick Hudson* has an artist as its central character. The novel asks what it takes for an American artist to survive as a creative talent. For James, always self-conscious in his role as an artist, and especially an American artist, this was a pressing question. So James's first novel, then, may be considered in many ways as a catalog of temptations, temptations which must be resisted if an artist is to survive and succeed.

It is Roderick's egotism and self-absorption that are ultimately fatal. In order to develop his talent, he must be exposed to the cultural experiences of the civilizations of Europe. At the same time, his selfishness makes him vulnerable to the temptation of Christina Light, and especially to the temptation of possessing her. Plunging into relationships in Europe separates Roderick from the healthy, stabilizing American influence of Mary Garland.

James argues that unless an American artist is able to preserve a certain simplicity and honesty, qualities associated with American civilization, he will be distracted and finally destroyed as a talent by European decadence. At the same time, it is clear from Rowland Mallet's experience, and the experiences of others like him in later works by James, that creative accomplishment also requires a sense of daring and risk. The unwillingness or inability to take those risks also dooms talent.

In *Roderick Hudson*, then, it is balance and poise which are crucial for artistic survival. One may also conclude that *Roderick Hudson* is not merely a prescription for survival in general but expresses James's strategy and hope for himself and reveals those temptations he felt were dangerous for his own development.

THE ROMANTIC COMEDIANS

Type of work: Novel
Author: Ellen Glasgow (1874–1945)
Type of plot: Humorous satire
Time of plot: 1920's
Locale: Richmond, Virginia
First published: 1926

Principal characters:

JUDGE GAMALIEL BLAND HONEYWELL, a widower of
sixty-five
ANNABEL, his second wife and a girl of twenty-three
MRS. UPCHURCH, Annabel's mother
EDMONIA BREDALBANE, the Judge's sister
AMANDA LIGHTFOOT, the Judge's childhood sweetheart

The Story:

As Judge Honeywell walked home from church on the first Easter morning after his wife's death, he was surprised by his own reactions to the Virginia springtime. He felt quite young, for sixty-five, and life with his wife, now dead, seemed so remote as never to have happened. In fact, he felt relieved, for his first wife had seldom let him lead an existence of his own.

The Judge hospitably looked after Mrs. Upchurch and her daughter Annabel because they were kinswomen of his late wife; but shortly after a memorable Easter morning, he began to think of twenty-three-year-old Annabel in quite another way. His changed attitude began because he was secretly sorry for her. She had been engaged to a young man who had left her almost at the altar. It had hurt her bitterly, as the Judge and her mother knew.

As time passed, Judge Honeywell found himself thinking more and more of Annabel Upchurch and of Amanda Lightfoot, his childhood sweetheart. Unfortunately, the Judge's sister, Mrs. Bredalbane, tried to convince him that falling in love with Amanda would be the sensible thing to do. The Judge promptly closed his mind to Amanda and began thinking more of Annabel, who had asked the Judge if he would help her to open a flower shop.

Soon the Judge had purchased a house with a large garden for Mrs. Upchurch and her daughter, so that Annabel might practice landscape gardening. When he told the girl, he added that he only expected the reward of seeing her happy; but when she left, he kissed her.

By the time that Mrs. Upchurch and Annabel were settled in their new home, the Judge knew he was in love with the girl, who was more than forty years younger than he. He bought new clothes and had his hair and beard trimmed to lessen the amount of gray which had appeared. He felt that he could give Annabel everything she needed—love, tenderness, security, and wealth.

The number and quality of the Judge's gifts soon made apparent to Annabel and her mother what was in the old man's mind. Annabel thought at first that it would be more suitable for him to marry her mother; however, as she informed her mother, marrying an older man was certainly better than living in an atmosphere of shabby gentility. Annabel decided to visit Amanda Lightfoot. Knowing that Amanda had never married because she had been in love with the Judge, Annabel wished to find out if the older woman still loved him. If she did not, Annabel decided, she herself would marry him, but the older woman almost refused to say anything at all. Annabel was disappointed but secretly relieved. When she arrived home, Judge Honeywell was waiting with a present for her, a sapphire bracelet. Before he left the house, he told her he loved her, and she accepted him.

After the marriage, the Judge and Annabel traveled in Europe and in England. The Judge felt that he was as fine a man as he had been at thirty-five, although his nerves were jarred a little when someone occasionally referred to Annabel as his daughter. That she often danced with young men did not bother him. He felt no envy of their youth; after all, she was his wife.

The Judge was glad to be back in his home in Virginia after the honeymoon. His dyspepsia soon disappeared after he began to eat familiar cooking once more, and he felt at peace to be living in the familiar old house which had not been refurnished in over thirty years.

The couple dined out frequently and went to many dances. The Judge, after noting how silly his contemporaries appeared on the dance floor, abstained from any dancing, but he encouraged Annabel to enjoy herself. He always went with her, not from jealousy but because he felt that he had to keep up with her life. It cost him a great deal of effort, for on those evenings he sometimes thought that he had never before known what fatigue was really like.

At home, Annabel had brought changes into the house. While he did not approve, Judge Honeywell said nothing until she tried to change the furniture in his own room. She learned then, although it cost him a ring she had admired, that he would not let her meddle with his own privacy.

When the Judge came down with bronchitis, Annabel proved an able and attentive nurse. During his convalescence, however, she found it difficult to remain at home reading night after night. He, noticing her restlessness, told her to begin going out again, even though he could not go with her. When Annabel went out, her mother or the Judge's sister would come to have dinner and stay with him during the evening.

The passing weeks brought a change in Annabel which many people noticed.

Noted for her boisterous spirits and lack of reticence, she surprised them by becoming more vague about her comings and goings. At the same time, they complimented the Judge on how happy she seemed. The compliments made the old gentleman content, for, as he said, Annabel's happiness was what he wanted most.

Slowly, Judge Honeywell began to feel that all was not right in his home. Annabel was distant in her manner. When he talked with his sister and Annabel's mother, both reassured him of the girl's devotion. Still, he knew something was not right. He received proof one day when he found Annabel kissing a young man. Dabney Birdsong belonged to an old family in the community. Annabel had resolved to have him, cost what it might. To the Judge, his greatest sorrow was that it might be only an infatuation which would not make Annabel happy. The girl, on the other hand, thought if she did not have Dabney, she would die.

Annabel and her lover ran away and went to New York. The Judge followed them to the city. Unable to understand his young wife, he felt sorry for her because she defied convention, and he thought that he himself was to blame for what had happened. After a talk with Annabel he left New York, defeated, to return to Virginia.

The rain and the draughty train gave the Judge a cold that turned into influenza, and he was in bed for several weeks in a serious condition. During his convalescence, he discovered that spring had once more arrived. With the stirring in nature, he felt a resurgence of life in his weary body. Like many an old man before him, the season of freshness and greenery gave him the feeling of youth that he had had on the previous Easter Sunday morning. He found himself beginning to look with new, eager interest at the young nurse who was attending him during his illness.

Critical Evaluation:

Ellen Glasgow has been largely overlooked by students of American literature. Her output was prodigious, and her penetrating analysis of the social history of Virginia from 1850 to 1930, her insight into the position of women, and her brilliant use of ironic characterization are qualities that set her apart from the mass of popular novelists of the first third of the century and necessitate a reevaluation of her work.

It was Glasgow's colleague, James Branch Cabell, who first called her a social historian; reviewing *Barren Ground,* he said that her books, taken collectively, were a "portrayal of all social and economic Virginia since the War Between the States." Other critics and Glasgow herself accepted the label; despite its accuracy, the phrase "social historian" is too narrow for the wide range of Glasgow's talents. She has also suffered from commentary by antagonistic male critics. Never one to accept a "woman's role," Glasgow often attacked those whose writing or person she did not admire. This penchant, as well as her creation of less-than-admirable male characters, has led to some highly questionable commentary about both her life and work. As late as 1971, one critic commented on her "anti-maleness," and then went on to contradict himself: "She continued to pursue the male of her own species with glee." Such unmeasured statements have not helped Glasgow's literary reputation.

Properly, Glasgow should be seen as an early member of the Southern Literary Renaissance. In 1931, she helped to organize a conference of Southern writers at the University of Virginia, attended by William Faulkner, Sherwood Anderson, and Allen Tate, among others. She was always interested in her native Virginia and wrote perceptively about various epochs and social classes. If her view is often an ironic one, it nevertheless helps the reader to see the love-hate relationship that she had with the South. She judges, but with a sympathetic voice.

The Romantic Comedians comes just after the more famous *Barren Ground* and is, like Glasgow's succeeding work (*They Stooped to Folly*), a novel of manners. Like all such works, *The Romantic Comedians* depends for much of its impact on tone and point of view, for neither plot nor characters are unique. The novel relies on the reader's knowledge of similar situations and characters in making its ironic commentary. From the outset, the narrator directs the reader's attitudes. Characters' names satirically reveal inner traits: "Bland Honeywell," "Upchurch," "Bredalbane," "Lightfoot." Judge Honeywell is seen as a slightly ridiculous figure, interested in the outward demonstration of his grief and unable to understand correctly his own emotions: "'I am a bird with a broken wing,' he sighed to himself." This romantic outward show of grief over his dead wife lacked sincerity, for simultaneously, he ". . . felt an odd palpitation . . . where his broken wing was helplessly trying to flutter." The narrator's voice is unmistakable, and Glasgow shows herself to be in the great tradition of Jane Austen and George Eliot, two other ironic critics of society.

Judge Honeywell is portrayed as a man of a bygone era, unable to understand or adjust to new ideas, yet somewhat naïvely excited by the prospect of Annabel's youth and beauty. He has firm beliefs which nevertheless do not alter his self-interested actions. His most endearing characteristic is his willingness to forgive Annabel, but this too he carries to excess, needlessly accepting the guilt for her unhappiness.

Not only is Judge Honeywell satirized but also all the characters are shown to be romantic or a bit ridiculous. Annabel is deluded by imagining that ultimate personal happiness is attainable and of primary importance. Her amoral attitude does, however, cut through the hypocrisy and moral sham of people like her mother and Amanda Lightfoot. Annabel asserts that perfect ladies "lie as perfectly as they behave." Edmonia Bredalbane carries her "scandalous" behavior to an extreme which, even in its refreshing lack of

convention, is shown to be silly. Glasgow reverses the generally accepted roles
in the relationship of the Judge and his twin sister; here the woman is eman-
cipated and the man tied by convention.

The theme of the novel is voiced by Mrs. Upchurch who muses on "the
popular superstition that love and happiness are interchangeable terms." She
notes that both old and young, old-fashioned and modern, are "enslaved" by
this illusion. The Judge, Amanda, Annabel, Dabney, "all this company of
happiness-hunters appeared to be little better than a troupe of romantic
comedians." This attitude seems to be the view of the narrator as well, but
Mrs. Upchurch is not always the narrator's mouthpiece. In fact, Mrs.
Upchurch's pragmatic morality, which shifts radically depending on the situation, is as often laughed at as the Judge's unyielding system. Mrs. Upchurch,
however, has a more realistic view of life than any other character.

Glasgow displays skill not only in the consistency of her tone but also in
her use of images to suggest character. The Judge always thinks of Annabel
in terms of nature—"fields and streams," "tall wind-blown grasses," the "April
mist" in her eyes; yet these very qualities in Annabel—her "natural" freedom
and amorality—doom their marriage; wild nature cannot become domestic
and maternal. As their relationship deteriorates, he begins to think of her in
terms of images of light without heat: she lacks the warmth he craves. She
is like "the fire at the heart of an opal"; her head is like "November leaves
in the sunlight"; after she runs off with Dabney, she looks alive "not as a
flower, but as a jewel."

Although the point of view is most often centered in Judge Honeywell's
consciousness, the narrator sometimes inserts commentary to make her attitude more obvious. Usually this is unobtrusive, but occasionally it becomes
an affectation of style or a violation of the convention already established.
An example would be the phrase, "like most lawyers and all vestrymen" in
beginning a comment on the Judge. In general, though, Glasgow's ironic tone
is consistent, pungent, and entertaining. The female characters—including
the dead Cordelia—each represent a distinctive way of dealing with the role
assigned to women in the South of the 1920's. These aspects make Glasgow
more than a social historian and suggest a higher place for her in the hierarchy
of American letters.

ROME HAUL

Type of work: Novel
Author: Walter D. Edmonds (1903–   )
Type of plot: Regional romance
Time of plot: 1850
Locale: Erie Canal
First published: 1929

Principal characters:

> DAN HARROW, a newcomer on the canal
> MOLLY LARKINS, his cook
> FORTUNE FRIENDLY, a canal character
> GENTLEMAN JOE CALASH, a canal highwayman
> JOTHAM KLORE, a canal bully

The Story:

It was early summer. A young man carrying a carpetbag was walking to Boonville, New York, when a peddler named Jacob Turnesa picked him up. The young man said his name was Dan Harrow, lately a farmhand and now looking for work on the Erie Canal. A farm woman stopped them for news and gave them some root beer. She and Turnesa talked about Gentleman Joe Calash, a highwayman on the canal.

While Dan was looking for lodgings in one of the taverns, he saw Gentleman Joe Calash quarreling with Jotham Klore, canal bully. The highwayman struck Klore with his revolver and rode off in the darkness. Dan made no effort to give the alarm, not even for the two thousand dollars reward. Inwardly, he felt sympathy for the robber, who was, like himself, alone and without friends.

Looking for work, Dan went to the *Ella-Romeyn*, the canal boat of Hector Berry. He found Berry playing cards with Sol Tinkle and Mrs. Gurget, Sol's cook. Mrs. Gurget was enormously fat and addicted to rum noggins with lots of lemon in them. Mrs. Berry was away, and so Hector, who could make no decisions without his wife, could only offer Dan a job for the short haul to Rome. Later that day, Mrs. Berry came aboard. She was suspicious of Dan because he was a stranger. Dan left the boat on reaching Rome.

At Rome, he went to Hennessy's Saloon to see Julius Wilson about a job. While he waited, he overheard more talk of Gentleman Joe Calash and of the reward for capturing him. Then Molly Larkins, a pretty canal cook, joined him. Molly cooked for Jotham Klore. When Klore came in, he accused Dan of getting too familiar with Molly. Angry, Dan hit Klore. Gentleman Joe

---

suddenly appeared, knocked out Klore, and held Molly and Dan with his weapon. When they promised not to give the alarm, he made his escape.

A little later, Wilson hired Dan for the haul to Albany on his boat, the *Xerxes*. Ben Rae was the captain and William Wampy, the cook and fiddler. Near Utica, they saw a tall thin man running from a crowd that chased him into a haymow. They learned that the man was a traveling preacher who had been paid for six sermons but had tried to sneak out without giving the last one. Cornered, the minister preached a fire-and-brimstone sermon from the mow. After he had finished, Ben Rae took the minister aboard. He explained that, though he had been trained for the ministry, he was not really a preacher. His name was Fortune Friendly.

At the next stop, Dan went ashore and encountered Molly Larkin again. She had given up her job with Klore and was going to Lucy Cashdollar's place to get a new position. Later that night, Dan got into another fight with Klore and was knocked out. When he regained consciousness, he found that someone had carried him to the boat. He caught a glimpse of Gentleman Joe.

At Albany, Samson Weaver, captain of the *Sarsy Sal*, hired him to drive his team. On the first day of their haul, they saw a burning canal boat condemned because of cholera. Samson claimed he was not afraid of cholera, but he began to drink hard. Ill, he asked Dan to use his money for a doctor, but before Dan could get one Samson died. While looking for an undertaker, Dan found a funeral director who offered him ten dollars for Samson's corpse. He took the money because he could not afford to pay for Samson's funeral.

Deciding to carry on alone, he headed for Lucy Cashdollar's agency. Lucy supplied girls as cooks for lonely canal men. Whether they married the canal men was no concern of hers, but usually she was glad if they did. By nightfall, Molly was installed as the cook aboard the *Sarsy Sal*.

Mr. Butterfield, the agent for whom Samson had worked, offered to keep Dan hauling for him at the rates he had paid Samson. Together they planned to reclaim Samson's body from the surgeon to whom the undertaker had sold it and give it a decent burial.

On the wharf, Dan saw old Fortune Friendly again and hired him as a driver. Molly and Friendly talked about Jotham Klore and agreed that, sooner or later, there would have to be a show-down fight between Klore and Dan. Molly and Dan found Samson's money hidden aboard the *Sarsy Sal*, more than eight hundred dollars. Dan thought it was enough to start a small farm.

When Dan decided to buy a pair of horses at the Utica fair, Molly, Sol Tinkle, Mrs. Gurget, Hector Berry, and Mrs. Berry went with him. While Molly and Dan shopped for a suit for Dan, the clerk treated them as man and wife. Dan almost asked Molly to marry him, but he lost his chance when Hector hurried them along so that his wife could witness the hanging of a woman who had browbeaten her husband and finally killed him. Hector hoped the hanging would be a lesson to his nagging wife. At the fair, Dan purchased two well-matched horses.

Autumn was in the air, and soon the canal would be closed for the season. Jotham Klore had not appeared. His fight with Dan would be postponed until spring. Dan and Molly saw Gentleman Joe again, and the highwayman gave them a jeweled pin as a memento. Dan had always linked himself with Gentleman Joe, feeling that neither he nor the highwayman was really part of the canal.

That winter, Dan and Molly realized that the initial warmth of their feeling for each other was over. Molly confided to her friends that she intended to stay on the canal and that if Dan decided to go back to the land she would leave him. When spring came, Dan received an offer to work on a farm, but the offer was good only if he were not married. Not knowing what to do and unwilling to desert Molly, Dan headed the *Sarsy Sal* west on the canal. At the Lansing Kill, they met Jotham Klore's boat coming toward the lock. Dan and Klore fought on a square of grass that the excited, shouting boaters marked off beside the locks. It was a battle that men talked about on the Erie for years afterward, Dan and Klore pummeling each other under the hot sunshine while Molly Larkin stood by to see what the outcome would be. Dan won, and he and Molly started west once more, but the feeling between them was no longer the same. Dan felt that she was pitying Klore, the beaten bully of the canal.

Then Gentleman Joe was caught and killed, and for the first time, Dan saw the highwayman's cruel, mean face. Somehow, he felt that the highwayman's death freed him from life on the canal. One day, Molly left him to go back to Klore. Dan took the farm job that had been offered him. He knew that he belonged in the farm country from which he had come.

Critical Evaluation:

Although Walter D. Edmonds had published several short stories, *Rome Haul* was his first novel, and it was quite successful with readers and critics. In an opening note, Edmonds describes the fun he had in writing it and how easily the writing progressed; however, he does not discuss the great amount of research he had done in preparation for this book.

There is a native tang and sharpness to this novel, which reclaims a segment of the American past in its picture of life along the Erie Canal. The book is vivid in its painstaking detail. The description of a flock of geese becomes more than description for pictorial effect; it becomes a symbol of the passing of a season and a passing of a way of life. There is poignancy and passion in the lives of people like Dan and Molly, Mrs. Gurget and Sol, and even Gentleman Joe Calash, who lived on the big ditch before the railroads destroyed its free, picturesque life.

Edmonds was already somewhat familiar with canal life, for he had lived in a small town on the Black Canal, and canal life had always fascinated him.

When he left the area to go to Harvard, his memories of the canal remained with him. To authenticate his account of the Erie Canal, he scrupulously studied records, listened to canal legends, and talked to the boatmen. This careful and thorough research is reflected in the realistic and minute detail of scene and action in *Rome Haul*. This is one of the strongest points of his writing, but he is also skilled in creating natural, vigorous dialogue which adds to the reality of the canal atmosphere.

Although Edmonds says that, in writing the book, he lost his earlier interest in the quaintness of the characters and began to see them as real people, a Dickensian touch remains—Dan Harrow is a farmer, Fortune Friendly is a would-be minister, and the enormously fat Mrs. Gurget, with her extreme fondness for rum noggins, immediately reminds one of the unforgettable Sairey Gamp of *Martin Chuzzlewit*. Edmonds, however, does not rely as heavily on caricature as does Dickens.

The plot is the major weakness of the novel, for it is quite loose in spots. As a narrative, the structure is weak, a fault Edmonds corrects in his most famous novel, *Drums Along the Mohawk*. Any lack of literary distinction in *Rome Haul*, however, is amply compensated by the sense of lusty life within the novel.

THE SACRED FOUNT

Type of work: Novel
Author: Henry James (1843–1916)
Type of plot: Psychological realism
Time of plot: 1890's
Locale: Newmarch, a British country estate, and the train from Paddington
   Station to Newmarch
First published: 1901

Principal characters:
   THE NARRATOR,
   GILBERT LONG,
   GUY BRISSENDEN,
   GRACE BRISSENDEN (MRS. BRISS), his wife,
   FORD OBERT, a painter,
   MRS. MAY SERVER, and
   LADY JOHN, all houseguests at Newmarch

To the mystification engendered by the late novels of Henry James, possibly
no work has contributed more spectacularly than *The Sacred Fount*, that
relatively slight book which falls between the weightier *The Awkward Age*
and *The Ambassadors.* The elaborate account of a weekend guest's attempt
to fathom the relations existing among his fellow guests, the novel baffles in
no small part because it is as short on facts—that Mrs. Server has "none too
much money" and has lost three children, and that Ford Obert is a painter
are virtually the only ones to which the reader is treated—as it is long on
speculation, so much so that the very concept of "fact" comes under question.
James has in this, more than in any other of his novels, ruthlessly stripped
away those historical and environmental encrustations that are ordinarily read
for clues to character, in order to concentrate on the central relationships.
That the narrator's speculations are finally refutable or, worse, uncorrobora-
ble is perhaps the ultimate mystification, one compounded even further by
James's feat in casting the ironic spotlight on this his sole novelistic first-
person narrator (and hence the reader's only source of information, other
than reproduced dialogue) in order to call both his motivation and his interpretation into question. Yet this extraordinarily modern opacity of the novel
anticipates Robbe-Grillet, even if antithetically, and is hardly attributable, as
has often been said, to a failure of James's imagination. For the book is itself
about the failure of the imagination. It is the fullest, wittiest, and darkest
development of that breakdown of consciousness which hovers behind all the
major James works, and its opacity is only the lucid rendering of such a
subject.

The Sacred Fount begins as the nameless narrator, said by many critics to

be a novelist—although the only evidence for his being so is the curiosity of
the typical Jamesian observer—encounters two former acquaintances, Gilbert
Long and Grace Brissenden, both of whom are also going to the party at
Newmarch, and both of whom appear to him considerably changed. Long,
who has previously struck him as a handsome clod, seems suddenly to have
become clever, and Mrs. Brissenden, who is supposedly at least forty, seems
to have grown younger, or at least not to have aged. In conversation with
Mrs. Briss, as she is called, the narrator receives the *donnée* for what is to
become his theory, that Gilbert Long's intellectual improvement is the result
of his having entered into a relationship with a clever woman, identified by
Mrs. Briss as Lady John, another guest at Newmarch, who is coming on a
later train with Guy Brissenden, her screen, as that gentleman's wife intimates,
for her affair with Long.

Arriving at the party, the narrator fails, just as he has initially failed in
the case of the wife, to recognize Guy Brissenden, who, though only in his
late twenties, looks older now than his wife—appears, in fact, "quite sixty."
This discovery completes his theory that as one party to a relationship gains,
either physically or intellectually, the other loses, is drained by the "sacrificer"
until quite depleted, a theory which he communicates to Ford Obert, who
has assumed Mrs. Briss to be considerably younger than her husband.

The remainder of the novel details the narrator's attempts to corroborate
his theory. His discovery that Lady John is as witty, and superficial, as ever
leads him to reject her, in a conversation with Mrs. Briss, as Long's "victim,"
for the partner to such a relationship would of necessity lack her former
attributes. At this juncture, the two conspirators discover in colloquy two
figures who prove to be Briss and May Server, the latter presumably using
Briss as a screen, just as Lady John was formerly said to have done. Mrs.
Briss happily proves to be the very woman for whom they have been looking
to serve as the replacement for the now unacceptable Lady John. Mrs. Server
is "all over the place," flitting from man to man in an attempt to mask the
loss of her faculties, Mrs. Briss confides to the narrator in their next interview
(which is their last, save for the extraordinary showdown between the two
which occupies the book's last three chapters), and her description tallies
remarkably with that given the narrator by Ford Obert, who sees Mrs. Server
greatly changed from the self-possessed woman she was when she sat for him
to have her portrait painted. By this time, the narrator, on the grounds of
both Mrs. Briss's and Obert's testimony and of an encounter with Mrs. Server
herself, has come around to accepting Mrs. Briss's account, but his tender
feeling for Mrs. Server, his sense that he and his collaborator are poking into
a matter which is none of their business, and perhaps also his pique that Mrs.
Briss is beating him at his own game, prevent him from acknowledging to
her fully the degree of conviction to which she has brought him around.

The amount of data with which the narrator is confronted becomes prodigious, but the theory expands to accommodate all of it: Lady John makes up to Briss to conceal the fact that she is in love with Long; Mrs. Server's single appearance with Long (the point is actually made by Mrs. Briss) is the exception that proves the rule; Mrs. Server's avoidance of the narrator, out of all the men at the party, indicates her awareness that he is on to her predicament (it never strikes him that she may find his patent inquisitiveness obnoxious); and Mrs. Server's frequent juxtaposition with Briss is less Mrs. Briss's postulated screen than the mutual tacit commiseration of the two victims, each conscious of the other's depletion (it has been the narrator's hypothesis that the two victims know while the two victimizers do not). A conversation with Briss, who tells the narrator that Mrs. Server has nothing to say and confesses a certain terror of, and yet fascination with, her, confirms his view of their condition and mutual relation—even though Briss's confusion might as easily be sincere, and Mrs. Server's evidently morbid state attributable to the loss of her three children. Briss, however, may be covering an actual affair which he is having with Mrs. Server and which prompts him to send Briss off in pursuit of her. In the next scene, the narrator himself engages in talk with Mrs. Server, hinting in a veiled manner at her relation with Briss and gleaning that she takes comfort in his awareness of her plight and his tolerant sympathy. Mrs. Server's participation in the dialogue is, however, so vague and so slight (most of the chapter is simply given up to the narrator's ruminations on the scene's meaning) that the reader can take it as evidence of everything or nothing.

In the ensuing scene, Lady John confronts the narrator with the fact that his supersubtlety and passion for reading meanings into everything have the rest of the company in mortal terror, and she chastises him for sending Briss off to Mrs. Server when it is perfectly obvious to everyone with what loathing she inspires him. The narrator, in an elaborate subterfuge, attempts to convince Lady John that as long as Long is in love with her and he himself with Mrs. Server, she ought to relinquish Briss so that the narrator might at least have the pleasure of seeing the woman he loves, Mrs. Server, get the man she loves, Briss. Their conversation is halted when they see Mrs. Briss and Long deep in talk, a fact which leads the narrator to speculate that Lady John benightedly and jealously conceives a liaison between the two, whereas he, by dint of his "superior wisdom," knows them now to have come to a knowledge, and by the very agency of his inquiries, of their "bloated" or victimizing conditions, and to be joining together for mutual protection. As their talk ends, Mrs. Briss approaches him and briefly informs him that she wishes to speak to him later in the evening, after the other guests have retired.

From here on, the narrator's theory begins to crumble into myriad shards. First, Ford Obert appears to inform him that Mrs. Server is no longer in her drained condition and that the man, whoever he may be, is out of the question since she has given him up. To top this blow, Mrs. Briss arrives to demolish what is left of the narrator's theory. There is nothing in what he says, she informs him, and she has speculated along his lines only under his spell. Mrs. Server is not the woman because there is no woman. Gilbert Long, as her conversation with him has amply testified, is as stupid as he ever had been. As a matter of fact, he and Lady John are lovers, a fact which squares perfectly with his theory because she is not drained (there being very little to drain) nor he improved. Moreover, she has it from Briss that Lady John and Long are intimate. What the narrator has thought he has seen is simply his insanity. Finally, to clinch her argument, to explain, in fact, her wriggling and self-contradiction throughout the course of the interview, Mrs. Server has not been using Briss as a screen; she has—and this from Briss's own lips—been making love to him. Also, Mrs. Server is sharply perceptive. At the narrator's amazed gasp, Mrs. Briss asks if that was not the very thing he had maintained. She then tells him he is crazy and bids him good night. And on this, the narrator can only wanly observe that she has had the last word.

The facts toward which the narrator works, then, are finally unknowable. Whether Mrs. Briss is telling the truth at the end, lying in collusion with Long to protect their status in the sacred fount relationships to which they are parties, or attempting to shield the fact that she is actually carrying on an affair with Long, cannot be resolved. Pointing toward the last interpretation are the "facts" that Mrs. Briss and Long happened to be on the same train for Newmarch, that Briss had been placed in bachelor quarters, the latter a circumstance peculiarly at odds with the narrator's belief that his wife's draining him is sexual in origin.

Such evidence is, like the rest in the book, more suggestive than conclusive. It is interesting to note that both Mrs. Briss and Long broach to the narrator the improvement in the other and that his theory thus receives its impetus and codification in terms which they provide but which she will, later, take great pains to deny. Even more interesting, perhaps, is the fact that the narrator's sense of Long's improvement stems from Long's cordially recognizing him instead of, as is his habit, snubbing him. Here is an indication of the tenuous and egotistical base upon which the entire theory possibly rests, especially as, outside of Mrs. Briss's initial testimony, there is no external evidence whatsoever of Long's presumed metamorphosis. Add to these a propensity and necessity to lie, surely almost as great on the part of the other characters as on the narrator's, and any theory as to the relations at Newmarch collapses because it is incapable of accommodating all the possibilities invoked.

What remains, then, is the discrimination between the narrator's method and Mrs. Briss's tone, his method itself the very preclusion of his sharing her tone, which is that of involvement in his theory. Not only is the possibility of participation in life as coincident with artistic creation called into question, but also art's validity in its own terms, for the novel's end relegates art and the creative imagination to the realm of delusion and madness, containing within themselves the principle of their own destruction.

The narrator is an example of the Jamesian creative imagination, reduced in this case to absurdity, and his theory a type of the work of art, the inclusive imaginative construct. Before his interview with Mrs. Server, the would-be ultimate test of his theory, he pictures himself at the center of the imaginative vision, where possibility looms in every direction and symmetry is achieved. His passion for symmetry even leads him to postulate that, should Gilbert Long change back to his old condition, Mrs. Briss would, in exemplification of the same law, change back too. But the inclusive theory must rest on exclusive facts, and the narrator, working inductively from presumed effect to presumptive cause which exemplifies a general law, must depend upon particulars that exclude other possibilities and alternative hypotheses. To be inclusive in application, the theory must be exclusive in exemplification. The antinomy is present in most of James's fiction and in the prefaces, but in *The Sacred Fount*, it receives its most desperate turn, for not only is the imaginative construct necessarily subject to limitation, but also its relevance to actuality is unknowable, perhaps a phantasm.

If, however, the limitations of artistic creation can be construed as analogous to those of actively living, the narrator's theory may be viewed as in some way figuring his own state. Early in the novel, Grace Brissenden tells him that he has affected her quite as Mrs. Server has affected Mr. Long, and at the end, he feels totally drained by her. This ironic application of the book's central image may be variously interpreted: perhaps Mrs. Briss is draining him by leading him totally astray; more likely, however, the efforts of the creative imagination drain him of vitality, rendering him incapable of life, and conversely, his imaginative strength is sapped in the presence of Mrs. Briss, life's indelicate child. Life is the sacred fount for art, but art is divergent from life. At one point, the narrator confesses that it would have been as embarrassing to reveal how little he knew of experience as it would have been to tell how much he had lived in fancy. He might well be summing up his entire condition, the condition of being thoroughly out of things, for which he tries to compensate in his hypothetical feeling for Mrs. Server.

In a much discussed scene early in the novel, the narrator and Mrs. Server pronounce antithetical views of a portrait of a young man holding what is presumably a mask. The scene is a nicely comic version—comic because, though his intent is to draw from Long a brilliant commentary which will corroborate his theory, the narrator proves himself so garrulous that Long is unable to get a word in—of the doubloon chapter of *Moby Dick* in that the external object, in this case an aesthetic object, is merely the receptacle for a solipsistic projection of individual consciousness. The narrator sees the mask, the work of art, as creating life, giving it meaning, but the book's final view is already latent here, that of the impossibility of ultimate knowledge or absolute meaning. Meaning is relational to the individual consciousness, and the creative consciousness collapses at the end—a method without meaning, a form without content. The "palace of thought" crumbles a "house of cards," not necessarily under pressure from the truth but of internal necessity. For his is the "imagination of atrocity" of which Lady John has accused him, an atrocity that of its own nature necessarily wreaks upon itself. If there is a Sacred Fount, it is inaccessible to the narrator, and his vision perishes of its own aridity and impossibility.

SANCTUARY

Type of work: Novel
Author: William Faulkner (1897–1962)
Type of plot: Psychological melodrama
Time of plot: 1929
Locale: Mississippi and Memphis, Tennessee
First published: 1931

> *Principal characters:*
> POPEYE, a racketeer
> HORACE BENBOW, a lawyer
> TEMPLE DRAKE, a girl attacked and held by Popeye
> TOMMY, a moonshiner killed by Popeye
> LEE GOODWIN, a moonshiner accused of Tommy's murder
> RUBY LAMAR, Goodwin's woman
> REBA RIVERS, the madam of a Memphis bawdy house
> GOWAN STEVENS, a college student

The Story:

Horace Benbow, on his way to Jefferson one afternoon, stopped to drink from a spring on the Old Frenchman place. When he rose, he saw an undersized man in a black suit watching him, the man's hand in a pocket that held his gun. Satisfied at last that the lawyer was not a revenue officer, Popeye led Benbow to the gaunt, gutted ruins of a plantation house. That night the lawyer ate with Popeye, several moonshiners, and a blind and deaf old man, the father of Lee Goodwin, one of the moonshiners. They were fed by Ruby, Goodwin's woman. Later, Benbow was given a lift into Jefferson on a truck loaded with whiskey on its way to Memphis.

The next afternoon, at his widowed sister's home, Benbow watched her walking in the garden with young Gowan Stevens. Stevens left that evening after supper because he had a date with a girl at the State University the following night. The girl was Temple Drake.

After a dance, Stevens got drunk. He awoke the next morning in front of the railroad station. A special train taking university students to a baseball game had already left. Driving rapidly, Stevens caught up with the train in the next town. Temple jumped from the train and climbed into his car. Disgusted with his disheveled appearance, she ordered him to drive her back to the university. Stevens insisted that he had promised to drive her to the game. On the way, he decided to stop at Goodwin's place to buy more whiskey.

Stevens wrecked his car when he struck a barrier across the lane leading to the house. Popeye took Temple and Stevens to the house. Temple went into the kitchen, where Ruby sat smoking and watching the door.

When she saw Stevens again, he was drunk. Then Popeye refused to drive them back to town. Temple was frightened. Ruby told Temple to go into the dining room to eat with the men.

One of the men tried to seize her, and Temple ran from the room. Tommy, one of the moonshiners, followed her with a plate of food. The men began to quarrel, and Stevens was knocked unconscious and carried into the house. Goodwin and a moonshiner named Van tussled until Popeye stopped them. When Van found Temple in one of the bedrooms, Goodwin knocked him down.

Then began a series of comings and goings in the bedroom. Ruby came to stand quietly in the darkness. Later, Popeye appeared and stood silently over the girl. After he had gone, Goodwin entered to claim a raincoat in which Temple had wrapped herself. Popeye returned once more, followed noiselessly by Tommy, who squatted in the dark beside Ruby. When the men finally left the house to load the truck for its run to Memphis, Ruby took Temple out to the barn and stayed with her until daylight.

Stevens awoke early and started out for the nearest house to hire a car. Feeling that he could not face Temple again after his drunken night, he paid a farmer to drive to the house for Temple, while he thumbed a ride into town.

Learning that Stevens had already gone, Temple went into the kitchen with Ruby. When she left the house again, she saw the shadowy outline of a man who was squatting in the bushes and watching her. She returned to the house. Seeing Goodwin coming toward the house, she ran to the barn and hid in the corncrib.

Watching, Popeye saw Goodwin looking from the house toward the barn. In the barn, Popeye found Tommy at the door of the corncrib. While Tommy stood watching Goodwin, Popeye shot him. A short time later, Goodwin told Ruby that Tommy had been shot. He sent her to the nearest house to phone for the sheriff.

Benbow stayed with his sister for two days. When Goodwin was brought in, charged with Tommy's murder, Benbow agreed to defend the prisoner. Goodwin, afraid of Popeye, claimed only that he had not shot Tommy. It was Ruby who told Benbow that Popeye had taken Temple away in his car.

Benbow attempted to trace the girl's whereabouts. State Senator Snopes told him that Judge Drake's daughter was supposed to be visiting an aunt in Michigan after an attempted runaway marriage.

A week before the opening of the court session, Benbow met Senator Snopes again. For a price the politician was willing to reveal that Temple was in Reba Rivers' bawdy house in Memphis. Benbow went at once to see the girl. Temple, although reluctant to talk, confirmed many details of Ruby's story. The lawyer realized that without the girl's testimony he could not prove that Goodwin was innocent of Popeye's crime.

One morning, Temple bribed Reba's black servant to let her out of the house to make a phone call. That evening she managed to sneak out again, just as a car with Popeye in it pulled up at the curb. When she refused to go back to her room, he took her to the Grotto, where Temple had arranged to meet a young man called Red, whom Popeye had taken to her room.

At the Grotto, she danced with Red while Popeye played at the crap table. She begged Red to take her away with him. Later in the evening, two of Popeye's henchmen forced Temple into a car waiting outside. As they drove away, Temple saw Popeye sitting in a parked car.

Red's funeral was held in the Grotto. For the occasion, the tables had been draped in black and a downtown orchestra had been hired to play hymns. Drinks were on the house.

The night before the trial, Benbow learned from Reba Rivers that Popeye and Temple had left her house. Ruby took the witness stand the next day, and she told the story of Tommy's murder. She and Benbow spent that night in the jail cell with Goodwin, who was afraid that Popeye might shoot him from one of the buildings across the street.

Temple, located through the efforts of Senator Snopes, was called to testify the next morning. She indicated that Goodwin was the man who had first attacked her on the day of Tommy's murder. Goodwin was convicted. That night a mob dragged the prisoner from the jail and burned him.

Popeye, on his way to Pensacola, was arrested for the murder of a policeman in Birmingham. The murder had occurred the same night that Red was shot outside the Grotto. Popeye made no defense, and his only claim was that he knew nothing about the Birmingham shooting. Convicted, he was executed for a crime he had not committed.

Judge Drake took his daughter to Europe. In the Luxembourg Gardens with her father, listening in boredom to the band, Temple sat in quiet, sullen discontent.

Critical Evaluation:

The sensationalism stemming from the lurid violence and carnality of *Sanctuary* helped make it a best-seller in 1931 and the first of William Faulkner's novels to reach a wide audience. Faulkner himself once claimed that the work was a potboiler written to make money. Despite his disclaimer, however, *Sanctuary* has since come to be considered an important continuation of the Faulknerian themes of the dillusionment and despair which results from a discovery of the pervasive reality of evil, and the subsequent spiritual collapse that follows the discovery.

Harsh and brutal, the book, on one level, reads like a sensational and motiveless recital of horrors enacted by a sinister cast of grotesques and perverts. Beneath its surface violence, however, the novel has a deeper meaning for which an interesting allegorical interpretation has been suggested: The social order of the old South has been corrupted and defiled by progressive modernism and materialistic exploitation, represented by Popeye and his bootlegging activities, so that historic tradition, symbolized by Horace Benbow, is powerless to act because it is opposed by middle-class apathy and inbred violence which victimizes both blacks and "poor white trash." Viewed in this light, *Sanctuary* is a social document that has its proper place in Faulkner's tragic legend of the South.

This drama of innocence and corruption, a theme that Faulkner also traces in *The Sound and the Fury*, in *Sanctuary* is delineated through the characters of Horace Benbow, Temple Drake, and Popeye. Benbow had been represented earlier by Faulkner in *Sartoris* (1929) as a naïve idealist and worshiper of spiritual purity and beauty in women. His illusions are shattered in *Sanctuary*, first by the realization that his marriage to Belle Mitchell has grown dull and routine, and then by the recognition that Little Belle, to whom he had transferred all his ideals concerning women, is actually no different than Temple Drake, or women generally. The conviction of Goodwin and his death at the hands of the mob undermine Benbow's idealistic beliefs in justice and mankind, just as his new contacts with moral and social hypocrisy, with perverted lust and cruelty, and with the blatant force of evil in the world take away his unrealistic idealizations of life.

Benbow discovers the fact of evil generally, but Temple Drake merely responds to the evil already inherent in her nature. This is what Benbow learns when he speaks to Temple at Miss Reba's. Her rape by Popeye and her subsequent moral degradation have only released in Temple the carnality that her virginity and background had previously checked. She is fascinated by and almost proud of her new moral role, once she has lost her innocence.

Neither good nor evil, Popeye's actions and personality are perverted beyond any moral scope. His sterile, pointless cruelties only emphasize the meaninglessness which Benbow comes to see in the universal order of things. In a world where the innocent are burned by mobs, where the guilty die for the wrong crimes, where public morality is more corrupt than that of a brothel, and where faded traditions are used to veil moral deterioration, a creature like Popeye not only belongs but also makes sense. There is no meaning in Popeye's actions, just as there is no meaning—as Benbow learns—in the "logical pattern" of evil or in life as a whole. Benbow underscores Faulkner's despairing view of the spiritual condition of modern man: There is no meaning.

SARTORIS

Type of work: Novel
Author: William Faulkner (1897–1962)
Type of plot: Psychological realism
Time of plot: 1919–1920
Locale: Jefferson, Yoknapatawpha County, Mississippi
First published: 1929

> *Principal characters:*
>> BAYARD SARTORIS, the son of John Sartoris and grandson of old Bayard
>> NARCISSA BENBOW SARTORIS, the second wife of Bayard and the sister of Horace Benbow
>> AUNT JENNY (VIRGINIA DU PRE), the sister of Colonel John Sartoris and Bayard's great-grandaunt
>> OLD BAYARD SARTORIS, Bayard's grandfather
>> OLD MAN FALLS (WILL), a ninety-four-year-old doctor-of-sorts and a close friend of the family
>> HORACE BENBOW, Narcissa's brother
>> HARRY MITCHELL, Horace's neighbor
>> BELLE MITCHELL, Harry's wife, who married Horace after divorcing Harry
>> BYRON SNOPES, a writer of indecent love letters to Narcissa
>> SIMON STROTHER, the black driver and helper for old Bayard and Aunt Jenny

Sartoris is the third of William Faulkner's novels but the first in which he established the family of Sartoris and the fictional Mississippian town of Jefferson, seat of Yoknapatawpha County, which remained his locale in most of the novels he wrote afterward. The principal character in the novel is Bayard Sartoris, a young man of twenty-six who has just returned from service with the British Royal Air Force in World War I. In a series of actions that reveal a compulsive, self-destructive lust for violence, the young veteran turns his homecoming into tragedy. He begins by purchasing a high-powered new car which he drives at a fanatical speed about the countryside, terrifying pedestrians and wagon drivers; he gashes his head in an attempt to ride bareback on an untrained stallion; he overturns the car into a creek and fractures his ribs in the process. After his bones are mended, he resumes his reckless driving habits, and on one wild ride he plunges over a cliff, causing the death of his grandfather. He flees abruptly from home and finally meets his own end as a test pilot, when he dies in the crash of a crackpot's experimental airplane.

This skeleton of the action in the novel can barely suggest the range and depth of its implications. Much of its power derives from an elaborate counterpoint between past and present. Bayard Sartoris' hunger for violence and recklessness is part of his ancestral inheritance, a kind of inborn fever that courses through his blood. At the beginning of the novel, readers learn that Bayard's wife has died in childbirth and that the war has recently taken his twin brother, John, who was shot down in a plane while fighting the Germans. John's death, however, a consequence of an action which Bayard himself thought foolhardy, is only a symptom of the desperate carelessness with which the Sartoris men have always lived. Young Bayard returns to a house that is still haunted by the ghosts of his great-grandfather, Colonel John Sartoris, and of his great-granduncle, who was also named Bayard Sartoris. The memory of Bayard is kept alive by young Bayard's great-grandaunt, Jenny, sister of the dead Colonel John, who never tires of telling, with romantic (and unconsciously ironic) reverence, the story of how her brother Bayard "gallantly" gave his life at the age of twenty-three during the Civil War; he was killed when he acted on a chance word from General Jeb Stuart and attempted to steal anchovies from a Federal encampment. On the other hand, the ghost of the dead Colonel John perseveres in the tireless recollections of Will Falls, an impoverished nonagenarian who subsists on regular handouts from young Bayard's grandfather, old Bayard, who is president of the local bank. In return for the banker's generosity, Falls sometimes provides a backwoods brand of medical care (he successfully removes a wen from old Bayard's face with an Indian salve considered wholly unacceptable by three doctors), but more often, he brings stories of Colonel John, old Bayard's father and Falls's contemporary. Falls recounts Colonel John's exploits in the Civil War, and he also tells of how the Colonel calmly shot two Yankee carpetbaggers who had tried to gain voting rights for blacks. It is Falls, too, who adverts to Colonel John's death at the hands of a man named Redlaw. One evening, without apparent provocation, Redlaw shot the Colonel in cold blood in the public square of Jefferson.

The Sartoris clan is distinguished, putatively, at least, for more than recklessness and violence. Through the history of its generations, transmuted into the shining gold of legend by the alchemy of Falls's admiration and Aunt Jenny's romantic imagination, are found a powerful strain of heroism, grandeur, nobility, and aristocratic elegance. This is the magnificent myth; and despite the fact that the Sartoris men often live violently and die absurdly, the myth survives. Young Bayard must somehow sustain the would-be tradition in a time of peace, and his extravagant exhibitionism with the wild stallion and the high-powered car is only his odd way of expressing an inherited compulsion. Indeed, although Aunt Jenny and old Bayard repeatedly warn him against the dangers of speeding, his wildness with the car becomes a kind of heroism in the eyes of Narcissa Benbow. She is a frail, quiet, frigidly self-conscious young woman (her name is a clue to her character) who still adores the memory of young John, but who gradually transfers her love to young Bayard. During his bedridden convalescence after he fractures his ribs in the automobile crash, she visits him faithfully, reads to him, and gently penetrates the hard surface of his bitter obsession with violence and with the only person he has ever loved, his dead brother, John. Gradually and delicately, she wins enough of Bayard's attention to become his second wife.

Seemingly, his marriage to Narcissa invests young Bayard's life with a kind of gentleness, dignity, and purpose. For a time at least, she is distinctly a stabilizing influence; she exacts from him a promise that he will curb his reckless driving. Narcissa, however, brings to Bayard her own pale shadow of sordidness, one that constantly threatens the tranquil elegance of the Sartoris home. Before her marriage, she had been receiving unsigned, semi-literate, indecent love letters that she has kept. The letters came from a man called Byron Snopes (again the Christian name is significant, this time iron-ically so), whose surname in the later novels of Faulkner comes to epitomize the crass rootlessness of a family that is the antithesis of the Sartoris clan. In addition, the end of the war has brought home Narcissa's beloved brother Horace, who lives ostensibly in a world of poetry, fine-spun rhetoric, and exquisite glass-blowing (he produces lovely vases from time to time), but who actually is conducting a rather sterile love affair with Belle Mitchell, the wife of his friend and neighbor, Harry Mitchell. Neither Horace Benbow's passion for Belle nor Byron's desperate yearning for Narcissa is satisfactorily resolved in this novel, nor does either man emerge here as a fully developed character. (Faulkner takes them both much further in his later work.) Yet, readers see enough of these men to understand the forces that mysteriously menace the apparent serenity of Narcissa's marriage to Bayard.

In spite of its occasional violence, *Sartoris* is not so terrifying or tragic in impact as several of Faulkner's greater novels, *The Sound and the Fury*, for example, or *Light in August*. His portrayal of the black characters who deco-rate the canvas of his tale in such rich abundance is witty, deft, and buoyant. Early in the novel, the reader meets Simon Strother, the garrulous and super-annuated family retainer, when he comes in a horse-drawn carriage to pick up old Bayard at the bank. Simon is filled with a sense of his own importance as the driver for the most aristocratic family in town, and he manages to give a kind of theatrical majesty to so prosaic an action as the departure of the carriage with the master inside. Readers learn, however, that Simon is just as venal and parasitical as many another black in the town, for it is discovered later that he has misappropriated the money entrusted to him by elders of the local black church. Claiming that he has lost the money in a bad invest-ment, he succeeds in persuading old Bayard to pay off the church elders; but he has actually used their money to keep a young mistress. One day, his body is found in her cabin, his head battered by an unknown assailant. He is a lesser victim of the violence that pervades the novel.

For all his inconsequence, however, what happens to Simon is a good example of what happens to the entire world of Sartoris, to the legend of heroism and majesty. With her brusque and candid insight, Aunt Jenny, herself the repository of the legend, knows only too well the disparity between the romantic ideals inherited from the past and the futile destructiveness of the present. Narcissa marries young Bayard in an atmosphere bright with peace and promise, and shortly afterward, she conceives his child. Marriage is not enough for Bayard; he reverts to his savagery behind the wheel of his newly repaired automobile, kills his grandfather when the car tumbles over a cliff, and promptly abandons his new wife. He seeks escape for a time in the company of the MacCallums, a country family with whom he and Johnny used to go hunting, but there is only pain in their talk of his grandfather or of old hunting days with Johnny, and soon he must be on his lonely way. Later Narcissa learns of his death in an airplane crash. The fatal accident seems to finish the Sartoris line.

The death of young Bayard is robbed of its finality by the almost simultaneous birth of his child, an event which lends a typical Faulknerian ambiguity to the conclusion of the novel. The Sartoris family has not yet succeeded in destroying itself wholly; in the birth of the child, a boy, there is hope for future generations of the line. Yet before he is born, the young boy's future is overshadowed by a fate that comes out of the past. Narcissa wants to christen him Benbow, but Aunt Jenny calls him Johnny while he is still in the womb, a name recalling the impulsive recklessness of the two John Sartorises who came before him. The final scene is ostensibly a peaceful one, with Narcissa softly and gently playing the piano for Aunt Jenny on a calm, windless night. The ghosts of past generations, however, still linger in the house, and through its rooms and hallways readers continue to hear the dark whisperings of disaster and fatality that have always intermingled themselves with the legendary glamour of the Sartoris name.

Indeed, in *Sartoris*, as in the great novels that follow it, no member of the mythic family dies an absolute death. His ghost remains, and his spirit fills the bones and bloodstream of each of his descendants. The novel in which Faulkner introduces this family is far from perfect; it is flawed with broken pieces and unassimilated parts, like the characters of Horace Benbow and Byron Snopes, or the visit of young Bayard to the MacCallums. In *Sartoris* Faulkner established the materials of his fictional world, and out of these materials, molded, shaped, and transformed into the shapes of his great novels, he created the work on which his reputation stands.

SATANSTOE
Or, The Littlepage Manuscripts, a Tale of the Colony

Type of work: Novel
Author: James Fenimore Cooper (1789–1851)
Type of plot: Historical romance
Time of plot: 1751–1758
Locale: New York State
First published: 1845

Principal characters:
>CORNELIUS (CORNY) LITTLEPAGE, the narrator
>HUGH ROGER LITTLEPAGE, Corny's grandfather
>DIRCK VAN VALKENBURGH, called Dirck Follock,
>   Corny's friend
>ABRAHAM VAN VALKENBURGH, called 'Brom Follock, his
>   father
>HERMAN MORDAUNT, a wealthy landowner
>ANNEKE MORDAUNT, his daughter
>MARY WALLACE, her friend
>GUERT TEN EYCK, Corny's friend, in love with Mary
>THE REVEREND THOMAS WORDEN, a clergyman
>JASON NEWCOME, a schoolmaster from Connecticut
>MOTHER DOORTJE, a fortune-teller
>MAJOR BULSTRODE, a British officer, in love with Anneke
>JAAP, Corny's black slave
>MR. TRAVERSE, a surveyor
>SUSQUESUS and
>JUMPER, Indian guides and runners

The Story:

As a lad, Cornelius Littlepage, usually called Corny, studied classics under the Reverend Thomas Worden at Satanstoe as a preparation for going to an American university. Satanstoe was owned by Corny's father and was so named because it was a peninsula shaped like an inverted toe. When Corny's father felt that he was prepared to attend a university, a discussion was held with Abraham Van Valkenburgh, or 'Brom Follock, as he was called, to decide on which university Corny was to attend. Follock also had a son, Dirck, the same age as Corny. After comparing the New England manners at Yale with the manners of Newark, later Princeton, it was decided to send Corny to Princeton.

Before settling at Newark, Corny went with his father to visit New York City. They arrived there during a holiday and toured the streets. Because the Patroon of Albany was visiting the city, a crowd had gathered. Corny noticed a beautiful girl named Anneke who had been insulted when a butcher's boy knocked an apple from her hand. Corny gave the boy a dig in the ribs and then exchanged blows with him. Turning to see the girl again, Corny found that she had disappeared.

In 1755, after completing the four-year course at college, Corny returned to Satanstoe. There he renewed his boyhood friendship with Dirck Follock and met Jason Newcome, the new schoolmaster from Danbury. Newcome took strong exception to New York habits and manners, as exampled by the Reverend Mr. Worden, who played whist with Corny's mother. Newcome, because of his Connecticut upbringing, was not as well educated as were the Littlepages, and he could not understand their leisure. He felt that Corny should work for a living.

When Corny was twenty, he and Dirck traveled to New York City. On the journey, Corny learned that their fathers had jointly purchased some land from the Indians and that probably, next year, they were to be sent to look over the land, which was not far from Albany. While on the road, Dirck pointed out Lilacsbush, the summer home of Herman Mordaunt, his mother's cousin. Corny suggested that they stop there, but Dirck explained that Mordaunt and his motherless daughter Anneke remained in their winter home in New York City until after the Pinkster holidays, around Easter time. Dirck declared that Anneke was one of the prettiest girls in the colony. The pair stopped at Mrs. Light's inn where they heard some gossip about Anneke's many admirers.

In New York City, Corny visited his aunt, Mrs. Legge, while Dirck stayed with relatives in the town. Jason Newcome, being on a holiday, also made his appearance. Soon after their arrival, the three young men went to the town common to watch the Pinkster frolics, a holiday celebrated by the blacks. There they met Anneke Mordaunt, Dirck's cousin, who remembered that Corny had fought the butcher's boy for her sake. The group visited a lion's cage, and Corny was able to save Anneke's life when the crowd pressed her close to the bars, and the animal seized her with one paw. In addition to Anneke's gratitude, Corny also earned that of her father, who invited Corny and Dirck to dine with him. At the Mordaunt house, Corny met several British officers who were numbered among Anneke's admirers. One, Major Bulstrode, asked Corny why he had not enlisted to fight in the war against the French. Corny replied that his grandfather would not have allowed him to join the colors. Later, he expressed his opinion that the war was not really the concern of the settlers but a quarrel between the English and the French.

During the stay in New York, Corny and Dirck frequently visited the Mordaunts. When the officers gave a dramatic performance to which the Mordaunts and their friends were invited, Bulstrode, the starring performer, was offensive to Anneke's sensitivities, theatrical performances not being highly considered in the Colonies. Corny and Dirck then rode with the Mordaunts and Mary Wallace to Lilacsbush. In spite of Corny's efforts to prevent him, Jason Newcome managed to travel with them on the journey back to Satanstoe. On their return home, Corny related the events of his trip, including his meetings with Anneke, to his mother, who was greatly pleased.

In the following March, Dirck and Corny traveled to Albany in order to inspect the land their fathers had bought. They carried with them a quantity of merchandise to sell to the army, which was stationed in Albany. At the inn where they stopped, they learned that the Mordaunts were also there as well as Bulstrode's regiment and that Herman Mordaunt wanted Anneke to marry Bulstrode. Corny and Dirck had the Reverend Mr. Worden and Jason as their companions, as well as Jaap, a faithful black servant. In order to reach Albany, they were forced to cross the Hudson on ice. Although many other wagons had made the crossing, Worden refused to ride in the sleigh and ran alongside, thus acquiring in Albany the title of the "loping Dominie." In Albany, Corny met Guert Ten Eyck, an irresponsible young man who took Corny sledding in the center of the town and humiliated him by guiding the sled to the feet of Anneke and her friend, Mary Wallace; sledding was considered a child's sport. Guert was in love with Mary, who admonished his action severely.

Guert, who helped Corny dispose of the goods he had brought from Satanstoe, invited his friends to dinner. Discovering that the army had stolen his dinner, he tricked Corny and Worden into helping to steal their dinner from the mayor. That official, learning of Guert's trick, invited them to a second dinner that night. Present at the mayor's house were the Mordaunts and Mary Wallace. That same night, Corny told Anneke that Guert loved Mary and then admitted that he loved her. Anneke, hearing his declaration, turned pale.

When Corny met Bulstrode in Albany, the British officer spoke of his love for Anneke and of his hopes of obtaining his father's permission for their marriage. They discussed the war and the relationship between England and the Colonies. Guert Ten Eyck, wishing to go riding with Mary, asked Corny to try to obtain Mr. Mordaunt's approval of a sleigh ride he was planning.

Mr. Mordaunt agreed to accompany Anneke and Mary on the sleigh ride with Guert, Corny, and Dirck on the following Monday. Then, over the weekend, the ice melted on all the roads because spring had arrived suddenly; Guert and Corny feared their trip would have to be postponed until the following year. The Hudson River was still frozen over, however, and Guert's suggestion that they go for a ride on the river itself proved a plan agreeable to the whole party.

The sleighs rode on the ice to Kinderhook without mishap. On the return trip, people frequently called out from the land, but the sleighs were going too fast for the occupants to understand what was being told them. Suddenly, to their dismay, they realized that the warm weather had caused the river to flood, breaking the ice apart and separating the sleighs from dry land. Fearing for the safety of the women, Corny promised to care for Anneke's life, and Guert promised to look after Mary. In their efforts to reach shore safely, the groups were separated, each attempting to save themselves by another route. Through courage and effort, everybody reached shore safely.

Because of their heroism on the ice, Guert and Corny became well-known in Albany. Bulstrode, congratulating Corny, learned for the first time that the young man was in love with Anneke. Although he received this news coolly, Bulstrode said that he saw no reason why he and Corny could not remain friends.

Disappointed in his courtship of Mary, Guert proposed that Corny accompany him on a visit to Mother Doortje, a fortune-teller. The Reverend Mr. Worden, not a strictly moralistic man, went with them, as did Dirck Follock. Although they disguised themselves, the seer recognized them and advised Guert to follow Corny into the woods during the summer. She also identified Worden as the loping Dominie and advised Jason Newcome to buy land for making a mill-seat. When Guert was told he might never marry, the fortune-teller's words caused him to give up almost all hope of winning Mary.

After the arrival of Lord Howe, the British troops moved northward. A short time later, Mr. Mordaunt announced that he was going to visit land of his own, a tract known as Ravensnest, which was very near the Littlepage and Follock property of Mooseridge. The group traveled together to Ravensnest. From there Corny, Dirck, Guert, the surveyor Mr. Traverse, two axmen, two chainbearers, Jaap, and Guert's black servant Pete set out to find Mooseridge. One the way, they met Jumper, an Indian whom they hired as a guide. Later a second Indian, Susquesus, or Trackless, was added to the party. Because of Susquesus' skill in woodcraft, they soon located the boundary marker and immediately began the work of surveying the tract. For shelter, they built a rude but comfortable log cabin.

Learning from the woods runner that the English were about to begin operations against Ticonderoga, Corny, Dirck, Guert, and Jaap, guided by Susquesus, set out to join the expedition. The British were badly defeated at the battle by a smaller force of French and Indians, and Lord Howe was killed. Under Guert's leadership, the volunteers escaped after learning that Bulstrode had been seriously wounded and sent to Ravensnest. Jaap had taken a Canadian Indian, Musquerusque, but he was forced to release his prisoner so that the group could make an escape. Jaap thrashed the Indian before freeing him; Susquesus warned that Jaap had done a very foolish deed. Guided by Susquesus, the party returned to Mooseridge, where they found the surveying party gone.

Susquesus, going to warn the surveyors of the danger of Indian raids, found strange Indian tracks and followed them. That night, the men returned from Ticonderoga, and all slept in the locked hut. In the middle of the night, Corny was awakened by Susquesus, who led him in the direction of cries for help. They found Pete, who had been with the surveyors, tortured and scalped. Later they found the body of one of the hunters and axmen and, a little farther on, the surveyor, his two chainbearers, and the second axman, also scalped and dead. Susquesus said that Musquerusque had taken his revenge for the beating.

Returning to Mooseridge, they found Jumper, the Indian scout, with a letter from Mr. Mordaunt inviting them to join him at Ravensnest. On the way, they came upon a party of Indians and dispersed them in a surprise attack.

At Ravensnest, Corny took the opportunity to press his suit. Anneke, in turn, confessed her love for him, adding that she had never loved Bulstrode. Mary Wallace, however, refused to marry Guert. During an Indian raid on the house, Guert fought with reckless courage. After he and Jaap had been captured, Mary realized that she loved him after all. Guert was mortally wounded, however, while escaping with Jaap from the Indians, and he died in Mary's arms. Bulstrode, confined to his bed because of his wound, did not learn until much later of Anneke's decision to marry Corny. When the two met again at Lilacsbush, Bulstrode offered his rival his hand and best wishes.

Corny's mother was overjoyed to hear of her son's approaching marriage, and Mr. Mordaunt, who had originally favored Bulstrode for his daughter's hand, decided to settle his property on Corny and his bride. After their marriage, Anneke and Corny settled at Lilacsbush. On the death of his grandfather, Corny acquired still more land. He and Anneke lived for many years in peace, and became the happy parents of a son whom they named Mordaunt.

Jason Newcome acquired a mill-seat from Mr. Mordaunt on a cheap lease. The Reverend Mr. Worden returned to Satanstoe. He had decided that missionary life was too difficult and that the only people who should be Christians were people who were already civilized.

Critical Evaluation:

To James Fenimore Cooper, who always felt himself to be a passionate advocate of democracy, property rights were vital to the democratic system. His most emphatic statements on the subject were made in a series of essays entitled *The American Democrat* (1838) where he stated: "As property is the base of all civilization, its existence and security are indispensable to social improvement." In the 1830's, he felt its "existence and security" were in grave jeopardy. In the 1840's the situation, in Cooper's view, became even worse and stimulated The Littlepage Trilogy, the first of which is *Satanstoe.*

The initiating events were a series of antirent wars which took place in upper New York State from 1839 to 1846. The issue involved attempts by the rich descendants of early Dutch settlers to collect long neglected rent payments from tenant farmers who held their land through perpetual or long-term leaseholds. The tenants reacted strongly, even violently, against what they felt to be a grossly unfair arrangement, eventually winning the right to purchase their lands outright. Although Cooper felt the long-term leasehold system to be archaic and inefficient, he saw the antirent agitation as a threat to the rights of property itself, and so he fought against this latest evidence of "leveling" with the only weapon he had, his pen.

It was Cooper's intention in the Littlepage Trilogy to follow a single family of landed gentry through four generations largely by concentrating on biography and realism rather than emphasizing plot and action. The three novels trace the family's fortunes from the establishment of the estate (*Satanstoe*), through the beginnings of social unrest and agitation (*The Chainbearer*, 1845), and ending with the contemporary antirent controversy (*The Redskins*, 1846). This chronicle thus establishes, in Cooper's view, the validity of the landed gentry position by demonstrating their long-term superiority.

In each of the novels, the issue of property rights and natural aristocracy versus forced equality and unmitigated majority rule is argued at great length, and these arguments represent one of the important debates in United States history. Unfortunately, Cooper was never able to integrate successfully his ideas into the action of the stories; the rhetoric remains just that, argument for the sake of argument; and since each novel in the trilogy is increasingly polemical, each is artistically inferior to its predecessor.

Therefore, *Satanstoe* remains the best of the Littlepage Trilogy because its rhetoric is the most muted. To be sure, it lacks the action, intensity, and firm plotting of many earlier Cooper novels. Except for a few incidents, such as the almost disastrous sleigh ride on melting ice, *Satanstoe* is a very leisurely, almost aimless book. The pleasures of the novel reside in the careful, accurate description of mid-eighteenth century life among the landed gentry—social customs, manners, rituals, tastes, courting behavior, life-styles—presented with a gentle, ironic humor. The most evident quality of this society is a sense of security derived from a fixed social order and a stable environment. The disruption of this security, only hinted at in *Satanstoe*, was to be the subject of the subsequent novels as well as the bane of Cooper's later years.

THE SCARLET LETTER

Type of work: Novel
Author: Nathaniel Hawthorne (1804–1864)
Type of plot: Psychological romance
Time of plot: Early days of the Massachusetts Colony
Locale: Boston
First published: 1850

> *Principal characters:*
> HESTER PRYNNE, a woman convicted of adultery
> ARTHUR DIMMESDALE, a minister of the community
> ROGER CHILLINGWORTH, a physician and Hester's
> husband
> PEARL, Hester's daughter

The Story:

On a summer morning in Boston, in the early days of the Massachusetts Colony, a throng of curious people had gathered outside the jail in Prison Lane. They were there looking for Hester Prynne, who had been found guilty of adultery by a court of stern Puritan judges. Condemned to wear on the breast of her gown the scarlet letter, the "A" which stood for adulteress, she was to stand on the stocks before the meetinghouse, so that her shame might be a warning and a reproach to all who saw her. The crowd waited to see her ascend the scaffold with her child in her arms, and there for three hours bear her shame alone.

At last, escorted by the town beadle, the woman appeared. She moved serenely to the steps of the scaffold and stood quietly under the staring eyes that watched her public disgrace. It was whispered in the gathering that she had been spared the penalty of death or branding only through the intercession of the Reverend Arthur Dimmesdale, into whose church she had brought her scandalous sin.

While Hester stood on the scaffold, an elderly, almost deformed man appeared from the edge of the forest. When her agitation made it plain that she had recognized him, he put his finger to his lips as a sign of silence.

Hester's story was well-known in the community. She was the daughter of an ancient house of decayed fortune, and when she was young, her family had married her to a husband who had great repute as a scholar. For some years, they had lived in Antwerp. Two years before, the husband had sent his wife alone across the ocean to the Massachusetts Colony, intending to follow her as soon as he could put his affairs in order. There had been news of his departure, but his ship had never been heard of again. Hester, a young,

THE SCARLET LETTER by Nathaniel Hawthorne. Published by Houghton Mifflin.

attractive widow, had lived quietly in Boston until the time of her disgrace.

The scaffold of the pillory on which Hester stood was situated next to the balcony of the church where all the dignitaries of the colony sat to watch her humiliation. The ministers of the town called on her to name the man who with herself was equally guilty, and the most eloquent of those who exhorted her was the Reverend Arthur Dimmesdale, her pastor. Still Hester refused to name the father of her child, and she was led back to the prison after her period of public shame had ended.

On her return to prison, Hester was found to be in a state of great nervous excitement. When at last medical aid was called, a man was found who professed knowledge of medicine. His name was Roger Chillingworth, he told the jailer, and he had recently arrived in town after a year of residence among the Indians. Chillingworth was the stranger who had appeared so suddenly from the forest while Hester stood on the scaffold that afternoon, and she knew him as her husband, the scholar Prynne. His ship had been wrecked on the coast, and he had been captive among the Indians for many months.

He also asked Hester to name the father of her child. When she refused, he stated that he would remain in Boston to practice medicine, swearing at the same time that he would devote the rest of his life to discovering the identity of the man who had dishonored him. He commanded Hester not to betray the relationship between them, and she swore she would keep his secret.

When Hester's term of imprisonment was over, she found a small house on the outskirts of town, far removed from other habitation. There with her child, whom she had named Pearl, she settled down to earn a living from needlework, an outcast from society and still wearing the scarlet emblem on her breast.

Hester Prynne dressed her child in bright, highly ornamented costumes, in contrast to her own sober dress. As she grew up, Pearl proved to be a capricious, wayward child, hard to discipline. One day, Hester called on Governor Bellingham to deliver a pair of embroidered gloves. She also wanted to see him about the custody of Pearl, for there was a movement afoot among the strict church members to take the child away from her. In the garden of the governor's mansion, Hester found the governor, Dimmesdale, and old Roger Chillingworth. Because the perverse Pearl would not repeat the catechism, the governor was about to separate the child from her mother. Dimmesdale saved the situation, however, by a persuasive speech which resulted in the decision to let Hester keep Pearl, who seemed to be strangely attracted to the minister.

Roger Chillingworth had become intimately acquainted with Arthur Dimmesdale both as his parishioner and his doctor, for the minister had been in ill health ever since the physician had come to town. As the two men lodged in the same house, the physician came to know Dimmesdale's inmost thoughts and feelings. The minister was much perturbed by thoughts of conscience and guilt, but when he expressed these ideas in generalities to his congregation, the people thought him only the more righteous. Slowly in Chillingworth, the conviction grew that Dimmesdale was Pearl's father, and he conjured up for the sick man visions of agony, terror, and remorse.

One night, unable to sleep, Dimmesdale walked to the pillory where Hester Prynne had stood in ignominy. He went up the steps and stood for a long time in the same place. A little later Hester, who had been watching at a deathbed, came by with little Pearl. The minister called them to the scaffold, saying that they had been there before when he lacked courage to stand beside them. Thus the three stood together, Dimmesdale acknowledging himself as Pearl's father, and Hester's partner in sin. This striking tableau was not unobserved. Roger Chillingworth watched them from the shadows.

Hester Prynne was so shocked by Dimmesdale's feeble and unhealthy condition that she determined to see her former husband and plead with him to free the sick minister from his evil influence.

One day, she met the old physician gathering herbs in the forest and begged him to be merciful to his victim. Chillingworth, however, was inexorable; he would not forgo his revenge on the man who had wronged him. Hester then advised him that she would tell Arthur Dimmesdale their secret and warn him against his physician. A short time later, Hester and Pearl intercepted Dimmesdale in the forest as he was returning from a missionary journey to the Indians. Hester confessed her true relation with Chillingworth and warned the minister against the physician's evil influence. She and the clergyman decided to leave the colony together in secret, to take passage in a ship then in the harbor, and to return to the Old World. They were to leave four days later, after Dimmesdale had preached the Election Sermon.

Election Day, on which the new governor was to be installed, was a holiday in Boston, and the port was lively with the unaccustomed presence of sailors from the ship in the harbor. In the crowd was the captain of the vessel, with whom Hester had made arrangements for her own and Dimmesdale's passage. During the morning, the captain informed Hester that Roger Chillingworth had also arranged for passage on the ship. Filled with despair, Hester turned away and went with Pearl to listen to Dimmesdale's sermon.

Unable to find room within the church, she stood at the foot of the scaffold where at least she could hear the sound of his voice. As the procession left the church, everyone had only words of praise for the minister's inspired address. Dimmesdale walked like a man in a dream, and once he tottered and almost fell. When he saw Hester and Pearl at the foot of the scaffold, he stepped out of the procession and called them to him. Then, taking them by the hand, he climbed the steps of the pillory. Almost fainting, but with a voice terrible and majestic, the minister admitted his guilt to the watching people. With a sudden motion, he tore the ministerial band from across his breast and sank dying to the platform. When he thus exposed his breast, witnesses said that the stigma of the scarlet letter "A" was seen imprinted on the flesh above his heart.

Chillingworth, no longer able to wreak his vengeance on Dimmesdale, died within the year, bequeathing his considerable property to Pearl. For a time, Hester disappeared from the colony, but years later, she returned alone to live in her humble thatched cottage and to wear as before the scarlet emblem on her breast. The scarlet letter, which was once her badge of shame, however, became an emblem of her tender mercy and kindness—an object of veneration and reverence to those whose sorrows she alleviated by her deeds of kindness and mercy. At her death, she directed that the only inscription on her tombstone should be the letter "A."

Critical Evaluation:

Since it was first published in 1850, *The Scarlet Letter* has never been out of print, nor indeed out of favor with literary critics. It is inevitably included in listings of the five or ten greatest American novels. Considered the best of Nathaniel Hawthorne's writings, it may also be the most typical—the strongest statement of his recurrent themes and an excellent example of his craftsmanship.

The main thematic emphasis in *The Scarlet Letter*, as in most of Hawthorne's work, is on sin and its effects upon both the individual and society. It is frequently noted that Hawthorne's preoccupation with sin springs from the Puritan-rooted culture in which he lived and from his awareness of two of his own ancestors who had presided over bloody persecutions during the Salem witchcraft trials. It is difficult for readers from a more permissive era to conceive of the heavy import that seventeenth century New Englanders placed upon transgression of the moral code. As Yvor Winters has pointed out, the Puritans, believing in predestination, viewed the commission of any sin as evidence of the sinner's corruption and preordained damnation. The harsh determinism and moralism of those early years, however, had softened somewhat by Hawthorne's day; furthermore, he had worked out, perhaps during the twelve years he spent in contemplation and semi-isolation, his own notions about man's will and his nature. Thus, *The Scarlet Letter* proves him closer to Paul Tillich than to Cotton Mather or Jonathan Edwards. Like Tillich, Hawthorne saw sin not as an act but as a state—that which Existentialists refer to as alienation, and which Tillich describes as a threefold separation from God, other men, and self. This alienation needs no fire and brimstone as consequence; it is in itself a hell.

There is a certain irony in the way in which this concept is worked out in *The Scarlet Letter*. Hester Prynne's pregnancy forces her sin to public view, and she is compelled to wear the scarlet "A" as a symbol of her adultery.

Yet, although she is apparently isolated from normal association with "decent" folk, Hester, having come to terms with her sin, is inwardly reconciled to God and self; and she ministers to the needy among her townspeople, reconciling herself with others until some observe that her "A" now stands for "Able." On the other hand, Arthur Dimmesdale, her secret lover, and Roger Chillingworth, her secret husband, move freely in society and even enjoy prestige: Dimmesdale as a beloved pastor, Chillingworth as a respected physician. But Dimmesdale's secret guilt gnaws so deeply inside him that he views himself with scorn as a hypocrite, and he is unable to make his peace with God or to feel at ease with his fellowman. For his part, Chillingworth has permitted vengeance to permeate his spirit so much that his alienation is absolute; he refers to himself as a "fiend," unable to impart forgiveness or change his profoundly evil path. His is the unpardonable sin—unpardonable not because God will not pardon, but because his own nature has become so depraved that he cannot repent or accept forgiveness.

Hawthorne clearly distinguishes between sins of passion and those of principle. Finally, even Dimmesdale, traditional Puritan though he is, becomes aware of the difference:

> We are not, Hester, the worst sinners in the world. There is one worse than even the polluted priest! That old man's revenge has been blacker than my sin. He has violated, in cold blood, the sanctity of a human heart. Thou and I, Hester, never did so.

Always more concerned with the consequences than the cause of sin, Hawthorne anticipated Sigmund Freud's theories of the effects of guilt to a remarkable extent. Hester, whose guilt is openly known, grows through her suffering into an extraordinarily compassionate and understanding woman, a complete person who is able to come to terms with life—including sin. Dimmesdale, who yearns for the relief of confession, but hides his guilt to safeguard his role as pastor, is devoured internally. Again like Freud, Hawthorne recognized that spiritual turmoil may produce physical distress. Dimmesdale's well-being diminishes, and eventually he dies from no apparent cause other than continual emotional stress.

The Scarlet Letter reflects a number of Hawthorne's shorter works. Dimmesdale reminds one of Young Goodman Brown who, having once glimpsed the darker nature of mankind, must forevermore view humanity as corrupt and hypocritical; and of Parson Hooper in "The Minister's Black Veil," who continues to perform the duties of his calling with eloquence and compassion but is forever separated from the company of men by the veil which he wears as a symbol of secret sin. Chillingworth is essentially like Ethan Brand, the limeburner who found the unpardonable sin in his own heart: "The sin of an intellect that triumphed over the sense of brotherhood with man and reverence for God, and sacrificed everything to its mighty claims!"

Hawthorne's craftsmanship is splendidly demonstrated in *The Scarlet Letter*. The structure is carefully unified, with three crucial scenes at the beginning, middle, and end of the action taking place on the scaffold. The scarlet "A" itself is entwined into the narrative repeatedly, as a symbol of sin or of shame, as a reminder of Hester's ability with the needle and her ableness with people, and in Dimmesdale's case, as evidence of the searing effects of secret guilt. Several times there is forewarning or suggestion that is fulfilled later in the book: for example, notice is made that Pearl, the impish child of Hester and Dimmesdale, seems to lack complete humanity, perhaps because she has never known great sorrow; at the end of the story, when Dimmesdale dies, readers are told that "as [Pearl's] tears fell upon her father's cheek, they were the pledge that she would grow up amid human joy and sorrow, nor forever do battle with the world, but be a woman in it."

Hawthorne's skill as a Symbolist is fully in evidence. As one critic has noted, there is hardly a concrete object in the book that does not do double duty as a symbol: the scarlet letter, the sunlight that eludes Hester, the scaffold of public notice, the armor in which Hester's shame and Pearl's elfishness are distorted and magnified—the list could go on indefinitely. The four main characters themselves also serve as central symbols in this, the greatest allegory of a master allegorist.

THE SEA OF GRASS

Type of work: Novel
Author: Conrad Richter (1890–1968)
Type of plot: Regional romance
Time of plot: 1885–1910
Locale: The Southwest
First published: 1936

> ### Principal characters:
> COLONEL JIM BREWTON, a pioneer rancher
> LUTIE, his wife
> HAL, his nephew
> BRICE CHAMBERLAIN, a lawyer
> BROCK, Lutie's son by Brice Chamberlain

The Story:

Hal Brewton never forgot the day he stood on the railroad platform at Salt Fork, where he waited to meet Lutie Cameron, who was arriving from St. Louis to marry his uncle, Colonel Jim Brewton, the owner of the vast Cross B Ranch. At present, Colonel Brewton was involved in a range war with nesters coming to rip the sod off the grazing lands in order to raise wheat.

On the day of Lutie's arrival, two of the Colonel's cowhands were being tried for shooting at a homesteader on the Brewton range. Although the Colonel's lawyer, Henry McCurtin, won the case, the opposition lawyer, young Brice Chamberlain, protested indignantly that the victory would not be permanent. Colonel Brewton was contemptuous of the lawyer's warnings.

Lutie Cameron was a lovely woman, too lovely for that still-wild territory. When men saw her, she won them completely. Only Hal refused to be moved by her charm. All that winter in an academy at Lexington, Missouri, he thought of her as part of the destruction coming from the East to destroy the sea of grass he loved.

The following summer, he returned to a changed ranch house. Lutie had filled it with furniture and flowers and had planted a row of cottonwoods and tamarisks about it. Guests from the whole territory came and went. Officers from the Army posts, officials of the railroad companies, and neighboring ranchmen all found ample welcome at the home of Colonel and Mrs. Brewton.

The old-timers who had known the Colonel before he had married Lutie hoped she would settle down after her babies came. The babies were born, two boys and a girl; however, Lutie did not settle down. The third baby was scarcely in its cradle before she was dancing with Brice Chamberlain as her favored partner. Colonel Brewton ignored the gossip that was whispered about Lutie.

Local politics shifted with the administration in Washington, for the territory depended upon appointments to its judicial staffs. For a while, Brice Chamberlain had influential support from Washington. Then, during another administration, the forces that backed Colonel Brewton were in power, and the incoming tide of settlers seemed to be checked. Hal read of the change with great pleasure, but when he returned to Salt Fork, he discovered that Chamberlain was still in his law office on the Salt Fork plaza. He learned that hundreds of settlers were waiting nearby for a change in government that would permit them to stake claims upon the miles of land held by men like Colonel Brewton.

Then Lutie calmly announced that she was leaving her husband and children. She explained that she had had enough of the flat grass country and the fighting between ranchers and homesteaders. She claimed she would be able to get possession of her three children, Jimmy, Brock, and Sarah Beth later, by court action.

The town was informed that Mrs. Brewton was leaving for a visit in St. Louis. Most of the people knew better. Their feelings were confirmed when they saw Brice Chamberlain with a bag packed, ready to head east on the same train; but the Colonel paced the station platform, a gun belt buckled under his broadcloth coat. Chamberlain did not board the train.

A few days later, the Colonel sent Hal to Denver, to give Lutie a thousand dollars—he knew that his wife's cowardly lover had no intention of following her—but Hal could find no trace of Lutie in Denver. At the same time, a new administration appointed Chamberlain a judge of the district court. Back in Salt Fork, Hal saw the white-covered wagons of the emigrant trains moving westward into the range country.

When Colonel Brewton planned to run the homesteaders off his land, a troop of cavalry from Fort Ewing was sent to guard him until all chances of his stopping the land grabbers were gone.

Studying for his medical degree, Hal spent three more years away from Salt Fork. When he returned, he discovered that his sea of grass had been hopelessly despoiled. His uncle seemed much older. The Brewton children were growing up wild, for their mother had never sent for them.

One day, Hal saw Jimmy and Brock fighting in the dusty Salt Fork street. Then a nester among the onlookers called out that he was betting on the Chamberlain brat. So Hal heard for the first time the rumor that Brock was not his uncle's son. Hal fired at the nester but missed. When Colonel Brewton appeared, the crowd, even the jeering nesters, grew quiet.

As young Brock grew older, he became the image of Brice Chamberlain. It was obvious that he realized the truth and resented it. He took to gambling, drinking, and barroom brawling. At last, he was caught cheating in a card game. For that disgrace Colonel Brewton could not forgive him, but he continued to indulge the boy and pay his debts.

By that time Hal was practicing medicine in Salt Fork. He was glad when Sarah Beth, who had been away at school, returned and began to look after her father.

One day, Brock shot and killed Dutch Charley, who had accused Brock of using a woman to help him cheat at cards. Brock was locked up, but Brice Chamberlain soon got him out of jail. When Brock returned home, he defied Colonel Brewton and said he was leaving the Brewton ranch to go to work for Brice Chamberlain's interests. This last blow to the Colonel's pride permanently wrecked his health.

Brock now took the name of Chamberlain, an act that cut the old Colonel still more. Brock began to ride wild, shooting up towns and staging reckless holdups. He became the talk of the Southwest for his daring lawlessness. At last, he was trapped by a posse of homesteaders and held at bay in a cabin by twenty or thirty vigilantes.

That same day, Lutie Brewton unexpectedly returned. She was fifteen years older, but she still carried herself with quiet self-possession. Lutie immediately assumed her place in her household as though she had been away fifteen days, not fifteen years.

Meanwhile, the Colonel rode out to the cabin where Brock was holding off the sheriff and the armed and angry nesters. With Hal, who had been summoned to attend a wounded deputy, he broke through to Brock, who lay dying from a bullet wound in his lung. They brought his body back across desolate country scorching in raw sunlight, with nesters' families huddled about sagging shacks and plows rusting in fields where wheat would not grow in hot, rainless summers. Sand was beginning to drift among dugouts and rotting fence posts.

Brock was buried on the Brewton ranch. The stone inscribed with the name "Brock Brewton" was the old Colonel's challenge to all gossip and speculation around Salt Fork. He and Lutie took up their life where she had broken it off years before, and no one ever dared ask either the Colonel or his wife where she had been. It seemed to Hal that the Colonel had found peace at last.

Critical Evaluation:

The Sea of Grass conveys within its brief framework the whole atmosphere of space and freedom of the West, the sweeping drama of the cow country at the end of the last century, when cattlemen fought to hold their free range against the homesteader's fence and plow. For a few years, an empire was available. Whether the ranchers had a greater right to it than the nesters is open to dispute, but the battle they fought was frontier history in brief passage. Employing an almost Homeric mode of narration and description, Conrad

Richter develops a view of the relationship between land and human personality that is quite reminiscent of Norris and Steinbeck.

In addition to the three main characters, there is the New Mexico prairie itself, which assumes an almost personal presence in the novel. The moral quality of the Colonel, Lutie, and Brock is revealed as they each establish their own particular relation to "the sea of grass." In the Colonel, an empathy for and long grappling with the land have produced immense courage, endurance, and directness. Lutie's own vitality and courage are, when tested by the range, found to spring from shallower sources. She must impose her own designs on frontier reality in order to survive psychologically. Ultimately, she cannot endure and escapes to "civilization," the essential qualities of which are embodied in Brice Chamberlain. Brock, who in effect has two fathers, is destroyed by his inability to resolve the conflict between nature (Colonel Brewton) and civilization (Judge Chamberlain).

This conflict is also played out in the struggle between the Cross B and the nesters. Chamberlain, with his cultivated abstractions, pictures the Colonel as merely greedy. In fact, the old pioneer wishes to protect the land from despoliation by the rootless, opportunistic farmers. He refuses to sympathize with their very real plight simply because he knows that the land bears them no such sympathy. The drought that drives them away proves the absurdity of Chamberlain's political machinations and vindicates the Brewton ethic of Stoic patience.

Richter envisions nature as a beautiful yet terrifying Presence which radically determines human destiny. In the novel, he communicates this view by giving the tale overtones of Greek epic poetry. The narrator, Hal Brewton, sings of a forgotten age of heroes. Like Homer, he repeats certain key poetic formulae again and again. Colonel Brewton, though a plain citizen, is really a New Mexico king, and Lutie, his venerated queen. Like classical myth, the plot of *The Sea of Grass* moves in great temporal circles, with new sons emerging to assume the old roles in the same fate-controlled drama.

THE SEA WOLF

Type of work: Novel
Author: Jack London (1876–1916)
Type of plot: Adventure romance
Time of plot: 1904
Locale: Pacific Ocean and Bering Sea
First published: 1904

Principal characters:

> HUMPHREY VAN WEYDEN (HUMP), an unwilling sailor
>   aboard the *Ghost*
> WOLF LARSEN, the captain of the *Ghost*
> MUGRIDGE, the ship's cook
> MAUD BREWSTER, a survivor picked up at sea

The Story:

When the ship in which he was a passenger sank in a collision off the coast of California, Humphrey Van Weyden was picked up by the crew of Wolf Larsen's ship, the *Ghost*, a sailing vessel headed for seal hunting ranges in the Bering Sea. Wolf Larsen was a brute. Van Weyden witnessed the inhuman treatment of a sick mate who died shortly afterward. He saw a cabin boy badly beaten. In his own interview with the captain, he fared little better. Instead of promising to help him return to San Francisco, Wolf demanded that Van Weyden sign as cabin boy and stay with his ship.

The crew set to work taking in the topsails and jibs. From that moment Hump, as the crew called Van Weyden, learned life the hard way. He had to get his sea legs, and he had to learn the stoical indifference to pain and suffering that the sailors seemed to have mastered already. As cabin boy, he peeled potatoes and washed greasy pots and pans. Mugridge, the cook, abused him and robbed him of his money.

Only one man, Louis, seemed to share Hump's feelings about the captain and his ship. Louis predicted many deaths would result from this voyage. He said that Wolf Larsen was a violent, dangerous man and that the crew and seal hunters were vicious outcasts. Wolf did seem mad. He varied from moods of wild exultation to spells of extreme depression. In his cabin were classic books of literature, and when he spoke, he chose either to use excellent English or the lingo of the sailors. Sometimes he amused himself by arguing with Hump. He claimed that life was without meaning.

During a southeaster, Hump badly dislocated his knee, and Wolf unexpectedly allowed Hump to rest for three days while he talked to him about philosophy and literature. When Hump returned to the galley, the cook was whetting his knife. In return, Hump obtained a knife and began whetting it also. His actions so frightened the cowardly cook that Hump was no longer the victim of his abuse.

Louis talked of the coming season with the seals. Moreover, he hinted that trouble would come if the *Macedonia*, a sealing steamer, came near. Captained by Death Larsen, the brother and enemy of Wolf, the *Macedonia* was a certain menace. As a prelude to things to come, an outbreak of fury took place aboard the *Ghost*. First, Wolf Larsen and the mate beat a seaman named Johnson to a pulp because he complained of ill treatment; then Leach, the former cabin boy, beat the cook. Later, two hunters exchanged shots, severely wounding each other, and Wolf beat them because they had crippled themselves before the hunting season began. Afterward, Wolf suffered from one of his periodic headaches. To Hump, life on shipboard was a tremendous experience in human cruelty and viciousness.

A few days later, the men tried to mutiny. In the row that followed, Johansen, the mate, was drowned, and Wolf was nearly killed. While Hump dressed Wolf's wounds, Wolf promoted him to mate in Johansen's place. Both Leach and Johnson would have killed Wolf in a second, but he remained too wary for them.

At the seal hunting grounds, a terrific storm cost them the lives of four men. The ship itself was beaten, its sails torn to shreds and portions of the deck swept into the sea.

When Leach and Johnson deserted in a small skiff, Wolf started out in pursuit. On the morning of the third day, an open boat was sighted. The boat contained a young woman and four men, survivors from a sinking steamer. Wolf took them aboard, planning to make sailors of the men as he had of Hump. Shortly afterward, the *Ghost* overtook Johnson and Leach. Refusing to pick them up, Wolf let them struggle to get aboard until their small craft capsized. He watched them drown without comment and then ordered the ship's course set for a return to the seal hunting grounds.

The woman survivor was Maud Brewster, a rich woman and a poet, as weak physically for a woman as Hump had been for a man. Wolf resented the intimacy that sprang up at once between Maud Brewster and Hump, but he took out his resentment by deciding to give the cook the first bath the cook had ever been known to take.

At his orders, Mugridge was thrown into the water with a towrope slung about his middle. First, however, the cook fled madly about the ship, causing one man to break a leg and another to be injured in a fall. Before Wolf was ready to bring Mugridge back aboard ship, a shark bit off the cook's right foot at the ankle. Dragged aboard, Mugridge in his fury tried to bite Wolf's leg, and the captain almost strangled him. Then Hump bandaged the wounded man's leg. Maud Brewster looked on and nearly fainted.

The *Macedonia* appeared one day and robbed Wolf's hunters of their day's catch of seals by cutting off the line of approach to the *Ghost*. In revenge, Wolf set his men to work capturing hunters from the *Macedonia*. When the *Macedonia* gave chase, Wolf sailed his ship into a fog bank.

That night, Wolf tried to seize Maud, but Hump, awakening, ran his knife into Wolf's shoulder. At the same time, Wolf was overcome by one of his headaches, this seizure accompanied by blindness. Hump helped him to his bunk, and under the cover of darkness, he and Maud made their escape in an open boat. After days of tossing, they came to a small island. Using supplies they had taken from the *Ghost*, they set about making themselves houses and gathering food for the coming winter.

One morning, Hump saw the wreck of the *Ghost* lying offshore. Going aboard, he discovered Wolf alone, his crew having deserted him to go aboard Death Larsen's ship. Wolf seemed nearly insane and had only a sick man's desire to sleep. Hump stole some pistols and food that he took to the island.

Hump, planning to repair the masts of the *Ghost*, began work on the crippled ship. That night, Wolf undid all Hump's work and cast the masts off the vessel.

Hump and Maud began anew to refit the ship. One day, Wolf attempted to murder Hump, but during the struggle, he had one of his spasms and fainted. While he was still unconscious, they handcuffed him and shut him in the hold.

Then they moved aboard the *Ghost*, and the work of refitting the vessel went forward. Wolf became more than a prisoner. He had a stroke that paralyzed the right side of his body.

Hump continued to repair the vessel. At last, it was able to sail. Wolf Larsen finally lost the use of his muscles and lay in a coma. When he died, Hump and Maud buried him at sea. By that time they were deeply in love. When a United States revenue cutter discovered them one day, they felt that their dangerous odyssey was at an end. They were, however, about to begin another, less perilous journey, together.

Critical Evaluation:
Jack London began his career as a sailor, and on shipboard, he observed the sea life that he later described. A teller of two-fisted yarns, he wrote brilliant description to go with tailor-made plots. Enormously popular with American readers, many of his books have been filmed and many of them republished year after year. In *The Sea Wolf*, London told an impossible story with such gusto and fervor that he created reality all his own within his limited, specialized world of violent action and masculine interests.

Published in 1904, the novel is still an exciting yarn; it can also be read as an allegory of the deepest hopes and fears of an age. The hopes were that mankind was becoming more spiritual, that his moral fiber was becoming stronger, his institutions enlightened, and his tastes elevated. The fears were that man's animal nature might frustrate his aspirations and that he might slip backward into a bestial state where his violence, greed, and lust would make a shambles of civilization. Such hopes and fears were a culmination of people's preoccupation with the theories of Charles Darwin (referred to by Wolf and Humphrey), who had shown man to be a product of evolution and a creature of nature.

London was well prepared to write about this tension between man's upward and downward possibilities. Reared in a knockabout way in the San Francisco Bay area, he was on his own at the age of fifteen, a drinking man and oyster pirate by sixteen, and a crewman on a sealing ship at seventeen. He knew the seamy side of life. He was also an avid reader, a man capable of strong romantic attachments, and a worker for social and economic justice. He aspired to a finer life.

In the novel, Wolf Larsen represents the primitive and feral in man and Maud Brewster, the spiritual. They stand, as Humphrey observes, at opposite ends of the ladder of evolution; both tug at him. Humphrey rejects Wolf's philosophy that life is a meaningless and brutal struggle, but he is toughened in body and mind by Wolf's harsh regimen. Maud's beauty and idealism fill Humphrey with love, tenderness, and chivalric courage. Readers may conclude that London was hopeful about man's future. Amoral Wolf's fierce vitality slowly ebbs. Ethereal Maud, brought at last to safety by Humphrey, unites with him in a chaste embrace. In this symbolic union, Humphrey as modern man rejects the cruel and brutish and dedicates himself to what is saving and civilized.

EL SEÑOR PRESIDENTE

Type of work: Novel
Author: Miguel Ángel Asturias (1899–1974)
Type of plot: Dark social satire
Time of plot: Early twentieth century
Locale: Central America
First published: 1946

    Principal characters:

THE PRESIDENT, dictator of a Latin American country
MIGUEL CARA DE ÁNGEL (ANGEL FACE), his crony
GENERAL EUSEBIO CANALES, a political rival
CAMILA CANALES, his daughter
ABEL CARVAJAL, a lawyer and a suspected Canales conspirator
AUDITOR GENERAL DE GUERRA, a Judge Advocate
DR. LUIS BARREÑO, the President's physician
LUCIO VÁSQUEZ, a member of the Secret Police
MR. GENGIS, a whiskey-drinking North American
MAJOR FARFÁN, a hatchetman for the dictator
CONCEPIÓN GAMUCINO (CHÓN GOLD TOOTH), Madame of El Dulce Encanto (The Sweet Enchantment)
COLONEL JOSÉ PARRALES SONRIENTE, a killer for the President
PATAHUECA (FLAT FOOT), a beggar
EL PELELE (ZANY), another beggar
MOSCO (MOSQUITO), a blind and legless beggar

Miguel Ángel Asturias, born in Guatemala, has spent much of his life elsewhere. Going to France in 1923, after finishing his studies as a lawyer at the University of Guatemala, he remained there for ten years, writing poetry in the French style and completing a novel about a Spanish American dictator that he had started before leaving home. He also wrote other fiction and served as Guatemala's diplomatic representative in France, Argentina, El Salvador, and Mexico. Following the increasing success of his writings, he retired to Buenos Aires with his wife and two sons.

It is chiefly for this bitter picture of a morally sick Latin American nation under dictatorship, a disease suffered by many of them, that he is recognized as an important New World author. The pictures of human misery in this novel make a powerful impression on even those critics who find it aesthetically weak. *El Señor Presidente* (English translation, 1963) is rather like that other picture of Central American dictatorships, an example of *esperpéntica*, a mixture of satire and the grotesque.

The novel provides no clue as to date or locale, beyond the mention, when Cara de Ángel was searching the pages of *El Nacional* for an announcement of his wedding, that he saw mention of the Battle of Verdun, at a time when Manuel Estrada Cabrera was the Guatemalan president. Apparently, Asturias had no special target in mind.

As if to lighten the unpleasant pictures of oppression and the exploitation of the poor, the author includes bits of folklore, references to Tohil, Giver of Fire, folk poetry, and descriptions that might have come from Asturias' earlier French Impressionist poetry period. Local color and regional words are so numerous in the novel that Asturias felt the need to include a vocabulary and glossary covering eight pages. The French version of the novel was awarded first place in the International Novel Competition in 1952.

The novel is concerned with the unnamed President of an unnamed Spanish American nation. He is a dictator who maintains himself in power by cruelty and ruthlessness, though his portrait, pasted everywhere, with punishment for its removal, makes him appear a youthful charmer wearing huge epaulets and about to be crowned with a laurel wreath by a smiling cherub. Judge Advocate de Guerra summed up the President's theory of control: never let anyone have grounds for hope; make them realize, by brutal beatings and kickings if necessary, that there is none. The President, lamenting the murder of his hatchetman, Colonel Parrales Sonriente, killed by a crazy beggar named Zany whom he had taunted on the cathedral steps, also revealed his philosophy by declaring that he had intended to make Parrales a general because of his ability to trample on the populace and humiliate them.

The killing of the officer provided the President with an excuse for getting rid of a political rival, General Canales, along with a fellow plotter, Lawyer Abel Carvajal. The Advocate General gathered up all the beggars from the cathedral door where the killing had taken place and beat them until they were willing to swear they had seen Canales commit the murder. The only one refusing to sign the accusation, Mosquito, the legless, blind beggar, was beaten to death. To prevent discovery of the true facts, Vásquez, of the secret police, came upon Zany, the real murderer, trying to flee, and silenced him with two bullets.

Further evidence of the merciless nature of the President is revealed as he orders the beating of his personal physician, Dr. Barreño, for uncovering political graft that had caused the death of soldiers at the hospital, poisoned by impure sodium sulphate. Even worse, he has his secretary whipped to death for spilling ink on a document. It is easy to understand how such a man could mark the innocent General Canales for death.

In order to carry out his scheme against General Canales, the President involved his crony, Miguel Angel Face, in an elaborate plot, first ordering the police to shoot the general if he attempted to flee, then sending Angel Face to warn him of his danger and urge him to escape. The crony, in love with the General's daughter, betrayed his master by getting his victim safely across the frontier. The General, however, died before he could recruit an army for invasion.

Complications, including the acceptance of bribes by the Judge Advocate to put Camila Canales into the Sweet Enchantment brothel, and her rescue by Angel Face, resulted in the arrangement of the marriage of Camila and Angel Face by the President to insure the loyalty of his crony, but through treachery, Angel Face was illegally imprisoned and soon died. Other rebels opposed to the President also died. As opposition continued, so did the atmosphere of terror that allowed the dictator's favorites to thrive in a generally corrupt society. With the Secret Police in power, El Señor Presidente continued to have his way.

A dictatorship in Spanish America may have several aspects. It is frequently viewed by the outside world as a sort of comic opera. O. Henry and others have written of its amusing moments and its romantic and adventurous episodes such as gun-running, but frequently it is much more tragic and cruel. The stakes are high and the financial returns enormous. History records many long-term Latin American dictatorships. Asturias' novel shows how fear and terror can make such longevity possible.

SET THIS HOUSE ON FIRE

Type of work: Novel
Author: William Styron (1925–   )
Type of plot: Psychological realism
Time of plot: Mid-1950's
Locale: Sambuco, Italy, and the American South
First published: 1960

Principal characters:

PETER LEVERETT, a young lawyer and the narrator
MASON FLAGG, a wealthy sensualist and sadist
CASS KINSOLVING, an American artist destroying himself
   with drink
POPPY, his wife
FRANCESCA RICCI, a young Italian servant
ROSEMARIE DE LAFRAMBOISE, Flagg's mistress
CELIA, another of Flagg's mistresses
LUIGI MIGLIORE, a humanistic young policeman

There are two kinds of fictional truth: the literal and the imaginative. The first is presented by writers who show a picture of the time and state of the world about them, and these novelists of the social point of view—Theodore Dreiser, Sinclair Lewis, Ellen Glasgow, Willa Cather—are given ungrudging recognition and belief. This, we agree, is the way people felt and thought and acted in particular times or places, and the stories these writers tell are a re-creation in art of all that is familiar in life.

There is another group of writers—Hawthorne, Melville, James, Hemingway, Faulkner, for example—in whose work readers find an atmosphere of the imaginative and strange, a reflection of reality from angles of vision that give some new or odd dimension to the nature and condition of man. Theirs is the way of distortion, fantasy, symbol, or myth, and the tensions of their books arise from interrelationships of an identifiable social scene and a more shadowy milieu in which artifice, metaphor, irony, and ambiguity replace the picture of life unselected and unarranged with a vision of life rearranged to show it in significant form and charged with moral vigor. One usually has these matters in mind when thinking of a writer's technique, his ability to present meaning achieved by his strategy with structure, image, and style.

William Styron's literary kinship with these latter writers who give experience an imaginative coloring and interpretation is shown by his preoccupation with innocence and guilt, illusion and reality, violence and order, good and evil. It was precisely his ability to give dramatic form to moral issues embedded in character and conduct that made *Lie Down in Darkness* so remarkable and compelling a first novel when it appeared in 1951. That fable of lost innocence and the wisdom generated by despair remains one of the impressive books of the decade, a work in which its Virginia-born author seems to have crossed at one jump the gap between the first novel as a chronicle of one's private loves, hates, and despairs, which most young writers make their starting point, and the work that does the harder job of bringing the imagination powerfully to bear on a world of external fact. A year later, Styron published *The Long Walk*, a novella dealing with military life. After that came eight years of silence, broken from time to time, however, by reports of an ambitious novel on which he was at work.

Set This House on Fire—the title comes from a passage in a sermon by John Donne—was the work in progress. Both its thematic proportions and the author's assured control of his material, aside from several minor flaws in the structure of the novel, should put to rest any interim doubts that admirers of *Lie Down in Darkness* may have had concerning Styron's literary resources or resiliency. The novel marks a considerable advance over its predecessor.

This statement is made in the knowledge that the reactions of the book's first reviewers were on the whole unfavorable. Comments ranged from charges that the novel is somehow meretricious in theme and design, as well as turgid or pretentious in its style, to suggestions that Styron had involved his characters in a mess of such moral nastiness that some of it was likely to rub off on the reader. The interesting thing was that most of this criticism was journalistic in nature and hastily written. Perhaps Styron had waited too long to publish his second book, and the reviewers had grown tired of waiting. Perhaps, too, the mood of the time has changed, and the evil in the world has become so commonplace that many can now think of it only as a force of general upheaval, a matter of little importance when found among the minute particularities of an obsessed and dislocated society. Whatever the reason, Styron nevertheless had his hearing in quarters where it counted for most, in the literary periodicals and the views of serious critics to whom a novel is not news for today or this week but to be read carefully, pondered over, adequately discussed. If one puts *Set This House on Fire* beside *Lie Down in Darkness* for the sake of comparison or contrast, the verdict is likely to be in favor of the later novel. It is a work of bold intent and powerful effect; otherwise, it would not have left as strong an impression on those who criticized it most sharply.

The theme of the novel is the corruption of personality that betrays and destroys, set against a colorful Italian background. Styron, however, has ingeniously reversed the situation central to so much of Henry James's fiction: the spectacle of the innocent American of good will confronting the disillusioning and perverse morality of the European and, in the process, acquiring wisdom and self-knowledge. In this novel, the force of evil is no product of European society or morality. It is the evil of rootless, traditionless American society transplanted to European soil, where it taints everyone it touches with its easy indulgence and lack of moral fiber. This is the significance of Mason Flagg's life as it is reconstructed, several years after his death, by the two men who had known him best.

The narrator is Peter Leverett, a young lawyer of Virginia ancestry, who has spent three years in Rome as a member of an overseas relief agency. About to return to America, he accepts Flagg's invitation to visit him in Sambuco, an isolated Italian village. Leverett had known Flagg in their preparatory school days as the handsome, spoiled son of a doting, alcoholic mother and a father who was too occupied with business to have much time for his wife or son. Years later, Leverett had encountered Flagg in New York, a meeting that revealed once more all that was flawed and phony in his friend's character. In this section of the novel, Styron may be making too much of Leverett's provincialism and Flagg's rather theatrical pursuit of vice—his smoking marijuana, the sex orgies of fabricated sin that he stages, his collection of pornography, his lies, his philosophy that the last frontier is sex. Such a view of Flagg's personality and activities, however, is necessary if readers are to understand the ambivalence in Leverett's attitude toward his former schoolmate. At the time, as he says, he saw Flagg's moral nihilism as not entirely evil because it showed a quality of imagination rare among most sons of wealthy men. Also, this early material helps to prepare readers for the nightmare of Leverett's visit to Sambuco several years later.

The all-night drive Leverett makes from Rome to Sambuco becomes a journey into chaos. Beyond Naples, he is involved in an accident in which an Italian is injured. His next encounter, just outside Sambuco, is with Cass Kinsolving, a young American painter making his last, despairing stand in an alcoholic flight from himself. Cass has lost the will to paint; some twist or warping of love and hate in his nature has made him drag his wife and four children halfway across Europe in his attempt to get away from his own sense of failure. Now he has found Mason Flagg an agent for the destruction he seems to anticipate and welcome. Exhausted and nerve-shaken, Leverett arrives in Sambuco to find a film company—all Flagg's acquaintances—on location there. The day ends with an orgiastic brawl revealing in all its hideous reality the nature of Flagg's hold over Cass and the perverse uses to which he puts the power he has gained over another man's mind and actions.

One of the victims of that terrible night is Francesca Ricci, a young peasant girl of great beauty and innocence in whom Cass is interested because of the simplicity of her youth and for whose father, dying of tuberculosis, he has been stealing medicines from Flagg. She is a servant in Flagg's establishment, and during the night, he pursues her and rapes her. Her shattered body is discovered on a mountain path next morning, shortly before Flagg's body is also found at the foot of the precipice from which he has either jumped or been thrown.

The story of that night of mystery and horror moves forward on three levels—the plane of reportage on which Leverett retells the sequence of events in which he was both spectator and participant; the flashbacks, skillfully controlled, which reveal Flagg's background and the story of his younger years; and the scenes in which Leverett and Cass Kinsolving, now living with his family in Charleston, South Carolina, and painting once more, share their knowledge of Flagg, unravel the mystery of his death, and round out the reader's understanding of what the events of that night signified for all concerned. The way in which two men meet, talk, and find out something gives *Set This House on Fire* its ultimate revelatory power as the themes of the story meet and join to support the vision of evil at the heart of the novel.

To achieve his full effect, Styron resorts to a device of dichotomy that criticism will have to resolve fully before final judgment of the novel can be made. Briefly, the writer has divided one man's experience between two men: Peter Leverett is the man who had fallen more or less under Flagg's corruptive charm when both were young and before circumstances separated them to let each go his own way; Cass Kinsolving, bedeviled, despairing, on the verge of moral as well as physical collapse, is what Leverett might have become under less happy circumstances. The clue to Styron's real meaning is so unobtrusively presented that the reader may overlook it in the scene in which it is presented. Leverett is reporting the episode in which the drunken artist is singing dirty songs and performing lewd antics for the amusement of Flagg's guests. Suddenly, as he says, the situation becomes vividly clear: Mason holds Cass in the same kind of guilty loyalty that Leverett had known as a boy and from which he had only narrowly escaped. Whether this division is justified in terms of character or structure is a matter of doubt. Certainly it adds to the reader's understanding of Styron's novel, but it does so at some cost to the inner harmony of the book.

Aside from this possible flaw in the otherwise beautifully achieved virtuosity of the novel, the novel is a work of considerable dramatic force and imaginative truth on a variety of modern themes: the corruption of power, the perversion of good, the burden of responsibility, the loss of self. *Set This House on Fire* presents unsparingly but compassionately the causes and configuration of man's guilt and the struggle of innocence and self to survive.

THE SEVEN WHO FLED

Type of work: Novel
Author: Frederic Prokosch (1908–   )
Type of plot: Exotic romance
Time of plot: c. 1935
Locale: China
First published: 1937

Principal characters:
LAYEVILLE, an English explorer
SERAFIMOV, a Russian exile
GOUPILLIÈRE, a Belgian criminal
HUGO WILDENBRUCH, a German geologist
JOACHIM VON WALD, an Austrian geologist
MONSIEUR DE LA SCAZE, a wealthy Frenchman
OLIVIA DE LA SCAZE, his Spanish wife
DR. LIU, a Chinese merchant

The Story:

Late one September night, a caravan crossed a dried riverbed and approached Aqsu from the direction of Kashgar. The members of the party were Dr. Liu, a wealthy and cultured Chinese merchant who had hired the caravan; seven Europeans, including one woman, whom he had permitted to join it; and a dozen or more Turki porters. The Europeans had been forced to leave Kashgar because of disturbances in Sinkiang Province. Before them lay an arduous, danger-filled journey of two thousand miles eastward to Shanghai.

Their troubles started early, at Aqsu. Local authorities mysteriously imprisoned the two young geologists, Wildenbruch and von Wald, the German and the Austrian. Two others were detained as hostages, the huge Russian Serafimov and the scarred, wiry Belgian, Goupillière. The remaining three were permitted to move on with Dr. Liu, but wealthy de la Scaze developed a fever and also stayed behind. His young and beautiful Spanish wife went on with the caravan, as did Layeville, the handsome English explorer. Layeville, inured to hardship, withstood imperturbably the rigors of desert heat and distance. The camels were less enduring; and finally, with only four of them left, the party was forced to halt. Fortunately, two caravans soon came into view, one headed eastward and the other toward Tibet. Dr. Liu and Olivia de la Scaze joined the former; but Layeville, to their astonishment, turned back toward Tibet. After weeks of travel, his caravan, misled by a treacherous

---

Tibetan, became hopelessly lost. Among the icy peaks which symbolized something remotely beckoning and unattainable, Layeville calmly awaited the experience he had been half-consciously seeking—death.

Back in Aqsu the hulking Russian exile began his interminable wait in the crowded *caravanserai*. Patient at first, Serafimov soon began to be tortured by physical desire. Hearing of a Russian prostitute who was supposed to possess wit and elegance, he went to her apartment, but she rejected him. Emotional and impulsive, Serafimov daily sank deeper into melancholy brooding. Soon his frustration found an outlet in hatred and jealousy of his cleverer fellow hostage. Eventually, he realized what he had to do—and one dark night, after Goupillière had slipped out to visit Madame Tastin, Serafimov awoke and followed him.

Goupillière had an unsavory past. Scheming and unscrupulous, his unusual beauty had allowed him to prey on women, robbing them of their virtue and jewels. Murder was added to the dark pattern of his crimes when, in blind fury, he strangled a Parisian grisette who had split his cheek with a pair of scissors. In newfound fear, he fled to Saigon—where he met de la Scaze and his wife—and thence to Kashgar and Aqsu. At Aqsu, his ability to torment the clumsy Russian had afforded Goupillière malicious pleasure. Now, however, the discovery of the menace lurking in Serafimov's eyes was turning the Belgian's amusement into fright. One night, coming from Madam Tastin's, Goupillière found the Russian waiting. A short flight, a game of frantic hide-and-seek in the dark, and he felt vast hands closing upon his throat.

Meanwhile Wildenbruch, with his Austrian companion, was still in prison. With Germanic thoroughness, he exercised, he counted passersby, he kept a journal. Finally the vigilance of the guards relaxed, and the prisoners escaped. After fleeing all night, they sighted a caravan which carried them into Mongolia and there abandoned them. They, however, were befriended by an old Russian, Mordovinov, who installed them in one of his two huts and helped them through the winter. During their stay in that frozen wasteland, Wildenbruch began to cough, and occasionally he found his handkerchief stained with blood. The discovery sent a chill of dismay through him, for his mother had died of tuberculosis.

Young von Wald did not find the long Mongolian winter irksome, although he was concerned by his friend's intermittent illness. High-spirited and hopeful, he attempted to encourage the despondent Wildenbruch. With the approach of spring, they decided to resume, once more, their eastward journey. Taking affectionate leave of Mordovinov, they traveled on foot for a few days until they reached a main road and fell in with a caravan of cattle and donkeys. Time passed, and they reached the coast, with Wildenbruch wildly anxious to sail for Germany; but von Wald, entranced with the East, decided to remain in Shanghai.

Shanghai was also the end of the trail for Olivia de la Scaze. Earlier, she had accepted Dr. Liu's hospitable invitation to break her difficult journey at his luxurious home in Lu-chow. It soon became clear, however, that he had no intention of allowing her to leave. Alarmed, she escaped one night and boarded a junk for Shanghai. During the voyage, she became feverish and listless, no longer caring what happened to her or that the Chinese captain and his handsome young pilot were obviously treating her as their virtual captive. Upon reaching Shanghai, she made no resistance when she was led into the street of the prostitutes and placed in a brothel.

A similar resignation to destiny had seized Olivia's husband, recuperating at Aqsu. His money ran low, but he made no effort to depart. Realizing that he had never utilized his powers of observation and understanding, he began to immerse himself in the sights and sounds of the East. The climax of his experience was reached when a beautiful dancing girl came to his apartment— but she brought with her the contagion of cholera. When de la Scaze fell ill, he made his way, like the natives, to the Dying Field. There he awaited, almost joyously, the purification of death.

A final three-cornered encounter took place in Shanghai. After saying good-bye to Wildenbruch, Joachim von Wald strolled back from the docks into the city. Resting at a café, he saw two people emerging from a doorway across the street. One was a prostitute, black-haired and beautifully shaped; she was Spanish, von Wald decided. Her companion was a huge Russian— Serafimov. A vague recollection stirred the Austrian, and he exchanged a few words with the man. Then they parted, and von Wald walked thoughtfully onward through the tangled maze of Shanghai streets.

Critical Evaluation:

Frederic Prokosch won international fame with the *Asiatics*, his first novel, which has been translated into more than fifteen languages. His subsequent works were praised by such writers as W. B. Yeats and Thomas Mann. He has been credited with inventing the "geographical novel" in which sensuality is mingled with irony and mystery. Albert Camus said that he "conveys a fatalistic sense of life half-hidden beneath a rich animal energy." His novels have a breadth of canvas and an inclusiveness which is more characteristic of European than American fiction, and many of his readers have not realized that he is an American. His poetry has received wide acclaim and a number of awards.

In *The Seven Who Fled*, Prokosch lays before the reader a reminder of *The Bridge of San Luis Rey* type of plot, bringing together varied individuals experiencing dangers in an exotic setting. There is more to this Harper Prize-winning novel, however, than the strange, surreal landscape writhing with humanity. Beyond the hallucinatory images of the prose, there is a concern with fundamental issues, with life and death. The episodic tale is told in a series of flashbacks; memory plays a vital role in the lives of these desperate, trapped people. Longings for a past and future are united in the crisis of the present.

Gradually, the portraits of the seven Europeans are filled in. They are not all admirable people, but they are very human. Prokosch's vision of life is grim; his people struggle but are doomed. Yet, at times, there is a strange victory in their damnation, a kind of transcendence for some of them. Nothingness, Prokosch implies, waits like a lover for all mortals. In these tales, death becomes an almost sexual consummation.

The characters suffer extremes of physical and emotional conditions. Stranded two thousand miles from the Caucasus and two thousand miles from Shanghai, they have no choice but to flee, but most of them find that they are helpless. As the events of their lives slow down, the actual pace of living seems to accelerate. A Balzacian vitality and lusty power pervades the descriptions of the low life encountered by the unfortunate seven.

The country itself, China and its borders, dominates the book. One of the characters comments that a landscape is a spiritual thing, a constant longing, a reflection of what is everlasting in human beings. One feels that the terrible deserts and mountains, the earth, the snows, all will remain after the seven Europeans are long forgotten. It is a gloomy message, but is unforgettably presented through dramatic scenes and dreamlike descriptions.

The gradual breaking down of the British explorer Layeville from the hardships of desert and mountains dominates the first half of the novel. His suffering, both mental and physical, his slowly ripening resignation, linger with the reader long after the book is put down. The other most vividly portrayed character in the first two hundred pages of the book is the half-mad Russian, Serafimov. A romantic, passionate man, he is tormented by memories and frustrations. He always felt that there were two people at war in him; a sly fellow and a wild one. He repeats to himself, "I'll survive," but his despair soon overwhelms him. He becomes an obsessed man, torn by an irrational hatred for another man. A strange, violent, almost homoerotic obsession grows between the huge Russian and the small Belgian, Goupillière. As their ardent fears and hates mount, the reader realizes that one of them must inevitably destroy the other.

Serafimov's obsession also includes the middle-aged prostitute Tastin, who desperately attempts to use her feminine wiles on the men who straggle to her door. Also an exile from Russia, she is caught in the web of the struggle for survival, doomed never to escape its sticky embrace.

The two Germans, Hugo Wildenbruch and Joachim von Wald, form another strange and passionate friendship, torn by an almost Dostoevskian perversity. The young Joachim, like the others, seems to be as drawn to death as he is repelled by it. Like the Frenchman de la Scaze, the geologists are filled with a longing for danger, pain, extremity—"to be captured by *reality!*" The wealthy and bored de la Scaze is thrilled even by the prospect of being tortured.

Monsieur de la Scaze wrote one day, as he waited for some change in his condition, that life can only be seen as tragic by a thoughtful and sensitive person. He divided evil into four types, pondering these with a perverse pleasure, only to change his mind and declare that evil cannot be explained at all. His thoughts centered not on his young wife, sent away because of the danger, but on his own past. Like the others, he found himself unable to act rationally, or even at all. He wallowed in a mire of aimless reflections and tangled memories and in vague observations of the strange world around him.

What had most impressed de la Scaze in all of China was its lack of pity. There was no room for pity in a place where the struggle for life was so intense. No longer sheltered by his wealth from the realities of existence, he was shocked by the self-centeredness of most people. Dr. Liu, the Chinese protector of Madame de la Scaze, however, told her that everyone lives on their own invisible pavilions, protecting themselves as much as possible from the stress of naked existence. It was no surprise to this elderly Chinese merchant that men are selfish. He would have been amazed if they were not.

Olivia de la Scaze finally fled from the sinister Dr. Liu, sailing downriver toward the sea, passing an almost mythical Chinese landscape. A lyric beauty and a sense of tragedy seems to flow across the page as the boat carries the young Spanish beauty to her destiny. At its best, Prokosch's style possesses a supple elegance which can transmit the immediate texture of an experience. At its worst, it becomes verbose and rather soft and flabby.

Unfortunately, a degree of posturing weakens the tone of the book. One might argue that the characters are all extremes, not like the normal mass of humanity. That the seven Europeans are consumed with their crazy rivalries, are egoistic and incapable of understanding their situation, is partly the theme of the novel, but they are too passive to be altogether successful as either symbols or heroes.

SEVENTEEN

Type of work: Novel
Author: Booth Tarkington (1869–1946)
Type of plot: Humorous romance
Time of plot: A summer in the early twentieth century
Locale: Small Midwestern town
First published: 1916

> *Principal characters:*
> WILLIAM SYLVANUS BAXTER, a seventeen-year-old youth
> MRS. BAXTER, his mother
> JANE BAXTER, his sister
> MISS PRATT, a summer visitor

The Story:

William Sylvanus Baxter had at last reached the impressive age of seventeen, and as he emerged from the corner drugstore after indulging in two chocolate and strawberry sodas, he tried to impress the town with his lofty air of self-importance. No one noticed him except his friend, Johnny Watson, who destroyed William's hauteur in one breath by calling him "Silly Bill." At that moment, William saw a feminine vision in pink and white. A stranger in town, she carried her parasol and her little white dog with easy grace. William, not daring to speak, managed only an insincere yawn. The vision, taking no apparent notice of William, spoke in charming lisps to her little dog Flopit and disappeared around the corner.

William went home in a daze, hardly bothering to speak to his outrageous little sister, Jane, who greeted him between mouthfuls of applesauce and bread. Scorning her, he went up to his room, his heart full of the mystery of love, and composed a poem to his new and unknown lady. He was interrupted by his mother, who asked William to go with Genesis, the black handyman, to pick up some laundry tubs from the secondhand store. The errand, to William, was worse than being seen in public with a leper, for he looked on Genesis as a ragged, bedraggled, down-at-the-heels pariah, whose presence was an unwholesome reproach to the whole neighborhood.

Genesis was in reality a wise old philosopher, despite his seminudity and the ubiquitous presence of his mongrel dog, Clematis; yet William was in no mood to be tolerant. His worst fears were realized when, on the way home, he heard behind him the silvery voice of the fair stranger referring to Clematis as a nasty old dog. William was hidden by the laundry tub he carried over his head, but his invisibility in no way diminished his growing horror at being taken for a companion of Genesis and the owner of the dreadful Clematis. Clematis, meanwhile, was fascinated by Flopit. When William heard the yips and barks of the two dogs, he ran away, still hidden under his protecting tub.

The young vision in pink and white was the summer visitor of May Parcher. Her name, William learned, was Miss Pratt. Soon the boys in the neighborhood collected on the Parcher porch and swarmed around the adorable girl every evening after supper, much to the disgust of Mr. Parcher, who lay awake for hours in his room over the porch and listened reluctantly to the drivel of conversation below. William had an advantage over the other suitors, for he borrowed his father's dress suit without his parents' knowledge and arrived each night in splendid attire.

During the day, William could not escape his sister Jane, who insisted on appearing in dirty summer sunsuits, her face smeared with her favorite repast of applesauce and bread, just at the moment when William would be walking by the house with Miss Pratt. His angry demands that his sister present a more ladylike appearance irritated Jane to a calm, smouldering intent to get even with William. She knew that William wore his father's dress suit every evening when he visited Miss Pratt. She also knew that Mr. Parcher was nearly crazy over the nightly sessions on his front porch. Putting these facts together, she coldly repeated to her mother some of Mr. Parcher's comments. Mrs. Baxter was horrified that William had worn out his welcome at the Parcher's, and when she discovered Mr. Baxter's dress suit under William's window seat, she took it to a tailor and had it altered to fit only Mr. Baxter. William could not go to see Miss Pratt without the dress suit. He was not among Miss Pratt's evening admirers thereafter.

As a reward to Jane, who had immediately told him of her part in decreasing by one the population of his front porch, Mr. Parcher sent her a five-pound box of candy, much to the amazement of the whole Baxter household. No one suspected Jane's perfidy.

Feeling herself to blame for William's gloomy moods, Mrs. Baxter decided to have a tea for some of her son's friends, with Miss Pratt as guest of honor. The great day arrived, swelteringly hot. Upstairs, William had no sooner broken his only collar button on his fifth and last white shirt than he had the misfortune to tear his white trousers. Another suit was splattered by Jane's paints. By the time he found a heavy winter suit in a trunk in the attic, the guests had gone. Angry and miserable, William sat down on Jane's open, wet paint box.

The time came for Miss Pratt to return home. As a farewell party, the relieved Parchers scheduled a picnic in their guest's honor. To impress Miss Pratt, William bought a package of Cuban cigarettes, but coy Miss Pratt gave all her attention to George, a braggart who stuffed himself with food to impress the beauty with his gustatory prowess. Lunch over, William offered George his cigarettes. Before long, he had the satisfaction of seeing George disappear behind a woodpile. William was blissful once more.

When Miss Pratt unexpectedly granted the weary Parchers the privilege of her company for another week, they gave a final farewell dance in her honor. Mrs. Baxter had her husband's dress suit again altered to fit William. Resplendent, but late as usual, William arrived at the dance to find all Miss Pratt's dances taken, and he was forced to spend the evening with a lonely wallflower. His dignity suffered another blow when Genesis, serving sandwiches, not only greeted William with familiarity but also chided him about the dress suit. His evening was a dismal failure.

The next day, William went down to the train to see Miss Pratt off. Laden with candy and lush poetry, he found her surrounded by her many admirers. He had the uncomfortable sensation that they were all laughing at him, for they were pointing derisively in his direction. Turning, he saw Jane, who had deliberately come to torment him in company with an equally disreputable female companion. The two pranksters were walking with a vulgar strut that William abhorred. So flustered was he that he merely waved to Miss Pratt and went sadly home, forgetting that he still carried under his arm the box of candy and the poem intended for the pink and white beauty who was going out of his life forever.

Critical Evaluation:

One reviewer of *Seventeen*, after its first publication in 1916, suggested that the only person who would not like or appreciate the book would be a seventeen-year-old. Even though the book is nearly half a century old, the story of youthful love is not. Booth Tarkington depicts the situation with skill and humor. He portrays William Sylvanus Baxter as a love-struck seventeen-year-old whose life, for one summer at least, revolves around the rather silly and childish Lola Pratt. Tarkington's humor is sympathetic and understanding, and because he does not take his hero seriously, the book remains light and funny. Seventeen is an age of extreme self-consciousness and portentous seriousness, not only for William Baxter, but for most boys his age, then and now. Tarkington knows this well and capitalizes upon the traumas of male adolescence. His sense of timing is perfect, and he uses his humor at exactly the right moment to achieve the maximum effect. For example, when Mr. Parcher is suffering from listening to the meaningless and saccharine conversations between "little boy Baxter" and Miss Pratt, William's description of his flame as "My Baby Talk Lady" is the last straw, causing him to explode and send volumes of Plutarch flying across the room.

The novel is full of all the characters necessary to make a believable situation comedy. On the one hand, there is the obnoxious and menacing little sister, Jane, to act as William's chief antagonist. Then there are his parents who seem to thwart his every attempt to appear grown-up and independent to his friends. Mrs. Baxter, true to form for a mother, understands her son better than anyone else and realizes that youngsters do strange things that they "get over" in time. In the end, she tries to make life easier for him by making his father's dress clothes conveniently available to William for Lola's farewell party. There are times, though, when she appears to William to be unsympathetic and completely against him. William's peers are all sketches of simple, believable buddies who are all after the same thing—Lola Pratt. There is a camaraderie among them in their attempts to share her for the summer, which seems to them the best possible arrangement under the circumstances. Genesis, the old hired hand, presents a different type of problem for William Baxter, whose relationship to the black man is one of the aspects of the story that date it.

On the whole, *Seventeen* provides light entertainment for the young reader. There are no complicated literary techniques (apart from Miss Pratt's rather ridiculous speeches), and the story is a straightforward, humorous, and accurate study of a boy in his teens.

SHADOWS ON THE ROCK

Type of work: Novel
Author: Willa Cather (1873–1947)
Type of plot: Historical chronicle
Time of plot: Late seventeenth century
Locale: Quebec, Canada
First published: 1931

> *Principal characters:*
> EUCLIDE AUCLAIR, the apothecary in Quebec
> CÉCILE AUCLAIR, his daughter
> COUNT FRONTENAC, the governor of New France and
> Auclair's patron
> PIERRE CHARRON, a Canadian woodsman

The Story:

Late in October of 1697, the last ship left Quebec to return to France, and the colony of New France was isolated from the world until the arrival of the fleet in June or July of the following year. One of the persons who watched as the last vessel passed out of sight down the St. Lawrence River was Euclide Auclair, the apothecary in Quebec.

Auclair lived on the street that wound up the slope and connected the Upper Town on the cliff with the Lower Town which clustered along the shore of the river at the foot of the mountain. In his home behind his shop, Auclair and his daughter Cécile did their best to re-create the atmosphere they had known in France. So successful were they that many people came to the shop merely to visit and snatch a breath of the France they had left behind.

Cécile was only twelve years old and her mother had been dead for several years. Although she was content to remain in Canada, her father seemed to live only for the time when he could return to France with his patron, the governor of the colony, Count Frontenac. Auclair, who had served the Count for many years, was a trusted friend of the governor as well as his apothecary.

A few weeks after the last ship had departed, Cécile went to see the Count to ask his aid in obtaining some shoes for a little orphan boy. The governor was glad to see her, for too many of the people who came to him were anxious only to help themselves. He said that when he made his will he would leave the girl a bowl of glass fruit that she had always admired.

The first days of December brought a heavy fall of snow which ushered in the deepest reality of life in Canada, the long, dark winter. The snow also reminded Cécile of the boxes of Christmas presents which had been sent to her by aunts in France the previous summer. On the twenty-fourth of December, the Auclairs brought the boxes out of their storage place. In one was a crèche to be set up in their living room. The crèche was the crowning point of Christmas for many of their friends, for the French colonists were, as a rule, very devout.

One day in March, Father Hector Saint-Cyr put in his appearance. The priest spent several evenings recounting to the Auclairs stories of the missionaries, the Indians, and the hardships of backwoods life. When he left, Euclide Auclair wondered if, after all, the gifts of an educated man like Father Saint-Cyr might not be going to waste in misplaced heroisms among the Canadian missions to the Indians.

About the middle of March, the weather changed. There was a continuous downpour of rain which the snow soaked up as if it were a gigantic sponge. Even the ice in the St. Lawrence broke up and floated downstream in huge gray blocks. It was a season of sickness, and the apothecary was busy from morning until night acting as doctor to many of the inhabitants of the town. Cécile herself caught a cold and was in bed for several days.

One evening while Cécile was ill, Auclair had a strange visit with a misshapen hunchback who secured water and wood for the Auclairs in return for a bowl of soup and a small glass of brandy each evening. Blinker, as the hunchback was called, told Auclair that as a boy he had been an apprentice to his father, one of the king's torturers at Rouen. Blinker had tortured an old woman into admitting that she had murdered her son. Some months after her execution, the son had returned. The shock of what he had done was too great for the apprentice. He ran away, took ship, and went to Quebec to begin a new life. Nevertheless, visions of the old woman haunted him so that he could not sleep. Filled with sympathy, the apothecary gave Blinker some laudanum so that he might have a little untroubled rest.

One day, while Cécile was regaining her strength, her father wrapped her in a blanket and carried her to the door. There, outside the door, Cécile saw the first swallow hunting for its old nest in the wall of the cliff that rose sharply to the chateau above. Delighted at this sign, Cécile had her father inform old Bishop Laval of the bird's appearance. The old man had kept a record of the changing seasons for thirty-eight years, and he had always included the date of the first swallow's arrival.

On the first day of June, the leaves began to bud, and the hunters arrived from the woods with their loads of pelts. Among the first hunters to reach Quebec was Pierre Charron, an old friend of the apothecary and his daughter. Pierre, the son of a rich family in Montreal, had been disappointed in love. His sweetheart decided to build a chapel with her dowry and enter the Church as a recluse. After she had taken her vows, Pierre had become a hunter traveling through the wilderness as far as Michilimackinac and Lake Superior in his quest for furs and forgetfulness. During the spring, Pierre Charron took Cécile with him to visit some friends on the Isle d'Orleans, in the St. Lawrence four miles below Quebec. The squalid and primitive life there disgusted Cécile.

Early in July, the ships from France arrived. The Count had requested the king to recall him from Canada, and he had promised that he would take the Auclairs back to France with him. As each ship arrived through the summer, the Auclairs looked for the governor's recall. When late October arrived, the Count called Euclide Auclair to the chateau to warn him that the king's request would never come. When the Count offered to send the Auclairs back to France, Euclide refused, assuring the Count that he could not leave while his patron was forced to remain in Quebec.

The last ship left Quebec in October. Shortly afterward, Count Frontenac became ill. Euclide Auclair knew that his patient could not live through the winter. When the Count died, Euclide carried out his patron's last wish. He sealed the Count's heart in a lead box and sent it with a missionary priest to the English colonies in the south. From there, it was returned to France for burial.

The death of the Count was a great blow to the Auclairs, for security seemed to have gone from their lives. Thinking of returning to France that year, they had not even laid in a proper supply of food to last through the winter. Fortunately for them, Pierre Charron arrived in Quebec with an offer of help. Later he married Cécile. Charron had not the authority of documents and seals which the Count had had to protect them, but he had his knowledge of the woods and the people, which was as good or better in the wilds of Canada. The future was safe.

Critical Evaluation:

Shadows on the Rock is a very human story about a little-known segment of North American history, the early colonies in Canada. Unlike many fictional French people in the literature of Great Britain and America, Willa Cather's characters maintain personalities and enlist the sympathies of the Anglo-Saxon reader. The author has divested them of any alien spirit so that they become members of the human family rather than members of a different national stock. The book is also a mine of information on life in Quebec at the end of the seventeenth century. The author noted in great detail the customs, habits, and daily routine of the people whom she described, even to the food they ate and the homes in which they lived.

The novel is a series of incidents set on the rock of Quebec in the late seventeenth century. It explores the qualities of the French civilization that grew up there through vignettes of simple people, their homes, labors, friendships, and desires. Cather explained that the title of this novel was significant, for the people of Quebec have long "cast their shadows" on the city: the people have changed, but the culture has endured.

The story revolves primarily around the widowed apothecary, Euclide Auclair, and his young daughter, Cécile; much of what the reader sees in this settlement is seen through the eyes of young Cécile. The simplicity of her viewpoint is refreshing as well as colorful. She is presented as dutiful and responsive to others, while her father is affectionate and thoughtful. All the characters are "types" that fit easily into the historical scenario; the sensitive and pitiful little Jacques, the strong and adventurous Pierre Charron, the noble but disillusioned old Count, and the flamboyant Bishop Laval. The characters lack great depth and dimension, but they fit carefully into their environment and contribute beautifully to the domestic picture of a French settlement. They are related to this rock, Quebec, to the world across the ocean in France, and to the challenge of the future. Cather draws a picture that emphasizes the hopes and expectations of the people in Quebec as her characters work to create order in a savage land.

One cannot look at this novel, however briefly, without noticing the innumerable descriptions of the religious traditions of the people. The colonists may be exiled from their homes in France, cut off from their families and friends, but they have brought their religious tradition and a great reverence for it with them. Cather spends the first three books emphasizing the religious foundations upon which the French colony was built. There are stories of saints and martyrs, such as the famous Montreal recluse, and involved explanations of the rivalry between the old Bishop and his successor. These narratives provide background and place the religious aspect in sharp contrast with the stories of adventure and bravery in the wilderness that follow in the last part of the book.

Through these vignettes, Cather created a mood, a picture of life that illustrates the virtues in the lives of proud people and how those virtues are symbolized in the enduring rock of Quebec.

THE SHELTERED LIFE

Type of work: Novel
Author: Ellen Glasgow (1874–1945)
Type of plot: Social criticism
Time of plot: Twentieth century
Locale: Virginia
First published: 1932

Principal characters:

> GENERAL ARCHBALD, a Southern gentleman
> JENNY BLAIR ARCHBALD, his granddaughter
> GEORGE BIRDSONG, his neighbor
> EVA BIRDSONG, George's wife

The Story:

The Archbalds and the Birdsongs were the last of the old families left on once-fashionable Washington Street, and they clung to it along with their passion for the gentility of the past decades in an effort to keep things as they had always known them. They not only disliked change; they also forbade it on their premises.

Jenny Blair Archbald was five years old when her father died. A short time later, her mother had gone to live with her husband's father and his two unmarried daughters, Etta and Isabella.

At the end of the block lived Eva and George Birdsong. Eva, after twelve years of marriage, was still the acknowledged beauty among her wide circle of friends. They had no doubt that, had she so chosen, she might have been a famous prima donna or a great actress. Her husband, however, was not successful; he lost his inheritance, he drank, and he was unfaithful to her.

Jenny Blair Archbald wanted new roller skates. Her grandfather, General Archbald, promised to give her a penny a page for reading *Little Women*, but Jenny Blair found the book dull reading. She would rather have been investigating Canal Street against her mother's wishes.

Aunt Etta was having one of her spells. Doomed to a single life by her unpopularity with men, Etta suffered all sorts of nervous disorders. Isabella, having just broken off an engagement, was currently allowing herself to talk frequently to Joseph Crocker, a carpenter.

Jenny Blair finally took her old roller skates and skated in the direction of Canal Street. There she stumbled and was taken in by Memoria, the Birdsongs' mulatto laundress. While she was recovering, she saw George Birdsong, who took her home but made sure that she promised to tell no one

---

where she had met him.

The Peytons were giving a ball which Jenny Blair was to attend, although she and young Bena Peyton were to keep out of sight and out of the way. Her aunts were preparing to go. Eva Birdsong was making over an old gown for the affair and was planning to dance only two dances, the first and the last, both with her husband. At the dance, Eva saw George walking in the garden with Delia Barron. She promptly fainted, recovered in the children's nursery, and had to be carried home by her husband.

Seven years passed. Old General Archbald, now eighty-three, mused over his life and that of his relatives. He had always surrendered the things he wanted most for the things he had felt were his duty. Now he wondered what he had done with his life. Isabella had broken two engagements to marry Joseph Crocker, a man socially beneath her. Jenny Blair's mother had loved his son, and his son had died while fox hunting. Eva Birdsong had given up everything for a husband who was indifferent to her beauty and wit. Now Eva, whom he admired greatly, was being operated on.

Eva was past the age when she was likely to have children, but she had hidden the nature of her illness as long as possible until now her life was in danger. For many long hours, the old General relived in his memories the fleeting events of his life.

The General visited Eva in the hospital. Eva seemed despondent. She made him promise to look after George and retold many amusing old tales about her life with her husband. As the General left the sick woman's room, the old man wondered how he could help her or if there were any help on earth for her.

Now old enough to make her appearance in the formal society of the dignified old city, Jenny Blair rebelled against her mother's formal plans. Instead, she and Bena Peyton hoped to go to New York. Jenny Blair thought that she wanted to be an actress.

One day, George Birdsong waited for Jenny Blair outside the hospital, where they talked as the sun was setting. Suddenly, before she knew what had happened, George seized her and kissed her. Jenny Blair was unsure of her emotions, although George pretended it was the kind of kiss he had always given her—a sort of little girl's kiss—but this kiss, she was positive, was different.

When she accompanied her grandfather home, she told him that she thought she would give up going on the stage or even going to New York.

The old man was puzzled and tired. Cora, Jenny Blair's mother, mixed a mint julep for him in an effort to revive him, but he felt that the drink had little effect. As he went upstairs to dress for dinner, he saw his sick daughter Etta reading in bed one of her endless French love stories. He wished in vain that she might have had some of Isabella's charm so that she might have married.

At the hospital the next day, Jenny Blair left a kimono for Eva to wear. Old General Archbald listened with disgust to George Birdsong's exhibition of grief for his wife's suffering. Then, just as the operation was about over, the old man had a heart attack which he kept secret.

Jenny Blair had become infatuated with George Birdsong, or thought she was, and to her, that was the same thing. She pretended to be angry with him, but when he took his wife away for a rest after her illness, Jenny Blair counted the days until he would return. She wondered why she had ever wanted to go to New York, and she decided that she hated Eva's cousin, John Welch, a doctor, because he seemed to understand her strange moods better than she herself understood them.

When George Birdsong returned alone, Jenny Blair sought him out and admitted she loved him. George, somewhat surprised, tried to put her off. Finally, he kissed her as she desired him to do, but he tried to make her see that she was being very foolish.

When autumn came and the Archbalds returned from their summer vacation, Jenny Blair was glad because she could see George Birdsong again. At the same time, she visited Eva, who seemed to get no better.

George had shot some ducks and tied cards to their necks with bits of Eva's green ribbon, for he intended to give them away to his friends. That evening, Jenny Blair and George stood together in the garden of the Birdsong home. As George bent to embrace her, they heard Eva, who had arisen from her bed. George went into the house at his wife's insistence. A few minutes later, there was a shot. When John Welch called Jenny Blair into the house, she saw George dead from a gunshot wound and Eva with a strangely vacant look on her face. The dead ducks and George's gun were lying in the hall. John insisted that the shooting had been an accident. Old General Archbald, when he arrived, asserted also that it had been an accident. Jenny Blair, in terror and shame, found refuge in hysteria.

Critical Evaluation:

Ellen Glasgow, at a time when many writers of her generation and section of the United States saw fit to write in experimental patterns, kept to established traditions of writing. The result was a lucid, realistic approach to the problem of Southern society in the early twentieth century. A tragedy that is the necessary outcome of folly is presented clearly and with distinction in *The Sheltered Life*. There can be no criticism of Glasgow's logic. The novel is a revealing picture of manners and morals.

As a Realist of the Southern regional school, Glasgow sought to depict the genuine, day-to-day actualities of Southern life without sentimental overlays. Although an American author and thoroughly imbued with American— and especially Southern—values, Glasgow was more nearly attuned to anachronistic Victorian British novelists of manners than has generally been recognized. While she precisely portrayed manners and mores of a particular age and place, Glasgow nevertheless fell prey to the fascination of her subject matter. Despite her skepticism, she thus presented the Southern class conflict from an overly favorable point of view, although *The Sheltered Life* ends tragically. In this sense, Glasgow accurately and valuably reflected a current trend.

The Sheltered Life is a satire of the genteel South trying to cope with modern industrialism. As such, the novel represents a fundamental class conflict between a conventional way of life and the necessary demands of progress. How to resolve the dilemma between traditional commitments and the requirements of modern life constitutes the fulcrum of *The Sheltered Life*, and the resolution of the problem is the resolution of the novel.

Yet, in a related vein, the plot revolves around a very timely issue of feminism, for the women in the novel assume roles of decision makers. With proper deference to the sly irony in the book's title, it is necessary to see the world as Glasgow would have one see it—through the eyes of affluent Virginia housewives in the early twentieth century. Such a point of view, radical for Glasgow's times, nevertheless presents a refreshing perspective on such universal and ubiquitous problems as socioeconomic conflicts, racial strife, and regional differences in approaches to reconciliation of disparate interests. Glasgow's novel also provides solid and compelling entertainment aside from its social significance.

SHIP OF FOOLS

Type of work: Novel
Author: Katherine Anne Porter (1890–1980)
Type of plot: Moral allegory
Time of plot: August 22–September 17, 1931
Locale: The North German Lloyd S.A. *Vera*, at sea
First published: 1962

Principal characters:

SHIP'S CAPTAIN THIELE, a pompous autocrat
DR. SCHUMANN, the ship's doctor
MARY TREADWELL, an American divorcée returning to Paris
DAVID SCOTT, a young American painter
JENNY BROWN, his mistress and an artist
WILLIAM DENNY, a young chemical engineer from Texas
HERR KARL BAUMGARTNER, a lawyer and an alcoholic
FRAU GRETA BAUMGARTNER, his wife
HANS BAUMGARTNER, their small son
HERR PROFESSOR HUTTEN, a retired teacher and a pedant
FRAU KÄTHE HUTTEN, his wife
FRÄULEIN LIZZI SPÖCKENKIEKER, a coquettish spinster
HERR SIEGFRIED RIEBER, a violently anti-Semitic trade magazine publisher
HERR WILLIAM FREYTAG, a young German engineer married to a Jewish wife
HERR KARL GLOCKEN, a hunchback
HERR WILIBALD GRAF, a dying religious fanatic
JOHANN, his rebellious nephew and nurse
HERR JULIUS LÖWENTHAL, a Jewish manufacturer of religious art objects
FRAU RITTERSDORF, a widow whose husband died during World War I
FRAU OTTO SCHMITT, a widow taking her husband's body to Germany for burial
HERR HEINRICH LUTZ, a Swiss hotelkeeper
FRAU LUTZ, his wife
ELSA LUTZ, their frumpish, frustrated daughter
LA CONDESA, a Spanish noblewoman and revolutionist deported from Cuba
ARNE HANSEN, a bitter, passionate, and violent Swede
AMPARO,
PASTORA,

CONCHA,
LOLA,
PEPE,
PANCHO,
MANOLO, and
TITO, members of a zarzuela troupe returning to Spain
    from Mexico
RIC (ARMANDO) and
RAC (DOLORES), Lola's six-year-old twins
SIX CUBAN MEDICAL STUDENTS, "Les Camelots de la
    Cucaracha"
ECHEGARAY, a Basque woodcarver drowned while saving
    a dog from the sea
FATHER CARILLO and
FATHER GARZA, Mexican priests
A HONEYMOONING COUPLE, Mexicans from Guadalajara
A RADICAL POLITICAL AGITATOR

The stories of Katherine Anne Porter are refractions of the visible world obliquely presented, works of observed reality and moral subtlety by a writer who has viewed life at close range but without commitment to its mass programs or dialectics. Early in her career, Porter made clear her position as a person and an artist faced by the spectacle of man obsessed by needs and fears of the inner self and shaken from without by the upheavals of his imperfect society. Commenting on the short stories in *Flowering Judas*, her first book, she wrote in the preface to the Modern Library edition of 1940 that her stories were parts of a design still incomplete but representative of vision and statement she had been able to achieve in a period of world crisis and disturbance. She added that her purpose as a writer was to trace to their sources the particular incidents of particular lives and to examine the scope and meaning of man's failure to live in the society he has created.

Such a statement could stand unchanged as the introductory note to *Ship of Fools*, for in the long-awaited and full-scale novel of Porter's career, readers have one more compelling instance of the earned knowledge which has solicited her attention and claimed her energies in fiction—the attempt on her part to confront the mystery of being, to uncover among the uncertainties, frustrations, and defeats of men's lives the causes of mankind's moral and spiritual failure—to find in the fabric of human society the flaw through which the concentration camp and the gas chamber entered history and gave the world a new dimension of bestiality and evil. The result of her labors is a book, rich in its variety of incident and character-drawing, in which the writer's outsights and insights are brought imaginatively to bear upon a circumscribed complex of personal relationships in such fashion as to point to something

universal and common to all people. As an example of structure and statement, *Ship of Fools* functions on more than one level of resonance and
meaning. Within limits of space and time determined by a sea voyage aboard
the ship *Vera*, which is Porter's image of the human community, it is a political
novel, a moral allegory, and a work of social criticism.

It is also a book with a history of its own. In 1931, Porter was a passenger
on a German ship bound from Veracruz, Mexico, to Bremerhaven, Germany.
It was her first trip to Europe, and her account of that experience, a travel
journal in the form of a letter to Caroline Gordon, a fellow writer, became
the starting point of her novel. In Switzerland a year later, while the impressions of the voyage were still fresh in her mind, she read Sebastian Brant's
Das Narrenschiff, a 1494 rhymed satire in which the writer pictured the world
as a ship carrying its human cargo of fools and madmen toward eternity. The
image of the world as a ship, already old when Brant used it, provided an
appropriate metaphor for the kind of story beginning to shape itself in Porter's
imagination. First called *The Promised Land*, it later became *No Safe Harbor*
and then *Ship of Fools*, all the while expanding under the dramatic and
symbolic power of its theme. Originally it was planned as a fourth novella in
Pale Horse, Pale Rider, but as it outgrew its intended proportions, it became
the long novel on which, from time to time, Porter was reported at work.
Years passed, a few short sections appeared in magazines, but the book itself
seemed no nearer completion. Announced for publication half a dozen times
and then withdrawn, it became the most famous unpublished novel since
James Joyce's *Work in Progress*.

Then, after twenty years of intermittent writing, the book appeared—497
pages long, handsomely bound, with a lavish cast of more than fifty cabin
passengers and ship's officers, not counting 876 unfortunate souls in the steerage and a doted on, seasick bulldog named Bébé, all embarked on a voyage
from Veracruz to Bremerhaven between August 22 and September 17, 1931.
The completed novel stands as a testament to time's insights and the craftsmanship of a dedicated artist.

In construction, *Ship of Fools* is divided into three sections: part 1, "Embar-
kation"; part 2, "High Sea"; part 3, "The Harbors." Each is introduced by
an epigraph relating its action to the larger thematic design of the novel, the
first, a line from Baudelaire, "*Quand partons nous vers le bonheur?*" (when
are we setting forth toward happiness?); the second, a phrase from a song
by Brahms, "*Kein Haus, Keine Heimat*" (no house, no home); and the third,
an incomplete quotation from St. Paul's injunction to the Hebrews, "For here
we have no continuing city." Porter's meaning is plain: man is constantly
setting out in search of happiness but discovers, instead, that he has no earthly
house or spiritual homeland and that his city is not eternal but threatened
with destruction. The title of the novel comes from Brant's fifteenth century
satire. In a brief foreword, Porter declared that she is a passenger on that

ship. By implication, so is the reader.

Although the title is symbolic, the story is rooted in recognizably human terms. A writer of sensuous detail and coloring, Porter builds her fictional world as solidly as the five senses re-create the world of man. The *Vera* is a real ship; the characters make the book. The novel contains no more plot than one would find in real life. Instead, the writer achieves her effects by skillful handling of parallels and contrasts—order and disorder, power and weakness, love and hate, deception and self-deception, individual and mass—shown in human relationships that are comic, abrasive, damaging, and deadly. People meet; they react to or upon one another; life is illuminated and truth revealed. In the process, a great deal is laid bare for the reader's understanding.

The characters represent a varied cross section drawn from different nations and races, and the arrangement by which they are presented is hierarchal. At the top stands Captain Thiele, the symbol of authority and order for which, as he believes, German culture stands. A petty, pompous tyrant living by rules and regulations, he expects everyone else to do the same. At the bottom of the scale are the steerage passengers, Spanish laborers, and their families being returned to their homes after the Cuban sugar crop has failed. Miserable in their squalor and hopelessness, they represent the blind, stubborn determination of mankind to stay alive at any price. If they cannot prevail, they can multiply. Seven children are born during the voyage. As some of the workmen disembark at Santa Cruz de Tenerife, a boy boasts that they are now more than when they started, and one of the new mothers shouts triumphantly that the newborn are all men. In between are the passengers and crew, all members of the middle class and the middle path in life. From time to time, they feel the weight of the Captain's authority from above—with repressed hate on the part of Jewish Herr Löwenthal, with eager submission by gentle Frau Schmitt—or peer down toward the steerage deck at the wretched creatures below.

Because the *Vera* is a North German Lloyd vessel, most of the passengers are Germans returning to the Fatherland after years of residence in Mexico or brief business trips there. These include Herr Rieber, a gross lecher and Jew-baiter and the publisher of a trade magazine; Fräulein Lizzi Spöcken-kieker, the cackling, vulgar owner of several dress shops; Professor and Frau Hutten, who lavish all the affection of their lonely lives on their pet bulldog; Frau Rittersdorf, who keeps a diary in which she records her impressions of those who fail to measure up to the standards of the master race; Frau Schmitt, a pathetic, helpless widow; Herr Baumgartner, an alcoholic lawyer and his family; Herr Graf, a dying mystic who believes himself gifted with the power of healing; Johann, his rebellious nephew and nurse; Herr Karl Glocken, a hunchback who has sold his newsstand in Mexico City; Herr Julius Löwenthal, a sullen Jewish manufacturer of religious relics; and Herr Wilhelm Freytag, a young oil executive secretly haunted by the fact that his wife is Jewish.

Four Americans are making the voyage. Mrs. Treadwell, recently divorced, has no real purpose in her life; for her, the promise of the past has been dimmed by the contradiction between hope and memory. William Denny is a young Texan engineer obsessed by status and sex. His guide in life is *Recreational Aspects of Sex and Mental Prophylaxis—A True Guide to Happiness*, and he judges the world by the standards of Brownsville, where a man knew who he was, and everyone knew his place and stayed in it. David Scott and Jenny Brown, young artists and lovers, are traveling in separate cabins; throughout the voyage, they approach each other with gestures of tenderness, only to be driven apart by the urge to possess or be possessed. With that hardness of heart often exhibited by the innocent and immature, they give only hurt where understanding and compassion are needed.

Other passengers are a Mexican bride and groom, absorbed in each other and remote from the life on shipboard; two priests; a raddled Spanish Condesa being deported from Cuba because of her revolutionary political activities; Herr Lutz, a Swiss hotel manager, his wife, and their frumpish daughter; Arne Hansen, a young Swede who finds relief from his existential despair in lust; six boisterous medical students from Cuba calling themselves "Les Camelots de la Cucaracha"; and a zarzuela troupe of Spanish singers and dancers. These entertainers are the most sinister of the travelers; the women are harlots, the men are pimps, and all are thieves. With them are two children, twins named Ric and Rac, creatures of natural depravity who become agents of even greater evil when they throw overboard the Condesa's stolen pearls and later hurl into the sea the Hutten's dog Bébé.

Mediating among the groups is Dr. Schumann, the ship's doctor, a man of warm and candid impulses beneath his detached professional manner. A Catholic, a scholar, a man of reason, he stands for the best in the German humanistic tradition, but he sees himself as old and tired. Aware of his serious heart condition, he knows that he is returning to Germany to die. During the voyage, he and the pathetic Condesa strip each other of pose. Although their encounter provides an opportunity for a love that makes no demands, imposes no obligations, he withdraws from emotional involvement. His training is too strong. Unable to dare enough, he remains the humane physician in his attempt to ease her addiction to drugs. The loss of illusions in the relationship of gentle Dr. Schumann and La Condesa is the most revealing and rending of all the unmasking that takes place aboard the *Vera*.

Porter sets her stage with great tact and skill, and almost everything that happens during the voyage is prefigured in image or incident against the sultry, violent background of Veracruz as the passengers prepare to embark. The screeching, chattering, yelping, spitting encounter of a parrot, a monkey, a dog, and a cat prepares readers for the knowledge that Fräulein Spöcken-kieker persists in shrilling like a peafowl; Herr Rieber's face is like a pig's pink snout; David Scott resembles a willful, high-spirited, blooded horse; a ranting political agitator has a voice like a bull's; and the women of the zarzuela company sound like a flock of quarreling birds. The morning newspaper contains a photograph of an Indian servant boy, accidentally killed in the bombing of the Swedish consulate, lying with one hand resting on his spilled entrails. Refused alms, a beggar woman pinches Mrs. Treadwell and leaves a discolored bruise on her arm. The Huttens feed sandwiches to their fat dog while an emaciated, ragged Indian sits nearby. When they leave, he ignores their abandoned food, but a horribly maimed beggar crawls across the square, guided blindly by his sense of smell, and gulps the sandwiches. Some armed men appear suddenly and hustle the impassive Indian away. Each of these details, presented so casually and with apparent irrelevance, points in some manner to the shape of things to come.

At the center of the novel stands a more compelling image fusing character, action, and theme, an incident viewed by Jenny Brown through the windows of a bus several years before: a glimpse of Indians surrounding a man and woman joined as if in physical, death-dealing combat, the man grasping a knife, the woman, bloody from her wounds, beating him over the head with a stone. Briefly seen, the incident left in Jenny's mind an impression of human cruelty and violence highlighted under a brilliant sun.

One by one, in their encounters with one another, Porter shows her people locked in a similar struggle between involvement and detachment within the cage of self. Here, in microcosm, is the world man has made, ridden by prejudice, filled with selfishness and greed, stupidly cruel, morally lost. Among so much, it is difficult to single out particular incidents that test these people by their participation in the common concerns of humanity, their moral flexibility, their humaneness of being. Most fail in their moment of crisis. After a disturbance in the steerage, Captain Thiele orders all tools and weapons taken away from the Cuban laborers. A Basque woodcarver, Echegaray, who makes his living by carving small animals, weeps when his knife is confiscated. Jenny Brown and David Scott discover hate in love and love in hate. Hansen, the victim of sterile lust, buys the favors of Amparo, one of the Spanish dancers. Arrogant William Denny is frustrated in his pursuit of Pastora, another dancer. When Ric and Rac throw the Hutten's bulldog over the side, Echegaray jumps into the sea and is drowned while trying to rescue the animal. During his funeral, which causes another riot in the steerage, three great whales appear spouting on the horizon. Frau Hutten finds the courage to interrupt her pompous husband's flow of words and contradict him. After Mrs. Treadwell innocently reveals Freytag's confidence that his wife is Jewish, the young man is banished from the Captain's table and the other diners close ranks against the outcast, the silence unbroken except for the sound of people lapping soup, motion suspended except for rising and dipping heads, on every face an expression of complacent unity. In a truly revealing episode, a mock fiesta is staged by the zarzuela troupe, ostensibly to honor the Captain but in reality to mock his authority, to parody the other passengers, and to turn the occasion into a *Walpurgisnacht* of weakness, pride, greed, and folly. Hansen breaks a bottle over Herr Rieber's head. When drunken Denny tries to force his way into Mrs. Treadwell's cabin, she discovers in herself unsuspected compulsions toward violence and beats him insensible with the heel of her evening slipper. The irony is that, after their shattering experiences, the passengers regain their composure, adjust their lives, and remain wrapped in their illusions of self. Only Mrs. Treadwell has a moment of illumination, the recognition of humanity's desperate need of understanding and the desolation of its absence, as she recalls the shamed and self-pitying manner of the Baumgartners and realizes that they have been silently, desperately pleading for love in spite of their fitness or unfitness, or even their ability, to give love in return.

This isolation of theme to a set of shipboard circumstances is a structural device admirably suited to Porter's purpose. The *Vera* leaves Mexico, a land torn by class strife and violence. It enters history again when it puts in at Bremerhaven. In the meantime, the story of the voyage has been surrounded by the space of silence that a true work of art requires.

In a novel like *Ship of Fools*, there can be no final resolution, with goodness rewarded and wrongdoing punished. The voyage ends, and the passengers go about their business, indifferent to everything except their private concerns. If readers remember the time of the story, they realize why the irresolution of the ending is necessary to Porter's design. Germany is preparing for the whole terrifying and obscene Nazi regime, the world for the violence and death of another great war. Trapped in their present, these people have no thought of the future they are helping to shape.

Porter says what she has to say with honesty and simplicity, with moral subtlety and stylistic evocation. In this novel, she shows that she is capable of keeping under control during the long flight the same qualities that readers find in her shorter fiction—the power of picture and symbol to probe deeply into human nature, the power of dramatic scene to illuminate a lifetime or an entire society, the power of language to create a world of sense impressions. Somber as it is in its insights and resonance, few novels of recent years have faced up to the problem of man's need for moral definition with greater reality of the imagination or authority of fact. *Ship of Fools* is a notable novel, perhaps a great one.

THE SHORT STORIES OF JOHN CHEEVER

Author: John Cheever (1912–1982)
First published: The Way Some People Live, 1943; *The Enormous Radio and Other Stories*, 1953; *The Housebreaker of Shady Hill*, 1958; *Some People, Places, and Things That Will Not Appear in My Next Novel*, 1961; *The Brigadier and the Golf Widow*, 1964; *The World of Apples*, 1973; *The Collected Stories of John Cheever*, 1978

John Cheever is an important short-story writer for a number of reasons, not the least of which is sheer staying power, longevity. His first stories appeared in print in the early 1940's, and they appeared regularly throughout his career. This is a remarkable record of continuous creativity and undiminished quality. Though he has won prizes and widespread popular recognition for his two novels, *The Wapshot Chronicle* (1957) and *The Wapshot Scandal* (1964), and high critical acclaim for his next two novels, *Bullet Park* (1969) and *Falconer* (1977), Cheever has always been primarily a story writer. There are any number of his contemporaries equally well-known and distinguished for their work in the short-story form, but none who has written stories regularly over such a span of time, a time which includes portions of at least three separate literary generations. Part of his success must be considered in terms of his long-standing position as one of the stable of contract writers for *The New Yorker*, a magazine that has always encouraged the short story, or a certain kind of short story, with high payment and the advantages of a large audience with definite expectations and conventions. This fact alone, however, cannot explain how Cheever managed to keep his gift for the short story alive and breathing while other, perhaps equally gifted writers for that magazine, though remembered and honored in short-story anthologies, became less vigorously productive. It is entirely possible that, weighing everything, Cheever was the finest story writer to have emerged from *The New Yorker*.

To place his work and to understand its development, it is first of all necessary to understand as clearly as possible what a *New Yorker* story is, for the vintage product has become to a great degree the accepted model for the modern American short story. Briefly, it is the maximum exploitation of a single, dramatically presented incident while more or less strictly observing the conventional unities of time and place, designed in its condensed form to gain by a richness of implication and by depth of characterization. Plot, in the old-fashioned sense, is absent and so are the moral dilemmas, middle-class, of slick fiction. In setting, the stories are usually regional—the East of suburbia and the City, the far and uncorrupted West, an updated version of the magnolia South and, often, foreign, aristocratic, and exotic. The stories have reflected the general moral views of the magazine and its audience. Its moral keystone is a gracious secular humanism coupled with a gentle intellectual skepticism. The virtues celebrated are all civilized virtues, sedentary, sophisticated, and rational, gently draped or camouflaged in veils of irony. The mortal sins are vulgarity without redeeming eccentricity, self-pity, stupidity, hypocrisy, bad manners, complacency, awkward excess of passion, and the absence of good health or physical beauty. In short, *The New Yorker* fiction has been a fiction of manners. The political orientation has been generally liberal, of the noblesse oblige variety, and as a magazine of manners, the aim has always been progressive. No matter how dark the present, how fraught with peril the future, or how quaint the past, the fiction and verse of *The New Yorker* have always gone hand in hand with the plentiful advertisements, the fine cartoons, and "The Talk of the Town," advancing toward a vaguely discernible horizon, the glow of which indicates a Jerusalem of "The Good Life" somewhere up there among idyllic Delectable Mountains, just beyond the reach of the clean, trimmed fingernails of the Ideal Reader.

To expect a great deal more than the competently second-rate from such a milieu would be folly, and to imagine that working in it a writer with the creativity of Cheever could emerge would demonstrate the gift of blind and pure prophecy. Readers have had enough fiction over a sufficient period of time to see that his stories, within the context of *The New Yorker* milieu, are original and independent. From the beginning with *The Way Some People Live*, the stories of Cheever in *The New Yorker* exhibited some independence of form. This may have been inevitable, for even then, the "single event" story was widely anthologized, beginning to be taught in schools, and becoming somewhat less than chic. Cheever's originality manifested itself in subject and treatment. Though part and parcel of the credible and suburban world, stories from *The Way Some People Live* and *The Enormous Radio* occasionally broke that orderly universe with the introduction of what used to be called "fantasy" but, more accurately, might be described as the introduction of some supernatural event or condition into an otherwise perfectly rational and realistic situation. In this sense, his fiction is often analogous to that of Marcel Ayme in France. Technically, the stories range rather freely and widely in time and space and point of view—even in tense, which is sometimes past, sometimes present, occasionally even future and conditional. There is often a cheerfully direct and open use of the narrator-writer of the story. He appears in the open like the chorus in an early Elizabethan play. As a narrator, he does his best to establish an air of intimacy and rapport with the reader, and then from time to time, he reenters, stopping the action, to point out significant aspects or to make intelligent comment. Like a cultivated and slightly condescending museum guide, this narrator is bright, clever, witty, yet always somehow sympathetic to the reader, perhaps because of his slight but pleasing smile, his habit of ironic self-deprecation, and his wry, worldly-wise shrug. The teller of the tale is always exact and up-to-date in his references and allusions, his knowledge of the things and habits of this world; and he can, when it is necessary, but never without a shared wink of misgiving, summon up a soupçon of the latest slang. The language of the stories is always a model of lucidity and decorum, free from the unrefined excess and extravagance of poetic frenzy, yet still able from time to time to climb toward a modest altitude on the slopes of Olympus, far below the sweaty chaos of the laughing and imperious gods and muses, but at least a place with a good view near the timberline, a place where a good gourmet picnic might be laid out and enjoyed.

Clearly, the form goes against the grain of the more typical, "dramatic" pattern of *The New Yorker* story, for most of these devices work to call attention to the story not as a happening but as artifice. The meaning of this relative freedom of form is equally clear. Cheever wants to say more, not only about persons, places, and things but also about what these may mean and the subtle patterns they make. Even in the earliest stories, for example, Cheever made frequent use of dreams. His characters dream and do so matter-of-factly. He has also permitted them and the narrator to digress, to reminisce, to imagine. Naturally this makes for a much more inclusive kind of fiction, at once deeper and more complex than the conventional dramatic method of telling a tale. It is one of his special gifts and artistic triumphs to be able to lead his characters and his readers with ease from an apparently realistic situation into realms of absurdity, nightmare, and farce. Perhaps this is what one reviewer meant when he tried to describe the singular qualities of Cheever. He was deeply interested in character, and he gave his characters depth and dimension, providing veils and layers of experience and being, and all the loose ends and untied laces of living, breathing human beings. Compared with most of his contemporaries, in or out of *The New Yorker*, Cheever had, as a result of his interest in and understanding of character, a good deal more sympathy and compassion for the people he created.

It is not easy to be a serious and, in a certain sense, an experimental writer and yet, at the same time, to share without much questioning the standards, rules, laws, and by-laws of a literary club as exclusive and cozy and proud as *The New Yorker*. It is more than difficult to make meaningful fiction, which was, after all, his aim, in the context of a moral world as bogus as a carnival and as insubstantial as cotton candy. For people do not live like characters in *The New Yorker*, try as they will, and its moral world is unique. In the world there may well be a system of election and damnation, but the elect are not necessarily immediately identifiable because they are charming, gifted, well-born, intelligent, eccentric, or even innocent. Nor are they children, cripples, blacks, or victims. The God that is predicated by *The New Yorker* and, so, in part accepted by Cheever, turns out to be a wise, well-to-do, old grandfather with a twinkle in his eye and stylish manners, lovable but a snob and not very likely of much help in times of trouble. Sheep and goats merge together in a glossy, nineteenth century pastoral scene.

Cheever's short fiction developed not in stages, in trials, and renunciations but in a fairly straight line. The stories of *The Brigadier and the Golf Widow* differ from the earliest stories only in a slightly freer form, a swifter move toward moral allegory, and a shade more impatience with the rules he was breaking; but after many years of considerable success, he was entitled to such liberty. The remarkable thing is how little he had changed over his long career. It appears that very early, he staked a claim, fenced it, and ever since had been exploring and exploiting it. This creates an apparent sameness about his work which might be called a disadvantage except that it must be balanced against the undeniable appeal of reliability. He did not, like some great writers, hit home runs or strike out. He was marvelously consistent and on a high level. Moreover, he did not, and did not need to, offend the reader. He wrote from conviction and certainty and—not the least of his virtues for his time—from a sense of contentment. The effect is at once entertaining and restful. Every sane human being is for courage and honesty, in favor of blue skies, trout streams, butterflies, and fine old houses full of lively and amusing people. Every sane person is against suffering, pain, hypocrisy, ugliness, and sordid behavior. No one speaks out in favor of sin, and no one, no matter how reactionary, is against progress or reform, though definitions may vary widely and deeply and behavior vary even more.

Cheever's fiction is, then, classical in orientation. (It is no wonder that he so frequently employed the great and timeless classical myths to heighten the implications of his stories.) He was a professional writer with an acceptable and decent point of view. If he had a dream, it was a dream of restoration and innocence, not a revolutionary and romantic vision. He conveyed no desire to run for public office or to be accepted as one of the unacknowledged legislators of the world. This attitude was important, for his long and distinguished career and the undeniable artistry of his short fiction give the lie to the notion that an artist must be a rebel, an outsider, and a boat-rocker to validate his claim to art. After all the qualifications are weighed and sifted, Cheever stands in the front rank, among the best of the short-story writers of the twentieth century. When all is said and done, for better or worse, it seems likely that his humane, graceful, and wistful stories will stand, if not for the best that artists have been able to achieve, then for the best hopes of civilization, its long dream of life and liberty, its aim and pursuit of human happiness.

THE SHORT STORIES OF ERNEST HEMINGWAY

Author: Ernest Hemingway (1899–1961)
First published: Three Stories and Ten Poems, 1923; *In Our Time*, 1924,
1925; *Men Without Women*, 1927; *Winner Take Nothing*, 1933; *The Fifth
Column and the First Forty-nine Stories*, 1938; *The Snows of Kilimanjaro
and Other Stories*, 1961; *The Nick Adams Stories*, 1972

Ernest Hemingway, who ranks with William Faulkner as one of the indis-
putable giants of twentieth century American fiction, wrote more than fifty
short stories. Together they constitute probably the greatest, certainly the
most widely known and influential, work in the genre during that period, and
a dozen or so, including "The Snows of Kilimanjaro," "The Short Happy
Life of Francis Macomber," "In Another Country," "A Way You'll Never
Be," "The Killers," "A Clean Well-Lighted Place," and "Big Two-Hearted
River," are unsurpassed and unsurpassable today or at any time. Perhaps
most at home in the short-story form, which in his case constitutes an unusually
large portion of a major writer's work, Hemingway used it for artistic purposes
and achievements of the highest order.

Hemingway's first short-story publication of note was *In Our Time*, a collection containing fourteen stories bounded and interspersed by brief inter-
chapters on violence coldly observed at bullfights, in World War I, and especially
in the Graeco-Turkish War, which Hemingway had recently viewed as a war
correspondent. Eight of the stories have Nick Adams for their protagonist—
a character Hemingway employed frequently, not only here but also in numerous later stories—and are arranged chronologically, tracing Nick's development from childhood to maturity. Because stories about Nick begin and end
the collection, and since the other six stories are placed so that the events in
them correspond temporally to stages in Nick's growth, *In Our Time* has a
narrative unity similar to that of an episodic novel. As a quasi novel, the
book belongs in a category with James Joyce's *Dubliners* and Sherwood
Anderson's *Winesburg, Ohio*. It belongs there not merely because of its narrative organization but also because, like them, it is thematically unified
around a concern with what Joyce called paralysis, the spiritual plight of
modern man; only where Joyce and Anderson chose a specific geographical
place, Hemingway, more ambitiously, chose "our time," a vague but readily
available temporal location, as the setting for that theme.

Though collected again in multiples of fourteen in *Men Without Women*
(1927) and *Winner Take Nothing* (1933), and then finally gathered in a largely
complete edition in *The Fifth Column and the First Forty-nine Stories* (1938),
a collection containing the first three collections plus seven other stories,
Hemingway's stories after *In Our Time* are not bound together chronologically
and narratively. Thematically and stylistically, they are, however, as collec-

tions or separate stories, continuations of *In Our Time*; all his stories, indeed his entire work, nonfiction as well as long and short fiction, are confined to a narrow range which is surveyed repeatedly and thoroughly. That narrowness is evident everywhere in his work, and so in his subject, which Hemingway defined in the introduction to *Men at War* (1942), a collection of war stories and accounts he edited, where he wrote:

> When you go to war as a boy you have a great illusion of immortality. Other people get killed; not you. It can happen to other people; but not to you. Then when you are badly wounded the first time you lose that illusion and you know it can happen to you. After being severely wounded two weeks before my nineteenth birthday I had a bad time until I figured it out that nothing could happen to me that had not happened to all men before me. Whatever I had to do men had always done. If they had done it then I could do it too and the best thing was not to worry about it.

The wound, that affliction through which man becomes aware of his mortality, of his finite limitations, or, in traditional Christian parlance, of his fallen state and spiritual futility, is the definitive encounter with reality upon which all Hemingway's short stories, and other fiction as well, are closely focused.

In Our Time initiates Hemingway's inquiry into this authentic and authenticating moment. In the first story, "Indian Camp," Nick is present when his father, a doctor, performs a Caesarian operation on an Indian woman who has suffered long, agonizing labor pains. Nick, unable to watch the operation after his first curiosity passed, rejects its relevance for himself, and instead, after the delivery, while crossing a lake in which he trails his hand, feels sure that he himself will never die. Since *In Our Time* is about love, not war, Nick's war wound is briefly and dryly treated in an interchapter. The more important wounds for him and in the book as a whole are the wounds of love, the pain of its effects and loss. Yet despite his being subjected to the consequences it leads to for the Indian husband, who, finding his wife's suffering intolerable, cuts his own throat, and Ad Francis, who goes insane when public pressure forces his wife to leave him, and his own disillusioning affairs with Marge in "An End of Something" and Luz in "A Very Short Story," Nick marries and gets his wife pregnant. When George, a friend with whom he is skiing in "Cross Country Snow," remarks on the hardship of life in general, Nick says it is not exactly that, though he cannot explain why. He only confesses that that is simply the way life is. In the last story of the collection, "Big Two-Hearted River," Nick moves through and beyond the burnt-out land to the river, completing a cycle wherein he progresses from innocence through experience via his wounds to self-renewal, from timelessness into time and mortality and back to timelessness again. Somewhat paradoxically, in the end, he chooses the high ground over the deep, dark, tragic water of the swamp, but in so doing, he rejects death, the impersonal, self-obliterating power in the universe. His war and love wounds have thrown him radically back upon himself, have defined his conditions as an individual human being, and he accepts those as necessary and even good. His bad times over, he has chosen to live within his human limitations and so has stopped worrying. Like a good soldier, he has learned to hold his imagination at bay and to live completely in the present as the meaningful essence of experience.

In later stories, Hemingway expands upon and clarifies phases in this cycle centering around the wound, with death moving into the foreground and love, when present, into the background. Though innocence does occur in its purest form on two later occasions in "The Snows of Kilimanjaro," where the protagonist's wife, sentimental and preferring illusion to reality, like so many women in Hemingway's fiction, fails to recognize the reality of death when her husband dies; and in "The Short Happy Life of Francis Macomber," the hero learns not to worry when he assumes his manhood by a sudden act which liberates him from the fear of death. Hemingway's imagination after *In Our Time* is absorbed with the effects resulting from a poignant consciousness of death or a wound received in war. Examples of the former are "A Day's Wait," in which a nine-year-old boy mistakenly waits all day to die, then has a rough time when he realizes that he will live; or "A Clean, Well-Lighted Place," in which an old man and a lonely waiter experience nothingness, the ultimate truth revealed by the wound about a world of death. "A Way You'll Never Be," which elaborates upon Nick's wounding related in an interchapter of *In Our Time*, and in *In Another Country*, are Hemingway's subtlest accounts of Nick's bad time resulting from his wound, which spreads its poison throughout his consciousness and destroys all his illusions—not only those of love and immortality but those of invulnerability, heroism, patriotism, comradeship, security, technology, and rehabilitation as well. The wound eventually strips away all grounds for certainty or hope and bares the reality of inexorable time and change.

"A writer's job," Hemingway repeatedly insisted, "is to write simple true sentences, to tell the truth so purely that it would be truer than anything factual, an absolute truth." This aspiration, inherited from Realism and disciplined by his training as a journalist, impelled him to report on the sorrowful loss that lies at the heart of love and death, with precision, economy, and clarity. He sought, above all, like Harold Krebs in "Soldier's Home" of *In Our Time*, to avoid the "nausea" that comes from untruth or exaggeration. He realized that this feeling depended upon his never lying, to others but most importantly to himself, about his own inner fears. The complete truth about himself, about his predicament as a man, must be faced honestly and without cowardice. His aesthetic aim, the moral and literary values to which he severely committed himself, his tough, realistic acknowledgment of man's deficiencies, coupled with a sane skepticism recognizing both the powers and limits of human intelligence and a sense that the highest, distinctive human enjoyment comes from understanding—simply knowing or being conscious—makes Hemingway the twentieth century's greatest scientific writer. That fact that he wrote in a scientific era makes his short stories, along with the rest of his work, the most accurate and profound statement of the way things are for scientific man.

Writing from the heart of his being, which throbbed in unison with the vital currents of Western culture, Hemingway founded his art upon a thoroughly integrated sense of life, so that despite his apparent mannerisms he has been and remains inimitable. At a time when Realism, committed to the dominion of the senses, matter, and environment, held the literary throne, and Romanticism, ex-royalty, was challenging Realism for the renewed supremacy of a passionate consummation with a self-transcendent ideal, Hemingway created the classic short story. A younger contemporary and friend of such foremost modernists as Ezra Pound, James Joyce, and Pablo Picasso, Hemingway learned his intellectualism and classicism from them but then went even further than they toward realizing them. Where their intellectualism and classicism tended to show itself somewhat gaudily in book learning, his was marked by an association of sensibility so subtle as to be seamless. His apparent anti-intellectualism actually signifies a completely successful pragmatic interfusion of thought into experience or consciousness. Hemingway's short stories, unlike Realistic ones, which are oppressive with their emphasis on the overwhelming details of the sensory world, and Romantic ones, which sob their cries of bitter, futile melancholy born of frustration, exemplify the active mind in quest of essences being nourished by its power to know and abide by the truth. Avoiding the tragic and extremes, deep, dark waters and the night, the unconscious and romantically ideal, Hemingway wrote stories by and for rational creatures who care about feeling cool and clear inside themselves, who care about a clean, well-lighted place for thought and action within the necessary human limitations. As long as anyone cares for these, the greatness and cogency of Hemingway's short stories will remain undiminished.

THE SHORT STORIES OF O. HENRY

Author: O. Henry (William Sydney Porter, 1862–1910)
First published: Cabbages and Kings, 1904; *The Four Million*, 1906; *Heart of the West*, 1907; *The Trimmed Lamp*, 1907; *The Gentle Grafter*, 1908; *The Voice of the City*, 1908; *Options*, 1909; *Roads of Destiny*, 1909; *Strictly Business*, 1910; *Whirligigs*, 1910; *Sixes and Sevens*, 1911; *Rolling Stones*, 1912; *Waifs and Strays*, 1917

The once inflated fame of O. Henry is no more. Today he is not only belittled by most critics of the short story but also practically ignored by writers on American literature in general. The *Literary History of the United States* (1946) mentions him twice, once as a user of slang and once as a writer popular in the U.S.S.R. *The Literature of the American People* (1951) ignores him altogether. Even Jay B. Hubbell's *The South in American Literature, 1607–1900* (1954) devotes less than two pages to him as a Southern writer and offers him only a sentence or two of subdued praise. Yet he continues to be widely read, as is clearly suggested by the inclusion of *The Best Short Stories of O. Henry* (1945) in the Modern Library, the reissuance of *The Complete Works of O. Henry* in two volumes (1953), and the publication of *The Pocket Book of O. Henry Stories* (1956). The last collection went into a second printing within a month.

The ingredients that appeal most in the typical O. Henry short story are usually a blend of humor and sentiment or sentimentality. There is no depth of characterization; O. Henry specializes in easily recognizable types. The story is neatly put together, and it moves rapidly. The style is breezy and slangy. Though the vocabulary may include a number of words unfamiliar to the reader of newspapers and pulp magazines (in which most of O. Henry's stories first appeared), there is enough of the American vernacular to sustain the story on a colloquial level. The unwary reader, in fact, may overlook the many humorous paraphrases from Shakespeare and other famous authors. The story characters belong either to the great American middle class or to a less exalted level of society. The author is obviously the friend of the "little man" and the enemy of those who would exploit him. There is a plentiful display of local color, especially in the many stories of New York life. There is a trick or surprise ending, often totally unexpected and illogical, but usually light and amusing. Though the surprise ending may be sentimental or even pathetic, it is never really tragic.

O. Henry has been compared to several of his predecessors and contemporaries from whom he may have learned something about story writing, among them Bret Harte, Guy de Maupassant, Mark Twain, and Frank Stockton. Many of the early stories are filled with the easy sentimentality of Bret Harte as well as Harte's editorial remarks about his characters. Maupassant's irony is often imitated, but the master's mordancy is missing, as well as his prevailingly serious view of life. O. Henry uses slang even more than Twain did, but where Twain's is integral, O. Henry's is gratuitous and frequently spoils what might have been some of his best effects. O. Henry is often credited with having introduced the trick ending into the short story, but Frank Stockton had already gained popularity with this type of ending several years before O. Henry's first story was published. Stockton's most famous story—"The Lady or the Tiger?"—had not even a trick ending; it had none at all, the reader being left to supply one for himself. The reader's choice ending of O. Henry's "Thimble, Thimble" is reminiscent of Stockton, who is specifically named as a model at the beginning of the story.

These facts show that O. Henry was, then, not so much an originator as a clever practitioner. Far more a craftsman than an artist, he was a close observer of the surfaces of life and character. In spite of his exaggerations and whimsicality, he remains an effective local colorist in his presentation of life in Bagdad-on-the-subway, as he called New York, in the first decade of the century. To read his stories of the metropolis is to enter in imagination a bygone era of gaslights, horse-drawn hacks, and rococo decor that was the delight of the rich and the envious dream of shopgirls and ill-paid clerks or sweatshop workers.

Reading "The Furnished Room" in *The Four Million* (1906), one senses how it felt a half century ago to be lonely in a gaslit furnished room filled with battered furniture and the scattered, forgotten mementos of former lodgers. One hears the distant, disquieting noises from other rooms and breathes the familiar odors of the dilapidated lodging house. In O. Henry's stories of the metropolis, one joins the strollers in Central Park or on Fifth Avenue, listens to tales told by drinkers in unobtrusive bars, inhales the garlic-rich atmosphere of a small Italian restaurant, or dines on lobster at fabulous Delmonico's.

Among the most famous of O. Henry's New York stories are "The Gift of the Magi" which, though somewhat hackneyed by many reprintings and a film version, still has its sentimental appeal; "The Cop and the Anthem," in which Soapy, after vainly trying to get himself jailed for the cold winter, hears church music and vows to reform, only to end with a three-month sentence for vagrancy; "The Romance of a Busy Broker," with the unbelievable revelation at the end that Harvey Maxwell has erred in proposing to his stenographer, because he has forgotten he married her the evening before; and "The Last Leaf," with its sentimental close that ironically counterbalances the saving of a young girl's life with the death of the kindly old artist who saved it.

Because O. Henry attained his fame while living in New York and because it is the scene of many of his stories, readers may forget that the author, like so many of the city dwellers he wrote about, was not a native. Born in North Carolina, he grew to manhood there. He lived for several years in Texas, and he stayed in Honduras for some months after having fled the United States to escape arrest for misappropriating funds from an Austin, Texas, bank. His life in the South, the Southwest, and Central America provided the backgrounds for numerous stories.

The more than twenty stories laid in the Southern states or employing distinctly Southern characters include several of his best. "A Municipal Report" is an excellent story of Nashville, Tennessee, written to answer an offhand comment by the novelist Frank Norris that Nashville was not a "story" city. The despicable Major Caswell of "A Municipal Report" is one of O. Henry's most vividly drawn characters, but he is matched by the very different Major Talbot of "The Duplicity of Hargraves," who romantically personifies the antebellum aristocrats of the columned mansions and great cotton plantations in the storied Old South. The faithfulness of former slaves to their former owners is shown in the devotion of Uncle Caesar to Mrs. Caswell in "A Municipal Report," the solicitude of Uncle Bushrod for the honor of the Weymouth family in "The Guardian of the Accolade." Other Southern stories are "The Whirligig of Life" (Tennessee), "The Rose of Dixie" (Georgia), "Cherchez la Femme" (New Orleans), "A Blackjack Bargainer" (North Carolina), and perhaps the funniest of O. Henry's stories, "The Ransom of Red Chief" (Alabama).

O. Henry's Texas years furnished him with both characters and atmosphere which he used for narrative purposes in *Heart of the West* (1907) and in scattered stories in other volumes. The leading character of "The Reformation of Calliope" delights in shooting rampages when drunk, like many a bad man in Western films. The Cisco Kid of "The Caballero's Way" is said to have been modeled after the notorious Texas killer, John Wesley Hardin. "The Passing of Black Eagle" is the story of another Texas desperado. "The Pimienta Pancakes" and "The Hiding of Black Bill" utilize O. Henry's knowledge of ranch life. It should be added, however, that the ludicrously polysyllabic language used by some of the characters in these Texas stories bears little relation to that ever used by any rancher or cowboy, O. Henry included.

For the loosely related series of stories in his first volume *Cabbages and Kings* (1904) and a few later stories, O. Henry drew upon his stay in Honduras and possibly upon tales he heard from the train robber Al Jennings and other friends he met there. Though some of these stories have comic-opera overtones, they probably reveal the same closely observed details of actual life that were later to appear in the New York stories.

O. Henry's life was marked by many vicissitudes, but he retained almost to the end a zest for living and a genuine love of people. Because of this and because his writing so frequently shows a humorous virtuosity of language and a facile playing upon the emotions of his readers, he seems likely to survive, even without benefit of criticism, for many years to come.

THE SHORT STORIES OF FLANNERY O'CONNOR

Author: Flannery O'Connor (1925–1964)
First published: A Good Man Is Hard to Find, 1955; *Everything That Rises Must Converge*, 1965; *The Complete Stories of Flannery O'Connor*, 1971

Criticism of Flannery O'Connor's two novels and two original collections of short stories notes the dramatic power of the nineteen stories in her two collections but is repelled by their shocking conclusions. If readers could narrow their application to the South from whence they come, as they can with *Tobacco Road*, for example, they would be much happier; but since her stories deal wholly with universals and are pervaded by an irony that seems both to involve and to mock, readers are forced to recognize that her vision encompasses the human condition, the naked spectacle of mortal man. O'Connor is not claiming so much as she is reminding that the human condition is fourfold: people are sinners, people shall die, people are equal in the sight of God, and people cannot expect to understand God's mercy but must recognize it in whatever outrageous form it appears, which is the beginning of salvation. Her term for that recognition is the "revelation" of sin, or death, or equality, and the beginning of "redemption." She does not follow the process of redemption, only its initiation through whatever unlikely instrument God chooses. Both O'Connor and her God are ironists, and readers and all her heroes are willful characters who must be humbled in learning that the will of God must prevail. This is the guiding vision in all her work.

Most of the titles in *A Good Man Is Hard to Find* are ironically intended and provide a key to the author's meaning. Three of the shortest stories show her intention most clearly: "A Stroke of Good Fortune," "A Late Encounter with the Enemy," and "A Temple of the Holy Ghost." The first describes the progress up four flights of stairs of Ruby Hill, who is terrified of having a baby and gradually realizes, as she climbs, that she is four months pregnant. This is the "stroke of good fortune" her palmist foretold; from the most unlikely sources comes the truth about Ruby's "condition." The second story shows how death and truth come to "General" Sash of the Confederacy at the late age of one hundred and four; he is no general but he is surrounded by false memories of the Confederacy, especially at the Atlanta premiere of *Gone with the Wind*, and he joins in the pretense. Death, the enemy, did not get him during the Civil War, but eventually he catches up, even with a Confederate general. In the last of the three stories, both a hermaphrodite and a platitudinous nun are shown to be "a temple of the Holy Ghost"; the outrageous and the comic are also clear signs of the truth for those who can both appreciate the ridiculous and get its message.

The other stories in the first collection fall into two groups: four independent stories that are related by theme; and three stories that use the same setting and similar cast. The latter group contains "A Circle in the Fire," "Good Country People," and the longest story O'Connor wrote, "The Displaced Person," which is the culmination of the volume. The common situation is an independent widow running a farm with the help of a succession of tenant farmers and some blacks. In the first two stories, the tenant farmer's wife acts as cool observer, like the black in *The Violent Bear It Away*, who offers a practical but unacceptable solution to the awkward situation which arises when an intruder arrives at the farm; in the last story, the tenant farmer's wife dies and becomes the motive for the "accidental" death of the "Displaced Person." The meaning of the stories seems to be that if one embarks on an act of charity one must be very sure of one's motives. Mrs. Hopewell, in "Good Country People," may be mistaken in her notions of country folk; certainly her ideas led her educated daughter astray and thus to a realization of the truth about herself, that she is in no way superior to what her mother calls "good country people." The play of ambiguity in these two stories is resolved in the last by identifying Christ as a person displaced from Mrs. McIntyre's heart; when He comes to her in the guise of a Displaced Person, she allows Him to be crucified again. It is not sufficient to be "nice"—a theme that recurs whenever this farm setting is used—one must be saved even at the cost of one's life. Mrs. McIntyre, like many of O'Connor's characters, is dying as the result of her revelation, the late reconciliation of word and deed.

The other group of four stories may be distinguished by the death or salvation of the protagonists. The stories are remarkable for the creation of a totally independent universe for each; "The River" and "A Good Man Is Hard to Find," contain the contrast between the well-to-do and the poor and end in death. The gentle death in the former of the four-year-old child seeking some meaning to his empty life is violently contrasted with the deaths of father, mother, baby, two children, and grandmother in the latter. O'Connor liked to read this story to her audiences, almost as if she were daring her hearers to face the truth in its most hideous manifestation. Solicitude for the family and the niceness of the grandmother notwithstanding, they will all perish at the hands of "The Misfit." The nickname is highly ironic: he is a "misfit" because he cannot find salvation or meaning to life and he knows his fallen condition. He is not, however, a "misfit" in a society of misfits who do not know their fallen condition and in turn call him a "misfit." A "good man" is not merely "hard to find"; without God he does not exist, and with God he knows he is a sinner.

The other two stories in this last group from *A Good Man Is Hard to Find* are "The Life You Save May Be Your Own" and "The Artificial Nigger." In the former, the revelation is accomplished by a road sign Mr. Shiftlet sees when he abandons his idiot bride; both the sign and the idiot are common devices in O'Connor's work to represent a truth beneath the surface. The latter story became the title of the English edition of this collection; O'Connor was displeased at the choice because of the inevitable and slipshod references to the South in her work and because, as in all her writing, the ironic meaning of the title belongs in the context of the story. In "The Artificial Nigger," the remark to that effect prompts the reconciliation between old Mr. Head and his estranged grandson, Nelson, whom he has denied. This is probably the happiest story O'Connor wrote, and it is important to her work in two ways: Nelson is the forerunner of the heroes of her two novels, and her guiding vision is most succinctly and clearly stated in the next to last paragraph where Mr. Head sees that God's mercy is not a soothing balm but a burning flame that purifies the sinner.

The stories in the second collection, *Everything That Rises Must Converge*, also fall into three groups. The first group comes early in the collection and in its material, corresponding roughly to the widow-farmer group in the first volume, seems to have come more directly from O'Connor's own experience. This first group includes the title story, "Greenleaf," "The Enduring Chill," and "The Comforts of Home." Each contains a spinsterish youngish bachelor and his mother; the Angel of the Lord appears as a bull, a black mother, a delinquent girl, and blasts the complacency of the young man or the mother.

The second group of stories—"A View of the Woods," "Parker's Back," and "Judgment Day"—corresponds roughly to the last group in the first volume. Each story has a world of its own which is vividly created, though all part of the same countryside, and the characters would seem remote from the writer's experience if one did not know that, like John Millington Synge, she liked to stand behind the kitchen door and listen to "good country people" yarn with her mother. In two stories, the meaning is clear: The saved and fearless soul so profoundly affects the hero's complacency in his way of life that, shaken, he tries to imitate the saved; his revelation is that he must seek his own way to God. In the last story in this group, "Judgment Day," the meaning is less clear; ambiguity plays around the central character and leaves the reader uncertain as to whether his way of life is that of salvation or not. One suspects the former because his antagonist is the city and a well-to-do daughter, and as far as O'Connor was concerned, both were passports to hell.

Two stories in the second collection complement each other in that their titles seem interchangeable. "The Lame Shall Enter First" is the best example of O'Connor's reworking of a situation, for the story is a rewriting and expansion of the second part of *The Violent Bear It Away*, omitting the preliminary farm and family history and the later return to the country. The infirmities of Rayber, the protagonist of the novel, are transferred to the protagonist of the story, Rufus Johnson, a boy with a clubfoot, a bad past, and not a trace of Southern charm. He remains a mystery to Sheppard, the welfare officer determined to rescue the boy's I.Q. from his circumstances and his religion; the attention is on Sheppard, an indictment of the intellect, or false education, as the chief begetter of complacency and "niceness." Although this view sometimes betrays O'Connor into a glorification of corn pone as the simple true bread of life, this lapse does not occur in "Revelation," a story that draws together many of her materials and states her own vision in that afforded Mrs. Turpin in the sunset by the hog pen. The tenant farmer's wife and the widow-farmer are brought together in Mrs. Turpin (though she is married), and the precocious or educated child becomes the messenger of her revelation in a typically clotted utterance which the protagonist must ponder until it is clarified in an awful moment of truth. Mrs. Turpin has to learn that in certain essentials she is a pig of a woman, less than the trash she so despises and that the "lame shall enter first" into Heaven, before the "nice" and capable. Mrs. Turpin thus brings up the procession of O'Connor's characters which began in "A Stroke of Good Fortune." So unified is her vision that the title of the first story discussed could be that of the last.

THE SHORT STORIES OF PETER TAYLOR

Author: Peter Taylor (1917–   )
First published: A Long Fourth and Other Stories, 1948; *The Widows of Thornton*, 1954; *Happy Families Are All Alike*, 1959; *Miss Leonora When Last Seen and Fifteen Other Stories*, 1963; *The Collected Stories of Peter Taylor*, 1970; *In The Miro District and Other Stories*, 1977

Peter Taylor's first published collection of seven short stories, *A Long Fourth and Other Stories*, was described by Robert Penn Warren as the product of a "disenchanted mind." This cool viewpoint has characterized much of his drama and short and long fiction. Taylor's increasing literary stature, however, is based chiefly on the skill with which that view is expressed and the flawless technique of his short fiction.

The world that Taylor views, and expresses just short of social satire, is chiefly the modern upper South in its small-town or equivalent suburban setting. His middle-class characters consider themselves a cut above middle class since, on a small-town social scale, they are sometimes the next best thing to gentry and are probably charter members of the town's first country club. They have, for example, the gentry's adherence to blood and bone and family; but their plantations are likely to be neat houses on green lawns, and their ancestral memories may be conveniently short. The Old South fabric of family is still there, but fading and threadbare, in imminent danger of being chopped up by modern scissors and sewed into something for practical usage around the house.

In fact, one might view Taylor's world as a recent island risen out of Faulknerian seas. The theme of land, that rural hold upon the heart, survives in Taylor; but the reader catches barely a sniff of the barnyard, now safely pushed beyond these city limit lines. The family, not merely falling into ruins now, is several generations along and better adjusted to commercialism, or at least it has more muted maladjustments. Tales of aristocracy and historical grief are still told by the old to the young but in a calmer voice. The role of the woman and the black in society remains unsettled, but in Taylor's world the terms in which each is discussed have become less simple, less basic, more "civilized." Taylor's characters suspect that there are no easy solutions to find, no such thing as "woman's role" or "black's place." The Faulkner themes have been updated, dragged forward a few years in time; and there is less despair when the Old Order clashes with the New in Southern society. It has already clashed and does clash, but despair slides over into what Warren called "disenchantment." Taylor's response to his contemporary South is less impassioned grief than melancholy, less rage than irony.

Some of these generalizations about Taylor's fictional world were justified in his earliest stories. In "A Long Fourth," the title story of his first book, a son brings into his Southern family household an "intellectual" New York girlfriend. The tensions of their holiday visit are set against the continuing hidden tensions between the mother and her black servant. Here is sentiment opposed to youth's embarrassment by sentiment, familiar attachments set against uneasy independence. The author deals almost tenderly with all his characters, including that generation which has not and never will catch up with the times. He describes Harriet's feeling that her children do not exist any longer; it is as if they died in childhood, never growing up at all.

Other stories that express this tangle of yesterday and today would include "A Spinster's Tale," the story of a motherless girl alienated in an all-male household; "The Scoutmaster," a picture of domestic crisis performed against a backdrop of Southern nobility (this story includes near-comic creation Uncle Jake, who bears a certain resemblance to Harriet), and "The Fancy Woman."

The latter story is probably Taylor's best-known and most widely anthologized story. Written in 1940, it is the funny, bittersweet, pitiful account of Josie Carlson's weekend stay on a plantation outside Memphis with an oaf named George. The "fancy woman's" visit is interrupted and altered by the arrival of George's two teenage sons and a set of shallow, good-time suburban friends. As one critic has said, this story holds intimations of a society disintegrating and of a tradition that was never wholly perfect or sustaining being replaced by something even less so.

The Taylor countryside, then, is one of Southern change. His characters are either changing or wearing under their refusal to do so. He picks up the Faulkner mood several degrees removed from violent upheaval and sets it down in a semi-industrialized, half-accepting, half-reluctant time.

It is not surprising that the style Taylor employs in his short stories should be consistent with their mood and setting. A reader's initial reaction may be almost negative; technically the stories seem at first notable for what they do not do, leave out, or conceal; but the threat of violence and upheaval exists under his smooth surfaces. Most of the violence and much traditional plot take place offstage. His technical skill in constructing a story, in weaving the rhythm of ordinary speech into narrative, in conveying character through meager but always pertinent bits of dialogue, is such that the technique seems to disappear. He sews up his story with an invisible seam.

One might almost say that Taylor's style is a studied avoidance of style. The statement demands amplification. For example, it is difficult to imagine Peter Taylor parodied, as Hemingway, Faulkner, François Sagan, or J. D. Salinger lend themselves to parody. There is little to be plucked from his prose as "pure Taylor." This lack of stylistic effect is partly the result of the way in which he casts many of his stories in easy-flowing narrative, the distilled reminiscence of a single character. The narrator may be identified ("Spinster's Tale," "Miss Leonora When Last Seen," "A Strange Story") or have no formal existence ("Rain in the Heart," "Fancy Woman," "Reservations," "An Overwhelming Question"). If he chooses, however, the reader can think back and mentally "retell" the story from a specific first-person viewpoint, such as Josie in "The Fancy Woman" or Helen Ruth in "A Wife of Nashville." The style of the story itself, on first reading, seems nearly neutral, taking its source from the story and not from a single mind or pair of eyes. Nothing blurs or refracts most of the told events—they are seldom handed out pre-digested or preinterpreted. Taylor is never spotted onstage adjusting the strings on the puppets. His narrative takes precedence over the language or the temptation to verbal flourishes. The style seems so natural, like conversation and the family tale, that it is clear window glass through which the action is purely seen.

Since there is so little intrusion of the author begging his case, an air of verisimilitude results. The "raisin-colored carpet," for example, simply is that color. The reader is both bemused and convinced by the quiet story told in the quiet parlor.

This apparent lack of effort and muting of drama works better for Taylor than italics or exclamation points. Such quiet understatement alerts the reader, who casts his mind back looking for all those implications woven almost invisibly into the story. When the reader does perceive, perhaps by hindsight, the delicate design, he halfway claims this as some kind of evidence of his own sensitivity.

This method enables Taylor to tell volumes through understatement. "Reservations," subtitled "A Love Story," follows a just-married couple from their bridal reception at the country club to a hotel where they will spend their wedding night. The bride accidentally locks herself in the bathroom and must be rescued by residents of an adjoining room, an embarrassed man and the woman he has purchased for the evening. Taylor, a serious writer who can be very humorous at times, conveys deftly a case of honeymoon jitters. While Dorothy Parker in "Here We Are" did much the same thing in sharp and witty dialogue, Taylor gives the reader, in very little more space, a full-length portrait of the nervous bride, her feeling that the prostitute is too familiar, and the harsh accusations she finally screams at the exasperated groom while he struggles with the locked door. Parker wrote of honeymooners; at the end of Taylor's story the reader knows what the whole marriage will be like. He makes what Hollis Summers once described as the effort to "realize simultaneously the tree and the forest of experience."

There is not a Taylor story which does not fulfill the dictum of short fiction to tell little but suggest much. In "Miss Leonora When Last Seen," Leonora Logan habitually dons dungarees, cardigan, and poke bonnet and drives her 1942 Dodge convertible through an assortment of states, orbiting Tennessee. The last time she drives away, unfortunately, she looks very much like a thousand others seen in small towns and on the highways. She is lost, out of eccentricity and into normality.

Aunt Munsie, in "What You Hear from 'Em?" gives up her hogs and slop wagon, but she also gives up really caring when the two Tolliver boys are coming home to live in Thornton. In "Allegiance," a Tennessee soldier in London goes to call upon an aunt with whom his family has quarreled and during the visit creates the whole microcosm of that family. In "An Overwhelming Question," a bizarre accident at the Hunt and Polo Club prevents the couple from living happily ever after, like a sleeping beauty and a sleeping prince awaking at the same moment in the same place. In these and in other stories, what distinguishes Taylor's fiction is, as Henry James suggested, "the power to guess the unseen from the seen, to trace the implication of things, to judge the whole piece by the pattern."

This is Taylor's special literary talent: to select, unerringly, the small seen moment which is a keyhole to an entire revelation. If the themes are, as suggested earlier, as broad as the changing, contemporary South, Taylor illuminates them with a single pencil-flashlight, and then another, and then another.

The change in one's homeland was expressed by William Faulkner in great intensity. Banners were furled and unfurled, and armor clanked, so much so that at first it may be hard to see that Taylor's is the same battlefield a few years later, coolly viewed, more quietly described. In literary time, if not chronologically, Taylor is much later than Faulkner; and where the Sartoris family bled, there is already a monument or so, encrusted with pigeon droppings. It is useful for the reader to remember, however, that between the older writer and the younger one, the issues differ less in substance than in approach, angle, and author's temperament in their presentations of a Southern region and its society.

THE SHORT STORIES OF JOHN UPDIKE

Author: John Updike (1932–   )
First published: The Same Door, 1959; *Pigeon Feathers and Other Stories*,
   1962; *Olinger Stories: A Selection*, 1964; *The Music School*, 1966; *Bech:
   A Book*, 1970; *Museums and Women and Other Stories*, 1972; *Too Far to
   Go: The Naples Stories*, 1979; *Problems and Other Stories*, 1979

John Updike is a prodigiously talented writer; he is a poet, parodist, critic, novelist, and short-story writer who achieved distinction and a very considerable reputation in the first half of the 1960's. His career is remarkable, indeed virtually unique among the serious writers of his generation. Perhaps equally remarkable—for there are limits to the most finely tuned imagination, and even though people tend to forget it they must inevitably judge others by their own experience—he gives evidence of enough self-transcendence to be aware of the surprising good fortune which has attended all his efforts. From the first, he has been a character in that rare thing: a genuine, American, real-life success story. It is the kind of thing that has not happened and does not happen to most serious American writers. One need only recall the story Robert Frost used to tell groups of eager young student writers, how a relative had offered him a living for a year, without worry or burden, to determine if he really were a poet. "Give me twenty," was Frost's reply to the astounded relative; it took twenty years of hard and lonely labor before Frost was able to convince a publisher to publish his poems. Equally familiar and typical is the example of William Faulkner, who wrote professionally for twenty-five years before anyone began to give him or his work any attention or to consider his work worthy of prizes and awards. Contemporary literary history would indicate that Faulkner's career and Frost's are typical, except, perhaps, for the happy endings.

Not only did Updike become a "writer" without prolonged struggle or delay, but, with the single exception of his first book of poems, *The Carpentered Hen*, he has remained with one publisher, and almost all of his work has been published in one magazine, *The New Yorker*. Both of these facts are extremely unusual for the times. Most serious writers, and especially the younger ones, move from publisher to publisher, not willingly perhaps, but compelled to by the complexities of the modern publishing business, which simply cannot allow a writer to grow and develop, acquiring an audience as he goes along, over any considerable period of time without demonstrable "success."

In a sense, Updike has been patronized by two strong and distinguished literary powers and, thus, given an opportunity to develop his talent under apparently almost ideal circumstances, saved from the simple, mundane, and frequently discouraging conditions which plague almost all other writers.

Moreover, his critical reception has been uniformly good. Surely he is one of the most encouraged writers of his time. It remains to be noted that he has made every effort to justify this extraordinary interest. He is obviously a prodigious worker. He has not wasted time, nor has he failed to make the most of his advantages. There is no doubt that he is a hard-working, highly gifted, and imaginative writer.

There are built-in dangers and disadvantages to this kind of success story. Talent, to be recognized easily and early, must inevitably be based upon precedent, upon a set of existing and accepted standards. For any establishment to offer rewards at the outset, the work of the neophyte must be acceptable to and, indeed, be complimentary to the establishment. Looking back in time, readers should have no cause to wonder why, for example, Lizette Reese was for so long considered a much better poet than Robert Frost, why Glenway Wescott was recognized as a literary artist while William Faulkner was not. In this era of intense self-consciousness, of continual agonizing reappraisal, it is highly unlikely that a decently educated and successful young writer would not be haunted by the specters of a recent literary past, troubled by the vague prospect that history may well be repeating itself in his case. The thought might well be inhibiting. Then there are the inhibitions that can so easily come from writing for particular patrons and an already existing audience. If these patrons are essentially conservative in literary matters, one would be disinclined to offend, to bite the hand that feeds. The mechanics of human rationalization are such that, in order to continue to create at all, a writer would have to believe in his patrons. To question would be crippling. To rebel might be disastrous.

It is, therefore, a tribute to the skill of Updike to report that in spite of all these factors and in spite of the fact that he has shown little interest in pioneering and innovation in any form, his work has continued to grow in stature and, so far, without the least sign of self-doubt or diminishing integrity.

It is by his short stories that Updike is best known, and it should be observed that chunks and sections of the novels have been originally published in somewhat different form as short stories. In this practical sense, Updike's fiction is the short story. *The Same Door* is a book of sixteen well-wrought stories, for the most part conventionally correct according to the familiar formula of *The New Yorker*, observing the taboos of that magazine, careful, restrained, controlled, and unemphatic in the smooth organization of subject, theme, and structure. Though they are not "autobiographical," they derive almost exclusively from the author's pragmatic rather than imagined experience, and they modestly do not aspire to extend beyond these self-imposed limitations. There are stories set in Olinger, which he acknowledges in the foreword to *Olinger Stories* to be an only lightly disguised reflection of his hometown, Shillington. There are school stories, stories of the pains and pleasures of adolescence, stories set in Oxford, and stories involving young married couples in New York. With the exception of the final story in the book, "The Happiest I've Been," each of these stories is almost a textbook example of *The New Yorker* story, the expanded anecdote, the significant sketch, told in a straightforward and uncomplicated manner, following the accepted convention of the dramatic presentation with a reasonable unity of time and place. Usually Updike employs a third-person narrator for whom, as a result of the things which happen, there is likely to be an ever so slight rearrangement of the structure of his sensibility. They are fixed in time, at once precisely and evocatively, by the convention of reference to things—the books, fads and fashions, brand names, and popular songs of a particular moment in time. Nevertheless, the essential mood of all the stories, in fact explicitly stated, is memory, unabashed nostalgia, of shards dug up, cleaned and polished, then elegantly displayed against the ruins of time. Time, mutability, the natural process of change and decay are the principal forces against which the human protagonists must wrestle. It is unfair to point out that this drama is a slight one, like the small child who cries against a rainy day, for it has a long and honored tradition, and great writers have made much of it. It is fair, however, to remark that such a theme allows for only small action and diminutive moral drama. Morality, good and evil, appears only insofar as it relates to the overriding concern of the single perceptive self in time. The moral world is, then, greatly simplified. What is bad is likely to be vulgarity, stupidity, ugliness, results of imposed conditions rather than active choices.

There is wit and some humor as well in this first book, but basically all of the stories are extremely serious, exemplary of high seriousness and earnestness applied to simple and commonplace experiences of life, at best succeeding in giving a glimpse of the extraordinary mystery at the heart of things, though always in danger, teetering close to the sheer edge of solemnity and the incorrigibly sentimental. It is this seriousness which has impressed Updike's enthusiastic critics most uniformly.

None of these items, however, would be enough to lift Updike to official stardom in the established literary firmament. There are a number of qualities that make *The Same Door* a good deal more significant than several other and roughly similar collections by young writers. His style and verbal felicity are vitally important to the overall effect. Updike is a poet and a good one. A poet's love of language and the exact shadings and connotations of the right word emerges in sentence after sentence. He displays, as well, a poet's ear, an aptness of dialogue, a breathtaking sense of the intricate rhythms of prose. Moreover, he demonstrates a superb visual sense, not surprising since he has studied art professionally, an ability to compose a scene or to evoke a person, place, or thing memorably with a few carefully sketched details. The final effect of all these virtues is a haunting quality of evocation, which fits his theme and mood with admirable decorum and, overwhelming all else, leaves a lapidary ambience, a feeling of great richness and beauty, a luminous purity brimming with an inner light.

The Same Door, however, is not the whole story by any means. *Pigeon Feathers* represents a new and expanded use of his talent. It is another example of the atypical quality of Updike's literary career. Many modern writers began with experiment and innovation and moved gradually toward the use of a developed style to explore other interests. Typically, *Pigeon Feathers* would be a first collection of stories, though, realistically, it would have been extremely difficult to publish as such. It is important that with *The Same Door*, Updike passed all the academic tests. He had "become a 'writer.'" With his chevron of achievement, he has been able to carry patron and audience with him into more adventurous directions in both form and subject matter. Again his basic theme, stated in a functional epigraph from Kafka, is memory, but now there is a difference. There are the apparently conventional stories, including the title story, which lead off the book, but even they are slightly off center when compared to the earlier stories. There are frankly, more explicitly autobiographical stories, and the first-person narration, used only sparingly in *The Same Door*, is here used freely and easily and often. Most significantly, there are varieties and exercises in the form and structure of the short story, which, while hardly new, are very new for Updike and quite new for *The New Yorker*. He has an epistolary story in "Dear Alexandros." He employs the method of dramatic monologue in "A & P," "Archangel," and "Lifeguard." There is a mild story of social consciousness in "The Doctor's Wife." There are, perhaps most successfully, a group of personal reminiscences which are transmuted into a form of fiction as in "The Crow in the Woods" and the almost essaylike concluding stories—"The Blessed Man of Boston, My Grandmother's Thimble, Fanning Island," and the second, "Packed Dirt, Churchgoing, A Dying Cat, A Traded Car." To make these work as stories requires all of his natural and acquired skill and, as well, requires of the reader a more than casual interest, not only in the perceptions of the author but also in his life. In fairness to the many fine contemporary story writers, it must be pointed out that his experiments are not radical and are, in large part, derivative. Yet they represent in many cases the first successful popularization of methods and techniques that have in the past been the exclusive domain of the little magazines. Other writers of the short story owe John Updike their gratitude even though he came late to the task; and even if his artistry has been overpraised by his admirers and often praised for the wrong reasons, there is no denying that Updike is a skilled and serious short-story writer.

THE SHORT STORIES OF EUDORA WELTY

Author: Eudora Welty (1909–   )
First published: A Curtain of Green and Other Stories, 1941; *The Wide Net and Other Stories*, 1943; *The Golden Apples*, 1949; *The Bride of the Innisfallen*, 1955; *The Collected Stories of Eudora Welty*, 1980

Eudora Welty is one of the best contemporary writers of short stories. A writer of novels as well, her reputation has been built upon her short fiction, especially that of her early collections, *A Curtain of Green and Other Stories*, and *The Wide Net and Other Stories*. Although somewhat restricted in setting, her short stories have demonstrated a wide variety in subject matter, ranging from the treatment of sideshow freaks in "Keela, the Outcast Indian Maiden" to that of the improvisations of a jazz musician in "Powerhouse." There is also a wide variety in moods, from the broad humor of "Why I Live at the P.O." and "Petrified Man" to the ironic and grim horror of "Flowers for Marjorie," from the fantasy of "Asphodel" to the devastatingly prosaic quality of "No Place for You, My Love." There is also a wide variety in time, for although most of the stories are set in the present, some like "First Love," "A Still Moment," and "The Burning" go back to the times of Aaron Burr, Audubon, and the Civil War.

However wide the variety of theme, mood, and time, the first thing that strikes the reader is Welty's absolute control over all her material. She is a master craftsman, and when her stories fail, as they sometimes do, it is often because her virtuosity as craftsman and experimenter overshadows the material on which she is operating. She has an uncanny ability to create a mood and setting for a story in a few sentences. "The Whistle" and "The Key" reveal in their opening paragraphs all there is to know about the story. Nothing is wasted, and all is used to make clearer the inevitable epiphany that occurs in her stories. Perhaps it is her interest in photography and painting that has sharpened this gift of observation. Her ear seems as sharp as her eye; the beauty parlor gossip in "Petrified Man" echoes diction, cadence, and tone brilliantly. The story called "A Memory" is a good illustration of this control, as the girl on the beach seems to be enacting Welty's own creative process. The girl makes frames out of her fingers and observes the world through them. Whereas the girl cannot include the disordered and grotesque in her framing vision, Welty is able to confine and fix all of life in her frame. An order is given to every "still moment" that her artistry captures, and the purely formal delight the reader experiences is one of the great pleasures her short stories afford.

There is, however, more than a caught moment in her stories. What gives them their solidity is that there is a caught place as well. Although her stories are mostly set in the present, they cannot really be called contemporary. For example, none of her stories in her first two collections has anything to do with World War II, although they were published at its height. The only sense in which the present is contemporary is that she has chosen to write of the contemporary South, more specifically the region of Mississippi. In *The Bride of the Innisfallen*, in particular, she has moved outside the South for her settings, and this move has not produced better work. In this volume, stories such as "Kin" and "No Place for You, My Love," which are set in the South, tend to be the best ones. This strong sense of place is closely tied to Welty's artistic control. It is the concrete reality to which her lyrical flights and moves toward fantasy must always return. Welty herself seems aware of the importance of place, and she has written an article called "Place in Fiction" that throws much light upon her own fictional achievements.

Moving inside this frame of artistic control and place, her short fiction reveals certain views and themes that seem to be characteristic of the stories as a whole. They are often an exploration of what it means to be isolated and set apart. In story after story, the leading character seems set apart or cut off from his world. His isolation is often marked by a peculiar grotesque quality, as if the spiritual and emotional separateness were symbolized by physical abnormality. Her stories are thus peopled with deaf mutes, Ellie and Albert in "The Key" or Joel Mayes in "First Love"; by deformed blacks, Keela in "Keela, the Outcast Indian Maiden"; by the feebleminded, Lily Daw in "Lily Daw and the Three Ladies"; by the very old and very small, Phoenix Jackson in "A Worn Path" or Solomon in "Livvie"; by the very young and very fat, Gabriella in "Going to Naples"; and by the frustrated and insane, Clytie in "Clytie" and Miss Theo in "The Burning."

Yet those who are isolated are most often people who seem more valuable than the world that isolates them. The reason is that Welty treats their separateness with sympathy and even with love. The isolation is what allows her to get inside her characters and, once inside, their shared isolation, with the reader and with the author, becomes a thing of beauty. Welty is very close to Sherwood Anderson in this aspect of her fiction. The "truth" in the grotesque is the special theme of *Winesburg, Ohio*, and the beauty, if not the truth, is the very thing Welty focuses upon. Because the abnormality is lovingly handled, the characters are invested with a certain beauty and mystery. Mr. Marblehall has a secret second life, with a second wife and child in another part of town. Ellie and Albert share a speechless communication that sets them apart from the others in the waiting room in "The Key," a communication that moves over into love as they discover the key on the floor. This mystery is often connected with a certain ritual, as it is in Phoenix Jackson's long trek along the "worn path" to get medicine for her grandson. Phoenix is as old as the land itself, yet the mysterious force that keeps her going, and over which she seems to have little control, gives her life a singular sort of beauty for those who see her life in its entirety and not in its isolation. Mystery is closely related to the lyrical quality as well as the ritualistic and almost mythical. As the couple in "The Whistle" silently burn all their furniture while the whistle blown when a freeze threatens is sounding outside, one senses the elegiac beauty created in their wordless act and the beauty revealed as this action enables them to speak with each other.

At times, the beauty is revealed by the fact of isolation. At other times, it comes as a result of the pathos created by the attempt to reach beyond the isolation. In other words, there are those cut off in place and those cut off from place. R. J. Bowman, in Welty's first published story, "Death of a Traveling Salesman," is an example of the latter. An outsider by occupation as well as nature, Bowman is a rootless salesman who stumbles onto a family in the middle of nowhere, Sonny and his pregnant wife, and in their prelapsarian, timeless familial bond of love, he sees all that his life has not been. Precisely because he sees, he achieves a certain human dignity even as he dies, somewhat ironically, of a heart attack. His heart fails but also succeeds. The same pathos is achieved in the treatment of Harris, another traveling salesman who in "The Hitch-Hikers" wishes people would call him "you" rather than "he." Then there is the Eastern businessman in "No Place for You, My Love" who travels south out of New Orleans with another stranger to the place, an unnamed woman, but goes to the end of the road and returns without ever knowing why he went or where.

As opposed to these figures cut off from place, there are those cut off in place, and these are more tragically and also more comically treated. There is, on the comic side, the humorously paranoic narrator of "Why I Live at the P.O." who escapes the isolation of living with her family by going to live at the post office. The tragic statement of the familial sort of isolation is found in the person of Clytie, who is so hounded by her family and the demands they make on her that she is driven to suicide. There are all the characters living in Morgana in *The Golden Apples* who feel the need to escape but who also know that there is no escape.

Indeed, it can be said that most of these characters who are caught in their isolation are torn by two forces and move toward a tenuous sort of resolution. Most often it is a movement from innocence to experience, the kind symbolized in "Livvie," in which the young black wife whose old husband, Solomon, is on his deathbed, moves from her sheltered existence to the flashy world of Cash McCord, the fieldhand who offers her all the pleasures of the world. The same conflict and process is present in Jennie in "At the Landing," when her quest for Floyd leads her from her sheltered home to the shack along the river where she is raped by Floyd's fellow fishermen. Yet her innocence seems to prevail, even as she is raped. The innocents are the blessed in Welty's fiction, and if to the world their innocence takes on a grotesque quality, they appear to be normal in the loving world of the inner heart that Welty explores so well.

Closely related to this theme of innocence and experience is the theme and structural device of the dream versus the reality, and the fusion that sometimes remains at the heart of life in general and life in Welty's fiction in particular. Although this is a theme and structural device employed more fully in Welty's later work, especially in "Music from Spain" in *The Golden Apples*, it can be seen in such early stories as "The Purple Hat," "Flowers for Marjorie," "Powerhouse," and "Old Mr. Marblehall." At times, when the dream is submitted to the reality, there is a shock, as in "Flowers for Marjorie" or "At the Landing"; but at other times, the dream and the reality seem inseparable, as in "The Purple Hat" and "Powerhouse," whose improvisations on the theme of his wife's death seem both real and unreal to the reader. What remains true is that most often it is the dream, the lyrical quality in which it is expressed, and the innocence that gives it birth that is beautiful. "Reality" is never beautiful in itself but is made so by its contact with the dream and the characters who reveal or embody it.

With such emphasis given to man in his particular environment, there is not much attention given to his place in the universe. Although there is little metaphysical speculation in Welty's stories, the presence of the universe and its reality is sometimes disturbingly felt. When perceived, the universe is at best indifferent and, more often than not, seemingly malevolent. Man is sometimes measured by his reaction to it, as in "The Whistle," where the warmth generated by the couple and their fire is equal to the chilling force of the unseasonal weather, but when special attention is drawn from man to the universe, man stands in a somewhat defeated posture.

A SIMPLE HONORABLE MAN

Type of work: Novel
Author: Conrad Richter (1890–1968)
Type of plot: Personal narrative
Time of plot: Early twentieth century
Locale: Pennsylvania
First published: 1962

>*Principal characters:*
>HARRY DONNER, a storekeeper who becomes a Lutheran
>   minister
>VALERIA DONNER, his wife
>JOHN,
>GENE, and
>TIM, their sons
>THE REVEREND ELIJAH MORGAN, Harry Donner's father-
>   in-law
>MIKE BARRETT, a dying Irish miner
>SALLY, his wife
>ISAAC GOTTSCHALL, a crippled miner
>EMMA SEVERN, a girl who marries unwisely
>PHILLIP RODEY, Harry Donner's friend and parishioner
>JENNY, his wife
>MRS. MCPHAIL, a woman grieving for her murdered son
>JAKE SCHNECKE, a murderer

In *The Waters of Kronos*, Conrad Richter told the imaginatively conceived and poetically textured story of one man's journey back to the lost times and landmarks of his youth, to remembrances recalled but now beyond his physical reach. For Unionville, the Pennsylvania community of his boyhood had been buried under the waters of a great hydroelectric dam, just as the years of his early life have been covered by the deep wash of time. What John Donner discovered at the end of that quietly told but deeply moving novel is the secret of his own mortality, the realization of how much in life is wasted and sad, how much that is beautiful and good is never recognized until it is past recall. In the end, man's death, half-welcomed and half-feared, is joined to his beginning, far back in the years of childhood and the place of his origins.

Although separate and complete in itself, *The Waters of Kronos* hinted at further disclosures in the Donner family, particularly of the father to whom John Donner, dying, becomes reconciled, and of the mother with whom a reunion has been promised. *A Simple Honorable Man* does extend the story of the Donners but on a different level of action and presentation. The earlier novel relied for much of its effect on time fantasy and suggestions from ancient myths. In this novel, however, the treatment is straightforward in chronology and structure.

The epigraph, taken from a letter by James Joyce, sets forth Richter's intentions to present a man of simplicity and honor. In *The Waters of Kronos*, there are hints that the younger John Donner never really understood his father and that there had been some kind of friction between them. A lack of understanding also appears in the relationship of father and son in this novel, but only because the boy cannot share his father's firm and joyous belief in the everlasting goodness of God. In the end, the father's example overwhelms, even if it never quite succeeds in erasing, his son's belief that the church maintains its authority by the "dark, theocratic gloom" of such phrases as "holiness," "original sin," "the blood of the lamb," and "eternal damnation." Words like these had chilled John Donner when he was a boy. To Harry Donner, however, church is a citadel of strength, and he lives the life of a clergyman with all the devotion of his passionate mind and heart. In his dealings with his fellows and with God he is, as his son eventually sees him, a simple, unselfish, honorable man.

Harry Donner's way of grace is not easy. He is almost forty, married, and the father of three sons when, about the turn of the century, he feels an irresistible call to the ministry. His father-in-law, the austere old clergyman whom John Donner calls Pap-pa, tries to dissuade him. Harry Donner is too old for such a step; he is a family man; he can never hope to obtain a charge in one of the better churches; he has his general store in Unionville and ought to be satisfied with the life he has. In the face of these arguments, however, he remains stubborn in his resolve. With a small legacy left to his wife and money from the sale of his store—the business had never been a success because he was unable to deny credit to the miners of the region—he goes off to West Shore College and from there to the seminary to prepare for the Lutheran ministry. In the next thirty-three years, he fills three parishes. The first is Mahanoy, about ten miles from Unionville. There he has his first experience in pastoral duties, not all of them pleasant. Perhaps he expects too much of his congregation, he decides. If the people of Mahanoy do not want to accept all that he is prepared to offer, the miners and poor people in the mining patch at Lost Run need him. There he visits the sick, comforts the dying, performs marriages, preaches funeral sermons, and in the end, builds at Lost Run the church of which he had dreamed. From Mahanoy, the Donners go to Wetherill, where the minister finds himself caught between opposing factions quarreling over building a new church or keeping the old one. While there, Harry Donner is offered the assistant pastorship of a large church in Brooklyn, but he refuses the call; he cannot believe that the people there really need him. So he goes off to a bleak parish at Paint Creek in Cambria County. There his sons grow up and leave home, and there his wife (the mother of *The Waters of Kronos*) dies, reliving in memory her early life with family and friends in Unionville. Harry Donner serves the Paint Creek parish until his retirement. When he dies his bank balance is one dollar and thirty-eight cents.

Harry Donner is the book. Other characters enter into his story briefly but memorably, figures like Mike Barrett, the tough old Irishman, who was baptized while he was dying of miner's asthma; Harry Gottschall, who had lost both arms in mine accidents; Mrs. McPhail, whose son had murdered his wife and child; beautiful young Emma Severn, who married a worthless fellow and paid the minister for the wedding with a bag of snitz; Dan Singer and Dolly, his common-law wife, who refused to get married, with Dan quoting the Bible to prove his point; Phillip Rodey, who was accused of stealing a pig, and his wife Jenny; the three Piatt brothers, who wanted all things their way; Jake Schnecke, who shot his best friend and then turned his gun on himself. Only in retrospect does the reader realize what a large and varied picture of experience Richter has distilled into his novel.

Tribulation, hardship, and strength of purpose fill Harry Donner's world, but humor is there as well. On one occasion, he mentioned David and Bathsheba in a sermon, only to be rebuked and threatened the next day by a backwoodsman named Dave Mace, who accused the minister of slandering him and his woman. As Dave explains it, he and Sheba are not living in sin; they merely have not yet got around to getting married. Harry Donner pays for the license, marries them, and baptizes their three children. Before long, he has performed four marriages in the community and has run out of baptismal certificates.

Richter makes the story of Harry Donner the record of a dedicated, proud, upright life, one rich in sustaining values. To his wife and sons, as to members of his congregations, he is at once a source of trial and a tower of strength. A man motivated by his strong yet unostentatious love for the meek and the lowly as much as by his religious zeal, he lives the life of a shepherd according to his own simple, unyielding belief and powers. He belongs to a time when right and wrong, good and bad, were still terms of meaning, before they were blunted by Freudian psychology and sociological cant. Harry Donner bases his life and his ministry on three simple premises. First, God forgives all sins if the sinner is repentant. Second, salvation is possible for everyone through God's grace. Third, all these things are wonderfully and meaningfully true.

Even though John Donner did not always understand his father, through his eyes that humble, earnest, dedicated man is brought warmly and movingly to life in this novel.

SISTER CARRIE

Type of work: Novel
Author: Theodore Dreiser (1871–1945)
Type of plot: Naturalism
Time of plot: 1889
Locale: Chicago and New York
First published: 1900

> Principal characters:
> CARRIE MEEBER, a small-town girl
> CHARLES DROUET, her first lover
> G. W. HURSTWOOD, Drouet's friend and Carrie's second
> lover

The Story:

When Carrie Meeber left her hometown in Wisconsin, she had nothing but a few dollars and a certain unspoiled beauty and charm. Young and inexperienced, she was going to Chicago to live with her sister and to find work. While on the train, she met Charles Drouet, a genial, flashy traveling salesman. Before the train pulled into the station, they had exchanged addresses, and Drouet promised to call on Carrie at her sister's house.

When she arrived at her sister's home, Carrie discovered that her life there would be far from the happy, carefree existence of which she had dreamed. The Hansons were hardworking people, grim and penny-pinching, allowing themselves no pleasures, and living a dull, conventional life. It was clear to Carrie that Drouet could not possibly call there, not only because of the unattractive atmosphere, but also because the Hansons were sure to object to him. She wrote and told him that he was not to call, and that she would get in touch with him later.

Meanwhile, Carrie went job-hunting and finally found work in a small shoe factory. Of her first wages, all but fifty cents went to her sister and brother-in-law. Then she fell ill and lost her job. Once again she had to look for work. Day after day, she trudged the streets, without success. It seemed as if she would have to go back to Wisconsin, and the Hansons encouraged her to do so. If she could not bring in money, they did not want her.

One day, while Carrie was looking for work, she met Drouet and told him her troubles. He offered her money which, with reluctance, she finally accepted. The money was for clothes she needed, but she did not know how to explain the source of the money to her sister. Drouet solved the problem by suggesting that he rent a room for her, where she could keep her clothing. A few days later, Carrie went to live with Drouet, who had promised to marry her as soon as he had completed a business deal.

In the meantime, Drouet introduced her to a friend, G. W. Hurstwood. Hurstwood had a good job as the manager of a saloon, a comfortable home, a wife, and two grown children. More than twice Carrie's age, he nevertheless accepted Drouet's suggestion that he look in on her while the salesman was out of town on one of his trips. Before long, Hurstwood was passionately in love with her. When Drouet came back, he discovered from a chambermaid that Carrie and Hurstwood had been going out together frequently. A scene followed. Carrie was furious when Drouet told her that Hurstwood was already married. She blamed Drouet for her folly, saying that he should have told her that Hurstwood was a married man.

Meanwhile, Mrs. Hurstwood had become suspicious of her husband. Drouet had secured for Carrie a part in a theatrical entertainment that a local lodge was presenting. Hurstwood, hearing that Carrie was to appear, persuaded many of his friends to go with him to the show. Mrs. Hurstwood learned of the affair and heard, too, that her husband had been seen riding with an unknown woman. She confronted Hurstwood and told him that she intended to sue for divorce. Faced with social and financial ruin, Hurstwood was in despair. One night, he discovered that his employer's safe was open. He robbed it of several thousand dollars and went to Carrie's apartment. Drouet had just deserted her. Pretending that Drouet had been hurt, Hurstwood succeeded in getting Carrie on a train bound for Montreal. In Montreal, Hurstwood was approached by an agent of his former employer, who urged him to return the money and to settle the issue quietly. Hurstwood returned all but a relatively small sum.

Under the name of Wheeler, he and Carrie were married, Carrie being all the while under the impression that the ceremony was legal. Then they left for New York. There Hurstwood looked for work but with no success. Finally, he bought a partnership in a small tavern. After a time, the partnership was dissolved, and he lost all his money. Every day he went looking for work. Gradually he grew less eager for a job and began staying at home all day. When bills piled up, he and Carrie moved to a new apartment to escape their creditors.

Carrie set out to find work and was lucky enough to get a job as a chorus girl. With a friend, she took an apartment and left Hurstwood to himself. Soon Carrie became a well-known actress, and a local hotel invited her to become a guest there, at a nominal expense. Carrie had many friends and admirers. She had money and all the comforts and luxuries that appealed to a small-town girl.

Hurstwood had not fared so well. He could find no work. Once he worked as a scab, during some labor troubles, but he left that job because it was too hazardous. He became a bum, living in Bowery flophouses and begging on the streets. One day, he went to see Carrie. She gave him some money, largely because she had seen Drouet and had learned for the first time of Hurstwood's theft in Chicago. She believed that Hurstwood had kept his disgrace a secret in order to spare her feelings.

Although Carrie was a toast of the town, she was not happy in spite of her success. She was invited to give performances abroad. In the meantime, Hurstwood died and, unknown to Carrie, was buried in the potter's field. As Carrie was sailing for London, Hurstwood's former wife, daughter, and son-in-law were in the city, eager for pleasure and social success, a success made possible by the daughter's marriage and by Hurstwood's divorce settlement, which had given the family all of his property.

Critical Evaluation:

Theodore Dreiser's first novel is, in some ways, somewhat superior to much of his later work. As usual his characters are vivid, lifelike, and sympathetically portrayed. Unlike some of the later novels, *Sister Carrie* is well-unified, the style more fluent and natural. A companion piece to Stephen Crane's *Maggie*—and a comparison between the two books is always interesting and revealing—it is also historically significant as a pioneer work of the Naturalistic movement in American literature.

Sister Carrie, like most of Dreiser's novels, embodies his Naturalistic belief that while men are controlled and conditioned by heredity, instinct, and chance, a few extraordinary and usually unsophisticated human beings refuse to accept their fate wordlessly and instead strive, unsuccessfully, to find meaning and purpose for their existence. Carrie, the title character, senses that she is merely a cipher in an uncaring world yet seeks to grasp the mysteries of life and thereby satisfy her need to matter. In pointing out "how curious are the vagaries of fortune," Dreiser suggests that even though life may be cruel, its enigmatic quality makes it all the more fascinating.

Despite its title, the novel is not a study of a family but of Carrie's strangely unemotional relationships with three men and of the resulting and unexpected changes which occur in her outlook and status. A "half-equipped little knight" with small talent, Carrie's instincts nevertheless raise her from a poor maiden to a successful actress. The novel traces the rise, through Carrie's increasing reliance on instinct, in a three-stage development. Initially, Carrie is at least partially ruled by reason, but by the end of the first phase of her rise—marked by her accidental second meeting with Drouet and her submission to his promises—Carrie begins to abandon the reason which has not served her well. During this second portion, her blossoming instinct pulls her to the material advantages offered by Drouet, and her life with him is evidence of her growing commitment to these instincts. Yet it is her almost unconscious and unplanned switch to Hurstwood that reveals how totally she is now following her instincts. Hurstwood offers finer material possessions and more emotional rapport, and Carrie drifts easily into his orbit. Now fully and irrevocably tied to her instincts, Carrie, throughout the rest of the novel, considers it an obligation to self to let these impulses lead her where they will. When a stage career and her association with Ames replace Hurstwood, she is merely proceeding further toward the end to which she is bound once she leaves Drouet and all trace of reason. As a plant must turn toward the sun, Carrie must feed her unsatisfied urge for happiness.

Closely related to Dreiser's belief that instinct must prevail is his thesis that man lacks responsibility for his fate, a thesis suggested by all three main characters. Drouet leads Carrie to what some consider her moral downfall, but, Dreiser states, "There was nothing evil in the fellow." His glands, not he, are to blame. Neither is there any question of guilt in Hurstwood's case. Since he rarely makes a choice, he cannot be expected to answer for what happens to him. Chance, not conviction, makes him a thief. His wife, not Hurstwood, ends their marriage. Even his attraction to Carrie is a thing of chance, for "He was merely floating those gossamer threads of thought which, like the spider's, he hoped would lay hold somewhere." Although merely a sham without true power or greatness (a fact Dreiser, dazzled by his own creation, seems to forget), Hurstwood, in his decline from semiprominence to degradation, reminds the reader that the forces which send Carrie to stardom can with equal ease reduce a man to nothing. Similarly, readers must neither praise Carrie nor be shocked because she is not punished for her sins.

Dreiser presents his ideas through many symbolic images, but most important are the city, the sea, and the rocking chair. The city, in the book represented by both New York and Chicago, is a microcosm of Dreiser's universe. Nature is grim and unfeeling; so is the city. Unless a man is strong, productive, and fortunate, he faces the world's indifference, a state magnified in the city where man is perhaps more isolated than elsewhere. When Hurstwood, for example, is dying, he does so alone despite Carrie's presence in a nearby apartment, Drouet's relative closeness in a hotel, and his wife's pending arrival on the train, for none know, nor care, about his tragedy. Dreiser's concept of an uncaring and ever-changing universe is equally conveyed by his use of the sea and the rocking chair. Again and again, Carrie is described as a "lone figure in a tossing, thoughtless sea." Like its counterpart, the city, the sea symbol suggests that only the strong or the lucky survive. The rocking chair hints at the futility of this constant flux, for a rocking chair is in continual motion but goes nowhere. Although Carrie's life would seem to improve, she is sitting miserably in the rocking chair not only at the novel's beginning but also at its end. While this circular development suggests that Carrie has small chance to become truly happy, the fact that she continues to rock provides evidence of her never-ceasing aspiration.

Part of the book reflects events from Dreiser's own turbulent life. In 1886,

L. A. Hopkins, a clerk in a Chicago saloon, took thirty-five hundred dollars from his employers, and with Emma Dreiser, one of the author's many troubled siblings, fled to New York. Using this incident as the genesis for his novel, Dreiser modeled Carrie on his sister and used Hopkins for aspects of Hurstwood's personality. By the time Dreiser finished the novel in 1900, however, he had gone far beyond the cheap story of adultery and theft and had created a work which presented complex questions of innocence and guilt.

Surrounding the publication of Dreiser's first novel were the controversy and confusion that were to mark the career of this man from a poor and disturbed Indiana family in whose plight he saw reflected much of the irony of the world. Apparently, the novel was accepted by Doubleday during the absence of Frank Doubleday, the senior partner, who upon his return expressed doubt about its content and style. Refusing to release the firm from its unwritten commitment, however, Dreiser demanded that the book be published, and it appeared in 1900. Although it sold poorly (earning for Dreiser only $68.40) and was not aggressively promoted by the publishers, stories relating Mrs. Doubleday's violent objections to its moral view and the resulting suppression of the novel are unverified legend. In his own typical confusion of fact and half-fact, Dreiser added to the myths by telling conflicting accounts of what had happened.

Reaction to the book was surprisingly widespread. Many critics attacked its philosophical premises as immoral. Such charges and those that the novel was poorly written, wordy, and melodramatic would later greet each of Dreiser's productions. Yet as Dreiser wrote book after book, exploring the yearning of the young for riches, position, and understanding, a yearning he personally experienced in an overwhelming form, readers were struck by the sincerity, powerful detail, and massive impact of his work. Especially known for *Jennie Gerhardt* (1911), and *An American Tragedy* (1925), Dreiser has a secure niche among top-ranking American Naturalists.

SO BIG

Type of work: Novel
Author: Edna Ferber (1887–1968)
Type of plot: Social chronicle
Time of plot: Early twentieth century
Locale: Illinois
First published: 1924

> *Principal characters:*
> SELINA PEAKE DEJONG, a woman of strong character and enterprise
> PERVUS DEJONG, her husband
> DIRK "SOBIG" DEJONG, her son
> AUGUST HEMPEL, a Chicago capitalist and later, Selina's friend
> JULIE HEMPEL, August's daughter and Selina's old schoolfriend
> SIMON PEAKE, Selina's father
> ROELF POOL, Selina's protégé
> MATTIE SCHWENGAUER, Dirk's one-time girlfriend
> PAULA ARNOLD STORM, Julie's daughter
> DALLAS O'MARA, an artist

So Big, considered by many to be Edna Ferber's best novel, won the Pulitzer Prize for fiction in 1925. This novel was, in a sense, what Edna Ferber had been preparing for through several volumes of short stories and a novel; in *Roast Beef Medium, Personality Plus, Emma McChesney & Co.,* and *The Girls,* she explored a new social phenomenon, the American woman in the business world. The story of *So Big* is the story of one woman who, like any Horatio Alger male hero, raises herself by her bootstraps and makes a place for herself in the world of trade and competition, although the world she conquers is but a microcosm of the great world of American business.

The title is not a reference to the major character but to the major concern of the novel. The task that Selina takes is typically assigned to the male tycoon, that of preparing an inheritance of education and sophistication for a son. Selina wants to guarantee that her son will have the opportunity to live the life of beauty and culture of which she has dreamed. The result is that there are two plots which merge to form the action of the novel. The first is the story of Selina's attempt to regain the magic she had known when her gambler father was alive, painting for her pictures of life as a great game to be played with zest. The life she is forced into after her father's death seems to promise nothing of magic, and it is only much later that she discovers that the true magic lies in the natural phenomenon of life itself. The second plot is the story of Selina's attempt to create the life of magic for her son, Dirk, and her ultimate realization that no one can create magic for someone else.

The novel can be said, in fact, to fall into two distinct parts, Selina's story and Dirk's story, but the character of Selina pervades and controls the entire novel. The point of view is in the third person, but all of the action is seen through Selina's eyes, so that the reader at length loses control of his own reactions; he is not sure if they are his own or Selina's. This is an effective technique, for without any direct description, Selina emerges as the clearest and most exactly drawn character in the novel. Hers, however, is not a complete characterization at the beginning; it is only after the entire action has been completed that her character has been fully revealed or has grown into its full realization.

The first step in Selina's development is her life with her father. He is a man who lives by the whims of fortune; when his gambling goes well, he and his daughter live in the best hotels, and when it goes badly, they barely get by in cheap boardinghouses. No matter where they live, they live every moment, savoring life as a fine meal. This ability to live is, in fact, the true legacy that Simon Peake is able to leave his daughter, and it becomes her most important possession. Her other legacy, after he is brought back to the boardinghouse dead from a bullet wound, is two diamonds and almost five hundred dollars in cash. With these, she is able to secure an education and find the means of earning a living for herself.

Simon Peake's death forces Selina to make the step into the next phase of her life, one that is to give shape to her future. She takes a teaching position in the Dutch farming country of Illinois. In her new job, she moves into an environment as different from that of her life with Simon Peake as the fine finishing school Selina attended in Chicago is different from the small country schoolhouse where she goes to teach. When Selina goes to live with the Pools, she sees a life that is not a game but an unending job. There is no time in the Pools' day for magic; every minute must be spent making a livelihood from the soil: in plowing and reaping, in repairing farm tools, and in cooking and mending clothes. The most striking aspect of life at the Pools', as far as Selina is concerned, is the fact that there is no time for beauty. Up to this point, Selina has had only to spend her time in the search for beauty; now she must devote herself to the problems of farming life, of teaching children whose parents are more concerned with their children's ability in the fields than with their ability in the classroom.

It is significant in Selina's development that, even in the midst of the drudgery of this life, she can find a source of beauty. Even among the hardworking Pools there is an artist. Selina gives herself to the task of introducing young Roelf Pool to the magic that life can have. She nurtures his native talents at handiwork and treasures the chest that he builds and carves for her.

The chest is the reminder that she keeps with her after Roelf leaves and goes to find his own life in the world outside Illinois. It is one of Selina's triumphs that Roelf ultimately becomes a fine and respected sculptor.

Selina's ability to find beauty even in the hard farm life becomes a kind of guiding principle for her life. She marries a beautiful man, capable of beautiful acts. Pervus DeJong may be the most unsuccessful farmer in the area, but he is a handsome man who recognizes the unusual beauty that marks Selina. When she is subjected to the embarrassment of having the "pretty" basket she prepares for the box supper laughed at, Pervus bids a precious ten dollars for her box, turning the laughter to amazement. While Selina's life with Pervus is not marked by beauty, she finds it a satisfying life. She becomes enamored of making things grow; her life becomes filled with "beautiful cabbages" and asparagus. When Pervus dies, she takes over the management of the farm and begins to build a future for her son.

With the aid of August Hempel, the rich father of Julie Hempel, one of Selina's former classmates at the finishing school, Selina is able to become a successful truck farmer, to send Dirk to good schools, and to give him the opportunity to find the life of magic and beauty of which she has always dreamed. It is at this point that Selina's story becomes Dirk's story. The first test of whether Dirk will be able to grasp the chance to pursue beauty occurs when he is at the University of Chicago. There he meets Mattie Schwengauer, an Iowa farmgirl who represents the innocent goodness of growing things. When Dirk rejects Mattie for the social life of the fraternities, where Mattie would not be accepted, Selina receives her first disappointment. Mattie represents the naïve appreciation of life that is the first step toward discovering the magic that life can offer. Dirk's inability to continue his relationship with her is a foreshadowing of Dirk's future life.

After Dirk becomes an architect, he meets Paula Arnold Storm, Julie's daughter, whom he had known when they were children. She is now a bored, sophisticated woman married to a man old enough to be her father. It is her influence that leads Dirk to leave his career as an architect, to leave his dreams of building beautiful buildings, to go into finance, where he is soon successful. To Selina's continuing disappointment, Dirk lives in a world of position and show. He takes a fashionable apartment and acquires an Oriental houseboy. He is, according to every conventional description, a success.

Then Dirk meets Dallas O'Mara, an artist who revels in life itself. For a time, it seems that she will be the force that may pull Dirk back to the course that Selina mapped for him. She fascinates Dirk, and he is as puzzled as he is charmed by her blithe rejection of the social standards that Dirk has come to accept. A battle between the attractions of Paula's world and those of Dallas' world develops. The situation is brought to a crisis when Roelf Pool returns to Chicago in the company of a French celebrity. Suddenly, the Illinois farmboy and his friend are the toast of Chicago society. Paula goes to all lengths to entertain the celebrated pair, and Dirk is drawn up short when he discovers that they prefer the company of Dallas. His world is further shattered when he finds that the person that Roelf most wants to see is Selina.

When Dirk sees Selina with Dallas and Roelf, all three laughing together, reveling in life itself, he realizes the emptiness of the life that Paula represents. He also realizes that he has irrevocably committed himself to Paula's world. Ironically, Selina discovers that her own life holds the magic she has always sought, for the magic lies in the seeking. Dirk, who earned his nickname by replying once to a question about how big he was that he was only "so big," discovers that there is not necessarily any magic in success. Perhaps the moral is that some people are only so big, and no bigger.

SO RED THE ROSE

Type of work: Novel
Author: Stark Young (1881–1963)
Type of plot: Historical romance
Time of plot: 1860–1865
Locale: Mississippi
First published: 1934

    Principal characters:
      MALCOLM BEDFORD, the owner of Portobello
      MRS. SARAH TAIT BEDFORD, his wife
      DUNCAN,
      MARY HARTWELL, and
      FRANCES, their children
      VALETTE, an adopted daughter
      MIDDLETON, an orphaned nephew
      HUGH MCGEHEE, the owner of Montrose
      AGNES MCGEHEE, his wife and Malcolm Bedford's sister
      EDWARD and
      LUCINDA (LUCY), their children
      SHELTON TALIAFERRO, a distant relative of the McGehees
      CHARLES, his son
      ZACH MCGEHEE, Hugh's nephew
      AMELIE BALFOUR, Zach's fiancée

The Story:

Malcolm Bedford was the owner of Portobello plantation, where he lived with his second wife, Sarah, and their three children, an adopted daughter, Valette, and an orphaned nephew, Middleton. Malcolm's sister Agnes had married Hugh McGehee, and they and their two children occupied a neighboring plantation, Montrose. Plantation life in Mississippi flowed easily in those days just preceding the Civil War, with frequent parties and visits between families to provide hospitality and entertainment. Other less pleasant happenings, however, intruded upon the serenity of plantation life. Talk of secession, states' rights, slavery, emancipation, Lincoln, and war began to be more seriously discussed and argued whenever a group of people assembled. Hugh McGehee and his son, Edward, discussed these problems and Edward's possible enlistment when the latter returned home for a short visit from the Louisiana Seminary of Learning and Military Academy.

Duncan Bedford was also in school at Washington College, Virginia. In love with Valette, he accused her of leading other young men on. When he went back to college, they were no longer on friendly terms.

Shelton Taliaferro, a distant relative of the McGehees, and his son Charles came to visit Montrose. Edward was home for a visit at the time, and the two young men became friends. They spent a short time together at the seminary until Charles resigned. It was this young man, to whom life seemed to flow generously, who attached himself to Edward. A year after his first visit to Montrose, he and Edward enlisted under General Beauregard. Shelton Taliaferro, his father, and Edward McGehee were the only two people for whom Charles cared, to the disappointment of Lucy, who had fallen in love with him. Duncan also enlisted, but without first coming home. He wrote a letter to Valette to tell her of his enlistment and to assure her that he still loved her.

About a year later, at the time of the battle of Pittsburg Landing, Agnes received a letter from her son. It was dated three days earlier, and according to his letter, the battle would be taking place at that moment she was reading the letter. Feeling instinctively that Edward was dead, she ordered William Veal, the butler, to hitch up the wagon so that they might set out for the battlefield and bring home the body of her dead son. When she returned, she brought with her Edward's body and those of two other boys of the neighborhood. She also brought word that the body of Charles Taliaferro had not been found, although it was almost certain that he was dead since he was not with the survivors of the desperate fighting. Lucy was heartbroken.

After the Emancipation Proclamation on January 2, 1863, many of the slaves deserted their former owners to flee to the Union lines. A short time later, Malcolm Bedford, who had been helping to strengthen the defenses at Vicksburg, came home with a very bad case of dysentery from which he never recovered. He died, on the day Vicksburg fell, claiming that with the fall of Vicksburg, the doom of the South was sealed.

Life went on at both plantations under much altered circumstances. Natchez, the nearest town, had been bombarded and occupied. Federal soldiers swarmed over the countryside, burning, looting, and carrying off horses, food, and clothing. More slaves ran away to the protection of Federal troops in Natchez, and many joined the Federal army to help fight against their former masters. When disease broke out in the Natchez stockades, where the blacks were confined, some of the former slaves, especially the older ones, began to return to the plantations, the only place they had ever known security.

Sherman, on a visit to Natchez, rode out to see the McGehees because he had known their son Edward when he was superintendent of the seminary that Edward had attended. He was very much an enigma to the McGehees, as he was to many. His kindness and personal interest could not be reconciled with his toleration of plunder and destruction by his troops. Shortly after his visit, Montrose was destroyed by a mob of former slaves under the direction of a few white officers. They burned the place to the ground, after permitting the family to save only what could be rescued in twenty minutes. After the fire the family moved into a five-room cottage on the plantation.

The Bedfords at Portobello were having their own difficulties. One night, a group of Confederate soldiers hanged three Federals on the trees not far from the house. A fourth soldier escaped, injured, and he was taken into the house and cared for until a way could be found to smuggle him out. The three Union soldiers were quickly buried to avoid reprisals.

There had been no word of Duncan for many months, and the Bedfords at Portobello believed that he must be dead. Now that the war was over, they thought that they should at least have a letter from him if he were still alive. Then one day Duncan, without any previous warning, walked in. He had been taken prisoner but had been booked for exchange soon afterward. A Union officer had spoken insultingly of General Lee, however, and Duncan had struck him. His order for exchange was immediately revoked, and he was placed in irons, charged with having struck an officer of the United States Army. When peace was declared and all prisoners were released, Duncan's charge still stood. At his trial, however, the judge, who felt that a great injustice had been done Duncan, dismissed the case.

The South was beginning to feel the vengeance of the North. Many of the plantations had been burned, and many of the men had been killed. The slave labor gone, there was no one to work the plantations. Heavy taxes were imposed to make the South pay for its military government. Blacks were insolent and destructive, and carpetbaggers were beginning to buy up mortgages on the plantations, thus gaining control of huge amounts of property. Mrs. Bedford and Duncan decided that they would not mortgage their property but would try to make the land productive once more. During those grim years, Duncan found Valette kinder and more understanding than she had been in the proud old days at Portobello.

Amelie Balfour and Zach McGehee, nephew of Hugh, were to be married. Amelie convinced Valette that they should make it a double wedding. Their plans were all made on the spur of the moment, and the next evening at Homewood, the home of Amelie's aunt, Duncan and Valette were married. They were to have a honeymoon in New Orleans and then return to Portobello to live.

Critical Evaluation:

This beautiful story is told tranquilly but deeply. It is tinged with yearning for life, for peace, and for an unrecoverable past when peach trees bloomed in April and loved ones who were destined to march off and die in war were still happily alive. *So Red the Rose* is a muted cry against war's stupidity, a lament over the passing of an idyllic way of life. It is also a philosophy of life for the future. In his unhurried narration, moreover, Stark Young not only shows the rosy side of life in the antebellum South, the dreadful war years, and the malicious brutality of Reconstruction, but also, almost with touches of the Spanish "Costumbrista" movement, he archives "pictures of customs," including details of dress, furniture, thought, imagery, psychology, and the way of life.

The novel's essence is in its final scene, where Agnes sits meditating at her son's grave in the Montrose family graveyard, with little Middleton at her side. Suddenly, she can feel the hard gravel under her feet at Shiloh, where she had sought Edward's body three years earlier. Now she reflects, sitting by Edward's grave (while little Middleton sits, staring at the foliage over the cemetery wall, where the sun's rays are slanting), on how Edward had died at Shiloh, where ranks of half-trained men and boys had been cut down on each side, epitomizing war's insanity and "the childish urges of men." She now grasps the interrelationship of war to men, and men to war, as contrasted with the same relationship for women. She concludes that the glory and folly and pain of war must remain for men even as women dream, delight, and are afraid when confronting childbirth. The rivers of red blood, soaked up by the earth on so many "Shilohs," must be born again in women.

Then again, trancelike, Agnes is back at Shiloh, listening to the wounded moan in the darkness ahead, and she discerns their shapes scattered on the battleground. Edward must be lying somewhere among them, but she considers all of the dead as hers. Suddenly now, at her side, Middleton is no longer gazing ahead but up at her, ecstatically, with pale face and rapt expression. She scarcely glances at him but is stirred by his expression. Tugged by memory back to her thoughts, she spiritually returns to Shiloh, amid the eerie silence, hearing only her heartbeat. The novel ends as she gazes over the gloomy field and the sleeping dead.

Agnes, however, now knows that a hallowed memory, living through time, is the finest learning to live by:

> I sometimes think that never blows so red
> The rose as where some buried Caesar bled;
> That every hyacinth the garden wears
> Dropt in her lap from some once lovely head.

THE SONG OF THE LARK

Type of work: Novel
Author: Willa Cather (1873–1947)
Type of plot: Impressionistic realism
Time of plot: Late nineteenth and early twentieth centuries
Locale: Colorado, Chicago, and New York
First published: 1915

> Principal characters:
> THEA KRONBORG, a young singer
> DR. HOWARD ARCHIE, her friend and adviser
> PROFESSOR WUNSCH, a music teacher
> ANDOR HARSANYI, a concert pianist
> FREDERICK OTTENBURG, a wealthy art patron
> TILLY KRONBORG, Thea's aunt

The Story:

Thea Kronborg was the daughter of the Swedish Methodist pastor in the small town of Moonstone, Colorado. A tall, fair girl with grave, candid eyes, her shy awkwardness hid restless depths of thought and feeling. Although she grew up in a lively household of brothers and sisters, she had no real friends among children her own age. Of her family, only her aunt, Tilly Kronborg, seemed to understand her; but Tilly was so ridiculous in her speech and actions that neighbors only laughed when she told them that the day was coming when Thea would make Moonstone sit up and take notice.

One of her few friends was Dr. Howard Archie, the town physician, who, when she was eleven, saved Thea's life during an attack of pneumonia. He was unhappily married to a mean-spirited woman who wanted only three things in life: to have her cigar-smoking husband away from home as much as possible, to keep her house closed against dust, and to live on food from cans. Having no children of his own, Dr. Archie loved Thea in a fatherly way, and he often wondered what would become of a girl so passionate and determined.

Another friend of her childhood was gruff, disreputable old Professor Wunsch, her music teacher. A drunkard, but at one time a talented pianist, he had drifted casually into Moonstone, and Fritz Kohler, the German tailor, had pitied him and given him a home. The two old men, both with memories of their younger years in Europe, became cronies. Fiercely resenting demands of family and school upon her time, he gave Thea her first glimpse of artistic endeavor, just as the Kohler house gave her a knowledge of true old-world simplicity and friendliness. Wunsch, unable to understand Thea's stubborn reserve, compared her to the yellow prickly pear blossoms of the desert.

Through these friends, she also knew Spanish Johnny from the Mexican settlement on the outskirts of town. He was another wanderer and drunkard, who always came back to Moonstone and his patient wife to recover from his debauches. The neighbors were scandalized when the minister's daughter went with the doctor and Wunsch to hear Spanish Johnny sing Mexican folk songs. Mrs. Kronborg, wiser than her husband, quietly allowed Thea to go her own way.

Still another man who took great interest in Thea was Ray Kennedy, a railroad conductor on the Denver run. He was waiting until she grew up; then he intended to marry her. In his own way, he was the most protective of all.

Thea was fifteen years old when old Wunsch, in a drunken frenzy, smashed the furniture in the Kohler house and left town. After his departure, Thea took over his pupils. A year later, Ray Kennedy, injured in a wreck, died, leaving Thea six hundred dollars in insurance. Dr. Archie advised her to take the money and study music for a winter in Chicago. After much discussion, the Kronborgs agreed, if the doctor would take her there and get her settled.

In Chicago, living in cheap rooms and earning extra money by singing in a church choir, Thea was homesick for the sand dunes and deep, silent snows of Moonstone. She hated the city, but she worked hard for Andor Harsanyi, under whom she studied. Like Wunsch, the brilliant young musician was baffled by qualities of Thea's imagination and will. He was almost in despair over her when he discovered that her real talent was in voice. Relieved yet sorry, he told her that she would never make a great pianist. She might, however, become a great singer.

The next summer, Thea went back to Moonstone. There she disturbed her family by refusing to sing at the funeral of Maggie Evans, a neighbor. Persuaded by her mother, she finally consented. Later, she shocked the town and disgusted her brothers and sisters by going to a party in the Mexican village and singing with Spanish Johnny and his friends.

Returning to Chicago, she studied under Madison Bowers, a teacher whom she both admired and disliked. At his studio, she met for the first time Fred Ottenburg, son of a rich brewer and an amateur musician. Bowers was cynically amused that the wealthy young man was attracted to the strange girl from the West. Through Ottenburg's influence, Thea was given singing engagements at the parties of his fashionable friends.

That winter, Thea caught a severe cold. Her convalescence was slow, and she felt weak and dispirited. Ottenburg, concerned for her welfare, urged her to go away for a rest at his father's ranch in Arizona. There Thea discovered a West different from the crude, vulgar Moonstone she had known. Prowling among the cliff dwellers' ruins in Panther Canyon, she felt herself part of an older West, a land closer to the everyday simplicities of sun, wind, and water. Thoughts of those primitive people aroused her own half-awakened nature; the desert country, ancient but filled with relics of human endeavor, gave her a realization of art as form given to hope and experience.

Rested, and grateful to Ottenburg, she accepted his proposal of marriage when he arrived at the ranch. On the way to Mexico, however, she learned that he already had a neurotic, invalid wife. Hurt and shocked, she refused his offers of assistance, borrowed money from Dr. Archie, and went to Germany for further study.

Years passed. By that time, Dr. Archie was a widower, his wife having been killed when some cleaning fluid exploded, and he had moved to Denver to take charge of some mining investments that had prospered. From time to time, reports reached him of Thea's progress abroad, and he was pleased when Ottenburg brought word that she had sung Elisabeth at the Dresden Opera. He alone understood why Thea, at a critical point in her career, had been unable to return to Moonstone for her mother's funeral.

He was in New York on that great night when the sudden illness of a famous singer gave Thea her chance to sing Sieglinde in *Die Walküre* at the Metropolitan Opera House. He and Ottenburg, whom Thea had forgiven, heard the performance together, both pleased and proud because they were the two men who had meant most in her career.

By 1909, Tilly was the last Kronborg in Moonstone. She never tired of boasting to her neighbors about Thea's successes and her marriage to wealthy Frederick Ottenburg after his wife's death. Best of all, she liked to remind the townspeople that Thea had once sung in Moonstone at Maggie Evans' funeral.

Critical Evaluation:

The West, the past—one is the physical background of Willa Cather's writing, the other its spiritual climate. Against her chosen backgrounds, she projected her stories of pioneers and artists, men and women of simple passions and creative energies. The very nature of her material determined her own values as an artist: to find in the people of her creation those realities of the spirit which have been almost overwhelmed in the complexity and confusion of the present. *The Song of the Lark*, which carries Thea Kronborg from an obscure Colorado town to the concert and opera stage, is a novel rich and sustaining in homely realism. The character of Thea was drawn in part from the late Olive Fremstad, but there is much of Cather's own story in the experiences of her heroine. Like Thea, she made common things and disciplined effort the shaping influences of her art. The story of the artist in America is usually sentimentalized or idealized. This novel is a notable exception.

Though it has never shared the success of some of Cather's other works,

The Song of the Lark is nevertheless a rewarding and significant part of the Cather canon. The novel has been criticized, and perhaps justly so, for its unselective use of detail and episode in developing Thea Kronborg's story; yet such thoroughness is also what has allowed Cather to convey so fully to the reader Thea's passionate spirit for living. Thea's growth as an artist is shown in the context of two themes which run throughout Cather's works: the invigorating, spiritual significance of the Southwest and its history, and the alienation of the artistic temperament from conventional life and values. *The Song of the Lark* is essentially a chronicle of the delicate awakening of the artistic sensibility and its consequent struggle to escape the limitations of a commonplace environment.

This theme is introduced in the novel through Thea's early opposition to the standards and values of Moonstone. The young girl's friends are those who, like Thea herself, display a quality of mind and spirit for life which Moonstone conventionality interprets as either wild and eccentric or blatantly selfish. The life-styles of Dr. Archie, old Wunsch, Ray Kennedy, and Spanish Johnny are in marked contrast to the provincial conformity and petty materialism embodied in the likes of Mrs. "Livery" Johnson or the community's endorsement of Thea's less talented rival, Lily Fisher. Though Thea's talent and ardent nature set her apart from the rest of her community, she finds happiness and fulfillment in expanding her awareness of things. Visiting the countryside with Dr. Archie, learning German from Wunsch, or singing songs with Spanish Johnny, she is progressively introduced to a broader sense of values and culture than the narrow environment of Moonstone can supply. Her later experience with the ancient pottery at the cliff dwellings in Arizona only makes Thea more conscious of the immense aspirations and possibilities within her own spirit and the human spirit in general.

Seeking to develop her own aspirations to their fullest, Thea becomes more and more dedicated to the disciplines of her art. By the end of the novel, her commitment has left almost no time in her life for other people, but she has fulfilled the artistic impulse that drove her beyond the limitations of a small-town environment and into a world of intense, rapturous feeling for the quality of life. Her disciplined, self-imposed isolation from the conventional world is the price the serious artist must pay for his expansive spirit.

When *The Song of the Lark* was reissued in 1932, Cather revised the novel rather heavily in an attempt to reduce wordage and tighten its style. Most of the changes occurred in the last two books, where the author felt that, because Thea's struggle was now over, the dramatic pull of the story necessarily lagged into the anticlimactic. None of these changes, however, appreciably affected the novel's content or thematic statement.

THE SOT-WEED FACTOR

Type of work: Novel
Author: John Barth (1930–   )
Type of plot: Historical parody
Time of plot: Late seventeenth and early eighteenth centuries
Locale: England and Maryland Province
First published: 1960

Principal characters:

EBENEZER COOKE, a young would-be poet
ANDREW COOKE, his father
ANNA COOKE, his twin sister
HENRY BURLINGAME III, an adventurer, tutor, and friend
    of Ebenezer
JOAN TOAST, a London trollop and, later, a wretched drab
    known as Susan Warren
JOHN MCEVOY, her usurped pimp
BERTRAND BURTON, Ebenezer's valet
CAPTAIN MITCHELL, a Maryland planter
MARY MUNGUMMORY, "the Traveling Whore o' Dorset"

The title of this extremely long, wholly outrageous, and cleverly executed novel may strike the reader as curious, and it should be explained before attempting to compass the work itself. A sot-weed factor may be defined as a merchant in tobacco. Not only does the term serve as the title of John Barth's book, but it is also the title of a satirical poem published in London in 1708 by an actual but obscure Ebenezer Cooke, "Poet & Laureate of the Province of Maryland": *The Sot-Weed Factor: Or, A Voyage to Maryland, A Satyr, in Which Is Describ'd the Laws, Government, Courts and Constitutions of the Country; and also the Buildings, Feasts, Frolicks, Entertainments and Drunken Humours of the Inhabitants of that Part of America. By Eben. Cooke, Gent.*

Poetry and innocence drive the principal character in John Barth's imaginative, ribald account of Ebenezer Cooke's character and adventures in Colonial America. Twenty-seven years old when he sets out to make his way in the world, Ebenezer simultaneously devotes his life to the twin ideals of chastity and art in an age when many men wooed the muse of poetry but very few regarded virtue as a possession to be preserved and even fewer thought of it as a matter for regret after its loss. His reason for his double dedication, as he frequently explains to unlikely listeners or under strange circumstances, is mystical rather than practical or moral: he has vowed to make purity the essence of his physical as well as his spiritual being. His resolve might have turned him into a Richardsonian prig. Instead, it transforms him into an innocent in the Shandean meaning of that term.

The son of a shrewd man, a planter and trader, he has suffered in his youth the not uncommon malady of sons of shrewd men. He cannot settle on an occupation; he is adrift. The principal cause of his indecisiveness is his inability to make up his mind. No one thing seems to appeal to him more than any other; all things are equal in his eyes. His is also the malady of the modern age—an existential vacuum.

Being an awkward fellow resembling a gangling flitch of bacon, he has failed not only his father's utilitarian goals but also the goals of manhood in his lack of sexual experience. He has pursued scholarship but cannot achieve it; he has tried business but is burdened by impracticality. Having been sent by his father to London and apprenticed to a merchant in order to learn the plantation trade, he has frittered away his time and remained a mere clerk on the bottom level of the countinghouse caste. In the meantime, because of his university background and the influence of Henry Burlingame III, his former tutor, he has drifted into the coffeehouse society of the period and become the hanger-on of a pseudoartistic circle presided over by Ben Oliver, Tom Trent, and Dick Merriweather, toss-pot poets and low wits. Then he is offered an opportunity to sully his virginity. The offer provides him with impetus into a vocation.

At this point, Barth begins to warm to, and give promise of, the Rabelaisian overtones laced throughout his novel. When, on a wager, Ebenezer is faced with the prospect of having sexual experience thrust upon him, the moment comes in the person of a rare and comely doxy of the taverns, Joan Toast. He fails to meet the test of his manhood, however, because he falls suddenly and completely in love with the bold young trollop. After much confusion, he hurries back to his rooms. There Mistress Toast pursues him, determined to perform her function in society and collect her rightful fee, only to learn that his love for her will not allow the occasion to be marred by the exchange of money. Either she must have him for his virginity alone, or she must leave. In the latter event, he will still adore her, even though his remains an unconsummated love.

Mistress Toast cannot understand this display of idealism, for her experience has conditioned her to complete pragmatism in matters of sex. A dispute follows. After her departure, Ebenezer composes a hymn to chastity and, in committing it to paper, discovers his true vocation—poetry. Awed by his discovery, he dedicates himself to purity and art.

Nevertheless, if Mistress Toast at the time of choice could not swallow so violent a change of diet, the cud softens in the chewing and even becomes tasteful. When she reports to her erstwhile truelove and pimp, John McEvoy, on her unprofitable hour with Ebenezer and McEvoy goes to collect a fee—whether or not she served Ebenezer carnally has no bearing in the matter; the poet has used her time—she is greatly displeased. Further, when McEvoy fails to collect and, as retribution, posts a condemning letter to Ebenezer's father, the girl decides in Ebenezer's favor, and McEvoy loses her.

McEvoy's letter hastens Ebenezer's departure for Maryland. Angered by the report, Andrew Cooke decides to send his son to Maryland for the purpose of overseeing the family tobacco plantation, Malden, on the Choptank River. Mistress Toast, now fully in love with Ebenezer's purity, vows to follow him. McEvoy himself is destined to be caught up in the web he has helped to spin, and he ends up in the New World. Ebenezer, unaware of those events, embarks for Maryland after obtaining from Lord Baltimore a commission naming him poet and laureate of the province, a commission that promptly involves the young man in political intrigues and that is eventually revealed as a bogus document devised by Henry Burlingame III.

Because he is the prime mover in the affairs of the novel, Burlingame deserves special attention. Among other things, he is at least part of the reason for Ebenezer's failure as a scholar and a businessman. In the boy's formative years, Andrew Cooke has Burlingame in his employ as a tutor to Ebenezer and his twin sister Anna. The unorthodox methods of the instruction they received and the tutor's unusual devotion to the world have left an indelible mark on Ebenezer and Anna. When Ebenezer decided, as a dutiful son, to follow a business career, Burlingame dropped out of the picture, but when the young man launches himself into his new fate by adopting poetry as his soul's profession and virginity as his body's handmaiden, Burlingame is ushered back into the thick of things. From this point on, the author used Burlingame for everything from scene revitalizer to *deus ex machina*.

The chief story line of *The Sot-Weed Factor* is simple. One of the book's delights is that it can be read on several levels at once. It is, on the surface, a bawdy journey through Colonial history and is vastly satisfying on this level as a good tale, well told. It is a farcical tour de force. With a plot more contrived than *Tom Jones*, it is an exaggerated burlesque of the picaresque novel. Barth is convinced that the novel is a dying literary form. If it is, *The Sot-Weed Factor* is its grandest requiem.

Implausible coincidence, Rabelaisian romps, and confused identities are all part of the story, as are tales within the tale, much in the manner of Chaucer and Boccaccio. The outline is the loss of Malden and the stratagems that bring about its recovery. However, Ebenezer's disillusionment with the New World is even more crucial to his own affairs than the Malden issue, as the laureate's rosy vision of writing an epic *Marylandiad* becomes incongruous with the realities of the rough and violent provincial life he encounters. The book can be read as a moral allegory, tracing the loss of innocence to the realities of life.

Ebenezer's vacillation between the extremes of angel and beast provides an area for the ribald humor that Barth sows throughout his book. The issue of the poet's moral struggle develops ironic perspectives. One example is Joan

Toast's career. In trying to change her life's work from that of sinner to that of saint, she is driven by the winds of mischance and paradox further into whoredom, and when Ebenezer meets her again, he does not recognize his real love in the person of Susan Warren, the swine tender on Captain Mitchell's plantation. Yet in the end, the author manages to marry her off to Ebenezer. By this development of the plot, the poet loses not only his treasured chastity but also his health, for Mistress Toast has become poxed on her way down the ladder of life.

Burlingame's search for the identity of Burlingame I and II leads to the discovery of the amazing "secret diary" of Captain John Smith. This outrageously comic secret journal details the "true" story of Captain Smith and Pocahontas; a story that should set them both twirling in their graves but makes for the most boisterously funny reading since Boccaccio.

Barth, in another of his works, has one of his characters remark that only in America can one have cheerful terrorism. This same theme shows up again about halfway through *The Sot-Weed Factor*, when Burlingame answers Ebenezer's question as to what he must do, and where he stands, by saying that man's sad lot is to be created by thoughtless man and birthed by thoughtless woman into a thoughtless world. Man is luck's fool, Nature's toy.

Candide had his Pangloss and Gargantua his Ponocrates; Ebenezer has his Burlingame. It is in the role of tutor that Burlingame reveals the real world to Ebenezer. In his many adventures, Ebenezer sees the world as cruel, stupid, intolerant, greedy, savage, selfish, rapacious, and unjust. Barth loves the dark, nightmarish comedy of Colonial history. He even bends history somewhat to suit his story, but it is this aspect of black humor that intrigues him most. In this absurd, meaningless, mechanized society, filled with its catastrophes and atrocities, man can only set up a howl of despair that comes out as laughter. Burlingame says at one point that the only things that can save man from madness are dullness and truth. Truth, being the common one, must be searched after before it can be found. Once it is found, it must be understood and shaped to the finder's will before it can bring about his ruin. Why, he asks, does Ebenezer put as much value in poetry and purity, or Burlingame in finding his father or fighting the marplot Goode? One must make and cling to his soul or go mad. He must choose what he will worship or hate, and he must tell the world that it is he who creates such a shadow. A man must assert himself or go mad. Burlingame knows no other course.

What basis for action is there, what justification or direction in a world such as this satire exposes? Through *Candide*, Voltaire came to know the blackness of nihilism. Barth's is a cheerful, even an optimistic nihilism, as near the end of the book, when Ebenezer explains to Anna that they must hold on to life even though they are searching all the time for a way to escape.

The Sot-Weed Factor in its final meaning is directed toward the ends of the antinovel. Barth has abandoned all allegiance to the novel's form and has shown up its deficiencies by overdoing them. His heroes are antiheroes; his humor is black; his form is outrageous. His commitment is exploration of the range beyond the novel.

THE SOUND AND THE FURY

Type of work: Novel
Author: William Faulkner (1897–1962)
Type of plot: Psychological realism
Time of plot: 1910–1928
Locale: Mississippi
First published: 1929

Principal characters:
MRS. COMPSON, the mother
BENJY, her idiot son
QUENTIN, another son
CANDACE, her daughter
JASON, another son
SYDNEY HERBERT HEAD, Candace's husband
QUENTIN, Candace's daughter
DILSEY, a black servant

The Story:

The Compson family had once been a good one, but the present generation had done everything possible to ruin the name of Compson for all time. In the little Mississippi town in which they lived, everyone laughed and made slighting remarks when the name Compson was mentioned.

Mrs. Compson had come from what she considered good stock, but she thought she must have sinned terribly in marrying a Compson and now she was paying for her sins. For eighteen years she had been saying that she did not have long to live and would no longer be a burden to her family. Benjy was her greatest cross. He was an idiot who moaned, cried, and slobbered all day long. The only person who could quiet Benjy was Candace, his sister. When they were small, Candace loved Benjy very much and made herself his protector. She saw to it that the other children of the family and the black servants did not tease him. As Candace grew up, she continued to love Benjy, but she also loved every man she met, giving herself freely to any man who would have her. Mrs. Compson thought Candace was another cross she had to bear and did very little to force her daughter to have better morals.

Quentin, another son, was a moody, morose boy whose only passion was his sister Candace. He loved her not as a sister, but as a woman, and she returned his love. Quentin was sent to school at Harvard. Although she loved Quentin in the spirit, Candace could not keep away from other men. Sydney Herbert Head was the one serious lover she had. He wanted to marry her.

Head, a banker, promised to give her brother Jason a job in his bank after they were married. When Quentin learned that Candace was in a condition that made her marriage necessary, he was wild. He lied to his father and told him that he had had incestuous relations with Candace and that she must not be allowed to marry. His father did not believe him, and the family went along with their plans for the wedding. At last, Quentin could stand no more. Two months after his sister's wedding, he drowned himself in the Charles River in Cambridge, Massachusetts. Mrs. Compson resigned herself to one more cross.

When Candace had a baby too soon, Head threw her out of his house with her child. Her mother and father and her brother Jason would not let her come home, but they adopted the baby girl, Quentin. Jason believed that Quentin was the child of his brother Quentin and Candace, but the rest of the family refused to face such a fact and accept it. They preferred to believe, and rightly, that Quentin was the child of some other lover who had deserted Candace. Candace stayed away from the little town for many years.

Quentin was as wild as her mother as she grew up. She, too, gave herself to any man in town and was talked about as her mother had been. Every month, Candace sent money to Mrs. Compson for Quentin's care. At first, Mrs. Compson burned the checks, for she would have none of Candace's ill-gotten money. When Mr. Compson died, Jason became the head of the family. He blamed Quentin for his not getting the job in the bank, for if the child had not been born too soon, Head would not have left Candace and would have given Jason the job. Hating his sister, he wrote checks on another bank and gave those to his mother in place of the checks Candace had sent. The old lady was almost blind and could not see what she burned. Jason then forged her signature on the real checks and cashed them, using the money to gamble on the cotton market.

Quentin hated her Uncle Jason as much as he hated her, and the two were always quarreling. He tried to make her go to school and keep away from the men, but Mrs. Compson thought he was too cruel to Quentin and took the girl's side.

A show troupe came to town, and Quentin took up with one of the performers. Her grandmother locked her in her room each night, but she climbed out of the window to meet her lover. One morning, she did not answer when old Dilsey, the black woman who had cared for the family for years, called her to breakfast. Jason went to her room and found that all her clothes were gone. He also found that the three thousand dollars he had hidden in his room had been stolen. He tried to get the sheriff to follow the girl and the showman, but the sheriff wanted no part of the Compson family affairs. Jason set out to find the fugitives, but he had to give up his search when a severe headache forced him to return home for medicine.

Jason felt more than cheated. His money was gone, and he could not find

Quentin so that he could punish her for stealing it. He forgot that the money really belonged to Quentin, for it was part of the amount he had saved from the money Candace had sent for the girl's care. There was nothing left for Jason but blind rage and hatred for everyone. He believed that everyone laughed at him because of his horrible family—because Benjy was an idiot, Candace a lost woman, Quentin a suicide, and the girl Quentin a village harlot and a thief. He forgot that he, too, was a thief and that he had a mistress. He felt cursed by his family as his mother was cursed.

When he saw Benjy riding through town in a carriage driven by one of the black boys, he knocked the black boy down and struck Benjy with all his force, for there was no other way for him to show his rage. Benjy let out a loud moan, and then settled back in the carriage. He very gently petted a wilted flower, and his face assumed a calm, quiet blankness, as if all the strife in the world were over and things were once more serene. It was as if he had understood what old Dilsey meant when she said she had seen the beginning and the end of life. Benjy had seen it all, too, in the pictures he could never understand but which flowed endlessly through his disordered mind.

Critical Evaluation:

After early undistinguished efforts in verse (*The Marble Faun*, 1924) and fiction (*Soldier's Pay*, 1926; *Mosquitoes*, 1927), William Faulkner moved suddenly into the forefront of American literature in 1929 with the appearance of *Sartoris* and *The Sound and the Fury*, the first installments in the artistically complex and subtly satirical saga of Yoknapatawpha County that would be spun out further in *As I Lay Dying* (1930), *Light in August* (1932), *Absalom, Absalom!* (1936), *Go Down, Moses* (1942), *The Unvanquished* (1938), *Intruder in the Dust* (1948), the *Hamlet-Town-Mansion* trilogy (1940, 1957, 1959), and *Requiem for a Nun* (1951)—the last an extension of materials in *Sanctuary* (1931). Chiefly in recognition of the monumental literary importance of the Yoknapatawpha saga, Faulkner was awarded the Nobel Prize in 1949.

The Sound and the Fury marked the beginning of the most fertile period of Faulkner's creativity, when he was in his early thirties. Yet, both for its form and for its thematic significance this novel may well be considered Faulkner's masterpiece. Never again would his work demonstrate such tight, precise structure, combined with the complexities of syntax and punctuation that became his most characteristic stylistic trait. Furthermore, the themes recorded in his simple but elegant Nobel Prize speech—"love and honor and pity and pride and compassion and sacrifice"—are already present in this novel with a forcefulness of characterization that could hardly be improved upon. It was in this novel that Faulkner found a way of embodying his peculiar view of time in an appropriate style, a style much influenced by Joycean stream-of-consciousness, and by Faulkner's own stated desire ultimately to "put all of human experience between one Cap and one period." That concept of time, most emphatic in Quentin's section, can be summarized by Faulkner's statement that "there is no such thing as *was*; if *was* existed there would be no grief or sorrow." The continuation of the past into the present, as a shaping influence that cannot be avoided, is the larger theme of Faulkner's life work.

In this novel, that theme is embodied specifically in the history of the decline of the once-aristocratic Compson family. Nearly twenty years after the original publication of the novel, at the instigation of his publisher Malcolm Cowley, Faulkner wrote the background history of the Compsons as an "appendix" that appears at the front of the book. The appendix records the noble origins of the Compson landstead, once the possession of a Chickasaw king named Ikkemotubbe, or "the man." After then proceeding through the Compson succession—beginning with Quentin Maclachan Compson, who immigrated from Glasgow, and proceeding to Jason III, the "dipsomaniac" lawyer who could not tear himself away from the Roman classics long enough to preserve the vestiges of his family's good name, Faulkner presents terse but invaluable insight into the chief characters of *The Sound and the Fury*. Candace knew she was doomed and regarded her virginity as no more than a "hangnail," and her promiscuity represents the moral sterility of the family. Quentin III, who "identified family with his sister's membrane," convinced himself he had committed incest with her, but really loved only death—in his sublimation of emotions into a kind of latter-day courtly love mystique—and found his love in June, 1910, by committing the physical suicide that the destruction of his grandfather's watch symbolized. Benjy, the "idiot" whose "tale" forms the remarkable first section of the novel, "loved three things: the pasture . . . his sister Candace (who 'smelled like trees'), and firelight" and symbolizes both the mental deterioration of the family and through his castration, its physical sterility. Jason IV, "the first sane Compson since before Culloden and (a childless bachelor) hence the last," commits Benjy to an asylum, sells the house, and displays the pathetically mediocre intelligence that alone is able to cope with the incursions of the modern world symbolized by the Snopes family. And, Quentin IV, the child of Candace, "already doomed to be unwed from the instant the dividing egg determined its sex," is the last Compson and the final burden destined for Mrs. Compson, the personification, to Jason, of all the evil and insanity of his decaying, decadent family.

Benjy's section takes place on April 7, 1928, the day before Quentin IV steals her uncle's money. It is written with incredibly delicate perception, pronouncing the lucidity of a simpleminded innocence that can yet be accompanied by a terrible sharpness and consistency of memory. In its confusion of his father's funeral with Candace's wedding, in its constant painful reactivation by the sound of the golfers crying "caddie" to cause him to bellow out his hollow sense of his sister's loss, Benjy's mind becomes the focus of more cruelty, compassion, and love than anyone but Dilsey imagines. Quentin

III's section, taking place eighteen years earlier on the day of his suicide at Harvard, is one of the most sustained lyrical passages of twentieth century prose. The concentration of Quentin's stream-of-consciousness around the broken, handless watch is one of Faulkner's greatest achievements. Just as the leitmotif of Benjy's section was the smell of trees associated with Caddy's loss, the recurring refrain of Quentin's is the desperate rhetorical question, "Did you ever have a sister?" Jason's theme is hate, a hate as pitiful as is the diminution of Compson pride into pathetic vanity; and this third section of the novel may be the greatest for its evocation of deep, moving passions from even the most mediocre. The last section is focused on Dilsey, who "seed de first en de last" and who represents, to Faulkner, the only humanity that survives the fall of the house of Compson—the only humanity to endure.

THE SPOILERS

Type of work: Novel
Author: Rex Beach (1877–1949)
Type of plot: Adventure romance
Time of plot: The Alaska gold rush
Locale: The Yukon
First published: 1906

Principal characters:

ROY GLENISTER, the owner of the Midas gold mine
BILL DEXTRY, Glenister's partner
MR. MCNAMARA, a politician
HELEN CHESTER, the girl with whom Glenister is in love
JUDGE STILLMAN, her uncle
CHERRY MALOTTE, a notorious woman in love with
    Glenister
MR. STRUVE, a dishonest lawyer

The Story:

Trouble began for Glenister and Dextry, the owners of the Midas mine, the moment they started from Seattle back to the frozen North. First of all, a young woman, Helen Chester, enlisted their aid in stowing away aboard their ship. Then Roy Glenister fell in love with her. After they were aboard, Dextry told Glenister that the government was sending a court to institute law and order in the gold country and warned him that they would have to be careful lest they lose their claim to the Midas mine.

In Nome, Helen delivered a packet of documents to the law firm of Struve and Dunham and then went with the two partners up to the Midas mine. There was no place else for her to go for the time being.

Two weeks later her uncle, Judge Stillman, arrived in Nome with a politician named McNamara. Stillman had been appointed the first Federal judge in Nome, Alaska. Trouble soon brewed for the owners of the mines on Anvil Creek, including Glenister and Dextry. Their claims were relocated, and possession of the mines was given to McNamara as a receiver appointed by the court until the claims could legally be cleared. Convinced that the receivership was dishonest, Glenister and Dextry robbed their mine of ten thousand dollars in gold with which to send their attorney to San Francisco. By the time the attorney had made the trip and returned, all the mine owners on Anvil Creek realized that there was collusion between Judge Stillman and McNamara. When the attorney tried to serve an injunction which would force the judge to return the mines to the owners, Stillman refused to recognize the writ from the San Francisco court. Glenister and Dextry immediately smuggled their attorney aboard a ship bound for San Francisco, with a request that United States marshals be sent to Nome to serve the writ and arrest Stillman for contempt of court.

Meanwhile, Glenister and Dextry spied on McNamara and discovered the part Helen Chester had played in bringing in the documents which had made possible the theft of the mines by McNamara. Cherry Malotte also told Glenister that Helen had informed McNamara of the money Glenister and Dextry had at their camp. The last straw for Glenister was the announcement that McNamara and Helen were to be married.

Deciding to repossess their mines by violence, the owners on Anvil Creek formed a vigilante committee with the intention of lynching McNamara and tarring and feathering the judge.

After spreading the word that troops were going to guard the mines, McNamara laid a trap for the vigilantes at his office in Nome. He thought that the mine owners, not daring to attack the troops, would attack his own office. To his surprise, the owners attacked the mines and seized them after a short, sharp battle. They discovered that the defending force had been only a few guards posted by McNamara.

In the meantime, Helen Chester had gone to Struve to discover what she could about the dealings of her uncle and McNamara. At a deserted hotel outside Nome, he tried to bargain with the girl for the documents he had, papers that would incriminate himself, the judge, and McNamara of collusion to rob the mines. After Helen had read the papers, he tried to attack her. As he was about to overpower her, a gambler—Helen's long-lost brother—appeared on the scene and shot Struve. Helen and her rescuer set out through a terrific storm to return to Nome and turn over the incriminating documents to Glenister and other mine owners.

A few hours after they had left, Glenister came to the hotel and discovered the wounded man. Struve told Glenister that Helen had left the hotel with a cheap gambler. Furious, Glenister rode back to Nome. He resolved to hunt down McNamara and the gambler and to kill them both.

When Glenister arrived in Nome early the following morning, he found McNamara alone in his office. Glenister laid aside his coat and gun to fight the man hand-to-hand. In their struggle, they demolished the office. A crowd gathered to watch them. Feeling himself slipping, McNamara tried to reach for a pistol. As he did so, Glenister seized him in a hammerlock and slowly broke his arm. At that moment, Judge Stillman arrived at the office with several soldiers and put Glenister under arrest.

As he was being led away to jail, a ship sailed into the harbor. Shortly afterward, Glenister's attorney came ashore with several United States marshals and the court orders from San Francisco. With Stillman's power broken,

Glenister was quickly released. When he returned to his cabin to rest, Dextry told him that his fight with McNamara was the talk of the town, for no one had ever seen a combat like it in all the rugged North country. Glenister, too tired to care, stumbled into his bunk and fell asleep.

He was finally awakened when Helen and her gambler brother entered his cabin. Helen told Glenister of the gambler's real identity and tried to prove to him that she had not willingly been a partner in the plot to rob the mine owners of Anvil Creek. What she told him convinced Glenister that she was telling the truth. She also told him that she had seen his fight with McNamara and that she could never marry a man who was more of a brute animal than a civilized human being.

The next day, all was again peaceful in Nome. Glenister planned to return to his mine and resume operations there. While he was preparing to leave, Dextry walked into his cabin. Dextry told him that he was going to sell his share of the Midas mine and leave Nome. His excuse was that law and order had finally come to Alaska, because the country was growing too civilized for an old frontiersman like himself.

After Dextry left, Glenister wandered down toward the beach, too downhearted to finish his preparations for going to the mine. Helen Chester saw him on the beach. Calling him to her, she told him that she finally understood why he could be as brutal as he was, for her own battle with Struve had shown her how thin the veneer of civilization was in the far North, where life had to be defended against both men and the elements. Glenister pretended not to understand what she meant and asked her when she was leaving. Her reply to him was that she did not intend to leave, unless he sent her away.

Critical Evaluation:

The Spoilers is a lusty book about a raw new land filled with adventurers and gamblers of all kinds. Blood and thunder leap forth from every page. The real fault of the novel is the number of coincidences. In his scenes of action, Rex Beach is at his best. His descriptions and dramatic incidents, like the battle at the mines or the epic bare-handed duel between the hero and the villain, are his best work. The merit of the book lies in such, not in the loosely planned plot or the love story.

Pure and simple, Beach is a master of physical violence. His novel abounds in terrifying fights, made doubly realistic by allusion in closest detail to crunching bones and tearing clothes. In the titanic duel that ends the novel—the final confrontation between Glenister and McNamara—both men turn into wild beasts. After the hero loses the use of his hand ("A sudden darting agony paralyzed Roy's hand, and he realized that he had broken the metacarpal bones"), boxing is discarded for brutal wrestling. Roy subdues the villain with a hammerlock and breaks his arm. The climax of the novel, this event gives the title to the penultimate chapter: "The Hammer-Lock."

Beach blends a vulgarized naturalism with adventure and romance. His hero's brutishness, though at first odious to Helen Chester, finally enthralls her because of its directness and honesty. "My pagan," she murmurs at the final embrace, somewhat cowed by the realization that all human beings have brutal instincts: "You told me once that the wilderness had made you a savage, and I laughed . . . when you said . . . that we're all alike, and that those motives are in us all. I see now that you were right and I was very simple."

It is Beach's context for this cardinal principle of Naturalism—the primitive streak in all human existence—that is simple. Naturalists like Norris and Dreiser demonstrate in such powerful works as *McTeague* and *Sister Carrie* that brutality and corruption are very near the surface in all people; what they do not do is suggest that the release of these forces can lead to adventure and romance. Quite the contrary. Naturalism often approaches tragedy by revealing the dark limitations of man, the obstacles that heredity and environment present to his happiness and moral health.

THE SPOILS OF POYNTON

Type of work: Novel
Author: Henry James (1843–1916)
Type of plot: Social morality
Time of plot: Late nineteenth century
Locale: England
First published: 1897

Principal characters:
MRS. GERETH, the mistress of Poynton
FLEDA VETCH, her companion
OWEN GERETH, her son
MONA BRIGSTOCK, Owen's fiancée

The Story:

While visiting one weekend at Waterbath, the country house of the Brigstock family, Mrs. Gereth met and was immediately drawn to a young woman named Fleda Vetch. The basis of the attraction was a mutual sensitiveness to beautiful things; each guessed that the other possessed such a feeling when they met one morning while obviously trying to escape the house and the rest of the party. Their aversion was caused not by the fact that Waterbath was exceptionally ugly, but rather because it was so very ordinary while pretending to be lovely. The house and the garden might have been quite attractive, and should have been so, but the Brigstocks, people without even a hint of feeling or taste, had had everything done over to fit the very latest fashion. It was this air of fashionable conformity to which Fleda and Mrs. Gereth objected. They recognized what the estate would have been naturally, and they could only be repulsed by what it had become.

Mrs. Gereth's horror of Waterbath was particularly acute because of the comparison she inevitably made between it and her own home at Poynton. Everything at Poynton was exquisite. She and her late husband had gradually furnished it after years of scraping and saving so that they might have the best. Every article in the house had been carefully chosen during their travels in various parts of the world, and she rightly considered it the most beautiful place in England. Unfortunately, the estate had been left to her son Owen, and she knew that she would have to give it up, along with her beloved treasures, when he married. Her secret dread was that he would marry a woman with as little a sense of the beautiful as he himself had. She therefore spent much of her time at Waterbath trying to turn his attention from Mona Brigstock, who personified everything she dreaded, to Fleda Vetch, the one person of her acquaintance who would appreciate and preserve Poynton as it was.

When Mrs. Gereth, with somewhat ulterior motives, invited Fleda to come to Poynton as a friend and permanent companion, Fleda, who had no real home of her own, readily accepted. To the chagrin of both women, Owen soon wrote that he was planning to marry Mona and that he was bringing her down within a week to see the estate. Mona, of course, approved. Although she failed to appreciate its beauty and immediately began planning certain changes, she did realize that every article in the house had some value, and she insisted that Mrs. Gereth leave all but her personal belongings as they were. Mrs. Gereth was to be given the smaller, but still charming, estate called Ricks.

At first, Mrs. Gereth refused to be moved, but she finally agreed to make the change when it was decided that she could take a few of her prized objects with her. Owen, who was very much disturbed at being pushed by Mona to the point of having a serious conflict with his mother, had solicited Fleda's aid in getting his mother to make the move quickly. This request only complicated matters, however, for Fleda soon fell in love with Owen and could not really be effective as an agent for both parties in the controversy. She encouraged Mrs. Gereth to move quickly and quietly, leaving Poynton essentially as it was; but, because of her feelings toward both her friend and the estate, she also encouraged Owen to give his mother more time.

During these negotiations, it became necessary for Fleda to go to London to see her father. While she was gone, Mrs. Gereth left Poynton. Her moving was quick and quiet. When Fleda rejoined her at Ricks, she found that the woman had moved virtually all of the furnishings from Poynton. Owen and Mona were less than pleased. In fact, Mona postponed the wedding; she refused to marry Owen until Poynton again held its rightful belongings. Again, Mrs. Gereth was stubborn, and more negotiations ensued, with both sides once more depending on Fleda for aid.

This time it was Owen's turn to fall in love. His strained relations with Mona, which caused a rather close relationship with Fleda, left him emotionally unstable. He had also lately come to realize how much Poynton, as he had always known it, meant to him and to appreciate anyone who understood its beauty and value as Fleda did. He knew that his life would have been much more satisfactory at this time if he were about to marry Fleda instead of Mona. Mrs. Gereth, who had always been willing to give up Poynton to anyone who could love it as she did, would gladly send back everything for Fleda. A realization of this fact finally caused Owen to declare his love for Fleda and to ask her to marry him.

Fleda, although she acknowledged her own feelings, would make no move until Owen had completely broken with Mona Brigstock, and it was to this end that she sent him away. When Mrs. Gereth heard of these developments, she thought that the situation had finally worked out to her liking, and she immediately sent everything back to Poynton. This act proved a mistake, however, for as soon as Mona heard that the furnishings had been returned, she immediately became her former charming self and again captivated Owen. Unfortunately, because of his honor as a gentleman, Owen could not break the engagement unless the lady demonstrated that she wished to do so; Mona Brigstock now made it clear that she did not wish to end the engagement. She quickly married him and moved at once to Poynton in order to acknowledge and secure her possession of the house and its contents. Soon, the couple began an extended tour of the Continent.

Fleda and Mrs. Gereth again took up residence at Ricks and succeeded in making a charming place out of it, in spite of having little to work with and of having to do it with broken hearts. Some time later, Fleda received a letter from Owen asking her to go to Poynton and take whatever object she most prized, and because of her love both for Owen and the estate, she resolved to do so. When she arrived at the station, still more than a mile from Poynton, she saw great billows of smoke rising from that direction. It was a porter who told her that everything was lost. Poynton and all its beautiful furnishings were destroyed in a fire, which was probably caused by a faulty lamp and aided tremendously by a strong wind.

Critical Evaluation:

According to Henry James in his preface to *The Spoils of Poynton*, he perceived the "germ" of the short novel in a friend's casual mention of an acrimonious conflict between a mother and her son over the disposition of the family furniture following the death of the father. "There had been but ten words, yet I recognized in them, as in a flash, all the possibilities of the little drama of my 'Spoils.'" "On the face of it," he went on to say, "the 'things' themselves would form the very center of such a crisis; these grouped objects, all conscious of their eminence and their price, would enjoy, in any picture of a conflict, the heroic importance."

The "things" alone, however, must not have been enough to provoke James to immediate creation, since he left the idea unused for almost two years. In 1895, however, needing a story to fulfill an obligation to the *Atlantic Monthly*, James returned to the "spoils" idea and added the necessary missing ingredient, the central character. "For something like Fleda Vetch had surely been latent in one's first appreciation of the theme."

Thus, James found the two lines of action that give the story its final shape: the conflict between Mrs. Gereth and her son, goaded on by Mona Brigstock, over the furnishings of Poynton and the romance between Owen Gereth and Fleda Vetch. The problem of who is to get the "spoils" dominates the first third of the book, but by chapter eight, the center of interest has shifted to the question of who will marry Owen. The two issues are completely intertwined since Owen is actually one of the "spoils" himself, and his marital decision also determines the disposition of the "things."

The dispute over the "spoils" is really a trial between two strong-willed, determined women, Mona Brigstock and Mrs. Gereth, who direct their strategies through Owen Gereth and Fleda Vetch. The contest becomes ambiguous and the outcome doubtful because the "agents" prove unreliable: Owen's emotional involvement with Fleda upsets Mona's calculations, and Fleda's ambivalent reactions threaten Mrs. Gereth's design.

It is unlikely that Mona cares much for the "things" of Poynton for themselves. After she finally wins Owen and Poynton, she flaunts her indifference to the house by not even living there. Her tenacity in seeking the "spoils" is a matter of willful pride: "Mona," wrote James, "is *all* will." She insists on the furniture because it "goes with the house"—and the house goes with Owen. In addition, it is probable that Mona sees the dispute as a "test" of Owen; or, rather, of her ability to control him. If she can force him to act against his mother's deepest wishes, then she can be confident of dominance in their marriage.

Even though Mrs. Gereth is no less strong-willed and ruthless in her passion to keep control of the artifacts of Poynton, she is a considerably more sympathetic figure. If her attitude toward Poynton reveals her to be a thorough materialist, she is at least a materialist with taste; Poynton, the fruit of her labors, is a fine art product, and her devotion to it is passionate and complete. If she is a snob, judging people solely in terms of their taste and "cleverness," she seems accurate in her judgments: Mona is vulgar, Owen is stupid, and Fleda is superior. If Mrs. Gereth's actions are arrogant and extreme, they are mitigated by her situation; the English law that grants all inheritance rights directly to the son, regardless of the widow's needs, is an unjust one; and, if she "collected" Fleda to use as part of a scheme to regain Poynton, she does, in the end, show genuine feeling and concern toward the girl as a person, not just a "piece of furniture."

The most sympathetic and interesting person in the story, however, is Fleda Vetch. In his preface, James identifies her as the only real character in the story; that is, the one figure of feeling and intelligence who is capable of development and change. It is through her perception and sensibility that the reader experiences the story and, in James's words, "the progress and march of my tale became and remained that of her understanding."

Not surprisingly, Fleda is the most complex and puzzling character in the book. Although her intelligence and moral superiority are evident throughout, her behavior frequently seems contradictory and self-defeating. Critics have disputed the motivations behind many of her actions and especially those during the crucial scenes that determine the outcome of her romance with Owen. The primary question is this: At the point where Owen says he loves her and wants to marry her, why does she send him straight back to Mona with "conditions" that virtually guarantee losing him? Or, to put it more generally, why does she throw away her one chance for happiness at the very time she seems to have it within her grasp?

In attempting to answer this question, three variables must be kept in mind: Fleda's relationship with Mrs. Gereth, her relationship with Owen, and her own aesthetic and moral values.

From the beginning, Fleda is flattered and awed by Mrs. Gereth's attentions and compliments. The older woman sees in Fleda the perfect protégée, a girl gifted with intelligence and intuitive good taste, but with little background experience, who can be influenced, even molded, by an astute mentor. Thus, Mrs. Gereth grooms a replacement for herself who can not only keep Poynton out of Mona's grasp but also minister to its treasures long after she, Mrs. Gereth, is gone. In matters of artistic taste, Mrs. Gereth probably has her way with Fleda, but after Owen becomes a factor her control over the girl becomes doubtful. In addition, as the book progresses Fleda becomes increasingly aware of being manipulated by Mrs. Gereth, and, while she may not personally object to being a "piece of furniture," she does feel quite guilty about being used as bait in a trap for Owen.

Fleda's relations with Owen are equally problematical. At first, she rejects him on the grounds that he is "too stupid," but even from the beginning, his amiable personality and physical desirability make a strong impression on her. As their relationship grows, Fleda's view of him becomes more and more clouded by self-deception. Her first impressions of him as "stupid" and "weak" are accurate, but, as she falls in love with him, she suppresses these obvious insights or rationalizes them into strengths. She insists that he act with "independence" and "maturity," yet, like Mona, she fully expects to dominate him after marriage ("It's because he's so weak that he needs me").

Fleda feels strongly attracted and obligated to both people, so she gives each of them the impression that she favors their cause. From these contending loyalties come such self-defeating acts as her persistent claim to Owen that she is winning his mother over and her lies to Mrs. Gereth regarding her emotions and, more important, Owen's feelings for her.

Thus, conflicting impulses probably determine her final self-defeating act. Because of her innate morality and her Victorian upbringing, Fleda is unable to accept the idea of winning a previously committed man away from his intended; she cannot act the part of the "designing woman"—especially in someone else's design. Given her tendency to self-deception, she probably convinces herself that Owen can, in fact, meet the conditions she imposes; unfortunately, "her Owen" is largely imaginary, and the real Owen cannot resist a fully aroused Mona Brigstock. Fleda seems to lack the emotional capacity, as Mrs. Gereth put it, to "let go."

These speculations, however, do not answer the central question about Fleda. Does her final act represent a failure of nerve, a running away from life and experience? Or, does it represent the moral victory of a woman too proud to jeopardize her ethics in return for a chance at happiness? Both views, and most positions in between, have been argued by the critics with little consensus. Each reader must make up his or her own mind on the point.

If Fleda's actions cost her a life with Owen, however, her reaction to that loss demonstrates her strength of character and her mature appreciation of life. It is she who senses the "meaning" of Ricks and brings a measure of solace to the defeated Mrs. Gereth. It is here that readers come really to understand Fleda's aesthetic sensibility; to her, objects have moral qualities and their beauty is a product of the human experience they reflect. If she can succeed in impressing that view on her companion, a mellowed Mrs. Gereth may find a measure of happiness at Ricks—even after the accidental fire which resolves forever the fate of the "spoils" of Poynton.

This novel, written in the middle period of James's career, shows the detailed character analysis, careful development, and acute insight into human affairs for which he has become famous. Here, one has a kind of tragedy, but not one in the classical sense. This novel is tragic first because many beautiful things are unavoidably given up to one who has no appreciation of them and, second, because these same objects are completely destroyed in a freak accident. The human emotions involved are seen to be somewhat mean in spite of the grandeur of the objects with which they are connected; and throughout the novel, readers have James's astute comments on, and impressions of, the society in which the action takes place.

THE SPY
A Tale of the Neutral Ground

Type of work: Novel
Author: James Fenimore Cooper (1789–1851)
Type of plot: Historical romance
Time of plot: 1780 and 1812
Locale: New York State
First published: 1821

Principal characters:
HARVEY BIRCH, a peddler
MR. HARPER, General George Washington
MR. WHARTON, a Loyalist sympathizer
FRANCES, his daughter
SARAH, another daughter
HENRY, his son
MAJOR PEYTON DUNWOODIE, an American officer
CAPTAIN LAWTON, another American officer
COLONEL WELLMERE, a British officer

The Story:

At the beginning of the Revolutionary War, Harvey Birch, a peddler, became a spy against the British. Because of the extremely secret nature of Birch's work, few Americans were aware of his true mission. As a matter of fact, they suspected that he was a British spy, and they denounced him as a bold and shameless Tory.

At the time, Westchester County in New York was considered common ground for both the rebels and the loyalists, and the inhabitants of the county affected a neutrality they did not feel. This was the case of Mr. Wharton, a British sympathizer, who at the outbreak of hostilities had retired to his country estate with his two daughters, Sarah and Frances, and their aunt, Miss Jeanette Peyton.

One evening as a storm was approaching, a horseman rode up to the Wharton house, The Locusts. He was a tall man of powerful frame, military in his bearing but plain and sober in his dress. After being let into the house by the Whartons' black servant, Caesar Thompson, the traveler introduced himself as Mr. Harper and asked for shelter from the storm. Mr. Wharton courteously granted the traveler's request, and the two men were soon engaged in conversation concerning the progress of the war. Mr. Wharton expressed his views cautiously in order to determine Mr. Harper's sentiments, but the stranger remained tight-lipped and uncommunicative in his replies.

The conversation between the two men was interrupted by the arrival of Henry Wharton, Mr. Wharton's son and a captain in the British army. The young man wore a disguise because he had been compelled to cross the American lines in order to visit his home. He was disconcerted when Mr. Harper recognized him, despite the disguise.

Later, Harvey Birch, the peddler believed by all in the neighborhood to be a Loyalist spy, came to the Wharton home, bringing with him laces for the ladies, tobacco for Mr. Wharton, and news of the war—news that included a report of the hanging of Major Andreé. During Birch's visit, Caesar remarked to his master that he had heard voices in Mr. Harper's room. There seemed to be no reason why the traveler and the peddler should have matters to talk over in private.

With the return of fair weather, Mr. Harper said good-bye to his host. Before he departed, he promised to help Henry Wharton, if the latter ever needed help, in return for Mr. Wharton's hospitality. Shortly after Mr. Harper left, the Wharton home was surrounded by a troop of Virginia cavalry looking for a man answering Mr. Harper's description. When the American soldiers entered Mr. Wharton's house, they discovered Henry, whose disguise was so hastily assumed that Captain Lawton, in command of the troop, was able to discover the deception. The Captain was certain that Henry was a spy because he knew that Birch, whom he believed a British spy, had recently been visiting the Whartons.

Not certain what course he should follow with Henry, Captain Lawton consulted his superior, Major Peyton Dunwoodie, who was interested not only in Henry Wharton but also in Henry's sister, Frances. She pleaded with her lover for Henry's release, but when Henry was found to have a pass signed by General Washington, Major Dunwoodie thought that the case warranted Henry's arrest.

Further investigation into the matter by Major Dunwoodie was halted by a report that British troops were in the neighborhood. The major rushed to his command, leaving Henry guarded by two soldiers.

In the confusion, Henry escaped. He reported to his superior, Colonel Wellmere, leader of the advancing British troops, who professed to be in love with Sarah Wharton. When Henry advised the Colonel to be wary of Major Dunwoodie and his Americans, Wellmere scorned the advice and determined to force a fight with the rebels. In the brief engagement that followed, the British were routed, and Captain Lawton succeeded in recapturing Henry, who was returned under guard to his father's home. Colonel Wellmere, also taken prisoner, was slightly wounded in the action. Chagrined by his defeat and capture, he gave the impression that his injuries were mortal, much to the distress of Sarah Wharton.

Birch was watching Major Dunwoodie's success from a distant hill when he was sighted by Captain Lawton, who determined to capture the spying peddler dead or alive. In the pursuit, Captain Lawton overtook Birch, but he fell from his horse and found himself at the peddler's mercy. Birch, however, spared Captain Lawton's life, and for that act of magnanimity, the Captain would not allow his men to overtake the peddler.

A price was put on Birch's head. One night, his house was ransacked and burned by a band of lawless men called Skinners, who surprised the peddler and his dying father. They then delivered Birch to Captain Lawton and claimed their reward. Major Dunwoodie, who was also present when the peddler was brought in, accused him of treason. Although Birch possessed a paper which would have cleared him of the charge, he swallowed it rather than betray the confidence of his secret employer. Captain Lawton paid the Skinners in gold for their captive, but he also ordered them whipped for burning, robbing, and murdering.

Birch was put in jail, but that night he escaped in the guise of a washer-woman who visited his cell. The next morning, on the outskirts of the American camp, he confronted Major Dunwoodie again. With a gun pointed at the officer, to prevent recapture, the peddler warned him to be on guard against danger to the Whartons. Major Dunwoodie was alarmed by the thought of danger threatening Frances Wharton. He was also disturbed because he felt that he could never win Frances if her brother were executed as a spy. Major Dunwoodie's troubles were magnified when, after assuring Frances that he would try to get General Washington's help for her brother, she turned from him coldly because she believed that he was in love with Isabella Singleton, the sister of an American officer who was recuperating at The Locusts from injuries sustained in the battle.

Meanwhile, Sarah Wharton had accepted Colonel Wellmere's proposal of marriage, and the date for the wedding had been set for the night when there was to be an exchange of prisoners at the Wharton house. Major Dunwoodie and Captain Lawton were among the guests during the truce arranged for the exchange and the wedding. The ceremony was suddenly interrupted, however, by the appearance of Birch, who told the Colonel that the Englishman's wife had crossed the ocean to meet him. Sarah fainted. Captain Lawton challenged Colonel Wellmere to a duel. The Englishman missed his mark, but Captain Lawton was prevented from killing his adversary when the Skinners leaped upon him and overpowered him. Colonel Wellmere fled the scene, and Captain Lawton was able to escape his enemies only after a fierce struggle.

The Skinners then proceeded to burn Mr. Wharton's house. Captain Lawton returned to the scene with troops he had met on the road, and after routing the Skinners, he rescued Frances from the blazing house. Birch rescued Sarah, and again, Captain Lawton permitted the peddler to escape. A bullet fired at Captain Lawton from the darkness, apparently by the Skinners, struck Isabella Singleton and wounded her mortally. On her deathbed, she confessed to Frances her love for Major Dunwoodie but said that he thought of her only as a friend.

At his trial, Henry Wharton admitted that he had used a disguise in order to pass through the American lines, but he insisted that his reason for doing so had been for the one purpose of visiting his family, especially his aged father. Major Dunwoodie himself vouched for Henry's character. Frances, however, ruined her brother's chances for acquittal when she confessed that Henry had had dealings with Birch, who, she told the court, had given her brother his disguise. Henry's fate seemed certain. He was found guilty and sentenced to be hanged on the following day.

Major Dunwoodie declared that he would go to General Washington to make an appeal for the life of his friend. His attempt was unsuccessful, however, for the commander-in-chief was not at his headquarters.

Soon afterward a tall, gaunt man in clerical dress appeared and announced himself as a minister from a nearby village who had come to offer spiritual comfort to the condemned man. Admitted to Henry's cell, he revealed himself as Harvey Birch. He helped Henry to disguise himself as Caesar Thompson, the faithful servant of the Whartons, and led the young officer past the unsuspecting sentinel with the remark that the black servant was being sent on an errand for his master.

Frances, hearing of the escape, thought that her brother and the peddler would probably hide in a cabin not far away. Stealing away from the American lines, she set out to join them, but to her surprise, she found the cabin occupied by Mr. Harper, who was poring over an outspread map. Recalling his promise to help her brother, she told him the whole story. He reassured her that all would be well and told her to return to headquarters to await Major Dunwoodie.

Orders from General Washington arrived in time to relieve Major Dunwoodie of the necessity of tracking down Henry, who was thus allowed to escape. Several days later, Birch saw him safely aboard a British man-of-war in New York harbor. Frances and Major Dunwoodie decided to be married immediately. Within a short time, however, their bliss was tempered by the news that Captain Lawton had fallen in battle with the British.

Some time later, Birch appeared at the headquarters of the American army in a New Jersey town. There he had a long interview with a grave and noble man whom the Whartons would have recognized as Mr. Harper. The peddler called him General Washington. During their talk, the General attempted to reward his faithful spy by giving him money. The peddler refused to accept payment for his services to his country, but he did welcome a letter of approbation from his commander-in-chief. It was agreed that the peddler's real mission as an American spy should remain a secret that only they would share.

Thirty-two years later, in the War of 1812, a gaunt old peddler appeared on the Canadian border and carried word of British troop movements to the American lines. There he met Captain Wharton Dunwoodie, the son of Major Peyton Dunwoodie and his wife Frances. To him, the peddler acknowledged his earlier acquaintanceship with the young officer's parents.

A few days later, during a battle, the old peddler threw away his pack and rushed into the fight with a musket seized from a fallen soldier. After the battle, Captain Dunwoodie found the old man's body and on his person a letter, signed by George Washington, which revealed Harvey Birch, not as a despicable spy but as a loyal, heroic, and long-suffering patriot.

Critical Evaluation:

Judged by modern standards, *The Spy: A Tale of the Neutral Ground* is still a satisfactory historical novel. As James Fenimore Cooper remarked in the introduction to his novel, however, his purpose in *The Spy* is frankly patriotic. If the reader bears this fact in mind, he can understand that Peyton Dunwoodie is supposed to represent the ideal American soldier and officer; Frances Wharton, the ideal of American womanhood; and Washington, the ideal father of his country, combining Roman strength and vigor with American humanity and humility. This understanding will help the reader to appreciate Cooper's point of view. The great historical novelist of the early nineteenth century was an intensely nationalistic individual who, conscious of the past achievements and potentialities of his country, eagerly looked forward to the development of a great nation.

The Spy is an important novel both in Cooper's career and in the history of American literature. For Cooper, *The Spy* represented a first success in a literary career which was to include thirty-three fictional works as well as a number of other writings over a period of thirty-one years. *The Spy*, however, also signifies the establishment of an independent American literature, a literature based on American life, American characters, and set in an American landscape. It is significant, then, that the novel which declared "independence" from European, and especially English, literature should take for its subject the American War of Independence.

In his preface to *The Spy*, Cooper showed that he was acutely conscious of being an American writer and of writing about American subjects. Still, there is no doubt that he was influenced by the major currents in literature written abroad; and, though in his preface he offers a tongue-in-cheek apology for not including castles and nobles, as Sir Walter Scott had done, it is certain that Scott influenced Cooper in *The Spy* and in his later career as well. Scott was a great pioneer in the art of the historical novel, and *The Spy* shows that Cooper learned much from Scott.

An important aspect of the historical novel are the historical types, characters who live in a specific historical period and in a particular place. One of the key differences between an authentic historical novel and a contemporary novel in a historical setting is characterization. Though one may argue that people are, in a sense, the same everywhere and at all times, it is apparent that the differences cannot be merely overlooked if one is mainly interested in accurately portraying a specific era. Thus, to capture a particular place at a particular time, the novelist must do more than merely dress his contemporaries in the clothing of days past. He must have a grasp of those human features and aspects which a historical period typically requires of men and women.

The Spy is full of historically typical men. The spy himself is a courageous and ingenious man able not only to affect the times in which he lives but permitted (and encouraged) by those times to display such qualities. Thus, another difference between an ordinary novel in a historical setting and a historical novel as such is that the characters help fashion history as they are fashioned by it.

In the War for Independence, fought on political as well as military grounds, involving civilians to a great extent and always posing the problem of divided loyalties, Cooper's choice of a spy is especially effective. The spy is not only a soldier in a war, but he must have a grasp of politics (and theater) as well.

Cooper discovered another advantage in the use of a spy as a central character. This advantage is connected to the subtitle of the novel, "A Tale of the Neutral Ground." Effective historical novels tend to focus on periods in which significant conflicts occur. Such conflicts as the War for Independence not only provide good dramatic material for the novelist but also offer later readers an insight into their own condition, since significant conflicts in the past have shaped their lives.

There is, however, an artistic problem in portraying such conflicts. To give a full picture of the clash of forces, an author must describe both sides in the fight (in Cooper's case, both the British and the Americans). Describing only one side tends to rob the novel of drama—but how is the novelist to show both and, at the same time, focus these forces on a single, central character?

Scott solved this problem by using figures of secondary historical interest as his primary focus of dramatic action. These secondary figures are able to move from one side to another as negotiators, go-betweens, and messengers. This movement back and forth allows scope for the novelist to show both sides of the conflict in a specific, concrete fashion.

Cooper has done this in *The Spy*. Instead of choosing Washington himself as a central character, Cooper has chosen a spy, a man able (and required) to move from one side to the other and yet a man who remains in the thick of the dramatic action. The "Neutral Ground," the space between opposing forces that Birch must cross and recross in his missions, the seam between the opponents, also reflects the need for an effective historical novel to move from one side to the other.

Other aspects of the historical novel are also significant. Besides the presence of other, minor "type" characters (the doctor, the housekeeper, the servant), there are the details of the warfare—the names, dates, places, and historical facts—that Cooper made a conscious effort to use; and *The Spy* reflects a degree of historical accuracy and fidelity to the facts which, despite moments of highly imaginative drama and humor, lend an air of reality to the action of the book as a whole.

Additionally, Cooper expends much print and dialogue on the arguments for and against the War for Independence. The revolutionaries argue with the counterrevolutionaries. Because he is able to show both sides dramatically, in real life, Cooper is able to describe the intellectual and political conflict of the era. In this way, Cooper avoids the trap of turning a historical novel into a mere adventure story; for in the course of history, and certainly in the course of the Revolutionary War, the battle of ideas deeply influences the physical battles. If Cooper is less successful in showing how arguments change individuals, he is still able to give a richer sense of the times and of the war than if he had concentrated entirely on physical action and adventure.

There are obvious weaknesses in Cooper's work. Cooper was, apart from being an opinionated man, one who shared many of the prejudices and preconceptions of his day. These views naturally affected the quality of his work.

One of his problems, for example, was that he seemed unable to characterize certain sorts of people in much depth. His attitude toward women and black people specifically is condescending. As a result, his portrayal of these figures is almost always superficial and unreal. Cooper's women in *The Spy* and elsewhere tend to be either precious darlings or selfish schemers.

Cooper also has a tendency to use a rather heavy-handedly ironic tone. In *The Spy*, Cooper follows a long tradition in English literature by making his comic characters members of the lower class. One senses that the class characteristics of those below him were humorous to Cooper. Corresponding to this general characterization of the lower orders (not true in every case, to be sure) is a general deference to those of higher rank.

Thus, in fully evaluating *The Spy* as literature, the reader is drawn to a central contradiction. On the one hand, Cooper clearly supports the American side and agrees with the arguments for independence, especially those arguments based on the God-given equality of men. In Cooper's mind, men *are* equal before God. At the same time, Cooper himself is a creature of his own time and upbringing. For him, though men may be equal under God, they are by no means equal to one another.

The conflict between ideals and reality is an old one in the United States, and it is no surprise that Cooper, declaring himself an authentic American novelist, should exhibit that conflict. Thus, *The Spy* is an informative historical novel both because it reflects a basic conflict in the history of a nation and because, as a work of art, it contains a basic conflict.

STATE FAIR

Type of work: Novel
Author: Phil Stong (1899–1957)
Type of plot: Regional romance
Time of plot: Early 1930's
Locale: Iowa
First published: 1932

Principal characters:
>ABEL FRAKE, a prosperous farmer
>MELISSA FRAKE, his wife
>WAYNE, his son
>MARGY, his daughter
>ELEANOR, Wayne's friend
>HARRY WARE, Margy's friend
>EMILY, a girl Wayne met at the fair
>PAT GILBERT, a newspaperman
>THE STOREKEEPER, a local philosopher
>BLUE BOY, a prize boar

The Story:

Abel Frake knew that this year Blue Boy would be judged the finest boar at the state fair. As he discussed his hog with the men loafing in the store one Saturday night, he found the storekeeper as pessimistic as usual.

The storekeeper believed that something intangible was always working to see that things did not go too well for most people. What it was he could not exactly say, but he was willing to bet Abel five dollars that it would either keep him from winning the blue ribbon or let him win because some other catastrophe would occur later. Abel, accustomed to the storekeeper's gloom, went home with his confidence in Blue Boy unshaken.

As Abel and his wife, Melissa, made plans for the next day's start for the fair, their son and daughter were not so carefree. Wayne was with Eleanor, home from her first year in college, but she was changed. Before she went away, she had always been his girl; now she did not want to be committed to any promises for the future. Wayne drove home in gloomy silence. When he pulled into the farmyard, he found his sister Margy and Harry Ware sitting in his convertible. Harry was begging Margy to marry him as soon as she came home from the fair. Margy, like Eleanor, did not know whether it was Harry she wanted.

Sunday was spent in making last-minute preparations for their departure.

Melissa checked the jars of pickles she intended to exhibit at the fair. Abel could do nothing except groom Blue Boy.

That evening, they started out in the farm truck. The pickles and Blue Boy were given most consideration in the packing, for they were to win honors for the family. Abel drove all night and reached the fairgrounds in Des Moines on Monday morning. Blue Boy was taken at once to the stock pavilion, and the family set up their tent in an area reserved for fair visitors.

As soon as Wayne could get away, he went to the fairgrounds to look for a barker who had cheated him the year before. During the past year, Wayne had practiced throwing hoops, and he almost cleaned out the barker before he stopped throwing. When the barker threatened to call the police, a girl who had been watching called his bluff and walked away with Wayne. Her name was Emily; she was the daughter of a stock-show manager. She and Wayne visited other booths together. In the afternoon, they went to the horse races, and Emily won some money for them to spend.

While Wayne was busy with Emily, Margy strolled around the fairgrounds and looked at the exhibits. That night, she and Wayne planned to visit the midway, but they became separated, and Margy went on alone. On the roller coaster, she met Pat Gilbert, a reporter for a Des Moines paper. Margy found that she could talk easily with Pat.

On Wednesday, Melissa's pickles won three blue ribbons. A photographer, who was with Pat, took pictures of Melissa and Margy. Neither Wayne nor Margy had told their family about their new friends, and Margy had to pretend that she did not see Pat at the exhibit. As soon as she could get away, she and Pat went again to the roller coaster. As they walked back to the tent grounds that night, they stopped in a grassy spot that was hidden from the walks and paths. Pat took Margy in his arms and kissed her, and she gave herself to him willingly.

On Thursday, the most important event was the judging of the hogs. Although Abel was nervous and at times had doubts of his victory, he was not really much surprised when Blue Boy had the blue ribbon pinned on his stall. The judges declared him the finest boar they had ever seen, and from then on, the fair was over for Abel. In fact, the judging over, he and Melissa had little interest in the remainder of the week.

That evening, Wayne and Emily went to a stage show in the city, and Wayne thought it the most wonderful show he had ever seen. Afterward, Emily took Wayne to her hotel room and gave him a drink of whiskey. He had never tasted liquor before; it gave him a wonderful, warm feeling inside. Emily went into another room to change from her evening gown. Wayne was not surprised when she returned wearing only a thin kimono. He had known what to expect when he had gone to the hotel with her.

On Friday evening, Pat asked Margy to marry him right away. He loved her and wanted to keep her with him. She knew, however, that a marriage between them would never work. Pat was restless and wanted to see the world. He thought now that he would gladly settle down in Des Moines for the rest of his life if he could have Margy with him, but she knew that he would grow restless again and be unhappy with her. When she told him good-bye, she knew she would not see him again.

That same night, Wayne told Emily that he loved her and asked her to marry him and go back to the farm with him. Emily also refused. She, like Pat, could never stand quiet life on the farm. She was not a wild girl, but she still wanted to enjoy the pleasures of youth.

The next morning, the family packed their truck and went back home. On Sunday, Eleanor and Harry came to dinner as though nothing had happened that made this Sunday different from any other. The storekeeper drove out and paid his five dollars to Abel, conceding that nothing would happen in the next two months to make him win the bet. Yet, as he looked at Wayne and Margy, he smiled, as if he saw that something had already happened.

Critical Evaluation:

Reviews of *State Fair* during the months following its publication in 1932 were unquestionably favorable. Critics agreed that Phil Stong drew an accurate picture of Midwestern life, especially as it related to that much revered event, the state fair. Stong was praised for his vivid descriptions of characters, young and old, and his ability to produce a novel that was robust and entertaining. Slight mention was made of the fact that there is no great depth or moral to the story beyond the dime store bits of philosophy espoused by the storekeeper. Reviewers at the time seemed to agree that Stong brought a certain degree of "city-slicker's knowingness and humor" to his sound understanding of farming life in Iowa. The novel is saved from being purely sentimental and superficially structured by Stong's style, which is full of assurance, ease, and grace.

One cannot help but notice the tight symmetry of *State Fair*. The novel revolves around a week which includes a five-day trip by car to Des Moines for the great "kermess." The Frake family is as closely knit as the novel itself. The four family members are constantly referring to what it means to be Frake and how their strength, inner conviction, and endurance help them to achieve all their goals. Mama is painfully committed to her pickles, and father Abel to his fattened, prizewinning boar, Blue Boy. Each character is sketched briefly but carefully early in the novel, to be picked up at greater length later in the book as he or she relates his experiences at the fair. Both Wayne and Margy, the young teenagers, leave sweethearts at home on the farm the night before they depart for the fair, and both have had an altercation of some sort with their sweethearts. The fair is a turning point for all the Frakes, and it transports the mother and father to glory that only prizewinning pickles and champion hogs can bring. The fair supplies Wayne and Margy with some exciting interludes, including a little behind-the-exhibits sex and perhaps some maturity. Margy meets Pat, the man-about-town newspaper reporter who makes her head spin and who wants to marry her at week's end. Margy, however, true to Frake form, realizes her allegiance to the farm and the life it offers and knows that Pat would soon be discontented. On the other hand, Wayne is wooed and seduced by the redheaded Emily who shows him how to bet on horses, dine fashionably in Des Moines, and take in the theater with style. Wayne falls for Emily in much the same way that Pat falls for Margy, but to no avail here either, for Emily also realizes that farm life is not for her. She anticipates many more experiences before she plans to settle down. Wayne and Margy learn much about life in general, and their goals in particular during that short week. They both return home to their former sweethearts, having taken some risks, suffered a little, but having grown a great deal.

The storekeeper's pessimism is apparent from the beginning of the novel when he says that all good is necessarily followed by some bad. In the end, one is found reflecting, momentarily at least, as to whether that is always true. For in the case of Wayne and Margy Frake, their salutary dip into pleasure brought them a week's worth of exhilarating happiness and fond memories that renewed their dedication to farm life.

THE STOIC

Type of work: Novel
Author: Theodore Dreiser (1871–1945)
Type of plot: Naturalism
Time of plot: Early twentieth century
Locale: Chicago, New York, London, and Paris
First published: 1947

Principal characters:
FRANK A. COWPERWOOD, a financier
AILEEN COWPERWOOD, his second wife
BERENICE FLEMING, his mistress
PHILIP HENSHAW and
MONTAGUE GREAVES, English engineers
BRUCE TOLLIFER, a Southern artist
LORD STANE, an English financier
LORNA MARIS, a dancer in Baltimore
MARIGOLD BRAINERD, Tollifer's friend
DR. JEFFERSON JAMES, Cowperwood's friend and doctor

The Story:

Frank Cowperwood, nearing age sixty, had just lost his long struggle to gain a fifty-year franchise to control the transportation system in Chicago. In addition, he and Aileen, his second wife, had failed to achieve the social prominence to which they felt their wealth entitled them. At the time of Cowperwood's defeat, Berenice Fleming, an attractive young woman whom he had loved for eight years, quite unexpectedly agreed to become his mistress. Berenice knew that Cowperwood intended to stay married to Aileen; Cowperwood agreed to continue to support Berenice and her mother.

Cowperwood, a vital man impatient for something to do, was interested in the proposition of two English engineers, Philip Henshaw and Montague Greaves. The proposition involved Cowperwood's help in financing the construction of the London underground. Henshaw and Greaves were interested in the line that ran from Charing Cross to Hampstead (each of the lines was originally planned by different organizations). Cowperwood, hoping to coordinate the separate lines, planned to go to England, with Berenice, to organize the financing and attempt to gain the controlling interest in the project.

On his way to England, Cowperwood stopped in New York to see Aileen in the palatial mansion he had built for her. First, he invited her to go to Europe; then he decided that he needed to keep her occupied socially so that he would have time for Berenice, and so he found an improvident artist, Bruce Tollifer, whom he hired to pursue and amuse his wife. Tollifer was to receive two hundred dollars a week plus expenses and was to meet Aileen in London. Not knowing of the arrangement and thinking of Tollifer as a friend, Aileen felt that, by asking her to come to Europe, her husband was finally settling down to one woman. The party left for Europe.

In London, Cowperwood discovered that he also needed control of the Central Loop line in order to solidify his interests. He met Lord Stane, a British financier, who helped him in both his business dealings and personal arrangements. Berenice rented a country house from Lord Stane. In the meantime, Tollifer persuaded Aileen to take a trip to Paris with him. He tried to make her more attractive (once pretty, Aileen had become middle-aged and overweight) by renewing her interest in clothes and exercise.

While Tollifer and Aileen were in Paris, Cowperwood and Berenice were free to live at Berenice's country house and tour the cathedral and university towns of England.

As Cowperwood's business interests expanded, he found it necessary to return to the United States to find more capital. He took Aileen and left her in New York while he toured the country raising money. In Baltimore, a beautiful young dancer named Lorna Maris came to his hotel room claiming that she was a distant Cowperwood relation. Lorna and Cowperwood began an affair, and he stayed in the United States longer than he had planned. Aileen, hearing of the affair through a newspaper item, sent the clipping on to Berenice; she had discovered the affair between Berenice and her husband before leaving Europe. Berenice was furious when she heard that Cowperwood and Lorna were having an open affair. Although she and Lord Stane, beginning to spend a great deal of time together, were finding that they had much in common, Berenice decided to remain faithful to Cowperwood; she found his vitality irresistible. Cowperwood broke off the affair with Lorna, returned to England, and was reunited with Berenice.

Cowperwood's trip was financially successful. Along with Lord Stane and several others, he now controlled the underground and the connected construction company. He had bought out Henshaw and Greaves. Aileen returned to Tollifer in Paris. However, while she had been in the United States, the artist had become friendly with Marigold Brainerd. At a party, Marigold, partly to protect her interest in Tollifer and partly because she was drunk, told Aileen that her husband had simply hired Tollifer to keep her occupied. Hurt and angry, Aileen returned to New York. Cowperwood, following her, announced that he planned to enlarge the New York house, fill it with more art treasures, and have it converted into a museum after they died. He wanted Aileen to supervise the new construction and to do it immediately, for after his death, much of his money was to go toward founding a hospital. He left Aileen in New York after promising to return as soon as he had completed his business in London.

Back in London, and ill, Cowperwood decided to hire a yacht and sail on a holiday to Norway with Berenice. Soon after he returned to work, constantly driving himself, he became ill once again, and the doctors told him he had Bright's disease. He decided to erect a tomb for himself and to wind up his business affairs as quickly as possible. During a weekend at Lord Stane's house, he suffered another attack and sent for his American physician and friend, Dr. Jefferson James. Dr. James took him on a boat trip to the Riviera, but once again the effect of the vacation was only temporary. Back at work in London, five months later, Cowperwood suffered another attack and decided to return to New York to see Aileen once more. Berenice was also to return to the United States and stay at the Waldorf-Astoria in order to be near him.

On the boat, Cowperwood suffered an even more serious attack and had to be carried off the boat on a stretcher. Because Aileen's house, in the midst of renovation, had no room for him, he was taken to the Waldorf-Astoria. Aileen came to the hotel to find Berenice caring for him in his room; her bitterness had scarcely abated by the time of Cowperwood's death a short time later. He was buried in the tomb he had built.

Although his financial position had seemed secure at his death, various lawsuits, deriving from some of his unsavory deals, plagued the estate. The lawsuits continued for five years, and Aileen, seeing Cowperwood's money vanish, was forced to sell her mansion and abandon all her plans for the museum and the hospital. A year after the mansion was sold, Aileen died and was buried in the tomb beside her husband.

After Cowperwood died, Berenice, at loose ends, traveled around the world. In India, she became fascinated with Hindu philosophy and stayed there for five years, regretting her past and developing a greater sense of humanity. She had her own income that Cowperwood had left her. When she returned to America, she heard that the rest of his money had been lost. She then decided to use her income to found a hospital, and she hired Dr. Jefferson James as the director.

Berenice herself began to work at the hospital where she found enormous satisfaction in dealing with handicapped children. Recognizing her very limited function in human affairs, she realized that the power Cowperwood had sought had not brought him happiness, peace, fame, or enduring power. A person could, she now knew, express himself effectively only in limited ways, such as helping a few handicapped children in a small hospital.

Critical Evaluation:

The Stoic, the third novel of the trilogy that includes *The Financier* and *The Titan*, completes the story of Frank Algernon Cowperwood. As in the other two novels, Cowperwood, a man of great force and vitality, is interested only in material things—making money, having attractive mistresses, and building monuments to perpetuate his name. Theodore Dreiser does not condemn this attitude morally, but he does point out that none of Cowperwood's relationships is lasting, none of his projects achieves permanence. For all of his power and strength, he is simply another man whose best efforts are cut down by time and the forces around him. Ironically, his cherished dream of founding a hospital is realized through Berenice, his former mistress turned Eastern philosopher, after his death; but the money Cowperwood left for the project is dissipated in endless lawsuits as shady as the deals by which Cowperwood got the money in the first place. Man, even the ruthless man of business, cannot, in Dreiser's world, impose his will on events for very long, and Cowperwood's ultimate ineffectuality, the difference between his desires and his real accomplishments, gives him a certain amount of sympathy. Dreiser never quite finished *The Stoic*; his wife wrote the final chapter, from his notes, before the novel was published posthumously in 1947. As a novel, it is not generally regarded as Dreiser's best, for the details of finance overwhelm the concept of Cowperwood's character, and the writing becomes more repetitious and uneven as it moves along. The nature of Dreiser's concept of human experience also made the struggles of his characters more interesting to most readers than the inevitable long conclusions concerning the worthlessness of the struggle.

A study of Dreiser's notes for *The Stoic* makes it clear that in the beginning, Dreiser saw Cowperwood as glamorous, richly dressed, good-looking, and in many ways enviable. Cowperwood triumphs, for Dreiser and for himself, when he faces a meeting of bankers who think he is short of funds as a result of a crisis in Chicago. He has foreseen their doubts and counters with a promise that he can repay every loan he has received, but that if they insist upon it, he will "gut every bank from here to the river." Cowperwood is in control.

Dreiser has built an indomitable figure for whom one must feel admiration, just as later one can only pity him. Cowperwood's methods consist in skillful manipulation, the greater power conquering little men at every move. He does not know what it is to fail or be insecure. Even when Cowperwood faces his darkest hour and is sentenced to jail (*The Financier*), he remains self-confident and optimistic. He feels that greatness is "inherent in him." Cowperwood reflects Dreiser's belief that men are instruments of higher forces, no more and no less than their natures dictate. Dreiser took the life of an American financier and economic manipulator, Charles Tyson Yerkes, and, through his genius, transformed it into a complex and dazzling study of the natures of success and failure. Cowperwood's successes are not always what he expects them to be, and his failures are integrally connected to his apparent successes. Although Dreiser's craftsmanship is often faulty in this last volume of the trilogy, the very force of his vision and the intensity of his convictions sweep the reader along. *The Stoic* is a weak novel that also happens to be an engrossing and great book.

STONE DESERT

Type of work: Novel
Author: Hugo Wast (Gustavo Adolfo Martínez Zuviría, 1883–1962)
Type of plot: Regional romance
Time of plot: Early twentieth century
Locale: Rocky tablelands of northern Argentina
First published: 1924

> *Principal characters:*
> DON PEDRO PABLO (PEPABLO) ONTIVEROS, an Argentine
>   landowner
> MIDAS ONTIVEROS, his nephew
> MARCELA, the daughter of Midas
> AQUILES and
> HECTOR, her brothers
> ALFONSO PUENTES, son of a neighboring farmer
> ROQUE CARPIO, a gaucho murderer and outlaw
> FROILÁN PALACIOS, an overseer
> DOÑA SILVESTRE, his wife

The Story:

One foggy April morning, a weary gaucho stopped at the house of Doña Silvestre and her husband, Froilán Palacios, an overseer on a ranch owned by old Pedro Pablo Ontiveros. The traveler's pallid face showed that he had recently been in prison. After receiving meat and bread, he betrayed his familiarity with the region around Real de San Eloy by starting out for the town of Canteros over a trail unknown to most of the natives.

Early the next morning, near the main ranch house on the Ontiveros estate, he found a girl's bare footprints in the sand by the river. A short time later, a boy appeared. He was Aquiles, a grandnephew of old Pepablo as everyone called Don Pedro. The boy said that the tracks had been made by his sister, Marcela. The traveler introduced himself as Juan-without-a-Country, but when he stopped at the tavern in Canteros, old Pepablo recognized him as Roque Carpio, a gaucho exiled to the Argentine penal colony at Ushuaia for killing his unfaithful wife twenty-five years before.

With old Pepablo was his nephew Midas. A failure in Buenos Aires, Midas had brought his daughter, Marcela, his sons, Aquiles and Hector, and his mother-in-law, Doña Claudia, to live on Pepablo's run-down ranch. Marcela wished to restore the property with the help of Leopolda, the mannish wife of Overseer Difunto. Pepablo scoffed at her plan. Hard work was for *gringos*

---

like his Spanish neighbor, Isidro Puentes, ambitious owner of a farm which had once belonged to Roque Carpio.

The old man did admire Marcela, however, and gradually turned the ranch over to her management. While searching for missing cattle, she had left the footprints seen by Roque. She found her cows in Puentes' barley field. The *gringo*, hoping to arrange a match between her and his son Alfonso, had let the starving animals graze. Marcela scorned Alfonso, partly because the neatness of Puentes' farm, in contrast with Pepablo's establishment, hurt her pride. Once, however, she asked his help when she ran a thorn into her arm.

Increasing drought brought death to Pepablo's cattle. Aquiles and Hector tried to bring rain by staking out a toad in the patio. A storm came, washing out Puentes' barley fields. Pepablo was delighted. When the *gringo* took advantage of the rainwater to drown burrowing hares that had been ruining his fields, Marcela wanted to follow his example. Pepablo was, however, too proud to imitate a *gringo*. Besides, the hares provided food for his dogs.

Marcela then suggested that they round up the remaining cattle and drive them to higher pastures. Pepablo promised her half the calves that could be saved. The score of neighbors she invited to the roundup spent the night at the house of Froilán Palacios at Real de San Eloy. Roque Carpio joined them for a cup of *mate* before he went home through a howling storm, leaving Marcela convinced that city dwellers were weak in contrast to rugged country people. A conversation she overheard later made her suspect that Roque was stealing and branding cattle.

Snow fell. Marcela hired Don Tertulio, a bonesetter and local treasure seeker, to make some repairs at the ranch house. At the feast of San Pedro and San Pablo, Pepablo was to carry the cross in the religious procession. When Marcela discovered that rats had eaten his best shoes, she got him a new pair. They were so stiff that Pepablo slipped them off during dinner, and the dogs gnawed them.

Midas, meanwhile, had been busy with a scheme to make church candles from beeswax. Failing in that venture, he threatened to take his family back to Buenos Aires. As a bribe, Pepablo unearthed some money he had hoarded and set his nephew up as an antique dealer. That project also failed. Midas' next plan was to cut down the algarrobo trees which were Pepablo's special pride and sell the timber. By cajolery and threats, he secured the old man's permission to fell the trees, but the sound of the woodsmen's axes was more than Pepablo could stand. He died, leaving the house and the trees to Midas and the rest of his property to Marcela.

Midas promptly sold his share to Puentes and moved his family to the overseer's house at Real de San Eloy. Marcela hoped that life on that rugged tableland would purge their blood of city-created decadence. After discharging Froilán, whom she suspected of conniving with Roque, she herself ran the ranch.

Froilán, with Doña Silvestre and their daughter Monica, opened a tavern and store. Roque and Midas were among his customers, and Midas discussed his grandiose schemes with the outlaw. He once asked Roque, jokingly, why he did not carry some girl away to one of his mountain caves.

The question turned Roque's thoughts to a plan to win Marcela. He killed a cow, making the death seem like the work of a mountain lion, so that Marcela would organize a lion hunt. His plan to steal her away at that time, however, was frustrated by the arrival of Melitón Bazán, a famous hunter who stirred Roque to rivalry by his claim that he carried only two cartridges because he never saw more than two lions at a time. During the hunt, Roque and Melitón each killed a lion. Alfonso Puentes shot Roque's dog in order to protect three cubs Marcela wanted. Only Marcela's quick defense saved the young man from the gaucho's fury. Roque left in anger.

Critical Evaluation:

Stone Desert—translated from the original *Desierta de piedra* in 1928—has been for Latin American readers a favorite among the thirty-two titles written by this most prolific of Argentine novelists. Afraid that his origins in Córdoba might handicap his sales, Gustavo Adolfo Martínez Zuviría hid his identity under a pen name when he published his first novel in 1911. Since that time his books, written under the name of Hugo Wast, have sold more than two million copies, with some three hundred editions in Spanish and seventy others in translation. In *Stone Desert*, Marcela speaks for the writer when she voices her opinion that a return to nature is the best cure for decadent city life. The novel also expresses the author's belief that the hope for Argentina lies in the toil of hardworking immigrants, combined with a change in the attitude of the country's easygoing, wasteful citizens.

Although not considered Wast's best novel, *Stone Desert* is remarkable for the number of themes that it handles well. One such theme has rarely been treated elsewhere in Latin American novels; namely, the alleged economic superiority of foreign immigrants to Latin America over the natives. This allegation is heard from Southern Brazil (where Italians, Portuguese, Japanese, Germans, Poles, and Lebanese have shown notable energy), to Venezuela (where Italians, Spaniards, and Portugese have done the same), to Uruguay and Argentina, where immigrants have renovated entire areas. In *Stone Desert*, Wast portrays the hard work done by Peninsular Spaniards in a far-off and rocky corner of the Argentine Republic. *Stone Desert* is one of the few Latin American novels to treat the important subject of ethnic minorities in Latin America and the contribution to their adopted lands.

Wast's novel is unusual in other ways. It is one of the relatively few Argentine novels set in the "lost" Northwest of the country, where Argentina fuses into Bolivia and Chile in the high, windy, cold, stony, and dun-brown Puna Atacama. *Stone Desert* also reflects the fact that Latin America's true vitality has sprung from the country and nourished the city. This has been notable in Argentine history, from the dictatorial days of Juan Manuel de Rosas to Juan Perón and has been at times a dominant note in national literature, including Argentina's two masterworks, *Martín Fierro*, and Domingo Sarmiento's great *Facundo* (although the latter views rural Argentina as a vigorous, barbaric drawback to progress and civilization).

It is noteworthy, then, that *Stone Desert* has also treated so many other themes, such as the nostalgic return home of Roque Carpio; the superstition of country folk (for example, the staking out of the toad in the patio to bring rain); the ruggedness of rural Argentines compared to city-dwelling "porteños," or inhabitants of Buenos Aires; and the return to nature as a cure for the decadence of urbanites.

THE STORY OF A BAD BOY

Type of work: Novel
Author: Thomas Bailey Aldrich (1836–1907)
Type of plot: Regional romance
Time of plot: Nineteenth century
Locale: New Hampshire
First published: 1869

Principal characters:

TOM BAILEY ALDRICH, the narrator
CAPTAIN NUTTER, his grandfather
MISS ABIGAIL, the Captain's sister
KITTY COLLINS, the Nutter maid
BILL CONWAY, and
SETH RODGERS, Tom's enemies
SAILOR BEN, Tom's friend and Kitty's missing husband
PHIL ADAMS,
PEPPER WHITCOMB, and
BINNY WALLACE, Tom's friends

The Story:

Tom, the son of a banker, was born at Rivermouth in New England. When he was eighteen months old, however, his family moved to New Orleans, and there he lived until he was ten, growing up in almost complete ignorance of everything that was not Southern. In his tenth year, he was sent North to live with his Grandfather Nutter. Tom soon learned to admire his hale, cheery grandfather and to respect his grandaunt, Miss Abigail. The fourth member of the household was Kitty Collins, the maid, an Irish girl happily married to a sailor until he sailed away one day and failed to return.

Tom's grandfather sent him to school immediately to keep him out of mischief. At the Temple Grammar School, he made friends with many boys and incurred the enmity of two, Bill Conway and Seth Rodgers. Tom's friends decided to put on a play, *William Tell*, in Tom's barn. Pepper Whitcomb, as Walter Tell, balanced an apple on his head, while Tom played the part of William. Tom's arrow missed the apple and struck Pepper in the mouth. The theatricals ceased abruptly.

Bill Conway's tyranny finally drove Tom to make preparations to fight his tormentor, and Phil Adams tutored Tom in the manly art of self-defense. The anticipated fight did not occur, however, until after Tom had experienced

---

several more adventures.

As the Fourth of July approached, the boys in the Temple Grammar School could not concentrate on their studies. One of the boys placed a torpedo under the cloth on the desk, at the exact spot where Mr. Grimshaw usually struck with his heavy ruler. The resultant explosion created a commotion and nearly caused the strangulation of Charley Marden, who was at the water pail getting a drink.

On the night before the Fourth of July, Tom slipped out of bed and used Kitty's clothesline to escape from his bedroom. He did not tie knots in the rope and, as a result, burned his hands in his descent. He went to the square, where a big bonfire was to be lit. When the fire burned down after a while, Tom and his friends took an old stagecoach from Ezra Wingate's barn and used the vehicle as fuel. The boys were caught and put in jail, but they escaped. The next day, Ezra collected three dollars from the family of each boy who had aided in the theft. Ezra made a good profit, for he had previously offered the coach to anyone who would pay seventy-five cents for it. During the celebration of the Fourth, Tom accidentally stepped on a mine and was blown into the air and knocked unconscious. As a result, he was a hero among his friends for about two weeks.

Shortly after this experience, Tom was initiated into the mysterious order of the Centipedes, an organization notorious for the pranks of its members. One of these pranks was the stealing of the druggist's gilt mortar and pestle, which the Centipedes placed over the Widow Conway's front door. On the drugstore window shutters, they tacked a sign advertising for a seamstress. The town laughed, because everyone except Mr. Meeks himself knew that Widow Conway had set her cap for the mild-mannered druggist.

One day after school, Tom found Bill Conway tormenting Binny Wallace. Tom lowered his head and swung right and left as he prepared to give Conway a thrashing. Tom pummeled the school pump for twenty seconds before he discovered that Conway had already retired.

Miss Abigail could not stand the odor of tobacco. When she took over as housekeeper for her brother, she restricted his smoking to the barn. One morning during a very cold winter, Grandfather Nutter descended the steps with a clay pipe in his mouth. Abigail objected strenuously, but the Captain merely removed the pipe from his lips and blew a cloud into the hall, where the temperature was two degrees below zero. Miss Abigail fainted. When she was revived, Grandfather Nutter told her that there had been no tobacco in the pipe and that she had seen only his congealed breath in the frosty hallway.

At Slatter's Hill, the North-End boys and the South-End boys met for a snowball fight at specified times during the week. The fights, however, became too dangerous because frozen snowballs were used, and parents and police put an end to the snow battles.

One summer, Tom bought a boat called the *Dolphin*, and he and three of his friends planned a day's trip to Sandpeep Island. When the boys landed on the island, they found that they had left the lemons in the boat. Binny Wallace volunteered to get them. The boat, after he stepped into it, broke loose from its mooring place and floated away. Binny drifted farther and farther out to sea. A rising squall developed into a full-sized storm, and the boys waited through it, hoping that Binny would be rescued. However, such was not to be. He was drowned.

One day, Tom saw Sailor Ben, whom he had met during his voyage north from New Orleans. The old sailor failed to recognize Tom because he had grown so tall. When Tom took Sailor Ben home with him, Kitty at once recognized the sailor as her long-lost husband and the two were reunited. Grandfather Nutter broke out a fresh decanter of Madeira, and they all celebrated the happy occasion. Deciding to quit the sea, Sailor Ben bought a small cottage near the wharf. Kitty remained as the Nutter maid but spent her free time with her husband.

Silas Trefethen bought all the cannon available in Rivermouth because he thought that war with England was imminent. When he died, still thinking so, the cannon rusted and became unfit for any use except as monuments. Tom and his gang decided to have some fun with the cannon after they found several pieces near the wharf and cleaned them. Everything went well with their plan to set them off, except that Tom and his conspirators could not make the proper fuse. Sailor Ben, learning of their plan, told them how to prepare the fuse. When everything was in readiness, the Centipedes drew lots to determine who would fire the cannon. The chance fell to Tom. That night he slipped out of bed, lit the fuse, and returned to his room before the first cannon went off. The operation succeeded as planned. Everyone was aroused from bed by the explosions. The only casualty was Sailor Ben's chimney. No one was ever able to solve the mystery of the explosions.

With Primrose Hall, a girls' school, close by, it was not surprising that Tom should fall in love, but he was unsuccessful with the girls attending the seminary. Tom finally fell in love with Nelly Glentworth, who came to visit his grandfather, but she scorned him, and so for some time, Tom rather enjoyed the pangs of unrequited love.

In New Orleans, the yellow fever broke out, causing the death of Tom's father. His mother came north and settled in New York, where Tom was offered a position with an uncle in his countinghouse. Ready at last to make his own way in the world, Tom left Rivermouth regretfully. He felt that the happiest days of his life were over.

Critical Evaluation:

He was, of course, not a very bad boy at all, and therein lies much of the story's charm. Boyhood, as any boy knows, looks best from the vantage point of maturity, and Thomas Bailey Aldrich tenderly and charmingly renders typical scenes of mischief and misdemeanor, friendship and puppy love.

The Story of a Bad Boy is one of the most fascinating and amusing accounts of the life of an American boy in the early part of the nineteenth century. Acknowledged by the author to be largely autobiographical, it is an adult recapture of childhood experience. The fictional Rivermouth is Portsmouth, New Hampshire, the author's childhood home.

The novel rises to no overall dramatic impact, but it is not without moments of heightened intensity. The tale of little Binny Wallace washing out to sea in a rowboat, never to be seen alive again, is narrated deftly enough to fetch a tear to the eye of the susceptible reader. There are memorable portraits of Tom's barnacle-ridden crony, Sailor Ben, and of that almost forgotten institution, The Oldest Inhabitant. Many of the adventures of Tom and his friends have that authentic ring of what nostalgia would like boyhood to have been.

The genteel sensibility which informs *The Story of a Bad Boy* helped insure Aldrich's literary prominence—he was editor of *Every Saturday* magazine while writing the novel and was to take over the reins at the prestigious *Atlantic Monthly* when William Dean Howells resigned in 1881. Other characteristics of the novel—the coy archness of its accomplished yet uninspiring prose style, the romanticizing of its subject matter, its loose, semiautobiographical structure, and lack of dramatic intensity and moral force—all help indicate why Aldrich gained prominence first as an editor and poet, second as a short-story writer, and only later as a novelist. Indeed, perhaps chief among the book's virtues is that it touched off among post-Civil War New England writers a whole series of "books about boys." Prominent among those that surpassed it in both popularity and literary merit are Howell's *A Boy's Town* (1890) and Mark Twain's *The Adventures of Tom Sawyer* (1876) and *The Adventures of Huckleberry Finn* (1884).

THE STORY OF A COUNTRY TOWN

Type of work: Novel
Author: Edgar Watson Howe (1853–1937)
Type of plot: Social criticism
Time of plot: Mid-nineteenth century
Locale: The Middle West
First published: 1883

Principal characters:

NED WESTLOCK, a boy on the Middle Border
REVEREND JOHN WESTLOCK, his father
JO ERRING, his uncle
MATEEL SHEPHERD, Jo Erring's sweetheart
CLINTON BRAGG, Jo Erring's rival for Mateel

The Story:

The Westlocks had gone west to grow up with the country. They lived first on a farm near a church where the father acted as the volunteer preacher. It was a life of toil and privation on the bleak prairie. Days began early and ended soon after supper, when fatigue drove the Westlocks to bed. There were four of them, John Westlock and his wife, their son, Ned, and Mrs. Westlock's younger brother, Jo Erring. The only real amusement Ned had was visiting a nearby miller with his young uncle. The miller, Mr. Barker, had been a sailor in early life, and he regaled the boys with stories of his travels.

When Ned was eleven years old, a minister was sent from the East to take charge of the country church where Mr. Westlock had been acting as preacher. Erring immediately fell in love with Mateel Shepherd, the daughter of the new preacher, but he found no favor in her eyes because he was uneducated and crude. With the miller's help, he began to improve himself. The miller became so fond of Erring that he took him on as an apprentice who would some day take over the mill. This was a great opportunity for the seventeen-year-old boy. The only flaw in his happiness then was that Mateel Shepherd was being courted by a young lawyer named Clinton Bragg.

Shortly after Erring left the farm, Mr. Westlock sold his farm and bought the almost defunct paper in the town of Twin Mounds. When the Westlocks moved into town, Ned went to the office every day to learn the printing trade and to help his father in the newspaper office.

Twin Mounds was an unprepossessing village with a post office, several stores, a jail, and about six hundred people. The only pleasures in which the people seemed to indulge, so far as Ned could see, were drinking, gossiping, and fighting. Although the Westlocks lived in a large stone house, the father had Ned stay at the newspaper office in the company of one of the printers, under whom he was learning the trade.

Erring, apprenticed to the miller, made such excellent progress that after a year or so the community subscribed to a fund so that he could build a mill of his own, the growing population justifying a second mill in the district. He was also successful in his suit with Mateel Shepherd, who had promised to marry him when his mill was completed and in operation.

One day, the quiet life of the Westlock family was rudely shattered. Mr. Westlock left the deeds to all his property in the custody of Ned and his mother and ran away with another woman. Ned took over the newspaper, which became more profitable under his management than it had been under his father, for the people in the community had not liked Mr. Westlock. He had been too solitary and strange to suit their natures.

The family gradually began to grow out of the feeling of disgrace that had fastened itself upon them when the father disappeared. Their friends did what they could for them and rallied in support of Mrs. Westlock and her son. At times, it seemed as if the disappearance of Mr. Westlock was of more benefit than harm. Ned was left with some valuable property and a chance to make a name for himself at a very early age.

The following Christmas Eve, Erring married Mateel Shepherd. Just before the marriage, he and Ned had a long talk, in which he told Ned that in some way he was not as anxious for the marriage as he had been when he first met Mateel. What Erring did not realize was that he had been so zealous in getting an education that he had not only reached Mateel's level, but he had already passed her. It was not a happy wedding. Only a handful of guests came to the wedding supper, and those who stayed away did not bother to send their regrets. The Shepherds were not popular in the community.

After the marriage of Mateel and Erring, life in the community of Twin Mounds settled into a quiet routine for everyone. Ned was more disappointed than ever in the town. Its people seldom thought out anything for themselves, and every opinion they had was made for them, often by Ned's own editorials. Their shallowness and smugness irked him.

One cold winter night, Erring appeared at the door of the Westlock home. Nervous and disheveled, he had come because he felt the need to talk to someone whom he could trust. He had found a letter which his wife had written to his rival before her marriage, a letter disclosing Mateel's belief that she could never love any man but Bragg. This idea rankled in Erring's mind. He had been thoughtful and tender with his wife, but she had always been distant and cool to him, in keeping with the vow she had made in her letter to Bragg.

Ned listened to his uncle's story and then took him back to the mill and Mateel. After Erring had confronted his wife with what he had discovered, he and Ned sat up all night, unable to sleep. Clinton Bragg disappeared from Twin Mounds within a few days, apparently afraid of Mateel's husband.

That same winter Ned's father returned to Twin Mounds and accidentally met his son on the street at a late hour. He told Ned that he had been faced with misfortune ever since he had left his wife and son. The woman with whom he had run away had not really loved him and had deserted him soon after she learned that he had left his money and property in Ned's hands. John Westlock was a pathetic and broken figure, unwilling to face the wife he had deserted. Ned gave him the little money he happened to have in his pocket, and the older man then turned away into the snowy night and was soon lost to sight. Ned knew that he had seen his father for the last time.

Meanwhile, matters between Erring and his wife had gone from bad to worse. He had taken a vow never to speak to his wife or touch her again, and Mateel began to fade quickly under his harsh treatment. At last, she asked Erring to let her return to her father's home. He agreed. A day later, Bragg drove up in a buggy to take the girl back to her father and mother. It was a bitter experience for Erring to see another man carry his wife away from his house. Ned was with his uncle and left only when the older man had fallen asleep, exhausted.

When Ned arrived home, he discovered that his mother had died in his absence. Always quiet and subdued, she had died as she had lived, asking nothing from anyone.

In the spring, Ned braved a heavy rainstorm to visit his uncle. He arrived to find the mill deserted. Suddenly the door opened, and Erring walked in, carrying Mateel, who was unconscious. In a calm voice, he told Ned how he had lain in wait along the road until Bragg and Mateel had come along in a buggy. He had dragged his rival from the vehicle and killed him with his bare hands while Mateel looked on. Then he had carried Mateel back to the mill. Unable to face the fact that Mateel had divorced him and married Bragg, he felt it was better to murder and then to die himself than to live with Mateel married to another.

Erring surrendered quietly to the authorities and was taken to jail. He was never tried, however, because one night he took poison. The jailer discovered him with a letter for Ned clutched in his hand.

After Erring's burial, Ned stopped at the Shepherd home to ask about Mateel. The poor girl was demented. While he was in the house, she came into the room and mistook Ned for Erring. She drew a dagger from her dress and told Ned she had gone by the mill that day to have one last look at the place where she had been happy. Now she intended to kill herself. Her mother led her away. That same night she died, shortly after telling her father and mother she hoped to see Jo Erring soon.

Critical Evaluation:

Howells and Twain praised Edgar Watson Howe's novel, and one early reviewer believed that at last someone had created the "great American novel." For the modern reader, however, its interest is historical rather than literary. Howe's style is often cumbersome with frequent errors of spelling, word usage, and construction.

Many reviewers have noted the novel's Dickensian tones. The most obvious influence is in the characters' names—Jo Erring, Ned's tragic, misunderstood uncle; the Reverend Goode Shepherd; the worthless but wordy philosopher, Lytle Biggs; and the boastful villain, Clinton Bragg. There is also the sense of melancholy Dickens gives to his child heroes. Ned resembles Pip and David Copperfield in the dismal circumstances of his early life. Dominated by work, death, religion, and rejection, Ned comes to a fatalistic acceptance that life is a wretched experience.

Unfortunately, the adult Ned is less interesting. His story is submerged as the book sinks into trite melodrama, and Ned remains important only as narrator of the misfortunes of Jo and Mateel. Another departure from Dickens is that there is no humor to relieve the book's starkness. The gray, wooden church with its graveyard dominates Fairview, and the Indian graves of Twin Mounds oversee the meanness of small-town culture.

Howe implies that country living makes men cruel. Trying desperately to wring an existence from the dry soil, the characters find the work ethic to be all-encompassing. Their only relief is religion, which is grimly Calvinistic. Ned begins his narrative by observing that his father's religion would have been incomplete without a hell, for Mr. Westlock hoped that everyone who did not share his piety would be punished. It is ironic that through the church Mr. Westlock meets Mrs. Tremaine, a temperance fanatic, with whom he elopes. When last seen, he is a broken, guilt-ridden old man who returns to Twin Mounds on the snowy eve of his wife's funeral.

This novel is the earliest of a number of books that sounded a revolt against the popular conception that the American small town was an idyllic place in which to live. In it, Howe drew a deadly picture of village life—the shallowness of thought, the materialism, the ever-present sense of failure and the under-lying spirit of petty and mischievous enmity. Through all of the book rings a note of sincerity which makes Howe's iconoclastic efforts valid, giving his novel depth and lasting value as a social document.

The melodrama and sketchy characterization weaken the novel, but the book is of definite value when seen as a precursor to *Winesburg, Ohio*; *Main Street*; and *Spoon River Anthology*.

STUDS LONIGAN
A Trilogy

Type of work: Novel
Author: James T. Farrell (1904–1979)
Type of plot: Naturalism
Time of plot: 1916–1931
Locale: Chicago
First published: Studs Lonigan: A Trilogy, 1935 (*Young Lonigan*, 1932; *The Young Manhood of Studs Lonigan*, 1934; *Judgment Day*, 1935)

Principal characters:

WILLIAM "STUDS" LONIGAN, a lower middle-class Irish-American
OLD LONIGAN, his father
MRS. LONIGAN, his mother
FRANCES LONIGAN, his sister
LUCY SCANLAN, the beloved of Studs Lonigan
CATHERINE BANAHAN, Studs Lonigan's mistress and fiancée
PAULIE HAGGERTY and
WEARY REILLEY, friends of Studs Lonigan

Studs Lonigan: A Trilogy, first published in separate volumes from 1932 to 1935, still appears to be James T. Farrell's major work, despite the long list of books—novels, collections of short stories, essays, and literary criticism—that have followed. Every significant critical work on the American novel published since 1935 has mentioned the trilogy. While critics have not always agreed on the merit of Farrell's work, the purposes behind it, or even the nature of the author's craft, they have all admitted that Farrell has contributed something of apparent but still unproved value to American fiction written in this century.

The three volumes about Studs Lonigan portray the disintegration, physical and moral, of a young Chicago Irishman during the period from 1916 to 1931, beginning with the protagonist's graduation from a parochial school on Chicago's South Side and ending with his death. Farrell himself has been explicit in pointing out that *Studs Lonigan* is not a story of the slums and that the tragedy of Studs Lonigan is not rooted in the economics of the community or nation. The trilogy was not intended to illustrate an economic thesis, nor does it. The downfall of Studs Lonigan is portrayed as the result of spiritual poverty in an Irish-American, lower middle-class neighborhood of Chicago. The elder Lonigan was a painting contractor who was successful enough that his family was not in want. The failure in the world of the Lonigans is a failure of moral sanctions. As Farrell himself has stated of that social milieu, there were important institutions which should have played a part in the education of Studs Lonigan and his friends; those institutions were the home, the family, the church, the school, the playground. When they failed, the streets and the poolroom took their place. Under these influences, young Lonigan, not an evil young man or a moral cripple, drifted into grim and dismal circumstances. To such an extent is the character of Studs Lonigan a social manifestation, as well as a fictional character.

The story of the growth of the trilogy has been told by its creator. While a student at the University of Chicago, Farrell took a course in advanced composition, apparently the only college course which he liked and in which he worked. In that course, he wrote a story entitled "Studs," which, shown to Professors James Weber Linn and Robert Morss Lovett, won encouragement for its author. Farrell then proceeded to construct a novel, which grew into a trilogy about the character of Studs, who came to be a symbol of the spiritual poverty of his neighborhood, his class, and his times. In a wider social sense, the tragedy of Studs may be also the tragedy of countless young Americans whose drifting, shattered lives have been, and still are, centered around too much sex, too much alcohol, too many automobiles, too many empty platitudes, too many empty social dogmas, and too little faith in themselves and human nature, lives ending in increasing numbers in alcoholism, drug addiction, delinquency, and crime. Farrell's portrayal of Studs Lonigan, ugly as it is in some respects, may have hit closer to artistic and social truth than the author dreamed of at the time.

Farrell's technique in the *Studs Lonigan* trilogy has been termed both Realistic and Naturalistic. Neither term, as it is traditionally used, fits Farrell's work, for he has gone beyond conventional categories. The primary reason for not regarding the *Studs Lonigan* trilogy as Naturalistic or Realistic is that Farrell has used determinism in a different fashion from that of earlier authors like Norris and Dreiser. Thus, the character of Studs Lonigan is not molded entirely by his environment; he knows, at least at times, where he is drifting. Farrell intimates in the novel that it was in his character's power not to have failed so entirely. Certainly Danny O'Neill, the hero of a later series of Farrell novels, and Farrell himself in real life, did not drift into the tragedy that becomes Studs Lonigan's lot. Unlike the earlier Naturalistic novelists, Farrell did not hold himself aloof, nor did he hold himself to an amoral view of his creations. To some extent, he asked for reform and improvement, as the traditional Naturalistic writer does not.

Another aspect of Farrell's work that has drawn comment, perhaps too much, is the selection of details and language in *Studs Lonigan*. The story is told in an idiom close enough to the original to be embarrassingly accurate for a person familiar with it, and yet the language is changed sufficiently to admit the expression of wider and deeper concepts than its culturally starved users normally can or wish to express. Readers who have never experienced this strata of society, however, may honestly feel shocked. Farrell has called his overall technique Social Realism, and certainly his language is part of that technique. Part of the objectivity, the realistic portrayal of both character and setting in the trilogy, would have been lost if the writer had employed any other style or selected his details differently. Farrell has chosen not to sentimentalize the world, not to romanticize it, nor to hide its real character in any other way. It should be noted, too, that from early in his career, which he has taken as seriously as his fictional Danny O'Neill takes his, Farrell has had confidence in his materials and in his methods. Many other writers of the same period became victims of adherence to left-wing brands of determinism in art. Those who did either changed or failed. Farrell did not fail, nor did he have to change, having evaded the trap from the beginning.

To summarize the total significance of the trilogy is difficult. Many readers misunderstand the purposes and the techniques, preferring the comfort of illusion to the pain of truth. Farrell himself has recognized this tendency. In *A Note on Literary Criticism* (1936), he said that art must flow from the reality of the writer's experience and that it cannot be better than life. The story of Studs Lonigan shows Farrell practicing what he expressed as his theory. Some critics and others who have admired Farrell's writings have defended the volumes by calling them sociological documents and making of Farrell a student of sociology rather than an artist in fiction. Farrell has not stooped to such subterfuge, deeming any such defense unwarranted and unnecessary.

THE SUN ALSO RISES

Type of work: Novel
Author: Ernest Hemingway (1899–1961)
Type of plot: Social criticism
Time of plot: 1920's
Locale: Paris and Pamplona, Spain
First published: 1926

Principal characters:
JAKE BARNES, an American newspaperman
LADY BRETT ASHLEY, one of the lost generation
ROBERT COHN, a young writer
MICHAEL (MIKE) CAMPBELL, Brett's fiancé
BILL GORTON, Jake's friend
PEDRO ROMERO, a Spanish bullfighter

The Story:

Jake Barnes knew Robert Cohn in Paris shortly after World War I. Somehow Jake always thought that Cohn was typical of the place and the time. Cohn, the son of wealthy Jewish parents, had once been the middleweight boxing champion of Princeton. He never wanted anyone to forget that fact. After leaving college, he had married and had lived incompatibly with his wife until she ran off with another man. Then in California, he met some writers and decided to start a little, arty review of his own. He also met Frances Clyne, who became his mistress, and when Jake knew Cohn, the two were living unhappily in Paris, where Cohn was writing his first novel. Cohn wrote and boxed and played tennis, and he was always careful not to mix his friendships. A man named Braddocks was his literary friend. Jake Barnes was his tennis friend.

Jake Barnes was an American newspaperman who had fought with the Italians during the war. His own private tragedy was a war wound which had emasculated him so that he could never marry Lady Brett Ashley, a young English war widow with whom he was in love. In order not to think too much about himself, Jake spent a lot of time listening to the troubles of his friends and drinking heavily. When he grew tired of Paris, he went on fishing trips to the Basque country or to Spain for the bullfights.

One night, feeling lonely, Jake asked Georgette, a girl of the streets, to join him in a drink at the Café Napolitain. They dined on the Left Bank, where Jake met a party of his friends, including Robert Cohn and Frances Clyne. Later, Brett Ashley came in with a group of young men. It was evident that Cohn was attracted to her, and Frances was jealous. Brett refused to dance with Cohn, however, saying that she had a date with Jake in Montmartre. Leaving a fifty-franc note with the café proprietor for Georgette, Jake left in a taxi with Brett for a ride to the Parc Montsouris. They talked for a time about themselves without mentioning what was in both their minds, Jake's injury. At last, Brett asked Jake to drive her back to the Café Select.

The next day, Cohn cornered Jake and asked him questions about Brett. Later, after drinking with Harvey Stone, another expatriate, on the terrace of the Café Select, Jake met Cohn and Frances, who announced that her lover was dismissing her by sending her off to London. She abused Cohn scornfully and taunted him with his inferiority complex while he sat quietly without replying. Jake was embarrassed. The same day, Jake received a telegram from his old friend Bill Gorton, announcing his arrival on the *France.* Brett went on a trip to San Sebastian with Robert Cohn. She thought the excursion would be good for him.

Jake and Bill Gorton had planned to go to Spain for the trout fishing and the bullfights at Pamplona. Michael Campbell, an Englishman whom Brett was to marry, had also arrived in Paris. He and Brett arranged to join Jake and Bill at Pamplona later. Because Cohn had gone to San Sebastian with Brett and because she was now staying with Mike Campbell, everyone felt that it would be awkward if Cohn accompanied Jake and Bill on their trip. Nevertheless, he decided to join them at Bayonne. The agreement was that Jake and Bill would first go trout fishing at Burguete in the mountains. Later, the whole party would meet at the Montoya Hotel in Pamplona for the fiesta.

When Jake and Bill arrived in Bayonne, they found Cohn awaiting them. Hiring a car, they drove on to Pamplona. Montoya, the proprietor of the hotel, was an old friend of Jake's because he recognized Jake as a true aficionado—one who is passionate about the bullfights. The next morning, Bill and Jake left by bus for Burguete, both riding atop the ancient vehicle with several bottles of wine and an assortment of Basque passengers. At Burguete, they enjoyed good fishing in the company of an Englishman named Wilson-Harris.

Once back in Pamplona, the whole party had gathered for the festival of San Fermin. The first night they went to see the bulls come in, to watch the men let the savage bulls out of the cages one at a time. Much wine made Mike Campbell loquacious and freed his tongue so that he harped constantly on the fact that Cohn had joined the group, although he knew he was not wanted. At noon on Sunday, the fiesta exploded. The carnival continued for seven days. Dances, parades, religious processions, the bullfights, and much wine furnished the excitement of that hectic week. Also staying at the Montoya Hotel was Pedro Romero, a bullfighter about twenty years old, who was extremely handsome. At the fights, Romero acquitted himself well, and Brett fell in love with him, a fact she admitted with embarrassment to Jake. Brett and the young man met at the hotel; Romero soon became interested in her.

Besides the bullfights, the main diversion of the group was drunken progress from one drinking spot to another. While they were in the Café Suizo, Jake told Cohn that Brett had gone off with the bullfighter to his room. Cohn swung at both Mike and Jake and knocked them down. After the fight, Cohn apologized, crying all the while. He could not understand how Brett could go off with him to San Sebastian one week and then treat him like a stranger when they met again. He planned to leave Pamplona the next morning.

The next morning, Jake learned that after the fight, Cohn had gone to Pedro Romero's room, where he found Brett and the bullfighter together. Cohn had beaten Romero badly, but that day, in spite of his swollen face and battered body, Romero performed beautifully in the ring, dispatching a bull that had recently killed another torero. That night, after the fights, Brett left Pamplona with Romero. Jake got very drunk.

As the fiesta ended, the party dispersed. Bill Gorton went back to Paris and Mike Campbell to Saint Jean de Luz. Jake was in San Sebastian when he received a wire from Brett asking him to come to the Hotel Montana in Madrid. Taking the express, Jake met her the next day. Brett was alone. She had sent Pedro Romero away, she said, because she thought she was not good for him. Then, without funds, she had sent for Jake. She had decided to go back to Mike, she told Jake, because the Englishman was her own sort.

After dinner, Jake and Brett rode around in a taxi, seeing the sights of Madrid. This, Jake reflected wryly, was one of the few ways they could ever be alone together—in bars and cafés and taxis. Both knew the ride was as purposeless as the war-wrecked world in which they lived, as aimless as the drifting generation to which they belonged.

Critical Evaluation:

Upon its publication in 1926, *The Sun Also Rises* was instantly accepted as one of the important American novels of the post-World War I period. Part of this recognition was the result of the superficial fact that sophisticated readers identified current expatriate celebrities among the book's characters, but, as most of these personages faded into obscurity, this *roman à clef* aspect of the novel soon lost its appeal. A more important reason for the book's immediate success is that it perfectly captured the mood and style of the American artistic and intellectual exiles who drank, loved, and searched for meaning on the Paris Left Bank in the aftermath of that first world struggle.

The overall theme of *The Sun Also Rises* is indicated by Ernest Hemingway's two epigraphs. Gertrude Stein's comment that "you are all a lost generation" suggests the ambiguous and pointless lives of Hemingway's exiles as they aimlessly wander about the Continent drinking, making love, and traveling from place to place and party to party. The quote from Ecclesiastes, which gives the novel its title, implies a larger frame of reference, a sense of permanence, order, and value. If the activities of the characters seem to justify the former quotation, their search for new meanings to replace the old ones— or at least to enable them to deal with that loss—demonstrates their desire to connect with the latter one.

Early in the novel the hero, Jake Barnes, declines to kiss Georgette, a prostitute, on the grounds that he is "sick." "Everybody's sick. I'm sick too," she responds. This sickness motif is opposed in another early conversation Jake has, this one with Count Mippipopolous, a most vivid minor character, who tells him "that is the secret. You must get to know the values." The search for values and the willingness to pay the price, first to acquire them and then to live by them, are what separates Hemingway's exiles, at least some of them, from simple, pointless hedonism.

At the center of this search for values is the Hemingway hero, Jake Barnes. As in all of Hemingway's important fictions, *The Sun Also Rises* is a novel of education—of learning to live with the conditions faced.

Jake's problem is complicated by his war injury. Having been emasculated in combat, Jake's "affair" with Lady Brett Ashley takes on a comical aspect— as he himself freely admits. Hemingway, however, has a very serious intention: Jake's wound is a metaphor for the condition of the entire expatriate group. They have all been damaged in some fundamental way by the war—physically, morally, psychologically, economically—and their aimless existence can be traced back to it. The real symbolic importance of Jake's wound, however, is that it has deprived him of the capacity to perform sexually, but it has not rid him of the desire. The people in *The Sun Also Rises* fervently want meaning and fulfillment, but they lack the ability and equipment to find it.

The heroes in Hemingway's major works learn the values in two ways: through their own actions and by contact with other characters who already know them. These exemplars understand the values either from long, hard experience, like Count Mippipopolous, or intuitively, automatically, like the bullfighter, Pedro Romero. Such heroes, however, never articulate these values; they only embody them in action. Indeed, once talked about, they become, in the Hemingway lexicon, spoiled. Jake's education can be most clearly seen in his relationship to three characters: Robert Cohn, Pedro Romero, and Lady Brett Ashley.

Critics have speculated on why Hemingway begins the novel with a long discussion of Robert Cohn, a relatively minor character. The reason is simple: If it is hard to say exactly what the values *are*, it is easy to say what they *are not* and Robert Cohn embodies the old, false, romantic values that Hemingway is reacting against.

In the beginning, Jake feels that Cohn is "nice and awful," but tolerates and pities him as a case of "arrested development." By the end of the book, he thoroughly hates him. Cohn's flaws include a false sense of superiority— reinforced by his pugilistic skills—and a romantic attitude toward himself and his activities that distorts his relationship with everyone around him. To reinforce this false romanticism, Cohn alters reality to suit his preconceptions. Falling in love with Brett, he refuses to see her realistically but idealizes her. When she spends a weekend with him, because she thinks it would be good for him, he treats it as a great affair and demands the rights of a serious lover, striking out at all the other men who approach her. In short, Cohn's false perception of reality and his self-romanticization underscore his chief fault, the cardinal sin in Hemingway's view: Cohn refuses to "pay his bill."

Cohn's romantic self-image is finally destroyed by the book's exemplar, the bullfighter Pedro Romero. After being introduced to Brett by Jake, Romero becomes enamored of her, and they go off together. Affronted that Brett has been taken from him, Cohn reacts predictably and forces the young man into a prolonged fistfight. Although totally outmanned as a boxer, Romero refuses to give in to Cohn. After absorbing considerable punishment, Romero, by sheer will, courage, and endurance, rallies to defeat and humiliate his opponent. His romantic bubble deflated, Cohn bursts into tears and fades from the novel.

It is appropriate that Cohn's false values be exposed by Pedro Romero, because his example is also central to the educations of both Jake and Brett. As an instinctively great bullfighter, Romero embodies the values in action and especially in the bullring. In a world bereft of religious certainties, Hemingway saw the bullfighter's performance as an aesthetic ceremony which substituted for obsolete religious ritual. Without transcendental meanings, man's dignity must come from the manner in which he faces his certain destiny; the bullfighter, who repeatedly does so by choice, was, for Hemingway, the supreme modern hero, providing he performs with skill, precision, style, and without falsity (that is, making it look harder or more dangerous than it really is). Shortly before the bullfight, Jake's group watches the local citizenry run with the bulls down the main street of the town. They see one man gored to death from behind. The following day, that same bull is presented to Romero, and he kills it perfectly by standing directly in front of it as he drives home his sword. This obvious symbolism states in a single image the most important of all the values, the need to confront reality directly and honestly.

It is not only Pedro's example that helps to educate Jake but also Jake's involvement in the Brett-Romero affair. His role as intermediary is the result of his would-be romance with her. They have long been in love and deeply frustrated by Jake's funny-sad war injury. Yet, despite the impossibility of a meaningful relationship, Jake can neither accept Brett as a friend nor cut himself off from her—although he knows that such a procedure would be the wisest course of action. She can, therefore, only be a temptress to him; she is quite accurate when she refers to herself as Circe.

The only time in the book when Jake feels whole and happy is when he and Bill Gorton take a fishing trip at Bayonne. There, in a world without women, they fish with skill and precision, drink wine, naturally chilled in the stream, instead of whiskey, relate to the hearty exuberance of the Basque peasantry, and feel serene in the rhythms of nature; but once they return and Jake meets Brett at San Sebastian, his serenity is destroyed.

Jake puts his group up at a hotel owned by Montoya, an old friend and the most honored bullfighting patron. Montoya is an admirer and accepts Jake as a true aficionado, that is, one who truly understands and appreciates bullfighting not only with his intellect but also with his whole being, his *passion*. Montoya even trusts Jake to the point of asking advice about the handling of this newest, potentially greatest young bullfighter, Pedro Romero. When Jake presents Brett to Pedro, fully understanding the implications of his act, he violates his trust with Montoya. His frustrated love for Brett exposes Pedro to her potentially corrupting influence. Jake's realization of his own weakness in betraying Romero, plus the fact that it has cost him his aficionado status, leaves him a sadder, wiser Hemingway hero.

Pedro, however, is not destroyed, because Brett sends him away before she can do any damage—yet, more than simple altruism is involved in her decision. Life with Pedro held the possibility of wholeness for her—as it held the possibility of dissipation for him. By sending him away, she relinquishes her last chance for health and happiness rather than risk damaging her lover.

Whether or not Jake's insights and Brett's final moral act give meaning to the lives of these exiles is problematical. During their Bayonne fishing trip, Jake's friend Bill Gorton sings a song about "pity and irony," and that seems to be the overall tone of the book, and especially of the ending: pity for the personal anguish and aimless searching of these people, but ironic detachment toward characters whose lives and situations are, at best, at least as comical as they are tragic.

SURRY OF EAGLE'S-NEST

Type of work: Novel
Author: John Esten Cooke (1830–1886)
Type of plot: Historical romance
Time of plot: 1861–1863
Locale: Virginia
First published: 1866

Principal characters:
LIEUTENANT COLONEL SURRY, the narrator
MAY BEVERLEY, later his wife
COLONEL MORDAUNT, an embittered, melancholy planter
FENWICK, his enemy
MRS. PARKINS, Fenwick's confederate
HARRY SALTOUN, a young officer and Mordaunt's son
VIOLET GRAFTON, an orphan
ACHMED, Mordaunt's Arab companion
GENERAL STONEWALL JACKSON
GENERAL J. E. B. STUART
GENERAL TURNER ASHBY
MAJOR JOHN PELHAM
CAPTAIN WILLIAM D. FARLEY, a Confederate scout

The Story:

Cavalier Philip Surry, who rode and fought under Prince Rupert in the English Civil War, escaped to Virginia when King Charles I was beheaded. Establishing a home, which he named Eagle's-Nest, on the Rappahannock River below Port Royal, he enjoined in his will that the oldest son of the family in each generation should sign himself "Surry of Eagle's-Nest."

The present Surry, who had attended the Virginia Military Institute for one session and had studied law at the University of Virginia, was in Richmond in April, 1861, when the State Convention passed its ordinance of secession. One evening at the Capitol Square, he saw with rapture a beautiful girl, whose dropped handkerchief contained the initials, M.B. On another day, in Hollywood Cemetery, he witnessed by chance a duel between a tall, bronzed stranger named Mordaunt and Fenwick, the encounter ending when Mordaunt put a pistol bullet through Fenwick's lungs. Surry left Richmond the proud recipient of a captain's commission in the Provisional Army of Virginia, and in his new gray uniform, he rode toward Harper's Ferry for duty under Colonel Jackson.

Losing his way in the Wilderness, which bordered the Rapidan River, he spent a night in a house where dwelt an insane woman in white, still possessing traces of youthful beauty, who was attended by her lovely young cousin,

Violet Grafton, and by a harridan, Mrs. Parkins. Surprisingly there appeared at this house Fenwick, whose duel wound had not been fatal. In the night, the "White Lady," tiptoeing into Surry's room, slipped into his coat pocket a package bearing the words, "Read these when I am dead—and remember . . . Your own Frances."

Further, while en route to Harper's Ferry, Surry was overtaken by a hurricane in a forest and was knocked from his horse by a large limb. He was stunned and his arm was broken. A female equestrian, whom the flying branches had spared, ordered her servant to take the injured man to her father's home, "The Oaks." There he convalesced under the eyes of Colonel Beverley and his daughter May, his rescuer and the owner of the handkerchief which he had picked up in Richmond. Surry's heart was fully captivated, but May was already bound by a between-fathers contract and a young-girl engagement to Frederick Baskerville. The fact that her new lover knew Baskerville to be a scoundrel made Surry's plight doubly bitter.

Fairly near "The Oaks" was the home of Mordaunt, which Surry visited. Its owner, who lived hermitlike with Achmed, a faithful Arab, was destined to become one of Surry's best friends. Mordaunt's air of melancholy indicated the gentleman's deeply tragic past.

After long delays, Captain Surry finally reported for duty to Colonel Thomas J. Jackson, who made him an aide-de-camp. Shortly afterward, the young staff officer met Colonel J. E. B. Stuart. The two colonels, soon to become generals, would be Surry's idols to the end of his days.

Before their first battle, Surry and Mordaunt, now a Confederate colonel, saw an eerie night burial in the garden of a stone house at Manassas. They observed on the scene Fenwick, the Parkins woman, and Violet Grafton. The dead person was the insane White Lady of the Wilderness. Again Mordaunt tried to kill Fenwick, but without success. Soon afterward, Surry delivered to Violet Grafton the package which her cousin had put in his pocket.

Wounded in the Battle of First Manassas, Surry was taken to the Fitzhugh home, "Elm Cottage," where he was well nursed. Mrs. Fitzhugh, charmed by Violet Grafton, gave the orphan girl a home.

In 1862, having recovered from his wound, Surry was with Jackson throughout his spectacular Valley Campaign and held General Turner Ashby in his arms when that "Knight of the Valley" expired on the battlefield. Briefly a prisoner, he met Sir Percy Wyndham, an Englishman wearing Federal blue. He also met and admired Captain Farley of Stuart's staff, an extraordinary scout. When Jackson joined General Lee near Richmond to defeat McClellan, Surry shared in that campaign; then he was back near Fredericksburg, in the Wilderness area.

There one night, peering through a window shutter at the house where he had first seen the White Lady and Violet Grafton, Surry heard Fenwick, while intoxicated, acknowledge himself to be a Yankee spy. Moreover, Fenwick reviewed to Mrs. Parkins the story of his and Mordaunt's enmity. Years before, Mordaunt and Fenwick, youthful friends, had become rivals for the love of Frances Carleton. When she married Mordaunt, Fenwick planned revenge. Still posing as a devoted friend, he utilized a trip of Mordaunt's to London to forge a letter which made Frances believe that her husband had landed in New York and was requesting her to let Fenwick escort her there to meet him. Aided by the easily bribed Mrs. Parkins, Fenwick abducted his friend's wife to Maryland, where she gave birth to a son, who was afterward reported dead, and where she contracted a fever which permanently affected her brain. Imitating Frances Carleton Mordaunt's handwriting, Fenwick perpetrated another forgery which duped Mordaunt into believing that his wife had forsaken him. Embittered, the young husband left Virginia for a long sojourn in Arabian lands. After drunken Fenwick's remarkable disclosure, Surry captured him, but the prisoner escaped after bribing a guard. At a later date, however, in a face-to-face combat, Mordaunt pinned his enemy to a tree with a thrust of his sword.

Surry, who, as the war continued, rose to be major and later lieutenant colonel, saw old Stonewall Jackson, Longstreet, and Lee defeat Pope at Second Manassas. In the Maryland campaign that followed, he was captured, interviewed by McClellan, and placed aboard a prison train headed for Baltimore; but he escaped by jumping through a window while the train was in motion. In December, 1862, he was present when Lee's two corps under Longstreet and Jackson repulsed Burnside at Fredericksburg. There he saw the youthful artillery genius, Major John Pelham, master-maneuver his guns. An ardent friendship between Surry and Pelham continued until the gallant young Alabaman was killed in battle.

The spring of 1863 brought Surry abundant joy. When Colonel Beverley's wealth at "The Oaks" was destroyed by invading armies, Frederick Baskerville lost interest in May so completely that he released her from her engagement. Consequently she married Surry, with her father's sanction.

Among Surry's friends was Harry Saltoun, a young Confederate lieutenant from Maryland. Fenwick, who repeatedly recovered from seemingly mortal wounds, by means of a lying anonymous letter, provoked Saltoun to challenge Colonel Mordaunt to a duel. Tragedy was averted, however, when Violet Grafton sent Mordaunt the paper in which the White Lady, Mrs. Frances Carleton Mordaunt, had recorded the whole truth about Fenwick and his evil deceptions. Also, through an affidavit of a Maryland woman, Harry Saltoun was proved to be Mordaunt's own son.

Fenwick's ultimate villainy was the abduction of Violet Grafton, but Mordaunt's devoted Arab companion, Achmed, trailed the knave to his hiding place. There Mordaunt and Fenwick had their final fight, but it was Achmed, not Mordaunt, who killed Fenwick with a gleaming dagger. Sadly, however, a ball from the dying villain's pistol wounded Achmed, who died in the presence of the two persons whom he loved, Mordaunt and Violet Grafton.

"Fighting Joe" Hooker, who had succeeded Burnside as commander of the Federal army of invasion, thrust at Lee in the Wilderness, on the south side of the Rapidan and Rappahannock rivers. In a brilliantly conceived surprise movement, Stonewall Jackson struck Hooker's right flank at Chancellorsville, to win a thrilling victory. This Southern triumph was dearly bought, for in the woods, on the night of May 2, 1863, Jackson was wounded by his own men, and on Sunday, May 10, that irreplaceable hero breathed his last.

Surry of Eagle's-Nest survived to tell his story and that of the war years. For him, only the ghosts of the past remained.

Critical Evaluation:

Surry of Eagle's-Nest remains of interest primarily as a romanticized version of John Esten Cooke's firsthand experiences as a Confederate officer during the Civil War—an ordeal that ranged from participation in the First Manassas to the final surrender at Appomattox Court House. While Cooke served primarily as a staff officer with J. E. B. Stuart's cavalry, he numbered Stonewall Jackson, Robert E. Lee, and other high-ranking Confederates among his personal acquaintances. Cooke published military biographies of Jackson (1863 and 1866) and of Lee (1871).

On the whole, *Surry of Eagle's-Nest*, a product of six weeks' work, is an uneven attempt to blend historical fact and fiction. The novel climaxes with a romanticized account of Stonewall Jackson's death in 1863, and, in its historical aspects, the novel draws upon the author's earlier military biographies of Jackson (just as *Mohun*, 1869, the sequel to *Surry of Eagle's-Nest*, parallels Cooke's later biography of Robert E. Lee). In *Surry of Eagle's-Nest*, Cooke merely combined the fictional trappings of conventional historical romance with real wartime events and experiences. The highly melodramatic aspects of the novel, particularly the purely Gothic subplot of the antagonists Mordaunt and Fenwick and the often confusing integration of historical and fictional characters, render the work less satisfactory than *The Virginia Comedians* (1854), Cooke's most successful historical romance. Cooke's idealization of antebellum Southern society and his acceptance of the myth of Cavalier origins of the Virginia aristocracy are also more prevalent in *Surry of Eagle's-Nest* than in his previous work. The novel was one of the earliest and most important contributions to the myth of the "Lost Cause" in the postwar South.

The novel, first published in 1866, found a receptive audience among celebrants of the "Lost Cause," and it has remained one of the most popular of Cooke's historical romances. Along with *Mohun*, *Surry of Eagle's-Nest* ranks as the best of Cooke's war novels, but neither possesses the unity or literary quality earlier achieved in *The Virginia Comedians*.

SWALLOW BARN

Type of work: Novel
Author: John P. Kennedy (1795–1870)
Type of plot: Comedy of manners
Time of plot: Early nineteenth century
Locale: Virginia
First published: 1832

> *Principal characters:*
> MARK LITTLETON, the narrator
> NED HAZARD, his cousin
> FRANK MERIWETHER, Ned's brother-in-law
> MR. ISAAC TRACY, a gentleman farmer
> BEL TRACY, his daughter
> HARVEY RIGGS, a Tracy kinsman

The Story:

After receiving many invitations from his cousin Ned Hazard, Mark Littleton at last felt that he could no longer put off a visit to Virginia. He left his mother and sisters in New York and began his journey south. At Swallow Barn, his cousin's home, Mark met or renewed acquaintance with a great many relatives and friends. Ned Hazard's sister had married Frank Meriwether, who was now the head of the family. The estate had been left to Ned. It had been heavily encumbered, and Frank had paid off the heaviest debts and put the plantation on a paying basis. The house was filled with Meriwether and Hazard relatives, all permanent guests. Some performed small functions as a pretense of paying their own way, but their tasks were no more than token duties kindly thought up for them so that they would feel useful.

Mark found life in Virginia restful and pleasant, for there was an unhurried rhythm about Swallow Barn that appealed to him. The plantation was filled with slaves and freed blacks who were fiercely loyal to Frank, a good master. Indeed, everyone loved Frank for his thoughtfulness and generosity. Mark's special favorite, however, was his cousin Ned Hazard. The two young men were inseparable companions. Ned was a man of excellent spirits, always indulging in pranks and jokes. Swallow Barn would one day revert to him, but he was content to let Frank use it as his own, wanting only to have a good time without the need of responsibilities. Ned took Mark on several excursions around the countryside and introduced him to local beauties of nature.

While Ned and Mark walked through the woods one day, they indulged in one of their favorite pastimes by singing their loudest, each trying to outdo the other. In one verse, Ned called out the name of Bel Tracy. He was deeply chagrined when that lady, having ridden up unnoticed, answered him. Bel

Tracy was the daughter of old Isaac Tracy, master of the neighboring estate, The Brakes. Ned's confusion at being discovered by Bel made Mark think that his cousin felt more than friendship for her. She teased him gently about his boisterous use of her name, leaving Ned stammering in confusion. Bel was accompanied by her sister and Harvey Riggs, a Tracy kinsman. Harvey joined in the teasing, but Mark saw at once that it was good-natured teasing and that Harvey felt great friendship for Ned.

The two parties went back to Swallow Barn, where Harvey delivered a letter from Mr. Tracy to Frank Meriwether. The subject matter was of long standing, and it afforded Frank some amusement. For many years, Mr. Tracy had imagined himself in possession of one hundred acres of marshland separating The Brakes from Swallow Barn. Every court in Virginia had denied his claim, but the old gentleman was adamant. Frank would long since have given him the land, for it was worthless, but he knew the old gentleman would be lost without the affair, which provided him with mental activity as he plotted ways to get possession of the land. In his letter, Mr. Tracy suggested that he and Frank let their lawyers go over the matter again, the two disputants to abide by the legal decision. Frank planned to ask his lawyer to arrange matters so that Mr. Tracy would win the suit after what looked like a difficult legal maneuver.

Old Mr. Tracy was a detriment to Ned, even though Ned loved the old gentleman. He was a gentleman of the old school, dignified and sober; Ned, on the other hand, could not repress his merry spirits. Bel, however, had absorbed some of her father's dignity and was usually not very receptive to Ned's foolishness. The poor young man tried hard to change, but his disposition was almost as firm as Mr. Tracy's.

After Ned had admitted to Mark that he loved Bel, the two friends mapped out a campaign to win her heart to Ned's cause. Their plans were temporarily postponed, however, by the arrival of the lawyers who would decide the disputed land claim.

The legal gentlemen afforded the young men much entertainment, one being a dandy known throughout Virginia. He was pursued by two of the maiden relatives, each of whom pretended to be pursued by him. When the dandy learned of their intentions, he finished his business and departed as quickly as possible. The settling of the suit gave everyone but old Mr. Tracy a lot of amusement. Because he was serious about the whole matter, Ned lost more ground in his suit when he unwittingly made light of the affair. It took a great deal of clever legal terminology to fool the old man, but at last he was awarded the land and convinced that justice had been done.

Sometimes Ned, Mark, and the others found entertainment in listening to the tales of goblins and ghosts told by old slaves on the plantation. The two families frequently gave large dinner parties, when the whole community would be invited to come and spend the day. Mark, thinking he would find it hard ever to return to New York and his own family, hoped to stay long enough to help Ned in his courtship of Bel. At one of the parties, Ned had a little wine and became more boisterous than ever, causing Bel to lose the esteem she had gradually been developing for him. He gained her good will once more by finding her pet falcon which had flown away, but later he lost her affection by engaging in a fistfight with a town bully. Harvey Riggs, joining Mark in attempts to help Ned with his suit, told Bel that Ned had fought the bully because the ruffian had cast slurs on her father. Pity at last entered Bel's heart, and she treated her suitor with more favor.

Mark at last left Virginia and went home to New York. Some months later, he learned that Ned had been successful; Bel had married him on New Year's Day. Ned wrote too that it was as Frank had feared. Old Mr. Tracy was sorry the land suit was settled and wished to open it again. Without the pending suit, he felt like a man who had lost an old and faithful friend.

Critical Evaluation:

Although John Pendleton Kennedy states definitely that *Swallow Barn* is not a novel, it is usually listed as such because of the continuous thread or theme running through it. In reality the book is a series of sketches or dramatic episodes concerned with plantation life and manners in Virginia during the early eighteenth century, sketches held together by a continuity of characters and events. *Swallow Barn*, the first work of popular fiction to be set in Virginia, was the forerunner of a large number of novels dealing with the historic background of that state.

Had Kennedy approached literature as a profession rather than an avocation, he might have become one of America's most important nineteenth century writers; but he felt his first obligation was to his career, initially as a lawyer in Baltimore, where his second marriage allied him firmly to the business community, and, subsequently, in the face of growing political and sectional unrest, as a man of public affairs, serving terms in the Maryland House of Delegates, the United States House of Representatives, and as the Secretary of the Navy. In between legal, business, and political commitments, he managed to write three very different novels: *Swallow Barn*; *Horseshoe Robinson* (1835), a historical novel about the Revolutionary War in South Carolina; and *Rob of the Bowl* (1838), a "Cavalier Romance" of Colonial Maryland. In addition, he wrote numerous essays, satires, and miscellaneous writings.

For all his lightness of touch, Kennedy had very serious motives in the writing of all of his literary efforts, especially in *Swallow Barn*. Having become progressively alarmed by the growing national tension and disunity, Kennedy hoped that this realistic, yet sympathetic portrait of Southern society might foster harmony by stimulating understanding.

In its own time, *Swallow Barn* was highly praised for its Realism, but

Kennedy's vision of the Old Dominion seems romanticized; indeed, the book's primary interest for a modern reader lies in the fact that it was the novel in which the "myth" of the old plantation South was first fictionalized. This atmosphere of serenity and pastoral elegance, described with affection and gentle, humorous irony, is based on a fixed, secure society without major social or political problems. In *Swallow Barn*, the most serious issue revolves around how to give away one hundred worthless acres in a manner that will not hurt the recipient's feelings. This uncomplicated vision of things was not, as Kennedy freely admitted, an unbiased one. The author carefully keeps the conflicts in the background—but he also makes sure they are there.

The primary conflict was, of course, the issue of slavery. The slaves at Swallow Barn and The Brakes conform to the plantation myth stereotype; they are well-treated, contented, amusing, and affectionate. At the same time, Kennedy acknowledges the basic injustice of the system. Far from being a Southern apologist, he was a mild Abolitionist, feeling slavery to be both immoral and inefficient, and he remained a Unionist throughout the Civil War. As a Southerner living in the midst of the situation, however, he saw and felt the complexity of the issue, and probably expressed his own sentiments through Frank Meriwether, who stated that it is wrong to keep slaves, but:

> We should not be justified in taking the hazard of internal convulsions to get rid of them; nor have we a right, in the desire to free ourselves, to whelm them in greater evils than their present bondage. A violent removal of them, or a general emancipation, would assuredly produce one or the other of these calamities.

To his own personal sorrow, Kennedy lived to see the worst of his expectations realized.

TALES OF SOLDIERS AND CIVILIANS

Type of work: Short stories
Author: Ambrose Bierce (1842–1914?)
First published: 1891

Ambrose Bierce wrote volumes of acid, satirical prose in his long career as a journalist and even managed to get a somewhat pretentious twelve-volume edition of his collected works published. Most of it, because of its time-bound nature, was doomed to oblivion by the time the edition appeared. The work that continues and promises to survive is the collection of short stories titled *Tales of Soldiers and Civilians*. Bierce's literary reputation rests essentially on this book.

The bland title of this collection stands in ironic contrast to the vision of life that informs the stories themselves. Indeed, Bierce seems to have striven for bland, noncommittal titles to most of his stories. Titles like "Chickamauga," "An Occurrence at Owl Creek Bridge," and "The Mocking-Bird" tell little of the macabre nature of these tales. Bierce seems to have chosen his mild titles with deliberate irony.

When this volume was reprinted in 1898, it was given a more meaningful title, *In the Midst of Life*. The irony is more obvious and more indicative of the true content of the book: in the midst of life is death.

Death is the sole absolute of this book, the common denominator of each story, and the final proposition in a logic of ruthless necessity. Each protagonist is part of a greater logic; each is subordinate to the plot, and each is cursed. Death is separated from life, is raised up as a separate principle antagonistic to life, and becomes an entity in its own right. Death is seen as a hostile specter, rather than a normal process of life. As such, Death seeks to conquer life rather than aid it. Death then becomes an inevitable victor that "has all seasons for his own," as Bierce was fond of remarking.

Against such a powerful antagonist, the heroes become victims in a web of cruel necessity, shadow figures drawn into the Valley of the Shadow; and as such, they are depicted with sharp, relentless strokes. Bierce's heroes are essentially lonely men who derive their reality from the fear they experience. These men are cursed and driven by the logic of their curse. Their strongest motivation is fear, an all-pervasive anxiety that frequently annihilates them. The success of each story depends on its ability to arouse this same fear in the reader.

In consequence, Bierce places a great value on courage, fearlessness in the face of death. He is acute enough, however, to see that courage is not so much fearlessness as it is a greater fear overcoming a lesser fear, in most cases a fear of dishonor overcoming a fear of death. Courage, then, is the faith that one's honor is more important than one's life. Frequently the heroes

Bierce admires court death with an awesome recklessness. His heroes are inevitably damned. There is no escape, no transcendence, and no salvation from the macabre situations into which they are drawn. Their dooms are inescapable facts; but the measure of their manhood is expressed in how they meet death.

Bierce's vision of life is fatalistic, but there is more to it than that. Avenging Furies hover about his stories, but they are not the same Furies that haunted Orestes. Bierce is nihilistic, but inevitably there is a macabre humor in his nihilism. The acid, satirical touch that colors the rest of Bierce's work is present here as well. Bierce's Furies are diabolical jesters, who love irony more than they love the wretched human spirit. His Furies are divine practical jokers, who drum "Dixie" and "John Brown's Body" on the human skull for laughs. One can scarcely tell whether the shriek one senses in Bierce's prose is that of humor or horror.

Bierce's grotesque wit serves as a relief from the horror of his situations. A related technique that serves the same purpose is his ironic stance, one which removes him from the petty human scene and separates him from the terror of his heroes. Bierce assumes a godlike attitude that determines the objective nature of his prose. He uses a naturalistic style that is precise in diction, spare in depiction, ironic in narration.

In effect, Bierce takes on the cruel role of the Furies in narrating his stories, and the tone of his prose is frigid, caustic, and inhuman. Yet it is precisely this emotional sterility, this godlike irony, that makes his stories so powerfully chilling. If, for example, Bierce were to sympathize with his heroes, readers would have pathos rather than terror. The very lack of an appropriate emotional response in the narration stimulates to an excessive degree the proper emotional response in the reader. The fact that Bierce himself was caustic, cruel, and sharp, demanding perfection of his fellow human beings, admirably served his limited artistic abilities and enabled him to focus his talent on evoking both terror and humor.

Tales of Soldiers and Civilians is divided into two parts, as the title suggests. There are the war stories and the mystery stories, and each type develops Bierce's vision of life in a different literary direction. The war tales anticipate Hemingway, while the civilian stories anticipate modern horror-tale writers like H. P. Lovecraft.

Beyond a doubt, Bierce reached his artistic peak in the soldier tales. War stories provided the perfect medium for someone of his character and experience. First of all, Bierce had served in the Civil War and undoubtedly his stories draw much of their vigor and reality from first-hand experience. His depiction of various battles and their effects have an unmistakable aura of reality. His description of war is hauntingly vivid and stands in marked contrast to the maudlin accounts given in the vast bulk of Civil War writings.

Secondly, war tales provided an acceptable outlet for his obsessions with fear, courage, and death. These leitmotifs could be presented naturally in tales of soldiers. Since war abounds in abnormal situations, Bierce could write naturally about a twin killing his twin, about a son killing his father, and about an artillery man killing his wife. In the context of their stories, these plots become necessary accidents, part of some divine causality.

Thirdly, Bierce's naturalistic style was admirably suited to describing the limited vision of the soldier in war, a vision which is not permitted the luxury of feeling pity and which must avoid all contemplation. It is a vision, moreover, that must concentrate on immediate objectives and on carrying out specific orders.

Finally, the army subjugates individuals to the mass. Deeds of fear and courage are the only acts by which a soldier is individualized and judged. Bierce's characters draw their reality from the way they face death. Each hero undergoes an ordeal, which means death either for him or for someone close to him, and that test determines his character. Apart from that ordeal Bierce's characters are lifeless puppets dancing to a meretricious plot.

Bierce's war stories are his best. Nowhere else did he achieve such a perfect fusion of form and content, except perhaps in his aphorisms. In quality, the tales are superior to about ninety-nine percent of the short fiction that was being written during the nineteenth century in America. In many instances, they anticipate or rival Hemingway's stories. Actually, many points of comparison can be drawn between Bierce and Hemingway; both show obsession with fear, courage, and death; both use a crisp, ironic prose to communicate their vision; both were to find happy expression in stories of war; both present character tested through some ordeal; and both possess a cruel and evocative power—a power that at times gives their fiction a haunting quality as vivid as a nightmare.

Bierce's war tales, particularly "Chickamauga," "An Occurrence at Owl Creek Bridge," "One Kind of Officer," and "Killed at Resaca," are first-rate for what they attempt to do. His civilian stories, however, fall somewhat short of the high standards he achieved in his war tales.

The reason for this diminished quality is that Bierce attempted to impose on his stories of civilians the same vision of life that pervades his soldier tales, and the grafting was not always successful. Pictures of war provided the perfect literary vehicle for his outlook, since war abounds in pathological situations. When he tried to impose this vision on civilian reality, however, the imperfections of plot, the implausibilities, and the grotesqueness showed up much more glaringly. The trick endings came off much worse. The characters and plots never matched those of the war stories. To inject a pathological fear into stories about civilians requires great skill.

What Bierce succeeded in doing in these stories was to extend a relatively new prose genre, the short mystery tale. In this lesser genre, Bierce came off rather well when compared with later writers who created in this vein. His stories continue to hold their own in the anthologies.

That Bierce was neurotic is beside the point. Successful in turning his neuroses into fine artistic stories, he has few equals in suspense, evocative power, clarity, and irony.

TALES OF UNCLE REMUS

Type of work: Tales
Author: Joel Chandler Harris (1848–1908)
First published: 1880–1910

An old black man sits talking to a little boy in his cabin on a cotton plantation not far from Atlanta, Georgia. The Civil War has not yet been fought, and the old man, a slave, belongs to the family that owns the cabin, the big house a few yards away, and the fine plantation. His loyalty is boundless to the parents of the little boy, the lady he calls "Miss Sally" and her husband "Mars John." He has known them a long time, and he shares their memories of earlier times. Occasionally he speaks of those old days, but it is more usual for him to tell of times far more distant, when "my great-grandaddy's great-grandaddy live nex' door ter whar ol' Grandaddy Cricket live at" or of "one time, way back yander, 'fo' you wuz borned, honey, en 'fo' Mars John er Miss Sally wuz borned—way back yander 'fo' enny un us wuz borned." When he talks to the little boy who sits beside him (and years later to the son of the first little boy), both he and his listener move in imagination into legendary eras which have no calendar dates and need none: The stories that Uncle Remus tells are drawn from the legends of many lands and ancient times.

Though Joel Chandler Harris wrote the tales of Uncle Remus, he laid no claim to having invented them. He looked upon himself as a mere recorder. A shy, modest, and somewhat diffident author who once described himself as a "cornfield journalist," Harris admitted, in the introduction to *Uncle Remus: His Songs and His Sayings* (1880), his indebtedness to the blacks from whom he heard the tales. In a later volume, *Nights with Uncle Remus* (1883), he gave credit not only to the Georgia blacks but also to the many correspondents who, having enjoyed his first Uncle Remus book, had supplied him with material which he embodied in later stories.

Harris was not certain where the Uncle Remus tales originated. Readers curious about possible origins may consult the introductions to the two volumes cited above and a number of articles listed in Lewis Leary's *Articles on American Literature, 1900–1950* (1954). Old tales like those told by Uncle Remus in the middle-Georgia black dialect and by his less-known friend Daddy Jake in the Gullah dialect of the coastal areas of South Carolina and Georgia have been found in Africa, Europe, South America, and the Orient.

Questions of origin are for specialists, however, not for lovers of the tales themselves. There are clear resemblances between the characters and the simple plots of many of the Uncle Remus tales and those in folktales from many nations. What gives these stories their special appeal is not their content but the manner in which they are told. (Mark Twain once wrote Harris: "In reality the stories are only alligator pears—one eats them merely for the sake of the dressing.") In addition, Uncle Remus himself is one of the most lovable characters in American literature. The sly humor of the old man, his pretended gruffness followed quickly by tender concern when he sees he has hurt the little boy's feelings, his ingenious parrying of the little boy's searching questions, his moralizing on the behavior of both children and adults, and his citing of ancient authority for the particular form of the tales ("de tale I give you like hit wer' gun to me")—all make him seem a very real person. Children see in him a kindly old man who loves to entertain children; to adults he is, in addition, a philosopher of life whose thoughts are based on close observation of people over many years. As to the origin of Uncle Remus, Harris replied when he was asked about it:

> He was not an invention of my own, but a human syndicate, I might say, of three or four old darkies whom I had known. I just walloped them together into one person and called him "Uncle Remus."

Though Brer Rabbit does not appear in all of the Uncle Remus tales, he is the hero of many of them. The reason was given by Harris in his first volume, when he said that ". . . it needs no scientific investigation to show why he [the Negro] selects as his hero the weakest and most harmless of all animals, and brings him out victorious in contests with the bear, the wolf, and the fox. It is not virtue that triumphs, but helplessness; it is not malice, but mischievousness." Moralists may complain that the mischievousness sometimes becomes cruelty and that Brer Rabbit is a remarkably accomplished liar, but to most adult readers, these would seem carping criticisms. Perhaps some of the children who have known the tales through three generations may have objected to a code of conduct in the tales which is very different from what they have been taught in Sunday School or at home. Most have probably thought that the world of Uncle Remus' animals and birds is simply a story world anyway, one in which many things seem all right that would not be so elsewhere. Even Uncle Remus suggests, now and then, that he does not entirely approve of what has been done in a certain tale, as when several terrapins have been used to make it seem that Brer Rabbit has lost his race with Brer Tarrypin, and the little boy objects, "But, Uncle Remus, that was cheating." The old man answers:

> Co'se, honey. De creeturs 'gun ter cheat, en den folks tuck it up, en hit keep on spreadin'. Hit mighty ketchin', en you min' yo' eye, honey, dat somebody don't cheat you 'fo' yo' ha'r get gray.

The black dialect of Uncle Remus presents a greater hindrance to readers today than it did when the tales first appeared. Even Southern black children have been known to ask in public libraries for a version of several of the tales simplified and "modernized." They complained that they could not understand the original tales. As the educational level rises for both whites and blacks in the Southern states and as Southern speech becomes more like that in other parts of the nation, the dialect of Uncle Remus may come to seem as foreign to Americans as the Scottish dialect of Burns, and perhaps not much more comprehensible than Chaucer's English. Uncle Remus' tales are essentially oral ones, and they are best when read aloud; but if future readers come upon the stories without ever having heard anyone talk like Uncle Remus, they will find it difficult to imagine the sounds, the inflections, and the easy flow of the old man's words in such a passage as the following:

> You kin put yo' 'pennunce in ole Brer Rabbit. . . . He wuz dere, but he shuffle up kinder late, kaze w'en Miss Meadows en de balance un um done gone down ter de place, Brer Rabbit, he crope 'roun' ter de ash-hopper, en fill Brer Coon slippers full er ashes, en den he tuck'n put um on en march off. He got dar atter w'ile, en soon's Miss Meadows en de gals seed 'im, dey up'n giggle, en make a great 'miration kaze Brer Rabbit got on slippers. Brer Fox, he so smart, he holler out, he did, en say he lay Brer Rabbit got de groun'-eatch.

Another barrier to comprehension of the Uncle Remus tales by future readers has been pointed out by Jay B. Hubbell in *The South in American Literature, 1607–1900* (1954). American life has become increasingly urban in the last half century, and many children now grow up with scarcely any knowledge of the ways of animals like the rabbit, the fox, and the wolf, or of what life is like on a farm. It is true that Uncle Remus does make some allowance, in several tales in *Told by Uncle Remus* (1905), for the ignorance of the second little boy, who has lived in Atlanta and whose actions Uncle Remus frequently contrasts with those of the first little boy a generation earlier. But most of the tales were told to the first little boy, and Uncle Remus makes no explanation, for example, of the "spring-'ouse" that Brer Fox and Brer Rabbit put some butter in, or of what the "go'd er water" is that Brer Rabbit gives Brer B'ar to keep him from "stranklin'" after he has bit all the hair off Brer Possum's tail.

It is to be hoped, however, that the reading handicaps of dialectal spelling and strange words, or of the frequent use of terms from Southern farm life before it was transformed by mechanization and electrification, will not be strong enough to prevent future generations of American children and adults from relishing the story of Brer Rabbit's escape in "How Mr. Rabbit Was Too Sharp for Mr. Fox," from secretly rejoicing at "The Awful Fate of Mr. Wolf," or from joining in the merriment at "Brother Rabbit's Laughing Place."

TAPS FOR PRIVATE TUSSIE

Type of work: Novel
Author: Jesse Stuart (1907–1984)
Type of plot: Regional romance
Time of plot: Twentieth century
Locale: Kentucky
First published: 1943

> *Principal characters:*
> GRANDPA TUSSIE, head of the Tussie clan
> GRANDMA TUSSIE, his wife
> GEORGE TUSSIE, his brother
> UNCLE MOTT TUSSIE, his son
> UNCLE KIM TUSSIE, his deceased son
> AUNT VITTIE TUSSIE, Kim's wife
> SID SEAGRAVES TUSSIE, a grandson

The Story:

There was trouble at Grandpa Tussie's. In the coal shed behind the school-house where the Tussies lived, Uncle Kim's body was beginning to smell. Kim Tussie had been killed in the war. The government had sent his body home, and now the Tussie clan had gathered for the funeral. Kim's folks, Grandpa and Grandma Tussie, comforted Aunt Vittie, Kim's wife, who was screaming and wailing. Uncle Mott, Kim's brother, was telling how he had identified the body. Sid, Kim's young nephew, was just excited. There had not been so much going on since he could remember. The noise the Tussie kin made as they carried the coffin up the mountainside could not soon be forgotten by a young boy.

Uncle Kim had left Aunt Vittie ten thousand dollars in government insur-ance, and the day after the funeral, she rented the Rayburn mansion and filled it with new furniture, all ready for Grandpa and Grandma, Uncle Mott, and Sid to move in. It was the biggest and best house any of the Tussies had ever seen. Uncle Mott flicked the electric lights off and on all day. Sid used the bathroom over and over. Aunt Vittie bought them all new clothes to go with the house. To Sid it was all wonderful, but his happiness was spoiled a little when he realized Uncle Kim had to die in order for the rest of them to have that splendor.

The next few weeks were really a miracle in the lives of the Tussies. Grandpa continued to get his relief groceries, and Aunt Vittie bought more groceries at the store. Grandpa began to look for more of the Tussies to come when they heard about the money. Grandpa thought his brother George would be the first. Brother George had been married five times. He could play a fiddle till it made a man cry.

Grandpa was right. When George heard about the money, he decided to come home to die. Uncle Mott hoped that that time would come soon, but Aunt Vittie looked at George and smiled. George played his fiddle far into the night, playing tunes Aunt Vittie asked for, and Grandpa knew George had come to stay. Aunt Vittie bought George new clothes, too, and Uncle Mott began to look mean.

Then more Tussies came, first Uncle Ben, then Dee, then young Uncle Ben, then Starkie, then Watt, then Sabie, then Abe, all with their wives and young ones. The mansion was ready to burst. Only Grandpa knew them all. When Grandma counted forty-six of them, she would stand for no more.

The money began to go fast. Sid knew now why Grandpa and Grandma had not cried at Kim's funeral. They had known Aunt Vittie would get the money, and all the Tussies would live high. Brother George's fiddle playing had Aunt Vittie looking as she had never looked before. Uncle Mott was losing out, and he looked dangerous.

Grandpa knew things were bound to change. He was right. First the government man came and stopped their relief. It hurt Grandpa to lose his relief. He had had it for years and had expected it to go on forever. Then George Rayburn came to inspect his house. When he saw the floor full of nail holes, the broken windowpanes, the charcoal and pencil marks on the walls, he threatened to bring suit if the Tussies did not leave at once. The uncles, the brothers, and the cousins twice removed, however, refused to leave. It was not until Sheriff Whiteapple came with the law papers that they knew they were whipped. That night there was the grandest dance of all. Aunt Vittie kissed Brother George and then she kissed Uncle Mott, but not very hard. It looked as if George were winning.

The next day, the Tussies began to leave. Grandpa and Grandma, Aunt Vittie, Brother George, Uncle Mott, and Sid were the last to go. Aunt Vittie had bought fifty acres of land and an old shack with the last of her money, and she put the farm in Grandpa's name. They had no furniture, no sheets, no dishes, since Rayburn had attached everything to pay for damages to his house. There was only Grandpa's old-age pension check to look forward to. Uncle Mott and Brother George made a table and sapling beds and Sid found their old dishes in the gully by the old schoolhouse, and the Tussies began living as they had always lived.

Then came the worst blow of all. Someone had reported that Grandpa now owned land, and his old-age pension was stopped. Sometimes there was not enough to eat. Uncle Mott and George began to look dangerous. Sid knew bad trouble was coming. After Brother George and Vittie were married, Uncle Mott usually stayed in town, drinking bootleg and getting mean drunk.

Grandpa knew his time on earth was about up, but he felt something was going to happen that he did not want to miss, and he was right again. Uncle Mott came home from town one day and told them that he had found young Uncle Ben and Dee and had shot them for reporting Grandpa to the relief agency. As Uncle Mott talked, Brother George began to stroke his fiddle, and he played a note of death. Uncle Mott, cursing the fiddle for being the cause of all his trouble, shot the fiddle from George's hands. George drew his gun and shot Uncle Mott through the head.

Aunt Vittie had been to town, too, begging food for Grandpa and the rest, and now they saw her coming, walking close beside a strange man. That is, he was a stranger until he came nearer, and then they saw that it was Uncle Kim, who was supposed to be buried on the mountainside. When George saw the ghost, he went through the windowpane; but it was simple for Sheriff Whiteapple, when he came a little later, to follow his footprints in the snow.

After Kim had explained that he had not been killed after all, they began to understand what had happened. Uncle Mott had always wanted Aunt Vittie, and it had been easy for him to identify a body as Kim's. Kim told Sid that he was Aunt Vittie's son, that she had been wronged by a rich man who paid Kim to marry her, and that now Sid would be their son.

That night, it was as if nothing had happened, except for Uncle Mott's body in the shack. To Sid it was like a dream, but a dream with life in it. For the first time he began to feel really good. Peace had come to the Tussies.

Critical Evaluation:

Jesse Stuart, who came into sudden fame with his book of Kentucky poems, *Man with a Bull-Tongue Plow*, continued to use this familiar background in the series of novels and short stories that followed. Stuart displays a great understanding for the people about whom he writes in *Taps for Private Tussie*. In this novel of the Kentucky mountain people, the plot is unimportant; the characters are the story. Stuart's treatment of this region grows out of his deep familiarity with the place and its people.

Although it may seem on the surface no more than the comic tale of the determination of the shiftless Tussie family to survive without work, *Taps for Private Tussie*, on subtler levels, encompasses serious literary and social dimensions which justify its reputation as Stuart's best novel. Like Mark Twain and William Faulkner, with whom he shares a number of qualities, Stuart wrote in the tradition of the frontier humorists of the past century, employing the vernacular style and episodic form to record the unique characteristics and folk customs of a dying culture. Also, as in the works of Twain and Faulkner, death and violence are just below the comic surface in Stuart's novels, mitigating his comic vision with a sense of the tragic in life.

Shiftless and lazy though they are, the Tussies are more victims than victimizers, and the reader's sympathy for them is based on this fact. On one level, their determination not to work parodies the traditional independence of the mountaineer who called no man master. Yet, the tragic cost of this false freedom has been their traditional integrity and heritage—the loss of which is implicit in the Tussies' support of the county Democrats in return for welfare groceries. As they become increasingly dependent upon a destructive welfare system (and increasingly shiftless), only Grandpa Tussie, the benign old patriarch who holds the clan together, keeps alive the mountaineer's traditional love of the land.

Ironically, when Grandpa Tussie finally achieves his dream of owning a farm, the clan is much worse off than before, as they lose their welfare benefits but can no longer resume the life of independence and dignity the farm once offered. As Twain saw romanticism destroying the South, and as Faulkner linked its fall to the "curse" of slavery, Stuart seems to have prophesied in 1943 the threat modern welfare systems would become to the traditional world of his Southern Appalachians.

THE TENANTS OF MOONBLOOM

Type of work: Novel
Author: Edward Lewis Wallant (1926–1962)
Type of plot: Humorous psychological realism
Time of plot: Early 1960's
Locale: New York City
First published: 1963

Principal characters:

NORMAN MOONBLOOM, a real-estate agent for four apartment houses

IRWIN MOONBLOOM, his brother and the owner of the buildings

GAYLORD KNIGHT, the janitor

BODIEN, an unlicensed plumber

EVA, MINNA, and LESTER BAILEY, two doting aunts and a nephew

ARNOLD and BETTY JACOBY, an aged couple

MARVIN SCHOENBRUN, a fastidious homosexual

STANLEY KATZ and SIDONE, bohemian jazz musicians

SHERMAN and CAROL HAUSER, a couple approaching middle age

AARON and SARAH LUBLIN, Jewish refugees

BASELLECCI, an Italian teacher

JERRY WUNG, a Chinese beatnik

BEELER, an elderly widower

SHERYL, his daughter

KRAM, a hunchback and a photograph retoucher

WADE JOHNSON, a schoolteacher

LENI CASS, a divorcée

J. T. and MILLY LEOPOLD, a retired carpenter and his wife

ILSE MOELLER, a German emigrant

KARLOFF, a hundred-year-old Russian immigrant

SUGARMAN, a philosophical candy-butcher

JOE PAXTON, a black homosexual writer

DEL RIO, a boxer

LOUIE, a bachelor

JIM and JANE SPRAGUE, a young expectant couple

Published posthumously (Wallant died of an aneurysm in December, 1962, leaving this and another novel in manuscript), *The Tenants of Moonbloom* is a profoundly humorous novel centering its focus on an awakening that exhibits the intensities and accents of a religious conversion to human dignity without ever departing from the secular indignities of the human condition. The acerbities of its plot, the grotesquerie of its characterizations, and the slyness of its humor are the marks of Edward Lewis Wallant's special talent, one removed from the current fashionable modes of writing. Although he was Jewish and specifically concerned with the treatment of Jewish themes, he is not a "Jewish writer" in the same sense as Bernard Malamud or Philip Roth. Although his work traffics at the very heart of the Existentialist intersection, he cannot be categorized with Heller, Pynchon, or Donleavy as practitioners of "the absurd." *The Tenants of Moonbloom* falls between both camps, occupying its own lonely place. It is possible, paradoxically, that this achievement of solitude is also the rare achievement of art, and the novel may continue to live after many changes in literary fashions.

As Wallant's third novel, it represents a distinct technical development over his earlier work. In particular, the major structural crudities that marred *The Human Season*, in 1960, and *The Pawnbroker*, in 1961, have been eradicated or bypassed. *The Tenants of Moonbloom* folds itself tightly within the arch of Wallant's sure capacities as a novelist. He discards both the flashback techniques of the earlier novels and the limiting constriction within the reflecting consciousness of an older broken personality.

The focusing figure of this novel is Norman Moonbloom, the agent of the convulsed miseries and frustrations of the four apartment houses which he serves. At the beginning of the novel, he is one of the unliving, moving through life inside an envelope of secure detachment. He is a thirty-three-year-old virgin—both physically and psychologically—unawakened, unhurt, and unjoying. Around him whirls the heterogeneous constellation of grotesques that are the tenants of his houses. They are sordid, posturing, desperate in their pain, and humorous and dignified in the artifices they erect to ward off an acceptance of total squalor. Moonbloom moves through them week by week, collecting the rents, hearing their human cries like "the ear of God," but without heed, without life.

The action of the novel is basically a chronicling of Moonbloom's reveille; a crude violent violation of his detachment which forces him to bear witness, to become alive himself. Like the ear of God, he is privy to all the petty complaints and profound disclosures of his tenants, and he suddenly finds himself listening. The envelope has been burst; he is no longer asleep, he is ravished by the shock of existence. "Otherness" crushes him into the private being of selfhood, and he discovers that being is unbearable unless it is put to some work. Perhaps, he explains to himself, he is attempting to find a name for what is happening, as he undertakes the gargantuan renovation program of painting, rewiring, repairing, cleaning, and ordering the four buildings in his charge. Nor does he fool himself as to the efficacy or motives of his actions. The child of one couple accidentally strangles to death, one tenant attempts suicide, another dies. Moonbloom himself is successfully seduced by one of the tenants for a reduction in the rent. All of his paint and carpentry will not alter a deformed physique, a remembered betrayal, an impossibly frustrated desire. His struggle for cleanliness and physical decency is only secondarily for the benefit of the tenants; it is primarily a means to work himself on the new calendar of his becoming.

The renovation of both Moonbloom and the houses reaches a climax in the rebuilding and plastering of the toilet wall in Basellecci's room at the end of the novel. Basellecci, dying of incurable cancer, had earlier blamed his disease on the tumorous bathroom wall; however, medical reports pointed to the true cause: he had succumbed to severe depression. Fortified on Strega and vermouth, Moonbloom, the plumber, and the janitor remake the wall in a drunken transcendent choreography of pain and joy, finding in a community of laughter a human acceptance and antidote to the inhuman absurdity of man's fated condition. The grip of the cancer is not denied, nor is the human fraternity assured any but the barest duration, but the wall shines with white plaster and the remembrance of a sacred joy.

However rich in grotesque density and humor *The Tenants of Moonbloom* is (the effects of the remodeling of the houses will be to make their assessed valuation prohibitively higher than Moonbloom's brother can afford), the aims and achievements of the novel go far beyond its restricting grotesqueries. Wallant's Realism is psychological and introspective, not reportorial, and this Realism is at the service of an evocative overarch of symbolism. The search for a name to what is happening is as much a description of Wallant's own building attempts in the making of his novel as it is for Moonbloom laboring in the cumulative filth and disorder of his Augean tenements. The reader is inexorably drawn into Moonbloom's metaphor, himself forced to burst the barrier of detachment and work at his own psychic renewal. On this level, the novel scores a signal success; within the severe aesthetic limitations in which such a statement can be true, Wallant's readers all become tenants of Moonbloom, exposed to the raw slash of "otherness" and led to a perverse joy in their own augmented selfhood.

It has been fashionable for fiction to be ambiguous, problematical, contemptuous of traditional pieties, and irreverent in its embracement of absurdism as the irrational rationale for everything. These may all be legitimate positions from which to write novels, but they also avoid resolving questions posed in a work. Wallant faces directly each of the problems that emerges from his work. The absurd and the problematic figure in his novel as inescapable but not dominating elements. He is able to wrest a form out of the chaos of contemporary experiences which goes beyond a queasy burlesque nihilism, which accents human possibilites rather than niggling determinisms, and which communicates itself in the tones of a sacred laughter that is within the reach of the human voice and spirit.

TENDER IS THE NIGHT

Type of work: Novel
Author: F. Scott Fitzgerald (1896–1940)
Type of plot: Social criticism
Time of plot: 1920's
Locale: Europe
First published: 1934

Principal characters:
DICK DIVER, a psychologist
NICOLE, his wife
ROSEMARY HOYT, an actress
TOMMY BARBAN, a professional soldier

The Story:

Rosemary Hoyt was just eighteen, dewy fresh and giving promise of beautiful maturity. In spite of her youth, she was already a famous actress, and her film *Daddy's Girl* was all the rage. She had come to the south of France with her mother for a rest. Rosemary needed relaxation, for she had been very ill after diving repeatedly into a Venetian canal during the shooting of her picture.

At the beach she met Dick Diver, and suddenly she realized that she was in love. After she became well acquainted with the Divers, she liked Diver's wife Nicole, too. Nicole was strikingly beautiful, and her two children complemented her nicely. Rosemary's mother also approved of Dick. When Rosemary attended one of the Divers' famous parties, she told Dick outright that she loved him, but he made light of her declaration.

During the party, Mrs. McKisco saw Nicole behaving hysterically in the bathroom, and on the way home, she tried to talk about it. Tommy Barban, a war hero, made her keep silent. Resenting Tommy's interference, Mr. McKisco provoked a quarrel with him. The quarrel ended in a duel in which several shots were exchanged but no one was hurt. Rosemary was greatly moved by the occurrence.

Rosemary traveled to Paris with the Divers and went on a round of parties and tours with them. Often she made advances to Dick. He refused, apathetically, until one day a young college boy told of an escapade in which Rosemary had been involved, and then Dick began to desire the young girl. Although their brief love affair was confined to furtive kisses in hallways, Nicole became suspicious.

Abe North, a brawling composer, offended two blacks and involved a third.

While Dick was in Rosemary's hotel room, Abe brought one of the black men to ask Dick's help in straightening up the mess. When Dick took Abe to his own room, the black stayed in the corridor. The two other black men killed him and laid the body on Rosemary's bed. When the body was found, Dick carried it into the hall and took Rosemary's bedspread into his bathtub to wash it out. Seeing the bloody spread, Nicole broke down and in an attack of hysteria accused Dick of many infidelities. Her breakdown was like the one Mrs. McKisco had previously seen in the bathroom at the party.

Some years before, Dick had been doing research in advanced psychology in Zurich. One day in the clinic he had met a pathetic patient, beautiful young Nicole Warren. Attracted to her professionally at first, he later learned the cause of her long residence in the clinic.

Nicole came from a wealthy Chicago family. When she was eleven, her mother died, and her father became very close to her. After an incestuous relationship with him, she suffered a breakdown. Her father, too cowardly to kill himself as he had planned, had put her in the clinic at Zurich. For many reasons, Dick became Nicole's tower of strength; with him she was almost normal. Finally, motivated by pity and love, Dick married her. For a time, he was able to keep her from periodic schizophrenic attacks, and the marriage seemed to be a success, aided by the fact that Nicole's family was rich; so rich, in fact, that Nicole's older sister was able to buy Dick a partnership in the clinic where Dick had first met Nicole.

For some time after the episode involving Rosemary, Nicole was quite calm but too withdrawn. Then a neurotic woman wrote her a letter accusing Dick of misdeeds with his women patients. The letter was the working of a diseased mind, but Nicole believed what the writer said and had another relapse. She left her family at a country fair and became hysterical while riding on the ferris wheel.

At one time, Dick had shown great promise as a writer and as a psychologist. His books had become standard, and among his colleagues, he was accounted a genius. It seemed, however, that after Nicole's hysterical fit on the ferris wheel, he could do little more real work. One reason was that Nicole was growing so wealthy that Dick did not have to work. At age thirty-eight, he was still a handsome and engaging man, but he began to drink heavily.

On several occasions, Nicole was shamed by her husband's drunken behavior. She did her best to make him stop; in so doing, she began to gain moral strength of her own. For the first time since the long stay at the clinic, she gradually came to have an independent life apart from Dick's influence.

Dissatisfied with the life he was leading, Dick decided to go away by himself for a while. He ran into Tommy Barban, still a reckless, strong, professional soldier. Tommy had just had a romantic escape from Russia. While still absent from his wife, Dick received word that his father had died.

Going back to America was for him a nostalgic experience. His father had been a gentle clergyman, living a narrow life; but his life had had roots, and he was buried among his ancestors. Dick had been away so long, had lived for so many years a footless, unfettered life, that he almost determined to remain in America.

On the way back to meet his family, Dick stopped in Naples. In his hotel, he met Rosemary again. She was making another motion picture, but she managed to find time to see him. Not so innocent now, she proved an easy conquest. Dick also met Nicole's older sister in Naples.

One night, Dick drank far too much and became embroiled with a chiseling taxi driver. When he refused to pay an exorbitant fee, a fight broke out, and Dick was arrested. The police captain unfairly upheld the taxi driver. Blind with rage, Dick struck a policeman and in return was severely beaten by the Fascist carabinieri. Thinking his eye had been gouged out, Dick got word to Nicole's sister, who brought all her influence to bear upon the consul to have her brother-in-law released.

Back in Zurich, Dick was busy for a time at the clinic. On a professional visit to Lausanne, he learned to his surprise that Nicole's father was there, very near death. When the dying man expressed a wish to see his daughter again, Dick sent for Nicole. Strangely enough, the weakened father still could not face his daughter. In a despairing frenzy, he escaped from the hospital and disappeared.

Dick continued to go downhill. He always drank too much. A patient, objecting to the liquor on his breath, created a scene. Finally, Dick was forced to surrender his partnership in the clinic.

With no job, Dick wandered about restlessly. He and his wife, he realized, had less and less in common. At last, after Dick had disgraced his family many times in drunken scenes, Nicole began to welcome the attentions of Tommy Barban. She confidently looked forward to an independent life with Tommy. She no longer needed Dick.

After the divorce, Dick moved to America. Nicole heard of him occasionally. He moved several times to successively smaller towns, an unsuccessful general practitioner.

Critical Evaluation:

In all of his literary work, F. Scott Fitzgerald proves to be a retrospective oracle. He describes an age of individuals who came on the scene and burned themselves out even before they were able to conceptualize themselves. His first published novel, *This Side of Paradise* (1920), is autobiographical and describes the early Jazz Age with its vague values of money, beauty, and a distorted sense of social propriety. His masterpiece, *The Great Gatsby*, came in 1925, and *Tender Is the Night* (1934) fictionalizes the personal and social disintegration that followed the success which *The Great Gatsby* brought Fitzgerald.

In addition to the glamour, the excitement, the frenetic pursuit of the good life between two world wars described in *Tender Is the Night*, the novel also contains a masterful attempt at thematic telescoping. The character of Dick Diver functions in a triple capacity: he is, on the largest scale, a mid-twentieth century American equivalent of the tragic hero; also, he signifies the complex disintegration of the American during this precarious point in time; and, by the close of the novel, the reader's attention is ultimately focused on Diver as a fictional character.

In many ways, Diver's fall follows Aristotle's formula for classical tragedy: He is an isolated hero upon whom an entire community of individuals depends for necessary form to their lives; he has a tragic flaw, since he is told by a classmate, "That's going to be your trouble—judgment about yourself," that is, he lacks perspective and introspection; he is a representative individual in that he is a psychiatrist expected to understand human motivation; he is at the mercy of fate, since the precipitating element, Nicole's case, "drifted into his hands"; and, his fall is monumental, from an elevated position in life into failure and anonymity. Most significant of all, however, Diver has a true sense of his own tragic importance; he realizes that he is losing his grip on situations, and, even though he recognizes some of the possible consequences of his actions, he is not equipped psychologically to combat them.

Dick Diver, however, is not the strictly tragic figure prescribed in *The Poetics*. Rather, he is at most the sort of tragic hero that America would allow in the 1920's, and it is in this capacity that Diver serves to describe the gradual disintegration of the American character. Dick is not simply symbolic of an American; his character is instead individualized to represent what an American with his exemplary vulnerabilities could become in a special set of circumstances. Diver and his companions create their own mystique to avoid the realities of a world thrown into, and later extracting itself from, war. Their frenetic rites and the aura in which the compatriots hide ultimately form the confusion that grows larger than Diver, unleashing itself and swallowing him. Diver and the American character at this time are incomplete; each is detrimentally eclectic and at the mercy of the props, such as music, money, and material possessions, upon which it depends for support. Incompleteness nourishes Diver's paternalistic assimilation of portions of the personalities that surround him and depend on him. His need to be needed, however, causes him to assimilate weaknesses more often than strengths; and the organic process is abortive. For the American character is a limited one, a possessive one, and there is a sense of something existing beyond Diver's intellectual and emotional reach that could have proved to be his salvation. Fitzgerald emphasizes the eclectic and incomplete nature of the American during this era by interweaving elements of the romantic, the realistic, and the didactic when describing actions and motivations of his characters. The result presents a severely realistic emotional conflict that sporadically explodes several characters, including Dick Diver, into psychological chaos.

Finally, Diver functions most specifically as the pivotal character of the plot itself. Given the demands of a novel of such scope, Fitzgerald relays Diver's decline quite convincingly. He succeeds by providing the reader subliminally with the correct formula for observing Diver's actions and their consequences. Within the first three chapters of the novel, the reader is taught, through Nicole's exemplary case, to appreciate the importance of psychological analysis and to isolate the "precipitating factor" in a character's development, and then to consider that factor's influence in subsequent actions. The reader is thereby equipped to transfer these premises to his observations of Diver. Throughout the duration of the novel, the reader realizes that Dick Diver is driven by a need to be needed; and it is this aspect of his personality that leads him increasingly into circumstances that involve him directly, causing him almost voluntarily to allow his energy to be sapped.

Tender Is the Night is above all a psychological novel that is more successful than most novels of its type. The device upon which the success of the novel depends is Fitzgerald's handling of time. Here, time serves both a horizontal and a vertical purpose. Horizontally, time is chronological, for chronological observation is an advantage the reader has—that Diver does not have— throughout the duration of the novel (this fact was not so in earlier drafts of the novel). The reader knows that Diver grows older; knows that Rosemary matures and finds other interests; knows that Nicole eventually recovers from her illness, and these are circumstances of which Diver is ignorant. For him, time is merely a psychological abstraction; only major events determine whether or not one is in stasis. Yet time also functions vertically, making the notion of thematic telescoping possible. Diver is not cognizant of the passing of time until his plunge is in its advanced stages. As Diver's gradual acknowledging of time and of the vast gap between his "heroic period" and his encroaching anonymity becomes increasingly important, one's awareness of Diver's thematic function passes from the purely tragic figure, through the import of the national character, and, toward the close of the novel, rests ultimately on the individual Dick Diver and his acceptance of his situation.

THEY SHOOT HORSES, DON'T THEY?

Type of work: Novel
Author: Horace McCoy (1897–1955)
Type of plot: Social allegory
Time of plot: The 1930's
Locale: An amusement pier near Hollywood, California
First published: 1935

Principal characters:
ROBERT SYVERTEN, a young contestant in a dance
    marathon
GLORIA BEATTY, his partner
ROCKY GRAVO, the master of ceremonies
VINCENT (SOCKS) DONALD, a promoter
MRS. LAYDEN, an elderly spectator

Horace McCoy's *They Shoot Horses, Don't They?* is an excellent example of the tough-guy fiction that flourished during the 1930's. Full of violence, sex, and hard-boiled talk, McCoy's five novels resemble the works of Hammett, Chandler, Cain, and B. Traven.

Robert, the young narrator who aspires to become a film director like Eisenstein, is no hoodlum. His tough tone simply reflects the effect a brutalizing experience has had upon him. An unemployed film extra in the middle of the depression, Robert meets Gloria, a not very attractive, unemployed extra who persuades him to enter a marathon dance contest as her partner. Both have come to Hollywood, glamour capital of the world, from small Southern towns, lured by the American dream of sudden success. After an unsuccessful suicide attempt before she left home, Gloria is now being "razzed" by an expert, God; but she lacks the courage to kill herself. Her verbal signature throughout the contest is some variation on the refrain, "I wish I was dead." Opposed to this total despair is Robert's typical American optimism, but he ends a victim of Gloria's nihilistic vision. Robert and Gloria exist only in terms of their situation as contestants; they have almost no past, and their future is violent death.

The contest is held on an amusement pier in an old building that was once a public dance hall. One hundred and forty couples enter: professional marathon dancers and amateurs, like Robert and Gloria. Floor judges, nurses, and a house doctor are in attendance; contestants are allowed to continue only if they are in good physical condition. The dancing area is thirty by one hundred feet; there are loge, circus, or general admission seats, and a bar. Contestants dance in one-hour-fifty-minute periods; during the ten-minute rest intervals between each, they sleep, eat, shave, bathe, excrete, change clothes. The trick is to learn to do several things at once. After the first week, contestants need not dance, they must simply keep moving; all employees of the hall must constantly be in motion. Local sponsors of individual couples provide equipment and costumes, the company name across the chest, the contestant's number on his back. Thus, Robert and Gloria become "Jonathan Beer." Specialty numbers draw a shower of silver; but one couple, who do a lifeless tap dance, declare that you are better off without a specialty. In the derby, a nightly fifteen-minute heel-and-toe endurance race, Robert soon stops trying to win and strives merely to keep from coming in last, to avoid being disqualified. If a dancer loses his partner, because of menstrual pains or a heart attack, for example, he may couple with another lone survivor; casualties are scarcely missed. A tub of ice water awaits those who faint; thus is Robert shocked out of a dream of being a film director. The main inducement for staying in the contest is that one knows from where his next meal is coming; food and bed are free as long as the contestant endures. For the winning couple, the purse is one thousand dollars, and every one has the same chance, according to Rocky Gravo, the master of ceremonies. There is also the chance of being "discovered" by a motion-picture producer, though after the second day, each contestant resembles a zombie. It is a contest of "endurance and skill"; one must have the skill to endure.

Gloria's attitude is overwhelmingly cynical. She and Robert are on a merry-go-round; when the dance is over, they will get off where they got on. Eating and sleeping are merely a postponing of death. Responding to Robert's expression of sympathy for one of the dancers who is arrested as a fugitive murderer, Gloria suggests that they are all condemned fugitives. "Socks," the promoter, appreciates the publicity; anything that draws the crowds is good. He asks Gloria and Robert to get married on the dance floor as a "high class" entertainment feature; they can get a divorce after the contest closes. Gloria refuses; Robert is afraid the angry promoter will disqualify them. Gloria, who wishes she had never been born, encourages one of the dancers who is pregnant to abort the child because it will only end up the same way.

In the 1920's and the 1930's, dance marathons, an import from Europe, were held in every major American city. Hollywood is a particularly apt symbolic setting for McCoy's marathon: it represents the public Eden to which few are admitted; the rejects end up on the dance floor. The roll call of actual celebrities among the spectators is effective, more so today since readers can see what fame comes to. In the context of the Depression, the spectators are the corrupt rich being amused by the antics of the workhorses, but ultimately spectator and dancer reverse roles. Just as the dance, symbol of the new postwar morality, became perverted by the marathon, sexual perversion is part of the experience. Gloria is about to submit to lesbians to get what she wants; Mrs. Layden, a wealthy old woman who comes every night to watch, lusts for Robert. Robert and Gloria are not in love; there is not even a sexual tie. About to do a favor for a nymphomaniac dancer under the bandstand,

Robert is interrupted by a voice in the dark; later, he learns that Gloria was nearby with Rocky. Rocky's monotonous exhortation to the orchestra, the dancers (especially the females), and the audience is "Give."

When a rich spectator finally shows an interest in her, Gloria, ironically, is too devoid of hope to respond. She declares that she is glad she is through with life. In the midst of a fight in the bar, the cause of which is never disclosed, five shots are fired. Mrs. Layden, on her way to the platform to judge the derby, is an accidental target. Ironically, old Mrs. Layden wanted to live to make love to young Robert, while Gloria wishes the bullet had struck herself. Without a winner, the marathon ends on the dictate of chance. Robert and Gloria walk out onto the pier. She persuades him that she is no good to herself or to anyone else, that she is better off dead. He shoots her to put her out of her misery. Ironically, his lawyer instructs Robert to throw himself on the mercy of the court; but the court gives him, against his will, what he gave Gloria at her own request—oblivion.

While the marathon dance symbolizes man's predicament in the 1930's, it is almost perfect as a symbolic expression of the universal human predicament. While McCoy's central symbolic action is realistically true and stark, and never literary, the dance draws to itself many traditional connotations that enhance the significance of the marathon. In mythic terms, the grinding dance is like Sisyphus' struggle to push his rock to the top of the mountain; the ten-minute rest periods are like his moment of freedom as he returns to his burden on the plain. In the simple event of the dance, readers experience a pure existential situation that exemplifies the absurd nature of life.

Among the most effective motifs, all of which McCoy develops quite naturally, is the incessant pounding of the ocean under the floor; like the slow ticking of the clock and the slow movement of its hands in relation to the movements of the dancers' legs, the surf counterpoints the dance. Robert used to love the ocean; now he hates it. Gloria observes that the waves have been moving for a million years; it is between the rising and falling of a wave that Robert honors her plea that he shoot her. Robert used to dislike the sun; now he tries to absorb every moment of sunlight that falls through a crack in the roof of the windowless hall. Gloria observes that he moves like a ballet dancer as he follows the dime-sized ray of sun. McCoy suggests the existential idea that man can expect only rare moments of natural bliss. Ironically, the brief respite, by allowing time to reflect on its context, is sometimes too bitter, and Robert is glad when the siren calls him back to the dance floor.

The form of this novel is strictly congruent with all its elements. Juxtaposition is McCoy's most effective technique for controlling and conceptualizing his raw material. Robert's story is presented as an interior monologue, the thirteen unlucky parts of which are juxtaposed to fragments of the sentence of death which a judge is pronouncing upon him. On the first page, a single statement directs the prisoner to stand. The next page begins as he stands up. The ironic immediacy of the sentence lends an immediacy to Robert's memory of the dance. The initial image is Gloria's face the moment after Robert fires the gun; at the end, the firing itself is depicted. Thus, the brevity of the novel gives the impression of a single juxtaposition. The marriage ceremony on the dance floor is juxtaposed to the Lord's Prayer, which is juxtaposed to the killings in the bar. Another graphic device is the score box that heads the last four chapters, showing: ELAPSED HOURS. COUPLES REMAINING. As the hours accumulate, the judge's words grow larger and larger on the page. On the last, he invokes God's mercy on the prisoner's soul.

As he tells it from the vantage of the prisoner's dock, Robert comments briefly (in italics) on his own story. Before he shoots Gloria, he recalls the shooting of his grandfather's horse when Robert was a child. Thus, the present was given in the past; the sentence he hears now, as he recalls the past, was passed during the dance, before the murder, because it is inherent in the nature of things. McCoy's structure gives a sense of the simultaneity of the sentence with the conditions that produced the "crime." Robert concludes that while the tune varies, the dance, one's experiences, are the same; nothing is new. The novel is superbly compressed: Robert's meeting Gloria is briefly described and their parting briefly depicted; the 879-hour-long dance is the large center of the action. The brevity of the killing and of the sentence, of the book itself, is an ironic comment on the length, the prolonged agony of the dance. It is singularly appropriate that dance-murder-trial be compressed within the judge's sentence.

THE THIN MAN

Type of work: Novel
Author: Dashiell Hammett (1894–1961)
Type of plot: Mystery romance
Time of plot: 1930's
Locale: New York
First published: 1934

>   *Principal characters:*
>   MIMI JORGENSEN, Clyde Wynant's former wife
>   DOROTHY WYNANT, her daughter
>   GILBERT WYNANT, her son
>   CHRISTIAN JORGENSEN, her present husband and
>   Wynant's former associate
>   NICK CHARLES, a detective
>   NORA CHARLES, his wife
>   HERBERT MACAULAY, Wynant's attorney
>   MORELLI, a gangster
>   ARTHUR NUNHEIM, a former convict

The Story:

Nick Charles, one-time detective and now a California lumberman, arrived in New York with his wife Nora for the Christmas holidays. He was drawn into investigation of a murder case because the dead woman, Julia Wolf, was the secretary of Nick's old client, a lunatic-fringe inventor whose wife had divorced him in order to marry a man named Christian Jorgensen. Clyde Wynant, the inventor, was reported to be out of town, working on some new project. Herbert Macaulay, attorney for Wynant, had told police that he had not seen Wynant since October, when Wynant had given the lawyer power of attorney.

Suspicion fell on Mimi Jorgensen, just returned from Europe, for she had gone to see Julia on the afternoon of the murder, had arrived, in fact, in time for Julia to die in her arms. She had wanted, she said, to get her husband's address, for she needed more money to support his two children, twenty-year-old Dorothy and eighteen-year-old Gilbert, since Jorgensen had spent the large settlement Wynant had made on Mimi at the time of their divorce.

Suspicion fell on Jorgensen, who turned out to be a man formerly known as Kelterman, with whom Wynant had worked several years before. He thought that Wynant had not treated him fairly. Then it was discovered that Jorgensen had a wife living in Boston and that he had married Mimi only to get Wynant's money.

Suspicion fell on Morelli, a gangster who had been fond of Julia. When he learned that Nick was on the case, Morelli went to Nick's apartment and, as the police arrived, shot Nick in the chest, a glancing shot that did not produce a serious wound. Nick told the police he would not press charges, because the man was apparently in enough trouble. Although the police beat up Morelli, they could find no reason for holding him. He was released the same day.

Suspicion fell on Gil Wynant, for the members of the Wynant family did not have much love for one another. Gil was an odd young man who asked Nick about bizarre subjects such as incest and cannibalism. He was frequently found at keyholes listening to private conversations.

Suspicion fell on Arthur Nunheim, who identified Julia Wolf's body. When Nick went with Guild, a detective, to see Nunheim, they found him living in an extremely untidy apartment with a big, frowzy blonde. In the presence of their callers, Nunheim and the blonde insulted each other until the woman left him. Nunheim escaped from Nick through a back window. He was reported murdered a little while later.

Suspicion fell on Wynant himself, for Macaulay reported that Wynant had made an appointment with him on the day the murder was committed but had failed to appear. During the course of the investigation, several people received communications from Wynant which seemed to throw suspicion on Mimi and Jorgensen. One day Wynant was reported to have tried to commit suicide in Allentown, Pennsylvania. The report was false, however, for the man was not Wynant.

Wynant had maintained a shop on First Avenue which the police had given a cursory examination. Nick insisted that they return and tear it apart if necessary, for he felt sure that some clue was to be found there. The police discovered a section of the cement floor newer than the rest. When they tore it up, they found the bones of a dead man, with a cane, some clothes apparently for a larger man than Wynant, and a key chain bearing the initials D.W.Q.

At last, Nick accused Macaulay of murdering Wynant, Julia, and Nunheim. He believed that Macaulay and Julia had joined forces to get Wynant's money, that Wynant had gone to Macaulay's house in Scarsdale to accuse Macaulay of the plot, and that Macaulay had killed his client there. Then, Nick reasoned, Macaulay had dismembered the body and brought it back to the workshop, where he discharged the two mechanics and buried the body under new cement. The cane, the large-size clothes, and the key chain were intended to prevent identification of the body.

Macaulay, according to Nick, had renewed the lease on the shop and kept it vacant while, with a forged power of attorney and Julia's help, he began to transfer Wynant's fortune to his own accounts. Then Mimi had come back from Europe with her children and had asked for Wynant. When Nick had arrived for the Christmas holiday and had agreed to help Mimi find the missing inventor, Macaulay felt he would be safer with Julia dead. Later he sent letters to members of Wynant's family, and even to himself, supposedly from Wynant. Nick thought Macaulay had killed Nunheim because the former convict had been near Julia's apartment and had probably heard the shots that killed her. When Nunheim had demanded hush money from Macaulay, the lawyer had murdered him also to keep him permanently quiet.

So Nick outlined his case; but on the day he made the accusation, Gilbert Wynant received a letter, supposedly from his father, telling him to use the enclosed key, go to Julia's apartment, and look for an important paper between the pages of a certain book. Following the instruction in the letter, Gilbert entered the apartment, where a plainclothesman struck him, handcuffed him, and took him to police headquarters. The boy showed the officials and Nick the letter that he had received. The book and paper had been invented. When Nick took Gilbert home, he learned from Mimi that Wynant had just been there to leave with Mimi ten thousand dollars in bonds.

As it turned out, Macaulay, knowing that the police would be in Julia's apartment, had sent the letter to Gilbert in an attempt to shift the suspicion back to Wynant once more. Also, Macaulay himself had brought Wynant's bonds to Mimi, making her promise to say that Wynant had brought them and thus give credence to his own story that Wynant was in town. Nick forced Mimi to admit the truth by explaining that Macaulay now had possession of Wynant's fortune and that, if she played his game, she would have to be satisfied with comparatively small sums occasionally, whereas if she were to stop shielding Macaulay—however innocent of Wynant's death—she would, through her children, have control of her former husband's entire fortune. Jorgensen, meanwhile, had gone back to his legal wife in Boston.

After Nick had explained the whole case to Nora, she could not help feeling that the business of a detective, based as it is on so much probability, is at best unsatisfactory.

Critical Evaluation:

As detective fiction, this novel presents a picture of sophisticated New York life at the end of the Prohibition era. The plot itself follows the pattern set by Poe in *The Murders of the Rue Morgue* in 1841 and by Arthur Conan Doyle in his Sherlock Holmes stories. Here are the astute detective, the somewhat obtuse and distrustful police, the questioning companion, the dropping of clues to give the reader a chance to solve the mystery, and the final explanation by the detective.

The Thin Man was the last and most popular of Dashiell Hammett's novels. In Nick and Nora Charles he created probably the most distinctive detective couple in the entire genre. Not only did the book do very well commercially, but it also spawned a radio program, television series, and an extremely successful sequence of films, in the 1930's and 1940's, starring William Powell and Myrna Loy.

Reasons for the popularity of the novel and its offshoots are not hard to find. It is the most briskly paced of Hammett's books, with an intricate plot that is ingenious and deceptive, although logical and believable. The action takes place among the denizens of New York café society during the Prohibition era, and Hammett portrays this frenzied, colorful world of money, corruption, sex, booze, and violence with accuracy and energy.

In addition, his characters are unusually vivid—the most memorable being, of course, Nick and Nora Charles. They give the novel qualities seen only occasionally in Hammett's earlier works: verbal wit and situational humor. As a former detective of obvious skill and experience, Nick is adroit enough in dealing with crime solving, but he is no aggressive, hard-boiled Continental Op, Sam Spade, or Ned Beaumont. He has retired from the business to manage Nora's not inconsiderable lumber interests, and, at least until his curiosity is aroused, has no desire to get back to his former occupation. Nick reluctantly becomes involved because Nora coaxes and dares him. Nick is a witty, cocky, charming man who would rather party than fight. Nora is equally fun loving. The mystery is, to her, an exciting game—until it gets dangerous. The best scenes in the novel are not those of action and violence, as in previous books, but those featuring witty banter and sexual byplay between Nick and Nora. Nick sums up this attitude at the end of the novel: "Let's stick around for a while. This excitement has put us behind in our drinking."

Yet, for all its ingenuity and charm, *The Thin Man* is one of Hammett's weakest novels and shows clear decline in his powers. The picture of New York in the 1920's is realistic and vivid, but superficial and cliché-ridden. The plot is clever and facile but has no implications beyond that of an interesting puzzle. The character of Nick Charles, while witty and charming, is relatively shallow and frivolous—and somewhat morally questionable. He is content to live off of Nora's money, indulge her whims, and drift from party to party and city to city. The intense personal morality of the earlier works gives way to a kind of lazy, benevolent hedonism in which nothing is more important than a 3:00 A.M. whiskey-and-soda. In short, the vital ethical and intellectual center seems replaced by slick, entertaining superficiality.

THE THREE BLACK PENNYS

Type of work: Novel
Author: Joseph Hergesheimer (1880–1954)
Type of plot: Period chronicle
Time of plot: c. 1750–1910
Locale: Pennsylvania
First published: 1917

Principal characters:
>HOWAT PENNY, the son of the owner of Myrtle Forge
>LUDOWIKA WINSCOMBE, a woman in love with Howat Penny
>JASPER PENNY, Howat Penny's great-grandson
>SUSAN BRUNDON, Jasper's sweetheart
>HOWAT PENNY, Jasper's and Susan's grandson
>MARIANA JANNAN, Howat's cousin
>JAMES POLDER, Mariana's lover

The Story:

The Penny family was English, except for a Welsh ancestor whose blood cropped out from time to time among his descendants. Those who showed the Welsh strain were called black Pennys by their relatives in an attempt to describe the mental makeup of individuals to whom it was applied. Howat was the first black Penny in more than a hundred years; the last one had been burned to death as a heretic by Queen Elizabeth, long before the family had emigrated to the Colonies.

Living at Myrtle Forge, on the edge of the Pennsylvania Wilderness, Howat Penny was far more interested in the deep woods than he was in becoming an ironmaster. Nor did the appearance of Ludowika Winscombe make him any more satisfied or contented with his life.

Ludowika Winscombe, the young Polish wife of an elderly British envoy, had been left at the Penny home while her husband traveled through the Colonies on the king's business. Before long, Howat Penny fell in love with her. Ludowika warned him, however, that she was a practical person who felt it was best that she remain married to her husband rather than to run away with a young frontiersman. Howat stubbornly told her that she would have to marry him, for he would permit nothing to stand in the way of their happiness.

Winscombe returned ill to Myrtle Forge, and Howat Penny found himself

---

acting as Winscombe's nurse. It was an ironic situation filled with tension. Howat Penny waited for the old man to die. Ludowika was torn between two desires. She wanted Howat Penny, but she hated to face a life with him in the wilderness. The climax came late one night while Howat and Ludowika sat by the sick man's bed while Winscombe made a gallant effort to remain alive. Howat and Ludowika dared not even look at each other for fear of what they might see behind each other's eyes. Early in the morning, the old man died. As they faced each other in the gray dawn, Howat and Ludowika realized that she was destined to remain with him in Pennsylvania and never to see London again.

Three generations later, the Welsh Penny blood again appeared in the person of Howat's great-grandson, Jasper. By that time the forge, which had been the beginning of the Penny fortune, had been replaced by a great foundry with many furnaces. Jasper Penny was a rich man, steadily growing richer by supplying the tremendous amounts of iron needed for the new railroads in the United States.

Jasper Penny had never married. Like his great-grandfather Howat, he was a man of great passions whose energies were spent in building up his foundry and fortune. He was still painfully reminded, however, of his earlier indiscretions with a woman who had borne him an illegitimate daughter. The woman hounded Jasper for money, and he found it easier to give her money than to refuse her demands.

He saw very little of Eunice, his daughter, for he assumed that she would be cared for by her mother as long as he paid all expenses. One day in Philadelphia, Jasper decided, on impulse, to visit Eunice. He discovered her, ill-clothed and underfed, in the home of a poor family, and, horrified, he took her away with him. Not knowing what to do with her, he finally placed her in a school in New York.

In Philadelphia, Jasper had also met Susan Brundon, mistress of a girls' school and friend of a distant branch of Jasper's family. Jasper fell in love with her and in his abrupt fashion proposed marriage. Being honest, he told her that he had an illegitimate child. Susan refused to marry Jasper because she felt that his first duty was to Eunice's mother.

Shortly after his proposal, Jasper was involved in a murder. Eunice's mother had killed another lover and suspicion fell on Jasper Penny. He hated to involve Susan Brundon in the sordid affair, but he found that the only way he could clear himself was through her testimony that he had been with her when the crime was committed.

After the trial, Susan told Jasper that she could not marry him until Eunice's mother was dead, that she could not have the past intruding itself upon her love for him after they were married. Almost a decade passed before they were finally able to marry.

The last of the black Pennys was also the last of the family name, for the family died out with the second Howat Penny, the grandson of Jasper Penny and Susan Brundon. Howat was a bachelor who lived alone in the country near the site of the original Penny forge. Interested in music and art, he had never married, and the management of the Penny foundries had gone out of his hands. Possessed of a comfortable fortune, he had in the closing years of his life the companionship of Mariana Jannan, a cousin. She was a young woman in her twenties and little understood by old-fashioned Howat.

He did not understand Mariana because he could not understand her generation. Because Jasper's son and grandson had never had anything to do with that branch of the family descended from Jasper's illegitimate daughter, Howat was horrified when Mariana told him that she was in love with James Polder, a distant cousin.

Howat thought that Mariana was mad to fall in love with James Polder, who had begun working in the Penny foundries as a boy. The fact that he had worked his way up to a position of importance failed to redeem him in old Howat's eyes.

Polder finally ran away with an actress. Three years after his marriage, Mariana and Howat Penny called on him and his wife. Polder, unhappy with his slatternly wife, had begun drinking heavily. Howat, at Mariana's insistence, invited Polder to visit his home in the country. Polder accepted. Shortly afterward, he learned that his wife had deserted him and returned to the stage. He no longer cared; in love once more, he and Mariana realized they should never have permitted family differences to come between them.

Mariana's relatives, shocked by the affair, protested to Howat. Howat himself said nothing, for he now felt that he was too old and understood too little of modern life to intrude in the affairs of Mariana and Polder. Although he was as much Mariana's friend as ever, he could not understand how she was able to live with Polder as his mistress while they waited for his wife to divorce him. Howat believed until the end of his life that women should be protected from reality. Even when he knew he was dying, he said nothing to Mariana, who sat reading by his side. The delicacy of his sensibilities prevented him from shocking her with the fact of his approaching death and kept him from saying good-bye to her when he died, the last of the three black Pennys.

Critical Evaluation:

Joseph's Hergesheimer's third novel, *The Three Black Pennys*, was published two years after D. H. Lawrence's *The Rainbow*. Lawrence's novel, suppressed in England, was declared obscene by the Bow Street Magistrate, who ordered police to seize copies at the bookstores and at the press. Hergesheimer's novel, on the other hand, was widely popular; together with *Java Head* (1919), it established for the author a major reputation during the early 1920's. Apart from their different publication histories, *The Three Black*

Pennys and *The Rainbow* are similar in many ways. Both treat the theme of mating—successful or unsuccessful—of three generations of a family, the Brangwens for Lawrence and the Pennys for Hergesheimer; both examine, almost as a mystique, a special quality of "blood" that distinguishes members of the family; both begin with a marriage involving a "mixed" bloodline from a Polish widow—Lydia Lensky in *The Rainbow* and Ludowika Winscombe in *The Three Black Pennys*—and show its effects upon the indigenous English or Welsh-American stock of the males of the family; both attempt, through symbolism concerning time, place, and character, to record the history of culture for their respective countries; both show, again through symbol and story, the diminishing vitality of the original family stock, from Ursula's failure in love (she marries in *Women in Love*) to the last Howat Penny's feeble bachelorhood that terminates his line; finally, both novels deal with the larger issues of vitality and degeneration, progress and decay.

Yet the novels, despite their remarkable similarities in theme, are markedly different in their effects. Lawrence's symbols, whether used on a conscious or subconscious Freudian-Jungian level, are worked integrally into the structure of his book; Hergesheimer's symbols—particularly those concerning the relationship between the men and the iron—are all quite obvious. They add substance to the narrative but do not provide additional levels of significance, nor do they turn the story into myth. Furthermore, Lawrence's concept of "blood consciousness," both a psychological and moral argument, is carefully elaborated in the lives of the Brangwens; Hergesheimer's treatment of the "black" strain (that is, the Welsh ancestry) in the Penny family's blood inheritance is superficial, a mere plot device with a psychological or moral frame of reference. Whether the "black" Welsh blood represents a behavioral atavism or is an odd coincidence of personality, its appearance over several generations is never fully explained. Finally, Lawrence's novel treats the partial or complete failures in sexuality as symbols for the disintegration of modern culture; Hergesheimer, however, treats the failures as isolated examples, without moving from the specific instance to the general malaise of American culture. Thus Lawrence's novel is clearly in the dominant tradition of modern psychological fiction. Hergesheimer's is a period piece, well crafted and entertaining, but not an innovative work of literature.

Nevertheless, critics in 1917 praised *The Three Black Pennys* for the author's accurate research into the history of the nation, for his mastery of prose style, and for his ability to create vigorous characters. As a chronicle, the novel contrasts with the popular sentimental romances of the time. In the reconstruction of three periods in America's past, the late Colonial period (concerning the first Howat Penny), the mid-nineteenth century (Jasper Penny), and the turn of the nineteenth century (the last Howat Penny), Hergesheimer is a Realist with a scrupulous eye for details. Dividing the novel into "The Furnace," "The Forge," and "The Metal," the author shows how the lives of the "black" Pennys and their contemporaries relate to the growth of industrial America.

Before the Revolutionary War, Gilbert Penny establishes in Pennsylvania the Myrtle Forge, a product of his own energy, persistence, and optimism. He and his rebellious son Howat are men of determination; their vision of America is one of struggle leading to power. Three generations later, Jasper Penny, Howat's great-grandson, inherits a mighty industrial complex built around the family's original forge. Like his ancestors, Jasper is concerned with power. A business magnate, he is accustomed to getting his way, but his own impetuosity nearly destroys his happiness. Entangled romantically with Essie Scofield, a worthless woman whom he had seduced and made pregnant while he was still a young man, he cannot in his mature years convince his true love, the idealistic Susan Brundon, to marry him. She insists that they wait until Essie's death. The child born of their middle age comes to represent the languishing vitality of the Penny family. By the time of the last "black" Penny, the effete second Howat, the family's failure to produce an heir corresponds with its decline from a position of industrial power. The foundry is silent, and Howat, merely the caretaker of the past, has memories of his energetic forebears to remind him of his own impotence.

To re-create a sense of the past, Hergesheimer unobtrusively works his research into the Penny chronicle. Without bogging down in the recital of historical facts, he allows the story to carry the reader forward. As a masterful stylist, he evokes setting with a few selective phrases, rather than a profusion of details. Compared to regional Realists like his contemporaries Ellen Glasgow or Willa Cather, rarely is he able to describe a setting so fully that it comes alive in all its parts. Even the description of the Myrtle Forge lacks a sense of immediacy. However, Hergesheimer does create an impressionistic feeling for the scene—not from the close observation of particulars but the careful choice of meaningful details which linger in the memory.

To be sure, Hergesheimer's command of style is more impressive than his characterizations. Although his early critics admired the first two romantic Pennys, they appear, in retrospect, deficient in psychological complexity. The first Howat Penny is described, at the beginning, as reclusive and tactless to the point of surliness—a kind of American Heathcliff mysteriously suffering from ambiguous passions. When he falls in love with Ludowika, he changes at once from a sullen misanthrope to an ardent, almost demoniac lover. Jasper, also driven by contradictory passions, is the philandering cad with Essie, the practical-minded and affectionate father with Eunice, and the gentle, diffident lover of Susan. The greatest problem in psychology, however, is the last Howat, the American Victorian. If the strain of "black" Welsh blood is said to distinguish those Pennys "impatient of assuaging relationships and beliefs," how can the feeble aesthete belong to the same strain as the impetuous first Howat or the ruthless tycoon Jasper? Apart from his inability to relate to the younger generation, particularly to Mariana Jannan, Howat appears to lack the element of violent, contradictory passions that sets the other "black" Pennys at odds with their peers. A touching, pathetic figure, he represents a dying breed. Yet the reader does not understand whether the fault for his failure lies in Howat's times or in himself. Nevertheless, the portrait of the last Howat, though psychologically blurred, is interesting enough to arouse the reader's sympathies. More than his cardboard-romantic ancestors, he resembles a Henry James hero, morbidly introspective, sensitive but fastidious, capable of tender emotions but little direct action. With him, the line of the "black" Pennys comes to an end.

THREE SOLDIERS

Type of work: Novel
Author: John Dos Passos (1896–1970)
Type of plot: Social criticism
Time of plot: 1917–1919
Locale: France
First published: 1921

> Principal characters:
> DAN FUSELLI, an American soldier from San Francisco
> CHRISFIELD, an American soldier from Indiana
> JOHN ANDREWS (ANDY), an American soldier from
>   Virginia
> GENEVIÈVE ROD, Andrews' friend

The Story:

Private Dan Fuselli was anxious to become Corporal Dan Fuselli. He had seen motion pictures of Huns spitting Belgian babies on their bayonets and then being chased like rabbits by heroic Yankee soldiers who were later rewarded with embraces by the pretty and picturesque Belgian milkmaids. He looked forward to the time when his girl, Mabe, writing from San Francisco, his hometown, would address her letters to Corporal Dan Fuselli.

Private First Class Fuselli of the Medical Corps hated the Army and everything about it, but he knew that to become a corporal he must keep clean, keep his mouth shut, obey the brass, and continually cajole the sergeant. He was infuriated one night when he went to town to see Yvonne and learned that the sergeant had taken her over. Then, when he returned to camp, he heard that the consumptive corporal was back, the one in whose absence Fuselli had been made acting corporal. Private Fuselli, however, kept his mouth shut. Someday he would be a corporal, perhaps even a sergeant; but now he kept his mouth shut.

Finally, after a setback doing endless K.P. and following his recovery from a venereal disease, after the Armistice he did become Corporal Dan Fuselli; but by that time, his girl had married a naval officer.

Matters worked out differently for Chrisfield. The Army was not as easygoing as life in the Indiana farm country had been. The officers shouted at the men and then made them do things that they hated, but it had to be withstood. One night, Chrisfield was so furious he pulled a knife on a sergeant named Anderson, but his friends held him back and nothing happened. In Europe, life was not much better. Occasionally, he had a talk about the stars

---

and the fields with his educated buddy, John Andrews. Mostly, however, the war was awful.

The marches were endless, and his shoulders ached from his heavy pack. When bombardments came, the marchers scattered face down in a field. Once Chrisfield asked Andrews to speak French for him to a French girl at an inn, but nothing came of it.

One day, walking alone through a wood near the front, Chrisfield found a dead German lying prone. When he kicked the body over, he saw that it had no face, only a multicolored, pulpy mass with green flies hovering around it. In the man's hand was a revolver—he was a suicide. Chrisfield ran off panting.

Chrisfield was high-strung. When he was sitting thinking, a soldier prodded him and asked him what he was dreaming about. Chrisfield punched the fellow in the nose. He and Andy hated the Y.M.C.A men who were always telling the men at the front what brutes the Huns were and urging them in the name of Old Glory to kill Germans. Chrisfield was court-martialed when he announced that he intended to kill Sergeant Anderson after the war was over. One day, he went wandering and made his way silently into the kitchen of a house near the front. Looking into the next room, he saw a man in a German uniform. He reached into his pocket, pressed the spring on the grenade he had, withdrew it, and tossed it into the room. Not long afterward he came across Anderson, now a lieutenant, seated wounded in a deserted section of the wood. Chrisfield had two more grenades in his pocket, and he threw them at the man he hated.

After the Armistice, the rumor that he had killed Anderson somehow leaked out. Afraid, Chrisfield went A.W.O.L. and became a refugee in France, eternally on the move.

John Andrews was a Harvard graduate and a would-be composer. The Queen of Sheba section of Flaubert's *Temptation of Saint Anthony* kept recurring to him as he washed the barracks windows, and he thought how fine the subject would be for a musical composition. He cursed the Army for slowly stamping him into its iron mold. Overseas, he saw action and was more convinced than ever that war was needless butchery. He felt happiest away from the regiment. One day, he walked away from his company in order to be alone. He was looking at little frogs in a pool when a shell burst near him. He awoke on a stretcher.

For a while, the hospital was a relief from the endless orders and general mechanization of Army routine. Lying in his bed, he began to realize that he had respect for himself only when he thought of rebelling against the system, of going A.W.O.L. Soon the tedium of the hospital began to gall him. After his leg healed, he rejoined his company reluctantly and full of rebellion. The Armistice had been signed. When he heard that he could go to a French university through a school detachment being set up, he lied, secured some recommendations, and found himself in Paris.

In Paris, he met Geneviève Rod, a young Frenchwoman who admired his piano playing and his artistic tastes. She thought of artists as men who, because of their special sensitivity, should be exempt from the horrors of war. Andrews disagreed; one worker was like another; it was the whole of humanity that should be exempt. One day, he left Paris without official leave for a country trip with Geneviève. An MP picked him up and took him to a local office where he was beaten by several MP's. He was sent to a labor battalion loading concrete for a stadium being presented by the Americans to the French. It was crushing work. Convinced that Army life was a menace to human freedom, Andrews decided to desert, for one man less in the system made it weaker by that much. One night, he leaped from a plank and swam out to a barge in the Seine.

The barge family cared for him for a few days. They sank his uniform in the river, bought him new clothes, and, as anarchists, proclaimed their solidarity with him. He went back to Paris to find Geneviève, and stayed for a while with Chrisfield and a group of other concealed deserters. Then, hearing that Geneviève was at her country place, he joined her there.

At first, he did not tell her of his desertion. He lived in an inn nearby and began composing, not about the Queen of Sheba, but about John Brown, liberator of slaves. When he finally confessed his plight to Geneviève, a noticeable reserve crept into her attitude toward him. Perhaps, she suggested, he should give himself up. She could not comprehend the social motive in his rebellion.

One day he heard an American officer's voice at the door of the inn below his window. He thought of the prison sentence he must face. Too late he discovered that the landlady, experienced in the ways of impecunious Americans who were possible deserters, had stolen his revolver. As the MP's took him away, the wind blew in through the window of his room, and the music papers on which he had been working fluttered one by one to the floor.

Critical Evaluation:

Three Soldiers is an early work by John Dos Passos and does not incorporate many of the original stylistic devices of his later work. The language and organization of the novel are conventional and straightforward. The central idea of the work, however, elaborated in three variations, is highly unconventional. Dos Passos tries to show the immortality and brutality in the organization of society and especially in a society mechanized, armed, and functioning for purposes of war. When John Andrews deserts the army at the end of *Three Soldiers* and indicts the army because it stifles the individual, a friend of his answers that an idea like that is "anarchistic."

Indeed it is. *Three Soldiers* is essentially an anarchistic novel, a dramatic polemic—using three exemplary lives—in which Dos Passos argues for a social-political vision. It is a classic anarchistic vision in which the supremacy of the individual over social organization is defended, even demanded.

In the case of Dan Fuselli, Dos Passos shows that the lure of advancement and rewards, a lure which uses arms to sustain discipline and therefore hierarchy, is both false and vicious. It is false because, in Fuselli's case, keeping his mouth shut and obeying orders achieved little for him. It is vicious because his superiors use that lure to take advantage of him; Fuselli's most tragic moment occurs when his girlfriend is stolen by a man from whom he hopes to gain a promotion.

Chrisfield is a second type of soldier and represents a second response to military life. He is a nervous, violent farm boy harassed by superior officers, one of whom takes inhuman advantage of Chrisfield's low rank. Finally, Chrisfield is driven to murder and desertion.

Andrews, the third character, like Dos Passos, is an artist. Andrews felt that burying his individuality in the mass of the army would somehow bring him peace—and an escape from the pains of creativity. Andrews finds, however, that no matter how much he tries, he cannot bury himself. Some elemental force asserts itself through him, and he realizes that above all he must remain a distinct individual. When Andrews deserts at the end of the novel, he is acting out of decency and integrity.

This novel attempts to do for World War I what Stephen Crane's *The Red Badge of Courage* did for the Civil War; that is, to destroy the myth of glamour and glory and to expose the brutal reality of war. Unlike the hero of *The Red Badge of Courage*, who deserts in fright and returns proudly to battle, John Andrews of *Three Soldiers* can only take a self-respecting step by deserting after months of ignominious conformity. The novel succeeds best in its presentation of the tedium, dehumanizing regimentation and the physical horrors of war. As such, it is a vividly realized social document.

THE TIME OF MAN

Type of work: Novel
Author: Elizabeth Madox Roberts (1886–1941)
Type of plot: Regional romance
Time of plot: Early twentieth century
Locale: Kentucky
First published: 1926

Principal characters:
ELLEN CHESSER, a farm girl
NELLIE, her mother
HENRY, her father
JASPER KENT, her husband
JONAS, her fiancé

The Story:

Henry and Nellie Chesser had been on the road a long time. People sometimes called the Chessers and their friends gypsies, and they did tell fortunes and swap horses and mules, but Henry liked the earth, and he worked as a tenant for different farmers from time to time. Only his restless spirit kept him from settling somewhere permanently.

One day Henry's wagon broke down. The others could not wait for the Chessers, and Henry haunted the smithy, hoping to speed repairs; but when Hep Bodine offered him twenty dollars a month, a tenant house, and a garden spot, he accepted. The house had only one room and a loft, but it was better than sleeping outside.

Henry's daughter, Ellen, was greatly disappointed. She hated to leave Tessie, her great friend, the fortune-teller. Ellen knew no one on the Bodine farm, nor did she make friends easily. Mrs. Bodine even ordered her out of the berry patch. Only Joe Trent, home from college, noticed her.

Joe was elegant, always wearing shoes and clothes of different kinds of cloth. He would joke with Ellen as she brought in the firewood. She was growing up, and Joe awakened some spark of longing in her thin body. Then one day, Joe drove past her with Emphira Bodine. He pretended not to see Ellen in her skimpy skirt above her bare feet and legs. After that, Joe would stand behind a big bush where the men from the house could not see him and call to Ellen. Ellen was ashamed. She was glad when her father decided to move over to the Wakefield farm.

Their new house was better; even the loft had once been papered. Miss Tod Wakefield let Ellen look after the turkeys for money wages. So with setting out tobacco plants, getting in the firewood, and going regularly to the big barnyard, she settled into a pleasant routine. By fall, Nellie was able to get Ellen a store dress and new shoes.

In an old abandoned barn where she went to look for turkey eggs, she often noticed Amanda Cain waiting in the hayloft for Scott MacMurtrie, who was married to Miss Cassie. All the field-workers knew of the affair, and they discussed eagerly how Miss Cassie would lay into Scott when she learned he was carrying on with her cousin Amanda, for Miss Cassie was strong and independent. One day, Scott and Amanda disappeared. That night Ellen was awakened by the tolling bell on the MacMurtrie place. She hurried over, outdistancing her father, who thought the barn must be on fire. Ellen found the old black woman pulling the bell rope in a frenzy. Miss Cassie had hanged herself.

Dorine moved into one of the tenant houses. She was merry and gay and attracted others to her. She and Ellen became friends. At her house, Ellen went to her first party. Shy, she hoped desperately that no one would notice her; but in her agony of timidity, she sang a ballad her father had taught her, and she was accepted as one of the group. At their dances and games and on their Sunday walks, she went sometimes with Jonas Prather but more often with Sebe Townley. Sebe was kind and gentle, but she liked Jonas better.

Jonas took little part in their gay dances. He would call the figures and then retire with the old folks. He seemed to withdraw from contact with girls; some even said he had got religion.

One night, Jonas told Ellen he wanted her to marry him. When he went away to work for wages, he promised to come back during the summer to get married. Ellen received a letter from him, and she wrote him a letter in return. The summer wore on, however, and Jonas did not come back. At last, she heard that Jonas had married Sallie Lou.

When Henry rented a patch of twenty-five acres called the Orkeys place, Ellen felt a sense of escaping from her troubles. Their new home had once been a tollhouse. It contained three rooms on one floor, and Ellen's bedroom was weathertight.

The nearest neighbors were on the Wingate place. Old Mrs. Wingate, half mad, sat suspiciously in her house all day long, and Jasper Kent worked her farm on half shares. Albert Wingate, the son, seldom came to the farm, and when he did appear, he would often be roaring drunk. He would beg or steal money from his mother and sometimes he would turn the house upside down looking for more. When he began driving off cattle in which Jasper had a half interest, Jasper felt his anger mount.

Although Jasper prudently kept his own pigs in a corral far from the house, Albert discovered them. One morning, Jasper found the corral empty; Albert had sold the pigs to a passing trader. That night Albert and Jasper fought in the barn. Jasper was stronger than his opponent. Then Albert drew a gun.

Jasper wrested it away and threw it in the brush. In the fighting, however, Jasper forgot his lantern on the barn floor. When the building went up in flames, Jasper fled. He had been in jail before, and he was afraid.

He found work on the Phillips farm. Joe Phillips offered a house to Jasper. Jasper and Ellen were married and set up housekeeping in their own place. Their house was tight, and Joe promised to add a room. Ellen was carrying her first child and was very content with her marriage.

The letter they had been dreading came, an indictment for arson drawn up against Jasper for the burning of the Wingate barn. Henry was Jasper's witness, and Jasper was freed. At last, Ellen and Jasper seemed to be free of all care; they had only to work the land and raise their family. Each year they had another child.

Following the custom of the migrant people, they left the Phillips farm. It became a matter of indifference to Ellen where she lived; a year on the Goodrich place, a year on the McKnight farm—it was all the same. Then they moved back to the Phillips farm. Joe Phillips, greatly attracted to Ellen, spoke sweet words to her. When Jasper began to go off for all-night carouses, Ellen accepted Joe's attentions. She did not tell Jasper right away about the new baby she was carrying. When she did, Jasper was bitter and swore it was Joe's. When the sickly child was born, however, Jasper was very fond of it. The baby died in its third year.

When a nearby barn burned, suspicion unjustly fell on Jasper. One night masked raiders came to their home, seized Jasper while he slept, and bound him with ropes. They beat him savagely. Ellen brought him in and washed his bleeding welts. Jasper was greatly shamed.

The family loaded all their goods on the wagon and set out. They scarcely knew where they were going, but it would be far away. As they went, they dreamed of a home and of a bit of land they could call their own. Perhaps they could even set out trees for an orchard, somewhere, someday.

Critical Evaluation:

The Time of Man is a farm story that strikes a nice balance between the sordid and the romantic. Here readers have the life of the migrant Kentucky farmer as it is, unvarnished and plain. Deeper in the work, the reader sees the springs from which these people draw their strength. They lived in poverty, with little hope of security; but in their love for the soil and in their fierce independence, they find meaning for their lives. To call this novel a story of local color would be true but inadequate. The regionalism of *The Time of Man* is but a convenient frame for the depiction of human and enduring values.

In the novel, Elizabeth Madox Roberts draws on her own firsthand knowledge of poor rural whites in Kentucky—where she was born and reared—to present a stark portrait of impoverishment balancing between hope and despair. The tenant farmer's lot has never been an easy one, but the field-workers and tenant farmers in Roberts' novel appear in especially dire straits. For them, it seems that each small advance is followed by a setback twice as large. In those days before government welfare programs, sheer endurance was their only defense against misfortune.

The wellsprings of their endurance, however, derive from complex sources. For the easy assumption is that the poor work only because of need. Although necessity is indeed a compelling motivation, the characters in *The Time of Man* work for other reasons as well. The Chessers, Ellen and Henry, and the others, for example, are psychologically and spiritually compelled to work: they get satisfaction from farming the land, and they believe unquestioningly in the virtues of work. Despite occasional straying, they are nevertheless devoted to their families and have a strong sense of responsibility toward them. It may thus be said that they embody some of the most powerful tenets of the Protestant work ethic—a startling testimony, under the circumstances, to the ubiquity and the force of middle-class values even among the poor.

The Chessers, the Kents, and their friends and neighbors are certainly poor, with a poverty that often extends to intellectual and emotional depri-vation as well. For they are so preoccupied with the struggle for survival that they rarely, if ever, question or challenge the assumptions upon which the social system, or even their own lives, is based. Essentially unsophisticated people, they have no anxieties in the modern clinical sense, for their view of the present and their vision of the future are geared to the basic necessities for survival. Hence, they have worries, and they have fears of the most primitive sort; and identity crises and abstract intellectualizing do not concern them. In this sense, therefore, the novel's title, *The Time of Man*, must be construed as ironic, for the novel itself deals with people who have been denied access to the dignity of being "Man," part of mankind, and part of the human race.

THE TITAN

Type of work: Novel
Author: Theodore Dreiser (1871–1945)
Type of plot: Naturalism
Time of plot: 1890's
Locale: Chicago
First published: 1914

> *Principal characters:*
> FRANK ALGERNON COWPERWOOD, a multimillionaire and
> financial genius
> AILEEN COWPERWOOD, his mistress and then his wife
> PETER LAUGHLIN, his business partner
> STEPHANIE PLATOW, Cowperwood's mistress
> BERENICE FLEMING, Cowperwood's protégée and mistress

The Story:

Released from a Pennsylvania prison in the 1870's, Frank Algernon Cow-perwood, still young and a millionaire, went to Chicago to begin a new life with Aileen Butler, his mistress. Within a short time, Cowperwood made friends among influential businessmen there.

Divorced by his first wife, Cowperwood finally married Aileen. He prepared to increase his fortune, to become a power in the city, and to conquer its society. To this end, he sought an enterprise which would quickly yield him heavy returns on his investment. His first battle among the financial barons of Chicago was to gain control of the gas companies.

At the same time, the Cowperwoods made their first attack on Chicago society, but with little success. Aileen Cowperwood was too high-spirited and lacking in the poise which would win her social success. Then Cowperwood became involved in several lawsuits and his earlier political-economic disgrace in Philadelphia was exposed in the Chicago newspapers. After a long battle, Cowperwood was able to force the rival gas companies to buy out his franchises at a profit to himself.

Unfortunately, the deal brought social defeat, at least temporarily, to the Cowperwoods, for his rivals in finance were the social powers of Chicago at that time. Cowperwood turned once again to a mistress, but the affair ended when Aileen attempted to kill her rival.

For several years, a cable-car system of street railways claimed most of Cowperwood's time. He bought control of the horsecar company which served the north side of Chicago. Then the naturally promiscuous temperament of

Cowperwood intruded itself when he met dark, lush Stephanie Platow. Ten years younger than his wife and interested in art, literature, and music, she was able to occupy a place in his life that Aileen could never fill.

While involved in that affair, Cowperwood coerced the west side street railway company into giving its franchise to him, but the sweetness of his victory was partially lost by the exposure of Stephanie as another man's lover. Meanwhile, financial forces were at work against Cowperwood. Through two city bosses, these forces hoped to play the city politicians against Cowperwood, for without the support of the city council to aid him with franchises and grants, the financier would find himself helpless to merge all the street railways of the city under his control.

The first battle was fought in an election to gain possession of the Chicago city council. It was far more painful for Cowperwood to learn at this time that his wife had been unfaithful to him than to discover that he had arrayed the whole financial and social element of the city against himself. The loss of the election proved no permanent setback to Cowperwood, however, nor did his wife's infidelity. From the latter he recovered, and the first was soon undone by his opponents because they did not pave the way with favors and money when they tried to push bills through the new reform council. Even the new mayor was soon an ally of Cowperwood.

Soon afterward, Cowperwood met Berenice Fleming, daughter of a procuress, who was being prepared in a fashionable boarding school for a career in society. Taking her and her family under his wing, Cowperwood became her lover with some misgivings, for the girl was but seventeen, and he was fifty-two at the time. By this time, his enemies were trying to gain franchises for elevated lines powered by electricity.

This new effort by his financial rivals meant that his own street railways had to be converted to electricity, and he had to compete for at least a share of the elevated lines to prevent his ruin. The south side "L" was already a tremendous success because of the World's Fair of 1893, and the whole city was now clamoring for better transportation service. Cowperwood's opponents held control over the city's banks, which prevented those institutions from lending him funds needed to begin his operations. When he attempted to secure funds in the East, Cowperwood discovered that his assets were in question. By one masterstroke, however, the financier wiped out any question of his ability and his credit; he donated three hundred thousand dollars to the local university for a telescope and observatory.

Even with unlimited credit, the problem of gaining franchises was not easy. He was determined to keep control of the Chicago transportation system, but he began to realize that neither he nor his wife could ever become socially acceptable there. He decided to build a mansion in New York to hold his collection of art and be his card of entry into society.

Meanwhile, having obtained his franchises, he began work on Chicago elevated lines. Cowperwood's enemies planned to let him overreach himself, so that they could force him out of Chicago financially as well as socially. Then the collapse of the American Match Corporation, partially engineered by Cowperwood, began a series of runs on the Chicago banks controlled by his enemies. When their attempts to recall the enormous loans made to Cowperwood failed, he emerged from the affair stronger than ever.

The final battle, the climax of Cowperwood's financial career in Chicago, was the one he waged to secure fifty-year franchises for his growing transportation system. This project was made doubly difficult because of Cowperwood's latest property, the Union Loop, by which he controlled the elevated lines. This loop of elevated track, encircling the downtown business district, had to be used by all the lines in the city. The moneyed interests opposed Cowperwood because he was not with them; the newspapers, because they wanted to see better and cheaper facilities. In the face of the opposition, even the most reckless of the city's aldermen feared to grant the franchises Cowperwood wanted, regardless of the money and the power he was prepared to give to them. Then his lawyers informed Cowperwood that the state constitution prevented the city from granting such long-term franchises, even if the city council could be coerced into approving them.

Cowperwood's next idea was to have a transportation commission set up by bribery in the state legislature. In the bill which set up the commission was a clause extending existing franchises for a period of fifty years. The bill, passed by the legislature, was vetoed by the governor.

Meanwhile, the New York mansion had been completed, and Aileen Cowperwood moved in. She met with no social success, except among the Bohemian set. Berenice Fleming was settled at the same time with her family in a mansion on Park Avenue. The next step in Cowperwood's personal affairs was to be his second divorce. Then Aileen heard of his affair with Berenice Fleming. When he asked her for the divorce, she tried to commit suicide but failed.

Cowperwood again tried to force his bill through the Illinois legislature, but the legislators returned it to the city council. There, as before, Cowperwood lost. The people and the newspapers frightened the aldermen so that they dared not grant what the financier wished, despite his fantastic bribes.

With his hope of controlling the Chicago transportation system gone, Cowperwood sold his interests. Admitting defeat, he and Berenice went to Europe. The Titan's empire had fallen.

Critical Evaluation:

Theodore Dreiser's full-length portrait of a great financial wizard is one of the triumphs of the Naturalistic school of writers. Between 1890 and the publication of this book, scores of novels dealing with the American financier were published but none approached the thoroughness and the psychological insight of *The Titan*, which continues the psychological and sociological study of Cowperwood begun by Dreiser in *The Financier*. While the man Dreiser portrays is wholly without a conventional moral code, he is nevertheless a strong man with a purpose. The author makes no effort to judge his character, and the reader feels that it is best if he, too, refrains from passing judgment.

The Titan is the second in Dreiser's trilogy of novels tracing the career of Frank Algernon Cowperwood. *The Financier* (1912) tells the story of Cowperwood's early successes in the financial world of Philadelphia, of the start of his extramarital affair with Aileen, and of his conviction and imprisonment for grand larceny. In *The Stoic* (1947), Cowperwood is again portrayed as shrewdly energetic and ambitious, now living abroad after his defeat in Chicago, and amassing a large but unneeded fortune in London. Estranged from Berenice, he dies a lonely death while his overextended empire finally comes to ruin.

Cowperwood's character is based upon that of Charles Yerkes (1837–1905), a nineteenth century Chicago financier whose life and personality supplied the framework for *The Titan* and the other two novels which Dreiser had planned to call "A Trilogy of Desire." Like Dreiser's Cowperwood, Yerkes was a shrewd schemer in business who made his fortune in Philadelphia public transportation, spent a short time in prison for illegal business manipulations, and then moved to Chicago and gained control of a gas trust. Yerkes later tried to monopolize the city's transportation system through long-term franchises, but finally failed and began new business interests in the London Tube. According to Richard Lehan's account in *Theodore Dreiser: His World and His Novels* (1969), several even more specific incidences in *The Titan* are taken directly from Dreiser's own exhaustive research into the life of Yerkes and the activities of the Chicago business world he came to dominate.

The Titan also demonstrates Dreiser's absorption with the ideas of Herbert Spencer, T. H. Huxley, and other nineteenth century social-Darwinists who viewed society as essentially controlled by the law of "the survival of the fittest." In Dreiser's view, it is the nature of the universe that "a balance is struck wherein the mass subdues the individual or the individual the mass." Cowperwood's struggle against Hand, Schryhart, and Arneel is one for survival in the financial jungle of Chicago big business.

For Dreiser, such a struggle is wholly amoral; there is no right or wrong because it is man's nature as well as his condition to have to struggle for power and survival. Cowperwood's cause is neither more nor less just than that of his antagonists, nor are his means any less scrupulous than their own. He may be said to be more shrewd than they, or to possess more ruthlessness in certain circumstances; but for Dreiser, his struggle is the elemental contest between the impulse-driven energies of the individual and those of others in his society.

The forces that motivate Cowperwood's ambitions, then, are actually larger than any mere individual desires on his part. Described in the novel as "impelled by some blazing internal force," Cowperwood is driven by instincts beyond his control. Caught up in a natural struggle for survival and for power over others, he is dominated by "the drug of a personality he could not gainsay." He can no more remain satisfied with the money and success he has already attained than he can stay content with one woman. Hence, the need to conquer, to dominate and control, characterizes both Cowperwood's financial and romantic interests in life. To both, he brings the same shrewd scheming and forcefulness needed for his success.

These two major plots—Cowperwood's business life and his romantic life—alternately mirror each other throughout the novel and prove to be integrally related. Cowperwood is as direct in his dealings with women as he is in his confrontations with men of business. Compare the frankness with which he first approaches Rita Sohlberg and his blunt way of attempting to bribe Governor Swanson. Moreover, many of Cowperwood's mistresses are related to the very men who, mainly as a consequence of his amorous trespassings, will oppose him most bitterly in Chicago. His affairs with Butler's, Cochrane's, and Haguenin's daughters—like his interlude with Hand's wife—not only lessen his circle of friends but also gain him a number of enemies who eventually group together to defeat him for business as well as personal reasons.

As the title of the novel suggests, Cowperwood is indeed a Titan among men, one striving after more and achieving greater victory because he is driven to do so by his very nature. As he had himself come to recognize, the "humdrum conventional world could not brook his daring, his insouciance, his constant desire to call a spade a spade. His genial sufficiency was a taunt and a mockery to many." Yet his is a lonely victory, a fact emphasized by his almost self-imposed alienation from the business community with which his life is so connected, and by his being socially ostracized in Chicago, despite his wealth, almost from the start.

In a sense, Cowperwood is as much a victim of his will to power as any of those he has defeated on the stock exchange. For such men as he, power is the very means of survival; and in the world of Chicago business, power generates money, which in turn generates more power. The cycle, as much as the struggle, is endless. If a balance is ever struck between the power of the individual and that of the group, it is, Dreiser suggests, only temporary: for "without variance, how should the balance be maintained?" For Dreiser, as for Cowperwood, this is the meaning of life, a continual rebalancing, a necessary searching after on the part of the individual to discover a means of maintaining or acquiring his own desires against those of his society. Man is but a tool of his own private nature, "forever suffering the goad of a restless heart."

For men like Cowperwood, then, defeat is no more final or settling than triumph. If he has won anything permanent by the novel's end, it is the love of Berenice. She is part, at least, of the whole that Cowperwood has been driven to seek after and attain. More than that, he will never achieve nor understand about life. "Thou hast lived," concludes Dreiser at the end of the novel, as if to say that the struggle and the searching after are themselves the whole and the balance men seek.

TOBACCO ROAD

Type of work: Novel
Author: Erskine Caldwell (1903–   )
Type of plot: Social melodrama
Time of plot: 1920's
Locale: Georgia
First published: 1932

Principal characters:
>JEETER LESTER, a poor white
>ADA, his wife
>DUDE, his son
>ELLIE MAY, his daughter
>PEARL, another daughter
>LOV BENSEY, Pearl's husband
>BESSIE, a backwoods evangelist

The Story:

Lov Bensey, husband of Pearl, the fifteen-year-old daughter of Jeeter Lester, felt low in his mind when he stopped by the Lester house on his way home with a bag of turnips. Pearl, he complained, refused to have anything to do with him; she would neither sleep with him nor talk to him.

The Lesters lived in a one-room shack which was falling apart. They had nothing to eat but pork-rind soup. Jeeter was trying to patch an inner tube so that the Lester car, a nondescript wreck which had been refused even by the junk dealer, could be used to carry firewood to Augusta. Jeeter's hare-lipped daughter, Ellie May, charmed Lov away from his bag of turnips. While she and Lov were dallying in the yard in front of the shack, the other Lesters pounced upon the bag of turnips. Jeeter grabbed it and ran into the scrub woods, followed by his worthless son Dude. Jeeter ate his fill of turnips. He gave Dude several and even saved a handful for the rest of the family. They returned from the woods to find Lov gone. Sister Bessie, a woman preacher, had come for a visit. Bessie, middle-aged, and Dude, sixteen, were attracted to each other. Bessie, upon leaving, promised to return to take Dude away to be her husband.

The Lesters were starving. Jeeter had long since been unable to get credit at the local stores in order to buy seed, fertilizer, and food. His land was exhausted, and there was no chance of reclaiming it because of Jeeter's utter laziness. Jeeter and his wife Ada had had seventeen children. Twelve of them survived, but all except Ellie May and Dude had left home.

Bessie returned and announced that God had given her permission to marry Dude, but Dude refused to listen until Bessie said that she was planning to buy a new car with some money that her late husband had left her. She and Dude went to town and bought a new Ford, the loud horn of which Dude highly approved. At the county courthouse, over the mild protestations of the clerk because of Dude's youth, Bessie got a marriage license. Back at the Lester shack, Bessie, using her authority as preacher, married herself to Dude.

The newlyweds went for a ride in their new car; they returned to the tobacco road at sundown with one fender of the car completely ruined. They had run into a farm wagon on the highway and had killed a black whom they left lying by the roadside.

Jeeter, anxious to get food and snuff, persuaded Bessie and Dude to take him to Augusta with a load of firewood. Their arrival in Augusta was delayed, however, by the breakdown of the car. A gallon and a half of oil poured into the crankcase enabled them to get to the city, where Jeeter failed to sell one stick of wood. The trio sold the car's spare tire, for which they could see no use, and bought food. They mistook a house of ill-repute for a hotel; Bessie was absent from Jeeter and her young husband most of the night.

During the return trip to the tobacco road, Jeeter unloaded the wood beside the highway and set fire to it. He was about to suggest another trip in the car, but Bessie and Dude rode away before he could stop them.

As the car rapidly fell apart, the warmth between Bessie and her young husband cooled. In a fight between Bessie and the Lesters over Jeeter's right to ride in the car again, Dude sided with his wife. After all, the car still ran a little.

Meanwhile, Pearl ran away from Lov; she had managed to escape after he had tied her to their bed. Jeeter advised Lov not to look for Pearl but to take Ellie May in her place. He asked Ellie May to bring back victuals and clothes from Lov's house. The grandmother, who had been run over by Bessie's Ford, died in the yard.

Jeeter anticipated seeding time by burning the broomsedge off his land. A wind blew the fire to the house while Jeeter and Ada were asleep. The destitute sharecroppers were burned to death on the land that Jeeter's family had once owned as prosperous farmers.

Critical Evaluation:

The uproarious, Rabelaisian episodes of *Tobacco Road* make the novel appear to be a burlesque on rural life of the southern United States. Granted the exaggeration for effect, the book deals truthfully, in the main, with a human element which is in evidence in the eastern piedmont from Virginia to Georgia. The character of Jeeter Lester, although repulsive in many respects, is nevertheless a curiously moving one. In creating Jeeter, Erskine Caldwell gave the world another minor hero, a man whose futile hopefulness attracts the sympathy of the sentimental and the social-minded.

Published in the midst of the Great Depression, the novel reflects the social and economic concerns of the 1930's, as well as principles of literary Naturalism. During the 1930's, a time of extreme economic hardship, novels such as *Tobacco Road* helped make Americans (and others) aware of the destructive poverty and alienation at the bottom of society.

Naturalism, a significant movement in American literature from before the beginning of the twentieth century through World War II, stresses the impersonal and powerful forces that shape human destinies. The characters of *Tobacco Road* are caught in the backwaters of industrialization, in the grip of irresistible forces. Unable to farm effectively, yet bound to the land, and so unable to migrate to the factories, they are trapped from one generation to the next. Jeeter, for instance, cannot farm his land, and yet instinct binds him (and, finally, his son) to it.

These characters are also prisoners of other forces, most notably the past and their sexuality. They find modern technology beyond their understanding, and they ruin a new car Bessie has managed to buy. Unable to use modern farming methods, Jeeter and Ada die trying to burn the fields to clear them for an imaginary cotton crop. Sexuality also operates powerfully on these characters. Bessie's marriage to Dude and Lov's attraction for Ellie May are based entirely on sex; and, in fact, the reader is left with the impression that the characters of *Tobacco Road* are as little able to cope with sexual forces as with economic forces.

The style of the novel, marked by simple, declarative sentences and catching the rhythms of the dialect used by poor white Southerners, is appropriate for the tragically self-destructive life Caldwell describes. This plain style, typical of Naturalism, corresponds to the basic drives for food, sex, and survival, drives that are not hidden or disguised by the demands of civilization but that Caldwell lays bare for all to see in the changeless lives of his characters.

THE TOWN

Type of work: Novel
Author: William Faulkner (1897–1962)
Type of plot: Psychological realism
Time of plot: 1909–1927
Locale: Jefferson, Yoknapatawpha County, Mississippi
First published: 1957

Principal characters:

FLEM SNOPES, the shrewdest of the Snopes family
EULA VARNER SNOPES, his wife
LINDA SNOPES, their daughter
MANFRED DE SPAIN, the mayor of Jefferson and Eula's lover
GAVIN STEVENS, a county attorney
V. K. RATLIFF, a salesman and friend of Gavin Stevens
CHARLES MALLISON, Stevens' nephew
MONTGOMERY WARD SNOPES,
WALLSTREET PANIC SNOPES,
BYRON SNOPES,
MINK SNOPES,
ECK SNOPES, and
I. O. SNOPES, Flem's cousins

The Story:

The Snopes family, which came out of nowhere after the Civil War, had successfully completed the invasion of Frenchman's Bend. Now Flem Snopes, son of Ab Snopes, a bushwhacker, sharecropper, and horse thief, was ready for the next goal, the domination of Jefferson, county seat of Yoknapatawpha County.

Flem Snopes was ruthless, shrewd, uneducated, and possessed of a fanatic belief in the power of money. The townspeople, who had seen him when he took over Frenchman's Bend and then left it under control of other family members, were wondering about Flem's next move. Among those interested were Gavin Stevens, a young lawyer educated in Heidelberg, and V. K. Ratliff, a good-natured sewing machine salesman, who made up for his lack of education with a great measure of common sense. Stevens felt a moral responsibility to defend the town against the Snopeses, and Ratliff was once the victim of Snopesism when, thinking that it contained a buried treasure, he bought worthless property from Flem for a high price. Another who became an assistant in the fight against Snopes infiltration was Stevens' nephew, Charles Mallison, who watched the Snopes invasion from his childhood through adolescence.

Flem Snopes realized that more subtle methods for conquering Jefferson were necessary than those he had used in Frenchman's Bend. The greatest advantage for him was his marriage with Eula Varner, daughter of Will Varner, chief property owner in that community. When Eula was pregnant, impotent Flem had married her after making a profitable deal with Varner, who despised Snopes but wanted to save his daughter's honor.

In a small rented house, Flem and his wife made a modest beginning in Jefferson by operating a small restaurant of which Ratliff had been a partner before he lost his share in the business deal with Flem. Later, the restaurant was transformed into a hotel. The first hint that Flem was aiming even higher came when he was appointed superintendent of the local power plant, before the people even knew that such a position existed.

As the new mayor of Jefferson, Manfred de Spain was not in favor with the town conservatives, but he had won the election in a landslide when he declared himself against an automobile ban imposed by the former mayor. Soon it became known in the town that Eula Snopes and the new mayor were lovers. No one had seen anything, but everybody seemed to know about the affair except her husband.

Shortly after the war, during which Gavin Stevens served overseas, the president of Jefferson's oldest bank was killed in an auto accident. De Spain, named president on account of the bank stock he had inherited, resigned as mayor. The election of a new president made necessary a routine check by government auditors, who uncovered the theft of a large sum of money by a defaulting clerk, Byron Snopes, who fled to Mexico. Announcement was made that the money had been replaced by the new president and that Mr. Flem Snopes had been made a vice president of the bank. Flem's appointment indicated to his opponents a new phase of Snopesism: the search for money power was now overshadowed by Flem's desire for respectability. This new tactic also became apparent when he rid himself and Jefferson of some undesirable kinsmen, like Montgomery Ward Snopes, who might have destroyed his efforts to make the name Snopes respectable. Montgomery Ward Snopes had returned from the war in France with a rich supply of pornographic pictures. A short time later, he opened a photographic studio and gave nightly slide shows for a large part of the male population of Yoknapatawpha County. Flem, not wishing to have his name associated with this shady enterprise, put bootleg whiskey in Montgomery Ward's studio to assure his arrest. When another Snopes, Mink, was jailed for murder, Flem failed to give him any assistance. There was also Eck Snopes, who did not fit into the Snopes pattern on account of his weak intelligence. Flem had no need to bring about his removal, for Eck removed himself. He had been hired to watch an oil tank.

While a search was being made for a lost child, Eck, trying to make sure that the child had not climbed into his oil tank, took a lantern and went to look inside the tank. After the explosion, only Eck's metal neck brace was available for burial. Meanwhile, the child was found safely somewhere along the road.

Flem's new desire for respectability also made him forget Wallstreet Panic Snopes, who had dared to become a self-made man without his kinsman's help. Wallstreet Panic, a successful grocer, introduced the first self-service store in Jefferson. Flem also disliked the outcome of one of his family projects with I. O. Snopes, who was trained to tie mules to the railroad track in order to collect money from damage lawsuits against the railroad. When I. O. Snopes was killed during one of these operations, Flem hoped to collect the indemnity. I. O.'s stubborn wife, however, kept all the money, and Flem, in order to avoid complications, was forced to pay off the man who had supplied the mules. Flem also tried to live up to his new social standing by letting a professional decorator furnish his house.

In the meantime, Gavin Stevens, who had never been able to rid himself of the attraction Eula Snopes held for him, concentrated his reform efforts on Linda, Eula's daughter. Linda, now in high school, did not know that Flem was not her real father. The lawyer loved Linda and tried to influence her to attend a northern college far away from Snopesism. Flem, however, needing a front of outwardly solid family life for his show of respectability, was opposed to the possibility of losing his control of Linda, especially since a will existed which gave the girl a great deal of Will Varner's estate. So Flem disregarded the pleas of his daughter because he still had one more step ahead of him to achieve the position he desired in Jefferson: his scheme to replace de Spain as president of the bank. When he failed in his first attempt to ruin the bank by instigating a run on it, he decided that the time had come to use his knowledge of his wife's adultery as a weapon. Acting as if he had just learned of the eighteen-year-old affair, and armed with a declaration from Linda that she would leave her part of her inheritance to her father, he visited Will Varner. Once more, in order to save the honor of his daughter and in return for Flem's promise to destroy Linda's note about the inheritance, Varner helped Flem to get rid of de Spain, and Flem became president of the bank. Hoping Eula would run away with him, de Spain sold his bank stock, but Eula, hoping to keep her daughter from ever learning of her affairs, remained in Jefferson. She committed suicide after securing from Gavin Stevens a promise that he would marry Linda.

Flem, having reached his goal, agreed to let Linda leave Jefferson. For a short interval, the ghost of old Snopesism came back to Jefferson, when bank thief Byron Snopes sent his four half-Indian children to stay with his kinsfolk. After a series of incidents in which the children terrorized Jefferson and Frenchman's Bend, Flem himself made sure that these last reminders of primitive Snopesism were sent back to Mexico. Meanwhile, he had bought the de Spain house, and workers were busy transforming it into a mansion suitable to Flem Snopes, president of the Bank of Jefferson.

Critical Evaluation:

It was in the 1920's that William Faulkner first conceived of the Snopes saga: a clan of crude, avaricious, amoral, unfeeling, but energetic and hard-driving individuals who would move into the settled, essentially moral society of the Old South and gradually, but inevitably, usurp the old order. To Faulkner, the Snopeses were not a special Mississippi phenomenon, but a characteristic evil of the mechanized, dehumanized twentieth century which filled the void left by the collapse of the agrarian pre-Civil War South. Flem Snopes is the supreme example of the type, and the Snopes Trilogy is primarily a chronicle of his career and its implications.

It was 1940, however, before Faulkner finished *The Hamlet*, the first book in the series (although several short stories appeared earlier), and not until the 1950's that he completed the trilogy with *The Town* and *The Mansion*. In the intervening time, Faulkner's vision of human morality and society had become more complex and, although the original design remained intact, the quest of the Snopes Clan became more devious and complicated, and "Snopesism" took on increasingly ambiguous meanings.

At the beginning of *The Town*, Flem arrives in Jefferson fresh from his triumphs in Frenchman's Bend, but with only a wagon, a new wife, Eula Varner Snopes, and their baby daughter, Linda. The book traces his rise in short order from restaurant owner to hotel owner, to power plant supervisor, to bank vice president, and finally to bank president, church deacon, and grieving widower. The book also describes the life of his wife, Eula, her lengthy affair with Manfred de Spain, her relations to the community, and her efforts for her daughter—all of which leads her, at last, to suicide.

If Flem is the embodiment of ruthless, aggressive inhumanity and devitalized conformity, Eula is the essence of warmth, emotional involvement, sexuality, and freedom. Although their direct confrontations are muted, *The Town* is basically about the struggle between these two characters and the contrasting approaches to life that they represent. The story is told by three anti-Snopesian citizens: V. K. Ratliff, the sewing machine salesman who previously tangled with Flem in Frenchman's Bend; Gavin Stevens, Heidelberg and Harvard educated County Attorney; and Charles Mallison, Stevens' young nephew. Although they confirm the essential facts, each speaker has a separate interpretation of the events. Thus, the reader must sift through their different attitudes and conclusions to arrive at the "truth" of the book. Frequently, it is the ironical distance between the events and the characters' interpretations of them that gives the book its bite and message—as well as its humor.

Mallison, who saw the events as a child but recounts them as an adult, is probably the most detached of the narrators. Ratliff is sardonic and realistic, but his bitter experiences with the Snopeses somewhat color his accounts. Gavin Stevens is the primary narrator and chief enemy of Flem, but the reliability of his statements is jeopardized by his lengthy, emotional, somewhat confused involvements with both Eula and Linda.

Stevens is a well-educated, sophisticated modern man who understands the complexities and difficulties of human relationships; but, at the same time, he is an old-fashioned Southern gentleman who clings to old attitudes and traditions. When Eula offers herself to him, it is not morality, but romanticism coupled with self-doubt that stimulates his refusal. He insists on viewing her through a romantic haze which prevents him from reacting realistically in the most critical situations. "What he was doing was simply defending forever with his blood the principle that chastity and virtue in women shall be defended whether they exist or not."

The same kinds of assumptions determine his relationship to Linda Snopes. Since he is nearly twice her age, he cannot imagine a sexual or marital arrangement between them in spite of the fact that he loves her and is encouraged by her mother. So, in the role of father protector and educator, Stevens reads poetry to Linda over sodas and feeds her dreams with college catalogs. Thus, because of his intense emotions, sense of morality, and traditional assumptions, Gavin Stevens is unable to deal either with Eula's simple sensuality or Flem Snopes's one-dimensional inhumanity.

In the final conflict between these two forces, Flem's ruthless rationality easily overcomes Eula's passionate free spirit. Being both physically and spiritually impotent, Flem can coldly and callously manipulate the sexual and emotional drives in others. Not only does he do so to thwart Stevens' anti-Snopes efforts, but more importantly to his plans, he also uses them to gain control over his primary Jefferson rival, Manfred de Spain.

Flem learns of his wife's affair with de Spain soon after his arrival in Jefferson, but he chooses to ignore it as long as it is profitable. It is even suggested that the two men work out a tacit agreement whereby Flem overlooks the affair in return for an appointment to the newly created job of power plant superintendent. De Spain's influence is later instrumental in securing Flem the vice presidency of the Sartoris Bank. After eighteen years, however, when Flem decides to make his move for the bank presidency, he suddenly becomes the outraged husband. He uses the threat of scandal to provoke Will Varner to action, to drive de Spain from the bank, to push Eula to suicide, and to coerce Stevens into unwilling complicity. Neither integrity nor sensuality can stop Snopesism.

As Flem succeeds in his drive to monetary wealth, another goal becomes predominant—"respectability." He learns from de Spain that in Jefferson one can become respectable without being moral—if one has the necessary money. So Flem systematically acquires all the requisite signs of success, and they, in turn, provide him with access to respectability. Only one last obstacle remains between Flem and complete social acceptance—the other Snopeses.

Consequently, it is Flem, himself, who finally rids Jefferson of the Snopeses. Using the same callous attitude and devious strategy on his kin that he used on other victims, he eliminates all of the lesser Snopeses who might pose a threat to his new status: Mink, Byron, Montgomery Ward, I. O., and, finally, Byron's brood of wild, half-breed children, "The last and final end of Snopes out-and-out unvarnished behavior in Jefferson."

So Flem becomes respectable. Faulkner's final question to the reader is this: Has Flem's drive to social acceptance weakened and narrowed him to the point where he is vulnerable, if not to the morality of the Ratliffs, Stevenses, and Mallisons, then to the latent vengeances of Snopesism? Faulkner answers that question in *The Mansion*.

THE TOWN

Type of work: Novel
Author: Conrad Richter (1890–1968)
Type of plot: Regional romance
Time of plot: Mid-nineteenth century
Locale: Ohio
First published: 1950

Principal characters:
SAYWARD WHEELER, a pioneer matriarch
PORTIUS, her husband
RESOLVE,
GUERDON,
KINZIE,
HULDAH,
SOOTH,
LIBBY,
DEZIA,
MERCY, and
CHANCEY, her children
JAKE TENCH, a steamboat operator
MRS. JAKE TENCH
ROSA TENCH, her child

The Story:

Three times in her life Sayward Wheeler had felt that her life was over and done. Not that it frightened her any; she figured she could do as well in the next world as in this. Once was the day before her father told her the game was leaving Pennsylvania. The next week, Sayward and her family traipsed west. The second time was the night she married Portius. This time she was not sure the feeling was more than that she would never have any more babies. She reckoned ten was enough, though one lay in the burying ground.

Her youngest worried her the most. All the others had been hearty enough, but Chancey was so frail that folks thought it would have been easier for him to die when he was born. When he was a little fellow, his heart flopped so much when he walked that he spent most of his time sitting on a stool in his daddy's office. He looked out of the window for hours, never opening his mouth. Chancey lived in two worlds, the earthy, boisterous one his family loved, and one in which he could float away and do wonderful things.

Sayward had fretted herself to raise him. To harden him, she always had guests sleep with him. She never knew how he shuddered lying next to most of them, but he liked the softness of the bride the time the bridesman got angry up in the loft with all of them and spent the night sitting in the kitchen.

Chancey was his father's favorite because his mind ran as clear as water. Often he rode his father's shoulders into town. He had an uncertain ride the day Portius took him to the hay scales. Portius had just returned from the state capitol where he had put through a bill calling for a new county for the township. With the making of the new county went four judgeships. Portius, because he was an agnostic, did not get an appointment as he had expected. It was given instead to a skinflint tax collector. Portius had come home, drunk and disheveled, minus his horse and saddle. Shortly afterward, the new judge came to deliver a load of hay which had to be weighed in town on the new scales. Portius, with Chancey on his shoulders, followed the wavering wagon tracks into town. With one eye on Portius' unsteady gait, the new judge stayed on the wagon while it was weighed in. They clinched their bargain at the inn, the judge demanding cash which Portius produced. When the judge started to leave, Portius claimed that he had bought the judge's person with the load of hay. Before he left the inn, the judge had given Portius the hay to avoid being hauled to court. Not many could get ahead of Portius; Sayward thought he had too much of the rascal in him himself.

Although he was not yet a judge, he was a popular lawyer, and he was the leader in the fight to have Americus named the county seat. Resolve had studied law with his father and also practiced at the courthouse. Sayward was pleased when he married a girl who was sensible, even if she did have a lot of money. Sayward felt at the time that things were going along too well and that the Lord would fetch her feet to the ground soon.

She was brought around feet first when Huldah disappeared. Sayward knew that black-eyed minx never fell in the river as some folks thought, but she was taken a little aback when she heard that Huldah had gone to a man's house stark naked, claiming the gypsies had taken her clothing. Sayward went after her. On the way home, the ferryman, muttering a coarse remark Sayward only guessed at, made them wait for a second crossing. Sayward would not wait; she drove her horse into the river and forded it instead. Huldah listened respectfully after that.

Her set-to with the ferryman settled in Sayward's mind. Next thing he knew, Portius was arguing for a bridge in town. When it was built, Guerdon worked on it, though he claimed all the while that it was too low for flood time. When the floods came, Chancey, running away, was caught on the bridge and washed down the river. He could not tell whether he was in a dream or not until some men rowed out after him. Guerdon came down the river later to take him home.

Guerdon married a slut and ran away after he killed her lover. Guerdon's daughter Guerda, a sprightly and prophetic child, became Sayward's favorite. Soon after, Guerda told Sayward that a good angel was coming for her, and the child died suddenly of a throat infection.

Of all the Wheeler children, Chancey always had the hardest row to hoe. He fell in love with Rosa, the child Mrs. Jake Tench had had by Portius. When Rosa realized that all chances were against her, she committed suicide.

After his Aunt Unity died and her Bay State furniture was sent to him, Portius persuaded Sayward that his position in town warranted a mansion on the square. Sayward was proud of the house, but comfortable only in the kitchen and the room where she kept her old cabin furniture. Oh, she never disgraced her family; she could keep up with folks, even when Resolve became state governor. Although she was the richest woman in town, her family said she was so common that she spoke to everyone she saw. The things she missed most at the townhouse were trees. She, who had sworn so often at the big butts, grew lonely for them. The first trees in town were those she planted in her yard.

She enjoyed having Portius' sister come to visit for a month, though the Bay State woman harped mostly on things and folks back east. Sayward could not help laughing when her old bushnipple of a pappy came in to see the woman and praised the old settlers skyhigh.

Her pappy had tracked down their lost Sulie. When Sayward and Genny went out to see her, they found her a squaw woman who would not admit she remembered them.

Chancey left home to become a newspaper editor, blasting the pioneers who slaved for their livelihood and praising the men who advocated the abolition of hardship. Sayward secretly supported Chancey's paper; she thought he had as good a right to say what he pleased as anyone. She missed him, but his newspaper pieces seemed to bring him closer. When he came back for Portius' funeral, Sayward guessed he really came to see if his father had left him any money.

Sayward was lonely. All the folks who had known her kind of life were gone. The children thought her mind wandered a little before she died. She talked to her trees and said in her will that they could not be cut down. When she finally took to her bed, she had it turned toward the trees outside.

Critical Evaluation:

As the third novel in a trilogy on early American life, *The Town* completes the story of Sayward Luckett Wheeler, her husband Portius, and their nine children. It depicts the settlement and growth of a town and describes the way of life experienced by the families who live and work in that period of American history when the frontier was closing down. In this historical novel, Conrad Richter gives sharp details about the everyday life and possessions of the early settlers. He uses authentic speech and describes their food, clothing, tableware, and furniture. Even accounts of medical practices and methods of printing are woven into the family experiences. Richter gives descriptions to fit each era of the trilogy, and much of the interest and warmth of the story comes from these ordinary aspects of daily life.

In addition to its value as history, *The Town* is also a commentary on progress and civilization. It compares the past, as in the Luckett's early years on the Ohio frontier, with the present in the town of Americus, Ohio. As participants in and builders of the new town, Sayward and the other old-timers wonder if the "easy life" they now have is really advancement or if it is the opposite—a demoralizing situation. The radical opinion, which Sayward's youngest son Chancey holds, is that pioneer times were brutal and wild and that true progress should continue. As times change, labor will not be necessary, and peace and happiness will flourish in a life of ease. Many of the discussions in the book concern the validity of each of these opposing ideas.

Richter, the son of a minister, was born in 1890 in Pennsylvania. At age fifteen, he finished high school and began a succession of jobs which included being a clerk, a farm laborer, and a county correspondent. He also reported on the Johnstown, Pennsylvania, *Journal*, and by age nineteen he was the editor of the weekly *Courier* at Patton, Pennsylvania. From there he went on to report for daily newspapers and then worked as a private secretary in Cleveland, where he sold his first fiction story.

In 1928 Richter moved to the West and began collecting materials on early American life. Not satisfied with his research into original sources, early rare books, newspapers, and manuscripts, he found and talked to early pioneers who were still alive. His lengthy visits with them provided much of the historical detail for his novels.

Richter published his first book in 1924, *Brothers of No Kin and Other Stories*. During his lifetime, he wrote approximately twenty-five books and published his last, *The Aristocrat*, shortly before his death in 1968. In 1950, he published *The Town* and in 1951 received the Pulitzer Prize for Fiction for that book.

Like the earlier novels in the trilogy, *The Town* is written in the third person, and much of it is from Sayward's point of view. In this last novel, however, the reader is also given the viewpoint of Chancey, Sayward's son. Even in Chancey's early years, his thoughts, feelings, and dreamworld are known to the reader.

As *The Town* begins, Sayward is in her late forties but remains the strong, practical woman she was in her earlier years. She represents realism, the acceptance of events as they happen. In character and determination, she is similar to the fictional characters of Scarlett O'Hara and Selina DeJong. She believes that physical work and hardship develop moral strength, healthy values, and happiness. Money and "society" mean nothing to her, although she is probably the richest and best-known person in town. She loves her simple cabin, built by her father when the Lucketts first moved to Ohio, and she moves to the mansion in town only when Portius insists on it. Sayward, who hated the trees when she first moved to Ohio and worked for years to clear away the growth and plant crops, now discovers she misses the huge old trees. She begins to see backbiting, pride, and greed for material things, attitudes she does not remember existing in frontier life. In Chancey and other town children, she discovers an aversion to work, and she considers this a weakness unheard of in her youth. It is these realizations that cause her to question the good of change and advancement.

It is also these observations that deepen the conflict between Sayward and Chancey. He is a dreamer, an idealist in a family of realists. Perhaps because he is weak and sickly, he has few friends and always feels misunderstood. Even Sayward, who has insight into her other children, lacks an understanding of Chancey's feelings and opinions. As a believer in progress, he stands against the brutal labor that opened the frontier. Although he ridicules her accomplishments and beliefs, she continues to support his newspaper work; this indicates her motherly love and her attempt to understand him. On his part, he feels only hate and does not accept or even tolerate another's opinions. Only at Sayward's deathbed does he even reconsider his attitudes toward her. Sayward's and Chancey's relationship illustrates the not-so-modern generation gap. As a real character, Chancey is not very believable, but as a representative of an idealistic and radical theory, he is a credible part of the story. Age versus youth and realism versus idealism are strong themes in this novel.

Minor issues in *The Town* include a conflict between a belief in God and agnosticism, exemplified by Sayward and Portius, and the Indian-white relationships. This novel tells of the white man's fears, friendships, and attitudes toward the Indians. Another of Richter's novels, *Light in the Forest*, discusses the relationship from the Indians' point of view.

When the novel ends, Portius and most of the old-timers are dead, and Sayward is dying. *The Town* has portrayed a family—its problems, joys, and adventures—but it has also told the story of a growing town and the changes in people, economics, and attitudes. It leaves the reader to draw his own conclusion about the advantages and disadvantages of progress.

Richter's purpose in writing these books was not a historical one. History for its own sake never enters into the story. Richter wanted, instead, to give to the reader the feeling of having lived with his characters, of being familiar with their colloquial speech, their habits, their clothes, their everyday problems, and their struggle for survival against nature, man, and beast. These are satisfying books, full of the love of the land, of earthy wisdom, and broad sympathy.

THE TRACK OF THE CAT

Type of work: Novel
Author: Walter Van Tilburg Clark (1909–1971)
Type of plot: Symbolic allegory
Time of plot: Early twentieth century
Locale: Sierra Nevada Mountains
First published: 1949

> Principal characters:
> ARTHUR BRIDGES, a dreamer
> CURT and
> HAROLD, his brothers
> GRACE, his sister
> MRS. BRIDGES, the mother
> MR. BRIDGES, the father
> JOE SAM, the Indian hired man
> GWEN WILLIAMS, Harold's girl

The Story:

Arthur Bridges, dreaming that he was caught in a blizzard in the Sierra Nevadas, could hear a loved one cry out to him, but he could not recognize the voice. He was afraid to move for fear he would fall off an icy cliff. He realized dimly that his left hand was bare and cold. As he put it in the pocket of his red and white cowhide parka, he felt the half-finished carving of a mountain lion that he was making for Joe Sam. Every year, he carved a cat for Joe Sam because the old Indian believed a black cat brought death with the first snow unless he could make medicine against it. This year the first snow had come early in October, and the carved cat was not finished. The black cat must be stalking some prey through the stormy night. As Arthur heard the scream again, he tried to get off the cliff. Falling, he screamed and woke himself up.

Finding himself in the bunk room of the ranch house, Arthur listened for a sound in the wind. When he heard it, he awoke his brothers, Curt and Harold. Curt thought Arthur was only dreaming until he also heard the scream of cattle being attacked somewhere in the storm. He rushed into his clothes to go out to the cattle.

The mother, having heard the screams, was making breakfast by the time the boys were dressed. Since it was dark and they could not see what was attacking, they ate while they made plans. Harold, the youngest, was to stay at home. Curt, always the boss, would take charge, but he would take Arthur along because he had dreamed that a black painter was at the cattle.

Arthur got out his whittling as they waited. Harold told him that Joe Sam had been up to his tricks that night. When something worried Joe Sam, he was likely to fall into a trance and go without eating or sleeping for days. Joe Sam always made medicine to his gods before the first snow and carried one of Arthur's carvings of a mountain lion in a little bag under his chin. The black cat was, to him, the height of evil. Bullets went through it so that it could never be killed. It was as big as a horse. It made no tracks; but it could kill viciously. The early October storm had caught them all unawares, with Joe Sam's cat still unfinished.

The mother had also dreamed something which she would not tell. She wanted Curt to take Harold with him instead of Arthur. But Harold's girl, Gwen Williams, had come to visit the night before, and Arthur thought Harold should stay with her. When the mother asked Harold his plans for marrying Gwen, he claimed that he had not gone that far. Arthur figured the valley could hold more stock out of which Harold could take a yearly cut. They all realized that Curt would object if he did not get his own way or if he saw money going outside of the immediate family, even if it were to a brother's family. Harold said he would arrange the matter with Curt when Gwen went home. They all knew the father, who lived now only to drink, would have no say in the matter.

Before Curt and Arthur left, the father and the girls, Grace and Gwen, came to breakfast. The father immediately started drinking. To spite Harold, Curt tried to impress Gwen. Although he made fun of Arthur's half-belief in Joe Sam's black cat, he admitted when he got the horses ready that they were spooky that morning.

Curt and Arthur took only one gun because Curt was sure the cat was in a box canyon where he could easily find and kill it; Arthur would not need a gun for his kind of cat. In the canyon, Curt found some of the cattle newly killed, obviously by a mountain lion. There were tracks nearby, but in his high-heeled boots he could not follow them through the snow. Leaving Arthur and the gun to hold the trail, Curt went back to the house for tracking boots and food.

Arthur, leading his pony, slowly followed the cat's tracks toward a half-dome where he had often sat, whittling his figures and admiring the view. Suddenly his pony neighed fiercely and jerked, throwing Arthur sprawling into the bushes nearby. As he looked up over his shoulder, Arthur saw the black cat leaping at him.

Curt dawdled at home. Trying to get a rise out of Gwen, he promised to bring her home the skin of the black cat to use as a blanket, or, if it should be a yellow one, to wear as a costume. Harold brought him a frisky horse. Curt, nearly trampling the Indian, asked Joe Sam whether he still believed in the black cat. Joe Sam only replied that the hunting would not be very good because of the heavy snow.

On the way back to the canyon, Curt saw Arthur's horse heading home. Disgusted because he thought Arthur had forgotten the horse as he day-dreamed, Curt followed the tracks until he found Arthur's body. While he exchanged his coat for Arthur's heavy parka and packed the body on his own horse, he swore to get the cat if he had to trail it to the Pacific. Then he headed the horse toward home with the body.

Arthur's death greatly upset the mother and Grace. Harold and Gwen had to keep things going at the ranch. The father was drunk and Joe Sam prac-tically hypnotized. A heavy snow settled in, delaying the burial. Afterward, they made a huge bonfire in front of the house in case Curt needed direction. He had been out more than two days since Arthur's body had come back on the horse. The mother told Harold he would have to go out after Curt and that he should take Joe Sam along to track.

The horses became spooky when Curt and Joe Sam came near the box canyon. Each man tracked one side of the creek. Harold found dead cattle, one heifer so freshly killed that the blood still spurted. Working carefully, he tracked the cat so closely that he was almost surprised when he saw it. As he shot, Joe Sam's bullet came from across the creek. The cat sprang away with a scream, but the men followed it and finished their job. Although it was almost all black, Joe Sam said that the cat was not his black painter. His was a devil killing all the time.

Harold found Curt's crumpled body under a cliff. Tracing back from the place above the body where the snow had been broken off, he guessed that Curt had rushed wildly about after leaving a fire and a pile of cut boughs higher up. There, where the fire had been, Harold found Curt's gun and snowshoes, but he could find no tracks except Curt's in all the clearing. Puzzled and a little terrified, Harold guessed that the dead black painter might as well be blamed for Curt's death after all.

Critical Evaluation:

Like his earlier novel, *The Ox-Bow Incident*, Walter Van Tilburg Clark's *The Track of the Cat* is a tragedy laid in Nevada, his adopted state. It is a long, psychological, and symbolic study of the effect of evil on a ranch family. The black cat means the end of everything to the Indian Joe Sam, whose animism, apparent in his recognition and acceptance of the primitive, mythic nature of Evil, affects the whole Bridges family for whom he works. Clark writes his story with his usual vivid contrasts between dream and fact, white man and Indian, tragedy and hope.

The novel falls into four parts: one for the testing of each of the brothers, and a fourth to show the state of life at the novel's psychological center, the ranchhouse kitchen. The kitchen, too, becomes a proving-ground for Gwen and Harold's love and, in a sense, a further test of Harold as a man.

The panther, the force against which each of the brothers is tried in turn, changes shape to meet the character of each antagonist. For Arthur, the mystic, it takes the form of malevolent reality, whose onslaught might easily have been parried by the most elementary precautions—reloading his gun and "keeping his eyes peeled." Practicality, however, is foreign to a man whose interior life is richer, more beautiful, and more hopeful than reality. For Curt, the cat assumes the mythic shape of the "black painter"; it means despair, a sense of the death of gods, or, as Arthur says, "the end of things." It means Curt's gods are his own strength and skill; when these fail him, he has no psychic resources on which to fall back and so falls into the grip of an egoistic mirage and dies. Harold, whose nature shows both mystical and practical elements, sees the panther complexly, both as wantonly destructive and harmful to the life of the ranch, but as beautiful in itself, a mysterious life force. He stalks it circumspectly and kills it reverently.

The novel seems to make the point that Arthur, identifying the cat as a brother-creature, is unable to kill it, while Curt in his self-absorption is unfit to kill it. Only Harold, whose compassion succors all the people of the ranch, and whose sense of human superiority and responsibility nurtures all the animals, is both fit and able to gain a victory over the wilderness of which the panther is a symbol. Fittingly, the cat's pelt will deck the marriage bed of Harold and Gwen, whose union is to renew the life of the ranch. The "end of everything" for Joe Sam, made all the more awful by being accomplished by the likes of Curt, is to some degree mitigated by this union of strong, earthy, yet sensitive natures.

THE TRAGIC MUSE

Type of work: Novel
Author: Henry James (1843–1916)
Type of plot: Social narrative
Time of plot: 1880's
Locale: Paris and England
First published: 1890

Principal characters:
> NICHOLAS DORMER, a young politician and amateur
> painter
> LADY AGNES DORMER, his mother
> GRACE DORMER, and
> BIDDY DORMER, his sisters
> JULIA DALLOW, their cousin
> PETER SHERRINGHAM, her brother
> GABRIEL NASH, a friend of Nicholas
> MIRIAM ROOTH, an actress
> MRS. ROOTH, her mother
> BASIL DASHWOOD, an actor

The Story:

Nicholas Dormer, a handsome young bachelor politician and amateur portrait painter, was vacationing in Paris with his formidable mother, Lady Agnes, the impoverished widow of a Liberal politician, and his two younger sisters, spinsterish Grace and lively, lovable Biddy. At an art exhibition, Nick met an old Oxford friend, Gabriel Nash, an aesthete and dilettante but sufficiently a gentleman to be introduced to the ladies. Another visitor in Paris was the Dormers' cousin, Julia Dallow, a rich and politically minded young widow, whose brother, Peter Sherringham, was at the British Embassy there. Nick's fondness for Julia, her devotion to his political career, Biddy's friendship with Julia and unrequited affection for Peter, and Peter and Nick's congeniality united the family group with particularly close ties.

While they were together in Paris, they heard that the member of Parliament for the constituency where Julia's estate and influence lay had died suddenly. Guaranteeing her financial as well as political support, Julia wanted Nick to stand for election. This family solidarity was threatened unobtrusively by Gabriel Nash's introduction of Mrs. Rooth and Miriam, typical Jamesian characters: respectively, the widow of limited means and vague claims to aristocratic connections in England, and the beautiful daughter who has been brought up in a succession of Continental pensions where living is cheap, superficially cultivated, and multilingual but without any real education or training. To promote Miriam's aspirations toward the stage, Nash had arranged an audition with a notable retired French actress whom Peter Sherringham knew through his passionate interest in the theater. Peter, also invited to the audition, persuaded Nick to join him and suggested that Nick should paint Miriam as the Tragic Muse. Although the audition was a fiasco, Peter was sufficiently intrigued to invite the Rooths to a party at his house. There Miriam recited again, met the ladies of the family, and made a bad impression on all but Biddy. Julia, disgusted both with Miriam and with what she considered the frivolousness of Nash, returned to England to organize the election campaign, and the Dormers followed soon after. Peter found himself increasingly involved with Miriam, to the extent of offering to pay for private lessons with the old French actress. At first, he assumed that his interest was in Miriam's potential as an actress, but he eventually realized that he had been in love with her all along.

At Harsh, Julia's principal estate, where Nick had just won the election, he proposed to Julia and was accepted. To their mutual happiness there was added an undercurrent of misunderstanding, his assurance that he would give up his painting, her incomprehension of what this would mean to him, and her refusal to set their wedding date. When Nick next went to see his father's old friend and political ally, Mr. Carteret, he learned that his prospects of being the rich old bachelor's heir depended on his marriage to Julia.

Peter Sherringham, meanwhile, returning to Paris after leave in London, found that Miriam had acquired another patron, an English actor named Basil Dashwood. Peter urged her to give up her theatrical ambition for a greater role as wife of a rising diplomat, but she said that she would accept him only as the husband of an actress. In London, the engaged couple faced similar difficulties as Julia planned to spend the Parliamentary recess on a round of strategic country-house visits, while Nick preferred to use his leisure painting in his studio. With the wedding date set at last, they separated and Nick retired to his studio, where his first visitor was Gabriel Nash, whom he had not seen since their meeting in Paris. Nash told him that Miriam had arrived in London after her first success in Paris and wanted Nick to make good his promise to paint her as the Tragic Muse. When Nash brought her to the studio the next day, Nick was excited about her possibilities as a portrait subject. Beginning to paint immediately, he waited until later that night to write Julia about it. Julia failed to get the letter because she returned to London unexpectedly, called to surprise Nick, and was so stunned to find him with an actress as a sitter that she left without a word and was not at home when he called that evening. When he finally saw her late at night, she broke the engagement on the grounds that his preference for the artistic life would never be compatible with her own interest in politics.

The next day, Julia left for the Continent. Stopping in Paris to see her brother and tell him what had happened, she also urged him to marry Biddy. Though he had determined to forget the actress, Julia's account made him more eager to see Miriam than Biddy. He found a pretext for a journey to London, where he went straight to Miriam's rented villa. Not finding her at home, he then went to Nick's studio and there found Biddy alone. Discussing the break between Nick and Julia with Biddy, who was loyal to and sympathetic with both her brother and her friend, Peter failed to understand either of them; but seeing the portrait of Miriam gave a deeper understanding of the actress' beauty and of Nick's talent. Peter gave Biddy a momentary thrill by inviting her to the theater that night to see Miriam act. During the rest of his visit, he spent most of his time with the coterie of Miriam's friends who met at her house to discuss the theater.

Nick was away from London on a visit to dying Mr. Carteret, to whom he confessed not only that the engagement was broken but also that he had just written a letter to his constituency resigning his seat in Parliament. Difficult as it was to disappoint his father's old friend, who had treated him like a son, Nick found it even harder to tell his mother, who believed that the sacrifice of his political career had betrayed his father's memory, while the dual sacrifice of Mr. Carteret's and Julia's fortunes had betrayed his sisters and herself. Only Biddy remained loyal to Nick; she spent more and more time at his studio, where she had taken up sculpture.

During Peter's prolonged stay in London, the central characters revolved around one another in a tantalizing minuet: Nick saw his devoted younger sister tortured by the knowledge that Peter was in love with Miriam, and Peter was tortured by Gabriel Nash's telling him that Miriam was in love with Nick. For the third time Nash, the detached observer of life, precipitated a crisis in the lives of others. Peter tried to maintain his equilibrium by calling on Lady Agnes and accepting an invitation to dinner, but he cancelled it at the last minute when he learned that the first night of Miriam's new play had been scheduled. Her superb performance increased his passion so much that he tried again to persuade her to give up the stage to marry him, but she repeated her original terms. Defeated by her determination, Peter accepted promotion to a higher post in some remote country and withdrew.

The next year, while Miriam established herself rapidly as a success on the London stage, Nick continued to paint her, though with no interest in her except as a subject. His own artistic career was not successful, and he was worried about debts. Biddy refused a rich suitor. Julia finally came back to England accompanied by rumors of romance with a leading politician. At this depressing period, Gabriel Nash reappeared and agreed to sit for a portrait, but after only one sitting disappeared again. His encouragement of Nick's artistic bent had a lasting influence, but the complications he evoked began to disappear when he did. Julia made overtures through Biddy with the suggestion that she wanted to sit for a portrait. While Nick and Biddy were discussing this proposal, they were surprised by the arrival at the studio of Miriam and her new husband, Basil Dashwood, both excited about Miriam's opening that night as Juliet. Although the house was sold out, they managed to get a seat for Biddy as well as Nick. At the theater, they saw Peter Sherringham, who had returned from abroad in time for the first night but too late to declare again his love for Miriam, who had married three days before.

With the Tragic Muse established as a public figure, Nicholas Dormer and Peter Sherringham brought their private affairs to a swift and easy conclusion. Peter arranged for an extension of his leave in order to return to his post with Biddy as his wife. Nick painted a portrait of Julia which attracted the favorable attention of critics at a private view. There were also rumors that Julia's other suitor was worried about her. Whether Nick would ever achieve success in the career for which he had sacrificed heavily, as Miriam and Peter achieved it in theirs, remained a provocative question for the future.

Critical Evaluation:

For Henry James, art was the supreme value to which a man might sacrifice himself, and, to some extent, James's own life was such a sacrifice. Few writers have been more fascinated by the artistic process and the artistic personality, and James dealt with these subjects again and again both as practicing critic and in his many stories of writers and artists. Though not his best writing on the topic, *The Tragic Muse* is nevertheless a significant example of James's concern with the relationship between the individual and his art.

Miriam Rooth—whose name may suggest the ruthlessness with which she is prepared to sacrifice everything for her career—is a symbol of the "tragic muse" as James perceives it. She is not tragic in the usual sense—her career is an uninterrupted rise to success—but her total dedication to the theater has its tragic aspect. For Miriam, art takes precedence over all else, and she willingly gives up for the stage any hope of happiness in the usual sense. In so doing, she dramatizes on one level the history of her own individual sacrifices and perhaps her alluring dehumanization as well. As the "tragic muse," she symbolizes the total dedication she demands of herself, and of anyone who would possess her.

Whereas Miriam never faced any real conflict in regard to her art, Nick Dormer is the dramatic center of the novel because he must choose between "art" and "life," between his career as a painter and the everyday world of political affairs. Unlike Peter Sherringham, who gives up pursuit of the "tragic muse" for his diplomatic career, Nick elects to make the personal, financial, and social sacrifices his art demands. For James, this is a right choice even if Nick never materially succeeds, because he will live at the higher level of consciousness characteristic of the artist.

The three central characters represent some aspect of the conflict between ordinary life and the demands of art. This theme predominates over the intrinsic interest of the characters themselves, with the result that the novel reveals more of James's preoccupations at a certain stage of his career than of his skill as a novelist. It was written at the beginning of a period in his life when he concentrated almost exclusively on the drama and attempted for five frustrating years to achieve success on the London stage. Although he considered drama the supreme literary form, he deplored the conditions of theatrical production, and this dilemma forms the subject of a considerable proportion of the conversation in the novel. The plot, developed in terms of the decisions each of the central characters makes about the sacrifices necessary for art, lacks the subtlety and complexity of the great novels of James's later years, when he turned from drama to perfect the dramatic method in the novel.

A TREE GROWS IN BROOKLYN

Type of work: Novel
Author: Betty Smith (1904–1972)
Type of plot: Domestic romance
Time of plot: Early twentieth century
Locale: Brooklyn, New York
First published: 1943

Principal characters:
>   FRANCIE NOLAN, a Brooklyn girl
>   NEELEY NOLAN, her brother
>   KATIE NOLAN, her mother
>   JOHNNIE NOLAN, her father

The Story:

For their spending money Francie and Neeley Nolan relied on a few pennies they collected from the junkey every Saturday. Katie, their mother, worked as a janitress in a Brooklyn tenement, and the money she and their father earned—he from his Saturday night jobs as a singing waiter—was barely enough to keep the family alive and clothed.

After their Saturday morning trips with the rags, metal, and rubber they had collected during the week, Francie would visit the library. She was methodically going through its contents in alphabetical order by reading a book each day, but on Saturdays she allowed herself the luxury of breaking the sequence. At home, sitting on the fire escape, she could look up from her book and watch her neighbors' preparations for Saturday night. A tree grew in the yard; Francie watched it from season to season during her long Saturday afternoons.

At five o'clock, when her father came home, Francie would iron his waiter's apron and then go to the dry-goods store to buy the paper collar and muslin dickey which would last him for the evening. It was her special Saturday night privilege to sleep in the front room, and there she could watch the people in the street. She got up briefly at two in the morning when her father came home and was given a share of the delicacies he had salvaged from the wedding or party at which he had served. Then, while her parents talked far into the night, Francie would fix Saturday's happenings in her mind and gradually drift off to sleep.

Johnnie Nolan and Katie Rommely had met when he was nineteen and she was seventeen, and they were married four months later. In a year's time, Francie was born. Johnnie, unable to bear the sight of Katie in labor, had got drunk, and when the water pipes burst at the school in which he was janitor, he was discharged. Neeley was born soon after Francie's first birthday. By that time, Johnnie was drinking so heavily that Katie knew she could no longer rely on him for the family's support. In return for free rent, the Nolans moved to a house in which Katie could be janitress.

Francie was not sent to school until she was seven, and Neeley was old enough to go with her. In that way the children were able to protect each other from would-be tormentors. Seated two-at-a-desk among the other poverty-stricken children, Francie soon grew to look forward to the weekly visits of her art and music teachers. They were the sunshine of her school days.

By pretending that Francie had gone to live with relatives, Johnnie was able to have her transferred to another school which Francie had seen on one of her walks. A long way from home, it was, nevertheless, an improvement over the old one. Most of the children were of American parentage and were not exploited by cruel teachers, as were those from immigrant families.

Francie noted time by holidays. Beginning the year with the Fourth of July and its firecrackers, she looked forward next to Halloween. Election Day, with its snake dances and bonfires, came soon after. Then followed Thanksgiving Day, on which the children disguised themselves with costumes and masks and begged trifles from storekeepers. Soon afterward came Christmas. The year Francie was ten and Neeley nine, they stood together on Christmas Eve while the biggest tree in the neighborhood was thrown at them. Trees unsold at that time were thrown at anyone who volunteered to stand against the impact. Bruised and scratched, Francie and her brother proudly dragged their tree home.

The week before Christmas, when Francie had just become fourteen, Johnnie staggered home drunk. Two days later, he was found, huddled in a doorway, ill with pneumonia. The next day he was dead. After the funeral, Neeley was given his father's ring and Francie his shaving mug, his only keepsakes aside from his two waiter's aprons. To his wife, Johnnie left a baby, due to be born the following spring.

In March, when their funds were running low, Katie cashed the children's insurance policies. The twenty-five dollars she received carried them through until the end of April. Then Mr. McGarrity, at whose saloon Johnnie had done most of his drinking, came to their rescue. He hired Neeley to help prepare free lunches after school and Francie to do housework, and the money the children earned was enough to tide them over until after Katie's baby was born.

Laurie was born in May. In June, after their graduation from grade school, Francie and Neeley found their first real jobs, Neeley as errand boy for a brokerage house and Francie as a stemmer in a flower factory. Dismissed two weeks later, she became a file clerk in a clipping bureau. She was quickly advanced to the position of reader.

In the fall, there was not enough money to send both her children to high school, and Katie decided that the more reluctant Neeley should be chosen.

With the money Francie earned and with Neeley's after-school job at McGarrity's saloon, the Nolans had more comforts that Christmas than they had ever known before. The house was warm; there was enough food; and there was money for presents. Fourteen-year-old Neeley received his first pair of spats, and Francie almost froze in her new black lace lingerie when they went to church on Christmas morning.

When the clipping bureau closed with the outbreak of the war, Francie got a job as teletype operator. By working at night, she was able to take advanced college credits in summer school that year. With the help of a fellow student, Ben Blake, she passed her chemistry and English courses.

Francie was eighteen when she had her first real date, with a soldier named Lee Rhynor. The evening he was to leave to say good-bye to his parents before going overseas, Lee asked her to marry him when he returned. Francie promised to write him every day. Three days later, she received a letter from the girl he married during his trip home.

Katie also had a letter that day. Officer McShane had long been fond of Katie. Now retired, he asked her to marry him. All the Nolans agreed to this proposal. As the time approached for the wedding, Francie resigned her job. With Katie married, she intended to go to Michigan to college, for with Ben Blake's help, she had succeeded in passing the entrance exams.

The day before Katie was to be wed, Francie put the baby in the carriage and walked down the avenue. For a time she watched the children carting their rubbish into the junk shop. She turned in her books at the library for the last time. She saw another little girl, a book in her hand, sitting on a fire escape. In her own yard, the tree had been cut down because the tenants had complained that it was in the way of their wash; but from its stump another trunk was growing.

Critical Evaluation:

With scenes recalling the photographic zeal of a Jacob Riis, this book is more than a television melodrama. It is an effective blend of romance and social criticism. Betty Smith gives the reader an imaginative re-creation of pre-World War I Brooklyn tenement life, and some of its residents—the permanent members, and those who escaped from this monotonous, demanding existence through premature death, or by moving elsewhere. Readers are returned to the days when bread was the staff of life for the masses, to the ethnic cultural richness of the Lower East Side area.

During the summer of 1912, as the story begins, Brooklyn was swollen with unwanted recent arrivals from Europe. Both young and old roamed the streets and alleys picking up rags and valuable junk, a humble testimony to the wastefulness of the modern economy, and the maldistribution of wealth. Teeming with life, with Irish Catholics, Russian Jews, and refugees from Poland and China, Brooklyn was never serene.

Timeless observations about cultural differences, a fundamental element of ethnocentrism, formed the backdrop for this book. Realism was important to the author; a pregnant Jewess waits for the Messiah, but the Irish women knew their babies would never make a Jesus. Francie Nolan was born in this milieu. She embodied the fundamental aspiration of tenement dwellers—to escape.

Francie's parents were of recent European stock. Katie Rommely was Austrian, and her husband, Johnnie Nolan, shanty Irish. Katie, a petite yet strong woman, was fiercely devoted to her children. Of limited ability, good-looking Johnnie resorted to drinking away his inadequacies, his inability to give his family a better life. Francie's father was the type of man about whom the temperance societies worried, and there were many such men. When he died, Katie, for the sake of her children's future, begged to have the cause of death recorded as pneumonia, which was the immediate cause, and not alcoholism.

Even with her valiant efforts, and those of her mother, who had through her self-deprivation attempted to get her offspring out of the ghetto, Francie never leaves. Through the subtle use of metaphor, Francie becomes the "Tree of Heaven," the tree that liked poor people. Her innocence and beauty survive. The tree that grew in her yard was chopped down, but new life sprouted from the trunk, symbols of poverty and hope.

THE TREES

Type of work: Novel
Author: Conrad Richter (1890–1968)
Type of plot: Regional romance
Time of plot: Late eighteenth and early nineteenth centuries
Locale: Old Northwest Territory
First published: 1940

> *Principal characters:*
> WORTH LUCKETT, a woodsy
> JARY, his wife
> SAYWARD,
> GENNY,
> ACHSA,
> WYITT, and
> SULIE, their children
> LOUIE SCURRAH, Genny's husband
> PORTIUS WHEELER, Sayward's husband
> JAKE TENCH, a white runner

The Story:

Worth Luckett was a woodsy with an itching foot. By the time he had five growing children and one left in its infant grave, he was ready to take off again. He had already been west when he was a boy with Colonel Bouquet. Jary, his wife, had never wanted to leave the settlements, but game was growing scarce in Pennsylvania; without food brought down by his gun, Worth could not see how he could feed his family. He was wary of telling Jary outright that he wanted to move on, but she knew what he wanted and was half resigned to it when she heard that the animals were clearing out of places where men lived.

Because Jary had the slow fever, the care of the younger children fell on Sayward's shoulders. She was nearly fifteen, a strapping girl scared of neither man nor beast. It was not beyond her strength to drown a white-faced buck when Worth had neglected to bring meat home. The girls, Genny, Achsa, and baby Sulie, and the boy Wyitt knew they had to step when Sayward spoke.

Worth led his family across the Ohio River and on until they came to a wilderness of trees that reached as far as the eye could see. Near a spot covered with deer antlers, Worth laid out a place for a cabin. He was handy enough with tools to have the shell of a cabin up quickly, but the game in

---

the woods drew him away so often that fall came before the cabin was finished. The darkness under the big trees had disheartened Jary so much that she did not even speak of the cabin, until one fall day when the leaves had fallen so that she could look up through the branches and see the sky again. Then she felt like a human being who wanted to live in a house. She sent Worth back to his job. The snow fell the day after they moved into their cabin.

A few Indians still followed the trace by the house. One came on a night when Worth was away. Sayward hid the ax under her bed to fell him if he made a move toward the children in the loft or came toward her bed. He got up at night to cook some of his own meat at the fire. Worth was disturbed when he came home and found the Indian still there, but he and the Indian roared with delight when Sayward showed them the hidden ax.

Jary had such a hankering after some bread that Worth walked six days to bring back some white flour, but she could not eat the bread after Sayward made it; the slow fever had nearly finished her. When she died, they buried her under one of the big trees outside the cabin. Worth went away for a while, leaving Sayward to take care of the others.

One day, for the first time since they had lived there, they heard another ax in the woods. The young ones investigated and found a cabin going up, a man and a boy working on it. The man was a tom thumb, Sayward thought, when he asked her father for Sayward as a wife. Sayward thought he might be the first around there to ask her to marry him but probably not the last.

Before long, a trading post was set up by the river. Wyitt could hardly wait to trade off some of his skins for a knife. Indians and whites were whooping it up while he was there. He never forgot the sight of the wolf they skinned alive and set free.

More people raised cabins nearby until the Lucketts had several neighbors within walking distance. Worth blamed them and their cutting of the trees for the swamp pestilence that brought down Achsa, who was as brown and tough as an Indian. While the fever was on her, Achsa begged for water, but that was the one thing she was not supposed to have. Late one night, Sayward awoke to see Achsa crawling into the cabin with the kettle. She had drunk her fill from the run and had brought water back in the kettle. After that Achsa got well.

As a child, Louie Scurrah had acted as a decoy for Delawares on the warpath. When he came back to a small cabin nearby, the Lucketts expected to steer clear of him. He charmed Worth first with his woodsy tales, then Genny and Achsa, but there was always unspoken enmity between him and Sayward.

Sulie never returned after the day she was separated from Wyitt as they drove in the neighbor's cows. Worth was away at the time, and the trail was cold when he and Louie gathered some neighborhood men to beat the woods. They found Sulie's tracks leading to a bark playhouse in a grove of trees, with a bit of her dress as a cover for a play trencher, but they could not find tracks leading out. Close by there were Indian trails, but they were also cold.

With Sulie gone, Worth went too. He thought he might follow the Indian tracks west.

The feeling between Louie and Sayward was not softened when Sayward, after finding Louie with Genny in the woods, told him it was time for him to marry Genny. He took Genny down the river and married her with good grace, but before long, his itching foot took him off more and more often.

Louie got Wyitt a rifle to help kill meat for Sayward's cabin. The first day he had it, Wyitt wounded a buck. Standing over the animal to slit its throat, he suddenly found himself hoisted aloft. The deer tried to shake him loose, but Wyitt was able to kill it when it tired. His clothes were torn to ribbons, and he was badly cut. Sayward, realizing that she had another woodsy on her hands and thankful for the meat he brought, said nothing.

Finally Louie went off to the English lakes with Achsa. Sayward did not know until later that they left the very night the painter tried to claw his way down Genny's chimney. Genny burned everything in the house that night to keep the painter from coming into the cabin. When Wyitt and Sayward found her, she did not recognize them. At last, under Sayward's care, Genny came back to her senses.

At a sober wedding of old folks, Jake Tench decided it was time to get a wife for solitary Portius Wheeler, a former Bay State lawyer. When the girl Jake picked shied off, Sayward told Jake that she would marry Portius. Jake brought Portius to Sayward's cabin where, under the influence of brandy, Portius went through the marriage ceremony. When neighbors tried to put him to bed with Sayward, however, he turned tail and ran. Jake brought him back at dawn. Although Sayward told him she would not hold him against his will, Portius stayed with her.

Together they cut down trees for a garden patch. The neighbors brought teams to snake out the logs and to plow. Portius treated Sayward with gentle deference, and she was happy when she looked forward to her firstborn.

Critical Evaluation:

As a lone novel, *The Trees* is an uncomplicated story of the life and feelings of an early pioneer family. When read with the other two novels of Conrad Richter's trilogy, *The Fields* and *The Town*, it becomes part of a commentary on progress in early America and its effects upon the land and its people.

Although written in the third person, much of the story involves Sayward's thoughts and feelings about her family and her home. Her attitudes and philosophy develop during three stages of her life: as a young, dutiful daughter, as a "big sister" in the role of mother, and as a wife to Portius Wheeler. Although illiterate, Sayward displays an understanding of people that even trained psychologists would find difficult. This perception enriches the portrayals of other characters and leaves no doubt that this is Sayward's story.

Although with less depth than with Sayward, Richter also gives considerable insight into the behavior and thoughts of the family's other members. Each individual represents a different response to life on the new and diminishing frontier. Jary cannot face the realities of pioneer life and gives up, physically and mentally; Worth and Wyitt are not satisfied to stay in one place, remaining only from loyalty to family; Genny is the gentle lady who insists that civilities can exist in the wilderness; Achsa is as wild, irresponsible, and stubborn as the thick forest growth; Sulie is the lost child, not quite old, wise, or strong enough to survive; and Sayward is the mainstay—dependable, hardworking, and accepting of her fate.

The trees, as representative of all nature, are the other leading characters in the story. To Worth and Wyitt, the forest is the home of animals to hunt and the only place of privacy for man; but, to Sayward and the other homesteaders, trees are villains preventing the easy cultivation of fields. *The Trees* traces Sayward's gradual victory over the stubborn growth around her. It is a story of a determined people and of their love, labor, and courage.

One of the most interesting characteristics of the book is the use Richter has made of early pioneer language as it was spoken, not as it was written. This is only one proof of the authenticity of the facts he used in writing a new and effective type of regional story. No other novel conveys so realistically what the first settlers must have felt when they faced the timbered wilderness on the frontier, the barrier of trees that shut out the sky and gave protection to animals and human enemies. *The Trees* is a pioneer story of simple human warmth and vigor.

TROPIC OF CAPRICORN

Type of work: Novel
Author: Henry Miller (1891-1980)
Type of plot: Humorous social history
Time of plot: 1920's
Locale: New York City
First published: 1939

Principal characters:

HENRY MILLER, the narrator and principal character
HIS WIFE,
HIS FATHER,
HIS MOTHER, and
HIS SISTER, all unnamed
GENE, Miller's cousin
AUNT CAROLINE, Gene's mother
JOEY KASSELBAUM, the slow-witted friend of Gene and
    Miller
STANLEY,
ALFIE BETCHA,
WILLIE MAINE,
JOE GERHARDT, and
JOHNNY GERHARDT, all boyhood friends of Miller
DR. MCKINNEY, the veterinarian
LOLA NIESSEN, Miller's piano teacher
VALESKA,
PAULINE JANOWSKI,
AGNES,
FRANCIE, and
RITA SCHNADIG, all women in his life

    Tropic of Capricorn is the third of the seven volumes in which Henry Miller proposed to tell the story of his life. In the first volume, *Tropic of Cancer*, published in 1934, Miller chronicled his lusty days as an uninhibited pauper in postwar Paris; in the second, *Black Spring*, which appeared in 1936, his treatment of his experiences in Paris is interspersed with sections on his boyhood in Brooklyn. The present book deals exclusively with New York, specifically with Miller's childhood, adolescence, and the years of his early manhood, before he took up residence abroad in self-imposed exile. Literally speaking, Miller describes his life as a boy in a small neighborhood of Brooklyn, his coming of age and the development of his sexual prowess, his numberless feats of copulation (beginning at the age of fifteen, when he seduced his piano teacher who was nearly twice as old), his exasperatingly hectic job as the employment manager for the Cosmodemonic Telegraph Company, and the inexhaustible indulgence of his friends, who subsidized his existence for much of the time. *Tropic of Capricorn*, however, is more than a simple recital of facts. It is actually an autobiographical novel, in which Miller reveals the emergence of his deepest, most vital self, and of that characteristically furious optimism with which he celebrates life and humanity in all its forms.

The book opens in a spirit of violent rebellion and denunciation. Miller recalls his childhood as a time of interior, philosophical reaction to the solidly established Nordic axiom that work, struggle, and effort, fortified by righteousness and cleanliness, are the pillars on which a man's life must rest. Against this doctrine, Miller set a creed of his own: that he would heed only the law of his personal independence, driven by the spur of caprice rather than the whip of compulsion. In the careful, cautious, foresighted restraint with which his parents labored for an ever-receding "tomorrow," Miller saw nothing but the paralysis of the inner self, the desiccation of life. Consequently, he developed a hatred of work, of conventional goals, of material success, of factories, of everything in America which destroys the human personality. He set out deliberately to establish himself as an anomaly, a voice of paradoxical joy and indignation crying out in a wilderness of spiritual death. This is really the key to Miller's philosophy—if one can use that term for the violent explosions of his mind. His defiant condemnation of conventional values is balanced by a rhapsodic yea-saying to life, a Whitmanesque celebration of the cosmos in its most primitive, barbaric, undisciplined variety.

Like *Tropic of Cancer*, the value of *Tropic of Capricorn* lies in the fact that Miller anchors his cosmological speculation to the solid ground of his own rich and intense experience. Early in his life, he claimed, he learned to maintain his personal independence by assuming an attitude of sublime indifference toward ordinary tribulations—death, for example. When he was about twelve years old, his best friend died after a long illness; but Miller wasted no tears at the young boy's bier; he rejoiced that the boy's death meant the end of suffering, for the boy and for those about him. From this incident, Miller jumps chronologically forward to the years of his early manhood during World War I (in which he did not participate), when he spent most of his time searching for a job. In this case, as in that of his boyhood friend, however, Miller looked upon his prospects with a kind of Olympian detachment. He did not care deeply about getting any job in particular, and it was only by the merest twist of chance that he secured a responsible position with the Cosmodemonic Telegraph Company of North America. He began by applying for a job as a messenger boy, but when the switchboard operator at the company's employment bureau turned him down, he became furious enough to take his case to the company's general manager. The result was an offer of a job as personnel manager, which Miller accepted.

The job turned out to be an almost crushing ordeal of constant chaos.

Only about twenty percent of the messenger force was composed of steady workers; the rest were drifters. This state of affairs meant that Miller was forced to hire and fire at a rapid rate; more important, it also meant that he was exposed to an extraordinarily varied collection of men and women from every part of the country and from virtually every part of the world. His applicants ranged from Hindus to prostitutes, from ex-convicts to Cherokee Indians. Miller treated nearly all of them as human beings in need, hiring with his heart rather than his head and thereby subverting company policy. The company often winced, but did not fire; in the end, after about five years, it was Miller himself who simply walked out.

After this, Miller subsisted principally on the generosity of his friends (who were legion, he says) and of his wife, who seems to have provided him with little besides money. What becomes important in Miller's universe, therefore, is not so much what he does as what he sees and feels. A great part of the experiences re-created in *Tropic of Capricorn* involve the people he meets and the books he reads. A chance encounter with a boyhood friend, just returned from Europe, for example, opened Miller's eyes to the exotic fascination of Capri, Pompeii, Morocco, and Paris, places he would later see for himself but which would always hold a special charm because of the way his friend described them. Later in the book, he tells of his response to Henri Bergson's *Creative Evolution*, a book which intoxicated him with the excitement of creativity and intensified his own sense of self. It made him feel, he says, as if he had crossed a boundary line into a mysterious new realm, where he felt alone, unknown, and foreign. It also gave him a new sense of order, an ability to understand virtually anything, even total confusion.

There are, however, more things in heaven and earth than are dreamt of in Bergsonian philosophy, and Miller is principally dedicated in this book to the reality of his own experiences—particularly of his encounters with the men and women who populate his unpredictable world. Needless to say, the women receive the lion's share of Miller's attention, for he is fascinated by them to the point of obsession. The opening chapter of *Tropic of Capricorn* is entitled "On the Ovarian Trolley," and it seems to set the tone for everything that follows. Miller's women wriggle through the pages of his book in a seemingly endless stream: Valeska, daughter of a prostitute and an anonymous black, who worked as Miller's secretary at the telegraph company and later committed suicide; Pauline Janowski, a homeless Jewess of about sixteen who read Balzac and yearned to be a writer; Monica, who came to New York from Buffalo with the body of her mother; Mara, an Egyptian Jewess; Francie, an accommodating Scottish girl whom Miller met in the Catskills; Agnes, her Irish-Catholic friend; and numerous others—whores, derelicts, anonymous ladies of the night. Few of these women assume distinctive personalities, and all tend to merge into the gigantic abstraction of sex, which is Miller's overriding concern. He cares little for their names or faces; he is simply mesmerized by their genitals, which he describes in exhaustive detail. Miller, of course, is more than an ordinary lecher, and there is a kind of metaphysical dimension to his mania for the female organ. Curiously enough for a man with his zest for life, it is not the generative power of the female organ which attracts him. He is fascinated instead with its sheer mystery, and he revels in the freedom and frequency with which he tears away the curtain of conventional reticence about it. It holds for him a kind of mystic significance which he celebrates with untiring energy. He seems, in fact, to derive as much pleasure from discussing what is normally forbidden or censored as he derives from his own amoral behavior; he luxuriates in the license which permits him to use the great triumvirate of Anglo-Saxon obscenities: the four-letter words for copulation, human excrement, and the female genitals. There is something of the bad boy run wild in Miller, gleefully scrawling his heart out on the lavatory wall.

It would hardly be fair, however, to dismiss the book as simply a lurid catalog of Miller's sexual adventures. Much of it is graphic and vivid evocation of his early years in the Brooklyn neighborhood where he was born as the son of a German tailor and grew up while he watched his environment change. The neighborhood that Miller describes exists now only in his memory, for it was, he says, deteriorating even as he passed his boyhood there; it was being radically altered by an invasion of Jews. When he returned to it as an adult, to the area of the little street called Fillmore Place which was once his entire world, he could no longer recognize it. The neighborhood he knew had been obliterated and nullified. It is precisely this feeling, perhaps, which lends a note of nostalgia to his re-creation of the past.

There is little of ordinary sentiment in his backward glance. He tells without remorse, for example, how he and his cousin Gene became embroiled in a rock fight when they were less than ten years old, and the two of them stoned another boy to death. Miller recalls the incident without the slightest tremor of guilt; in his account of it, what emerges in boldest relief is not the act of murder but the spontaneous generosity of his Aunt Caroline, who greeted the boys when they returned home with two large slices of sour rye spread with fresh butter and sugar. The gift of the bread was for Miller something like an act of grace—unearned, unmerited, and therefore purer than any bread that he would later gain by the sweat of struggle. In retrospect, the bread assumes a sacramental significance in his mind.

The canvas of these early years is painted with bright if sometimes garish colors. Miller writes of his boyhood chums—of the slow-witted Joey Kasselbaum, whom he and Gene humored in their games of marbles; of Stanley, a Polish boy with a violent temper who would help young Miller to raid Aunt Caroline's icebox; of Alfie Betcha and a crazy boy named Willie Maine, both of whom got drunk at a neighborhood party and fell to biting one another; of a part-Irish youth named Johnny Gerhardt, who beat another boy senseless and then ran away from home; and of Johnny's brother Joe, who distinguished himself by the delicate act of apologizing to the beaten boy. Miller writes too of Dr. McKinney, the local veterinarian, who castrated stallions in public and let the blood run into the gutter; and he speaks with bitterness of his father's final illness, induced by his decision to renounce liquor. In the face of impending death, it seems, the old man suddenly acquired an astonishing piety; but this effort collapsed upon the departure of the local Congregationalist minister (whom Miller's father had come to worship), and the experience left him a broken, empty, disillusioned man. The interior life had been drained out of him, and Miller, remembering happier days with a lighthearted father, mourns the loss.

There is little in his past that Miller mourns. On the whole, his book is an emphatic celebration of life, a paean to vitality. From the sordid sensuality of the Broadway dance hall to the heights of his mystic communion with Bergson, from the spasms of his copulative moments to the depths of his cosmological speculations, Miller is the apostle of the living self.

THE TURN OF THE SCREW

Type of work: Novella
Author: Henry James (1843–1916)
Type of plot: Moral allegory
Time of plot: Mid-nineteenth century
Locale: England
First published: 1898

Principal characters:
THE GOVERNESS
MRS. GROSE, housekeeper at Bly
MILES and
FLORA, the two children of the house
MR. QUINT and
MISS JESSEL, two apparitions

The Story:

It was a pleasant afternoon in June when the governess first arrived at the country estate at Bly where she was to take charge of Miles, aged ten, and Flora, eight. She faced her new position with some trepidation because of the unusual circumstances of her situation. The two children were to be under her complete care, and the uncle who had engaged her had been explicit in the fact that he did not wish to be bothered with his orphaned niece and nephew. Her uneasiness disappeared, however, when she saw her charges, for Flora and Miles seemed incapable of giving the slightest trouble.

The weeks of June passed uneventfully. Then, one evening, while she was walking in the garden at twilight, the governess was startled to see a strange young man at a distance. The man looked at her challengingly and disappeared. The incident angered and distressed the young woman, but she decided the man was a trespasser.

On the following Sunday evening, the young woman was startled to see the same stranger looking in at her through a window. Once again he stared piercingly at her for a few seconds and then disappeared. This time the governess realized that the man was looking for someone in particular and that perhaps he boded evil for the children in her care. A few minutes later, the governess told the housekeeper, Mrs. Grose, of the incident and described the appearance of the man. Mrs. Grose told her that it was a perfect description of Peter Quint, the valet to the governess' employer but that Mr. Quint was dead.

One afternoon shortly afterward, a second apparition appeared. This time the ghost of Miss Jessel, the former governess, appeared in the garden to both the governess and the little girl, Flora. The strange part of the situation was that the little girl refused to let the governess know that she had seen the figure and knew who it was, though it was obvious that she had understood the appearance fully.

The governess learned from the housekeeper that the two apparitions had been lovers while alive, though the girl had been of a very fine family and the man had been guilty of drunkenness and worse vices. For what evil purpose these two spirits wished to influence the seemingly innocent children, neither the housekeeper nor the governess could guess. The secrecy of the children about seeing the ghosts was maddening to the two women.

They both felt that the boy was continuing to see the two ghosts in private and concealed that fact, just as he had known of the illicit affair between the valet and the former governess in life and had helped them to conceal it. Yet, when in the presence of the children, the governess sometimes felt that it would be impossible for the two children to be influenced into evil.

The third time, the ghost of Quint appeared to the governess inside the house. Unable to sleep, she had sat reading late at night. Hearing someone on the stairs, she went to investigate and saw the ghost, which disappeared when faced by her unflinching gaze. Each night after that, she inspected the stairs, but she never again saw the ghost of the man. Once she glimpsed the apparition of Miss Jessel as it sat dejectedly on the lowest stair. Worse than the appearance of the ghosts was the discovery that the children had left their beds at night to wander on the lawn in communication with the spirits who were leading them to unknown evil. It became apparent to the governess that the children were not good within themselves. In their imaginations, they were living in a world populated by the evil dead restored.

In such an atmosphere, the summer wore away into autumn. In all that time, the children had given no sign of awareness of the apparitions. Knowing that her influence with the children was as tenuous as a thread which would break at the least provocation, the governess did not allude to the ghosts. She herself had seen no more manifestations, but she had often felt by the children's attitude that the apparitions were close at hand. What was worse for the distressed woman was the thought that what Miles and Flora saw were things still more terrible than she imagined, visions that sprang from their association with the evil figures in the past.

One day, Miles went to her and announced his desire to go away to school. The governess realized it was only proper that he be sent to school, but she feared the results of ghostly influences once he was beyond her care. Later, opening the door of the schoolroom, she again saw the ghost of her predecessor, Miss Jessel. As the apparition faded, the governess realized that her duty was to stay with the children and combat the spirits and their deadly influence. She decided to write immediately to the children's uncle, contra-dictory to his injunction against being bothered in their behalf. That night before she wrote, she went into Miles's room and asked the boy to let her help him in his secret troubles. Suddenly a rush of cold air filled the room, as if the window had been blown open. When the governess relighted the candle blown out by the draft, the window was still closed, and the drawn curtain had not been disturbed.

The following day Flora disappeared. Mrs. Grose and the governess found her beside the garden pond. The governess, knowing she had gone there to see the ghost, asked her where Miss Jessel was. The child replied that she only wanted to be left alone. The governess could see the apparition of Miss Jessel standing on the opposite side of the pond.

The governess, afraid that the evil influence had already dominated the little girl, asked the housekeeper to take the child to London, and to request the uncle's aid. In place of the lovable angelic Flora there had suddenly appeared a little child with a filthy mind and filthy speech, which she used in denouncing the governess to the housekeeper. The same afternoon, Mrs. Grose left with the child as the governess had requested.

That evening, immediately after dinner, the governess asked Miles to tell her what was on his mind before he left the dining room. When he refused, she asked him if he had stolen the letter she had written to his uncle. As she asked the question, she realized that standing outside the window, staring into the room, was the ghost of Peter Quint. She pulled the boy close to her, shielding him from any view of the ghost at the window, while he told her that he had taken the letter. He also informed her that he had already been expelled from one school because of his lewd speech and actions. Noting how close the governess was holding him, he suddenly asked if Miss Jessel were near. The governess, angry and distraught, shrieked at him that it was the ghost of Peter Quint, just outside the window. When Miles turned around, the apparition was gone. With a scream, he fell into the governess' arms. At first, she did not realize that she had lost him forever—that Miles was dead.

Critical Evaluation:

One of the world's most famous ghost stories, *The Turn of the Screw* was first published serially in *Collier's Weekly* from January 27, 1898, to April 16, 1898), and in book form, along with a second story, *Covering End*, late in 1898. In 1908, Henry James discussed at some length the origin and nature of the tale in the preface to volume 12 of *The Novels and Tales of Henry James*. Considerable critical discussion and controversy have been devoted to the story, especially since Edmund Wilson's 1934 essay on "The Ambiguity of Henry James," in which Wilson argues that "the governess who is made to tell the story is a neurotic case of sex repression, and that the ghosts are not real ghosts but hallucinations of the governess." Since many critics have taken issue with Wilson and since Wilson later modified his interpretation, it is important to note briefly what James himself says about his story, his characters, and his theme in the preface. He calls *The Turn of the Screw* "a piece of ingenuity pure and simple, of cold artistic calculation, an *amusette* to catch those not easily caught . . . the jaded, the disillusioned, the fastidious." He terms the governess' account "her record of so many anomalies and obscurities." He comments that he purposely limited his revelation of the governess' character: "We have surely as much of her nature as we can swallow in watching it reflect her anxieties and inductions." He says he presented the ghosts as "real" ones, and he describes them as

> my hovering prowling blighting presences, my pair of abnormal agents . . . [who] would be agents in fact; there would be laid on them the dire duty of causing the situation to reek with the air of Evil. Their desire and their ability to do so, visibly measuring meanwhile their effect, together with their observed and described success—this was exactly my central idea.

Concluding his discussion of "my fable," James explains that he purposely did not specify the evils in which the ghosts either attempt to or actually involve Miles and Flora: "Only make the reader's general vision of evil intense enough, I said to myself . . . and his own experience, his own imagination, his own sympathy (with the children) and horror (of their false friends) will supply him quite sufficiently with all the particulars."

Thus, readers see that James conceived of the tale as one in which the governess, a young woman with limited experience and education but high moral principles, attempts to protect two seemingly innocent children from corruption by the malign ghosts of two former servants who in life were evil persons. His capitalizing of "Evil" and his use of the term "fable" to describe the story suggest a moral as well as an aesthetic intent in writing it. To interpret *The Turn of the Screw* in terms of Freudian sex psychology, as Wilson and some other critics have done, is to go beyond James and to find what he did not put there—consciously anyway. Admittedly, some of the "anomalies and obscurities" which puzzle and trouble the governess do lead the reader in the direction of a Freudian interpretation. The account is the governess' alone, and there is no proof that anyone else actually saw the ghosts though she believes that the children saw them and lied to her or tried otherwise to hide the truth from her. Before his reading of the governess' journal, Douglas admits that she was in love with her employer, the children's handsome uncle who showed no personal interest in her. Within the account itself, the reader who hunts may find apparent Freudian sex symbolism. For example, the male ghost, Peter Quint, first appears standing on a *tower* when the governess has been deeply longing for her employer to appear and approve her care of the children. The female ghost, Miss Jessel, first appears by a *lake* and watches as little Flora, also watched absorbedly by the governess, plays a childish game:

> She had picked up a small flat piece of wood, which happened to have in it a little hole that had evidently suggested to her the idea of sticking in another fragment that might figure as a mast and make the thing a boat. This second morsel . . . she was very markedly and intently attempting to tighten in its place.

Ten-year-old Miles's repeated use of the word "dear" in speaking to the governess may suggest a precocious boy's sexual interest in his pretty governess.

One can go on, but it is important to remember that James's story was published in 1898 and that Freud's first significant work explaining his sexual theory did not appear until 1905. Perhaps it is best to regard such details in the story as those cited as no more than coincidental, though they may seem suggestive to the post-Freudian reader of *The Turn of the Screw*.

Among the most difficult facts to explain away in developing the theory that the ghosts are mere hallucinations of a sexually frustrated young woman, is the governess' detailed description of a man she has never seen or heard of:

> He has no hat. . . . He has red hair, very red, close-curling, and a pale face, long in shape, with straight, good features and little, rather queer whiskers that are as red as his hair. His eyebrows are, somehow, darker; they look particularly arched. . . . His eyes are sharp—awfully. . . . His mouth's wide, and his lips are thin, and except for his whiskers he's quite clean-shaven.

Mrs. Grose easily identifies him as the dead Peter Quint. She just as easily identifies Miss Jessel when the governess describes the person she later saw: " . . . a figure of quite an unmistakable horror and evil: a woman in black, pale and dreadful—with such an air also, and such a face!—on the other side of the lake." It is difficult to argue convincingly that Peter Quint and Miss Jessel are not "real" ghosts.

The Turn of the Screw will continue to fascinate and to intrigue because James's "cold artistic calculation" has so filled it with suggestiveness and intentional ambiguity that it may be read at different levels and with new revelations at each successive reading. As Leon Edel has said, "The reader's mind is forced to hold to two levels of awareness: *the story as told*, and *the story to be deduced*."

TYPEE

Type of work: Novel
Author: Herman Melville (1819–1891)
Type of plot: Adventure romance
Time of plot: Mid-nineteenth century
Locale: Marquesas Islands
First published: 1846

Principal characters:
HERMAN MELVILLE (TOM), an American sailor
TOBY, his friend
MEHEVI, chief of the Typees
KORY-KORY, a native servant
FAYAWAY, a native girl
MARNOO, a native taboo man

The Story:

The whaler *Dolly* had been long at sea, and the men were discontented and restless when the captain finally gave orders to put in at Nukuheva, one of the Marquesas Islands. This was the chance for which Tom and Toby, two young sailors, had been waiting. Even though the natives of the island were known to be cannibals, Tom and Toby deserted the ship and fled inland, planning to hide until the *Dolly* sailed. Then they hoped to sign aboard another ship where they would get better treatment.

Tom and Toby began their flight with only a few biscuits for food. On the first night away from the ship, Tom contracted a disease which caused his leg to swell, and he was in much pain. Nevertheless, he and Toby went on. At last, when their food was all gone, they realized that they could stay alive only by giving themselves up to one of the savage tribes that inhabited the island.

They discovered too late that the natives to whom they surrendered themselves were the Typee tribe, the most ferocious cannibals on Nukuheva. Tom and Toby were treated with respect, however, and were given food and comfortable quarters. All the natives came to see the strangers. Mehevi, the king of the Typees, appointed Kory-Kory as personal servant to Tom. The captives went to live in the home of Tinor, Kory-Kory's mother. Mehevi had a medicine man examine Tom's swollen leg, but the native remedies had no effect on the disease.

Tom, unable to walk, spent most of his time reclining in the house while Kory-Kory attended to his needs. A beautiful young maiden, Fayaway, was also his constant companion. She, among all the Typees, seemed to understand the painful situation of the two captives.

Toby convinced the Typees that he should be allowed to return to the main harbor on the island to seek medical aid for Tom. On the trail, he was attacked by hostile warriors from a neighboring tribe, and he returned to the Typees with an ugly head wound.

A few days later, Toby discovered a boat offshore. He was allowed to go down by the beach, but Tom was detained in his house. Toby promised to bring medical aid to Tom within three days, but the three days passed without the return of Toby. Tom could learn nothing from the natives; he realized that now he was the single captive of the Typees. Somewhat recovered, he was allowed to roam almost at will within the country of the Typees; but he was always accompanied by Kory-Kory, and there was no chance for escape.

As Tom's leg improved, he began to indulge in the pleasures allowed him and to observe the native life with interest. The Typees seemed to exist in a perpetual state of happiness, interrupted only by skirmishes with neighboring tribes.

One of Tom's greatest pleasures was to paddle a canoe about a small lake in company with Fayaway. For the privilege of taking Fayaway with him, he had to ask special permission, since entering a canoe was ordinarily taboo for a woman.

One day a handsome stranger appeared among the Typees bearing news from other parts of the island. He was Marnoo, a taboo man, who was free to go among all the tribes without harm. When Tom learned that Marnoo knew English, he asked the native to help him escape. This Marnoo could not do for fear of arousing the anger of the Typees.

The daily life of the natives was extremely regular. Each morning they bathed and ate breakfast. After the meal, they smoked their pipes. The rest of the morning they spent sleeping, conversing, or doing odd jobs about their houses. The men often spent the afternoon in the large meetinghouse of Mehevi; there they relaxed and joked in a sort of bachelors' club. Before the evening meal, they bathed again. After the meal, the young girls entertained the rest with dancing. Everyone retired at an early hour.

Tom was present at the Feast of the Calabashes. It seemed to have some religious significance, but most of the time was spent in eating and drinking. During the two days of the festival, Tom decided that the natives did not take their religion seriously. They possessed many idols not treated with any high degree of respect. The most universal religious observance was that of tattooing; everyone was tattooed upon the face, even the women. The bodies of some of the men were completely covered with intricate designs.

Since the men outnumbered the women in the tribe, the women often had two or three husbands, but the men never had more than one wife. All in the tribe seemed happy with the various aspects of their social organization. Private property was limited to household goods; food was common property. All understood and followed the laws and customs of the tribe; there were never disputes among the Typees.

One day, a battle was fought between the Typees and a neighboring tribe. Afterward, the bodies of the dead enemies were taken to the ceremonial feasting place. For the next day or two, Tom was not allowed to leave the vicinity of his house. He suspected that the Typees were making a meal of their dead enemies. Later he discovered the remains of the meal and found that he was correct, though the Typees denied they were cannibals.

A few days later, Marnoo again appeared among the Typees. This time he told Tom to try to escape by means of the same path by which he left. Tom was unable to leave the village, however, for Kory-Kory kept close watch on him day and night.

Not many days after Marnoo had left, the Typees excitedly announced the approach of a boat. Tom argued with the natives and finally persuaded them to let him go to the beach. He had some difficulty in getting there, since his leg had begun to swell again.

At the beach, Tom found a boat from an Australian ship standing just outside the surf. Marnoo had told the Australian captain of Tom's trouble, and he had sent a boat loaded with presents to obtain Tom's release. The Typees, however, had no wish to release their captive. In desperation, Tom broke away from the guard which had been placed around him and plunged into the surf. He managed to reach the boat, and the sailors pulled away from shore.

Thus ended Tom's captivity among the Typees. His only regret was in leaving the faithful Kory-Kory and the beautiful Fayaway.

Many years later Tom again met Toby and learned from him that he had intended to return to the aid of his injured friend, but he had been tricked into boarding a vessel which sailed from Nukuheva the following day. It was only long after Toby had given Tom up for lost that the two friends learned of each other's fate after their separation.

Critical Evaluation:

Herman Melville's assertion in *Moby Dick* that a whale ship was his Yale and Harvard reminds readers of how central to his development the sea adventures of his youth were and how strongly they would shape his writing. It was from the whaler *Acushnet* that Melville jumped ship in the Marquesas to spend a few weeks among the Nukuheva natives. The episode ended, sooner and less dramatically than in *Typee*, when he departed the island on another whaler, eventually to join the American warship, *United States*, for a voyage back to Boston. Though the adventure had ended in actuality, it only began imaginatively for Melville when he sought to discover its meaning in the fictionalized account of his sojourn among the cannibals which he called *Typee*. Though actually a novel based upon experience, *Typee* was regarded generally as simply a travel narrative when it appeared, and the work's reputation since has had to fight against that classification. In fact, *Typee* contains more of the basic elements of Melville's later fiction than its detractors have realized, and it deserves a primary place among such other early works as *Redburn* and *White-Jacket* which give meaning to the idea of Melville's education on board the ships he sailed as a young man.

The essential facts of *Typee*, except for the time which Melville considerably exaggerates, are true: he did jump ship in company of a friend named Toby Greene and spent a few weeks among the natives of the Typee valley where he enjoyed a somewhat ambiguous status as a prisoner-guest; Melville did injure his leg escaping the *Acushnet* and allowed Toby to go for medical supplies; Toby failed to return, having been shanghaied by another whaler; and, after a few weeks, Melville was taken off the island by a whaler in search of crewmen. The novel, however, is more than the sum of these few facts, and it cannot be done justice by a reading which regards it as no more than a slightly fictionalized autobiographical narrative. Far from simply recounting his adventures, Melville is, in *Typee*, discovering the fundamental ambiguities in man and nature which would characterize his best work as the basis for the unanswerable questions his novels propose.

From its very beginning, the boys' journey into the Typee valley promises to be more than it seems. Running not only from the ship and its cruelly authoritarian master, but from the world of the coast natives which has been hopelessly corrupted by sailors, administrators, and missionaries, these adventurers make their way down a precipitous route which carries them metaphorically backward in time as it takes them beyond the reach of civilization. Eventually reaching the valley floor, the boys initially encounter Typee (which they still believe to be Happar) as a new paradise. Not only the fecundity and lushness of the rich valley but also the young lovers who are the first inhabitants encountered, point to the discovery of a South Sea Eden. This vision of innocence and beauty in the South Sea islands was, to some extent, typical of nineteenth century Romanticism with its recurrent theme of the Noble Savage, but Melville, even this early in his career, was no typical Romantic writer.

From the time Tom (now renamed Tommo) settles, albeit unwillingly, into life with the Typees, Melville begins to develop around him a series of symbols which point to the fundamental ambiguity that lies at the heart of the island "paradise." On the one hand, the simplicity, loyalty, and unself-conscious devotion offered by Kory-Kory, and, more particularly, the innocent love and natural sexuality of Fayaway, keep alive the vision of an Edenic garden. On the other hand, Tommo's discovery that he is in the land of the dread Typees rather than among the peaceful Happars leads to his fear of cannibalism, the most dread of all man's aberrations. Tommo's injured leg, which mysteriously grows worse as his suspicions of cannibalism near confirmation, becomes an objective correlative for his sick spirit which, cut off from the civilization it sought to escape, languishes. Tattooing also develops a symbolic value, since it would complete the initiation into the Typean world begun with the ritual name-change. Once tattooed, Tommo would never again be able to return to his own world.

The essential ambiguity in *Typee* centers around the prospect of a paradise corrupted at its heart by the horror of cannibalism. In later years, Melville would assert that he could look upon a horror and be familiar with it, but this is not so of Tommo, who cannot reconcile himself to this discovery. More generally, the implications of the innate evil of *Typee* seriously challenges the view of optimistic philosophers of Melville's period who argued that the universe, and man, were essentially good, evil being only an appearance rather than a reality. Tommo might like to think that he, as a civilized human being, somehow transcends the essentially savage nature of man, but Melville will not have it so. In the escape scene, Tommo repays the hospitality of his hosts by driving the boat hook into the throat of one of his recent friends. Even as Tommo feels the horror of his violent act, readers feel the horror of Melville's world in which the savage impulse dwells even in the most civilized breast.

Though perhaps less orderly than this reading suggests, Melville's symbols are clearly present, and they serve to put his vision in a direct line of descent from that of his Calvinist forebears who endorsed the doctrine of the essential depravity of man. It is only because the symbols are tentative and nascent, rather than fully developed into Melville's mature symbolism, that *Typee* must be seen more as an anticipation of later Melville than as a fully realized work of art in itself. *Typee* does reveal, however, how early Melville began to develop the symbolic mode which would become the hallmark of his greatest romances, and how soon he began to discover those unsolvable questions of the nature of good and evil that would preoccupy him throughout his career.

UNCLE TOM'S CABIN
Or, Life Among the Lowly

Type of work: Novel
Author: Harriet Beecher Stowe (1811–1896)
Type of plot: Sentimental romance
Time of plot: Mid-nineteenth century
Locale: Kentucky and Mississippi
First published: 1852

Principal characters:
UNCLE TOM, a black slave
EVA ST. CLARE, daughter of a wealthy Southerner
SIMON LEGREE, a planter
ELIZA, a runaway slave
TOPSY, a black imp

The Story:

Because his Kentucky plantation was encumbered by debt, Mr. Shelby made plans to sell one of his slaves to his chief creditor, a New Orleans slave dealer named Haley. The dealer shrewdly selected Uncle Tom as part payment on Mr. Shelby's debt. While they were discussing the transaction, Eliza's child, Harry, came into the room. Haley wanted to buy Harry too, but at first Shelby was unwilling to part with the child. Eliza listened to enough of the conversation to be frightened. She confided her fears to George Harris, her husband, a slave on an adjoining plantation. George, who was already bitter because his master had put him to work in the fields when he was capable of doing better work, promised that some day he would have his revenge upon his hard masters. Eliza had been brought up more indulgently by the Shelbys, and she begged him not to try anything rash.

After supper in the cabin of Uncle Tom and Aunt Chloe, his wife, the Shelby slaves gathered for a meeting. They sang songs, and young George Shelby, who had eaten his supper there, read from the Bible. In the big house, Mr. Shelby signed the papers making Uncle Tom and little Harry the property of Haley. Eliza, learning her child's fate from some remarks of Mr. Shelby to his wife, fled with her child, hoping to reach Canada and safety. Uncle Tom, hearing of the sale, resigned himself to the wisdom of providence.

The next day, after Haley had discovered his loss, he set out to capture Eliza; however, she had a good start. Moreover, Mrs. Shelby purposely delayed the pursuit by serving a late breakfast. When her pursuers came in sight, Eliza escaped across the Ohio River by jumping from one floating ice cake to another, young Harry in her arms.

UNCLE TOM'S CABIN by Harriet Beecher Stowe. Published by Houghton Mifflin Co.

Haley hired two slave-catchers, Marks and Loker, to track Eliza through Ohio. For their trouble, she was to be given to them. They set off that night.

Eliza found shelter in the home of Senator and Mrs. Bird. The senator took her to the house of a man known to aid fugitive slaves. Uncle Tom, however, was not so lucky. Haley made sure Tom would not escape by shackling his ankles before taking him to the boat bound for New Orleans. When young George Shelby heard Tom had been sold, he followed Haley on his horse. George gave Tom a dollar as a token of his sympathy and told him that he would buy him back one day.

At the same time, George Harris began his escape. White enough to pass as a Spaniard, he appeared at a tavern as a gentleman and took a room there, hoping to find before long a station on the underground railway.

Eliza was resting at the home of Rachel and Simeon Halliday when George Harris arrived in the same Quaker settlement.

On board the boat bound for New Orleans, Uncle Tom saved the life of young Eva St. Clare, and in gratitude, Eva's father purchased the slave. Eva told Tom he would now have a happy life, for her father was kind to everyone. Augustine St. Clare was married to a woman who imagined herself sick and therefore took no interest in her daughter Eva. He had gone north to bring back his cousin, Miss Ophelia, to provide care for the neglected and delicate Eva. When they arrived at the St. Clare plantation, Tom was made head coachman.

Meanwhile, Loker and Marks were on the trail of Eliza and George. They caught up with the fugitives, and there was a fight in which George wounded Loker. Marks fled, and so the Quakers who were protecting the runaways took Loker along with them and gave him medical treatment.

Unused to lavish Southern customs, Miss Ophelia tried to understand the South. Shocked at the extravagance of St. Clare's household, she attempted to bring order out of the chaos, but she received no encouragement because the slaves had been humored and petted too long. Indulgent in all things, St. Clare was indifferent to the affairs of his family and his property. Uncle Tom lived an easy life in the loft over the stable. He and little Eva became close friends with St. Clare's approval. Sometimes St. Clare had doubts regarding the morality of the institution of slavery, and in one of these moods, he bought an odd pixielike child, named Topsy, for his prim-and-proper New England cousin to educate.

Eva grew more frail. Knowing that she was about to die, she asked her father to free his slaves, as he had so often promised. After Eva's death, St. Clare began to read his Bible and to make plans to free all his slaves. He gave Topsy to Miss Ophelia legally, so that the spinster might rear the child as she wished. Then one evening, he tried to separate two quarreling men. He received a knife wound in the side and died shortly afterward. Mrs. St. Clare, however, had no intention of freeing the slaves, and she ordered that

Tom be sent to the slave market.

At a public auction, he was sold to a brutal plantation owner named Simon Legree. Legree drank heavily, and his plantation house had fallen to ruin. He kept dogs for the purpose of tracking runaway slaves. At the slave quarters, Tom was given his sack of corn for the week, told to grind it himself and bake the meal into cakes for his supper. At the mill, he aided two women. In return, they baked his cakes for him. He read selections from the Bible to them.

For a few weeks, Tom quietly tried to please his harsh master. One day, he helped a sick woman by putting cotton into her basket. For this act, Legree ordered him to flog the woman. When Tom refused, his master had him flogged until he fainted. A slave named Cassy came to Tom's aid. She told Tom the story of her life with Legree and of a young daughter who had been sold years before.

Then she went to Legree's apartment and tormented him. She hated her master, and she had power over him. Legree was superstitious. When she talked, letting her eyes flash over him, he felt as though she were casting an evil spell. Haunted by the secrets of his guilty past, he drank until he fell asleep. He had forgotten his fears by the next morning, however, and he knocked Tom to the ground with his fist.

Meanwhile, far to the north, George and Eliza and young Harry were making their way slowly through the stations on the underground railway toward Canada.

Cassy and Emmeline, another slave, were determined to make their escape. Knowing the consequences if they should be caught, they tricked Legree into thinking they were hiding in the swamp. When Legree sent dogs and men after them, they sneaked back into the house and hid in the garret. Legree suspected that Tom knew where the women had gone and decided to beat the truth out of his slave. He had Tom beaten until the old man could neither speak nor stand.

Two days later, George Shelby arrived to buy Tom back, but he came too late. Tom was dying. When George threatened to have Legree tried for murder, Legree mocked him. George struck Legree in the face and knocked him down.

Still hiding in the attic, Cassy and Emmeline pretended they were ghosts. Frightened, Legree drank harder than ever. George Shelby helped them to escape. Later, on a riverboat headed north, the two women discovered a Madame de Thoux, who said she was George Harris' sister. With this disclosure, Cassy learned also that Eliza, her daughter, was the Eliza who had married George and with him and her child had escaped safely to Canada.

These relatives were reunited in Canada after many years. In Kentucky, George Shelby freed all his slaves when his father died. He said he freed them in the name of Uncle Tom.

Critical Evaluation:

It has been suggested that Mark Twain wrote the first book in the American idiom, but surely Stowe's powerful novel introduces the reader to an in-depth use of a regional dialect from an earlier period. The author intentionally created the characters of Tom, Legree, Eva, and Sambo, all of whom subsequently became the stereotypes of various slave personalities, the brutal slave owner, and white southern womanhood, because these features were a part of the conventional wisdom of antebellum America. These characters were convenient, effective agencies to warn the Christians of the nation of an impending doom: "every nation that carries in its bosom great and unredressed injustice has in it the elements of this last convulsion." God would certainly punish such a nation.

First published in book form in 1852, this book attracted millions of readers then, and is now often required reading in high schools and colleges. This work will always provide an added dimension to an understanding of the spiritual crisis of pre-Civil War America. The human tragedy in the story symbolizes the moral decay of the country. Simon Legree becomes the manhood of white America that supported slavery, feared hell, yet was more concerned with the material world. Tom lost his wife, children, and life to the ravages of the "peculiar institution." The collective guilt of the nation could only be cleansed by the abolition of slavery.

The fate of the nation and the role of Christian churches in perpetuating slavery were topics of great concern to the author: "And yet, O my country these things are done under the Shadow of thy laws! O Christ! Thy Church sees them, almost in silence." The author observed and wrote about the crisis that divided Protestantism into sectional churches, a spiritual antecedent of the war. Clearly, the moral regeneration of the individual would lead to the abolition of slavery. Seeking support for her cause, the author admonished the reader to pity "those mothers that are constantly made childless by the American slave trade."

The author was a colonizationist, but she believed deeply that white America must first pay reparations to the nation's enslaved blacks. Once freed, the author points out, blacks needed and desired education and skills. She hoped that her testimony might bring an end to man's inhumanity to man. Little wonder, then, that President Lincoln, upon meeting the author, remarked, "So you're the little lady who started the war."

THE UNDERDOGS

Type of work: Novel
Author: Mariano Azuela (1873–1952)
Type of plot: Social and historical chronicle
Time of plot: 1914–1915
Locale: Zacatecas, northern Mexico
First published: 1915

Principal characters:
DEMETRIO MACÍAS, a poor Indian of Jalisco
LUIS CERVANTES, an opportunistic journalist and political
    turncoat
CAMILA, a village girl
LA PINTADA, "The Painted Lady," a prostitute and camp
    follower
WHITEY MARGARITO, a sadistic soldier

The Story:

Demetrio Macías was a peaceful Indian who knew nothing about revolutions. When as a follower of Madera he was hounded by the political leader of Jalisco, he fled with his wife and child to the mountains. There, some Federal soldiers came upon the fugitives at breakfast and sent Demetrio flying. Wild and lawless, they would have raped his wife if he had not returned with a gun. Being no killer, the Indian let them go free, only to have them come back with reinforcements and burn his fields. Demetrio then joined a band of sixty sharpshooting rebel outlaws and helped them to drive off twice that many soldiers. During the fighting, two of the rebels were killed, and Demetrio was shot in the leg.

For two weeks, the outlaws remained hidden in a native village, looked after by Indians who hated the government. Venancio, a barber-surgeon, tended Demetrio's wound. The village women also used poultices of laurel and fresh pigeon blood to heal him. An attractive young girl named Camila was his nurse.

One day, the pseudo-intellectual Luis Cervantes blundered into the village and explained that he had deserted the government forces because his commanding officer had assigned him to menial duty. Distrusting Cervantes' glib tongue and big words, the rebels pretended to condemn him to death. One outlaw dressed in a priest's robes and pretended to hear the deserter's last confession in order to determine whether he was a spy. Accepted eventually as a revolutionist, Cervantes then urged the rebels to join the great revolu-

THE UNDERDOGS by Mariano Azuela. Translated by E. Munguia, Jr. By permission of the publishers, Coward-McCann, Inc. Copyright, 1929, by Coward-McCann, Inc.

tionary leaders of Mexico. Camila fell in love with him. Although she made her feelings evident, Cervantes never encouraged her, not even on the night of the outlaws' departure. The girl had never responded to Demetrio's love-making; he was only an Indian.

Hearing from messengers that Huerta's Federalists had fortified the city of Zacatecas, Cervantes urged the band to hurry to join the besiegers and be in at the capture. He also flattered Demetrio by telling the Indian that he was more than a common rebel, that he was a tool of destiny to win back the rights of the people.

Demetrio planned a surprise attack on one of the towns along their march, but an Indian guide betrayed the scheme, and the Federalists were prepared to resist. A friendly citizen showed the rebels a back way into the town, however, and the garrison was overwhelmed. The rebels found and stabbed the treacherous guard and killed the Federal soldiers who had survived the attack.

By the time General Natera arrived in the district, Demetrio's reputation had grown so great that he was made a colonel in the revolutionary army. Failing to take Zacatecas, the rebels were forced to retreat, discarding their booty along the road. Demetrio thought of going back to Camila, until news of Villa's coming excited the rebels and gave them a fresh incentive.

During the next battle, Cervantes and Solis, an idealist, took refuge in a place where they thought they would be safe. While they discussed the significance of the revolution, a stray bullet killed Solis. Demetrio's gallant charge turned the tide of battle for Villa and won him promotion to the rank of general.

While drinking and boasting in a tavern after the battle, Demetrio met Whitey Margarito and La Pintada, a prostitute with whom he went looking for a hotel room. Her insistence that, as a general, he should occupy a house of his own made him decide to commandeer a fine residence. During the ransacking, Cervantes found a valuable diamond ring. The soldiers tore the pictures from books in the library and sold the ruined volumes. Whitey, joining Demetrio's forces, ran off with Cervantes' girl while Demetrio was arguing the matter of taking her instead of La Pintada, of whom he had tired.

Soon afterward, the rebels raided the house of Don Mónico, Demetrio's landowning enemy, and burned the estate. Cervantes, having collected much loot, suggested that he and Demetrio hide it in case they were forced to leave the country. Demetrio wished to share it with the others. Still an idealist, he believed the rebel cause would triumph. Because he wanted only Camila, Cervantes promised to get her for his leader.

Cervantes went to the village and persuaded the girl to return with him. Believing that Cervantes was in love with her, she was surprised to find herself in Demetrio's bed. The next morning, La Pintada discovered Camila and offered to help her escape. Camila refused. She had found that she liked

Demetrio, and she decided to stay with him and the army.

During the march against General Orozco at Jalisco, Whitey showed his cruelty when he tortured a prisoner by tightening a rope around the man's neck until his eyes bulged. Later, when kindhearted Camila persuaded Demetrio to return ten bushels of confiscated corn to a starving villager, Whitey gave the man ten lashes instead. Camila's protests at the incident won her the enmity of La Pintada, who had taken up with Whitey after Demetrio and Cervantes had discarded her. When Demetrio, siding with Camila, ordered the camp follower away, La Pintada became enraged and stabbed Camila.

By the time Demetrio and his men reached Aguascalientes, they found Villa and Carranza, once allies, fighting each other. The Federal forces, taking advantage of the disunity, defeated Villa at Celaya. The defeat was a terrible shock to Demetrio's followers, who could not bring themselves to believe that their idol had been beaten. The rebels were forced to retreat.

Cervantes escaped safely across the border. From El Paso he wrote to Venancio, the barber-surgeon. He said that Whitey had shot himself, and he invited Venancio to join him in Texas, where with the barber's money they could open a Mexican restaurant.

After Villa's defeat, Demetrio found the villagers no longer willing to help the rebels. To them, he and his followers had become outlaws once more. Somewhat discouraged, he decided to return home. He had been away two years and had seen much, but he could not answer his wife's questions when she asked him why he kept on fighting. He lacked Cervantes' glib tongue to put his true feelings into words.

Trying to pacify the landowners of the region, the government sent troops into the uplands after the outlaw band. Once more the rebels and the Federal troops clashed. Outnumbered, the outlaws perished on the spot where two years before they had won their first victory. After the fighting had ended, the soldiers found the body of Demetrio Macías. His eyes, forever fixed, still sighted along the barrel of his gun.

Critical Evaluation:

Mariano Azuela knew at firsthand the materials of this novel, for he had served as a military doctor with Pancho Villa's Golden Boys. His vivid account of revolutionary Mexico was first published serially in a small El Paso newspaper. Almost forgotten, it was revived in 1924 and won immediate fame for its author. Pessimism marks this story of those coming up from below—*Los de abajo*—at the beginning of the Mexican Revolution. This is no overall picture of the struggle but a blending of excitement, cruelty, and beauty as seen through the eyes of a man practically pushed into the struggle, a soldier who fought because the enemy was in front of him. Best known of Azuela's sixteen novels, *The Underdogs* has appeared in dozens of Spanish editions and has been translated into many languages.

    This old favorite of the 1910–1917 Mexican Revolution still merits its international fame. Vivid and deep, it has literary and sociological worth. Azuela's honesty glitters in it, since he does not overly caricature his Porfirista enemy even while lampooning him, but bares the hypocrisies of his own side with the skill of a surgeon's scalpel. His characterization is true to life, and his action scenes are fast and clear. Violence, pathos, beauty, and tragedy are etched against Jalisco's night-blackened hills, so that the reader receives an indelible image of revolutionary pageantry with its women soldaderas, bandoleered rebels, uniformed federales, and greedy nouveau riche who muddy the pond of revolutionary ideals. Thus, while painting only local vignettes of a nationwide holocaust, *The Underdogs* presents the seedy as well as inspiring aspects of the entire contortion well enough to be a historical document.

    The genuine worth of this novel was not recognized until almost a decade after its publication. By the mid-1920's, however, it had been translated into various languages and was considered a Latin American as well as a Mexican classic. It was written almost literally amid powder smoke, when Azuela was in black despair because he saw that the revolution was drowning some injustices in blood only to spawn others as bad and as self-perpetuating. The virtue of the novel thus lies in its taut swiftness, in its throbbing heartbeat, and its eyewitness impressions of intense, futile events. Azuela captured the excitement of times when bandoleered peons rode and marched off to war to the strains of the "Zacatecas March" or "La Cucaracha," when the Victorian, Bourbonic, ordered age of Don Porfirio Diaz was dying. Lamentably, it was being supplanted by a violently conceived but stillborn new order that was not even to attempt many of its reforms until many dismal years later.

    Noted for its "Mexicanness," and still ranked internationally as the best novel of the Mexican Revolution, *The Underdogs* helped transform the Latin American novel (which before 1910 had inspired few translations or fame beyond the local region that had produced each novel) into the most important literary genre of Latin America. *The Underdogs* is also possibly the first Latin American novel whose singular literary style was deliberately engendered by the subject matter. For example, time is telescoped to reflect the rapidity of events, while linguistic nuances tinge different aspects of the novel, including characters, scenes, and episodes. Individual members of Demetrio's command symbolize certain features of Mexican society—one soldier is a former barber, others are peons, both poor and prosperous, and there are also prostitutes, virtuous countrywomen, a former waiter, and many other types. Each such individual also has a personality representative of those to be found frequently in Mexico. Although venal characters are city dwellers, never country folk, the latter are sometimes ignorant.

    An elliptical style selects and spotlights a few specific characteristics of a person, a scene, or a situation so as to describe it deftly. Disjointed scenes are thus used, rather than systematic chapters, so as to strengthen the overtone of violent eruption. Selfishness wins, idealism is crucified, and the novel's true protagonist—Mexico's poor—does *not* march out of misery into a sunny horizon.

Although fragmented into many swift scenes, the novel is divided into three basic sections. The first section has twenty-one chapters and reflects hope; the last two sections have a total of twenty-one chapters and reflect failure. It is in the latter two portions of the novel that the filth, nastiness, lewdness, and garbage of war are best painted, when personalities such as Cervantes realize that the revolutionary issues will not be decided by logic or delicacy but by brute power as symbolized by self-made, upstart generals who care little for ideals.

Azuela used colors and details well. The natural dialogue is regionalistic but not difficult and, even though each personality uses special shades of language that subtly characterize him, there is a high percentage of standard Spanish.

It is sometimes felt of Azuela that he saw the Revolution coming like a silver cloud of hope, next as a black tornado; but then he watched it hit destructively, unleashing the contorted features of primeval chaos. It finally disappeared without having helped but having further flagellated the common people who needed help. Azuela's sympathy in *The Underdogs* is thus always with the poor, whom he neither idealizes nor attacks. For the opportunists who betrayed the revolutionary ideals, he reserves a special spleen, a sour sarcasm.

Azuela's masterpiece became the standard-bearer of the novel of the Revolution of 1910–1917, the first significant socioeconomic upheaval in Latin America. Most other revolutionary movements of the preceding years had not sought to aid the submerged masses, the mestizo, the Indian, the laborer, "the underdog" in general. Following Azuela's example, many Mexican and other Latin American novelists took up the fight for reform, denouncing tyranny and championing the cause of the "forgotten man." Since 1916, hence, numerous starkly realistic novels have been published in Mexico and throughout Latin America that defend the underdog, whether he lives in the pampa, the llanos, sierra, jungle, city slum, or desert areas of this hemisphere.

THE UNVANQUISHED

Type of work: Novel
Author: William Faulkner (1897–1962)
Type of plot: Psychological realism
Time of plot: 1863–1874
Locale: Jefferson, Yoknapatawpha County, Mississippi
First published: 1938

Principal characters:

BAYARD SARTORIS, a boy and later a young man
MISS ROSA MILLARD (GRANNY), Bayard's grandmother
COLONEL JOHN SARTORIS, Bayard's father
MARENGO SARTORIS (RINGO), Bayard's black playmate and servant
DRUSILLA HAWK, John Sartoris' cousin and, later, his wife
VIRGINIA SARTORIS DU PRE (AUNT JENNY), John Sartoris' widowed sister and Bayard's aunt
COLONEL DICK, commander of an Ohio regiment
AB SNOPES, a horse and mule trader and Rosa Millard's killer
MAJOR GRUMBY, a bushwhacker Southerner and also Rosa Millard's killer
BENJAMIN J. REDMOND, a Jefferson lawyer, at one time John Sartoris' railroad partner, later his killer

Most of William Faulkner's novels have an individual and unconventional form, but two share a common formal distinction: *Go Down, Moses* and *The Unvanquished* appear at first glance to be collections of short stories. The chronology in both, like that of the conventional novel, is strictly observed, but the exact order of composition of the episodes, first published as separate short stories, has not been determined.

At least three stages appear to have occurred in creating the novel from the stories. First, Faulkner's imagination played freely on real and remembered incidents that became a set of anecdotes about the adventures of the Sartoris women and children during the Civil War. Next, these were arranged in order to provide a family chronicle from the moment the first Union troops appeared near Jefferson, with resulting disruption of Sartoris family life, until its tentative reestablishment at the Sartoris home during the Reconstruction. Last, the chronicle was given both the perspective and larger meaning that a novel offers by writing a new story, "An Odor of Verbena," set some years later than the rest, in which the role of Bayard is clarified as "the unvanquished." This concluding story was necessary because there is no separate story or chapter so called in the book, though the story "Riposte in Tertio" originally bore that title. Five of the stories were published in chronological order in *The Saturday Evening Post* between September, 1934, and December, 1936; "Skirmish at Sartoris" appeared in *Scribner's Magazine* during that period. Very few changes in text were made between periodical and book publication. "An Odor of Verbena" was printed for the first time in the novel.

The Unvanquished is, therefore, an interesting example of how Faulkner could mine his Sartoris material for a number of anecdotes which, as they were gradually assembled, he shaped into a novel by writing a conclusion that would transfer the attention from Granny Millard (who, with Ringo, dominates the first four stories) to Bayard, who completed Granny's history in the fifth story. At the same time Faulkner explored the whole Southern code and came up with a different ending to the series of episodes in the new story he wrote. The imposition of this conclusion is Faulkner's clearest statement about the origins and foundations of the Southern code, and this fact makes *The Unvanquished* not only the best introduction to his work and the earliest in the Yoknapatawpha saga but also the most important to an understanding of all his writings.

At the start of the novel, the "unvanquished" are three of the four recognized constituents of a Southern Civil War novel: Southern men, women, children, and blacks: in turn, the first two are vanquished not by the Union but by inherent weakness in the Southern code; the child grown into a man remains unvanquished by North or South; the black looks on and survives. Certain unifying features bring out these distinctions. All seven stories or chapters are told in the first person by Bayard, so that the book could be considered a child's testament to the War; the setting is held to Jefferson as much as possible, but the homestead serves largely as a point of departure and return; even when the house has been burned to the ground, the chimneys will not fall, and the cabins are used for shelter. The events take place between the fall of Vicksburg in 1863, when Bayard is twelve years old, and 1874, when he is twenty-four. The first six stories, however, take place in the three years after the novel opens; "An Odor of Verbena," separated by more than time from the others, serves as an epilogue to the volume.

The progression of events leading to the last story is based on shootings and deaths; at the end of the fourth story, "Riposte in Tertio," Granny has been shot by Major Grumby, a renegade Southerner and leader of Grumby's Independents, with the apparent connivance of Ab Snopes, historically the first of the Snopes in Yoknapatawpha County. At the end of the fifth story, "Vendée," Grumby has been shot in revenge by Bayard; before the beginning of the last story, Colonel Sartoris has been shot by Benjamin J. Redmond, his former partner in a railroad-building venture. The structure of the novel depends on a similar parallelism of characters, situations, and events, with the movement of the Union troops precipitating most of the action. Bayard, for example, is accompanied or paralleled by Ringo; the action of the first four stories is based on the struggle between Union troops and Confederate raiding parties, such as that of Colonel Sartoris, to hold or control Mississippi, but for every triumph of the former, the populace in that section of Mississippi, led by Granny Millard, score a victory over the invaders. When that struggle concludes, another begins between Granny and the harsh conditions of the Reconstruction: her death at the hands of Major Grumby and Ab Snopes causes the death of Grumby at the hands of Bayard and Ringo. A third struggle between the returned Southerners and the carpetbaggers begins in the sixth story, "Skirmish at Sartoris." The last confrontation, between Bayard and the Southern code, is the final story.

This is also a progression from the high comedy of the two boys, Bayard and Ringo, blindly shooting at Yankees in the first story, through the various shootings and killings until Bayard is grimly face-to-face with Redmond in the last story; Redmond, like Grumby, shoots twice at Bayard, misses, and leaves town. Bayard, unarmed, has brought the cycle of violence, initiated by his own act in shooting at the Yankees, to a Christian close. Accompanied by Ringo, escorted by the Colonel's old troop, challenged by Drusilla, Bayard manages to withstand all these encouragements to violence, thus gaining the approval of his father's sister, Aunt Jenny Sartoris, who takes the place of dead Granny Millard as the voice of good conduct. Granny Millard was killed because she had been compelled to violate her own standards: in the first story, "Ambuscade," she lies to Colonel Dick to protect Bayard and Ringo; in the second, "Retreat," she swears as the Union troops burn the Sartoris house; in the third, "Raid," she steals from the Union troops by forging copies of the official order that generous Colonel Dick gave her to make up for her original loss of slaves, mules, and silver. Her habit had been to punish the boys for such transgressions, and she tried to keep up such a code of punishment, but at the end, Bayard and Ringo were unable to stop her trying one last theft and lie. In the fourth story, she meets worse liars and robbers in Ab Snopes and Grumby; they add murder to these crimes.

The accretion of parallel events and the final moral decision confronting Bayard—whether to shoot Redmond as Redmond shot his father—give the novel both epic and ethical dimensions. The epic dimension is shown in the way Granny Millard comes to stand for all Southern womanhood, fighting with wit and grit, and apparently, overwhelming forces—and winning. Most of the exciting passages, such as the great river of freed slaves "going to Jordan" or the trailing of Major Grumby are associated with the epic of Granny Millard and Ringo, in which Bayard is largely a bystander. The ethical dimension comes from the three occasions on which Bayard handles a gun: first, when he shoots at the Yankees; second, when he kills Grumby; third, when Drusilla presses on him the dueling pistols with which she intends he shall shoot Redmond. Greater than the courage of pistols, however, is the courage of endurance, which must be the total meaning of the Civil War to the South. The power of the pistol failed, but the power to endure carried the South on. This latter power is represented as "the odor of verbena," and in the last story so named, Drusilla, the toughest battler of them all, comes to recognize that Bayard deserves this accolade.

Although Colonel Sartoris was eventually vanquished by Northern arms and even more by the triumph of total war as practiced by Sherman, and although Granny was eventually vanquished by the desire to loot, but for the highest and most unselfish motives, Bayard has been able to escape the fever of killing, break the chain of shootings, and in doing so offer a way of escape to the South and from the past. He could not do so without the example of Granny and his father. He is "unvanquished" because he did not allow the Southern code to negate the universal law against killing. The tragedy of the South, as Faulkner explores it in his work, is that it could not see that Bayard, the Christ-figure, had come to redeem the South from itself.

U.S.A.

Type of work: Novel
Author: John Dos Passos (1896–1970)
Type of plot: Social chronicle
Time of plot: 1900–1935
Locale: The United States
First published: 1930, 1932, and 1936

Principal characters:

FAINY MCCREARY (MAC), a labor organizer
JANEY WILLIAMS, a private secretary
JOE WILLIAMS, her brother
J. WARD MOOREHOUSE, a public relations executive
ELEANOR STODDARD, an interior decorator
CHARLEY ANDERSON, an airplane manufacturer
RICHARD ELLSWORTH SAVAGE, Moorehouse's assistant
EVELINE HUTCHINS, Eleanor Stoddard's partner
ANNE ELIZABETH TRENT (DAUGHTER), a relief worker
BEN COMPTON, a radical
MARY FRENCH, a labor worker
MARGO DOWLING, a film star

The Story:

The Spanish-American War was over. Politicians with mustaches said that America was now ready to lead the world.

Mac McCreary was a printer for a fly-by-night publisher in Chicago. Later he worked his way to the West Coast. There he got work as a printer in Sacramento and married Maisie Spencer, who could never understand his radical views. They quarreled, and he went to Mexico to work in the revolutionary movement there.

Janey Williams, growing up in Washington, D.C., became a stenographer. She was always ashamed when her sailor brother, Joe, showed up, and even more ashamed of him after she became secretary to J. Ward Moorehouse. Of all Moorehouse's female acquaintances, she was the only one who never became his mistress.

J. Ward Moorehouse's boyish manner and blue eyes were the secret of his success. They attracted Annabelle Strang, the wealthy nymphomaniac he later divorced. Gertrude Staple, his second wife, helped to make him a prominent public relations expert. His shrewdness made him an ideal man for government service in France during World War I. After the war, he became one

---

of the nation's leading advertising executives.

Because Eleanor Stoddard hated the sordid environment of her childhood, her delicate, arty tastes led her naturally into partnership with Eveline Hutchins in the decorating business and eventually to New York and acquaintanceship with J. Ward Moorehouse. In Europe with the Red Cross during the war, she lived with Moorehouse. Back in New York in the 1920's she used her connections in shrewd fashion and became engaged to a member of the Russian nobility.

Charley Anderson had been an aviator in the war. A successful invention and astute opportunism made him a wealthy airplane manufacturer. He married a wife who had little sympathy for his interest in mechanics. In Florida, after a plane crash, he met Margo Dowling, an actress. Charley Anderson's series of drunks ended in a grade crossing accident.

Joe Williams was a sailor who had been on the beach in Buenos Aires. In Norfolk he met Della, who urged him to give up seafaring and settle down. Unable to hold a job, he shipped out again and almost lost his life when the ship he was on was sunk by a German submarine. When Joe got his third mate's license, he and Della were married. He was ill in the East Indies, arrested in New York for not carrying a draft card, and torpedoed once more off the coast of Spain. Della was unfaithful to him. Treated coldly the few times he looked up his sister Janey, he shipped for Europe once more. One night in St. Nazaire he attacked a huge Senegalese who was dancing with a girl he knew. His skull was crushed when he was hit over the head with a bottle.

Teachers encouraged Dick Savage in his literary talents. During his teens, he worked at a summer hotel, and there he slept with a minister's wife who shared his taste in poetry. A government official paid his way through Harvard, where Dick cultivated his estheticism and mild snobbery before he joined the Norton-Harjes ambulance service and went to Europe. There some of his letters about the war came to the attention of censorship officials, and he was shipped back to the United States. His former sponsor got him an officer's commission, and he returned to France. In Italy, he met a relief worker named Anne Elizabeth Trent, who was his mistress for a time. When he returned to the United States, he became an idea man for Moorehouse's advertising agency.

Eveline Hutchins, who had a small artistic talent, became Eleanor Stoddard's partner in a decorating establishment in New York. All her life she tried to escape from boredom through sensation. Beginning with the Mexican artist who was her first lover, she had a succession of affairs. In France, where she was Eleanor's assistant in the Red Cross, she married a shy young soldier named Paul Johnson. Later she had a brief affair with Charley Anderson. Dissatisfied, she decided at last that life was too dull for endurance and died from an overdose of sleeping pills.

Anne Elizabeth Trent, known as Daughter, was the child of moderately wealthy Texans. In New York, she met Webb Cruthers, a young anarchist. One day, seeing a policeman kick a woman picketer in the face, Daughter attacked him with her fists. Her night in jail disturbed her father so much that she returned to Texas and worked in Red Cross canteens. Later she went overseas, met Dick Savage, became pregnant by him, and learned that he had no intention of marrying her. In Paris, she went on a drunken spree with a French aviator and died with him in a plane crash.

Benny Compton was the son of Jewish immigrants. After six months in jail for making radical speeches, he worked his way west through Canada. In Seattle, he and other agitators were beaten by deputies. Benny returned East. One day police broke up a meeting where he was speaking. On his twenty-third birthday, Benny went to Atlanta to serve a ten-year sentence. Released after the war, he lived for a time with Mary French, a fellow traveler in the party.

Mary French spent her childhood in Trinidad, where her father, a physician, did charity work among the native miners. Mary, planning to become a social worker, spent her summers at Jane Addams' Hull House. She went to Washington as secretary to a union official and later worked as a union organizer in New York City. There she took care of Ben Compton after his release from Atlanta. While working with the Sacco-Vanzetti Committee, she fell in love with Don Stevens, a fellow party member. Summoned to Moscow with a group of party leaders, Stevens returned to New York with a wife assigned to him by the party. Mary went back to her committee work for laboring men's relief.

Margo Dowling grew up in a rundown house in Rockaway, Long Island, with her drunken father and Agnes, her father's mistress. At last, Agnes left her lover and took Margo with her. In New York, Agnes became the common-law wife of an actor named Frank Mandeville. One day, while drunk, Mandeville raped the girl. Margo ran off to Cuba with Tony, an effeminate Cuban guitar player, whom she later deserted. She was a cheerful companion for Charley Anderson, who gave her a check for five thousand dollars on his deathbed. In Hollywood, she met Sam Margolies, a successful producer, who made a star of her.

Jobless and hungry, a young hitchhiker stood by the roadside. Overhead droned a plane in which people of the big money rode the skyways. Below, the hitchhiker with empty belly thumbed cars speeding by. The haves and the have-nots—that was America in the depression 1930's.

Critical Evaluation:

John Dos Passos' statement at the beginning of *U.S.A.* that America is, more than anything else, the sounds of its many voices, offers several insights into the style and content of the trilogy. The style, for example, reflects the author's attempt to capture some sense of characteristically American "voices," not just in the idiomatic narration of the chronicles (or novel sections), but in the "Newsreels," "Biographies," and "The Camera Eye" as well. While these sections reflect, respectively, the public voice of the media and popular culture, the oratorical and eulogistic voice of the biographies, and the personal and private voice of the artist, the most important voices in the trilogy are those of the chronicles in which Dos Passos introduces a cross-section of American voices ranging from the blue collar worker to the professional and managerial classes, and representing a variety of regional and ethnic backgrounds. Like Walt Whitman, who profoundly influenced him, Dos Passos takes all America as his subject matter as he tries to capture through the sounds of the many voices which characterize its people and institutions the meaning of *U.S.A.*

Many people have associated the social, political, and economic views expressed in *U.S.A.* with Marxism—as leftists in the 1930's liked to believe this important author made common cause with them—but it is really the American economist, Thornstein Veblen, rather than Marx, who seems to have shaped Dos Passos' thinking about the economic and political situation in the United States during the first quarter of this century. Dos Passos had read Veblen's *The Theory of the Leisure Class*, *The Theory of Business Enterprise*, and other writings, and it was from these sources that his attack on the American business economy stemmed. In *The Big Money*, Dos Passos offers a "Biography" of Veblen in which he summarizes this economist's theories of the domination of society by monopoly capitalism and the sabotage of the workers' human rights by business interests dominated by the profit motive. According to Dos Passos, the alternatives Veblen saw were either a society strangled and its workers destroyed by the capitalists' insatiable greed for profit or a society in which the needs of those who do the work would be the prime consideration. Veblen, writing just at the turn of the century, still held out hope that the workers might yet take control of the means of production before monopoly capitalism could plunge the world into a new dark age. Dos Passos further develops the idea that any such hope died with World War I and that the American dream of democracy was dead from that time forward.

Against the background of Veblen's ideas, *U.S.A.* can be seen as a documentary chronicling the growing exploitation of the American worker by the capitalist system and a lamentation for the lost hope of Veblen's dream of a society which would make the producer the prime beneficiary of his own labor. The best characterization of the blue collar worker is Mac McCreary— a rootless laborer constantly searching for some outlet for his idealistic hope of restoring power to the worker. Certainly one of the most sympathetic characters in *U.S.A.*, Mac dramatizes the isolation and frustration of the modern worker, who is only a human cog in the industrial machine, unable either to take pride in his work or finally to profit significantly by it. Other characters as well fit within the pattern of the capitalist system as Veblen described it, or else, like Mac, revolt against the injustice of the system. There are the exploiters and the exploited, and there are some few, like Mary French and Ben Compton, who make opposition to the system a way of life. Equally prevalent are those characters who dramatize Veblen's theory of conspicuous consumption by serving as playthings (Margo Dowling), lackeys (Dick Savage), or promoters (J. Ward Moorehouse) for those who control the wealth and power.

Throughout the trilogy, the essential conflict is that between the business interests who control the wealth and the workers who produce it, but Dos Passos is almost equally concerned with the way in which the system of monopoly capitalism exploits and destroys even those of the managerial class who seem to profit most immediately from it. Dick Savage, for example, starts out as a talented young writer only to be corrupted by the system. Charley Anderson, who early could be seen as typifying the American Dream of success through ingenuity and imagination, dies as much a victim of the system as any of its workers. J. Ward Moorehouse, on the other hand, makes nothing and produces nothing, but his is the talent that can parlay nothing into a fortune and the mentality that can survive in the world of *U.S.A.*

The two national historical events to which Dos Passos gives most attention are World War I and the execution of the anarchists Sacco and Vanzetti. The war, as Dos Passos saw it, under the pretense of making the world safe for democracy, gave the capitalists the opportunity they needed to solidify their power by actually crushing the democratic spirit. For Dos Passos, democracy was dead in America from World War I, and the Sacco and Vanzetti case proved it. The death of these two immigrant Italian radicals on a trumped-up charge of murder was, in Dos Passos' eyes, the ultimate demonstration of the fact that traditional freedoms were lost and that monopoly capitalism had usurped power in America. When, in his later and more conservative years, Dos Passos was accused of having deserted the liberal positions of his youth, he maintained that his views had not shifted from those he argued in *U.S.A.* The evidence of the novel would seem to bear him out. The *U.S.A.* trilogy is a more nostalgic than revolutionary work, and it looks back to that point in American history before the options were lost rather than forward to a Socialist revolution. His finest work shows Dos Passos as a democratic idealist rather than as a Socialist revolutionary.

THE VELVET HORN

Type of work: Novel
Author: Andrew Lytle (1902–   )
Type of plot: Lyrical melodrama
Time of plot: August, 1879–April, 1880
Locale: The Peaks of Laurel, presumably in Tennessee
First published: 1957

Principal characters:

LUCIUS CREE (or LEGRAND), the son of Julia Cree
JULIA CREE (née CROPLEIGH), later Julia Legrand
JOE CREE, Julia's husband and cousin and Lucius' father
JACK CROPLEIGH, Julia's older brother
BEVERLY CROPLEIGH, the oldest of the Cropleighs
DUNCAN CROPLEIGH, Julia's youngest brother
AUNT AMELIE CROPLEIGH, Duncan's widow
PETER LEGRAND, Lucius' real father
EDDIE DUNBAUGH, kin to the Cropleighs
FRANKIE DUNBAUGH, Eddie's wife
JEFF DUNBAUGH, the son of Eddie and Frankie
ADA RUTTER, a sharecropper's wife
ADA BELLE RUTTER, her older daughter and Lucius' wife
RUTHY RUTTER, her younger daughter and Jeff's wife
OTHEL RUTTER, her son

In Andrew Lytle's first book, *Bedford Forrest and His Critter Company*, General Forrest became, in Lytle's hands, the symbol of the Mississippian South and its best illumination, next to Lytle's "The Hind Tit," his essay in *I'll Take My Stand*, the manifesto of the Southern agrarians. The passionate portrait of primal simplicity in both works is fascinating and frustrating; the same reaction meets most of Lytle's work—certainly *The Velvet Horn*—and is probably the truest measure of the novelist.

The novel, dedicated to John Crowe Ransom, joins a distinguished company of works acknowledging his influence, and it is this agrarian viewpoint which both attracts and repels in the novel. The lyrical description of the lost simplicity of the Garden summons up the old Adam in the reader, only to make the reader reject the vanished vision when he raises his eyes from the page. In this novel, as in Faulkner's "The Bear," the Garden is the unspoiled forest, here the Wilderness and specifically the Peaks of Laurel. It comes equipped with game, cover, and water, even with a Cooperesque secret entrance through a waterfall; but this is only the starting point of the novel, the setting for the story of the Cropleigh brothers and their sister Julia which precipitates years later the events that affect Julia's son, Lucius, the apparent hero. The agrarian point of view is in the custody of the most impressive character, Uncle Jack Cropleigh. The tension between the agrarian base and the Reconstruction events is complicated by the poetic language in the lyrical description of the wilderness life and by the twists of the interconnected plots. This is a highly wrought novel.

Although the simplistic agrarian cosmos is shattered by the mercantilism of those who prospered in Reconstruction days and by the necessity for Lucius finally to make a living cutting virgin timber from the wilderness, the difficulty of facing up to such a resolution is shown in the length and occasional turgidity of the novel. When the action becomes static, the language becomes overwhelming, and there are several set scenes in which this sometimes happens, as in the first meeting between Ada Rutter and Jack Cropleigh, or at Captain Cree's wake. Lytle's solution is to underwrite such set pieces with a current of tension derived from the plot or plots.

The first meeting with Ada Rutter, for example, is tense because Uncle Jack is trying to drink the dwarf-child, Othel, under the table, to keep him from shooting Eddie Dunbaugh for watering his cattle on the Peaks of Laurel during the drought with which the novel opens in August, 1879. This would give time to dig the well which Uncle Jack has already divined; but Eddie prefers to steal the water so that he can fornicate with Ruthy, Ada's younger daughter, who has also been seduced by Eddie's son Jeff. Frankie, Eddie's wife, knew what was keeping Eddie on the Peaks but did not foresee Jeff's interference. At Frankie's insistence, Jack divined the well. The whole incident, the major portion of the first part, "The Peaks of Laurel," ends even more unexpectedly in the seduction of Lucius by Ada's older daughter, Ada Belle Rutter.

Lucius had originally been called away by his mother from helping his father cut Aunt Amelie's timber tract to drag Uncle Jack up the Peaks and thus help out Cousin Frankie, and incidentally Eddie. Worst of all, news of the event with which the novel opens, the apparently accidental death of Captain Cree under the falling white-oak tree, finally reaches Lucius at the Peaks, and he returns to his father's funeral on the day he becomes eighteen. Such complexity of event is achieved by a number of flashbacks which carry the story back to two earlier events in the history of the Cropleighs, the family that dominates the novel. When Jack was eighteen, his mother and father were blown up in a steamboat explosion, leaving the four Cropleigh boys and little Julia under the guardianship of their cousin, Joe Cree. Some eight years later when the youngest boy, Duncan, is almost eighteen, the last hunt is held on the Big Meadow at the Peaks of Laurel before Peter Legrand turns it to plow. In those eight years, Beverly, the oldest brother, and Duncan had taken to the forest, often accompanied by Julia, leaving Jack to run the farm and put a younger brother through medical college. During the hunt, Julia and Legrand find the secret entrance to Beverly's game sanctuary and sleep together.

When the Cropleigh brothers find them, Duncan knifes Legrand, the medical brother sews him up, and the others marry Julia smartly to Joe Cree. Lucius arrives nine months later in August, 1861.

This deception haunts the events of the novel and is complicated by two further developments. During the Civil War, Duncan and Beverly kill each other in blowing up the secret entrance, and Duncan's widow, Amelie, vows long revenge against Joe Cree, as the captain of their troop, for sending Duncan to his death. She has to wait until 1879 when Cree, in financial desperation, agrees to cut her timber tract under nearly impossible conditions. When it looks as if he may succeed, Aunt Amelie springs her trap and tells him about Lucius; Cree walks under the tree. When Lucius takes over his father's contract, she tells him the same news—that he is really Lucius Legrand; then she hands him the deed to the timber tract to make his fortune. The deed is made out to Lucius Cree.

Although this is the barest outline of the main plot, it is obvious that it bears a remarkable similarity to the Victorian melodrama that unravels the parentage of the foundling and leaves him secure in his fortune. The resemblance comes from the family feuding involved. Of the principal characters, leaving aside faithful retainers who play a considerable role in the embellishment of this story, all but one belong to one of three families, the Cropleighs, Dunbaughs, and Rutters. The outsider is Peter Legrand, whose story is told largely in the third part, "The Passionate Husk"; it is he who marries Julia and finances Lucius in the timber business. The Dunbaughs are related to the Cropleighs and Crees (who form one family) but serve mainly to pry Lucius away into the hands of Ada Rutter, an awful and portentous character whose full evil is seen only at the end of the novel. The Rutters are, in two senses, what their name implies; sharecroppers who rut the land and women who behave as expected. In the last part of the novel, "The Night Sea Journey," the Rutters and Dunbaughs change situations, the former taking the place of the latter at the tollgate and the Dunbaughs retiring to farm the Peaks. When Ada sees that Lucius knows his parentage, a secret she guessed long ago, she presses home her advantage. Lucius abducts Ada Belle, marries her, and returns to Uncle Jack for help. To them enter both Julia and Ada Rutter, accompanied by menacing Othel, who shoots Uncle Jack while aiming at Lucius. Although Uncle Jack tries to sum up in a dying speech some sort of meaning from the whole affair, it is not clear what the novel is really saying. The tension between Beverly's mode as "keeper" or maintainer of the wilderness and Legrand as the "husk" of progress is resolved in the latter's favor and apparently to the author's displeasure.

A possible source of enlightenment is found in the rhetoric and the poetry of the speeches, of which, since the book is mostly in direct speech or unspoken thought, there is an abundance. The most obvious feature, apart from Jack's astoundingly free associations, is the symbolism. The velvet horn, in view of

Lucius' experiences with Ada Belle and Aunt Amelie, is comprehensible, but it also refers to the unicorn Jack thinks he sees during Captain Cree's wake.

The falling white-oak tree is not necessarily symbolically related to Lucius' fall with Ada Belle; it seems to enclose the action of the plot, for at the end of the novel, Lucius is to live in a house built of the planks of the tree that killed his father. Other symbols dominate the sections of the novel, generally aspects of nature such as the drought with which the novel opens and the flood with which it closes.

Neither Lucius nor Julia seems to come alive, but readers are meant to sympathize with the boy and therefore possibly favor the denouement. Uncle Jack and several minor characters dominate the novel yet lose out to Legrand. It is possible that this is more a *roman à thèse* than appears on the surface and only placing it in its full agrarian context would illuminate its meaning.

THE VENETIAN GLASS NEPHEW

Type of work: Novel
Author: Elinor Wylie (1885–1928)
Type of plot: Fantasy
Time of plot: 1782
Locale: Italy and France
First published: 1925

Principal characters:
> PETER INNOCENT BON, an unworldly cardinal
> VIRGINIO, his Venetian glass nephew
> ROSALBA BERNI (SAPPHO THE YOUNGER), Virginio's bride
> MONSIEUR DE CHASTELNEUF, the Chevalier de Langeist
> ANGELO QUERINI, a philosopher and scholar
> COUNT CARLO GOZZI, a writer of fairy tales

The Story:

The heart of Peter Innocent Bon, cardinal prefect of the Congregation of the Propaganda, was filled with happiness that was almost childlike in its simplicity. After thirty years, he was to see his native Venice once more, for brilliant, vain Pius VI, about to visit its lagoons and golden palaces, had named the aged cardinal a member of his suite. Peter Innocent, in 1782, was in the eighty-first year of his life. A shy, mild man, he seldom appeared in the rich vestments of his office, but went inconspicuously about Rome in the gray-brown garb of the Franciscan Friars Minor, a robe suited to the humility of a follower of St. Francis.

Only one small regret marred Peter Innocent's pleasure as he viewed again the city of his youth. Pius was traveling in state, and he and many of his suite were accompanied by their nephews. Peter Innocent had no nephews; his brother had fathered only daughters and his sisters were in holy orders. Seeing the satisfaction that other churchmen found in the company of their young kinsmen, he wished that he too might have enjoyed such comfort in his old age. Prayers, fasting, and pilgrimages to holy shrines, however, had given him no nephew of his own, and the thought of parenthood would have been as foreign to the chastity of his mind as to that of his body.

During the Venetian visit, Pius treated Peter Innocent with particular graciousness and asked him to represent the pontiff at the singing of a new cantata at the Incurabili. Listening to the music, the cardinal felt that its subject, the return of Tobias, was appropriate to his own situation.

As he left the Incurabili, a hand touched his shoulder. He turned to find Alvise Luna, the famous glassblower of Murano, at his elbow. Luna, whom the cardinal had known in earlier days, complained that he had fallen upon evil times. Willing to help his old friend and not knowing that the man was under suspicion as a sorcerer, Peter Innocent went with him to his cellar workshop. There he met a masked stranger whom Luna introduced as M. de Chastelneuf, Chevalier de Langeist. Peter Innocent was amazed when the men displayed their miraculous wares, a flying golden griffin, a glass stag that walked, and glass birds that sang. When they asked if they might execute a commission for some bauble he had in mind, Peter Innocent reached a sudden decision. He asked modestly if they could make him a nephew such as he had always desired.

At Luna's warning glance, Chastelneuf repressed the smile and the ribald comment that rose to his lips. Solemnly he assured the cardinal that such a work of art was difficult but not impossible. If he would return in three days, he could see for himself the result of their labors.

Peter Innocent went to Luna's cellar three nights later. In a chamber scented with spices and incense, Chastelneuf brought to life a figure of Venetian glass that lay upon a covered bier. The cardinal's nephew stood revealed as a handsome young man of nineteen or twenty, of complexion so fair as to seem translucent, with yellow hair as fine as spun glass. He was dressed completely in white and wore a strange ring of crystal. Peter Innocent baptized him Virginio.

The cardinal, as much concerned for his nephew's mind as he was for his person and his soul, decided to send him to Altichieri to study under the noble Angelo Querini, who had been Voltaire's friend. On his arrival, Virginio met Rosalba Berni, Querini's lovely ward. Some thought her a descendant of Francesco Berni, the poet; others whispered the name of Cardinal de Bernis. At eighteen, she was a prodigy of learning and a poet known officially as Sappho the Younger. Virginio had never seen anyone so beautiful, and Rosalba was not so engrossed in the classics as to fail to notice how handsome he was. Scholarly Querini, always indulgent toward Rosalba, gave them his blessing when they announced their desire to wed.

Meanwhile, Peter Innocent had gone to consult Count Carlo Gozzi, his longtime friend and a writer of fairy tales, on matters connected with Virginio's future. He found Chastelneuf closeted with the Count; the chevalier had come to discuss the match between Rosalba and Virginio. He explained the reason for his interest in the girl to Peter Innocent and the Count. Years before he had loved Caterina, Rosalba's mother, but because of his attachment to another woman, he had callously relinquished his innocent beloved to Cardinal de Bernis, a notorious libertine. The cardinal had loved Caterina faithfully, however, and Rosalba was the daughter of that affectionate union. After the mother's death, de Bernis had been summoned to Rome. Rosalba, already famous for her beauty and learning, had become the spoiled darling of French scholars and philosophers. After Voltaire's death, Querini had become her guardian.

As Chastelneuf finished his story, Rosalba and Virginio appeared, having driven from Altichieri in the chevalier's carriage. Seeing their happiness and youthful high spirits, Peter Innocent and his friends decided that the wedding should take place at once.

The marriage of Virginio and Rosalba, however, did not end as happily as one of Count Gozzi's fairy tales. Chastelneuf had seen to it that Virginio could play the part of a tender and devoted husband, but there had been no provision for the contingencies of daily association with a hoyden such as Rosalba had suddenly become. He splintered too easily; sometimes, after a hearty embrace, Rosalba found particles of glass in her palms. Games like hide-and-seek and blind-man's-buff, in which she sportively delighted, were impossible for him. Privately, she and Virginio were unhappy, and, realizing their unhappiness, Peter Innocent, Querini, Chastelneuf, and Count Gozzi were wretched as well.

At last, after Rosalba had tried to end her misery by leaping into a bonfire, Chastelneuf made a desperate suggestion. If she were willing to endure the agony of fire, she could be changed into a woman of the finest Sèvres porcelain. Rosalba agreed for Virginio's sake and because of her own love. Through winter snows, she and Chastelneuf and Peter Innocent traveled to the ancient town of Sèvres, in France. While Peter Innocent, in an inn at Versailles, read aloud from the life of St. Francis, she and Chastelneuf went to the abandoned Dubois factory, and there she was transformed into a proper bride for a Venetian glass lover.

So Virginio and Rosalba returned to Venice in the twilight of a dimming century to live happily in a delicate, beautiful world of porcelain and Murano glass. There Pietro Longhi painted them in his old age. With fragile grace, the lovers look out from the miniature he made, and reflected in the mirrors that surround them are the faces of Peter Innocent Bon, Angelo Querini, and Count Carlo Gozzi. M. de Chastelneuf is not in the antique miniature; it is believed that he had retired to Bohemia.

Critical Evaluation:

Elinor Wylie came to fiction writing late in her career. In her poetry, her famous intensity had been controlled though spectacular, but in her novels it took on a feverish and artificial quality. She did not have to strain to write well, for her feeling for style was instinctive, but she was obsessed with the need to create ornate pictures out of words. She became part of the group of "Exquisites" of the 1920's which included Joseph Hergesheimer, James Branch Cabell, and Carl Van Vechten. The shadow behind *The Venetian Glass Nephew*, however, is the Oscar Wilde of *The Picture of Dorian Grey*.

Both novels deal with artificially created beauty and both convey, beneath their baroque surfaces, a moral lesson.

The Venetian Glass Nephew is the most completely realized of Wylie's novels, reflecting the qualities of her poetic imagination and style. A subtle fable of life and art, it marches with minuet grace and precision along its fantastic course. Virginio, the man of glass, and Rosalba, his flesh-and-blood bride, are more than figures in a romance which seems on the surface as slight and fragile as its spun-glass hero. Under the brittle brilliance of this novel, there is a darkly personal note of mocking irony and almost silent grief. What might have been a slight work of artifice becomes, through its underlying meaning, a work of limited but authentic art. M. de Chastelneuf, idealist, cynic, and charlatan, is the famous Casanova under thin disguise.

A decadent eroticism (especially in the character of Chastelneuf) pervades the book. The question raised by Gozzi stands at the center of the novel: Can this artificial youth be "better than human"? Chastelneuf, who stage-manages the entire drama, cannot be concerned with ordinary moral questions. He is insistent upon carrying human passion and curiosity to the limits of possibility. Yet, it appears, at last his heart is touched by the plight of Virginio, composed of magic and glass, and Rosalba, that "burning and spiritual child of love."

Wylie's novels seem to invert Hemingway's aphorism: "Prose is architecture, not interior decoration," but there are in *The Venetian Glass Nephew* a gaiety and erudition that give the book a lovely, amused formality that the reader cannot easily resist. The tale poses a contest between Christian art and pagan nature, and in this conflict, there can be only one result: nature must yield. Venice is the appropriately artificial setting for the story, and the eighteenth century, the Age of Reason, the inevitable setting for this moral romance of "exquisite monsters" and alchemists and brittle lovers.

THE VICTIM

Type of work: Novel
Author: Saul Bellow (1915–   )
Type of plot: Modernist
Time of plot: Several weeks during a hot summer in the 1940's
Locale: New York City
First published: 1947

Principal characters:
ASA LEVENTHAL, the protagonist
MARY, his wife
MAX, his brother
ELENA, Leventhal's sister-in-law and Max's wife
PHILIP, Elena's elder son, perhaps twelve or thirteen years old
MICKEY, Elena's younger son, eight or nine years old
KIRBY ALLBEE, an acquaintance who plagues Leventhal by forcing him to examine the meaning of certain events in his life
DANIEL HARKAVY, Leventhal's friend
STAN WILLISTON, Allbee's friend

Like all good fiction, the novels of Saul Bellow are founded upon solidity of character and authenticity of event. This is not to say that they are always realistic; obviously the Africa of *Henderson the Rain King* is to be found nowhere beyond the boundaries of Bellow's imagination. The people, places, and events in these novels, however, have an intensity of presence that forces them upon the reader's senses and causes them to lodge in his memory. Despite the elements of fantasy, the peculiar twists of character, the disquieting failures of modulation (the excessive agonizing, for example, of some of the early works), there is never in Bellow's fiction an air of contrivance. This last, however, can be said of a number of writers of lesser stature. The distinguishing quality that gives these works their unique pressure is their depth of moral implication. Many writers are interested in moral issues, but few are able to enter that awesome territory of confusion and paradox in which moral concern can have its only real trial. In a world where the consequences of an act are severed from its motive, Bellow's characters seek, often unconsciously, for a mode of behavior that will restore the link, bind intention to effect, and thus create the possibility of moral choice—or at least of potency. Instead of issues, which at least would be clear in their terms, they face a confusion, a turmoil, a darkness noisy with unforeseeable moral collisions.

For Asa Leventhal, the protagonist of *The Victim*, the question of a man's responsibility for his actions is personal, immediate, painful, and as insistent as a wound. It is, in fact, hardly a question at all but rather a pathology, something to be healed more than answered. On the one hand, he is plagued by a sense of persecution, a conviction that others are consciously and deliberately responsible for his sufferings, that society is joined in a total effort to exclude him from its graces. On the other, he is infected with an increasing sense of culpability by the woes of those around him. His condition is aggravated by an inability to measure either his virtue or his potency. Though afflicted by an image of himself as inconsequential, a reject destined to dwell forever on the fringes of possibility, Leventhal nevertheless has a megaloid streak: he fears his own powers and sees himself as a man who cannot budge without visiting disaster upon his fellows.

Involved in Leventhal's consciousness of himself are three areas of action. First, there is his past, presented retrospectively in the novel. It is from the shocks of this personal history that his tenuous relation to the present derives. His mother having died in an insane asylum when he was eight, Leventhal, after finishing high school, left Hartford and went to New York where he worked as the assistant to an auctioneer. When the auctioneer died, he lost the job and began to drift, living in a dirty room on the lower East Side, working at odd jobs. The job that affected him most was a clerking position in a flophouse on lower Broadway, the ruined and outcast transients representing for him a condition that was a constant threat in his own life. After several years of this borderline existence, he took a civil service job in Baltimore, where he found a girl and became engaged, an event that promised to ameliorate his fears. But he was fated to suffer shock and delay before his marriage could come into being with any degree of security. Though he had in effect rediscovered his mother—this time young, attractive, eminently sane— in the person of his betrothed, he found that she had continued, during the engagement, a lingering affair with a married man. The result was immediate trauma and several years of separation before they finally married.

The crucial elements in that history, all reflected in his present phobic sense of being, are insanity, infidelity, and poverty. Together these represent for him the ingredients of disaster in his relations with the world. The threat of insanity, a heritage from his mother, is in effect a threat of lost control, that state in which he may unintentionally bring harm to others. It evokes fears of personal irresponsibility, of the arbitrary, the disordered, the perilous within the self. Infidelity implies the antithesis of this: deception by others, the conscious attempts of the world to smash personal defenses. Finally there is poverty, the potential effect of aimless forces, accidents of circumstance which seem always to Leventhal to exert a downward pressure, a thrust toward calamity. He sees himself as perpetually at the point where all of these possibilities intersect. Everywhere, within and beyond the shell of his being, is peril.

In the present time of the novel, Leventhal's frighteningly delicate condition is further elaborated through two involved situations, one happening at a distance, the other up so close that it is as much a manifestation of his frenzied consciousness as of realistic circumstance. His wife having gone to Maryland for several weeks to visit her mother, he is thrown into a period of isolation in the oppressive heart of New York, the stifling solitude of their Manhattan apartment, the opiate routine of his job on a trade paper. His sister-in-law on Staten Island, desperately worried during this time over the sickness of her younger boy, makes repeated demands upon Leventhal's attention, and he finds himself impelled to take on the emotional responsibilities of his brother, who has left his family in order to work somewhere in the West. Simultaneously, he is visited again and again in his apartment by an old acquaintance, Kirby Allbee, who accuses him of having wrecked Allbee's life. Like the heat, these oppressions are constant, debilitating, and disorienting.

Whereas Allbee's visits seem almost unreal, the hallucinations of a lonely mind, the events in Staten Island are in no important sense projections of his fear but disturbing occasions in the world beyond. His sister-in-law, an Italian, is a woman with alien responses. Fearing hospitals, she resists sending her child to one despite the seriousness of his condition. Thus she is, for Leventhal, an outsider, a stranger dwelling in a different set of attitudes, a different locale of consciousness. All strangers signify to Leventhal's paranoid spirit an accusation, a proclamation of his difference and therefore his error and guilt. When her child dies in a hospital to which Leventhal has urged her to commit him, this sense of accusation oppresses him despite the absence of vindictiveness, of any charge from his sister-in-law. A victim of outer circumstance and inward predilection, Leventhal stands accused of the sins, the enormities, of chance.

It is in the central situation of the book, the encounters with Allbee, an experience at once literal and fantastic, that the ordeals of Leventhal's conscience are most strikingly elaborated. Allbee, his accuser, is the personification of everything that Leventhal is oppressed by. Shabby, penniless, half-deranged, he evokes images of all those broken creatures in the flophouse of Leventhal's past. Allbee's accusations—that Leventhal had lost him his job by being rude to his employer, had thereby indirectly caused his wife to leave him, was even somehow responsible for the death of that wife in an automobile accident—are like dream representations of the vague but deep-seated guilt dragging constantly at Leventhal's life. Despite Leventhal's confused attempts to remove this specter from his consciousness as well as from his presence, Allbee presses closer, forcing a kind of intimacy that fuses the two in a grim relationship of hatred and compassion. Prevailing upon Leventhal to let him move into the apartment, he takes to wearing Leventhal's robes, to reading postcards from Leventhal's wife on which are intimate references to details of their sex life, even brings a woman into Leventhal's bed and locks his harried host from the apartment. It is as though he has taken Leventhal's wife and is absorbing his existence. The result of this strange pattern of circumstances is that Leventhal—victimized, driven, tormented by Allbee's transgressions—finally comes to acknowledge his own complicity in his tormentor's plight. However inadvertently, he had initiated the chain of events that led to Allbee's disintegration. Allbee, his tormentor, is his victim and is also himself.

In the end, the increasing fusion of identities, Allbee's complete failure to distinguish between himself and his surrogate, brings the erratic relationship to a conclusion. When Allbee attempts suicide by turning on the gas in the middle of the night, an act that will of course destroy Leventhal as well as himself, Leventhal drives him from the apartment and shuts him from his life. Through the experience with Allbee, he seems to have sensed not only the necessity of recognizing one's part in the trials of his fellows but also the near madness of that lingering self-renunciation which obliterates the borders of identity. To be totally victimized by the sense that one has victimized others is to bring ruin not only upon the self but upon one's victims as well. When Leventhal encounters a somewhat regenerated Allbee several years later, this implicit lesson is reinforced by the happier circumstances of each. Though no man is an island, neither is mankind an indivisible continent. Unchartable, the topography of human relation is a paradox as deep as time.

THE VILLAGERS

Type of work: Novel
Author: Jorge Icaza (1906–1978)
Type of plot: Social criticism
Time of plot: Twentieth century
Locale: Ecuador
First published: 1934

> *Principal characters:*
> ALFONSO PEREIRA, a debt-ridden landowner
> BLANCA, his wife
> LOLITA, his daughter
> DON JULIO, his uncle
> POLICARPIO, an overseer
> ANDRÉS CHILIQUINGA, an Indian laborer
> CUNSHI, his wife
> PADRE LOMAS, the village priest
> JUANCHO CABASCANGO, a well-to-do Indian tenant
> farmer

The Story:

Alfonso Pereira was an Ecuadorian landowner plagued by domestic and financial troubles. His wife, Blanca, nagged him, and he was worried about his seventeen-year-old daughter Lolita, who wanted to marry a man who was part Indian. Don Julio, his uncle, added to his difficulties by demanding repayment of a loan of ten thousand sucres, a debt already three months overdue.

When Pereira confessed that he was unable to pay the loan, Don Julio suggested that his nephew try to interest Mr. Chapy, a North American promoter, in a timber concession on Pereira's mountain estate. Privately, the old man suspected that Mr. Chapy and his associates were on the lookout for oil and used their lumber-cutting activities in the region as a blind. In order to interest the North Americans, however, it would be necessary to build fifteen miles of road and get possession of two forest tracts. Also, the Indians must be driven off their *huasipungos*, the lands supplied to them in return for working on the master's estate.

Pereira assured his uncle that such a course would be difficult. The Indians, having a deep affection for their lands along both sides of the river, would never willingly relinquish them. Old Julio ridiculed Pereira's sentimentality and told him to return to the estate at Tomachi and build the road.

Back home, Pereira discussed his problem with Padre Lomas, the village priest. The padre agreed to persuade the Indians to work on the road: he would tell them that the labor was the will of God. They also tried to determine how many *mingas*, brawls in which Indians were plied with drink to make them willing to work, would be necessary before the road could be completed. Jacinto Quintana, proprietor of the village store and saloon, promised that he and his wife, Juana, would make the home-brew for the first of the *mingas*.

Andrés Chiliquinga, an Indian workman, was unhappy because Pereira had returned, for he had gone against his master's and the priest's wishes by taking Cunshi as his wife. He was one of thirty Indians sent to start cutting wood and clearing the roadbed.

To find a wet nurse for her baby, Blanca Pereira examined some of the dirty Indian mothers. Their undernourished babies were diseased, some with malaria or dysentery; others were idiotic or epileptic. Policarpio, the overseer, finally chose Cunshi, mother of the healthiest child in the village, and took her to the Pereira house. The master, seeing the young Indian woman, forced her to sleep with him.

One night, Andrés made the long trip home to see his wife. Finding no one in their hillside shack, he became suspicious and angry. The next day, he deliberately let his ax fall on his foot. The Indians treated the cut with spiderwebs and mud, but when the bandage was removed, three days later, the foot was so badly infected that Andrés was sent home. A medicine man who poulticed the sore saved Andrés' life, but the wound left him lame.

One day, while Pereira and the priest were at the Quintana store discussing the building of the road, they sent Jacinto on an errand. After his departure, both men forced Juana to sleep with them.

Pereira gave Padre Lomas' one hundred sucres for a big mass. Then he held a *minga* and work on the road was accelerated. Storms made life miserable for the Indians, unprotected as they were in their camps. Some died when they tried to drain a swamp. Others perished in quicksands. Pereira, choosing to risk the Indians rather than follow a longer, safer route, kept the workmen drunk and entertained them with cockfights. The ignorant laborers continued to toil.

The priest went to Juancho Cabascango, an Indian with a prosperous *huasipungo* beside the river, and asked for one hundred sucres to pay for another mass. When the Indian refused, Padre Lomas cursed him. A short time later, a flash flood drowned some of the Indians and their cattle. Blaming the disaster on Juancho, his superstitious neighbors beat him to death. The priest declared the affair the will of God and easily collected several hundred sucres for his mass.

At last, the road was completed, but the Indians received none of the benefits Padre Lomas had promised. He himself bought a bus and two trucks that took away all transport from those who used to drive mule teams into Quito with the products of the region. Young Indians rode the bus to the city and, there, became criminals and prostitutes.

Because of easy transportation and the possibility of a profitable sale in Quito, Pereira decided not to give the Indians their customary grain from his plentiful harvest. Policarpio's protests did no good. When the hungry Indians went to Pereira's patio and begged their master to relieve the hunger of their families, he told them that their daily pay of fifty centavos was generous enough. Besides, the ton and a half of corn needed to feed the Indians would help considerably in reducing his debts. He did, however, heed his overseer's warning and asked that guards for his estate be sent from Quito.

Hunger stalked the region and babies and old people perished. When one of Pereira's cows died, the famished Indians begged for the carcass. He refused, because they might be tempted to kill other cows, and ordered Policarpio to bury the dead animal. Desperate, Andrés uncovered it; after he and his family ate some of the meat, the tainted flesh killed Cunshi. Padre Lomas demanded twenty-five sucres, more than the Indian could ever earn, in payment for burying the dead woman. That same night, Andrés stole one of his master's cows and sold it to a nearby butcher. Tracked down by dogs, the Indian was captured and flogged in Pereira's patio. There was no one to protest except his small son, who was almost killed by the white men when he tried to help his father.

A score of foreigners arrived in Tomachi. The Indians welcomed them timorously, thinking that these new white men could certainly be no more cruel than their Spanish masters. Mr. Chapy's first act, however, was to order the Indians driven from their *huasipungos* to make room for company houses and a sawmill.

When Andrés' son brought news of the order, the Indians rebelled. They had stolidly accepted the white man's cruelty, even his lechery toward their women, but they felt that the land was theirs. Jacinto vainly tried to stop them when they marched on the village. The enraged Indians killed six of the white men. The others, including Mr. Chapy, fled in their automobiles.

They returned, over the road the Indians had built, with three hundred soldiers under a leader who had killed two thousand Indians in a similar rebellion near Cuenca. Troops hunted down and machine-gunned Indians of all ages and sexes. The few survivors, taking refuge in Andrés' hillside shack, rolled rocks down on the soldiers and shot at them with birdguns. Finally, the soldiers set fire to the thatched roof. When the Indians ran from the burning house, the troops shot them without mercy.

Critical Evaluation:

This brutal novel flows swiftly. Technically, it is one of the better Spanish-American novels. Its virtues are legion, as are its defects, and among the former are interesting dialogue, bitter irony, sardonic humor, interesting plot, effective use of detail, exposure of social injustice, and crispness of style with short sentences that get to the point. *Huasipungo* (1934; *The Villagers*, 1964) presents the Ecuadorian Andes so clearly that readers see them in stark detail. Even the sounds of the sierra are heard, while the odors, temperature changes, and direction of the night wind are experienced. Nevertheless, *The Villagers'* crowning virtue is its defense of Ecuador's oppressed Indians. For this reason it has been considered Jorge Icaza's most significant novel, and has attained Continental prestige. It helped launch the cycle of so-called *Indianista* novels, which are devoted to telling the story of the long-abandoned Indians. The novel's protagonist, thus, is the Indian, who is characterized collectively but clearly, even to the peculiar flavor of his Spanish.

Decay is a prominent and depressing note in *The Villagers*; images of garbage, filth, mold, slime, and rotten meat are frequent. Trash, dirt, and profanity are always present; everything is sloppy and unkempt, reflecting life's hopelessness. Depression is thus a constant note, accentuated by dismal mountain fogs, clammy cold, foul speech, and superstition. *Soroche* (altitude sickness) occasionally strikes, as do other afflictions. Alcoholism is the Indian's bane, for the *huasipunguero* abandons everything—chickens, corn, potatoes, children—for alcohol.

The characters in the novel generally fail to change or develop. At the novel's end, they are almost the same personalities and characters that they were at its start. The principal exception is the Indian community itself, for "from all corners of the soul, from every pore, grow the secret rebellions of a slave." Icaza also implied that the mestizo or mulatto suffers from a psychological inferiority complex in Ecuador, as is exemplified by Juana la Chola's (Juana the Half-breed) inert submission to rape by a landowner and a cleric. The latter villains, unfortunately, are crudely drawn. Don Alfonso Pereira is a second-rate Simon Legree, a consistent rascal, self-server, hypocrite, and uncomplicated brute from start to finish of the novel. He snarls, curses, and brutalizes Indians but cringes from those above him. The priest is worse; he is so utterly depraved as to be comical. He extorts money from hungry Indians, sells passages out of purgatory or burial plots "close to Heaven" at alarming prices, builds a lucrative trucking business on ill-gotten money, and commits ridiculous rascalities too numerous to mention, including the drunken rape of Juana the Half-breed. Referred to as "the Cassocked One," the priest is a symbol of Icaza's disenchantment with religion, and it is puzzling that this "larger-than-life" caricature has not aroused disdain or even criticism from many generations of students and professors.

Other ogres in *The Villagers* are wealthy people, businessmen, whites, property owners, and Gringo capitalists. The Gringoes careen about in Cadillacs, oblivious to Indians; they relish money and lack human feelings. It is possible that they were grotesquely overdrawn by Icaza to appeal only to readers blinded by prejudice, but it should also be recalled that the novel was intended as a tirade against the social injustice that then blighted Ecuador. Icaza possibly had the illusion that his novel would bring a better life to the Indians, but initially his work was better received and lauded abroad than it was in his own country. In any event, Icaza exposed the plight of Ecuador's peons and also the decay of the rural aristocrats, who had left the work of their fathers to live luxuriously in the city. The novel also promotes the conflict of red race against white. White aristocrats are portrayed as hard, unfeeling, and cruel. They are contemptuous of Indians and exploit the poor. Some critics feel that Icaza's work had political motivations; others compare him to John Steinbeck (*The Grapes of Wrath*) and consider him a social reformer.

No one in *The Villagers* apparently wishes to live in the country, since life in Quito is much richer. The countryside is backward, isolated, and uncomfortable; the city is cultured and far superior. Nature is unattractive; its beauties are unmentioned and unextolled. Nature's dangers are stressed, however, such as the scene where a man dies horribly by drowning in mud. Little interest is shown in animals, birds, or plants. The novel is almost devoid of color. Tints of sunrises, sunsets, mountains, skies, fields, or towns are generally lacking, and even the grayness of the constant mountain mist is assumed rather than described. The author's treatment of color is a deliberate stylistic device to increase the feeling of dismal hopelessness.

Although of Spanish blood and comfortable background, Icaza decided as a youth to champion Ecuador's poor of all races. Having attracted international attention, his novel eventually won acceptance in Ecuador and undoubtedly helped the Indian. It has therefore helped to implement some social reform and to attract attention to the cause of the Indian. Some of the political attention has been lip-service, but the life of Ecuador's highland Indians has improved over that described in *The Villagers*. Thus, like *Uncle Tom's Cabin*, Icaza's novel has, in spite of its propagandistic qualities and superficial characterization, attracted much attention through its literary readability and has made considerable impact on Ecuador and Spanish America in general.

THE VIOLENT BEAR IT AWAY

Type of work: Novel
Author: Flannery O'Connor (1925–1964)
Type of plot: Gothic
Time of plot: 1952
Locale: Tennessee
First published: 1960

Principal characters:

FRANCIS MARION TARWATER, a fourteen-year-old boy
    trained to be a prophet
MASON TARWATER, his granduncle and a mad religious
    fanatic
GEORGE F. RAYBER, the boy's uncle
BISHOP RAYBER, George's idiot son
BERNICE BISHOP RAYBER, George's wife
BUFORD MUNSON, a black farmer
MEEKS, a copper flue salesman

Flannery O'Connor, the gifted author of *A Good Man Is Hard to Find*, displays in *The Violent Bear It Away* some of the same qualities that made the short stories of that volume so memorable: a sharp eye and ear, a dazzling combination of the humorous with the macabre and grotesque, and profound interest in the inner lives of men, women, and children. The surface of her prose is deceptively easy, straightforward, and simple-seeming. Actually, she is a deft handler of the flashback, the direct interior monologue, and the matter-of-fact presentation of the strange and bizarre which, at its best, suggests the technique of Franz Kafka.

Printed large across the title pages of the novel is the passage from Matthew, 11:12, from which the title is taken: "From the days of John the Baptist until now, the kingdom of heaven suffereth violence, and the violent bear it away." This much-interpreted passage has meant to some that violence has been done to the kingdom in the form of that meted out to its members; to others, it has meant that only to those former sinners such as harlots and tax-gatherers, whose vociferous acceptance of redemption caused the righteous to exclude them, would the kingdom in fact be opened. The intent of the novel seems closer to the first interpretation than the second, for here violence and fanaticism triumph, and love and understanding are defeated.

The novel follows fourteen-year-old Francis Marion Tarwater as he flees from his home, ventures out into the big world, is tried in soul and mind, and returns briefly to his home to prepare for his special mission in life. The reader would be wrong to assume this is another adolescent like Huckleberry Finn or Holden Caulfield, although like them, he is deprived of parental love and forced to make his way in an adult world he never made. Unlike them, he is a murderer. The son of a tramp and foster son of a madman, he can neither make his way toward maturity, as does Huck, nor give love to the world that torments him, as does Holden.

The figure looming almost larger than the protagonist is that of Mason Tarwater, Francis Marion Tarwater's eighty-four-year-old granduncle, whose death is announced in the novel's first sentence. His baleful influence on the boy is made clear in the flashbacks that describe their life together from the time, fourteen years before, when Mason Tarwater had abducted him from George R. Rayber, the old man's schoolteacher nephew, himself the uncle of the boy. The old man works the land on his remote farm to provide an abundant diet for himself and his grandnephew, but farming is not his chief concern. He is a self-styled and self-anointed prophet who, when the spirit comes upon him, speaks in tongues, prophesying to the wicked the intent of the Lord and the events that He will cause to come to pass.

Mason Tarwater's influence persists after his death, and the central and final portions of the book recount the struggle of Rayber to counteract it. Himself twisted by the fanatic indoctrination imposed upon him in childhood by the old man, Rayber hopes to help the boy to find freedom but at a lesser cost than his own years of struggle. Francis Marion Tarwater fights him, however, fiercely resentful of any attempt to shape or guide him, repeating the saws and phrases of his granduncle. Ironically, Rayber is still suffering from the influence of Mason Tarwater. Listening to the exhortations of a crippled child preaching in a squalid tabernacle as her missionary parents look on, he dreams of sheltering all the exploited children of the world in a hidden garden where their minds would be open to sunshine and truth. But Rayber resists the lingering effects of the old man's conditioning, and he uses all the persistence and tact he can muster to induce the difficult boy to do the same. Intent on doing it in his own way, the boy fiercely resists almost all the attempts Rayber makes.

The climactic action of the novel centers around a character who seems as symbolic, as much a judgment upon his family, as Benjy Compson in Faulkner's *The Sound and the Fury*. This character is Bishop Rayber, for this strange child, like Benjy, is an idiot. Abandoned by his social-worker mother, he is cared for by his father, who, in his intense love for the boy, alternately feels that he should perform a mercy killing and that he would be unable to go on living if he did. Rayber has always refused to baptize the child, saying that this is one travesty he will not perform. Before his death, Mason Tarwater has charged Francis Marion with this responsibility. A sensible, kind, and rational voice within the boy tells him that if he can resist the desire to complete this act, he will be able to free himself from the twisting and misshaping spirit of the old man. Rayber tells him the same thing. Exhausted and at the end of the tether, Rayber allows Francis Marion to take Bishop for a boat ride on the lake in the gathering darkness. There Francis Marion baptizes him, but when Rayber hears Bishop's bellows (the same word Faulkner uses for Benjy), he realizes that Francis Marion has followed the first ritual act with a second: he has drowned Bishop.

At the end of the novel, the boy returns to the isolated farm where the charred remains of the house he burned still stand. He touches a flaming branch to bushes and trees as he goes. Then, awaiting a sign or portent, he looks back to see a tree of fire behind him; he knows that it is the fire which protected Daniel, lifted Elijah to glory, and spoke to Moses from the burning bush. Lying on his granduncle's grave, he hears a command telling him to warn God's children that mercy is terrible and swift. He sets out for the dark, sleeping city to carry this message of terror and love.

The Violent Bear It Away, so permeated with the grotesque and the macabre, has numerous flashes of humor deriving from acute observation of human crochets and even from speech patterns, particularly those of the boy and his granduncle, who place much store upon—among other things—minding one's own "bidnis." Its most powerful effect, however, comes from its examination of the impulses of religion and of love and the strange and terrible forms which they can assume.

THE VIOLENT LAND

Type of work: Novel
Author: Jorge Amado (1913–   )
Type of plot: Historical romance
Time of plot: Late nineteenth century
Locale: State of Bahia, Brazil
First published: 1942

Principal characters:

COLONEL HORACIO DA SILVEIRA, a cacao planter
COLONEL SINHÔ BADARÓ, another planter
DOÑA ESTER DA SILVEIRA, Colonel da Silveira's wife
DOÑA ANA BADARÓ, Colonel Badaró's daughter
CAPTAIN JOÃO MAGALHÃES, in love with Doña Ana
DR. VIRGILIO CABRAL, Doña Ester's lover and da
    Silveira's lawyer
MARGOT, a prostitute
JUCA BADARÓ, Colonel Badaró's younger brother

The Story:

In the minds of most Brazilians, the São Jorge dos Ilhéus was a semibarbarous country ruled by a handful of rich planters who styled themselves colonels. These men had risen, almost without exception, from humble origins by means of courage, bravado, and murder. The two most important planters were Colonel Horacio da Silveira and Colonel Sinhô Badaró. Between their lands lay a large forest, upon which both men had long cast covetous eyes. The forest, actually a jungle, could be cleared to uncover an almost fabulous cacao-growing soil.

Among the strangers who poured into the region in search of wealth at the time were several people who were to range themselves on one side or the other in the coming struggle. Dr. Virgilio Cabral, a cultured and talented lawyer, was to ally himself with da Silveira. With the lawyer came Margot, a beautiful prostitute who had fallen in love with him and become his mistress while he was a student. Another arrival was Captain João Magalhães, a professional gambler and a courageous opportunist who called himself a military engineer. Among his admirers were Juca Badaró, Colonel Badaró's younger brother, and Doña Ana Badaró, the colonel's daughter, who was also the heiress to the Badaró fortunes.

Soon after his arrival, Cabral fell in love with Ester, da Silveira's beautiful wife. The woman, who hated her semibarbarous husband, quickly returned

---

the affection of the more cultured man. When she became his mistress, both knew that they would be killed if the husband found them out. As his ardor for Ester da Silveira increased, the lawyer's affection for his former mistress waned, and soon Margot found herself unwanted by her lover. In retaliation, and because she needed someone to support her, Margot became the mistress of Juca Badaró. Out of spite, she also furnished him with scandal about the opposition, gossip that he turned to account in the newspaper which favored the Badarós.

Professionally, as well as amorously, Cabral was a success, for he found an old survey of the contested lands and registered the title in da Silveira's name after he had bribed the registry officials. The Badaró family quickly retaliated by burning the registry office and all the records on file. In addition, the Badarós hired Magalhães to run a survey for them. He made the survey, even though he lacked the proper knowledge to do so. His presence at the Badaró plantation earned him the respect of the Badaró brothers and the love of Doña Ana Badaró. The self-styled captain, always an opportunist, permitted himself to fall in love with the girl and pay court to her.

Because the Badaró family was the more powerful of the two factions, da Silveira went to several small planters and promised to let them divide half of the forest land if they, as a group, would help him hold it against the Badarós. There was bloody fighting on both sides of the forest and within it, for both factions hired many assassins and bodyguards to back up their interests with bullets. The Badarós controlled the local government, and the state government was in opposition to the federal government of Brazil.

Juca Badaró was assassinated by a hired gunman after he had insulted Cabral. Juca had found the lawyer dancing with Margot, at the girl's request, and had insulted the lawyer for daring to do so. On the other side, too, there were disappointments and deaths. Both Cabral and da Silveira were deterred in their plans when the Colonel fell ill with a fever. The planter recovered, but his wife, the lawyer's mistress, became ill as a result of nursing her husband. Her death removed one incentive in the efforts of both her husband and her lover, but they stubbornly continued the fight.

As the struggle in the courts and in the fields continued, the Badarós spent more and more money. They not only sold their current crop of cacao pods but also sold their next year's crop in order to raise funds immediately. Before his assassination, Juca Badaró had seen to it that his niece, Doña Ana, was married to the gambler, for he saw in Magalhães an ambitious man willing to fight for money and power. So tempting was the proposal the Badarós made that the captain agreed to take his wife's name, her father insisting that he do so in order to carry on the Badaró line.

At first, by tacit consent, the contending parties did no damage to one another's cacao trees, but as the Badarós became desperate, they instructed their desperadoes to burn the cacao groves. Their opponents saw that the matter had to be settled at once, lest both parties be irretrievably ruined and become victims of someone stronger than they. Colonel da Silveira and his henchman, along with their paid gunmen, attacked the Badaró plantation in force and drove off the family, after killing all the men except a handful led by Magalhães.

Da Silveira and his men thought that the women of the Badaró household had been sent away, but the attackers were greeted by gunfire from Doña Ana herself as they entered the house. When she ran out of ammunition, she gave up, expecting to be killed. The attackers let her go, however, because she was a woman.

The Badaró rout was completed by an announcement from the Brazilian capital that the political party favoring da Silveira had come into power and was sending troops and government agents to the district to quiet the violence. The jungle lands were ceded to the da Silveira faction by the government's action. Da Silveira was forced to stand trial for the murder of Juca Badaró, but the trial, having been staged more to clear the Colonel than to find him guilty, was a mere formality.

The district quickly settled down after the great feud had ended and the new government had started its operations, but there was to be one more assassination. While going through his dead wife's effects, da Silveira discovered the letters Cabral had written to her. He was horrified and embarrassed to learn of her infidelity, which he had not suspected, and his lawyer's duplicity. After thinking about the matter for some time, he sent a gunman to clear his honor by killing the man who had made him a cuckold.

To symbolize the new peace that had come into the frontier district, the Church made the city of Ilhéus the seat of a newly created diocese and sent a bishop to officiate as its representative there. As if to show the value of the former jungle land, the cacao trees planted there produced a crop in the fourth year, a full twelve months earlier than usual.

Critical Evaluation:

Jorge Amado's novel is titled *Terras do sem fin* (the endless lands) in Portuguese. This story is the standard-bearer of the cacao cycle in Brazilian literature, a series of novels exposing exploitation of cacao workers. Brazilian novelists have long been making a huge mosaic of Brazil with their novels, each novel being a tiny stone in the literary mosaic of that subcontinent, and Amado's work is a worthy one and his masterpiece.

The Violent Land (first published in English in 1945) is the story of Bahia's Panhandle, where a balmy climate, fertile soil, and lack of high winds make it one of the few areas on earth well suited for chocolate trees, whose weak stems and heavy pods need heat but cannot stand strong winds. Amado's characterization is particularly representative of the raw frontier that the Panhandle of Bahia (a narrow strip stretching southward toward the mountains of Espirito Santo) has been for so long. The reader thus sees not only an area where "the Colonels" and their heavily armed cohorts oppress the weak, but also the Bahian *sertão* (backlands) in general, brimming with blood, old feuds, religious messianism, and fanaticism. Even today, the colonels, cowboys, professionals, and workers that sprinkle the novel's pages can be seen around the old town of Ilhéus and elsewhere in the Panhandle. Amado's characters are thus not larger-than-life but authentic, flesh-and-blood realities from rural Bahia. His principal characterization flaw is an error of omission, for the warmly human types so common everywhere in Brazil, including Bahia, are lacking in the violent pages of *The Violent Land*.

This novel refreshingly explodes the oft-heard myth that Brazil, unlike Spanish America, is a bland and frivolous land not given to violence. Amado's novel bristles with the violence and mystery endemic to the *sertão*, and it is for this reason that Amado's true title of *The Endless Lands* has been changed for the book's English translation into *The Violent Land*. Amado paints a land fertile with blood, as his preface indicates. Set about the turn of the twentieth century, when cacao was power, wealth, and life, the novel's action portrays the enslavement of everything and everyone to the cacao pod. The shadow of cacao darkens every heart. It smothers finer instincts and levels all characters from aristocratic Colonel Horacio da Silveira to the more common Badarós. Nothing washes away the cacao stain. Workers in the orchards have a thick crust of cacao slime on their boots, while everyone from colonels to lawyers, merchants, and *jagunços* (hired killers) have cacao slime in their hearts.

The Violent Land reflects progress, however, for the colonels are drawn as a crude but civilizing force in Brazil's historic "march to the west" that is opening up the once trackless *sertão*. Amado himself was born on a cacao plantation in 1912 and admired the *fazendeiros* (ranchers), such as his own father, who settled the raw Panhandle, crossed *sertões*, built roads, and founded towns, all this through heroic strength and what Amado terms "the poetry of their lives." The novel's first scene, symbolically enough, is aboard a ship drawing away from the black-tile roofs of the baroque city of São Salvador de Bahia. The passengers aboard are immigrants to the rich but violent lands of the Panhandle and are discussing lands, money, cacao, and death. They sing a sad song that presages disaster, but that night, in their staterooms and steerage quarters, they dream of laden cacao trees.

Landscape is an important factor in *The Violent Land* and reflects Brazil's intrinsic beauty. Amado paints the golden mornings dawning over green palms, the red soil under the cacao trees, the blue-green waves of the sea, and indigo skies. One also sees stormy nights, wild Brahma cattle, birds, and snakes. Trees are almost idolized, especially the cacao. Above all, Amado lyrically paints the forest in the uninterrupted sleep that it enjoyed before the colonels came. Days and nights pass over the virginal expanses of trees, along with winter rains and summer suns. The waiting forest is like an unexplored sea, locked in its own mystery: virginal, lovely, and radiant. Amado also presents the varied Bahian racial types from Scandinavian-like blondes to Latin brunettes and Hamitic blacks. One also sees the colonels in khaki trousers, white hats, and gun belts, as well as the leather-clad *jagunços*, legendarily ferocious *onças* (wild cats), ranch tools, and folklore.

Fear is an additional element in the story. The forest's mysteries incite fear—Ester hysterically fears snakes and is haunted by the phobia that they will one night invade her house en masse. The backlanders tell many snake stories, while dogs howl at night, rain clouds are dark, and nights are jet black; but the violent Badaró family and the *jagunços* do not know what fear is. The Badarós even read the Bible daily for they, like the endless lands that they are so ruthlessly penetrating, are many-sided.

Lamentably, the storied and colorful old city of São Salvador de Bahia does not loom in *The Violent Land* as Atlanta does in *Gone with the Wind*. But little, pastel São Jorge dos Ilhéus, "a city of palms in the wind," is well depicted. Its streets are lined by palms, but it is dominated by the cacao tree, for the scent of chocolate is in every conversation, and each colonel's fortune can be measured by the size of his mansion. Inland from the pastel town, on every red-dirt road leading into the cacao lands, are crosses without names.

Brazilian novelists complained for decades that the harsh, nasal, Germanic-sounding Portuguese language in which they wrote was "the Graveyard of Literature," a literary cul-de-sac. *The Violent Land*, however, was translated into more than twenty languages, and translations of other novels into foreign languages have since been opening Brazilian literature to the world. Amado's masterwork also helps reveal that the key to Brazilian literature is not chronology, nor style, nor study of influences, but geography. Brazil is a literary archipelago with six literary "islands," and *The Violent Land* is to be read and regarded as a work of the "island" of Bahia.

THE VIRGINIA COMEDIANS

Type of work: Novel
Author: John Esten Cooke (1830–1886)
Type of plot: Sentimental romance
Time of plot: 1763–1765
Locale: Colonial Virginia
First published: 1854

Principal characters:
CHAMP EFFINGHAM, foppish scion of a wealthy planter
BEATRICE HALLAM, a young actress with whom
    Effingham falls in love
CLARE LEE, Effingham's cousin and fiancée
CHARLES WATERS, Effingham's rival for Beatrice Hallam
CAPTAIN RALPH WATERS, Charles Waters' brother
JACK HAMILTON, a friend of Effingham and his sister's
    fiancé

The Story:

In the spring of 1763, Williamsburg, the colonial capital of Virginia, was treated to its first professional dramatic presentation by an English company called The Virginia Comedians. The colony, rich and poor, was highly excited in anticipation of the event. The day the company was to arrive in Williamsburg, young Champ Effingham, son of a wealthy planter, rode to town for a holiday. Young Effingham, educated at Oxford, had taken up the ways of the London fops while in England. His dress was extraordinary; his manners were artificial.

On the way to Williamsburg, he met a beautiful young woman on horseback who asked him the way. When questioned by him, she refused to give her name, stating only that she was unknown to him because she was not a lady. The mystery was solved the next day at the play, when Effingham discovered that the girl was an actress with the traveling company. Despite the fact that he was engaged to marry one of the most beautiful and wealthy of the Virginia girls, Effingham became infatuated with the actress, whose name was Beatrice Hallam. She was the daughter of the manager of the company.

There was scandal in the neighborhood when it became known that Champ Effingham was paying court to the actress. Everyone among the gentry was perturbed, for actresses were considered low in the social scale. When word came to Effingham's father, the old gentleman ordered his son to desist. The son's answer was to leave the house and take up residence at the inn in Williamsburg where the players were lodging. Effingham had little success with Beatrice Hallam, however; she despised him because of his artificial manners and his condescending attitude. She was really in love with a commoner, a young man named Charles Waters, who had rescued her from the James River on a stormy day when she had fallen overboard while boating.

Beatrice's father, on the other hand, wanted his daughter to encourage young Effingham. Mr. Hallam saw in Effingham a chance for his daughter to marry into a wealthy family, thus gaining an honest reputation for herself and a comfortable life for him.

At the opening of the session of the House of Burgesses, the governor gave a ball for the gentry of the colony. When an invitation was sent to Effingham, he resolved to take Beatrice to the ball, but his friends warned him not to do so because of the scandal. Although Beatrice did not want to go with him to the ball, her father finally browbeat her into agreeing. Effingham, daring his friends to prevent his appearance with an actress, vowed to fight duels with all who tried to hinder him or who insulted the girl.

At the ball, everything went smoothly, because the Virginians, too well-mannered to make a disturbance over Effingham's actions, were all coolly polite to the actress. Their coolness only made the girl miserable, however, particularly when she knew how she was hurting Clare Lee, to whom Effingham had been engaged.

After the ball, Effingham resolved to turn actor and join the company under the direction of Mr. Hallam. The manager was happy to have the young Virginian. In trying to find a costume for himself, Effingham inadvertently uncovered a little girl's dress and a letter, both of which he dropped in Beatrice's room. The dress and letter proved to her that she was not Hallam's daughter, and that her name was really Beatrice Waters. After some investigation, she learned that she was the cousin of the Charles Waters who had rescued her from the river and death by drowning.

Effingham was furious when he discovered the relationship between Beatrice and Charles Waters. Rather than fight a duel with the girl's cousin, he kidnaped her and took her away on his boat. Charles and a friend followed, however, and boarded Effingham's craft. In the fight to rescue Beatrice, Effingham wounded his rival. Thinking he had killed him, Effingham, in his extremity, went home to his father, who arranged for his son's escape to Europe.

After Effingham left for Europe, Beatrice nursed her cousin and restored him to health. Before long, they were married and moved to a home in the uplands of the Piedmont region of Virginia. They left behind Captain Ralph Waters, Charles's brother, who had vowed to fight a duel with Champ Effingham on his brother's behalf. The planters were glad to see Charles Waters leave for another area; he had been heard to speak against the British government and to advocate a revolution.

Two years passed before Champ Effingham returned to Virginia, after learning that his sword thrust had not killed Charles Waters. Young Effingham, thoroughly cured of his infatuation for Beatrice, had also lost his foppishness of dress and manner. Although he returned a changed and acceptable young man, he was given to periods of moodiness, and nothing his family could do restored him to mental health. Then his boyhood friend, Jack Hamilton, secretly engaged to Effingham's sister, resolved to try to restore the young man. He encouraged and even forced Effingham to ride out to hounds and to visit other houses. He brought Captain Ralph Waters and Effingham together and made them friends. Still, young Effingham remained moody and gloomy.

At last, Hamilton resolved to try the power of jealousy, for he knew that Effingham was still very much in love with Clare Lee, whom he had thrown aside in his infatuation for Beatrice. In addition, Hamilton knew that Clare still loved Effingham and would accept him as her husband, in spite of all that had happened. Hamilton pretended to be in love with Clare; he even talked to Effingham about his suit for her hand. Such talk was too much for Effingham, who stirred himself to threaten Hamilton until he learned that Hamilton was really engaged to his sister. His sister and Hamilton finally persuaded him to go see Clare, who readily accepted his suit and promised to become Mrs. Champ Effingham.

Happiness reigned in the colony. Hamilton and Effingham's sister were married a few days after the wedding of Effingham and Clare. Captain Ralph Waters and Clare's sister were also married. The marriages seemed to mark the end of an era, however, for at the time of their celebration, news came to the colony of the passage of the Stamp Act, which everyone hated. Before long, many began to speak of revolt against the British Crown. A leader of the agitators was Charles Waters, who returned to Williamsburg after the death of his wife, Beatrice.

Critical Evaluation:

John Esten Cooke was one of the last of the historical romanticists who followed the footsteps of James Fenimore Cooper. He was also the first of a long line of authors who continued to idealize the pre-Civil War South. Unlike some of the imitators of Cooper, Cooke wrote books which are well grounded in the history of Virginia, especially that of the James River section, in which most of them are laid.

By his own account, Cooke conceived and wrote *The Virginia Comedians* in a few weeks during the winter of 1853–1854. Its publication by D. Appleton and Company in two volumes in 1854 brought immediate recognition to the twenty-four-year-old author. In the opinion of John O. Beaty, his biographer, the novel was "by far the finest" of his more than thirty published volumes.

The enduring value of the novel lies beyond its maze of intricate subplots, melodramatic intrigues, multiple love affairs, and diffusive colloquies—the conventional trappings of popular nineteenth century historical romances. Cooke's avowed intention was to present "some view, however slight, of the various classes of individuals who formed that Virginia of 1765." Critics agree that the novel remains important for its realistic portrayal of the various elements in Virginia society on the eve of the American Revolution. The life-style, and the manners and morals of the aristocratic Effinghams, the middle-class Waters, and the itinerant Hallams are particularly well delineated. Less satisfactory are Cooke's descriptions of the characters on the lower rungs of society, and, to a degree, he perpetuates the myth of the Cavalier origins of Southern aristocracy, but this fault is more pronounced in his post-Civil War works.

By choosing a transitional period for the novel's setting, Cooke, through the character of the revolution-fomenting Charles Waters, also injects an element of historical drama and a foreboding sense of coming change into the work. The novel climaxes with Waters whipping a crowd of disgruntled citizens into a frenzy with his denunciation of the recent Stamp Act. Watching approvingly is Waters' mentor, the mysterious "man in the red cloak," whose identity is finally revealed as Patrick Henry.

Cooke never again matched the overall quality attained in *The Virginia Comedians*, although he attempted to exploit its successful formula in several additional novels before his death in 1886. The novel remains credible social history, and for this, and his subsequent work, Cooke became one of the most popular Southern novelists in the nineteenth century.

THE VIRGINIAN
A Horseman of the Plains

Type of work: Novel
Author: Owen Wister (1860–1938)
Type of plot: Regional romance
Time of plot: Late nineteenth century
Locale: Wyoming
First published: 1902
Principal characters:
> THE VIRGINIAN, a cowboy
> JUDGE HENRY, the Virginian's employer
> TRAMPAS, a cowboy and the Virginian's enemy
> STEVE, a cowboy friend of the Virginian
> SHORTY, a cowboy at Judge Henry's ranch
> MOLLY WOOD, a young schoolteacher at Bear Creek,
>   Wyoming

The Story:

The Virginian had been sent by his employer to meet an Eastern guest at Medicine Bow and escort him the two hundred and sixty miles from the town to Sunk Creek Ranch. While the Virginian and the guest were awaiting the arrival of the Easterner's trunk on the following westbound train, the cowboy entered into a poker game. One of the players, a cowboy named Trampas, accused the Virginian of cheating. The man backed down, however, before the gun of the cowboy from Sunk Creek. It was apparent to everyone that the Virginian had made an implacable enemy.

A few months later, in the fall, a schoolmistress came West from Vermont to teach in the new school at Bear Creek, Wyoming. All the single men, and there were many of them in the territory, anxiously awaited the arrival of the new teacher, Molly Wood. The Virginian was fortunate in his first meeting with her. A drunken stage driver tried to ford a creek in high water and marooned his coach and passenger. The Virginian, passing by, rode to the stage, lifted out the young woman, and deposited her safely on the bank of the stream. After he had ridden away, Molly missed her handkerchief and realized the young cowboy had somehow contrived to take it.

The next time the Virginian saw Molly, she was a guest at a barbecue. The cowboy had ridden his horse for two days for an opportunity to see her, but she coquettishly refused to notice him. The Virginian and another cowboy, piqued by her attitude, got drunk and played a prank on all the people who had brought their children to the barbecue. They switched the babies and their clothing, so that when the barbecue was over, many of the mothers carried off the wrong babies. Before he left for Sunk Creek, the Virginian warned Molly that she was going to love him eventually, no matter what she thought of him then.

During the next year, the Virginian began to read books for the first time since he had left school in the sixth grade. He borrowed the books from Molly in order to ride to Bear Creek to see her at intervals. In the meantime, he had risen high in the estimation of his employer. Judge Henry put him in charge of a party of men who were to escort two trainloads of steers to the Chicago market.

On the trip back to the ranch, the Virginian's men threatened to desert the train to go prospecting for gold which had been discovered in the Black Hills. The ringleader of the insurgents was Trampas.

The Virginian saw that the best way to win over the men was to make a fool of Trampas. His chance came when the train stopped near a bridge that was being repaired. Since there was no food on the train, the Virginian went out and gathered a sackful of frogs to cook. Then he began a story about frogs, a tall story by which Trampas was completely taken in. As soon as the rest of the cowboys saw how foolish Trampas appeared, they were willing to return to the ranch, much to the discomfiture of their ringleader.

Back at Sunk Creek, the Virginian found a pleasant surprise awaiting him. The foreman of the ranch had been forced to leave because of an invalid wife, and the judge had made the Virginian his foreman.

Trampas had expected to be discharged from his job as soon as the Virginian became foreman at the Sunk Creek Ranch. The Virginian, however, decided it was better to have his enemy in sight, and so Trampas stayed on, sullen and defiant in his behavior.

The following spring, the Virginian made a trip to a neighboring ranch. On the way back, he was attacked by Indians and severely wounded. He managed to escape from the Indians and make his way to a spring. There he was found, half dead, by Molly Wood. The girl stayed with him at the risk of her life, for the Indians were still in the vicinity. She then bound his wounds and took him back to her cabin and called a doctor.

Molly, meanwhile, had packed her possessions, for she was preparing to leave for her home in the East. By the time the Virginian had recovered sufficiently to go back to work, she had decided not to leave Wyoming. She was sure by then that she was in love with the cowboy foreman. When the Virginian left her cabin for Sunk Creek, Molly had promised to marry him.

Upon returning to work, the Virginian found that his enemy, Trampas, had disappeared, taking another of the cowboys, Shorty, with him. About the same time, the ranches in that territory began to lose cattle to rustlers, and a posse was formed to track down the cattle thieves. After several weeks of searching, two of the thieves were caught. Since the rustlers had somehow managed to gain control of the local courts and had already been freed on one charge, the posse hanged both of them. It was a terrible experience for the Virginian, because one of the men, Steve, had been a close friend. The Virginian hated to think he had hanged his friend, and the hurt was made worse by the fact that the condemned man had refused to say a word to his former companion.

On his way back to Sunk Creek, the Virginian came across the trail of the other two rustlers. They were Trampas and Shorty. Because they had only one horse between them, Trampas murdered Shorty in order to escape.

When Molly Wood heard of the lynching and the Virginian's part in it, she refused to marry him. After a conversation with Judge Henry, however, she realized that the Virginian had done no more than his duty. She and the Virginian were reconciled, and a date was set for their wedding.

On the day before their wedding, Molly and the Virginian started to ride to Medicine Bow. On the way, they met Trampas, who galloped ahead of them into the town. Molly questioned the Virginian about the man and discovered the enmity between the two. When they arrived in town, they were warned that Trampas had said he would shoot the Virginian if he were not out of town by sunset. Molly told him that she could never marry him if he fought with Trampas and killed him. The Virginian, knowing that his honor was at stake, left her in the hotel and went out to face his enemy. Trampas fired first and missed. Then the Virginian fired and killed Trampas.

When the Virginian returned to the hotel, Molly was too glad to see him alive to remember her threat. Hearing the shots, she had been afraid that the Virginian had been killed. They were married the following day, as they had planned, and spent two months of their honeymoon high in the Rocky Mountains where no other humans ever went.

Critical Evaluation:

This book appeared in 1902, some ten years after the closing of the frontier and shortly after Frederick Jackson Turner explained in his famous "safety-valve" thesis the function that the frontier had performed in American history. Perhaps *The Virginian* is an expression of the need, once the frontier was gone, to experience a frontier that never was. This book is one of the first serious novelistic treatments of the American cowboy, if one excludes the dime novels that had dismayed parents for almost the previous fifty years. When the open range was gone, the cowboy came into his own as a literary figure, and there seems to be more than coincidence in the two facts. The end of the frontier era and the beginning of the cowboy novel meld too closely for there to be much accident about it.

This book is not set in the American West so much as in a country called Cattle Land, where men are men, and they possess all the virtues and characteristics popularly associated with Horatio Alger. Owen Wister associates one more element to this mythical character about whom he is writing— primal man. Wister very often describes the Virginian as "wild" or "natural," and the two words are seemingly interchangeable. The East is decadent, and the American virtues have their last home in the West.

Tied up with this idea of primal innocence is the concept of an Americanism that is itself primal, free of the decadence of Europe. Decadence, however, has swept westward, as Wister sees it, and has pushed Americanism in front of it. The only Vermonter, back in Molly's home state, to approve of her new husband is the grandaunt who sees in the Virginian the spirit of her own husband, a general in the Revolutionary War. This theme of Americanism as a primal, Adamic innocence and as found only in the West is brought out most forcefully when Judge Henry tries to explain to Molly why the Virginian and others had to lynch a cattle rustler. Molly objects that they took the law into their own hands. The Judge's reply is that the law came originally from people who delegated this responsibility to their representatives; in turn, they established in the Constitution machinery for administering the law; but in Wyoming, the hands of the law were weak and could not do the job that had been delegated them. So the Virginian had only been taking back what had been his own. The delegates to the Constitutional Convention, then, were in spirit to be found in the far West, ironically at a Wyoming lynching party.

This is Wister's world and it is, as he said in his foreword to the novel, one that no longer exists. He was wrong when he said this in 1902, for men like the Virginian, although less romantic when seen in the flesh, are spread over the country. Many Americans would agree with much that the Virginian says and represents, and in that respect, the cowboy has not vanished from the land any more than the belief that the primal innocence of America has lessened. He may have changed, perhaps become urbanized, but many contemporary Americans continue to live with the Virginian's values.

THE WAPSHOT CHRONICLE

Type of work: Novel
Author: John Cheever (1912–1982)
Type of plot: Humorous regional chronicle
Time of plot: 1890's–1950's
Locale: St. Botolphs, Massachusetts; Washington; New York; and a
rocket-launching station
First published: 1957

Principal characters:

> LEANDER WAPSHOT, a Yankee skeptic, philosopher, and
>   skipper of the launch *Topaze*
> SARAH WAPSHOT, his brisk, practical wife
> MOSES and
> COVERLY, their sons
> MELISSA, Moses' wife
> BETSEY, Coverly's wife
> HONORA WAPSHOT, a wealthy cousin and the family
>   matriarch
> JUSTINA WAPSHOT MOLESWORTH SCADDON, another
>   wealthy cousin
> ROSALIE, a wanton

The Wapshot Chronicle is a novel created wholly in its own image and
nothing else; therefore, it is to be apprehended only in terms of its innocent
ribaldry, sad knowledge, and comic invention. The secret of the book's appeal
and power is something each reader must decide for himself. For some, the
work will take shape as a pungent regional narrative, richly flavored with the
oddities of New England life and character. Others will read it as a rueful
lament for an uncramped way of life rapidly disappearing from the American
scene. Many readers will undoubtedly view it as a bright comedy of manners.
Still others will relish John Cheever's lively satire on a variety of topics, among
them bossy old women, the social brutality of the very rich, and psychology's
invasion of personal privacy in modern industry.

Beneath and beyond these matters, however, is the functioning of the
author's wryly comic point of view. Like a number of his contemporaries who
deserve to be called serious writers, Cheever chose to cast his fiction in the
mold of comedy. In fact, the presence of the comic spirit in the novels of the
1950's and later was a sign that a literary movement of sorts was under way.
In no sense, however, were these writers to be thought of as a school. At the
same time, collectively, they suggest that the comic vision may be the best
angle from which to view the existential concerns, hostile realities, and moral
ambiguities of the world. (It was Kierkegaard who said that the humorous

interpretation is always the final one.) Tragedy instructs people in the nature of death, the Dionysian, fated end of man; but in a world darkly overshadowed by threats of violence and disaster, tragedy has lost much of the meaning and force it held in earlier, more ordered times. Comedy, on the other hand, consoles one with the grace of innocence and the power of love for the cold fact of mortality. This is its function in Cheever's novels and short stories where the comic vision is largely of a conditioning order, mediating between a quality of truth that life reveals and a quality of the imagination at work reshaping the familiar world into something strange and new.

Used in this manner, the comic mode serves Cheever's purposes admirably. As a picture of the way people lived, *The Wapshot Chronicle* is witty, sad, whimsical, outrageous, fantastic, and rich in its flow of invention. As a novel, it is episodic, relaxed, modestly proportioned but generous in implication and precisely styled. Plainly, here is a writer with little patience for the closed point of view or the closed structure of the well-made novel. He works within an open form giving him greater opportunities for improvisation, relevance beyond mere reporting, and easy accommodation to the eccentric or the grotesque in human character and conduct. This freedom allows him to write about almost everything that falls within the scope of his observation, imagination, and talent. His effects are unpredictable. A situation may begin on a level of earthy realism and then turn aside into a region of pure comedy overshadowed by fantasy. Fragments of myth as well as suggestions of the supernatural turn up in the most unexpected places. These matters are interesting in themselves as qualities of vision or devices of technique, but they do not explain Cheever's special power as a writer. That comes from the broader human significance achieved in his work by joining two forces usually not found together: an upward thrust of joy in man's fruitfulness, the promise of his continuity, and a sense of moral structure in the universe. His people are all veterans of the ancient conflict between spirit and flesh. In their efforts to define themselves, to communicate with one another, to find some road back into a past of innocence and promise, to face the future, they stand or fall simply because they are human, as vulnerable to the blunders, absurdities, lusts, and cruelties of mankind as they are capable of goodness and compassion and grave commitment to life's portion of delight or dismay. In Cheever, readers confront a moralist.

On still another level, *The Wapshot Chronicle* is a delicate probing into the anatomy of love. For Cheever's people are also possessed by love in most of its forms and occasions: love of place, of the fireside and the hearth, of the ties of kinship; carnal love, the stirrings of the old Adam to plague and goad human flesh; love that is gentle and good, asking nothing except the simple joy of giving; love that is protective and kind; love of the ancestral past, of the living for the dead; love that can be funny or hopeless or perverted or cruel. It is plain that to Cheever the capacity to love and be loved helped to compensate man for his mortality; it is the bridge on which he kept his precarious balance between the mysteries of birth and death. In this story of Leander Wapshot and his sons, the ordinary routines of living and private fantasies of desire combine to convey a sense of generations passing and to celebrate in man's fruitfulness the promise of continuance.

The story is presented through a series of loosely threaded episodes that sometimes give the impression of being unrelated but which have been cunningly devised for juxtaposed or contrapuntal effect.

One may begin, as Cheever does, with the place. St. Botolphs had been a bustling, prosperous river port in the days of the Massachusetts clipper fleets. Now it is kept alive by a few small industries and summer visitors, a moribund port town replaced by a tourist center of antique stores, gift shops, and tearooms quaintly decorated by the handcrafted artifacts of an older seafaring and agricultural America.

Leander's home, West Farm, cluttered like an old attic with the memories and the possessions of dead and gone Wapshots, is another image of a good past and an uncertain present. The Wapshots, like the village, have come down in the world. The older generations of the family had been seafaring wanderers in their youth, and they had come back to St. Botolphs with their manhood seasoned by the hardships and perils of their calling, with wits sharpened by the strategies of trade in foreign ports, with memories of lovely, naked brown girls in the islands of the Pacific. Leander has never known adventure in far places or a sultry paradise of love. Failing fortunes and changing times beached him inland, a spiritual castaway on the shores of Wapshot tradition and a dependent on Cousin Honora's charity.

Nominally, he is the head of the family, but the real power is Cousin Honora, a matriarch who speaks and acts with the authority of one who holds the purse strings. In her eccentric way, she regards Leander and herself as the holders of a family trust, Leander because he has fathered two sons, herself because she controls the fortune which she intends to pass on to the boys when they marry and produce sons of their own. Meanwhile, she pays the bills and bullies Leander as her whims dictate. He has never been provident, and now he is old. Because a man should be useful for something, however, Cousin Honora has bought the *Topaze*, a battered old launch that Leander ferries daily between Travertine and the amusement park at Nangasakit across the bay. In Honora's opinion, the *Topaze* keeps Leander out of other mischief and satisfies his taste for romance and nonsense. Leander's wife is Sarah, a brisk, practical woman who indulges her husband, looks after her sons, and, as president of the Women's Club, works energetically for the civic improvement of St. Botolphs.

In spite of his failings, old Leander, with his regard for the ceremoniousness of things, the idea of life as a process of excellence and continuity, dominates the book; in his zest for life, he is the guardian of tribal rituals and masculine skills which he hopes to pass on to his sons. What Moses and Coverly absorb from his examples of parental love and wisdom shows them to be true Wapshots in kind if not in degree. Although the family fortunes depend on proof of their virility, they cannot take to wife an ordinary mortal after they have heard in dreams the pagan sirens singing on distant beaches—certainly not Rosalie, the waif catapulted into the Wapshot household from a blazing car in which her lover died. Rosalie is lost between the power of loneliness and the power of love, and her giving herself to Moses is merely a gesture of her inner despair. Her brief passage through Leander's world serves chiefly as an excuse for Cousin Honora's decision that the time has come for Moses to go out into the world to seek his fortune in the approved Wapshot manner.

When Moses leaves home, Coverly also runs away. First a government employee in Washington, Moses later finds his place in a New York fiduciary house. Coverly's adventures are more varied and include failure to get a job in a carpet factory because the company psychiatrists find him psychologically unstable, work as a department store clerk, night school, civilian status in a secret government project in the South Pacific, and a position on a rocket-launching project in the West. Each in the end finds the object of his seeking. Moses' choice is Melissa, the penniless ward of another Wapshot cousin, the parsimonious widow of a five-and-dime store tycoon, who lives in ugly baroque discomfort on the Hudson. For Melissa's sake, Moses can even put up with Cousin Justina's penny-pinching and nagging. Coverly's fate comes to him in a sandwich shop in the Forties, in the person of Betsey, a lonely Southern girl as unpretentious as corn pone and as nourishing. So the Wapshot fortunes are made secure, for with the birth of sons to Melissa and Betsey, Cousin Honora proves as good as her word and turns her money over to Moses and Coverly.

Meanwhile, Leander's world has fallen apart. He had wrecked the *Topaze*, and Cousin Honora refused to pay for the repairs. When Sarah Wapshot converts the old craft into "The Only Floating Gift Shoppe in New England" and opens the establishment with a gala tea and a sale of Italian pottery, Leander is heartbroken. At first he tries to keep busy writing his memoirs but remembrance proves too painful for him to continue. At last, disgusted with the ugliness of life, he drowns himself. Moses and Coverly, returning to St. Botolphs to buy their father a new boat, hear instead the burial service for those who have perished at sea.

Yet the final work is Leander's. On a later visit home, Coverly finds in a copy of Shakespeare a note of advice bequeathed by Leander to his sons, a litany of idiosyncratic personal belief and homely folk wisdom. Like his protagonist, Cheever did not blink at the chaos of human existence. He accepted it and, in the process, made of its truths and joys and terrors a gift of the imagination, leavening his picture of human folly and failure with a comic vision capable of seeing as well those consoling virtues that make life bearable.

THE WAPSHOT SCANDAL

Type of work: Novel
Author: John Cheever (1912–1982)
Type of plot: Humorous regional chronicle
Time of plot: Early 1960's
Locale: St. Botolphs, Massachusetts; Proxmire Manor, a Westchester
  suburb; and Talifer, a missile research base
First published: 1964
        Principal characters:
          HONORA WAPSHOT, matriarch of the Wapshot clan, a
              Yankee individualist, and an anachronism in the modern
              world
          COVERLY WAPSHOT, her good-hearted, well-meaning
              nephew, a public relations worker at the Talifer Missile
              Site
          BETSEY WAPSHOT, his wife, a woman of whims
          MOSES WAPSHOT, another nephew, a stockholder and an
              alcoholic
          MELISSA WAPSHOT, his wife, a modern Circe disguised as
              a suburban matron
          EMILE CRANMER, the grocery boy who becomes Melissa's
              lover
          DR. LEMUEL CAMERON, the atomic scientist in charge of
              the Talifer Missile Site
          MR. APPLEGATE, the rector of Christ Church in St.
              Botolphs, also an alcoholic
          GERTRUDE LOCKHART, a Proxmire Manor matron driven
              to drunkenness, promiscuity, and suicide by the failure
              of her household appliances
          NORMAN JOHNSON, an agent of the Internal Revenue
              Service

John Cheever's *The Wapshot Scandal* chronicles the decline and collapse of an ostensibly staid, prestigious, wealthy, and morally irreproachable New England family. It is first of all the story of Honora Wapshot, eccentric spinster and septuagenarian guardian of the Wapshot treasure trove, oldest living descendant of a family that settled in the fictional town of St. Botolphs, Massachusetts, in the seventeenth century. From her vantage point in this ancestral hamlet, Honora supervises—but mainly underwrites with quarterly checks from a trust fund—the lives of her two young cousins, Moses and Coverly Wapshot. At the beginning of the period traced by the novel, the two brothers have lost both their mother, Sarah, and their father, Leander, who drowned while swimming (the often-facetious mythic allusion is a Cheever trademark), but who left behind him two sons of whom he was proud and a world which appeared to be orderly and sane. What happens to that world is revealed in the separate but intersecting lines of three stories—each in its own way crystallizing the grotesque dissolution of the Wapshot probity.

The novel begins and ends on Christmas Eve in the town of St. Botolphs, but the piety suggested by such a parenthesis is undercut by the fact that on both occasions, the minister who conducts the Episcopal service is an alcoholic. The corruption of these ancient, holy rites is the first of many indications that the stability of St. Botolphs, and particularly the stability of one of its oldest families, is gravely threatened. The first readers see of St. Botolphs is its railway station, and the town itself is the alpha and omega of the novel; but between these terminal points, the Wapshots travel far, gradually losing all that is sacred and valuable in their birthright and returning to the town like wasted prodigals, impoverished, exhausted, and desolate, in a kind of parody of the traditional Christmas homecoming. The ordered world has been destroyed.

The novel begins with the story of Coverly Wapshot. After a Christmas visit to Honora, where he is haunted by the ghost of his high-minded father, Coverly travels west. He returns to a world that would have baffled his father, the Talifer Missile Site. At this top-secret complex of experimental laboratories and space equipment, some irrevocable error by a personnel-selecting machine has recently placed Coverly in the department of public relations, even though he is trained for computer programming. He lives in Talifer with his wife Betsey and their son Binxey, but their social life in the community is a little bleak. One day Betsey, after watching with bland indifference as a neighbor falls to his death on a cement terrace, neglects to notify anyone because of her vague fear that she might violate security regulations. Coming home one day, Coverly learns that their garbage pail has been taken by the wife of another neighbor, and the two men come to blows and bites over the incident. Shortly afterward, Betsey and Coverly attempt to meet their neighbors (who have never called on them since their arrival) by inviting twenty-five people to a cocktail party; but the plan is aborted when no one appears. Betsey is shattered, and her reaction takes the form of a lasting resentment of Coverly, whom she blames for making her live in Talifer.

Through a strange accident in circumstance, Coverly is offered a position on the personal staff of Dr. Lemuel Cameron, the egomaniacal titan of the missile complex. Coverly, however, is entirely at the mercy of Cameron's caprice, and soon discovers that he is nothing more than a chauffeur for the great man, a glorified attendant. Also, beneath the surface of Cameron's brilliance and cultural pretensions (he is capable of quoting a little poetry) Cheever exposes the viciousness of a man who professes a belief in the blessedness of the universe, but who talks with perfect equanimity of the destruction of the world, who suffers agonies of lust which can be satisfied only by a mistress in Rome, who beats his subordinates in ferocious outbursts of temper, and who has driven his son to insanity by practicing hideous extremes of cruelty under the name of "discipline." In a short time, therefore, Coverly finds that he has hitched his wagon to a rather sinister star. When his security clearance at the missile site is withdrawn because of Honora's delinquency on her federal income tax, Coverly expects that Cameron will get him reinstated. When he goes for that purpose to Washington, where Cameron is being questioned by a Congressional Committee, he is witness to a rather startling phenomenon: as a result of his savage temperament, Cameron's own security clearance is withdrawn.

Moses Wapshot has trouble with his work but far more with his wife Melissa. He works at a brokerage house (in, presumably, New York), and the couple live with their son in an affluent little suburban cocoon called Proxmire Manor, where the only thing that occupies the police is the memory that once, several years prior to the time of the novel, a woman was arrested for tearing up a parking ticket. The community makes a pretense at maintaining rigid moral standards; on the afternoon when she is first seen, Melissa is learning that a certain couple is being expelled from Proxmire Manor because the wife had been flagrantly promiscuous, notably with grocery boys and deliverymen. Melissa is bored with such standards, and she becomes a little unhinged when she stumbles across evidence of lesbianism at a local dance that very evening. Shortly thereafter, she herself develops a fondness and then a passion for Emile Cranmer, the boy who delivers her groceries. She seduces him without much difficulty. They begin with a weekend at her house in Nantucket, followed by a rendezvous in Boston, in New York, and eventually, in a little shack outside the town of Proxmire Manor. Emile engages in the affair with little compunction; Melissa's money buys him food to satisfy an insatiable appetite and supplies him with expensive baubles, such as an eight-hundred-dollar sapphire ring; but Melissa pays much more than money to maintain the affair. After meeting Emile for the third time, she is tortured with remorse and seeks release in drunkenness. When she goes to a doctor for a physical examination, she becomes so aroused that she ends up by fornicating with him. As a last resort, she seeks the counsel of the minister, who can do nothing but refer her to the town psychiatrist. Melissa, however, will not settle for the explanation that she is simply sick (and therefore irresponsible); so she has only one place left to go, back to Emile.

Moses learns of his wife's infidelity from Emile's mother. The impact of the news is explosive. He nearly strangles his wife, then leaves his home and turns to drink and dissipation. By a series of bizarre and elaborate maneuvers, Melissa manages to meet Emile in Italy, where she goes with her son; she buys him at an auction in Ladros for a hundred thousand lire, they retire to her luxurious villa, and they are last seen together in Rome. For his part,

Moses abandons himself completely to sex and alcohol. On Christmas Eve, at the end of the novel, Coverly finds him in the upstairs room of the St. Botolph's hotel drunkenly wallowing in the embrace of an equally inebriated and licentious widow. Moses comes home with Coverly to Honora's house, but the next morning he shuts himself in a closet full of bourbon. That is the last readers see of him.

During all of this action, Honora has been steadily losing her grip. She seems at first incapable of any serious wrong, but early in the novel, the old woman learns that because she has never paid any federal income tax, she faces a criminal indictment. Her friend, Judge Beasley, recommends that she take her money out of the bank and leave the country. She follows his advice and decides on a ship to Europe, but this move is scarcely the end of her troubles. On the ship she is flattered by the attentions of a nice-mannered young man who helps her to get around the decks; when he tells her that he is a stowaway, she arranges for him to be fed regularly in her cabin, and she develops enough interest in him to be capable of jealousy when she sees him in the company of another woman. One morning, however, in the early hours, he attempts to steal her money belt, and she strikes him over the head with a brass lamp. Though she thinks he is dead, he survives the blow and pursues his calling elsewhere; just before the ship docks at Naples, he strolls by Honora with another aging victim on his arm. Her only way of releasing her fury is by striking out at the entire ship; she does so by the simple expedient of plugging her curling iron into an outlet in the bathroom of her cabin. This, as she has already discovered, has the effect of blowing out the ship's generators.

Honora enters the Bay of Naples, therefore, on a ship in darkness. In Italy, she finds little to brighten her world. She visits the Pope in the Vatican, but his rather precarious command of the English language frustrates communication between them and only sharpens her nostalgic yearning for the familiar territory of St. Botolphs. A short time later, her wish to return is satisfied, but in a cruelly unexpected way. Norman Johnson, an agent of the Internal Revenue Service who had visited her first in St. Botolphs, now comes to her calmly and politely (a fine ironic touch) with extradition papers, a criminal indictment, and an order for the confiscation of all her property. She returns to St. Botolphs immediately and spends the last of her days immured in her old house, consuming nothing but bourbon. Shortly before Christmas, she is pronounced dead of starvation; but there is a final, posthumous twist. She has left Coverly with a command to hold a Christmas dinner in her house for the inmates of the local institute for the blind. Coverly executes her wishes.

The stories of Honora, Moses, and Coverly Wapshot are separately developed in the unfolding of the novel. Each character sinks and collapses in a different way; but the power of the novel derives from the skill with which Cheever has joined these stories. Thematically he forges links between Honora's impending bankruptcy, the erosion of Moses' marriage, and the reverses in Coverly's career, so that all three stories reveal the undoing of the sane, orderly world that Leander Wapshot left behind him. For generations, the family had stood together; now it falls together, and Cheever traces the decline with a striking, often chilling mixture of derision and compassion. This is a novel so intensely comic that it hovers on the edge of tragedy.

WASHINGTON SQUARE

Type of work: Novel
Author: Henry James (1843–1916)
Type of plot: Psychological realism
Time of plot: About 1850
Locale: New York City
First published: 1881

> *Principal characters:*
> DR. SLOPER, a prominent New York doctor
> CATHERINE SLOPER, his daughter
> MRS. PENNIMAN, his sister
> MORRIS TOWNSEND, Catherine's suitor

The Story:

Peace, especially of the domestic variety, was becoming increasingly important to Dr. Sloper as he entered his fifties. Intelligent, poised, distinguished in his profession, he was accustomed to meeting life on his own terms. Not entirely unscarred by fate, he had suffered the loss of his wife and a young son many years before; but the passage of time had helped to soften even this blow. Now he dwelt quietly and comfortably in his mansion on Washington Square with his only remaining child, his daughter Catherine, and his widowed sister, Mrs. Penniman.

Neither of these companions, oddly enough, inspired the doctor with any great fondness. His sister had just the sort of nature, incurably romantic and deviously feminine, to set his teeth on edge; he saw her presence in his establishment as merely an inconvenience to be overlooked in the interest of providing female supervision of his growing daughter. Nor, regarding the daughter herself, was Dr. Sloper any less candid in his private appraisal. Catherine was a good girl, he thought, but incurably dull. Entering her twenties, she had never had a romantic interest or a prospect of any. She was shyly fond of her father and very much afraid of him, especially when an ironical tone crept into his voice. However, he was generally kind and courteous to her, even if more self-contained than an adoring daughter might always wish.

Catherine's taste for ornate dress was one of the characteristics which her father found especially trying. She had long cherished this taste without venturing to express it, but when she reached the age of twenty, she bought a red satin gown trimmed with gold fringe. It made her look like a woman of thirty, and her father inwardly grimaced at the thought that a child of his should be both ugly and overdressed.

Catherine was wearing her red gown on the evening when she first met Morris Townsend. The occasion was a party, given by her aunt, Mrs. Almond.

Catherine became quickly convinced that she had never met a young man so handsome, clever, and attentive. When his absorption with Catherine began to attract notice, Townsend quickly shifted his attentions to Mrs. Penniman, whose romantic sensibilities were soon aflutter with delight and anticipation. Before the evening ended, she had managed to intimate to this agreeable young man that he would be welcome to call in Washington Square.

The visit soon occurred, to be quickly followed by another; and presently young Townsend was in regular attendance upon Catherine. This development was far from unobserved by the other two members of the household, though their reactions were entirely different. Mrs. Penniman, undertaking the role of a middle-aged Cupid, pressed Townsend's claims and assisted his cause as ardently as she dared. Dr. Sloper, on the other hand, became first skeptical and then concerned. An interview with the young man strengthened his conviction that Townsend's charming manner was only a mask for irresponsibility and selfishness. He suspected that Townsend was living off the meager resources of the latter's sister, a widow with five children, and the doctor determined to investigate the matter. Before he could do so, however, Catherine brought him word that Morris Townsend had proposed to her and that she was anxious to accept him.

His suspicions confirmed by a talk with Mrs. Montgomery, Townsend's sister, the doctor came away from his call more convinced than ever that Catherine's young man was a fortune hunter. For once, however, his objections failed to sway the infatuated girl. As a last resort, Dr. Sloper declared that if Catherine married Townsend he would disinherit her. This measure would not leave her penniless by any means, since an inheritance from her mother would still supply her with a comfortable income. Nevertheless it would reduce, by two-thirds, the amount Catherine could eventually expect; and the doctor's announcement gave both Townsend and Mrs. Penniman, also the object of her brother's displeasure, something to think about.

Mrs. Penniman, alarmed, counseled delay, and Townsend agreed to part with Catherine while she accompanied her father to Europe. Both Townsend and Mrs. Penniman hoped that the passage of time would soften the doctor's obdurate opposition to the match. Catherine, while agreeing to make the trip, cherished no such illusions. After several months the travelers returned, but the situation remained unchanged. Catherine was determined to go ahead with the marriage; Townsend kept putting her off. Suddenly he vanished from New York altogether.

Years passed before she saw him again. In the meantime, Dr. Sloper had died and, fearful to the end that Townsend might reenter Catherine's life, had left his own fortune to charity. One night while Catherine was sitting quietly at home, there was a ring at the door. Morris Townsend had come back, secretly encouraged by the unwearying Mrs. Penniman. Bearded, heavier, and forty-five years of age, he was still fluent and personable; his whole manner made it clear that he expected to be made welcome in Washington Square. The lapse of twenty years might have taken much from him, including the European wife of whom Catherine had vaguely heard, but he had not lost the bright assurance with which he now waited for his words to work their old-time magic on Catherine's heart.

He stood, hat in hand, murmuring his warm phrases, but Catherine did not ask him to sit down. She looked at him as if he were a stranger, repelling all advances and brushing off all explanations with a cool imperturbability which would have been worthy of the old doctor himself. With Catherine there was no longer any question of yielding to his charm: she had suffered too much. This time it would be she who sent him away; and she gave him his dismissal with a finality which he had no choice but to accept and understand.

Critical Evaluation:

The publication of *Washington Square* marked the end of what has been called the first period of its author's work. At that time, Henry James was still twenty or more years away from the three great novels which climaxed his artistic efforts: *The Wings of the Dove* (1902), *The Ambassadors* (1903), and *The Golden Bowl* (1904). In spite of its early date and its differences from these later and more ambitious books, however, *Washington Square* has been called a work of great genius. The plot of the book, simple as it is, still appeals to a considerable audience. Nor are its merits visible only to readers of intellectual pretensions, as in some other novels of James. A short novel, with a style much less involved than that which James was later to develop, *Washington Square* can be read in two or three hours. It is one of the few of the author's earlier works with scenes laid in America. It is also one of the few which are not preoccupied with the contrast existing between the civilization of Europe and that of America. Laid in New York City around the middle of the nineteenth century, it explores a family situation ruffling the peace of a rich and respected New York physician.

With characteristic skill, James explores the complex relationship between Dr. Sloper, disappointed because his plain and somewhat dull daughter cannot replace either his deceased wife or his lost son, and Catherine Sloper, whose essential goodness makes her one of James's most appealing heroines. Catherine, surviving and growing through the callous treatment by her father and her great disappointment in Morris Townsend, gradually develops a stoic strength and dignity which give her a tragic quality.

When readers first encounter Catherine, she is torn between the extremes of her aunt's foolish romanticism and her father's hardheaded realism. In the course of the novel, she will move from one extreme to the other, but James does not present her growth as necessarily a victory of knowledge over naïveté. From the start, Dr. Sloper recognizes Morris' motives, but his handling of the situation borders on the sadistic. He neither tries to understand Catherine nor to consider her feelings or happiness. Rather, he devotes his attention to causing Morris finally to reveal his mercenary plans, thus making marriage impossible for his daughter. One wonders if marriage to Morris could have been worse than the lonely spinsterhood to which Catherine finally comes.

Catherine reveals her strength and pride in defying her father's demand that she renounce Townsend. Though, purged of her girlish romanticism, she undoubtedly knows already that she will never marry Morris, she nevertheless retains her autonomy by refusing on principle to submit to Dr. Sloper's demands. Unfortunately, however, neither the loss of romantic dreams of happiness nor the development of real inner strength has offered Catherine a fuller or richer life. At the end of the novel, she is alone, facing an empty future.

THE WATERS OF KRONOS

Type of work: Novel
Author: Conrad Richter (1890–1968)
Type of plot: Symbolic fantasy
Time of plot: 1960's and the past
Locale: Unionville, a town lost beneath the waters of time
First published: 1960

> *Principal characters:*
> JOHN DONNER, an old man
> HARRY DONNER, his father
> GREAT-AUNT TERESA
> AUNT JESS
> RICHARD RYON, Aunt Jess's husband
> MRS. BONAWITZ, a neighbor of the Donners

Conrad Richter is a writer apparently haunted by a sense of the past. In his early novels he re-created with quiet and assured art some spacious landscapes of an older America, regions widely separated in geography and time: the American Southwest in *The Sea of Grass*, *Tacey Cromwell*, and *The Lady*; the growth of a settlement on the Ohio-Pennsylvania frontier in the trilogy of *The Trees*, *The Fields*, and *The Town*; the period of the American Revolution in *The Free Man*; bucolic comedy in *The Grandfathers*; life in a small Pennsylvania city in the years following the Spanish-American War in *Always Young and Fair*; and the romance of the pioneer wilderness in *The Light in the Forest* and *A Country of Strangers*. These books are fresh and authentic in their presentation of regional and historical themes. In *The Waters of Kronos*, he gives a picture of a different kind of past, the story of one man's pilgrimage back to the lost times and landmarks of his youth. In the process, Richter deals expertly with two matters of great concern in modern fiction, the problem of time and the enigma of man's identity.

These, after all, make up the modern subject: the search for self and the exploration of consciousness, which is man's measurement of the nature and duration of time, as memory and history are its deposit. The crisis for personality is the challenge of the age, for in a world as fragmented and confused as the earth is, the private sensibility is no longer self-contained, and man's search for identity and wholeness takes on the form of a despairing quest. Leopold Bloom and Stephen Dedalus wandering the streets of Dublin, Proust's narrator confronting his unrecognized figure in the mirror, Eugene Gant's search for the father, Camus' Jean-Baptiste Clemence in the Amsterdam bar, Saul Bellow's Henderson shouting his "I want, I want" toward the African sky—these are the images of alienated, divided man trying to define himself in space and time. In a special way, Richter presents a variation on this universal quest, which in *The Waters of Kronos* is a return to a lost and buried past.

The fantasy of time travel is not new; it was as useful to Mark Twain as it was to H. G. Wells. The works of these writers, however, were based on what is called the mathematics of a space-time continuum; Richter's novel, on its metaphysics. There is no book quite like this anywhere in American literature. In fact, the only two works which suggest any comparison in either quality or kind are Thornton Wilder's play *Our Town*, and Robert Frost's poem "Directive." As in Wilder's play, readers watch events unfolding with a knowledge of how much of the life presented will be wasted and sad, how much of the beautiful and good will go unrecognized until it is past all recall; and readers look on helplessly, not with anticipation, but with foreknowledge of what the future holds for the people involved. *The Waters of Kronos* suggests "Directive" also in that it conveys with quiet tenderness and sad wisdom a sense of the inevitability of things: the loneliness of being, the awkwardness of communication, the fact that life wears away to a death that is half-welcomed and half-feared, the knowledge that the waters of time wash over the years of childhood and in the end man goes back to the depths where he began. These matters are the substance of old myths that express the fundamental common experience of the race. They shaped the strange adventure of John Donner when he went back to the place of his origins.

To begin with, it was a useless pilgrimage, as he knew, for Unionville, the town where he was born, is now buried under the waters of a huge hydroelectric dam. Donner is an old man who has lived in the West for many years. He has been ill also, and during his sickness his desire for many things now vanished from his life prompted him to make the long trip back to the Pennsylvania countryside of his ancestors. On his arrival, he finds everything as he knew it would be. The town is gone, deep under the dark waters. Only the bodies of the dead have been saved from the flooding. In the new cemetery to which they have been removed, they are all that remains of the past. Donner is deeply affected. Then as memories of the lost town close in about him, a miracle occurs. A man driving a miner's wagon comes down the remains of an old road and gives him a lift. Donner finds himself back in Unionville as he had known it when he was a boy.

Now, however, the situation is reversed. He is an old man walking the familiar streets, peering into the houses, meeting old friends and relatives all younger than he. The time is 1899, the day before his grandfather's funeral. He talks to his father but cannot reveal himself. He goes to the home of Great-Aunt Teresa and Aunt Jess, his childhood favorites, but all his relatives are busy with preparations for the funeral, and he is turned away. Wandering through the town, he sees people whose future he already knows. When he comes to the Flail house, he remembers that the father, a butcher, would kill his wife, their four children, and himself a short time later; he frightens Mrs.

Flail when he calls out to her to leave her husband. That night, he sleeps in a covered bridge. The next day, he attends his grandfather's funeral. Unrecognized, he sees himself as a boy. He sees his mother, but she is surrounded by relatives. When he goes to his father's house later on and asks to see her, he is again turned away. Only Great-Aunt Teresa notes a family resemblance; she thinks he is the dead grandfather buried that day.

That night, he is taken in by Mrs. Bonawitz, a neighbor of the Donners, after he has lost consciousness and fallen. During the night, he meets his own boyhood again when young John Donner comes bringing word that the mother for whom old John Donner has asked will come to see the stranger the next day. Later, awake, he finds the answers to the two questions that have haunted his life. He is his father's true son, he realizes, and the face of the great frightener who had disturbed the dreams of his childhood was really himself, as old as he is now, the specter shape of man's mortality in the moment of death.

This realization joins reality and dream, part of the scheme of things that gives man his deepest knowledge, but too late. For John Donner, at the end, is dying. Reconciled with his father, he looks forward to reunion with his mother. "He could scarcely wait. She had promised yesterday that he would see her 'tomorrow' and she had never told him a falsehood yet." This conclusion suggests that Richter has further disclosures to make from the deep wash of time's waters, the fulfillment of continued life suggested by the promise of the mother.

Part of the effectiveness of *The Waters of Kronos* comes from the device of superimposing one image upon another, past and present, youth and age, life and death. This dualism extends even into the dialogue, in which Conrad Richter's people say one thing but seem to suggest other meanings, thus setting up a resonance which readers are more likely to find in poetry than in fiction. The novel, imaginatively conceived and beautifully styled, is a work of quiet hints and gentle persuasions. Conrad Richter is a writer who knows his own powers and thus is able to suit them admirably to the uses which the moral occasion demands.

THE WEB AND THE ROCK

Type of work: Novel
Author: Thomas Wolfe (1900-1938)
Type of plot: Impressionistic realism
Time of plot: 1900-1928
Locale: North Carolina, New York, and Europe
First published: 1939

Principal characters:
GEORGE WEBBER, a young writer
ESTHER JACK, his beloved

The Story:

George Webber's childhood was one of bleakness and misery. He was really a charity ward, even though he lived with his aunt and uncle. George's father had deserted him and his mother and had gone off to live with another woman. After the death of George's mother, her Joyner relatives took George into their home, where the boy was never allowed to forget that he had some of the blood of the Webbers mixed with his Joyner blood. Strangely, all his good and beautiful dreams were dreams of his father, and often he hotly and passionately defended his father to the Joyners. His love for his father made his childhood a divided one. George hated the people his aunt and uncle called good; and those they called bad, he loved. A lonely child, George kept his thoughts and dreams to himself rather than expose them to the ridicule of the Joyners; but the picture of that happy, joyful world of his father, and others like him, stayed with him during those bleak years of his childhood.

When George was sixteen, his father died, leaving the boy a small inheritance. With that money, George left the little southern town of Libya Hill and went to college. There he found knowledge, freedom, and life. Like many other young men, George wasted some of that freedom in sprees of riotous and loose living, but he also used his freedom to read everything he could get his hands on, and he was deeply impressed with the power of great writers. George was beginning to feel the need of getting down some of his thoughts and memories on paper. He wanted to write of the two sides of the world—the bright, happy world of the people who had everything and the horrible, dreary world of the derelicts and the poor. His college years ended, George fulfilled the dream of every country boy in the nation; he went to the city, to the beautiful, wonderful enfabled rock, as he called New York.

The city was as great and as marvelous as George had known it would be.

He shared an apartment with four other boys; it was a dingy, cheap place, but it was their own apartment, where they could do as they pleased. George, however, found the city a lonely place in spite of its millions of people and its bright lights. There was no one to whom he was responsible nor to whom he belonged. He thought he would burst with what he knew about people and about life, and, since there was no one he could talk to about those things, he tried to write them down. He began his first novel.

The next year was the loneliest one George had ever known. He drove himself mercilessly. He was wretched, for the words torturing his mind would not go on the paper as he wanted. At the end of a year, he took the last of his inheritance and went to Europe. He hoped to find there the peace of mind he needed to finish his book. The cities of Europe did not hold his salvation. He was still lonely and bitter because he could not find the answer to the riddle of life. He went back to New York, but the city was no longer an unfriendly enemy, for George had found Esther.

They had met on the ship bound for New York. Esther was Mrs. Esther Jack, a well-known and successful stage set designer. She was fifteen or twenty years older than George, but she was also younger in many ways, for Esther loved people and believed in them. Where George was silent and distrustful, Esther was open and trusting. George sometimes felt that theirs was the greatest love of all times, at once brutal and tender, passionate and friendly, so deep that it could not last. For the next three years, however, he was the king of the world. To Esther, George told all his dreams, all his memories, and all his formerly wordless thoughts about life and people.

George failed to realize at first that Esther meant more than a lover to him. Gradually he came to know that through her he was becoming a new person, a man who loved everyone. For the first time in his life, George Webber belonged to someone. Since he was no longer lonely, the torture and the torment left him. At last his book began to take shape, to become a reality. George Webber was happy.

Slowly, however, the magic of his affair with Esther began to disappear. He still loved her more than he believed possible and knew that he would always love her; but they began to quarrel, to have horrible, name-calling scenes that left them both exhausted and empty, even the quarrels that ended with passionate lovemaking. At first, George did not know the reason for those scenes, although he always knew that it was he who started them. Slowly he began to realize that he quarreled with Esther because she possessed him so completely. He had given her his pride, his individuality, his dreams, his manhood. Esther had also unknowingly been a factor in his disillusionment, for through her he had met and known the great people of the world—the artists, the writers, the actors—and he had found those people disgusting and cheap. They had destroyed his childhood illusions of fame and greatness, and he hated them for it.

When his novel was finished, Esther sent the manuscript to several publishers she knew. After months had passed without his hearing that it had
been accepted, George turned on Esther in one final burst of savage abuse
and told her to leave him and never return. Then he went to Europe again.

Although he had gone to Europe to forget Esther, he did nothing without
thinking of her and longing for her. Esther wrote to him regularly, and he
paced the floor if the expected letter did not arrive; but he was still determined
to be himself and to accomplish his purpose he must not see Esther again.

One night in a German beer hall, George got into a drunken brawl and
was badly beaten. While he was in the hospital, a feeling of peace came over
him for the first time in ten years. He looked into a mirror and saw his body
as a thing apart from the rest of him. He knew that his body had been true
to him, that it had taken the abuse he had heaped upon it for almost thirty
years. Often he had been almost mad, and he had driven that body beyond
endurance in his insane quest—for what he did not know. Now he was ready
to go home again. If his first novel should not be published, he would write
another. He still had a lot to say. The next time he would put it down right,
and then he would be at peace with himself. George Webber was beginning
to find himself at last.

Critical Evaluation:

In *The Story of a Novel* (1936), Thomas Wolfe responded to critics' complaints that he could write only about his own life and that his Scribner's
editor, Maxwell Perkins, was responsible for organizing the material of his
first two novels, *Look Homeward, Angel* (1929) and *Of Time and the River*
(1935). He promised to write in a more "objective," disciplined style; and to
prove that he could structure his sprawling fiction without assistance, he
severed his professional association with Perkins. In July 1938, two months
before he died following a brain operation, Wolfe submitted to his new editor,
Edward C. Aswell, the manuscript from which his last two novels, *The Web
and the Rock* and *You Can't Go Home Again*, were assembled. Although
somewhat more objective and more finely controlled than his earlier fiction,
the novels continue the supreme subject of all his work: the story of his own
life reshaped into myth.

Critics have said that *The Web and the Rock* is at once the best and the
worst novel that Wolfe wrote. Certainly the first part of the book, that describing George Webber's childhood in a Southern town, is an excellent regional
chronicle. Here Wolfe's genius with words reaches new heights. The rest of
the novel, however, drags somewhat from overdone treatment of a love story
in which similar scenes are repeated until they become monotonous.

George Webber, described as monkeylike with long arms and an awkward,
ambling gait, scarcely resembles the tall, hawklike Eugene Gant of *Look
Homeward, Angel*. Yet he is surely another psychological portrait of Wolfe,

the tormented artist among Philistines. In the first part of *The Web and the Rock*, the author attempts to provide for his hero a new family and social background, but the Joyners, despite their vitality, are mere copies of the Pentlands; Libya Hill resembles Altamont; and the moody, romantic Webber recalls the young Eugene. Some of the minor characters, notably the baseball hero Nebraska Crane and Aunt Maw, are brilliantly drawn; and the chapter "The Child by Tiger," originally published as a short story, reveals Wolfe's great power to create tragic myth. Above all, the strength of the first part of the book rests upon the author's heroic vision of the townspeople and the mountain folk of North Carolina—a stock of enterprising, stubborn, passionately independent souls. They represent the mysterious "web" of the earth. Like Webber, a child of the mountain folk, they are tied by threads of destiny not only to the land but also to the seasons, the workings of time. As an artist, Webber understands intuitively the heart of things, the patterns of life and dreams.

In roughly the second half of the novel, Wolfe contrasts the "web" of the earth with the "rock" of the city of New York. At this point in his writing, he abandons, for the most part, his scheme of objectivity and deals with the experiences of his own life. Webber meets and falls in love with Esther Jack (the same Esther who first appears to Eugene Gant in the "Faust and Helen" chapter of *Of Time and the River*)—in real life the stage designer and artist Aline Bernstein. With remarkable frankness, Wolfe describes the tragic course of the affair between these markedly different personalities: the egotistic, brilliant, despotic provincial-genius and his mistress, a sophisticated, sensitive, upper-middle class Jewish wife and mother. As a Realist, Wolfe is at his best detailing scenes of lovemaking and eating, of tempestuous quarrels and passionate reconciliations. Throughout the extended part of the book dealing with the love affair—for all its excesses and absurdities—Wolfe is able to touch the reader: George and Esther truly care about each other. They try desperately to make their fragile relationship endure.

Yet the theme of the novel is the fragility of all dreams. The "rock" of New York, which George once loved as well as feared, begins to crumble in this novel; it will betray its fullest stresses in *You Can't Go Home Again*. The city, founded upon greed and selfish power, has no soul. To escape from his own sense of ruin, George visits pre-Nazi Germany, already ripe for the advent of a Hitler. George hopes to recapture, among the drunken revelers at a Munich Oktoberfest, the sense of joy of his own manhood; but he becomes violent, a savage fighting the beer hall swaggerers and is terribly beaten. By the end of the novel, he wishes to return to America so that he might establish his dreams once again upon a foundation that will endure: upon the "web" of his failing sense of the earth, and upon the "rock" of an already insecure civilization. In the last chapter, "The Looking Glass," Webber comes to understand the futility of these dreams.

WHAT MAISIE KNEW

Type of work: Novel
Author: Henry James (1843–1916)
Type of plot: Social morality
Time of plot: 1890's
Locale: London, Folkestone, and Boulogne
First published: 1897

Principal characters:

MAISIE FARANGE, the daughter of divorced parents
IDA FARANGE, her mother
BEALE FARANGE, her father
MISS OVERMORE, a governess and, later, the second Mrs.
  Beale Farange
MRS. WIX, a governess
SIR CLAUDE, Ida Farange's second husband

The Story:

Beale and Ida Farange were divorced with much publicity. At first, each fought to possess their daughter Maisie, but at last it was arranged that the girl should spend six months with each in turn. The first period was to be spent with her father.

Maisie was confused by the divorce. At first, she truthfully reported to her parents what they said about each other, but finding that her candor provoked furious outbursts and that she was being used as an innocent messenger, she soon became silent on the subject of the absent parent and appeared to absorb no knowledge during her visits.

Ida engaged Miss Overmore, a pretty governess, for Maisie, and Maisie was unhappy to leave her when she returned to her father. Soon, however, Miss Overmore went to Beale Farange's house where she was, to Ida's fury, also engaged as Maisie's governess. Upon her subsequent return to Ida, Maisie was placed in the care of Mrs. Wix. She learned no lessons from Mrs. Wix but adored her conversation and felt comfortable and secure with her.

During Maisie's next stay with Beale, he went for a few days to Brighton with Miss Overmore. When the governess returned, she found Mrs. Wix waiting for her. Mrs. Wix alone was preoccupied with Maisie's welfare and was outraged by the child's environment. She announced to Miss Overmore that Ida was about to remarry, and she gave Maisie a photograph of Sir Claude, her future stepfather. Miss Overmore outdid her, as it were, by announcing that she had just married Beale Farange.

Some time after his marriage, Sir Claude called and was received by the new Mrs. Beale Farange. Maisie was delighted by their apparent understanding and declared that she had brought them together. Sir Claude won Maisie's love by his gentleness toward her and by his declared intent to make her his responsibility. In spite of the pain of leaving the new Mrs. Farange, the girl was pleased to go home with him. Ida's love for her new husband, however, soon waned, and she had several lovers. When she accused Sir Claude of basely stealing Maisie's affections and threatened to drive Mrs. Wix out of the house for supporting him, Maisie felt that she belonged nowhere. In this disturbed situation, Mrs. Wix was determined to meet her responsibility for Maisie, and she desired to "save" Sir Claude from Mrs. Beale Farange, whom he frequently visited. Also, fearing the loss of her livelihood, she wished that Sir Claude would take a house for himself where she and Maisie would also live.

On one outing, Sir Claude took Maisie to her father's new house, which she was afraid to enter for fear of losing him if she remained there. Once in the house, however, she was again enthralled by Mrs. Farange's beauty and was interested to learn that Beale mattered no more to his wife than Sir Claude did to Ida. Maisie remained happily with her stepmother after Sir Claude had assured her that he would provide for Mrs. Wix and visit her frequently.

After a long absence, Sir Claude visited Maisie again. While they were walking in the park, they met Ida with an unknown, military-appearing man. Ida and Sir Claude were immensely angry at their meeting, and Maisie was sent to talk with Ida's escort, whom her mother had called the Captain, while they finished their argument. Maisie, who was by that time thoroughly aware that neither parent loved her, wept when the Captain praised her mother highly and was eager to agree that she was "good." After this episode, Sir Claude, unable to learn from Maisie what the Captain had said to her, sent her home alone in a cab.

Mrs. Farange told Maisie that she met Sir Claude away from her home, but that he was reluctant to visit them and thus compromise Maisie. The three hoped to meet at a London exhibition; instead, they unexpectedly encountered Beale Farange. After a subdued but violent quarrel, Maisie was whisked away by her father to the house of his mistress. There he offered, in such a way that Maisie could only refuse, to take her to America with him.

Sir Claude, encouraged by Mrs. Wix, took Maisie to Folkestone as the first step toward making a home for them in France. There Ida arrived suddenly and surrendered Maisie to Sir Claude's guardianship. The following day, they crossed to France, where Mrs. Wix joined them. Sir Claude was to return to England and to Mrs. Beale Farange, when Maisie's father had finally left. Sir Claude confessed that he feared Mrs. Farange as he had formerly feared Ida. Mrs. Wix, still strongly opposed to Mrs. Farange, asked to be sent to England to sever their relationship. This request was refused by Sir Claude, who went off to England alone.

While he was away, Mrs. Wix explained to a bewildered Maisie that she refused to condone the immorality of Mrs. Farange and Sir Claude in living together with them. Also, she declared that she would never again leave Maisie. After several walks and much thought, the full implications of what this situation might mean became apparent to Maisie. She realized, too, that she had no moral "sense," and having rapidly absorbed the idea of such a sense from vague but emphatic conversations with Mrs. Wix, she decided to show in her future responses that she did indeed possess it.

When they returned to their hotel after a morning walk, Maisie was unexpectedly greeted by her stepmother. Mrs. Wix's own "moral sense" was nearly destroyed by Mrs. Farange's charm and, further, by her determination to have the governess-companion as an ally. According to Mrs. Farange, now that the girl's father had left, Maisie was her own daughter. In this way, she intended to hold Sir Claude, through his devotion to the girl. Mrs. Wix wavered, but Maisie declared that she would stay with Sir Claude only if he were alone.

The next morning, Mrs. Wix awakened Maisie with the news that Sir Claude had arrived. When Maisie breakfasted alone with him, he asked her if she would leave Mrs. Wix and live with him and Mrs. Farange. She asked to see Mrs. Wix before deciding. Later, while walking with Sir Claude, she said she would give up Mrs. Wix only if he would give up Mrs. Farange. Maisie made her decision when the four people confronted one another in a final struggle at the hotel. After she had failed in her appeal to have Mrs. Farange give up Sir Claude, Maisie decided to stay with Mrs. Wix.

Critical Evaluation:

Henry James is credited with freeing fiction from a "moral" purpose. His influential theories on point of view and scenic power educated succeeding generations of writers to the formal capacities of the novel. The ultimate purpose of his dismissal of a simpleminded didacticism from fiction, however, was not the eradication of moral vision as such. On the contrary, as his "technique" grew more subtle, the result was an increasingly profound exploration of human values and motives. He was reluctant to judge, which was probably the outstanding Naturalist trait in his fiction, but he nevertheless served an ethical muse by demonstrating and revealing the moral realities of life.

What Maisie Knew has often been singled out as a neglected masterpiece; neither early nor late James, it is credited with combining the storytelling virtues of the earlier novels with the psychological complexity of the later. The truth is that its central position in James's canon invests it with almost more weight than it can bear. As the psychological intensity grows, the plot is contorted to keep up. Maisie's parents divorce, remarry, and *their* new spouses become lovers and finally surrogate parents to Maisie. It is diabolically neat but almost farcical—and farce is not what James wants as a background for his moral and psychological development of Maisie.

The point is that Maisie herself is not always a convincing protagonist, especially as a vehicle for the novel's intricate, and often tortured, shifts in point of view: " . . . if he [Sir Claude] had an idea at the back of his head she had also one in a recess as deep, and for a time, while they sat together, there was an extraordinary mute passage between her vision of this vision of his, his vision of her vision, and her vision of his vision of her vision." Unlike Mrs. Wix, who never loses her "wonder" over what Maisie knew, the reader sometimes doubts that James was sure what she knew. He could, of course, experiment very freely with her capacity to know: she is only a child and therefore has an open-ended mind, but her child's identity is never adequately established. It is revealing that readers never have a clear idea of her exact age. Lewis Carroll's Alice is a real child in an imaginary world; James's Maisie is an imaginary child in a moral jungle.

WHERE THE AIR IS CLEAR

Type of work: Novel
Author: Carlos Fuentes (1928–   )
Type of plot: Symbolic realism
Time of plot: 1910–1954
Locale: Mexico City
First published: 1958

Principal characters:

IXCA CIENFUEGOS, a curious, visionary spectator of life
FEDERICO ROBLES, a wealthy industrialist and former
   revolutionary
NORMA LARRAGOITI DE ROBLES, his wife
HORTENSIA CHACÓN, his blind mistress
MANUEL ZAMACONA, a poet
MERCEDES ZAMACONA, his mother
RODRIGO POLA, a literary dabbler
ROSENDA ZUBARÁN DE POLA, his mother
GERVASIO POLA, his father, executed during the
   Revolution
PIMPINELA DE OVANDO, an impoverished aristocrat
TEÓDULA MOCTEZUMA, an aged widow
ROBERTO RÉGULES, a business opportunist
SILVIA RÉGULES, his wife
BETINA, their daughter
BOBÓ GUTIÉRREZ,
PEDRO CASEAUX,
CHARLOTTE GARCÍA,
NATASHA, and
CUQUIS, the members of the fashionable set
GABRIEL, a young wetback
BETO, a young tough
FELICIANO SÁNCHEZ, a labor leader
JUAN MORALES, a taxi driver
JAIME CEBALLOS, an ambitious law student

Nature—forests, mountains, rivers, plains—seemed to have thematic preference among Spanish-American novelists of the twentieth century. The great masters of fiction, such as Mariano Azuela, José Eustasio Rivera, Rómulo Gallegos, Ricardo Güiraldes, and some of his followers, such as the Peruvian novelist, Ciro Alegría, undertook to depict the landscape more than the men, or better written, to crush the human being under the burden of telluric forces. As one of Ciro's titles suggests, the world is too wide and alien for man; he has no room in this planet in spite of its magnitude.

A new trend, however, began to emerge in the fictional field of the Spanish American republics. Nature and its inhabitants have now become a secondary subject, their places in fiction replaced by the city and its dwellers. The work of God has now given way to the works of men; the rural setting has been forgotten, and the urban environment grasps the preoccupations of the writers of fiction. Instead of the objective presentation of farmers, settlers, and Indians, who struggle in vain against a jungle of greenness and obstreperous rivers, the narrator of today inserts his characters amid a jungle of iron, cement, and rivers of light. Juan Carlos Onetti, Eduardo Mallea, Julio Cortázar, Mario Vargas Llosa, among others, exemplify the trend through dynamic, complex, bitter novels.

In Mexico, Carlos Fuentes inaugurated the new urban novel. Born in Mexico City, resident in many major cities of the American continents—Rio de Janeiro, Montevideo, Washington, Santiago, Lima, Buenos Aires—he chose the city as his main concern in his writings. This city is his city: Mexico, an urban conglomerate often visited and departed from, tasted and remembered, lived in and yearned for because of his frequent trips abroad accompanying his father, a Mexican diplomat. Very often, after beginning his literary career, he wanted to concretize and condense the multiform, variegated, tumultuous, vital stream of Mexico, a city basically disorderly, but he could not organize a fit scheme. Finally, through *La región más transparente* (*Where the Air Is Clear*, 1960), his first novel, Fuentes was able to seize upon and bring into being his desire.

The title of the novel corresponds to a phrase taken from the *Visión de Anáhuac*, a study written by the Mexican essayist Alfonso Reyes, who described the high Mexican plateau as the clearest region of the air. Fuentes, however, gives a different, almost sarcastic interpretation to the phrase. The moral and physical atmosphere of Mexico, as seen by Fuentes, is quite contrary to that contemplated by Reyes. It is hard to think of a darker environment than this one, involving all the characters in a cloud of fumes, rain, dust, corruption, and frustration.

This novel constitutes a vast, chaotic synthesis of the society of the Mexican capital. It is written with demolishing impetus, dialectic assumptions and modern formal techniques; through its pages the reader attends, in a criss-cross itinerary and with accelerated movement, to the drama of the urban inhabitants. All of them are marked with a deterministic sign—they cannot act in a different way or escape their environment and past. They were born in Mexico City, in a given spot, and have to be submissive to their destiny. Immersed in this geographic fatalism, Fuentes creates a great fresco depicting men and women, real or semifantastic, belonging to different ethnic characteristics, social and economic strata, attitudes, professions, environments. About them and at the same time partially constituted by them, solemnly and cruelly stands the city, with its "three navels"—Indian, Spanish, and cosmopolitan—its antiquity, its height, its "mineral" rain, its unquenchable thirst for human lives, its old mythology, its irrationality.

The characters of the novel are prostitutes, snobs, pseudointellectuals, aristocrats, international opportunists, cab drivers, *braceros*, underdogs, nouveau riche, politicians, social climbers, and, in one way or another, their lives are linked together by a character of penumbral profile, Ixca Cienfuegos. This is the only figure who escapes undamaged from the physical or moral disaster, and he does so because he is more a symbol than a real entity. He ubiquitously appears everywhere, is known by most of the characters, talks with them, listens to their autobiographical confessions, and expresses the voice of the old, instinctive Indian ancestry. He, perhaps, represents the anonymous, the people, the Mexican.

In spite of the concreteness and turpitude of many pages, the novel cannot be classified as belonging to the realistic tradition, taking this term in its traditional connotation. Fuentes belongs, as do other Mexican writers of his generation, to the so-called Symbolic Realism. He tries to perceive, behind the feel of things and situations, a reality closer to truth than the evident daily reality, as he states. This view makes his novel a surrealistic and naturalistic story, with characters close to fantasy as well as life, well-known places and others without local fixation, dialogues made of uncommon words and others built up with platitudinous and cheap sentences, temporal situations of today and of the time past. The reader feels that he is amid a sad, rotten, turbulent, intemporal carnival, in which every character is merely a player acting a prefixed role.

The technical aspect of the novel is basically that of the masters of the twentieth century: Faulkner, Dos Passos, Lawrence, and Huxley. This means that the stream of consciousness, dislocation of time, social protest, interference of characters, and crudity of expressions are omnipresent. Moreover, there is not a plot, a development, a climax. It could be said that Fuentes wrote a novel of fragments, linked together with very circumstantial vinculum, with the intention of creating a kaleidoscopic panorama of men, environments, and situations.

The book is divided into three parts of different lengths. The first presents the most important characters, Ixca Cienfuegos, Manuel Zamacona, Federico Robles, his wife Norma Larragoiti de Robles, Rodrigo Pola, Hortensia Chacón, the Ovando family. In the second, the largest section of the book, the lives of these men and women meet, intermingle, interfere, collide. In the third, the shortest section, new though secondary characters appear. The book closes with an intent to synthesize Mexican history.

Ixca Cienfuegos opens the book. He is the spokesman of the city or perhaps the city itself, as is suggested almost at the end of the book. From his words, readers know that the ancient Indian spirit remains always and everywhere present in all phases of Mexican life. The ancestral forces operate mainly in the city of Mexico, cradle of the strongest old Indian culture. The old gods have not died; they look upon the people of every condition and sooner or later devour them all. From this initial monologue of Ixca, the parade of characters begins to defile in a tumultuous, contrapuntal way, sometimes in a consecutive linkage, sometimes with abrupt jumps. Beginning with the first matutinal hours of the day, Gladys García, a poor but not depraved prostitute, seeks for food and while roaming downtown starts to remember her life, her parents, her lovers. On the night of the same day, she sees a group of fashionable, snobbish people—corrupted, pseudointellectual—who engage in a wild party. Federico Robles, lawyer and banker, then appears in the book. He is a nouveau riche, despotic man, with no social concerns, who has climbed to high social esteem by cunning and wealth obtained through dishonest means during the days of the Mexican Revolution. He was pushed to enter this movement without consciousness of what it was for, but at the end of it, he found himself with money, prestige, pride, and reasons to justify his holdings. Later, he marries Norma Larragoiti, an unscrupulous, status-seeking woman who thinks she is doing a permanent favor to her husband because of her marriage to him. Robles has a lover, Hortensia Chacón, a long-suffering woman, blinded by her first husband, who loves Robles without self-interest and with compassion. Another jump in the plot sends the reader to meet Rodrigo Pola, son of a revolutionist shot to death without knowing his child. Just as abruptly, other characters are introduced: the Ovandos, an aristocratic family of the past days of Díaz, who struggle to no avail to keep their haughtiness and money; Manuel Zamacona, an idealist, original thinker, and poet, and many other people of lesser importance. All of them are met by the omnipresent Ixca Cienfuegos, who appears in the crucial moment of frustration or confession of the characters.

The second part of the book constitutes the section of the frustration. All the main people of the novel, Ixca excepted, fall into disaster. Robles becomes bankrupt and is repudiated by his wife; Norma perishes in a blaze in her home; Pola climbs the social staircase but is unhappy; the Ovandos are forced to work in the humblest jobs and live in secluded and poor rooms; Manuel Zamacona is killed in a bar. In this way, Fuentes proves that the ancient Mexican deities, always in control, and hatred of human lives have taken their revenge. Every life has been little more than a hideous play, as in the past days of human sacrifices.

The last pages of the book are perhaps the most successful. They are a tight, energetic synthesis of the tragic, painful history of the Mexican people. There appear many people of decisive importance upon the Mexican country and its society: the conquerors of wealth, the elected, those who have a name, and finally the common people, the anonymous names, the "you," the poor, the ever-suffering. And there stands also Gladys García, the first-appearing character, and Ixca Cienfuegos, symbol of the city and of Mexican history who would like to say fatalistically that these things have happened, that they could not be avoided or halted, in the most transparent region of the air.

Without doubt, Fuentes has written a singular novel, a story, or collection of interlinking stories, told in an overflowing, contrasted, negative, black protesting tone. It cannot be denied that *Where the Air Is Clear* is also a book born out of compulsory passion and love for his city and country. To echo the words of one of his characters, when a person writes about Mexico, the work must be done with joy, anger, compassion, hatred, and the fire of passion. The novel is a work of genuine, if undisciplined, achievement.

WHITE-JACKET
Or, The World in a Man-of-War

Type of work: Novel
Author: Herman Melville (1819–1891)
Type of plot: Adventure romance
Time of plot: 1840's
Locale: A vessel of the United States Navy
First published: 1850

Principal characters:

WHITE-JACKET, a sailor on board the U.S.S. *Neversink*
JACK CHASE, the captain of the maintop in the ship
CAPTAIN CLARET, the commander of the vessel

The Story:

White-Jacket, as he was later nicknamed, was a common sailor, a member of the crew of the United States frigate *Neversink* on a cruise of the Pacific Ocean during the 1840's. After the ship left Callao, Peru, the sailor tried to purchase a heavy jacket, needed protection when the *Neversink* passed into the colder climate off Cape Horn. Because a heavy jacket was not available from the ship's purser, the vessel having been at sea for more than three years, the sailor had to make a canvas jacket for himself.

The jacket was full of pockets and quilted with odds and ends of rags and clothing for warmth. When the maker requested some paint to make it waterproof and to darken its color, he was told that no paint was available for the purpose.

As the ship moved southward toward the Antarctic, the sailor gradually came to be called White-Jacket by the crew because of the strange garment he wore. Some of the sailors, superstitious as old wives, disliked him because of the jacket; they said that White-Jacket was too much like a ghost as he went about his duties high in the rigging of the frigate.

The offensiveness of White-Jacket's strange apparel was revealed only a few days after the ship's anchor had been weighed at Callao. White-Jacket was forced to leave the mess group to which he had been assigned, for the sailors told him openly that anyone who wore such a weird garment was unwelcome. That White-Jacket had proved himself a very poor cook during his tour of duty for the group had not helped his cause.

Forced from his original messmates' company, White-Jacket was taken into the mess to which belonged the petty officer of the maintop under whom White-Jacket served. The petty officer was Jack Chase, a gentlemanly Britisher who shared White-Jacket's love of literature. Chase, who had returned to the *Neversink* after an absence of months, during which he had served as an officer on a Peruvian insurrectionist vessel, was admired by the rough sailors and respected by all the officers aboard the ship.

As the *Neversink* sailed southward along the western coast of South America the general ship's duties continued. White-Jacket and his fellows set sails and took them in, washed down the decks, stood their watches, and prepared for colder weather. To relieve the tedium of the long voyage, Captain Claret gave out word that the men would be permitted to stage a theatrical entertainment. The Captain had permitted such entertainments in the earlier stages of the cruise, but he had discontinued them because one of the actors had behaved in an objectionable manner. White-Jacket noted that before the play, the Captain perused and censored the script. Neither the Captain nor the Commodore who was aboard the *Neversink* dignified the men's entertainment by being present.

During the coastal voyage, a man fell overboard and was drowned. The incident demonstrated to White-Jacket how risky life aboard a ship was and how quickly a lost man was forgotten.

The *Neversink* was becalmed in the waters off Cape Horn. After three days of cold and calm, the Captain gave the unusual order for the crew to "skylark." The men gave themselves over to all kinds of activity and games of a rougher sort, all in an attempt to keep warm and to prevent frozen hands and feet. Shortly thereafter a wind came up. The ship rounded the Cape and began to cruise steadily northward.

One day the lookout sighted a number of casks floating on the ocean. Word was given that they should be picked up, and when they were hauled aboard, it was discovered that they contained very fine port wine. The discovery caused great joy among the crew. In the 1840's the navy still clung to the custom of serving spirits to the men twice a day, but the *Neversink*'s steward, for some unaccountable reason, had neglected to replenish the ship's supply of rum during the stop at Callao.

The most significant happenings during the run from Cape Horn northward to Rio de Janeiro, so far as White-Jacket was concerned, were a series of floggings. At that time the American navy still made flogging a punishment for offenses at sea. White-Jacket hated the cruel whippings, which all crew members and officers were forced to watch. White-Jacket reflected that even in Rome no citizen could be flogged as punishment and that the great naval officers of the nineteenth century were opposed to a practice so brutal and unnecessary.

The *Neversink* finally reached Rio de Janeiro. During many days in port, the men were not to be permitted ashore. At last, the petty officers appointed Jack Chase, the captain of the maintop, to request shore leave for the men. At first, the Captain was unwilling to grant leave, but the Commodore interceded and gave his approval to sending the men ashore. Once again, Chase was the hero of the men aboard the vessel.

One day the Emperor of Brazil was expected to visit the vessel. White-

Jacket, amazed at preparations made by men and officers for the royal visit, wondered how men from a democratic nation could so easily fawn upon royalty. He decided the men would have made fewer preparations to receive the President of the United States.

On the voyage northward along the eastern coast of South America, one of White-Jacket's shipmates fell ill and died. White-Jacket watched the preparations for burial, including the traditional final stitch of the shroud through the nose, then stood by during the service. That event was as moving to him as an amputation demonstrated by the ship's doctor while the *Neversink* lay in the harbor at Rio de Janeiro. The operation was performed, White-Jacket believed, because the surgeon wished to show off to colleagues from other vessels anchored there at the same time. Convinced that the operation was unnecessary, White-Jacket was very bitter when the injured man died of shock.

White-Jacket himself had a close escape from death when the ship was off the Virginia capes. Sent aloft to reeve a line through some blocks, he lost his balance and fell from the rigging a hundred feet into the sea. He had to cut away his white jacket in order to keep afloat. He was barely out of his garment when a sailor, mistaking the jacket for a white shark, threw a harpoon into it. White-Jacket, rescued from the sea, was sent aloft ten minutes later to complete his task. White-Jacket was content to close his story of the voyage with the loss of his unlucky garment.

Critical Evaluation:

White-Jacket, Herman Melville's fifth book, reflects the experience Melville had when he returned to America on board the U.S. frigate *United States* from Honolulu in 1843–1844. The loosely knit narrative was thus formed from experience as well as fiction. The novel gives an astonishing portrait of life in an American naval vessel at the time, astonishing because of the detail and because of the practices then in vogue. The actual purpose of the novel was to help correct some of the vicious practices which Melville had seen firsthand. Flogging, tyranny of commanders, issuance of spirituous liquors to sailors, and the poor messing facilities of naval vessels of a century ago were all condemned by Melville in vivid terms. Authorities have conceded that Melville's novel did more than any other single source to abolish at least one of those practices, the flogging of enlisted men.

Beyond an autobiographical exposé of the abuses against crewmen aboard American naval vessels in the 1840's, *White-Jacket* also contains essential elements of a novel of initiation into a complex world of good and evil. White-Jacket's bizarre garment develops into a symbol of the naïve innocence of its wearer, who, through his adventures on the *Neversink*, comes to a knowledge of the real world as represented by the man-of-war. The boy's final plunge into the sea as a result of having become entangled in his white coat represents his baptism into the world of adult knowledge and the shedding of his childhood innocence.

Although not clearly developed in novelistic form, a number of themes in *White-Jacket* tie this novel to Melville's more mature works. The evil resulting from insecure authority and arbitrary laws underlies much of the abuse of power aboard ship, for example. In fact, Melville seems to suggest a distinction along class lines of the problems resulting from an abuse of power by the officers and the "sins" of the sailors, both seen as resulting from the inhumane conditions aboard ship. While these forms of physical abuse account for one type of evil aboard ship, and the behavior of the sailors at their worst represents another, however, a typically Melvillian suggestion of innate evil can be seen in certain characters. The inhumanity of Cadwallader Cuticle, M.D., who murders a sailor in the name of science, and the master-at-arms, Bland, said to be "without a soul," are manifestations of such innate evil.

Melville's world, however, is always ambiguous. Thus, in *White-Jacket*, the evil represented by Bland and the doctor is balanced by Jack Chase, who epitomizes all that is best in man.

WICKFORD POINT

Type of work: Novel
Author: John P. Marquand (1893-1960)
Type of plot: Social satire
Time of plot: Twentieth century
Locale: New York and Wickford Point
First published: 1939

> *Principal characters:*
> JIM CALDER, a writer
> MRS. CLOTHILDE WRIGHT, his cousin, formerly Clothilde
> Brill
> BELLA BRILL, her daughter
> MARY BRILL, another daughter
> PATRICIA LEIGHTON, Jim's friend
> JOE STOWE, Bella's former husband

The Story:

Jim Calder made his living by writing fiction for popular magazines. For this reason, the contradiction between the actual life of his relatives at Wickford Point and the fiction he was required to write was extremely obvious. His relatives, the Brills, were a group of New Englanders who had little money but who were disinclined to make a living. Being himself close to the Brills, he had attempted to escape from them and the enervating atmosphere of Wickford Point. He was only a second cousin to the Brill children, but his continual association with them in his early life produced bonds that were exceedingly hard to break. No matter how many times he left Wickford Point, he always returned. No matter how many times he returned, he always planned to get away again as soon as possible.

Jim attended Harvard and there met Joe Stowe. Harry Brill also attended Harvard, where he made sure that he knew the right people. Throughout his life, Harry was concerned with meeting the right people, but he never did make the right connections. Jim and Joe were fortunate in the fact that they became fast friends and were never elected to the right campus clubs. This polite ostracism served only to strengthen their friendship and to bring with it the assurance that they at least would be more successful than many of their snobbish classmates in their dealings with people.

When World War I arrived and America became involved, Joe and Jim were among the first to go into service, and they were shipped overseas as first lieutenants before they had completed their officers' training. After the war, they went to China and served with the forces of General Feng. Some years later, Jim returned to America to find a new way of life; Joe went to Italy. Both decided upon writing as a career.

When Jim returned to Wickford Point, he found the Brills just the same and as inconsequential as when he had left. Cousin Clothilde was still unable to manage finances satisfactorily. When she received her check on the first of the month, her children all raced to get their share of the cash, the first one arriving getting the greater share. Cousin Clothilde was always broke within a few hours after receiving her money.

Bella had grown into quite a beautiful young woman during Jim's absence from America, and at the moment of his return, she was involved in a rather serious affair with a nice young man named Avery Gifford. Jim, who had always been Bella's confidant, continued in this role when Bella sought advice from him. Since she was not sure that she loved Avery, it was decided that she should wait until her return from Europe to decide whether she would marry him. She went to Italy with her stepfather, Archie Wright, and while there, she met Joe Stowe and eloped with him.

Their marriage was doomed to failure from the start, and after some years, it ended in divorce. Bella never really knew what she wanted. She seemed to want everything but could never be satisfied with anything she had. She went from one affair to another because she was extremely attractive to men, but her affairs always remained platonic. Sometimes Jim felt that he was Bella's only friend, for none of her other friendships ever lasted, and she made new friends as fast as she lost old ones. She was always confident that whenever she got into difficulties she could fly to Jim and he would straighten out the situation for her.

Jim met Patricia Leighton, a woman of great executive ability who had a penthouse in New York City and an income of several thousand dollars a year. Jim's affair with her was a lasting one, each party contributing equally to the relationship. At first, Jim went to Pat to escape the inanities of his relatives at Wickford Point. Pat was a very understanding woman who realized clearly what Jim's problem really was, and she tried in an unobtrusive manner to help him make the final break with his family background.

In spite of their divorce, Bella and Joe thought often of each other, even though they both realized that to remarry would lead only to another divorce. Joe, since his divorce, had become a famous novelist, well off financially. Bella expressed her selfishness to Jim in her regretful admission that when she divorced Joe she had no idea that he would ever be so successful.

Bella went from one contemplated marriage to another, led her admirers on, and finally put herself into a rather delicate situation with Avery Gifford and Howard Berg. When she called upon Jim to rescue her once more, Jim decided that this time Bella would have to extricate herself, his refusal being motivated by his memory of recent conversations with Pat. Into the midst of these misunderstandings and resolves came Joe as a result of a telegram sent to him by Bella. At first, Bella and Joe seemed likely to try marriage once more, but as a result of Jim's attitude toward her, Bella accomplished the first generous deed in her life; she told Joe that she would not marry him again.

Jim took Bella back to changeless Wickford Point to find the place, as usual, thronged with visitors. Pat Leighton, as had previously been arranged, came down to Wickford Point to visit. Allen Southby, a friend of Jim's and a professor of English at Harvard, came to stay with the Brills while gathering material for his novel about Wickford Point. Mary Brill looked upon Allen as her own particular conquest until Bella's arrival. All her life Bella had been stealing Mary's eligible young men.

With the arrival of Pat, she and Jim once more faced the problem of getting Jim to break away from Wickford Point and the Brills. Jim finally made the decision to leave, after telling Pat that a part of him would always remain at Wickford Point and that he would always have to return occasionally for short visits. Under the circumstances, Pat agreed. Seeing Southby's apparent willingness to marry Bella, Jim felt free of Wickford Point and the clinging past. He began to pack his bags to return with Pat to New York.

Critical Evaluation:

John P. Marquand has said that he started writing *Wickford Point* from memories of his childhood and adolescence that centered around a country home once owned by his great-grandmother. He then added to these memories patterns of relationships observable in any family. This family chronicle of the old Brill homestead at Wickford Point, north of Boston, is told by a cousin, Jim Calder. Jim is loyal to this self-satisfied and inefficient family, but he struggles to keep clear of their strangling affection and dependence. The novel's social implications are true and unpretentious. It is written with a brilliant manipulation of scenes and incidents. Marquand's literary workmanship and intelligence are unobtrusively evident everywhere. The prose seems informal but is actually artful in the best sense. The satire and irony are never heavy-handed but are blended slyly with wit and a nice touch of sentiment. Although somewhat repetitious, the novel nevertheless maintains the reader's interest.

The nuances of life in and around Boston are intricately detailed and often are as amusing as scenes from Jane Austen or Anthony Trollope. Nobody ever does anything about anything at Wickford Point. Jim Calder understands the chaotic Brill clan, but he still loves one of its members, the wicked and delightful Bella. This conflict between mind and emotion provides a humorous and touching struggle within the hero-narrator. The narration usually avoids the archness that often distorts satire. This is because Marquand *cares* about the people he chooses to portray.

Wickford Point does not have the unity of *The Late George Apley* (1937), but its portrayal of clan snobbishness is even more pointed than in the earlier novel. The true worth of *Wickford Point* lies below its satiric surface. It is a novel of importance because its underlying emphasis is upon the motivations of human behavior.

Marquand's technique here is marked by the use of flashbacks to make the present meaningful and to explain the motives of his characters. His touch is deft, his theme well-handled, his story interesting, and his irony amusing. The impact of the outside world upon the little, complacent society of Wickford Point is admirably demonstrated.

WIELAND
Or, The Transformation, an American Tale

Type of work: Novel
Author: Charles Brockden Brown (1771–1810)
Type of plot: Mystery romance
Time of plot: Eighteenth century
Locale: Pennsylvania
First published: 1798

> *Principal characters:*
> WIELAND, a madman
> CLARA, his sister
> CATHARINE PLEYEL, his wife
> HENRY PLEYEL, Catherine's brother
> CARWIN, a ventriloquist

The Story:

In a long letter to a friend, Clara Wieland told the story of the tragedy of her family. Her father had been almost a religious fanatic, a strange man who feared some dreadful punishment because he had not answered a call to the mission field. He became more and more depressed and withdrawn until his life ended in a horrible fashion. One night, he visited a temple he had built for solitary meditation. His wife, fearing the appearance and manner of her husband, followed him and saw his clothing suddenly go up in flames. She found him insensible, muttering incoherently about having been struck down by an unseen hand. Soon afterward, he died. Within a few months, the mother followed her husband to the grave, leaving Clara and her brother orphaned but wealthy. They were happily reared by an aunt who gave them love and comfort and a good education.

One of their companions was Catharine Pleyel, a rich and beautiful girl with whom Wieland fell in love when he reached young manhood. Catharine returned his love, and when Wieland came of age they were married. Wieland took possession of the family house and half of the fortune, Clara the other half of their inheritance. Since she and Catharine and Wieland were beloved friends as well as relatives, Clara took a house only a short distance from her brother and sister-in-law. The three spent much time together. Clara and Catharine were frank and cheerful, but Wieland was more somber and thoughtful in disposition. He was, however, always considerate of their happiness and nobly devoted his life to it. His melancholy was not morbid, only sober. The temple in which their father had met his strange fate was used by the three as a setting for long and delightful conversations, although Wieland's talk dwelt too often on death to suit Clara and Catharine.

Their circle was soon augmented by the addition of Catharine's beloved brother Henry, who had been for some time in Europe. His boisterous mirth enlivened the little group. Henry and Wieland found one great difference in their beliefs: Wieland built his life on religious necessity; Henry, on intellectual liberty. Their fondness for each other, however, allowed them to differ without altering their mutual affection.

Wieland's family was enlarged during the next six years by four natural children and a foster child whose mother had died while under his aunt's protection. About that time, another strange occurrence took place in the Wieland family. One day, Wieland went to the temple to pick up a letter which would settle a minor dispute. Before he reached the temple, he was stopped by his wife's voice, telling him that danger lay in his path. Returning quickly to the house, he found his wife there. Clara and Henry verified her statement that she had not left the room. Although the others soon dismissed the incident from their minds, it preyed on the already melancholy Wieland to the exclusion of everything else.

Not long after that incident, Henry Pleyel learned that Wieland had inherited some large estates in Europe, and he wanted Wieland to go abroad to claim them. Henry would accompany his friend because he had left his heart with a baroness, now widowed and willing to accept his suit. When Wieland seemed reluctant to make the journey, Henry, in an effort to persuade him, asked him one night to go for a walk. Their walk was interrupted by a voice telling them that the baroness was dead. Again, the voice was Catharine's, but again Catharine had been nowhere near the men when the voice was heard. More frightening was the verification of the baroness' death given to Henry a few days later. Some dread supernatural power, Wieland believed, had spoken to them.

Shortly after these two mysterious occurrences, a stranger appeared in the neighborhood. He was dressed like a clown or a pathetically humorous beggar, but his voice had the musical ring of an actor. Clara, who saw him before the others knew of his existence, was strangely drawn to him.

She forgot him, however, because of another frightening incident. One night, alone in her room, she heard two voices in the closet planning her murder. One voice advised shooting; the other, choking. She fled to her brother's house and fell at his door in a faint. Wieland and Henry came to her rescue in answer to a summons from an unknown source, a voice calling that a loved one lay dying at the door.

Henry insisted upon occupying a vacant apartment in Clara's home in order to protect her from her unknown enemies. Clara was beset with nightmares, the mystifying voice having warned her of danger from her brother. Soon after the affair of the voices in the closet, she met the stranger she had seen and to whom she had been unaccountably drawn. His name was Carwin, and he had known Henry in Spain. His intelligent conversation and his wide travels made him welcome in the little group, and he joined them frequently. When they discussed the supernatural voices they had all heard, Carwin dismissed the voices as fancy or pranks.

Clara, beginning to feel herself in love with Henry, believed that he returned her love but feared to tell her of it because he did not know her feelings. Then he confronted her with the accusation that she was a wanton. He said that he had heard her and a lover, Carwin, talking and that her words made her a sinner and a fallen woman. Henry had also learned that Carwin was wanted for murder, and he heaped abuses on the innocent Clara for consorting with such a man. All her pleas of innocence went unheeded, and she was thrown into despair. Thinking that Carwin had set out to ruin her, she was enraged when she received a note in which he asked for an interview. Reluctantly, she agreed to meet him and hear his story. He was to come to her home, but when she arrived there she found only a note warning her of a horrible sight awaiting her. In her room, she found Catharine on the bed. She had been murdered.

Wieland entered her room, his manner strange and exulted, and begged that this sacrifice not be demanded of him. Before he reached Clara, however, others came into the house. From them she learned that her brother's children were also dead, killed by the same hand that had murdered their mother.

Clara was taken by friends to the city. There, after a time, she learned the tragic story. The murderer had been Wieland, his hand guided, he said, by a voice from heaven demanding that he sacrifice his loved ones to God; but he felt no guilt, only glory at having been the instrument through whom God worked. Twice Wieland had broken out of prison, his belief being that he must also kill Clara and Henry. Clara suspected that Carwin had somehow influenced Wieland to kill.

Carwin went to Clara and protested his innocence of the crime. He admitted that his had been the other voices heard. He was a ventriloquist who had used his tricks either to play some prank or to escape detection while prying into other people's affairs. Clara refused to believe him. While they talked, Wieland entered the apartment. Prepared to kill Clara, he had again broken out of prison to fulfill his bloody destiny. This time Carwin, using his skill to save Clara, called out to Wieland that no voice had told him to kill, that only his own lunatic brain had guided him. At his words, Wieland regained his sanity and seemed to understand for the first time what he had done. Picking up a knife, he plunged it into his throat.

Three years passed before Clara knew peace. Her uncle cared for her and arranged a meeting between Carwin and Henry so that Carwin might confess his part in the defamation of Clara's character. Carwin had been jealous and thus tried to destroy Henry's affection for her. Henry also learned that his baroness was not dead; the report had been another of Carwin's tricks. Henry married the baroness and settled down near Boston. Carwin, not a murderer but the victim of a plot, escaped to the country and became a farmer. Henry's wife died soon after their marriage, and he and Clara renewed their love. Their later happiness was marred only by sad and tragic memories.

Critical Evaluation:

Charles Brockden Brown has been called the Father of American Literature, and rightly so, for his was the first truly native American literature in the field of the novel. Undoubtedly the best of Brown's works is *Wieland*, a romantic tragedy in a genre of horror and remorse, which Poe was to cultivate later. Brown was a careless writer, never revising, but submitting manuscripts with mechanical errors as well as cumbersome sentence structures. In spite of his faults, the macabre effects of his writing can still stir readers curious enough to read the now old-fashioned romances of this forerunner of Poe and Melville.

Although badly flawed in plot and characterization, *Wieland* deserves a higher place in American literature than that accorded a historical curiosity. In this novel, Brown initiates the characteristically American use of the fantastic and grotesque Gothic tale to explore the moral and psychological dimensions of experience. Poe, Hawthorne, and Melville would refine the Gothic mode into the American romance, but it was Brown and *Wieland* that first introduced the genre into American literature and demonstrated its possibilities.

Like most romancers, Brown had little interest in such concrete details as time and place. His locales are generalized, and he offers little in the way of observation about manners in Pennsylvania society of the eighteenth century. Rather, his characters occupy a landscape of the mind, more symbolic than real, in which their actions dramatize basic human hopes, fears, and passions rather than realistic situations. The Gothic horrors that abound in *Wieland* are not introduced for the sake of sensationalism. They represent symbolic dramatizations of aspects of the human condition and the American experience.

The two most memorable characters to emerge in *Wieland* are the religious fanatic, Wieland, and the mysterious Carwin. The latter character is only partly responsible for Wieland's dementia. Driven by the madness of a monomaniacal religious obsession to commit unspeakable crimes upon his loved ones, Wieland anticipates the obsessed characters of Poe, Hawthorne, and Melville. Carwin, on the other hand, represents the man whose cold, scientific curiosity impairs his humanity, so he experiments with human subjects without regard for the consequences. Frequently in later writers, these two figures merge into one to create such monomaniacal seekers after knowledge as Hawthorne's Ethan Brand or Melville's Ahab.

Other writers would take the American romance to greater heights than Brown could achieve, but they would do so within the tradition he established on American soil.

THE WILD PALMS

Type of work: Novel
Author: William Faulkner (1897–1962)
Type of plot: Tragicomedy
Time of plot: 1927 and 1937
Locale: The United States
First published: 1939

> *Principal characters:*
> HARRY WILBOURNE, a twenty-seven-year-old intern
> CHARLOTTE RITTENMEYER, a young married woman
> FRANCIS "RAT" RITTENMEYER, her husband
> THE TALL CONVICT, a man serving a ten-year term for
> train robbery
> THE PALE CONVICT, his work partner in the flood
> THE WOMAN, pregnant and stranded in the flood

Often considered to be an inferior novel even by William Faulkner's better critics, *The Wild Palms* has had a curious history, for it has most often been reprinted as two short novels (*Wild Palms* and *Old Man*), sometimes in the same volume and even more often as two separate books. That it has been so casually treated is unfortunate, because structurally it is perhaps the most subtle and demanding of Faulkner's novels, and it is also his best approach to the comically absurd world of male-female relationships.

Most of the misunderstanding of the novel grows from its unique structure. The two short novels, either of which appears to be able to stand alone, are presented in alternating chapters in the novel. Their plots never cross or relate directly to each other; but they are so deeply involved in theme and symbolic and imagistic texture that apart each seems almost a thematic contradiction of the other. Together, however, they form an organic unit in which contrasts form parallels and contradiction becomes paradox. The novel demands of its readers an imaginative commitment beyond that of a more conventionally constructed novel, for its paradox, of both meaning and structure, must be solved by the reader willing to read the book with the attention to rhythm and form that he would normally give to a piece of music and the attention to images and words that he would normally give to a poem.

The pattern of events of the two parts of the novel are relatively simple. "Wild Palms" takes place in 1937, in the heart of the Depression, and is the love story of Harry Wilbourne and Charlotte Rittenmeyer. Charlotte leaves her husband for Harry who, not having finished his internship, is incapable of gaining any steady work. They wander from New Orleans to Chicago to Wisconsin and even to a remote mining camp in Utah until Charlotte becomes accidentally pregnant; their journeys, too, have carried them deeper into squalor and their love from romance into the physically sordid. Urged by Charlotte, Harry performs an unsuccessful abortion which results in her death; but in prison, he refuses suicide, choosing grief to nothing.

The events in "Old Man" take place ten years earlier during the great Mississippi River flood of 1927, and they compose the chronicle of a comic hero in a physical world gone quite as mad as the social world of the Depression in "Wild Palms." A young convict is sent out onto the flooded Mississippi in a skiff with another convict to rescue a woman stranded in a tree and a man on a cotton house. He loses the other convict, rescues the woman who proves to be very pregnant, and is carried downstream by a wild flood. Battered by gigantic waves, he is offered three temptations for escape; but after a time killing alligators with a group of Cajuns, he returns the boat and the woman with her safely born child and is given an additional ten-year sentence for attempted escape.

Neither of these brief descriptions even approaches the complexities of the two stories, separately or as a unit, for theirs is an artistic value of reflection and texture in which event is but an item of form, and form a vehicle for imaginative idea. "Wild Palms" is a tragicomedy, a parody of Hemingway's romantic "anti-Romantic" ideas (particularly those in *A Farewell to Arms*), a parable of a fallen world in which agape is lost to an eros made perverse by the forces of a society built on money and sexually inverted by the "freeing" of woman. "Old Man" is also a bitter comedy, but one in which the comic hero, God's fool, bears the burdens of the world and finds his victory in seeming defeat, his reward in the last ironic slap of "risible nature." "Wild Palms" resolves itself in onanistic frustration, and "Old Man" discovers the rewards of struggle in this life to be only the peace of being allowed out of life. The novel is a product, then, of the same era that produced *The Waste Land*, but its Chaucerian comic sense makes it more than an existential lament for a meaningless world, transforms its madness and ugliness into a Christian comedy of human folly which shows man at his worst, only to remind him of the necessity of striving toward his best. The novel is not a moral allegory, although "Old Man" often seems to be, but a parable of the vanity of human wishes and the follies of this earth.

The primary themes of both parts of the novel are those of human folly: the tragic consequences of romantic but earthly ideals and the failure of sex as the essential element of human fulfillment. Both Harry and the convict are victims of romantic ideals: the convict was sent to prison for an attempted train robbery inspired by reading dime novels and intended to impress a girl; Harry was betrayed into his affair with Charlotte by his ascetic student's life and his belief (fostered by Charlotte) in physical love and the value of physical permanence in a spiritless world.

If the heroes of both stories are innocents in a confusing world, women offer them little aid or solace. The women in the novel represent the two emasculating extremes of the female character, isolated with the simplicity of parable. Charlotte is the defeminized female artist of masculine mind and manner, the aggressor in the sexual act and in life; the woman in "Old Man" is simple nearly to mindlessness, for she is the mother, the primitive force of life to be borne by man as the weight of his duty. Charlotte is destroyed by the sex which she attempts to use as a man uses his, but cannot because she is what she wishes to deny—a woman, a vessel, and bearer of man's seed and progeny. The woman in "Old Man" realizes and fulfills her proper role as mother, but in this comic world fails as a romantic sexual figure even as she succeeds; she lives on but without her man, the convict who had complained that she, of all the women in the world, is the one with whom he has been thrown by chance.

The men are innocents; the women are failures with them. "Old Man" ends with the convict's brief, violent summation of his feelings about the world of sex and women. "Wild Palms" ends with Harry's refusal to kill himself only because in his grief he can find the onanistic solace of the memory of Charlotte's flesh. Both stories end in hollowness and ugliness. Each, taken by itself, presents a vision of frustration and despair, yet the novel itself has no such effect.

The two stories present opposing accounts of the nature of failure and comic success which, if seen in the perspective that their juxtaposition in an organic whole imposes upon the reader (a perspective similar to that formed by the shifting points of view in *As I Lay Dying*), cancel each other. This is a vision which causes the reader to apply his own norms to the events and to see the exact nature of the folly of both extremes, of sex and sexlessness, of romantic and anti-Romantic ideals shattered. The world of *The Wild Palms* is a mad world, but its madness casts bright light upon our own world, mad in its own right but alive with balances which may be found with comic and artistic perspective.

Faulkner does not explicitly offer his reader the moral of his novel, but it is there to be drawn. That the reader can find it by an imaginative and creative act of his own synthesis is the true power of the novel. When man can laugh for joy even as he weeps in sorrow, he can survive and prevail. Such was the intention of this novel which, for all of its difficulty, is an extraordinary example of the variety of Faulkner's ability, of his artistic genius.

WINESBURG, OHIO
A Group of Tales of Ohio Small Town Life

Type of work: Novel
Author: Sherwood Anderson (1876–1941)
Type of plot: Psychological realism
Time of plot: Late nineteenth century
Locale: Winesburg, Ohio
First published: 1919

Principal characters:

GEORGE WILLARD, a young reporter
ELIZABETH WILLARD, his mother
DR. REEFY, Elizabeth's confidant
HELEN WHITE, George's friend
KATE SWIFT, George's former teacher
THE REVEREND CURTIS HARTMAN, Kate's unknown
   admirer
WING BIDDLEBAUM, a berry picker

The Story:

Young George Willard was the only child of Elizabeth and Tom Willard. His father, a dull, conventional, insensitive man, owned the local hotel. His mother had once been a popular young belle. She had never loved Tom Willard, but the young married women of the town seemed to her so happy, so satisfied, that she had married him in the hope that marriage would somehow change her own life for the better. Before long, she realized that she was caught in the dull life of Winesburg, her dreams turned to drab realities by her life with Tom Willard.

The only person who ever understood her was Dr. Reefy. Only in his small, untidy office did she feel free; only there did she achieve some measure of self-expression. Their relationship, doomed from the start, was nevertheless beautiful, a meeting of two lonely and sensitive people. Dr. Reefy, too, had his sorrows. Once, years ago, a young girl, pregnant and unmarried, had come to his office, and shortly afterward, he had married her. The following spring she had died, and from then on, Dr. Reefy went around making little paper pills and stuffing his pockets with them. On the pieces of paper he had scribbled his thoughts about the beauty and strangeness of life.

Through her son George, Elizabeth Willard hoped to express herself, for she saw in him the fulfillment of her own hopes and desires. More than anything, she feared that George would settle down in Winesburg. When she learned that he wanted to be a writer, she was glad. Unknown to her husband, she had put away money enough to give her son a start; but before she could realize her ambition, Elizabeth Willard died. Lying on her bed, she did not seem dead to either George or Dr. Reefy. To both, she was extremely beautiful. To George, she did not seem like his mother at all. To Dr. Reefy, she was the woman he had loved, now the symbol of another lost illusion.

Many people of the town sought out George Willard; they told him of their lives, of their compulsions, of their failures. Old Wing Biddlebaum, the berry picker, had been a schoolteacher years before. He had loved the boys in his charge, and he had been, in fact, one of those few teachers who understood young people. One of his pupils, however, having conceived a strong affection for his teacher, had accused him of homosexuality. Wing Biddlebaum, though innocent, was driven out of town. In Winesburg, he became the best berry picker in the region, but always the same hands that earned his livelihood were a source of wonder and fear to him. When George Willard encountered him in the berry field, Wing's hands went forward as if to caress the youth; but a wave of horror swept over him, and he hurriedly thrust them into his pockets. To George, also, Wing's hands seemed odd, mysterious.

Kate Swift, once George's teacher, saw in him a future writer. She tried to tell him what writing was, what it meant. George did not understand exactly, but he understood that Kate was speaking, not as his teacher, but as a woman. One night, in her house, she embraced him, for George was now a young man with whom she had fallen in love. On another night, when all of Winesburg seemed asleep, she went to his room, but just as she was on the point of yielding to him, she struck him and ran away, leaving George lonely and frustrated.

Kate lived across the street from the Presbyterian church. The pastor, Reverend Curtis Hartman, accidentally had learned that he could see into Kate's room from his study in the bell tower of the church. Night after night, he looked through the window at Kate in her bed. He wanted at first to prove his faith, but his flesh was weak. One night, the same night Kate had fled from George Willard, he saw her come into her room. He watched her. Naked, she threw herself on the bed and furiously pounded the pillows. Then she arose, knelt, and began to pray. With a cry, the minister got up from his chair, swept the Bible to the floor, smashed the glass in the window, and dashed out into the darkness. Running to the newspaper office, he burst in upon George. Wild-eyed, his fist dripping blood, he told the astonished young man that God had appeared to him in the person of a naked woman, that Kate Swift was the instrument of the Almighty, and that he was saved.

Besides Kate Swift, there were other women in George's life. There was Helen White, the banker's daughter. One night, George and Helen went out together. At first, they laughed and kissed, but then a strange new maturity overcame them and kept them apart. Louise Trunnion, a farm girl, wrote to George, saying that she was his if he wanted her. After dark, he went out to the farm, and they went for a walk. There, in a berry field, George Willard enjoyed the love that Helen White had refused him.

Like Louise Trunnion, Louise Bentley also wanted love. Before going to live in Winesburg, Louise had lived on a farm, forgotten and unloved by a greedy, fanatical father who had desired a son instead of a daughter. In Winesburg, she lived with the Hardy family while she went to school. She was a good student, praised by her teachers, but she was resented by the two Hardy girls, who believed that Louise was always showing off. More than ever, she wanted someone to love. One day, she sent young John Hardy a note, and a few weeks later, she gave herself to him. When it became clear that she was pregnant, Louise and John were married.

John reproached her for cruelty toward her son David. She would not nurse her child, and for long periods of time, she would ignore him. Since she had never really loved her husband, nor had he loved her, the marriage was not a happy one. At last, she and John separated, and shortly afterward, her father took young David to live with him on the farm.

Old Jesse Bentley was convinced that God had manifested himself in his grandchild, that the young David, like the biblical hero, would be a savior, the conqueror of the Philistines who owned the land Jesse Bentley wanted for himself. One day the old man took the boy into the fields with him. Young David had brought along a little lamb, and the grandfather prepared to offer the animal as a sacrifice to the Almighty. The youngster, terrified, struck his grandfather and ran away, never to return to Winesburg.

The time came when George Willard had to choose between staying in Winesburg and starting out on his career as a writer. Shortly after his mother's death, George got up early one morning and walked to the railroad station. There, with the postmistress' expression of good luck in his ears, he boarded the train and left Winesburg behind him.

Critical Evaluation:

Winesburg, Ohio has the stature of a modern classic. It is at once beautiful and tragic, realistic and poetic. Without being a novel in the usual sense of the word, the connected stories have the full range and emotional impact of a novel. In simple, though highly skillful and powerful language, Sherwood Anderson has told the story of a small town and the lonely, frustrated people who live there. Though regional in its setting and characters, the book is also intensely American. No one since Anderson has succeeded in interpreting the inner compulsions and loneliness of the national psyche with the same degree of accuracy and emotional impact.

Using young George Willard both as protagonist and observer, Anderson creates his probing psychological portrait of small-town America. Though his characters outwardly seem dull and commonplace, Anderson is acutely tuned to the tensions between their psychological and emotional needs and the restrictions placed upon their lives by the small-town atmosphere of Winesburg. Though not methodically psychoanalytical, Anderson's work probes deeply into the psychic lives of these "grotesques" to discover the emotional wounds which have been inflicted by the Puritan attitudes of the midwestern village. Though Anderson may not have been directly influenced by Freud or Jung, his interests clearly parallel those of the depth psychology which became popular with American intellectuals during the first quarter of the century. In this respect, Anderson can legitimately be called America's first psychological novelist.

Anderson believed the traditional forms of the novel were too restrictive and formal to adapt well to his American subject matter, so *Winesburg, Ohio* represents in part an experiment in form. Rather than unifying his work through a plot in the usual sense, Anderson uses patterns of imagery, tone, character, and theme to achieve a sense of wholeness. It is, however, George Willard's narrative voice and presence as either observer or protagonist in the stories which ultimately unify them. As a small-town reporter, Willard can credibly serve as a confidant for his townspeople. Also, he is a kind of professional observer recording the surface lives of his people for the newspaper. At the same time, readers must see him as the budding artist who is interested in discovering the deeper and more meaningful truths of peoples' lives than those seen at the surface. Eventually, George must make his own choice as to which of these roles he will elect, and his function as the central consciousness of the book is vital to its aesthetic success.

Winesburg, Ohio also follows the classic pattern of the *Bildungsroman* or "portrait of the artist as a young man" as it traces George Willard's growth from adolescence to maturity. Central to this aspect of the novel is George's relationship with his mother whose death eventually frees him to escape from Winesburg. Mrs. Willard is the first person to see, in George's ambition to write, a potential release for her own inarticulate suffering, so she encourages his ambition partly to fill her own needs. As George comes into contact with other characters in the novel, they too see in him a way to make their voices heard, so they tell him their stories so he might write them down.

Part of George's growing maturity results from the understanding he finds as a result of his willingness to listen, but this passive development is paralleled by more overt experience. In particular, sexual initiation is an essential part of George's learning and growth, as is his coming to understand something of the nature of love in its various aspects. Through this combination of active and passive experiences, George eventually comes to the realization that isolation is an essential part of the human condition. People, George realizes in the sketch called "Sophistication," must learn to live with the limited relationships possible in a world which must isolate them, and they must develop the strength not to be destroyed by loneliness. This knowledge gives George the maturity he needs to break with Winesburg and face the future as an adult and an artist. In "Departure," the final sketch, he goes toward that responsibility.

Anderson's introduction to *Winesburg, Ohio*, called "The Book of the Grotesque," suggests yet another way in which this work is unified. Conceived as a whole within which the sketches and stories are pulled together by the idea of the grotesques, the work can be seen as a group of stories connected by a central thematic concern. Anderson defined his grotesques as people who had seized upon some aspect of the truth which so dominates their lives as to distort their entire beings. This definition, however, only loosely fits the characters actually encountered in the novel. Rather, the failure in some way of emotional life seems to account for the twists of character which lead Winesburg's citizens to their universal sense of failure and isolation. In spite of apparent differences, virtually all of Anderson's figures suffer from a deep sense of failure—frequently of material failure as well as emotional—and from a frustrating inability to express their pain and rage in a meaningful way. Essentially, they are emotional cripples who must turn to George Willard in search of a voice to articulate their suffering.

Paralleling that level of *Winesburg, Ohio* which is concerned with individual psychology is a general reaction against the American small town and its atmosphere of Puritanical repression. Although Anderson is not without some nostalgia for the village life which was already passing from the American scene when *Winesburg, Ohio* was published in 1919, he does not allow his sentiment to stand in the way of a powerful condemnation of the cultural and spiritual sterility characteristic of the American village scene. While other writers were mourning the passing of the nation's innocent youth by sentimentalizing the small agrarian community, Anderson reveals its dark underside of destroyed lives, thwarted ambitions, and crippled souls—all of which resulted in part from the repressive atmosphere of towns like Winesburg. Thus, even while *Winesburg, Ohio* marks the end of an era of agrarian order in America, it raises the very real possibility that an innocent past was less of a paradise than the sentimentalist would have one believe.

Studies of the modern American novel tradition often begin with *Winesburg, Ohio* which, by its pioneering of new techniques, introduction of new subject matter, and development of new attitudes and ideas as well as a new frankness, changed the course of American literary history. In addition, Anderson's generous help to such younger writers as Hemingway and Faulkner, who would continue to shape the course of the American novel, justifies his position as the father of the modern American novel.

THE WINGS OF THE DOVE

Type of work: Novel
Author: Henry James (1843–1916)
Type of plot: Psychological realism
Time of plot: c. 1900
Locale: London and Venice
First published: 1902

Principal characters:
MILLY THEALE, a rich American girl
MRS. SUSAN SHEPHERD STRINGHAM, an American friend
of Milly Theale
MRS. LOWDER, an English friend of Mrs. Stringham
KATE CROY, Mrs. Lowder's niece
MERTON DENSHER, Kate Croy's fiancé
LORD MARK, another suitor for Kate Croy's hand
SIR LUKE STRETT, an eminent British doctor

The Story:

Kate Croy was dependent upon her aunt, Mrs. Lowder, because Kate's own father was a ne'er-do-well. Mrs. Lowder had great plans for her niece, and she encouraged Lord Mark as a suitor for Kate's hand. Kate's own mind was set on a young reporter, Merton Densher, who worked on one of the London papers. While Mrs. Lowder liked Densher, and even invited him to her home, she did not want him to marry her niece, for he had no apparent prospects of money or a place in society. Mrs. Lowder breathed easier when she learned that the young man was being sent by his newspaper to America, to write a series of articles on life in the United States.

While he was in New York, Densher made the acquaintance of a pretty young American, Milly Theale, who had recently inherited a large fortune through the death of her parents.

A few weeks later, Milly Theale asked a Boston friend, Mrs. Susan Stringham, widow and a writer, to go with her to Europe. Within a matter of days, they had taken passage on a liner and soon arrived in Italy. They traveled up the Italian peninsula and into Switzerland. Restless, Milly soon decided that she would like to go to London.

When they had arrived in England, Mrs. Stringham sent word of her arrival to Mrs. Lowder, the one real acquaintance she had in that country from her school days many years before. Mrs. Stringham and Milly Theale immediately

---

became familiar callers at Mrs. Lowder's home. Because of her beauty, money, and attractive personality, Milly was a great success. Lord Mark became infatuated with her. Milly and Kate Croy became fast friends.

Aware that she was ill, Milly went to see Sir Luke Strett, an eminent surgeon who informed her that there was nothing surgery or medicine could do to save her, and he advised her to make the best of the time she had left. Although Kate Croy, Mrs. Lowder, and Mrs. Stringham knew that she had only a few months to live, Milly requested them to keep silent in the matter. Her intention was to enjoy herself as much as possible.

Great friends as Kate Croy and Milly Theale were, they never mentioned their mutual acquaintance, Merton Densher. One day, while walking in the National Art Galleries, Milly saw him and her friend Kate together. Kate and Densher enlisted the aid of Mrs. Stringham and Milly to further their courtship. Milly, herself a little in love with Densher, was only too glad to help him be near Kate.

Soon Kate hit upon a way to bring her affair with Densher to a happy conclusion. She told the young man to marry Milly, thus making her happy for the few remaining months of her life. Kate had seen clearly that Milly was falling in love with Densher. Kate realized that Milly's fortune would be left after her death to Densher, who would then be free to marry Kate and would have sufficient money to allay any objections Mrs. Lowder might have to the match. Kate was sure that Mrs. Lowder or Mrs. Stringham would not try to prevent a marriage between Milly and Merton Densher, for she knew that the two older women loved Milly enough to go to any lengths to make her final days happy.

The four women, accompanied by Densher, went to Venice for the winter months, Milly on the advice of Sir Luke Strett. Densher made little headway with his plan to marry Milly until Mrs. Lowder and Kate returned to England for a few weeks. Before they left, Kate made Densher promise that he would do as she had planned. Densher's conscience rebelled at the duplicity of the scheme, and he was not sure that when the plan was worked out to its finish Kate would still want him. As a sign that there was mutual trust between them, he asked Kate to go to his rooms with him. She did so the day before she left Venice, leaving her lover honor-bound to try to marry another woman.

One day, as Densher approached the house Milly had taken for the winter, he saw Lord Mark leaving. He soon found out from Mrs. Stringham that Lord Mark had proposed to Milly and had been rejected because the girl had detected unwanted sympathy in his proposal and had suspected that he was after her money rather than her love. Densher believed, rightly, that Lord Mark's rejection gave him some reason to be hopeful. He informed Milly that she was the only reason he was neglecting his work. She was highly pleased and hoped that he would propose.

Lord Mark disappeared from Venice for almost a month. Then Densher discovered him in a café, shortly after Densher had been refused admittance to Milly's house. Immediately, Densher knew what had happened. Lord Mark had, in some way, discovered the engagement between Densher and Kate and had informed Milly. Densher attempted to hit upon some plan to right the situation. Three days later, Mrs. Stringham came to him and told him what had happened. It was as he had guessed. What he had not guessed, however, was that Milly had ceased to take any interest in living and was refusing to eat or talk to anyone. Mrs. Stringham, desperate, had sent for Sir Luke Strett.

Densher returned to London but did not, at first, go to see Kate. He could not face her after the turn which their plans had taken, and he could not bear the idea of having hurt Milly as he had done. Finally, on Christmas Day, he had a premonition. He hurried to Sir Luke Strett's residence. There he found Mrs. Lowder, who told him that she had received a telegram the previous day telling of Milly's death. A few days later, a letter arrived from Venice. Without opening it, Densher knew what the message was, for it was addressed in Milly's handwriting. He went immediately to see Kate, who also guessed that it was a letter informing Densher that she had left him part of her fortune so that he and Kate might marry. Neither of them dared to open the letter because they were ashamed of their conduct toward Milly. They burned the letter in the fireplace.

Within ten days, another letter came from a New York law firm. Densher did not open it but sent it with a short note to Kate. She came to his rooms with it. She wanted to know why he had sent it on to her. He replied that it was up to her to answer whether he should take the money that was offered by it, for he could never marry her with the money Milly had left him.

Kate refused to answer him or to open the letter, lest the large amount of the fortune tempt either of them into accepting it. Finally Densher said he wanted to marry her, but only as they had been before the arrival of Milly Theale. Kate left, after reminding him that they could never be the same, that such was impossible, for the events pertaining to Milly Theale had embedded themselves into their souls.

Critical Evaluation:

Henry James came of a family whose members considered themselves viewers of, rather than participants in, society. Their wealth enabled them to remove themselves from the common rout, and Henry and his father both suffered from physical disabilities which to some degree enforced this detachment, which was emotional as well as physical. The family traveled continually during the author's youth; as an adult he lived chiefly in Europe, though nevertheless maintaining close relations with his parents and siblings. The ties of blood, for him, took the place of national feeling. He considered himself a citizen of the world and took of the life of his countrymen the same objective, albeit curious and sympathetic, view as of society in general. Coming as he did of parents whose chief business in life was the cultivation of their own and their children's sensibilities and sharing the family's strong if eccentric religious bent, he took it as his artistic mission to examine the condition of human society at large as that condition manifested itself in the most subdued and civilized of human milieus.

The specifics of the plot of *The Wings of the Dove* were suggested to the author by the premature death of his cousin Mary Temple, called Minny. The girl had charm, beauty, money, and love. She had, as it is said, everything for which to live and grimly resisted her fate to the end. After her death from tuberculosis in 1870, James was, as he later wrote, "haunted" by the tragedy of her situation. Two of his most appealing heroines take their essential lines from her: Isabel Archer of *The Portrait of a Lady*, and Milly Theale.

James wrote three of his best novels in quick succession shortly after 1900. As the new century began, he produced *The Ambassadors* (1902), *The Wings of the Dove* (1903), and *The Golden Bowl* (1904). These three novels represent the highest expression of the ideas of art and life gleaned over nearly six decades of observation and analysis of European and American mores. According to critic Robert E. Spiller, the three themes that impel these novels, as well as most of his previous works, are: "the contrast of American sincerity and crudity with European deceit and culture, the conflicting realities of life and art, and the substitution of psychological for ethical measurements of good and evil." *The Wings of the Dove* treats all three.

The first is most neatly illustrated by the counterpoise of Mrs. Maud Lowder and Mrs. Stringham. Aunt Maud's wardship of Kate has a monetary quality made explicit in her remark to Merton Densher: "'I've been saving [Kate's presence] up and letting it, as you say of investments, appreciate, and you may judge whether, now it has begun to pay so, I'm likely to consent to treat for it with any but a high bidder.'" Mrs. Stringham's attachment to Milly, on the other hand, takes for her the shape of a holy mission to shepherd through the hazards of the world a being so exalted that the heroines of literature pale beside her. Her view of Milly is essentially romantic; she calls her "an angel," "a princess in a palace," and ironically "the real thing"; ironically, because *real* is exactly what Milly is not for her companion, any more than Kate is at bottom anything more than a marketable commodity to Mrs. Lowder. The difference in the characters of Kate and Milly enlarges on this theme; Kate accepts that definition of herself, using it to her own purpose, but succumbs at the last to its corrupting influence in using Densher as just such another counter, thus losing both love and honor. Milly, resisting the dehumanizing effects of both hero-worship and pity, works her own salvation as well as Densher's.

The life that Milly makes for herself, knowing her days are numbered and knowing, almost, their number, comprehends abysses both sublime and terrible. She recognizes, from the first, the effects of her money on the company into which she is betrayed by her shepherd, so graphically if unintentionally particularized for her by kind, corrupt Lord Mark, who brings her before the Bronzino portrait; so like her but, most poignantly to Milly's sense, "dead, dead, dead." She has, even before she hears her sentence pronounced by Sir Luke Strett, a trick of deferring judgment, of not permitting the baseness of others to circumscribe or debase her experience. Afterward, this tendency flowers into a kind of divine duplicity, a double reverse which consists of her keeping from everyone but Mrs. Stringham the fact that she is dying. Readers are to keep in mind that after a certain point in the story, she must inevitably see everyone else as acting in the light of this knowledge of her limited future. Yet she makes no move to defend herself; she simply, profoundly, trusts. In short, she offers herself as a dove for sacrifice, a gesture that parallels the willingness of others to sacrifice her to their own designs. All her putative friends deceive themselves in regard to her, acting for their own good but in the name of her happiness; but Milly does not deceive herself. Her surrender is deliberate. In this she is a supreme artist; she makes of her life an instrument for Mrs. Stringham's gratification, for Kate's enlightenment, and for Densher's redemption, a creative act of the highest kind.

All this great work, as well as diverse strokes of wickedness, is done in a few murmured words, a nod or a look, an invitation accepted or declined, gestures always within the bounds of propriety. Such an exposition of the instincts of the jungle expressed in the manners of the salon generates, in the end, more force than many a less subdued narrative. For the reader is treated not only to the powerful spectacle of Kate Croy prowling her situation with the disciplined rage of a caged tigress but also to the glorious vision of Milly Theale, triumphant over betrayal and death, fulfilling her extraordinary nature to its highest potential.

WISE BLOOD

Type of work: Novel
Author: Flannery O'Connor (1925–1964)
Type of plot: Gothic
Time of plot: Mid-twentieth century
Locale: Taulkinham, a Southern city
First published: 1952

        Principal characters:
        HAZEL MOTES, a twenty-two-year-old preacher
        ENOCH EMERY, an eighteen-year-old zoo attendant
        ASA HAWKS, an itinerant blind preacher and beggar
        SABBATH LILY HAWKS, his daughter
        HOOVER SHOATS (also ONNIE JAY HOLY), a religious
          racketeer
        MRS. FLOOD, Hazel's landlady in the city
        MRS. LEORA WATTS, a prostitute

The directions for reading this novel are given in the short, dryly ironic note Flannery O'Connor prefaced to the second edition. Like the directions for getting places in *Through the Looking-Glass and What Alice Found There*, they warn the reader that he must cope with the opposite to whatever he expects in fiction; what in life may appear tragic is here comical triumph— Hazel Motes's self-blinding—and the hero, like every character in the book, is a most unattractive person.

Where he is not laughable, he is pitiable. The novel is thus a comic and wholly serious presentation of the painful inevitability of becoming a Christian in the absolute sense O'Connor intends, however much readers are offended by the lack of humanity in the characters and their creator. Hazel achieves the integrity and hence the dignity of the human soul by giving up the struggle to escape redemption by Christ, and for most of the time that he wriggles on the hook of his destiny, he looks undignified.

The novel is simply constructed of fourteen chapters, most of them episodes in Hazel Motes's unwilling quest for the true Jesus through an assortment of false prophets. The complexity of the novel comes from the novelist's intention. O'Connor is herself a prophet warning by lurid exempla of the wrath to come. Hazel Motes is surrounded by people who think they act reasonably, especially in allowing a comfortable religious feeling a small part of their existence; operators such as Hoover Shoats and Mrs. Flood do not know that they are swine about to be deluged. They are in hell and do not know it, unlike the damned—Sabbath Lily Hawks—who do know it and do not care. Hazel thinks he has shaken off any fooling about with the religion of his grandfather and mother and is thus clean of hypocrisy; he can sleep nights with a prostitute, Mrs. Leora Watts, and not imperil his soul. He learns better by the end of the novel, and it is, as it must be, an agonizing experience. He has to blind himself with quicklime before he can see clearly his redemption by Christ. The irony of the novel consists in showing that every step Hazel thinks will take him farther from Christ simply brings him closer to his Redeemer.

Such irony would be objectionable if it were possible to treat Hazel Motes as contemptible in his mad goings-on, or, remembering Christian charity, as deserving of sympathy, a welfare check, and a course of analysis. Motes, however, is eventually superior in man's only proper business of holy living and holy dying and a martyr for the reader's edification. One also feels that O'Connor has martyred him in mortification of her own ego. This novel could stand as her New Testament to the necessity of forgetting self in the service of God, even to mutilation if that is necessary, just as her second novel, *The Violent Bear It Away*, seems to recover for her the meaning of the Old Testament.

Hazel Motes is either repulsively or ludicrously grotesque from his first entrance in the train on his way to the city; he has just been discharged from Army service at the age of twenty-two and has kept himself clean all that time; he returns to Eastrod, Tennessee, only to find that dwindling hamlet vanished. Now he is free of his Christian past and proceeds to the city to sin, which he accomplishes with Mrs. Watts. He buys a car as well and thus joins the gallery of O'Connor's characters for whom the city and the automobile are symbols of corruption. In the third chapter, he meets the false prophets: Asa Hawks, who says he has blinded himself for his belief in redemption by Christ, and Enoch Emery, the young man of eighteen, country-bred like Hazel, who lives by the "wise blood" he inherits from his daddy. Thereafter, Hazel becomes more involved with both these prophets of a false way of life and has to shake himself free of each. It is not until four events happen that he is freed from the false trail he is following, summarized in the novel as the "Church of Christ Without Christ" which he preaches before movie houses: he sees that Asa Hawks is not blind; he rejects the false god (a mummified man) that Enoch worships and Sabbath Lily Hawks adopts; he kills the image of himself that Hoover Shoats has hired to preach the false or imitation "Church of Christ Without Christ"; and his car is deliberately wrecked by a policeman. The last two episodes probably repel us more than the fantastic doings of Enoch, Asa, and Lily. Someone should bring the policeman to justice for smashing the boy's car, even if Hazel did not have a driver's license; at the same time, someone should charge Hazel with murder.

Another justice, however, is at work here, the swift and terrible speed of mercy. Hazel Motes has been mercifully delivered by God from his false prophets, and he proceeds to blind himself in accordance with the policeman's dictum that those who have no license need no car: those who have a "mote" in their eye must cast it out; they that have no eyes for the true God need no sight. Hazel spends his last days in the hands of Mrs. Flood, who is indirectly responsible for his murder by two casual policemen, until, having escaped her and life, he is at last composed in death. In the final paragraph of the novel, Mrs. Flood glimpses the vision that his actions are governed by a secret which could be the light of her life. Her tentative achievement of this diminutive revelation could be the meaning of Hazel's life and death.

The possessor of the "wise blood," Enoch Emery, plays a subordinate but integral role in the novel; in the fifth, eighth, and eleventh chapters, his story is told independently and then related to that of Hazel Motes. Although O'Connor began in the third chapter by letting Enoch tell his history to Hazel, in the later chapters she lets Enoch go his own way, guided by the "wise blood" which tells him that Hazel is important to him. This intuition is confirmed when Hazel seeks him out before he begins to preach "The Church of Christ Without Christ," and Enoch shows Hazel the mummified man that fascinates him in the run-down museum attached to the zoo, which places are symbolic of man's animal nature and dead past.

When Enoch hears Hazel preaching, he determines to steal the mummified man and give the figure to Hazel as his new "Christ"; but after doing so, his "wise blood" takes charge again and leads him to seize the gorilla suit of a fake "gorilla" film star, Gonga, and try to make friends in this rig-out. The whole of the twelfth chapter is devoted to this episode which leaves "Gonga" Emery alone and puzzled on the highway: it contains some of the most comic writing of O'Connor, partly verbal, partly comedy of situation, and at the same time profoundly meaningful. This is man as man alone, a "bare, forked animal" thinking he can be a success in life by following his "wise blood." Enoch is thus a more direct contrast to Hazel than Asa Hawks or Hoover Shoats ("Onnie Jay Holy"), who simply use religion to make money and thus confirm Hazel's disgust with institutional or evangelical Christianity. Theirs is a false way to salvation, but Enoch's is equally profitless in his determination to get on in the world at all costs, and his is the more prevalent code.

The many minor characters are not all condemned by O'Connor, as is shown by their treatment of Hazel Motes. Those who cheat him—the car salesman, the hat salesman, Mrs. Flood—are clearly vicious, though the way they gull poor simple Hazel is richly comic. On at least three occasions, however, someone tries to tell Hazel the truth about his Essex car, and he will not listen, leading to its destruction at the hands of the policeman. Swift sketches of the physical appearance and nature of the minor characters, such as the woman at the swimming pool, reveal O'Connor's remarkable gift for caricature.

Striking similes and other tricks of style—elliptical country speech, in which so much is left unsaid, the rapid succession of events in the narrative—carry the story along at a fast pace. The narrative is brief and the meaning clear.

Granted the initial stance of high irony in which everything is at once itself and its opposite, there is no difficulty in realizing that Hazel Motes and O'Connor are preaching "The Church of Christ with Christ."

The writer's gifts amply ensure the reader's understanding of the story's meaning. There remains a final hesitation for those readers whose Christ is a tender and loving spirit. When Hazel's mother reminds him that Christ died to redeem him from sin, he replies that he did not ask Christ to do that. There is no freedom for the individual in this novel because, as O'Connor suggests in her introductory note, man's free will is simply a conflict of many wills or desires in man; this conflict is resolved only when a man abandons his desires and accedes to the will of God and allows it to be imposed on him. This is the "jealous" God of the Old Testament who in the New Testament sent his Son to be crucified for man. One must expect to be equally crucified in his turn, as Hazel Motes is in this novel.

WORLD ENOUGH AND TIME

Type of work: Novel
Author: Robert Penn Warren (1905–   )
Type of plot: Philosophical romance
Time of plot: 1801–1826
Locale: Kentucky
First published: 1950

Principal characters:
   JEREMIAH BEAUMONT, an idealist
   COLONEL CASSIUS FORT, a frontier politician and
      Jeremiah's benefactor
   RACHAEL JORDAN, a woman betrayed by Fort and, later,
      Jeremiah's wife
   WILKIE BARRON, an opportunist
   DR. LEICESTER BURNHAM, Jeremiah's teacher
   LA GRAND' BOSSE, a river pirate

The Story:

Jeremiah Beaumont was born in Kentucky in 1801. His father was Jasper Beaumont, one of the first settlers in Glasgow County, and his mother was the disinherited daughter of a wealthy planter. Jasper Beaumont never prospered as he had hoped, and his unfulfilled ambitions bred in him a strain of awkward moodiness which was reflected in his son.

Jasper died, debt-ridden, when Jeremiah was thirteen. Before that time, the boy had been put to school with Leicester Burnham. Hoping for a better life than his father's, Jeremiah was diligent in his studies. He was also stubbornly independent, for he refused to become his grandfather's heir because the old man insisted that he take his mother's maiden name, Marcher. When he was seventeen, Dr. Burnham introduced him to Colonel Cassius Fort, a famous frontier lawyer and politician who was looking for a young man to train in his law office at Bowling Green. Jeremiah was eager to accept Fort's offer but could not do so because of his ailing mother. Fort said that he was willing to wait for anyone Dr. Burnham recommended so highly.

In the next spring, Mrs. Beaumont died, and Jeremiah went to Bowling Green to study law, not in Fort's office, however, for the lawyer had returned to Congress. Jeremiah's only friend in the town was Wilkie Barron, another law student, from whose mother Jeremiah rented a room. Fort returned from Washington in 1820 and took the young man under his patronage. From him, Jeremiah learned to look on the law not as a collection of dry statutes but

---

as man's agent of truth and justice. Times were hard in Kentucky following the Panic of 1819, and the legislature had passed a law allowing a twelve-month stay of sale for debt. Fort was on the side of the Relief Party, as those who supported the measure were called.

Wilkie Barron first told Jeremiah of a scandal linking Fort's name with that of Rachael Jordan, daughter of a planter who had died heavily in debt. Called in to help settle the estate, Fort was supposed to have seduced the girl and fathered her stillborn child. Grieved by that story of innocence betrayed, Jeremiah decided to have nothing more to do with his benefactor. In a letter he informed Fort, who was away at the time, of his decision. Fort wrote in reply, but before his letter reached Bowling Green, Jeremiah had gone to visit Wilkie's uncle, old Thomas Barron, in Saul County. The Jordan place was only a few miles away from his host's. There he met Rachael Jordan, won her confidence, and, after hearing from her own lips the story of her shame, married her. She accepted him on the condition that he kill Fort.

In the meantime, he had become involved in local politics. Wilkie Barron and Percival Scrogg, fanatic liberal editor of a Frankfort newspaper, arrived to take part in a disputed election. After a riot at the polls, in which he and Wilkie fought side by side, Jeremiah was dismayed to learn that his friend was working for Fort. Wilkie advised him to put aside personal grudges for the public good.

Jeremiah and Rachael Jordan were married in 1822. At the time, Fort was away on private business. Taking over the Jordan plantation, the young husband devoted all his energies to making the place productive. Sometimes he felt that he had his father's score to settle as well as his wife's, that his hard work would vindicate his bankrupt father against men like Fort, to whom wealth and fame came easily. Ambitious for the future and foreseeing expansion of the settlements, he formed a partnership with Josh Parham, a rich landowner, and, with Parham's son, Felix surveyed town sites in the unclaimed western lands. The venture in land speculation fell through, however, when Desha, the Relief candidate, was elected governor in 1824. Parham, an anti-Relief man, swore that he would never spend money opening up land in Kentucky while the Relief Party was in office.

Rachael and Jeremiah were expecting their first child when Fort returned from the East. Rachael, begging her husband to give up his intention of killing Fort, persuaded him that his first duty was to her and the unborn child. A week later, Wilkie arrived at the plantation with a handbill in which Fort, announcing his candidacy for the legislature, disavowed membership in the Relief Party. Urged by Wilkie, Jeremiah also became a candidate for office. The campaign was a bitter one. Unknown to Jeremiah, the Relief Party printed a broadside in which the scandal involving Fort and Rachael was revived. Jeremiah, to his wife's relief, was defeated by Sellars, the candidate he opposed.

Two months later, Rachael had a miscarriage. On the same day, a handbill was mysteriously delivered to the house. Signed by Fort, it refuted the campaign slanders against him and accused Rachael of having her first child by a mulatto slave. That night Jeremiah reached his decision to kill Fort. As soon as he could leave his wife in a neighbor's care, he rode to Frankfort. Disguised, he went at night to the house in which Fort was staying, called him to the door, and stabbed him to death. He then rode home and told Rachael what he had done.

Four days later, officers appeared and summoned him to Frankfort for examination in connection with the murder. Believing that there was no evidence against him, he went willingly; but his enemies were already busy manufacturing false clues, and to his surprise, he was held for court. By the time of his trial bribery and perjury had done their work. In spite of the efforts of Dr. Burnham and other loyal friends, his case was lost when Wilkie appeared to testify against him. Although many believed him innocent, Jeremiah was sentenced to be hanged on August 20, 1826. Meanwhile, Rachael had been arrested and brought to Frankfort, where she and her husband shared the same cell. Jeremiah's lawyers appealed the sentence. When they failed to produce one of the handbills defaming Rachael, the appeal was denied.

Two days before the execution date, Wilkie Barron and several men broke into the jail and freed the prisoners, who were taken secretly to a refuge ruled over by La Grand' Bosse, a river pirate. There, from one of Wilkie's former henchmen, Jeremiah learned that Scrogg and Wilkie had forged the handbill responsible for Fort's death. In despair, Rachael killed herself. Realizing how he had been duped, Jeremiah tried to return to Frankfort and reveal the truth. Wilkie's man overtook him and cut off his head.

Wilkie went into partnership with the Parhams and became rich. Still politically ambitious, he was elected senator. One night in Washington, he shot himself. Among his effects, to be uncovered in an old trunk years later, were some letters and a manuscript in which Jeremiah Beaumont, during his months in prison and in the outlaw camp, had written his story of deceit and betrayal. No one would ever know why Wilkie had kept those incriminating papers. Unable to destroy the truth, he had tried to conceal it. Perhaps at the end, like Jeremiah, he wondered whether the striving, pride, violence, agony, and expiation had all been for nothing.

Critical Evaluation:

Colonel Solomon P. Sharp, Solicitor General of Kentucky, was killed by a masked assassin in 1825. Shortly afterward, Jeroboam Beauchamp, a young lawyer and a member of the political party opposing Sharp, was arrested and charged with the crime. During the trial, it was revealed that Beauchamp had married a planter's daughter whom Sharp had seduced. Found guilty and awaiting execution, Beauchamp was visited in his cell by his wife. The husband and wife stabbed themselves after a dose of laudanum failed to kill them. The wife died in her husband's cell. Beauchamp was hanged. The Kentucky Tragedy, as this story of intrigue and revenge was called, became a popular subject during the nineteenth century, among writers as dissimilar as Edgar Allan Poe, Charlotte Barnes, Thomas H. Chivers, Charles F. Hoffman, and William Gilmore Simms. Robert Penn Warren, reworking the old tale, has filled it with philosophical speculation and symbolic moral overtones. His Jeremiah Beaumont is an idealist confronted by the realities and compromises of the world, a man betrayed not only by an acquisitive and self-seeking society but also by the very idealism that sustains him in loneliness and doubt. The plot, centering about a theme of community guilt and expiation, illustrates the complex moral issues of the era.

Given his lifelong preoccupation with Southern history, it is not surprising that Robert Penn Warren was attracted to the Kentucky Tragedy as a vehicle for expression of his thoughts and feelings about idealism, fanaticism, politics, love, sex, and violence. In adapting this historical event—almost a folk legend— Warren begins with a story of innocence violated, villainy rewarded, revenge, political corruption, and backwoods violence. The raw material is, therefore, highly dramatic—almost too much so. Warren's first problem is how to tell the story without descending to sentimental romance or lurid melodrama.

In the first place, he mutes the obvious sensationalism of the events through his handling of point of view. An unnamed historian, having pieced together the story from Jeremiah Beaumont's "confession" and other data, narrates the events with scholarly objectivity and frequent moralizing in an ornate prose style. This elaborate, indirect approach, with the highly charged dramatic scenes, gives the book both historical distance and dramatic intensity.

Second, Warren shifts the usual focus of the tale from the sentimental, revenge-seeking woman, Rachael Jordan, to her idealistic but confused lover, Jeremiah. Therefore, the novel takes on a shape not unlike Warren's earlier masterpiece *All the King's Men*. As in the previous book, the novel centers around the relationship between a young man (Jeremiah), a powerful father figure (Cassius Fort), who combines idealistic good with pragmatic evil and who inspires worship as well as revulsion, and the woman (Rachael) who is the victim both of the older man's attractiveness and his ruthlessness. Again the father figure is murdered by the young man to avenge the honor of the woman.

Warren's analysis of the political context of the act further differentiates his handling of the Kentucky Tragedy from previous ones. The results of Jeremiah's act demonstrate the potential dangers of fanatical idealism in conflict with corrupt pragmatic politics. He is finally convicted not because he committed the crime but because his guilt serves the selfish needs of those in power.

Warren's biggest deviation from the original events, however, lies in the novel's resolution. The historical couple attempted mutual suicide; the woman died, and the man was hanged. In Warren's version, an escape is arranged. In the course of their flight, Jeremiah and Rachael learn the truth of their situation, which drives Rachael to suicide and Jeremiah to an attempt at public confession. The important thing to Warren is not Jeremiah's legal punishment but the growth of his personal awareness. Jeremiah, like other Warren protagonists, must finally accept responsibility not only for his own deed but also for the sequence of turbulent events provoked by that first act of violence.

THE YEARLING

Type of work: Novel
Author: Marjorie Kinnan Rawlings (1896–1953)
Type of plot: Regional romance
Time of plot: Late nineteenth century
Locale: The Florida scrub country
First published: 1938

Principal characters:
JODY BAXTER, a young boy
PENNY BAXTER, his father
ORA BAXTER, his mother
FODDER-WING FORRESTER, Jody's crippled friend
OLIVER HUTTO, Penny's friend
GRANDMA HUTTO, his mother
TWINK WEATHERBY, Oliver's sweetheart

The Story:

The Baxter family consisted of Penny Baxter, his plump wife Ora, and their boy Jody. They lived in a simple cabin in the Florida scrub, where patient, hardworking Penny eked out a meager living by farming and hunting.

Young Jody still saw life through the eyes of a child and found a boy's pleasure in building a flutter mill at the spring when he should have been hoeing the garden patch.

One spring morning, the family discovered that Betsy, their black brood sow, had been killed by a bear. Penny recognized the tracks as those of Old Slewfoot, a giant black bear with one toe missing. Determined to be rid of this offender, he cornered the animal in the scrub, but his old gun would not fire, and the bear escaped.

Unable to afford a new gun, Penny traded a worthless feist to his neighbors, the Forresters, for a new double-barreled shotgun of fine make. The Forrester family consisted of the old parents, six gigantic, lawless sons, and Fodder-wing, a deformed and crippled son who was Jody's best friend. Penny was reluctant to dupe his neighbors, but his very living depended upon Old Slewfoot's destruction. He eased his conscience by telling the Forrester boys truthfully that the feist could not be trained for hunting. His words convinced the suspicious Forresters that the dog was even more valuable than they had thought, and it was they who insisted on the trade.

After the old gun had been repaired, it became Jody's great pride. One day, while hunting with his father, he shot a buck which Penny sold at the store in Volusia. After selling the venison, Penny and Jody went to see Grandma Hutto, at whose house they spent the night. In the morning, everyone was made glad by the unexpected arrival of Oliver Hutto, Grandma's son, just home from sea. Later that day, Oliver went downtown, where he met Lem Forrester. Both of the men were courting a yellow-haired girl, Twink Weatherby. When the two started to fight, all of Lem's brothers joined in against Oliver Hutto. Wiry Penny and small Jody also entered the fight with Oliver, since the odds against him were so heavy. Oliver left the fight badly battered. Jody had been knocked unconscious. To keep people from talking, Twink Weatherby left town on the riverboat the next morning.

A short time later, Penny discovered that his hogs had disappeared. He suspected the Forresters of having trapped them in order to get revenge for the shotgun deal, and he and Jody started to track the hogs. As he searched, a rattlesnake bit Penny on the arm. He saved himself by shooting a doe and applying the liver to the bite to draw out the poison. Even in the excitement, Jody had noticed that the doe had a fawn. While Penny staggered homeward, Jody went to the Forresters to ask them to ride for Doc Wilson.

The Forresters, with the exception of Lem, evidently held no grudge over the trading of the dog and the fight in town, and they did all they could for the Baxters. One of the boys brought Doc Wilson to the cabin. Later they rounded up the hogs and returned them, and Buck Forrester stayed on at the Baxter cabin to help with the work.

While Penny was still desperately ill, Jody returned to the place where his father had been bitten, and there he found the helpless young fawn. He was so eager to have it for his own that his parents allowed him to bring it home as a pet. Rations were scarcer than ever at the Baxters during Penny's illness, but Jody was willing to share his own food and milk with the fawn. Fodderwing gave the fawn its name. He called it Flag.

In September a great storm came, destroying most of the Baxter crops. About a month later, Old Slewfoot visited the Baxter land again and killed a fat hog. Penny, who was in bed with chills and fever, was not able to follow the great black bear. Later, wolves killed one of the calves, and with the Forresters, the Baxters hunted down the whole pack which had been bothering all the neighborhood. During the hunt, they found ten bear cubs, left motherless by the plague and hunters after the storm. Two of the Forresters took the cubs to Jacksonville and sold them. Penny and Jody's share of the profits bought the necessities which would tide the Baxters over the coming winter.

The Baxters had planned to spend Christmas in Volusia with Grandma Hutto and to attend the town's festivities on Christmas Eve; but a few days before Christmas, Old Slewfoot again appeared and killed a calf. Penny swore that he would kill the raider, and after several days of determined hunting, he found and shot the five-hundred-pound bear.

The Baxters joined Grandma Hutto at the Christmas party. During the evening, Oliver Hutto arrived in town with his wife, Twink. To get revenge, Lem Forrester and his brothers fired Grandma Hutto's house and burned it to the ground. Without Oliver's knowing that the house had been fired by the Forresters, Grandma Hutto, Oliver, and Twink left town the next morning on the riverboat. They had decided to go to Boston to live.

Back in their cabin, the Baxters settled down to a quiet winter of fishing and hunting. Flag, the fawn, had grown until he was a yearling. The fawn had never been a favorite of Ma Baxter because she begrudged him the food and milk Jody fed him, and because he was a nuisance around the cabin.

In the spring, while Jody was helping his father plant corn, Flag got into the tobacco field and destroyed about half of the young plants. One day, while trying to pull a stump out of the ground, Penny ruptured himself and afterward spent many days in bed. Then Jody had to do all of the farm work. He watched the corn sprouting through the ground. One morning, he found that Flag had eaten most of the tender green shoots. Mrs. Baxter wanted to kill the fawn at once, but Penny suggested that Jody build a fence around the corn to keep Flag out. Accordingly, Jody spent many days replanting the corn and building a high fence around the field. When the new planting of corn came up, Flag leaped the high fence with ease and again nibbled off the green shoots.

Her patience exhausted, Mrs. Baxter took Penny's gun and shot the fawn. Unhappy Jody had to shoot his pet again because his mother's aim was so poor. Jody felt that the family had betrayed him. He hated them. He left the clearing and wandered into the scrub. With the vague idea of running away from home to join the Huttos in Boston, he headed for the river and set out in Nellie Ginright's dugout canoe. After several days without food, he was picked up by the river mail boat. He returned home, ashamed and penitent, but a yearling—no longer interested in the flutter mill, which now he considered only a plaything for children.

Critical Evaluation:

The Yearling, a classic of juvenile romantic fiction, appeals to both young and adult readers. As a novel of development, the book treats a "rite of passage" from the carefree pleasures of childhood to the more sober stage of responsibilities that come with growth—a subject that interests as well as educates children. At the same time, Marjorie Kinnan Rawlings' careful observation of people and setting in rural Florida entertains mature readers. Life is hard for the Baxters. Although Jody is reared close to nature with a joyous appreciation for beauty and is secure in the affection of his family, his parents have to struggle to make ends meet. Theirs is a marginal existence from a stubborn soil; and Rawlings constantly reminds the reader of the Baxters' empty woodbox, the water barrels that need filling from the sink hole, the privations of the scrub-farmers' toil. Without glossing over the hardships of the Baxters and their neighbors, the author also shows her love for the land and its creatures, her admiration for the rugged honesty and perseverance of the farmers, and her sense of wonder at the beauty of Florida's vanishing wilderness.

The plot of *The Yearling* falls into two main narratives that treat the two important actions: the first is the bear hunt that culminates with the killing of Old Slewfoot; the second is the story of Jody's affection for the fawn Flag, the yearling. The first narrative reminds the reader of Faulkner's novella *The Bear*. Like the Faulkner story, the bear hunt is a ritual involving not only the boy and his family but also neighbors of all sorts, representing rural society. In both stories, the bear at first escapes from the hunters; in both, a feist— a small aggressive hound—is important either to make the hunt possible or to corner the bear; finally, in Faulkner as well as Rawlings, the bear is considered to be an extremely capable, sly, and dangerous foe. Beyond this point, the resemblance between the stories cannot be extended. Faulkner's bear is clearly a metaphysical force as well as an animal; Rawlings' bear is only a powerful creature.

The second narrative concerns Jody's discovery of the fawn, his growing sense of identification with the animal, and his terrible grief when the yearling is slain. This action resembles some parts of the first section of Steinbeck's *The Red Pony* (1937): "The Gift." In both stories, a boy (each named, coincidentally, Jody) receives for his particular care an animal—Flag for Jody Baxter, the pony Gabilan for Jody Tiflin; in both, the raising of the animal is difficult yet emotionally rewarding for the boy; in both, the animal does not survive, and the boy is heartbroken. To be sure, in Steinbeck's novel the pony is not slain by man. The special poignancy of the conclusion of *The Yearling* is the manner of Flag's death. To protect her corn from the fawn's ravages, Mrs. Baxter has to shoot the animal; when the job is botched, it is Jody who must finish off his beloved pet. This necessary but agonizing chore estranges the boy from his parents. Torn by grief, Jody flees them as betrayers— then returns. By the end of the book, Jody has learned to make compromises with reality. It is a bitter lesson, but young readers understand that it is an essential part of one's education in growing up.

The book introduces the reader to a way of life that is new and strange. Because of the author's sympathy and understanding, her pleasant interest in nature and wildlife, her deep knowledge of human nature, reading *The Yearling* becomes a highly personal experience.

THE YEMASSEE
A Romance of Carolina

Type of work: Novel
Author: William Gilmore Simms (1806–1870)
Type of plot: Historical romance
Time of plot: Early eighteenth century
Locale: South Carolina
First published: 1835

Principal characters:

SANUTEE, a Yemassee chief
MATIWAN, his wife
OCCONESTOGA, his son
GABRIEL HARRISON, a young settler
HECTOR, Gabriel's black slave
PARSON MATTHEWS, a minister
BESS MATTHEWS, his daughter

The Story:

The English settlers, who at first had to accept aid from the Yemassee Indians when the white men landed on the South Carolina shores, had become quite powerful by 1715. No longer did they have to be careful not to offend the Indians; instead, they continually set up farms on the wrong side of the boundary lines between white and Indian territory. Sanutee, one of the Yemassee chiefs, had become suspicious of the colonists; he was afraid that they would soon take over all the Yemassee land. In order to keep them from occupying Indian territory, he had made treaties with other tribes and with the Spanish, who were willing to help the Indians defeat the English. Sanutee's life was made unhappy by his son, Occonestoga, who had been tempted by liquor to become a close friend of the whites. Sanutee was too proud of his ancestry and his position to call a drunkard his son, and it was only by constant pleas that his wife, Matiwan, was able to keep him from completely disowning Occonestoga.

One of the recent settlers was Gabriel Harrison, a strange young man whose commanding presence and jolly manner made him both admired and disliked. Among those who liked him was Bess Matthews, the daughter of old Parson Matthews, and Walter Grayson, an honorable young farmer. Parson Matthews disliked Harrison because he was too gay and worldly in his manner, and Walter's brother, Hugh, disliked Harrison because he was also an admirer of Bess. Harrison had brought with him a fine black slave named Hector, who was his constant companion, and a strong and faithful dog named Dugdale. With these two companions, Harrison wandered about the district.

One day in the forest, Harrison came upon Sanutee fighting with a stranger over the carcass of a deer. He arrived in time to save Sanutee's life, but the proud Indian expressed no gratitude. Harrison learned that Sanutee's opponent was a sailor named Dick Chorley, who had recently arrived on the coast. Although Chorley said that he had come to trade, Harrison rightly suspected that he was really a Spanish agent who had come to arm the Indians against the English. Harrison sent Hector to spy on Chorley and Sanutee, who had been joined by Ishiagaska, another Yemassee chief.

Hector, hiding in the brush, overheard Chorley's declaration that he had come to South Carolina to arm the Indians. Displaying the wampum belt of an Indian treaty, he asked the Yemassee tribe to join the tribes who were willing to fight the English. Before Hector could return to tell Harrison what he had learned, the slave was captured and taken aboard Chorley's ship.

Harrison guessed what had become of Hector. He found Chorley in the Parson's cabin and, by threats, forced the seaman to sign an order freeing Hector. His action angered the Parson, who refused to suspect Chorley of treason. He denied Harrison the right to wed his daughter Bess.

In the meantime, the Yemassee chiefs were called to a council and asked to sell more land to the English. Most of the chiefs were willing to sell, but Sanutee, who arrived late at the meeting, made a stirring speech against the sale. Interrupted by his drunken son, the old Yemassee almost killed Occonestoga. When he heard that the chiefs intended to sell the land over his protests, Sanutee left the meeting and went to arouse the people against their chiefs. With the aid of an Indian prophet named Enoree Mattee, he so infuriated the crowd that they repudiated the other chiefs and punished them by having the tribal mark cut from their skins, so that they became outcasts from the tribe. Only Occonestoga escaped this punishment.

Occonestoga hid in the woods. One day, he saved Bess Matthews' life by killing a rattlesnake that was about to strike her. For his deed, Harrison rewarded the young Yemassee with his friendship. Soon afterward, he sent Occonestoga back to the Indian stronghold to learn what the Indians were planning. Occonestoga secretly made his way to his mother, Matiwan, who hid him in her tent. By chance, Sanutee discovered the boy and ordered that he be killed after having the tribal mark cut from his skin. In desperation, Matiwan killed her son before the sentence could be carried out, for the tribal mark could not be cut from a dead man.

Harrison, realizing that Sanutee was about to lead the Indians against the whites, did his best to get all the settlers to go to the blockhouse for protection. Parson Matthews insisted that the Indians had never been more friendly, and he refused to leave his cabin. Harrison, while scouting in the woods, was captured by Indians. With the aid of Matiwan, who had heard of his kindness to her dead son, he escaped. In his attempt to save Bess before the Indians could seize her, he was almost recaptured. Hector and his dog Dugdale arrived just in time to save him.

Meanwhile, Chorley had led a party of Indians and sailors to the Parson's cabin and had captured both Bess and her father. Harrison was able to rescue them and lead them to the blockhouse before the Indian attack began. A furious struggle took place, with even the women aiding in the fight to hold off the Indians. Both the Grayson brothers became friendly with Harrison because of the bravery he had shown in saving their families, and together they fought valiantly to save the community. At last, the Indians were forced to withdraw.

Harrison made plans to send many of the settlers to Charleston, where they would be safe until troops could be mustered to defeat the Indians permanently. After winning the Parson's permission to marry Bess, consent freely given after his heroic defense of the colony, Harrison astonished the group by announcing that he was in reality Charles Craven, the new governor of the province. He had come to the region in disguise so that he could see for himself the true state of affairs on the frontier. He made Hugh Grayson commander of the garrison forces. When he offered Hector his freedom, the old slave refused to be parted from his kind master.

In Charleston, Craven raised a considerable fighting force and returned to battle with the Yemassee Indians on the banks of the Salkehatchie River. When the Indians attacked the camp of the white men, the governor's troops, firing from ambush, shot them down. Sanutee fell, mortally wounded, and Craven saw Matiwan run upon the field and fall weeping by her husband's body. The last of the Yemassee braves was dead.

Critical Evaluation:

In early American frontier novels, the Indian was inevitably characterized in one of two ways, either as a noble savage, a natural primitive untainted by civilization's corrupting influences, or, more commonly, a savage barbarian who took pleasure in cruelty and violence toward innocent white settlers. Even America's most famous author of historical romances, James Fenimore Cooper, divided his Indians into absolutely good and bad types and developed his novels accordingly. Perhaps only William Gilmore Simms in *The Yemassee* succeeded in creating believable, human Indians with mixed qualities, natures, and potentials; and that is the primary reason why *The Yemassee*, in spite of severe artistic flaws, must be acknowledged as one of the best nineteenth century frontier novels.

Through the first third of the book, the action is seen primarily from the Indian viewpoint. Simms carefully describes the Yemassee tribe as they plan and attempt to execute an uprising against the white settlers. Their motives, however, spring not from innate hostility or cruelty but from a realization that the powers and needs of the white man make the conflict—and their own ultimate defeat—inevitable. Thus, Simms imports to the Yemassee a kind of doomed, almost tragic grandeur.

It is in his presentation of the intimate life of the Indian that Simms is most impressive. Unlike Cooper, Simms describes the natives in their own environment and shows their daily routines, tribal mores, rituals, and politics in minute, careful detail. This Indian culture is presented with respect, and individual tribe members are presented as fallible, but admirable human beings.

The most vivid portraits are those of Chief Sanutee, his wife, and their son. Sanutee is a proud, intelligent, brave but flawed leader, who understands and accepts the unavoidable dissolution of his tribe, but who, nevertheless, inspires his men to heroic resistance. His wife, Matiwan, shares her husband's courage and insight, but her compassion elevates her above racial identity to become a kind of Earth Mother figure. Their son, Occonestoga, contaminated by contact with the white man's whiskey and promises, finally finds his courage and nobility in a time of crisis, although too late to salvage his tribal status. Few scenes in nineteenth century fiction are as powerful as the one in which, during the ritual that is to strip Occonestoga of his tribal identity, Matiwan kills her own son before the assembled Indians to save his honor and dignity.

Had Simms been able to sustain the insights and intensity of the first third of the book, *The Yemassee* might have been a great novel. Unfortunately, once the focus of the novel shifts to the white man's world, the characters, both Indians and whites, become stock characters, and the novel degenerates into a clichéd chase-capture-escape romance.

Simms's sympathetic treatment of the Indians, however, does not mean that he considered them the white man's equal. Even Sanutee "well knew that the superior must necessarily be the ruin of the race which is inferior." As a staunch upholder of the Southern position in the pre-Civil War South, Simms firmly believed in racial superiority and what he and others called an "organic society." In Simms's view, the Indian was doomed because he was an inferior race and culture and, unlike the black, could not be fit into a useful place in the white man's world. However tragic and seemingly unjust the displacement or destruction of the red man might be, it was, to Simms, the necessary price that had to be paid in order to establish the superior society.

YOU CAN'T GO HOME AGAIN

Type of work: Novel
Author: Thomas Wolfe (1900–1938)
Type of plot: Impressionistic realism
Time of plot: 1929–1936
Locale: New York, England, and Germany
First published: 1940

Principal characters:
GEORGE WEBBER, a writer
ESTHER JACK, the woman he loves
FOXHALL EDWARDS, his editor and best friend
LLOYD MCHARG, a famous novelist
ELSE VON KOHLER, a woman also loved by Webber

The Story:

As George Webber looked out of his New York apartment window that spring day in 1929, he was filled with happiness. The bitter despair of the previous year had been lost somewhere in the riotous time he had spent in Europe, and now it was good to be back in New York with the feeling that he knew where he was going. His book had been accepted by a great publishing firm, and Foxhall Edwards, the best editor of the house, had been assigned to help him with the corrections and revisions. George had also resumed his old love affair with Esther Jack, who, married and the mother of a grown daughter, nevertheless returned his love with tenderness and passion. This love, however, was a flaw in George's otherwise great content, for he and Esther seemed to be pulling different ways. She was a famous stage designer who mingled with a sophisticated artistic set. George thought that he could find himself completely only if he lived among and understood the little people of the world.

Before George's book was published, he tried for the first time to go home again. Home was Libya Hill, a small city in the mountains of Old Catawba. When the aunt who had reared George died, he went back to Libya Hill for her funeral. There he learned that he could never really go home again, for home was no longer the quiet town of his boyhood but a growing city of money-crazy speculators who were concerned only with making huge paper fortunes out of real estate.

George found some satisfaction in the small excitement he created because he had written a book which was soon to be published. Even that pleasure was not to last long, for when he returned to New York and the book was published, almost every citizen in Libya Hill wrote him letters filled with threats and curses. George had written of Libya Hill and the people he knew there. His only motive had been to tell the truth as he saw it, but his old friends and relatives in Libya Hill seemed to think that he had spied on them through his boyhood in order to gossip about them in later years. Even the small fame he received in New York, where his book was favorably reviewed by the critics, could not atone for the abusive letters from Libya Hill. He felt he could redeem himself only by working feverishly on his new book.

George moved to Brooklyn, first telling Esther good-bye. This severance from Esther was difficult, but George could not live a lie himself and attempt to write the truth. In Brooklyn, he did learn to know and love the little people—the derelicts, the prostitutes, the petty criminals—and he learned that they, like the so-called good men and women, were all representative of America. His only real friend was Foxhall Edwards, who had become like a father to George. Edwards was a great man, a genius among editors and a genius at understanding and encouraging those who, like George, found it difficult to believe in anything during the Depression years. Edwards, too, knew that only through truth could America and the world be saved from destruction; but, unlike George, he believed that the truth could not be thrust suddenly upon people. He calmly accepted conditions as they existed. George raged at his friend's skepticism.

After four years in Brooklyn, George finished the first draft of his new book. Tired of New York, he thought that he might find the atmosphere he needed to complete his manuscript in Europe. In London, he met Lloyd McHarg, the embodiment of all that George wanted to be. George yearned for fame in that period of his life. Because his book had brought him temporary fame, quickly extinguished, he envied McHarg's world reputation as a novelist. George was disillusioned when he learned that McHarg thought fame an empty thing. He had held the world in his hand for a time but nothing had happened. Now he was living feverishly, looking for something he could not name.

When his manuscript was ready for publication, George returned to New York, made the corrections Edwards suggested, and then sailed again for Europe. He went to Germany, a country he had not visited since 1928. In 1936, he was more saddened by the change in the German people than he had been by anything else in his life. He had always felt a kinship with the Germans, but they were no longer the people he had known before. Persecution and fear tinged every life in that once proud country, and George, sickened, wondered if there were any place in the world where truth and freedom still lived.

There were, however, two bright horizons in his visit to Germany. The first was the fame which greeted him on his arrival there. His first book had been well received, and his second, now published, was a great success. For a time, he basked in that glory, but soon he, like McHarg, found fame an elusive thing that brought no real reward. His other great experience was his love for Else von Kohler. That was also an elusive joy, for her roots were deep in Germany, and George knew he must return to America to cry out to his own people that they must live the truth and so save America from the world's ruin.

Before he left Germany, he saw more examples of the horror and tyranny under which the people existed, and he left with a heavy heart. He realized once more that one can never go home again.

Back in New York, he knew that he must break at last his ties with Foxhall Edwards. He wrote to Edwards, telling him why they could no longer travel the same path. First, he reviewed the story of his own life, through which he wove the story of his desire to make the American people awake to the great need for truth so that they might keep their freedom. He told Edwards, too, that in his youth he had wanted fame and love above all else. Having had both, he had learned that they were not enough. Slowly he had learned humility, and he knew that he wanted to speak the truth to the downtrodden, to all humanity. Because George knew he had to try to awaken the slumbering conscience of America, he was saying farewell to his friend. For Edwards believed that if the end of freedom was to be the lot of man, fighting against that end was useless.

Sometimes George feared that the battle was lost, but he would never stop fighting as long as there was hope that America would find herself. He knew at last the real enemy in America. It was selfishness and greed, disguised as a friend of mankind. He felt that if he could only get help from the little people, he could defeat the enemy. Through George, America might go home again.

Critical Evaluation:

In May, 1938, having broken with his first editor and mentor Maxwell Perkins ("Foxhall Edwards" in the novel), Thomas Wolfe deposited an unfinished manuscript of perhaps a million words on the desk of his new editor, Edward C. Aswell of Harper and Brothers, and left for a tour of the West. In Vancouver he contracted pneumonia, in Seattle it worsened, and finally, after he had been moved to Johns Hopkins in Baltimore, it was found that the illness had triggered the release of previously latent tuberculosis bacteria in his lungs which had gone to the brain; he died on September 15, 1938.

Thus, it was left to Aswell to assemble, organize, and edit Wolfe's admittedly unfinished material into publishable fictions. The major results of Aswell's efforts were the two massive novels that chronicle the life and artistic development of George Webber, *The Web and the Rock* (1939) and *You Can't Go Home Again*. Consequently, the episodic, fragmentary, sometimes even arbitrary structure of these books and the unevenness and occasional excessiveness of the writing must in part be the result of the compositional problems—though these flaws also exist in his two prior works. There is no way of knowing what the final form of the novels would have been had Wolfe lived to complete them to his own satisfaction.

It has been said that Wolfe wrote only one book during his career, a thinly disguised autobiography. In a sense this is true, but, like Walt Whitman, the American author who seems most like him in artistic intention and attitude, Wolfe saw his own experience as the focal point for the experience of a nation in the process of becoming. Thus, as the major character in Wolfe's novels strives for experience, personal meaning, and a means of artistic expression, he is also trying to seize and formalize the nature and direction of nothing less than American society itself.

You Can't Go Home Again is the most external and social of his four major novels. The title sets the theme and action line of the novel. George cannot go "home" to any of the old places, experiences, or ideas that have formed him, because every time he attempts to do so, he either finds a corruption that has destroyed the thing he would return to, or he finds that he has gone beyond that particular experience and has neither the need nor the desire to repeat it. Metaphorically, "home" is the naïve, idealized vision of America and of his potential place in it that he had held as a young man but now learns no longer exists and perhaps never did.

When George returns to his hometown of Libya Hill to attend his aunt's funeral, he finds the old rural values gone and a new corrupt speculative fever running rampant. Then he sees the collapse of this greedy dream in the beginnings of the Depression. He cannot go back to his physical home because it no longer exists and he is repelled by what has replaced it. Libya Hill, however, is only a microcosm, a foreshadowing of what he is to encounter. As America enters into the Depression, George comes into painful contact with both the results of the American economic and social system as he intimately observes both its victims and its victimizers—and he seeks to disassociate himself from both.

It is Europe and especially Germany, however, that brings George to his final understanding. The notion that artistic success and fame will bring him satisfaction is destroyed by his meeting with the famous novelist Lloyd McHarg (a fictionalized Sinclair Lewis), who finds only bitterness, loneliness, and alcohol in his success. George then completes his education in Germany when he is exposed to the horror of the newly powerful Nazi regime. The Nazi horror, thus, is the logical extension and end result of the greed and corruption George has observed in America, perhaps even the America of the not too distant future.

Yet *You Can't Go Home Again* is not a despairing book. It ends with an exhortation. For all the evil and pessimism he has encountered in his education, George continues to feel that mankind in general and America in particular still have the potential to assert their positive capacities and realize the ideals they once possessed. That is where, as an artist in Whitman's bardic tradition, George sees his place in America to be—as a spokesman for that vision.

YOU KNOW ME AL
A Busher's Letters

Type of work: Epistolary novel
Author: Ring Lardner (1885–1933)
Type of plot: Humorous satire
Time of plot: c. 1915
Locale: Chicago
First published: 1916

Principal characters:
JACK KEEFE, a ball player
AL BLANCHARD, his correspondent
FLORRIE, Jack's wife
ALLEN, Jack's brother-in-law, also a ball player
MARIE, his wife

The Story:

When Jack Keefe, a pitcher, was brought up from the minor leagues by the Chicago White Sox, he began writing a series of letters to his hometown friend, Al. It was a peculiar friendship, however, for Jack was basically incapable of any of the emotions real friendship requires. He patronized Al and used him. Jack was a braggart and a chronic self-excuser, and the letters gave him a chance to exercise his ego. Al apparently never saw through Jack.

So sublimely self-confident that he felt every trifling detail of his life was important, Jack wrote full accounts of his adventures. Having neither modesty nor shame, he even included episodes in which he appeared foolish.

When Jack reported to training camp on the West Coast, he immediately annoyed the manager by his overeating, refusal to take orders, and laziness. Though a powerful right-handed pitcher, he was an indifferent fielder and careless about base runners. The manager tried to handle Jack with irony, but it was lost on him. Whenever he had a bad day, he alibied that his arm was sore. Any hit made against him was the fault of the fielders, the umpires, or the scorers. Jack also believed that he was irresistible to women. In training camp, he met a girl from Detroit named Violet, and he planned to romance her when the White Sox were playing Detroit.

Jack did well enough in spring training to be included on the White Sox roster. In his first starting assignment against the Tigers, he played miserably. The manager left him in the game as punishment, and sixteen runs were scored against him. Ty Cobb stole four bases. As usual, Jack complained that his arm was sore. By now, the manager was thoroughly disgusted with him, and Jack was sent to San Francisco. He sulked and said he would quit baseball, but he went. Violet called him a busher.

In San Francisco, he won eleven straight games and became engaged to a girl named Hazel. Recalled by the White Sox at the end of the season, he pitched well enough to be used in the City Series between the White Sox and the Cubs. Hazel asked him for one hundred dollars to pay her fare to Chicago for their wedding. He sent her thirty, and she married a boxer instead. Jack then attempted to marry Violet, but she married another ball player. Jack married Florrie, the sister-in-law of a White Sox left-hander named Allen.

When Florrie refused to spend the winter in Bedford, Jack's hometown, they rented an apartment across the hall from the Allens. There were many quarrels between the two families, most of them occasioned by Jack's stinginess. Jack had always been convinced that all left-handers were crazy; his trouble with Allen only served to strengthen his conviction. Allen was taking his wife Marie along to spring training. Florrie wanted to go too, but Jack felt that he could not afford to take her. Since he felt that he was underpaid, he tried to get a raise from the club, even though he had already signed a contract. Charles Comiskey, the owner of the White Sox, had already had contract trouble with Jack and refused to grant him any concessions. Jack then tried to join the Federal League, a third major league that was hiring players away from the American and National Leagues; however, the Federal League would have nothing to do with him because he had signed a contract with the White Sox. Then his team learned about this attempted defection. Hog-fat after gorging himself on food and liquor all winter, he was sold to Milwaukee as a disciplinary measure. Florrie left him. Jack, protesting that he would not go to the minors again, borrowed money from Al to return to Bedford. The White Sox were forced to keep him, however, because of a technicality in the waiver rule.

The manager limited Jack's diet, and he got into shape good enough to be given another chance with the White Sox. Florrie and Jack were reconciled because she was pregnant, and she soon presented him with a son. At first, Jack worried because the baby appeared to be left-handed. Florrie named the baby Allen after her brother-in-law, but Jack insisted that the baby was named for Al. Although he continued to display the same old patterns of bragging and complacency, Jack turned out to be a doting father in his own fashion.

After a successful season, he was selected to pitch in the City Series, a cause of fresh strife with Florrie because she wanted to attend the games, and he wanted her to stay home with the baby. Jack was not concerned about the money for a babysitter as much as he was worried about the welfare of his son. When the team bribed Florrie to stay home, she used the money to hire a babysitter. Jack then decided to leave her but changed his mind when he learned that she would have custody of the child. After another argument with the Allens, Jack moved his family out of the apartment which they shared and for which Allen paid the rent.

The White Sox wanted Jack to join the world tour the team was making with the Giants, but he did not want to be away from the baby. The real reason for taking him was to keep him in shape, but Jack believed that baseball fans in other countries wanted to see him. They coaxed him to Canada because Christy Mathewson was going that far. Then they told him that President Wilson was afraid Japan would declare war if Jack did not go there to play. Convinced at first, he later began to worry about the dangers of the ocean voyage and backed down, but when he was told that Allen would be taken in his place, his vindictiveness triumphed over his fear. He sailed away boasting of triumphs to come.

Critical Evaluation:

Ring Lardner was the first important American author to write seriously about sports. As a young sportswriter, his constant association with athletes strongly influenced his notions about American character and society. As early as 1914, Lardner understood what other mainstream American writers did not realize until the 1950's and later—the importance of big sports in the emotions, imaginations, and needs of the public and the extent to which it embodies some of the most basic assumptions and myths of the culture.

Sports is one area where pursuit of the American Dream can still be seen in its purest form. According to this myth, any man with the requisite talent and drive can compete openly and fairly for the best rewards society has to offer: money, status, and adulation of the people. The best man necessarily wins and goes directly and quickly to the "top."

Lardner also saw the distance between dream and reality, so he chronicled this incongruity in a series of vivid, funny, sad, biting, and often bitter works of fiction—notably "Champion," "Alibi Ike," "My Roomy," and especially *You Know Me Al.* He described the mean, dreary, crude, and often vicious world of professional athletics with humor, honesty, and realism—without sentimentality, but not without compassion. Although he largely abandoned sportswriting as a profession and sports as a subject matter after 1922, these stories still form the backbone of his reputation.

Jack Keefe is both an exploiter of the American Dream and its victim. He imagines himself a hero—invincible on the diamond, shrewd and popular off of it, applauded by fans, adored by women, destined to "greatness." In fact, Jack is mocked and taken advantage of by most people he meets: teammates, opponents, employers, women in general, and his wife, Florrie, in particular. For all of his faults—his bragging, his alibiing, his self-indulgence, laziness, stinginess, beer-swilling, and crudity—he is still the more sinned against than sinner. It is this ironical distance between Jack's self-image and the reality of his situation that gives *You Know Me Al* its rich humor and poignancy.

Jack is an especially American comic type: The boastful loser who is too naïve and pugnacious to realize that he really is a loser. It is this dogged, optimistic pursuit of his false image and improbable dream that makes Jack Keefe most human and most American.

Although Lardner's reputation is based on the high level of achievement in his short stories, *You Know Me Al*, his first novel, is a major document in American humor. Several streams of American comic tradition merge in this work: the comic letter, the wisecrack, the braggart character, the use of sporting vocabulary and fractured English, and the general debunking mood. The letters are hilarious for their verbal wit, but Lardner also achieved comedy through his use of character and situation. The novel, more than a loosely organized series of humorous letters, achieves unity through the characterization of Jack Keefe. As he egotistically describes his experiences, he inadvertently exposes himself. The bitterness of this portrait is foreign to American humor. Apart from the later works of Mark Twain, its parallels must be sought in Swift or Smollett. Lardner does not appear to hate Jack, however; instead, he despairs for him and perhaps pities him.

YOUMA
The Story of a West-Indian Slave

Type of work: Novel
Author: Lafcadio Hearn (1850–1904)
Type of plot: Exotic romance
Time of plot: 1840's
Locale: Martinique
First published: 1890

Principal characters:

YOUMA, a young black slave
GABRIEL, another slave, in love with Youma
MAYOTTE, a white child entrusted to Youma's care
MONSIEUR DESRIVIÈRES, Gabriel's master
AIMÉE, wife of M. Desrivières and Mayotte's mother
MADAME PEYRONETTE, Youma's owner and Mayotte's grandmother

The Story:

Youma was a pet slave and the godchild of Madame Peyronette. Youma's mother had been the nurse of Madame Peyronette's only daughter, Aimée, and the two children, white and black, had grown up together almost as sisters. Even when Aimée was sent to a convent to have her manners finished off according to Creole custom, the vacations she spent at home were always in the company of the young black slave.

As the girls grew to womanhood, Aimée begged her mother on several occasions to give Youma her freedom, but Madame Peyronette felt that she was guarding Youma by keeping her in slavery. Privately, Madame Peyronette had decided first to find the girl a good husband and then, after she was safely married, to grant her freedom. Before Madame Peyronette could carry out her plan, Aimée married Monsieur Desrivières, son of a wealthy old Creole family. Upon her marriage, Aimée asked that Youma be permitted to serve for her in the new household, a request speedily granted by her mother.

Thirteen months after Aimée's wedding, a baby girl was born to her and her husband. The child was named Marie, which the blacks made into the diminutive Mayotte. Tragedy struck the household a year later when Aimée, who had been caught in a chilling rain while riding in an open carriage, fell ill and died within twenty-four hours. Before she died, Aimée begged Youma to assume the duties of a nurse for little Mayotte. Youma, recalling the kindnesses she had received at the hands of Aimée, vowed to do the best she could for the motherless child.

Monsieur Desrivières went to his sugar plantation at Anse-Marine, in another section of the island, for he could not remain in the same house after his wife's death. Not long after, little Mayotte being in delicate health, Madame Peyronette sent her, in Youma's care, to the plantation. The grandmother thought that the climate at the plantation would be better for Mayotte.

The little girl and Youma loved the life at the plantation; for both, it was an experience in people. Little Mayotte was irked at times because she was not permitted to mingle freely with the little black children. This was not caused by difference in race but by fear that she was in danger of sunstroke while participating in their games. To pass the time, Mayotte and Youma went on walks in shaded places or sat on the verandas while Youma told folktales of her race.

One afternoon, Youma warned Mayotte that if she heard so many tales during the day she would see zombies at night. Mayotte laughed and asked for another story, but that night, she screamed to Youma that something was in her room. As Youma stepped into the room to calm the child, she felt a tremendous snake under her foot. Keeping the snake imprisoned beneath her foot, Youma called for help as the serpent writhed itself about her legs and body. When Monsieur Desrivières and the servants arrived with a light, they found Youma holding down a large and poisonous reptile. One of the slaves, Gabriel, swung a cutlass and lopped off the snake's head. Fortunately for the girl and the child, Youma had stepped on the snake immediately behind the head, and it had not been able to strike at her with its fangs.

The incident earned for Youma the respect of everyone at the plantation. Gabriel, in particular, showed his admiration by bringing gifts of fruit and spending the hours of early evening listening to her tell stories or sing to little Mayotte. He even made a rustic bench which he placed beside the little pool where Youma took Mayotte to play in the water. Finally, Gabriel gave her a pair of earrings; when she put them on, he knew that she was willing to marry him. Gabriel, wishing to marry Youma, was told that Madame Peyronette's permission was necessary, since Youma belonged to her. When asked, Madame Peyronette refused to give permission; she felt that it would be wrong to permit Youma, who had been brought up almost as a white girl, to marry Gabriel, who, although a fine specimen of manhood, was only a field hand.

Gabriel and Youma were grievously disappointed at the denial of their request. When Gabriel, a resourceful fellow, proposed that he and Youma elope and cross the channel to a British-held island where slavery had been abolished, Youma almost succumbed to his temptations, until she remembered her promise to care for Mayotte. With that promise in mind, she refused to desert her charge.

Within a few days of the refusal, Youma and Mayotte were sent back to the city. Not long after, the year being 1848, word spread through the West Indies that a republic had been proclaimed in France and that slavery would soon be abolished in Martinique. Feeling ran high, for there were only twelve thousand whites on the island and more than a hundred and fifty thousand blacks. The whites, knowing full well of the troubles in Haiti years before, were extremely cautious in dealing with the black people. Even so, rumors began to spread that the whites were conspiring to retain slavery. An outbreak began over the imprudent whipping of a slave on the very eve of emancipation. Thousands of slaves poured into the city from the country.

Madame Peyronette, Youma, and Mayotte, after taking refuge with another family in a large, well-built stone house near the army barracks, believed that they would be safe from the mob. When the hordes of slaves poured into the city, however, a crowd gathered in front of the house and finally broke in. Since the whites on the second floor were temporarily out of their reach, the slaves set fire to the house. When some of the whites tried to escape by leaping out of windows, the mob killed them immediately.

Youma, in an effort to save Mayotte and herself, went out on a balcony and identified herself as a slave. Gabriel, who happened to be in the crowd, tried to save them, but the bloodthirsty blacks refused to let the white child be spared. Youma, rather than leave Mayotte to die alone, stood on the balcony with the child until the walls of the house collapsed and killed them both.

Critical Evaluation:

This book is an understanding story of life in the West Indies, written essentially from the black's point of view. Whites enter the story only as they are forces or background figures for the lives of the blacks who are the principal characters. That this novel should have come from the pen of Lafcadio Hearn is not surprising, for he had spent months in the West Indies and had seen for himself the life and personality of the black people. Even more important, Hearn had been aware of the black and his problems in the United States, particularly in Louisiana. Like much of Hearn's work, *Youma* is filled with pictures of exotic scenery and life. A story of West Indian slavery, the novel is also a vehicle portraying the life, customs, folklore, and lush scenery of a beautiful island.

Reportedly based on a true incident that occurred during the Martinique rebellion, *Youma* is also an example of Hearn's lifelong fascination with the exotic and his carefully delineated translations of truth into fiction. The story reveals the degree of Youma's attachment to her white foster family.

Orphaned Youma was accorded many of the same privileges as her mistress' daughter during the children's early years. Although Youma was not taught to read and write and was not sent away to school with the daughter, she was well aware that she received far better treatment than most slaves.

Youma, however, was unaware that her mistress planned to arrange a suitable marriage for her with a black freedman and then to free her. Thus, she saw no deterrent to a marriage with Gabriel and was stunned when permission was not granted. She might have fled with Gabriel, but her affection for the white family, and especially for Mayotte, to whom she was a foster mother as Madame Peyronette had been to her, outweighed her resentment and prevented such a course of action.

Had Madame Peyronette acceded to the young couple's wishes, Youma and Mayotte would have remained safely on the plantation. Unfortunately, the romance precipitated obedient Youma's return with the child to the city at a time when tensions were running high among slaves fearful that their masters might attempt to prevent black emancipation. The action of one white man then set the stage for Youma's final act of devotion. His cruel punishment of a slave incited the rebellion.

Youma could have lived by abandoning Mayotte; but neither her fear of death, nor her dislike of slavery, nor the prospect of freedom could induce her to leave the child. Martyred in the flames, Youma represents the epitome of altruistic love.

EL ZARCO

Type of work: Novel
Author: Ignacio Manuel Altamirano (1834–1893)
Type of plot: Romantic tragedy
Time of plot: 1861–1863
Locale: Province of Morelos, Mexico
First published: 1901

> *Principal characters:*
> NICOLAS, an Indian blacksmith
> EL ZARCO, a bandit
> MANUELA, a woman in love with El Zarco
> DOÑA ANTONIA, her mother
> PILAR, Doña Antonia's godchild, in love with Nicolas
> MARTÍN SÁNCHEZ, a rancher and El Zarco's enemy
> EL TIGRE, El Zarco's lieutenant

The Story:

During the War of Reform, and after, bands of robber outlaws took advantage of the troubled times to overrun those districts of Mexico where the local authorities, in a land still disturbed by civil war, were powerless to make effective reprisals against them. Roaming the countryside in armed bands, the *plateados*, as they were called, waylaid and murdered travelers, kidnaped wealthy estate owners for ransom, and levied tribute on the villages and haciendas. For their amusement, they often wantonly burned the cane fields and inflicted brutal tortures on their prisoners.

A town terrorized in this fashion was Yautepec, a pleasant village of the *tierra caliente* in the province of Morelos. By day, the people maintained lookouts in the church towers to give warning of approaching marauders; at night, they barricaded themselves in their houses, so that after sunset the little town in the middle of its circling orange groves resembled a place of the dead. The bandits, some five hundred strong, had their headquarters at Xochimancas, a nearby ruined hacienda from which they made forays to ravage the whole district. Their leader was El Zarco, a man of savage temper and cruel disposition whose bloody exploits caused all respectable and decent people to fear him. The bandits sometimes entered the town and rode boldly through the streets.

On an evening in August, 1861, Doña Antonia sat in the inner courtyard of her house with her daughter Manuela and Pilar, her godchild. The two girls were plaiting flower garlands for their hair. After a time, Manuela began

---

to tease Pilar because her friend was making a wreath of orange blossoms, the flower of weddings; Manuela was twining a circlet of roses. When Manuela complained pettishly of her dull life, her mother rebuked her sharply, saying that the girl ought to forget fiestas and dances, and take a husband who would protect her. Doña Antonia's choice was Nicolas, the sober and industrious blacksmith of the estate at Atlihuayan. At this suggestion, Manuela began to speak scornfully of the Indian, as she called him, and declared that she would rather have El Zarco as a suitor. She added that Nicolas might be good enough for Pilar, but she herself would never have him. Pilar blushed but said nothing.

Before Doña Antonia could reprove her daughter further, Nicolas, a nightly caller, arrived with the news that the night before the *plateados* had robbed and killed an English family traveling to Acapulco and that a cavalry detachment was being sent from Cuernavaca to pursue the bandits. Alarmed at this latest outrage, Doña Antonia decided that she and Manuela would go to Mexico City until times grew better; they would travel with the troops as their escort for part of the dangerous journey. Nicolas thought her decision a wise one for Manuela's sake.

Later, while Nicolas was on his way back to Atlihuayan, another rider was traveling toward Yautepec. The horseman was El Zarco. In the village, he turned down a dark lane that led to a stone wall surrounding Doña Antonia's orange grove. Drawing rein beneath a giant sapota tree, he whistled twice. An answering whistle came from the darkness under the tree where Manuela was waiting for her lover.

El Zarco had met Manuela in Cuernavaca during a brief period when he and his men were aiding the government forces, and the two had been strongly drawn to each other. After he had established himself at Xochimancas, the bandit learned that the girl and her mother had returned to Yautepec. Through his spies in the village, he had arranged to see her regularly. El Zarco found her wholehearted devotion flattering to his vanity. Manuela, refusing to believe the stories of his violence and cruelty, saw him only as a handsome, brave caballero. Now, unwilling to leave Yautepec, she told him of Doña Antonia's plans and asked him to take her away. Before they parted that night, they had arranged for him to carry her off to Xochimancas. In parting, El Zarco gave her several small boxes for safekeeping. After his departure, she saw that one was bloodstained. The boxes contained a diamond ring, two bracelets, and earrings. Putting them on, she went to a pool in the garden and looked at her reflection by the light of a lantern. She buried the jewels with other gems and money that El Zarco had already entrusted to her.

The next night, Manuela fled with El Zarco to his hideout, leaving behind a note in which she told her mother good-bye. Heartbroken, Doña Antonia asked Nicolas to go with her to beg that the cavalry troop from Cuernavaca would hunt down the bandits and rescue Manuela. When the commander refused, Nicolas charged the officer with shirking his duties. The blacksmith was placed under arrest and ordered held for trial.

Pilar, upset by the news of Nicolas' arrest, tried to visit him in prison but was turned back by his guards. Nicolas, hearing her pleas, realized that it was Pilar and not Manuela whom he truly loved. The authorities of Yautepec and the manager of Atlihuayan were indignant over the treatment Nicolas had received. When the commander set out to take his prisoner to the capital, a large party accompanied the troops to see that the blacksmith received full justice. Through the intercession of the owner of Atlihuayan, Nicolas was finally released. He returned to Yautepec in time to see Doña Antonia on her deathbed, for the poor woman was dying of grief over her daughter's disgrace. After her death, Nicolas continued to ride into the village each evening, but now he went to visit Pilar.

Meanwhile, at Xochimancas, Manuela lived a different and sordid life of lawlessness and violence. Forced to associate with the disreputable women of the *plateados*, ogled and showered with lewd compliments from the men, she was at first terrified by her new surroundings. She realized at last that she had been attracted to El Zarco by infatuation and greed, not love. In particular, she was horrified by the condition of a French prisoner, tortured daily to extort from him a greater ransom. At a fiesta to celebrate one of El Zarco's raids, she was forced to dance with El Tigre, a repulsive creature who told her that El Zarco would tire of her eventually and turn her over to one of his lieutenants. El Tigre intended to be the man.

A short time before, El Zarco had killed the father and son of a rancher named Martín Sánchez. Swearing revenge, Sánchez sold his property and bought arms and equipment for twenty men he recruited to track down the bandits. After he had made several successful raids on the outlaws, other men were roused from their apathy and fears to join him. In an encounter at La Calavera, in which Nicolas took part, El Zarco was wounded and taken prisoner. With him was Manuela.

In spite of Martín Sánchez' protests, El Zarco cleverly arranged to have his trial held in Cuernavaca. While the prisoners were being taken there, bandits fell on the escorting troops and set El Zarco and Manuela free. Sánchez, determined to end lawlessness in the region, obtained from President Juarez authority to hang without trial any bandit who fell into his hands.

The wedding day of Pilar and Nicolas arrived at last. After the mass had been said, they started by coach for Atlihuayan with friends invited to the feast to be held there. On the way, they met a troop of horsemen led by Martín Sánchez, who asked the party to drive on without stopping. At that moment, Manuela appeared from behind the horsemen and begged help of Nicolas and his bride. El Zarco and El Tigre, she said, had been captured and were to be executed. Martín Sánchez told how he had saved the wedding party from an ambush. Pilar, filled with pity for Manuela, wanted to take that unfortunate creature into the coach, but the distraught girl cried out that she would rather die with El Zarco than see Pilar in her wreath of orange blossoms. Saddened, the wedding party rode on.

Shot down by a firing squad, El Zarco's body was then hung from the branch of a tree. Manuela, seeing her lover dangling there, gave a loud cry and fell to the ground. Blood ran from her mouth. Several men tried to lift her, but she was already dead.

Critical Evaluation:

Ignacio Manuel Altamirano is the first Mexican who may truly be called a novelist, working with an awareness of and within limitations imposed by a clearly defined literary form. A patriot and a veteran of the War of Reform, he found the materials of his fiction in the life of that turbulent period. *El Zarco* illustrates his expressed intention to present Mexican life and to interpret faithfully the spirit of the people. It is a somber work, historical in background, deeply probing in psychological depth, and suffused with the beauty of the Mexican landscape. Two characters stand out from the background against which they move: Manuela, an impulsive, headstrong girl brought to folly and ruin by infatuation and greed, and Nicolas, an Indian representative of the class in which Altamirano saw a bright promise for the future of his nation. Completed shortly before the writer's death, the novel appeared posthumously eight years later.

El Zarco has beauty, action, and clarity. It paints the subtropical mountains of Morelos between 1861 and 1863, when political conditions were chaotic, a potentially rich economy stagnated, and social justice was unknown. Readers thus see the traditional reasons for Mexico's sluggish progress, which stemmed basically from bad government, but which has been blamed too exclusively on the rich, on bloated landlords, on narrow-minded priests, and other prototypes of the oppressor.

El Zarco sketches folklore, human types, and the Mexican psychology of the time. Above all, it clearly depicts the dichotomy between a virtuous social element—as represented by Nicolas, Antonia, and others—and the various corrupt types that were crippling Mexico through laziness, greed, and dishonesty. As in the times of *El Zarco*, the negative minority is sometimes in sociopolitical control today while the healthier majority is excluded from the levers of control. The same theme appears often in Mexican literature, implying that Mexican revolutions have often been meaninglessly destructive, and that even some of the glorified patriotic victories (such as the defeat of Spain, 1810–1822; the defeat of Maximilian soon after the time of *El Zarco*; and of Porfirio Diaz in 1910–1911) have blocked as well as unleashed progress. This, for example, is a theme of Mariano Azuela's *The Underdogs* (*Los de abajo*), which, in describing the civil strife that took place half a century after *El Zarco*, condemned the nouveau riche of a popular revolution as much as it did their opponents.

El Zarco suffers from the inevitable limitations of the nineteenth century in which it was written. Some of its characterizations are simplistic—Nicolas, for example, seems too faultless and is not presented convincingly, while Antonia, Pilar, and El Tigre are rather one-dimensional figures. Nevertheless, El Zarco himself was presented in greater depth, since his motivations for vengeance and power—that stemmed from his sorry past as a stable boy and menial drudge on large estates—are convincing. Altamirano even makes it clear that El Zarco's menial tasks were given to him because he was too worthlessly lazy to learn higher skills, and that El Zarco simply belonged to that inherently unblessed type of revolutionary who is ever ready to be whistled out of the mesquite at the wave of a sombrero to murder and plunder for "La Causa."

Manuela is initially callous, greedy, spoiled, and even deliberately evil. Sorrow, frustration, and total defeat finally goad her into psychological transformation. Disillusioned and hapless, knowing that she has sinned, she receives the attendant punishment without self-pity as she dies at the foot of El Zarco's corpse.

The real person that Altamirano was in his daily life stalks through the pages of *El Zarco*. The novel reflects his impoverished youth—for which he yearns, oddly enough—and its memories of slights, offenses, and the indifferences of calculating women who were frivolously incapable of seeing in him anything more than an impoverished youth. Yet Altamirano's novels, even while reliving the memories that make these novels authentic, are not basically autobiographical. Typically, El Zarco's reaction to his humble past is opposite that of Altamirano's, while Nicolas' reaction to life is Altamirano's since he does not live as an abject and servile Indian but as a cultured man dignified by work and conscious of his own personal worth.

Altamirano was one of the most complete men of action and letters of his time in Mexico. He did not view the novel as a pastime for lazy souls, but "as a treasury whose disguises could be penetrated" to find jewels of historical fact, political doctrine, social reality, and character-building morality. He also felt that the novel should be used to present the beliefs of specific political parties or religious denominations, or even other entities. He considered it, in short, the genre par excellence of the masses, comparable to popular music, mass circulation magazines, or the orator's podium.

Altamirano thus used the novel as he used the sword in favor of his liberal views, which were liberal in a nineteenth century sense. He thus followed the tradition of Argentina's Domingo Sarmiento and Bartolomé Mitre, who were literary presidents of the Argentine Republic. Like them, Altamirano was politically active as a theoretician and campaigner; he also served in three of Mexico's wars—the War of Ayutla, the War of the Reform and the War of French Intervention during Maximilian's time. He was also a parliamentarian and journalist, pouring the wisdom of his rich experiences into his novels. In *El Zarco*, as in all of his other novels, he deliberately ripped back the curtain of Mexican history, highlighting the evils that lacerated the flesh of his country.

Altamirano stated that he finished *El Zarco* at exactly eleven-twenty on the night of April 6, 1888. He first titled the novel "Episodes of Mexican Life in 1861–63" and had sold it for two hundred dollars when it was barely half-finished. The novel's stated goal was to be a clear mirror of Mexico, and a compass revealing the advisable path, as well as the erroneous one, for his bleeding nation to follow. For this goal, he dedicated the simple fluidity of his style and the wisdom of his years.

MASTERPLOTS

AMERICAN FICTION
SERIES

TITLE INDEX

I

TITLE INDEX

TITLE INDEX

V

AUTHOR INDEX

AGEE, JAMES
  Death in the Family, A, I-269
ALCOTT, LOUISA MAY
  Little Women, II-687
ALDRICH, THOMAS BAILEY
  Story of a Bad Boy, The, III-1227
ALEGRÍA, CIRO
  Broad and Alien Is the World, I-144
ALLEN, HERVEY
  Anthony Adverse, I-58
ALTAMIRANO, IGNACIO MANUEL
  Zarco, El, III-1480
AMADO, JORGE
  Gabriela, Clove and Cinnamon, I-425
  Violent Land, The, III-1383
ANDERSON, SHERWOOD
  Dark Laughter, I-255
  Poor White, II-961
  Winesburg, Ohio, III-1440
ASCH, SHOLEM
  Apostle, The, I-62
  Nazarene, The, II-837
ASTURIAS, MIGUEL ÁNGEL
  Señor Presidente, El, III-1110
AZUELA, MARIANO
  Flies, The, I-395
  Underdogs, The, III-1349

BALDWIN, JAMES
  Go Tell It on the Mountain, I-458
BARRIOS, EDUARDO
  Brother Ass, I-149
BARTH, JOHN
  End of the Road, The, I-339
  Sot-Weed Factor, The, III-1188
BEACH, REX
  Spoilers, The, III-1198
BELLAMANN, HENRY
  Kings Row, II-636
BELLAMY, EDWARD
  Looking Backward, II-702
BELLOW, SAUL
  Adventures of Augie March, The, I-7
  Henderson the Rain King, II-547
  Victim, The, III-1371
BIERCE, AMBROSE
  Tales of Soldiers and Civilians, III-1252
BIRD, ROBERT MONTGOMERY
  Nick of the Woods, II-841
BORGES, JORGE LUIS
  Ficciones, I-375

BOYD, JAMES
  Drums, I-313
  Marching On, II-761
BRACKENRIDGE, HUGH HENRY
  Modern Chivalry, II-806
BROMFIELD, LOUIS
  Green Bay Tree, The, II-509
BROWN, CHARLES BROCKDEN
  Wieland, III-1433
BUCK, PEARL S.
  Dragon Seed, I-309
  Good Earth, The, I-478

CABELL, JAMES BRANCH
  Cream of the Jest, The, I-231
  Jurgen, II-626
  Rivet in Grandfather's Neck, The, III-1058
CABLE, GEORGE W.
  Grandissimes, The, I-483
CAIN, JAMES M.
  Postman Always Rings Twice, The, II-978
CALDWELL, ERSKINE
  Tobacco Road, III-1299
CATHER, WILLA
  Death Comes for the Archbishop, I-264
  Lost Lady, A, II-706
  My Ántonia, II-823
  O Pioneers!, II-856
  Professor's House, The, II-994
  Shadows on the Rock, III-1126
  Song of the Lark, The, III-1184
CHEEVER, JOHN
  Short Stories of John Cheever, The,
    III-1141
  Wapshot Chronicle, The, III-1396
  Wapshot Scandal, The, III-1400
CHESNUTT, CHARLES WADDELL
  Conjure Woman, The, I-211
CHURCHILL, WINSTON
  Crisis, The, I-235
CLARK, WALTER VAN TILBURG
  Ox-Box Incident, II-892
  Track of the Cat, The, III-1313
CLEMENS, SAMUEL L. See TWAIN,
  MARK
COOKE, JOHN ESTEN
  Surry of Eagle's-Nest, III-1244
  Virginia Comedians, The, III-1388
COOPER, JAMES FENIMORE
  Chainbearer, The, I-191
  Deerslayer, The, I-286
  Last of the Mohicans, The, II-639

AUTHOR INDEX

MASTERPLOTS

X

WRIGHT, RICHARD
Native Son, II-832
WYLIE, ELINOR
Venetian Glass Nephew, The, III-1367

YÁÑEZ, AGUSTÍN
Edge of the Storm, The, I-331
YOUNG, STARK
So Red the Rose, III-1180

ZUVIRÍA, GUSTAVA ADOLFO
MARTÍNEZ. *See* WAST, HUGO